The Yale Scene

University Series, 3

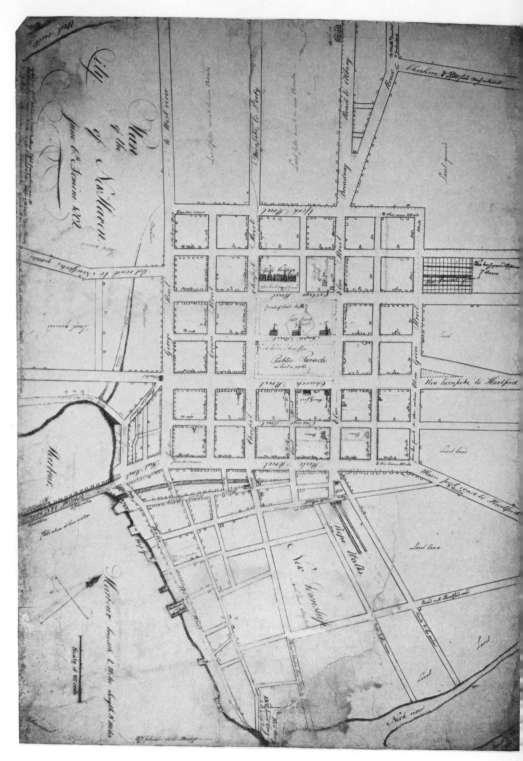

NEW HAVEN IN 1802

YALE

A HISTORY

BROOKS MATHER KELLEY

New Haven and London : Yale University Press

1974

Library of Congress catalog card number: 73-86902
International standard book number: 0-300-01636-0

Designed by John O. C. McCrillis
and set in Baskerville type.
Printed in the United States of America by
The Vail-Ballou Press, Inc., Binghamton, N.Y.

Published in Great Britain, Europe, and Africa by
Yale University Press, Ltd., London.
Distributed in Latin America by Kaiman & Polon,
Inc., New York City; in Australasia and Southeast
Asia by John Wiley & Sons Australasia Pty. Ltd.,
Sydney; in India by UBS Publishers' Distributors Pvt.,
Ltd., Delhi; in Japan by John Weatherhill, Inc., Tokyo.

Published with the aid of funds
given in memory of Norman Vaux
Donaldson.

*To my mother
and the memory of
my father*

Contents

Maps

Preface

During a brief stint as University Archivist in the mid-1960s, it was constantly brought home to me that no general history of Yale had been attempted since the end of the nineteenth century. After I resigned as Archivist in 1966, I determined to write a brief overview of the university's long history. Within a few months of embarking on my project, I decided that, since Yale had never had a full-scale single-volume account of its history, it really deserved something more than a one-hundred-page survey. This book is the result of that decision.

It is probably fortunate that the study grew in the way it did. Had I realized at the outset the size and complexity of the undertaking, I might never have begun. I should make it clear, however, that this book is only a "first approximation" at a history of Yale. In order to spend just years instead of decades preparing it, it was necessary to depend on the numerous published sources and secondary materials available. I went to the massive manuscript resources only when absolutely necessary. It was possible to follow this procedure because so much had already been written about Yale, but obviously the technique risks error. I took the chance because it seemed to me most important to get in print a history of Yale that would be generally accurate and would correct many of the mistaken views of the university's history, and that would at the same time, as I hope, spur others to do the basic studies from which another, far more nearly complete volume will emerge.

While this is in no way an "authorized" history, I owe a great deal to official Yale and to many individuals at the university for assisting me with it. My first and perhaps greatest debt is to all those who have written about Yale. Among them, special acknowledgments are due to certain early workers in the vineyard: Franklin B. Dexter's enormously productive labors on the eighteenth century are invaluable; nineteenth-century Yale has not yet received the attention it deserves, but to William L. Kingsley and those who contributed to his two massive volumes on Yale history, I owe many credits; Lyman Bagg deserves a special bow for his unique volume on life at Yale in the nineteenth century. Professor George W. Pierson, the University

Historian, has assisted me so much with his excellent two-volume study of Yale College, 1871–1937, as well as through his careful readings of this manuscript, that words cannot do justice to my debt to him.

Deepest thanks are due to the many others who have read part or all of this book as it evolved over the years (as well, in many cases, as writing important works about the institution): Professors Roland Bainton, Thomas Bergin, Edmund Morgan, Rollin Osterweis, Norman Pearson, Gaddis Smith, Robert Stevens, Richard Warch, and John Whitehead, my wife, Jean Kelley, and Elizabeth Thomson, Research Associate in the History of Science and Medicine. Many others have shared with me their thoughts about various aspects of Yale history. Some of the individuals whom I interviewed are mentioned in the footnotes; a few did not wish to be identified; to all I owe profound gratitude. Each of those named or unnamed helped save me from mistakes; none agreed entirely with all my interpretations; the errors that remain are my own.

The stimulating conversation and wide knowledge of various aspects of Yale's history of the Fellows of Jonathan Edwards College were invaluable. My teacher and friend, Daniel Boorstin, Director of The National Museum of History and Technology of the Smithsonian Institution, and my former colleague and guide at Yale, Professor William Goetzmann of the University of Texas in Austin, have constantly encouraged me and given me good advice. I want to give special credit to Brooks, John, and Todd for spurring me on when my spirits flagged by constantly asking, "When are you going to finish?"

The Yale University Library has been my most important aid. To that great institution and its devoted staff, and especially to Judith Schiff, Chief Research Archivist, Manuscripts and Archives, I send heartfelt thanks. So also, my gratitude is due to the copy-editor of this volume, Cynthia Brodhead, who showed me so well the value of a skillful and understanding editor, and to Henrietta Else, who typed the entire manuscript and put up with my illegible interlineations. My son, Brooks R. Kelley, read proof with me and helped make that dreary task almost pleasant.

Yale has been a part of my life, at one time or another, for nearly seventeen years. For six years it was almost my only interest. Since the days in Gstaad, Switzerland, during the winter of 1967, when I set the first tentative words to paper (and where I learned, for the first time, a bit about the great respect with which Yale is held outside the United States) my admiration for the university has steadily increased. More and more I have learned the truth of William A. Brown's statement, "Institutions, like individuals, are not made, they grow. They are living things that have souls as well as bodies." Certainly, despite the increasing similarity of American universities, Yale has retained a body and a soul which are uniquely hers and which bear the unmistakable imprint of her long history. Despite attacks from conservatives and radicals, and despite misunderstandings about the university's role in society which exist both within and without the institution, Yale remains a place where the pursuit of light and truth goes forward unchecked.

New Haven, Connecticut   B. M. K.
July 1973

Part One

The Critical Years

1701–1739

1

Founding a College

For a moment, the Western world was at peace. England and France had reached one of the quiet intervals in the series of wars they fought from 1688 to 1815. In 1701, during this brief pause, a college was founded in the wilderness of Connecticut by a small group of ministers.

The dream of establishing a college in this little corner of the earth was an old one. It had originated with John Davenport, a founder of the New Haven Colony and first minister to the New Haven congregation. Davenport had been one of the original overseers of the "colledge at Newetown," later called Harvard, and when he came to the mouth of the Quinnipiac River in 1638 to establish a new and more perfect holy commonwealth it seems probable his plan to start a college had already been formulated.[1]

The New Haven Puritans, like those at Massachusetts Bay, depended on an educated ministry for the preservation of their religion. Learned ministers were necessary for the interpretation of the Bible. Without them error would creep in and soon the pure religion would cease to exist. This was the prime reason for their desire to found a college. But there were other motives as well. The new colony could not exist, Davenport and the other settlers knew, without a continuous supply of educated laymen. But the trip to the struggling little college in the Massachusetts Bay Colony was long, arduous, dangerous, and expensive. It would be better to have a college nearer home. Finally, Davenport may have wished the education of future religious and lay leaders of the colony to take place under his eyes, so he could be sure that education remained orthodox.[2]

Periodically during Davenport's years in New Haven (1636–67) it appeared the colony would establish a college. The nearest approach to fulfillment of the dream came when Edward Hopkins, friend to Davenport, onetime governor of Connecticut, and husband of Anne Yale (aunt of Elihu), left a sizable bequest to Connecticut and New Haven for the founding of a college. Because of the imprecise wording of the will and the demands of Connecticut and Massachusetts, the generous gift was ultimately divided and went to launching grammar schools named after the donor in New Haven, Hartford, and Hadley, Massachusetts. A considerable amount, many years later, went to Harvard.[3]

In 1665, the New Haven Colony was absorbed by Connecticut, and two years later an embittered John Davenport departed for Boston. His plan for a separate colony had been defeated by politics, financial failures, and a meager population. But the proposal of a college for New Haven did not die with the removal of its most active proponent. Young ministers who also saw the need for a college arrived on the scene, and finally, after many more years of effort, they made the dream a reality.[4]

The actual steps that preceded the founding of Yale, and even the individuals involved, are uncertain. Myth, tradition, wishful thinking, and fact have been so mixed over the years that it is now difficult to separate truth from fiction. Little in the way of documents, letters, and the like has survived. Nevertheless, the bare outlines of the story can be discerned.[5]

It seems clear that after the departure of Davenport nothing of significance in the attempt to found a college took place until the Treaty of Ryswick ended King William's War in 1697. In the period of peace that followed, serious discussion of the need for a college probably began again. The rationale had changed little since Davenport's day, but to the original reasons had been added the fear that Harvard was falling away from the true, pure religion. Even in Connecticut, it was felt, all was not well. If the religion of their forefathers was to be preserved uncorrupted, a learned ministry and magistrates well-schooled in theology must be provided. As Roland Bainton so concisely put it: "Yale was conservative before she was born."[6]

The main question facing the ministers who were behind this new attempt was what legal course to follow to establish a college. The answer was by no means clear-cut. In England, for example, colleges were residences or places of instruction but gave no degrees. That right was reserved to the two universities. Yet in Massachusetts Bay, Harvard College had been blithely granting degrees, without the legal right to do so, since 1642. Harvard had not even been chartered by the colony until 1650, and then it had lost that charter when the Dominion of New England was created in 1686. Harvard had been trying to get a new, permanent charter ever since, but without success.

If Harvard's situation was insecure, so was Connecticut's, for the Lords Commissioners of Trade and Plantations had recommended an end to all corporate and proprietary colonies in March 1701, and a bill to that effect went before Parliament in April of that year. A further problem was that if a colony overstepped its own charter by incorporating a college, it might bring down upon it the wrath of the crown, for no colony had the explicit legal right to create corporations.[7]

In this confused and uncertain situation five Connnecticut ministers—James Pierpont, Thomas Buckingham, Abraham Pierson, Israel Chauncy, and Gurdon Saltonstall—sent out a letter in early August 1701 to certain important men in Connecticut and Massachusetts, asking a series of practical questions about how legally to set up the school so that it could not be dissolved by the crown, how to secure and manage donations, entitle the master of the school, give degrees, and the like. They feared that the General Assembly of Connecticut might not have the right to grant a charter, while it seemed very possible that the crown would refuse to do so.[8]

The replies the ministers received contained mixed advice, but apparently the case for asking the colonial assembly to charter the college was strongest, for during the month of September they hastened ahead with their plans in order to be ready for the October meeting of the General Assembly in New Haven. In the course of these preparations it appears that some of the ministers—exactly who we do not know—may have held a meeting at the end of September or during the first days of October at Branford in the Reverend Samuel Russell's house. At this meeting, according to Thomas Clap in his *Annals of Yale College,* "Each . . . brought a Number of Books . . . ; and laying them on the Table, said these Words, or to this Effect; *I give these Books for the founding a College in this Colony."* [9]

This is a charming story, much cherished in the mythology of Yale and often repeated by the *Yale Alumni Magazine* and the university's fund raisers. Unfortunately, it seems unlikely that it ever happened. President Clap in the original draft of his college history said that the books were given in 1702. His later version, which puts the event in 1700, was written with the desire to prove to the General Assembly that the founding actually preceded the chartering of the institution (see p. 68). Since Clap's account is the sole basis of the story, it must be discounted. There is evidence to indicate that at some point in 1701 several of the founders appear to have said they would give books to the college. They may have made their pledge at Branford that fall, but it is unlikely that anyone actually gave books until somewhat later.[10]

Whatever may—or may not—have happened at Branford, some of the founding ministers were present in New Haven when the governor and General Assembly met there for the first time (the town had just become a co-capital, with Hartford, of the colony) on 9 October 1701. James Pierpont and James Noyes were certainly there, and undoubtedly others as well, for the meeting of the Assembly was one of the great events of the year. With no time to spare, a draft charter arrived that had been prepared at the behest of Pierpont by two Massachusetts men, Chief Justice Samuel Sewall and Secretary of the Province Isaac Addington. Quickly the ministers went over the draft, Pierpont wrote in the various changes desired, a revised copy was prepared, and the document was presented to the Assembly.[11]

What debates took place over the act we do not know. We do not even know exactly when it was passed; but probably on 15 or 16 October 1701 "An Act for Liberty to Erect a Collegiate School" was approved by the General Assembly. The act is interesting in several ways. First, it avoided the issue of incorporation and merely gave certain ministers of the colony the right to found a "collegiate school," hold its property, and direct its affairs. It skirted the issue of the nature of the institution by giving it, as Sewall and Addington said, "as low a name as we could that it might the better stand in wind and weather," and failed to incorporate it so it would not "be liable to be served with a Writ of Quo Warranto." Sewall and Addington had written into their draft the right to grant degrees such as those given by Harvard, but the act as passed only granted the trustees the right to make such rules as they wished.

In addition to these important legal features, the act granted the

ministerial undertakers £120 "Country Pay" a year for the college.*
Furthermore, it broadly defined the collegiate school as a place
"wherein Youth may be instructed in the Arts and Sciences who
thorough the blessing of Almighty God may be fitted for Publick
employment both in Church and Civil State." Thus from the very
beginning the college was viewed as more than just a school for ministers.[12]

A further feature of the act, as Frederick Rudolph has noted, was
that it "inaugurated a type of governing board which would become standard American practice—the single absentee body." This
means, as Richard Hofstadter and DeWitt Hardy have observed,
that

constitutionally, the American teaching profession is thus potentially subject to government by an oligarchy of laymen. In this respect American
higher education is a deviant among the educational systems of the Western world, a thing "without parallel outside the North American continent." It is also without parallel among the other learned professions
within the United States.[13]

In later years in the attempts to show that the founding actually
preceded the charter a good deal of stress has been laid on the fact
that, whereas Sewall and Addington called their draft "An Act for
Founding," the final version was entitled "An Act for Liberty to
Erect." Professor Dexter claimed that the ministers changed the title
because they had already founded the college. But while Pierpont
made many alterations in the draft, he left the title as it was.[14] The
change seems to have been made in the Assembly in order to have
the title coincide with the form usually used in Connecticut for such
legislation.[15]

This act for the Collegiate School is usually taken as marking the
beginning of Yale, but in fact only the right to found a college existed, so this attempt (like so many earlier ones) could still have
failed. But on 11 November 1701 the new trustees met at Saybrook
to found the collegiate school that the General Assembly had given

---

Country pay referred to certain products upon which the General Assembly had
fixed a monetary price and which would be accepted in lieu of money as payment for
taxes. A clear explanation of country pay may be found in Richard Warch, *School of
the Prophets: Yale College, 1701–1740* (New Haven, 1973), p. 43. Warch figures that
the college grant was worth £80 in New England currency in 1701. From other figures
he gives, it appears that the grant was worth slightly less than £64 sterling.

them permission to establish. Present at the meeting were the Reverends Samuel Andrew of Milford, Thomas Buckingham of Saybrook (in whose house they probably met), Israel Chauncy of Stratford, James Pierpont of New Haven, Abraham Pierson of Killingworth, Noadiah Russell of Middletown, and Joseph Webb of Fairfield. Reverend Samuel Mather of Windsor, a Harvard classmate of Samuel Sewall, who was "little and feeble" and had been "ill of late," was absent, as were Reverend Timothy Woodbridge of Hartford, who was recovering in Boston from a "humor" in his leg, and Reverend James Noyes of Stonington, who had been in New Haven when the General Assembly met but found himself exhausted after that trip. To excuse his absence, he wrote the trustees, "I am aged crazie my will is more than my streneth. We rod early & late coming home & I haue not been well since I came home." [16]

Of those present and absent, the most important in the movement to establish the college appear to have been James Pierpont, Thomas Buckingham, and Israel Chauncy, members of the original board, Samuel Russell, who was soon to be elected to that body, and Gurdon Saltonstall, who was never a trustee. Of these, the surviving documents clearly indicate that James Pierpont was foremost. He more than any other individual deserves the title of founder of Yale.[17]

There was nothing especially striking about the men who created the college that later became Yale. They ranged in age from James Noyes, who was sixty-one, to Joseph Webb, who was thirty-five. All of them had been born in either Massachusetts or Connecticut except Timothy Woodbridge, who had been born in England. All of them had gone to Harvard except Thomas Buckingham, who never attended college. Three of them, Samuel Russell, James Pierpont, and Noadiah Russell, had graduated in the class of 1681. One, Joseph Webb, had been expelled for abusing freshmen, but after a full confession and apology he had been readmitted and had graduated in the class of 1684 with Gurdon Saltonstall. Others were even more closely related than through their college experiences. As Charles Thwing noted in his *History of Higher Education in America:* "Mather and Andrew married sisters; Webb and Chauncy also married sisters; Pierpont was the nephew of Pierson by one marriage, and the stepson by another; Noyes and Woodbridge were cousins."

Beyond the relationships of college, marriage, and blood, all of

the founders were ministers and three, Pierpont, Andrew, and
Woodbridge, had been ordained by Connecticut congregations in
the same year, 1685. By virtue of their ministerial positions they
were all influential men in the colony. In general, their lives do not
make exciting reading; nonetheless, they were strong men and could
act decisively. James Noyes, for example, had been present in April
1676 when the chief sachem of the Narragansetts was captured near
Pawtucket. The chief had been a warlike man and had made much
trouble for the settlers, so "Mr. Noyes . . . advised to despatch him
there and prevent all further evil consequences that might ensue
through his means." Thereupon the chief had been executed on the
spot as the good reverend watched.

The only founder who was much more than a simple minister
during his life was Gurdon Saltonstall. Governor Fitz-John Winthrop was a member of his congregation in New London. Saltonstall
became his closest adviser, and when Winthrop died in 1707, Saltonstall was elected to succeed him. As governor he assisted the college in every way he could until he died, still in office, in 1724.[18]

Most of the original trustees were from villages bordering Long
Island Sound, but three, Timothy Woodbridge, Samuel Mather, and
Noadiah Russell, were from towns on the Connecticut River. The
"sea-side" promoters of the venture appear to have intentionally
added "up-river" ministers to the board to make sure all parts of the
colony were represented in the new endeavor. But the inclusion of
up-river trustees was soon to lead to strife and the near destruction
of the college.[19]

When the trustees gathered in Saybrook for their first official
meeting they knew it was a historic moment. So they recorded at the
start of the minutes of the meeting—as their first official act—that
their fathers had come to America to plant and propagate "the
blessed Reformed, Protestant Religion," and that to perpetuate this
design a "Liberal and Relligious Education of Suitable youth" was
"a chief, and most probable expedient." Therefore they ordained
and appointed "that there shal, and hereby is Erected and formed a
Collegiate School, Wherein shal be taught the Liberal Arts, and
Languages."

Having set forth the reasons for founding the college, they moved
on to the details. They laid down rules for their proceedings and for
the college; selected Saybrook at the juncture of the Connecticut

River and Long Island Sound for the location of the institution because it was convenient to both the shore and river towns; established entrance requirements; elected Abraham Pierson as rector
(after Chauncy refused); ordered that "A Diploma or Licence for
Degrees of Batcheler or Master" be given in September each year;
and took care of many other lesser matters necessary to getting the
college started.[20]

In this way, at a four-day meeting which had begun on 11 November 1701, the Collegiate School that later became Yale College was
founded. It was the third college—after Harvard (1636) and William and Mary (1693)—to be established in England's American colonies. Yale has the second longest record for the continuous granting of degrees, since William and Mary was forced to close at least
twice.[21]

The new institution that came into the world in the fall of 1701
was hardly noticeable outside New England, just as the founders
wished. It was not an incorporated body but merely a group of partners or undertakers who, by the charter, had to be Connecticut ministers. As the Collegiate School, it had a "low" and somewhat ambig-
uous name. The head of the school was to be addressed as "rector,"
and while that was not an uncommon title in England and Scotland,
it did follow John Eliot's advice of earlier that fall: "As to the Title
of the Master of the said Scool . . . That which shows Least Grandeur will be Least obnoxious." [22]

This new and insignificant college was the product of two generations of hopes and dreams, but it was still little more than a proposal. The next few years would be critical in its struggle for life.

2

Wanderjahre

The task facing the trustees and the new rector was a staggering one: to build a college in a colony that was still largely wilderness. In all of Connecticut there were only about 30,000 people, living in widely separated communities scattered along the shore of Long Island Sound and up the Connecticut River. Nor were they a wealthy people. They had to struggle hard for whatever they had—farming the meager, rocky soil and trading their few products beyond their borders. To support a college they would have to sacrifice, but that they seemed willing to do. Many years before, when the New England Confederation had asked settlers to contribute a quarter bushel of wheat or its equivalent in money to Harvard, the people of New Haven and Connecticut had been more generous, proportionately, in giving this "college corn" than the citizens of the Massachusetts Bay Colony itself. And now, when chartering the Collegiate School, the General Assembly voted an annual subvention of £120 in country pay. Without this grant, one may wonder if the college could have begun at all.[1]

Private individuals, too, contributed to the new college, and thus began a cooperation of state and individuals which has continued throughout Yale's history. It cannot be stressed too much that the college has never been wholly a private institution. At first it was the beneficiary of aid from the colony and the people of Connecticut. Throughout the eighteenth century Connecticut's contribution amounted to more than one half the total gifts to the college. Gradually Yale became a national institution, until today it receives nearly a third of its income directly from the people of the United States through the Federal government. Since 1745 it has been indirectly subsidized, to one degree or another, by city, state, and nation through its exemption from taxation.[2]

But all that was in the future as Rector Pierson made his way from Saybrook over the rough trail that wandered through the woods, fields, and marshes of the shore to his home in Killingworth (now Clinton). Abraham Pierson had been elected rector after Israel

11

Chauncy, the youngest son of President Chauncy of Harvard, had rejected the position because of "His age And other Circumstances." [3] No doubt among Chauncy's considerations were the need to leave the comfortable circumstance of ministering to his congregation in Stratford, where he received steady pay, for the uncertainty of leading a scarcely existent and doubtfully financed college. Abraham Pierson at fifty-six was only a year younger than Chauncy, and he too must have hesitated over leaving his congregation under such circumstances.

The new rector had been born in 1645, probably in Southampton, Long Island, where his father was minister. The elder Pierson was an unbending man. When Southampton became part of Connecticut, he left. Believing that church and state should work more closely together than the laws of Connecticut provided, he moved his family to Branford in the New Haven Colony, where ideas congenial to his on the relationship of church and state prevailed.

Young Abraham Pierson was at Harvard when the New Haven Colony in its turn was absorbed by Connecticut and his father again chose to move to a more congenial place. Pierson senior and a large part of his Branford congregation went to Newark, New Jersey. There Abraham joined them after he graduated from Harvard in 1668. He studied with his father and in 1669 he was officially called by the Newark congregation to assist the older man. After his father's death in 1678 he became sole pastor of the congregation. But there must have been in Abraham Pierson the younger some of the same unwillingness to compromise that there was in the father, for, after some disagreement with his congregation, he was dismissed in 1692. He then returned to Connecticut and preached in Greenwich until called to Killingworth.

Unfortunately there are no portraits of Abraham Pierson. The statue that now stands in Clinton and the copy on the Old Campus at Yale are imaginative recreations. President Stiles was once told by a very old woman who had been only a child when Pierson died that "he was something taller than a middle size, a fleshy, well-favoured, and comely-looking man." And President Clap collected the information that he was "a hard Student, a good Scholar, a great Divine, and a wise, steady and judicious Gentleman." Whatever else Rector Pierson was, he was a practical man, as the attempts of his fellow trustees to get him to move to Saybrook from Killingworth clearly showed. [4]

When Pierson returned to his home, he carried a letter from the trustees asking Killingworth to dismiss their minister so he could move to Saybrook to conduct the college. To the town this was a most serious matter. When a minister was called, it was in the belief that he would remain for life, and thus a house and land were given him. Pierson, in the negotiations with the town that proceeded until his death, insisted that he would not leave his congregation unless he had their cordial support, clearly shown. That approval was to be indicated by their unanimity and, even more important, one feels, their willingness to buy back from him the house and lands they had given him. Naturally, some of his congregation balked at doing quite so much for him, so that practical Puritan refused to move. The result was that though both the trustees and the townspeople of Killingworth were discontented, Abraham Pierson kept his solid house, his pleasant fields, and his ministerial robes.[5]

These arguments over the intended move to Saybrook, accompanied by town demands that he give up the school, punctuated Pierson's entire term as rector, but despite them the little college began and prospered under his sensible rule. The first student, Jacob Heminway from East Haven, arrived at Rector Pierson's house in March 1702. He may have been the only student for the rest of that first academic year (which lasted into September), but tradition has it that he was joined toward the end of the year by Nathaniel Chauncey.[6] This young man had been raised and probably educated by his uncle, Israel Chauncy, one of the founders of the college. As compensation for this service, Israel got the use of his brother's library. Tradition further relates that when young Nathaniel was examined for the degree of Bachelor of Arts, he was found so well prepared that the trustees decided to give him his M.A. as well. Only a cynic would suggest that this might have been done to flatter his uncle—the trustee, founder, and son of a former president of Harvard. In addition, since Stephen Buckingham, also the son of a trustee, was getting his M.A. at the same ceremony, it may have been thought diplomatic to treat both young men alike.

In any case, Chauncey received his degree at the first commencement on Wednesday, 16 September 1702, at the home of the Reverend Mr. Buckingham in Saybrook. Following the rules of the college, the ceremony was small and private so that no unnecessary expense would be entailed by student, parent, or college. The trustees did not want the commencement to be like Harvard's, which had taken on the atmosphere of a great country fair—with the concomitant cost. The practical men of Connecticut wished to avoid both show and expense at their college ceremony.[7]

Along with Nathaniel Chauncey, four Harvard graduates received Master of Arts degrees.* Only Chauncey is listed as a Bachelor of Arts graduate—the first Yale graduate—in this class, since it is assumed that to have received the M.A. degree he must have been granted his B.A. as well. Chauncey's M.A. diploma, one of Yale's cherished possessions, is now in the University Archives.[8]

Immediately after commencement, the new school year began, for it was not the practice for some years to give the students any regular vacations. College kept throughout the year.[9]

During the second year several new students arrived to join Jacob Heminway at Rector Pierson's house. The first tutor was hired to assist the busy rector, and the first real B.A. was awarded to John Hart of Farmington. Hart had studied for two years at Harvard and then spent a year at the Collegiate School.[10] Under the first college rules, which lasted only a few years, he could receive his B.A. after three years of study. It was hoped that this, like the private commencements, would help to lower the cost of a college education. Hart was the lone graduate in 1703 and his B.A. diploma—probably the first —is also preserved in the archives of the University.[11]

Even before Hart graduated, the moment of peace during which the college had been founded came to an end when Queen Anne's War, or the War of the Spanish Succession as it was called in Europe, broke out in May 1702. This did not halt the growth of the college, however, and John Hart was appointed tutor immediately after his graduation.[12]

Because of the war and because the colony needed and valued educated men, the General Assembly in October 1703 passed a law exempting scholars in the Collegiate School from taxation and "watching and warding and all other such publick service." While these exemptions were customary rights in English colleges and had been granted in Harvard's charter of 1650, they had not been included in the Yale charter.[13]

With the assurance that its students would be able to continue

---

* These, then, were the first men to enjoy what President John F. Kennedy described as the happy circumstance of having the best of both worlds—a Harvard education and a Yale degree.

their education, the next few years were relatively quiet and prosperous for the little school. The students studied in the rector's house close by the Killingworth meetinghouse. Every day there were prayers morning and evening, and twice each Sunday the boys made their way up the small hill to the meetinghouse, whence they could see as they went in and out the rustling marsh grass and, at a small distance, the glinting waters of Long Island Sound.[14]

This quiet existence was broken by the sudden death of Abraham Pierson on 5 March 1707. Though the number of students had remained small, though there had been minor disciplinary problems, and though the people of Killingworth had grown increasingly annoyed by their minister's second job, none of these problems had become critical. The college would not, in fact, know such peace and prosperity again for almost two decades. President Clap rightly wrote of Abraham Pierson, "He instructed and governed the Infant College with general Approbation." The college would sorely miss his firm and practical guidance.

Abraham Pierson was buried within sight of his old meetinghouse in what remains a still, quiet spot. Not far from him lies his most famous student, Jared Eliot. Pierson's grave is marked with a small stone which reads

> Here lieth the
> Body of ye Rev^d
> Mr Abra^h Pierson
> The First Rector
> of ye colledge
> in Connecticut
> who deceased
> March ye 5th 1706/7
> Aged 61 years [15]

The trustees turned immediately to the necessary arrangements for continuing the college year. They selected one of their number, the Reverend Samuel Andrew of Milford, as rector *pro tempore,* and packed the seniors off to live and study with him until commencement. Andrew was the obvious choice for this position since he had been a tutor at Harvard and had been given charge of that college, with another tutor, after the sudden death of President Oakes. The lone tutor of the Collegiate School and the remainder of the students were sent to Saybrook, which from the first the trustees had intended as the location of the school.[16]

The seniors remained in Milford only until commencement in 1707 and thereafter all the students seem to have resided in Saybrook. This is uncertain, however, for very little information survives about this period in the history of the college.[17] We do not even know the school's exact location in Saybrook. The scholars seem to have boarded around the town, and the tutors may have done the same. It is also possible that the tutors lived and held classes in a house given to the college by its first treasurer, Nathaniel Lynde.[18] It is the approximate location of this house that is now marked by a stone near the old burying ground on Saybrook Point. But those who return to this spot seeking some feeling for the old college will have to use a great deal of imagination, for Saybrook moved, as did the Collegiate School, and the town green and the old houses are gone. All that exists to remind one of the past is the cemetery, a few names, such as Church Street, and the geography of the area: the neck of land leading to the point remains, marsh is still visible, and the water of the Connecticut River continues to lap on three sides.

The years the Collegiate School spent in Saybrook were not happy ones. At first the difficulties of the situation were probably eased by the presence of the Reverend Mr. Buckingham, whose house was nearby and whose meetinghouse the boys attended. But Buckingham died in 1709 and Saybrook called to fill his place Azariah Mather, son of the always absent, somewhat demented trustee. Young Mather, a graduate of the college in 1705, was a tutor when he was selected to minister to the town. Clearly, he could not replace for the college the age and experience of Buckingham.[19]

Mather had been junior tutor with Phineas Fiske (B.A. 1704), who was a tutor from 1706 to 1713 and whose relatively long term of service in that position gave some stability and continuity to the college. When Fiske departed—still with no full-time rector appointed —the college entered on an even more perilous period. Though the class of 1714 with nine members was the largest to graduate until 1718, the class of 1715 amounted to only three. With such a small number of students and lacking a resident rector, the college struggled to survive.[20]

One auspicious event did occur, however, to brighten these dark days. Early in September 1714 the news came to Saybrook that nine boxes of books for the college had arrived in Boston. These were the first shipment of over 800 volumes that Jeremiah Dummer had collected in England, many from the authors themselves, for the college.

Dummer, a Harvard graduate in the class of 1699, was the agent of Massachusetts and Connecticut in England. First employed by the Collegiate School to pursue its interest in the Hopkins estate, he felt it necessary to advise the college to drop the case, since he feared a court fight might eat up what remained of the legacy. Perhaps to counterbalance that bitter pill, he began to seek donations of books —and possibly money as well—for the college. It was Dummer who first suggested, in 1711, that "Mr. Yale" might profitably be approached on the subject of giving to the school. Mr. Yale did give a few books at this time, as did Isaac Newton and Richard Steele, who contributed their own works.

The importance of the Dummer collection to the college was immeasurable. One student who graduated in 1714 said that the library prior to Dummer's gift contained only books "100 or 150 years old such as the first settlers of the country brought with them." The Dummer books added works by Boyle, Locke, Newton, Halley, Raleigh, Steele, Chaucer, Milton, and Bacon, among others. As one historian has said, "The collection included practically all of the important current books on medicine and philosophy, and representative works on science and in history and literature." [21]

This splendid acquisition, which gave Yale in some ways the finest library in New England, seemed to signify an upturning in the affairs of the college. It was offset shortly thereafter, however, by the death of James Pierpont. Franklin B. Dexter, whose years of work on the early history and graduates of the college give authority to his words, called Pierpont "the most earnest promoter of the scheme" for the college. Dexter considered it "not unlikely that, if he had been spared a few years longer, the course of our history would have run more smoothly." [22] The evidence seems to support this conclusion. Pierpont appears to have been the first among equals on the Board of Trustees, and without his guidance that group began to disintegrate into factions.*

---

* It is unfortunate that Yale has never seen fit to create a distinguished memorial to James Pierpont, the founder of Yale. One might, in fact, even call him its progenitor,

The proximate cause of the differences among the trustees that now surfaced and that were soon to come close to destroying the college completely seems to have been a grant of money from Connecticut. In 1714 the General Assembly had refused to provide any money for a new building that was needed to house both the students and the books received from Dummer; but in 1715 the Assembly found an easy way to vote funds. In the settlement of a dispute with Massachusetts, Connecticut received 100,000 acres of land. The General Assembly then voted to give the college £500 from the proceeds of the sale of this land. Fortunately, no one realized that the colony would receive only £683—a ridiculously low price even in 1715—for the whole parcel, or the Assembly might not have been so generous.[23]

Nevertheless, when the trustees met in April 1716, it was with the knowledge that they would soon receive £500. The expenditure of that sum on a house in Saybrook would tend to establish the college there permanently. The trustees also had to deal with disorders among the students who claimed that their tutors were so young and inexperienced that they could get better instruction nearer their homes. The students had a point. The tutors were only twenty-one and twenty-two years old and had only one and two years' experience.[24]

There is no record of the discussions among the trustees at this meeting, but we know that they decided to build a house for the college, a house for a rector as well, and to hire a resident rector at a salary of £100 a year. The trustees also voted to hire a third tutor and to allow the seniors to finish their studies elsewhere. Unfortunately, the other students chose to interpret this vote as applying to all classes, and they too departed for more pleasant places. Thus it may have appeared to some observers that the Collegiate School was well on the road to complete disintegration.[25]

In these circumstances the two Hartford trustees, Reverend Timothy Woodbridge, one of the original trustees, and Reverend Thomas Buckingham, who had been recently elected to the board and who was a nephew of the founder of the same name, in May submitted to the General Assembly a petition signed by many peo-

---

for his great grandson, his great, great grandson, and his great, great, great grandson were all distinguished presidents of Yale: Timothy Dwight, Theodore Dwight Woolsey, and the second Timothy Dwight.

ple from the Hartford area. This document stated that the college was about to fail completely and that the people of Hartford were ready to finance the school fully if the General Assembly would "fix" it in Hartford.[26]

It is questionable whether the General Assembly had the right to "fix" the college anywhere, but upon receipt of this petition that body called upon the trustees to meet in Hartford on Wednesday, 23 May 1716.[27] The other trustees seem to have had no warning of what Woodbridge and Buckingham were up to. Since the college was soon to receive £500 and they had just recently voted to build in Saybrook, they must have been somewhat surprised to hear the opinion that the college was about to fail completely.

Six of the trustees met in Hartford on the twenty-third and voted that the General Assembly should do nothing immediately, that the trustees should try to reach a unanimous decision, and, if they failed, that the General Assembly at its October meeting should name a place for the college to settle.[28] Then the trustees went home and a spirited competition began among the residents of Hartford, Saybrook, and New Haven to raise money to help attract the college to their community.

On 12 September 1716 the last commencement was held in Saybrook and three young men received B.A. degrees. The trustees met the same day to try to decide the crucial question of the location of the college. A series of votes was taken and only Woodbridge and Buckingham favored Hartford. Only those two opposed New Haven. It was then decided to meet in New Haven in October to attempt to reach a final—and, they hoped, unanimous—decision, but Woodbridge and Buckingham even voted against this. They had embarked on a course of opposition and harassment which would nearly wreck the college.[29]

The trustees reconvened in New Haven on 17 October and held a series of meetings during the next few days. The first formal vote taken was on the question whether they should settle in New Haven, since it was a convenient location and had made "the Most Liberal Donations" to the college. Four trustees favored this alternative; one approved if the college did not stay in Saybrook; Woodbridge and Buckingham opposed it.

Since the trustees were divided, we may assume that the next few days saw a good deal of jockeying, many meetings with members of the General Assembly, which was then in session, and numerous attempts to settle upon a place. In a sense, the trustees who favored New Haven triumphed in this politicking, for the General Assembly did not name a location for the college. Buckingham and Woodbridge were not persuaded to drop their opposition to New Haven, but the group that favored that town moved ahead with their plans. Although the students were scattered during the school year 1716–17, with fourteen in Wethersfield, four in Saybrook, and thirteen in New Haven, the decision was made to hold commencement in New Haven.[30]

Despite the fact that it was the largest town in Connecticut, New Haven was a very small place then. In 1748 it would still be possible to make a map of the place and label most of the houses, while as late as 1761 the population would be only 1,500. The main public building in 1716, and for forty years thereafter, was the old, square, unpainted, wooden meetinghouse on the Green. Also on the Green were the graveyard, the jail, the shelter for the night watch, and the grammar school. All in all, the Green was not a very pretty place with its rustic buildings, rotting tree stumps, and even a small swamp. Nevertheless, it was the center of the town, and here, in the ramshackle meetinghouse, the first New Haven commencement of the college was held on 11 September 1717.[31]

No description of that ceremony has come down to us, but if it was like the other early commencements the following account may not wander too far from the truth.[32] Though the service was now public, the crowd probably was not large—some neighboring ministers, as many trustees (not opposed to the move) as could come, perhaps a few members of the colonial government, parents and other relatives, and any holders of B.A. or M.A. degrees who were interested. The ceremony began with a prayer. Then the audience was greeted by George Griswold, a candidate for the bachelor's degree, who delivered in Latin the salutatory oration.[33] This was followed by syllogistic disputations, also in Latin, by the candidates for the first degree on such esoteric subjects as "The universe is not infinite, but extends indefinitely." [34]

After the Bachelors disputed, the audience went out for lunch, but soon all were back to see the Masters perform. These were young men who had taken the bachelor's degree (and thus were called "Sir"), lived godly lives for at least three years, and were now going to show the knowledge they had acquired since receiving the B.A. In later years, the M.A. was given automatically on application three years after graduation to any alumnus who had merely avoided conduct of which the college authorities disapproved. But the requirements had not yet become so minimal. Most graduates studied divinity after college; all who applied for the M.A. were supposed to present "a written synopsis either of logick or naturall phylosophy or metaphysicks as also a Common place on some Divinity thesis" and solve several problems posed by the rector; and at commencement they had to demonstrate their advanced knowledge in response to Quaestiones similar in nature to the B.A. Theses of the morning but treating more important and complex subjects.[35]

After the Masters of Arts were finished, Rector *pro tem* Samuel Andrew turned to the trustees and said in Latin (for the whole ceremony was in that language) something like, "Reverend Ministers, I present to you these youths, whom I know to be sufficient in learning as in manners to be raised to the First [or Second] Degree in Arts. Doth it please you?" This question in Latin was "Placetne vobis," to which the trustees replied, "Placet, placet." Then the rector gave the degrees by saying, still in Latin, "I admit thee to the First Degree in Arts and I hand thee this book, together with the power to lecture publicly on any one of the Arts which thou hast studied, whensoever thou shalt have been called to that office." When the rector came to the words "this book," he handed them a volume, which they handed right back. Diplomas were not, at first, presented at the ceremony, but were given a month or so later. By 1737, however, a Harvard graduate reported after viewing the Yale ceremony, "The Custom of giving Diploma at the time of giving the Degree is most fit and proper in my Eye and what I could wish our College would come to." [36]

After the degrees were conferred, one of the new Masters of Arts delivered "a grateful and pathetic Valediction to all the Members of the Society" and a closing prayer was pronounced. Thus ended the ceremony, a direct descendant of the procedures of the Middle Ages.[37]

The dispute over the location of the college continued: at the same time that four young men received the B.A. in New Haven, one lonely soul, Isaac Burr, was taking his first degree in Wethersfield from the unbending Mr. Woodbridge.[38] But the New Haven trustees, undaunted by his perseverance, on 26 September 1717 purchased from the New Haven congregation a lot given to it by Mrs. Hester Coster. For £26 in bills of credit, which were worth about ten shillings sterling on the pound, the college got an acre and a quarter facing the Green at the corner of Chapel and College Streets (though they were still unnamed then) where Bingham Hall now stands. And on 8 October the building of the college's first real house began.[39] Since the death of Abraham Pierson over ten years before, the college's site and sometimes its very existence had been uncertain. Now at last it must have seemed that the wanderings and divisions and uncertainties were almost over. A majority of the trustees had bought land and begun to build; surely, all would now unite to push the Collegiate School forward.

3

The College Gets a Name

If the trustees who favored New Haven expected that all opposition would cease after holding a commencement and beginning the construction of a house for the college, they were sadly mistaken. The General Assembly, which tended to favor the up-river trustees, was angered by what it felt was the New Haven group's failure to consult before acting. When the legislature met in New Haven on 10 October 1717, the lower house called the trustees to appear before it to show the reasons for their proceedings "and Particularly Why they or any of them Have Ordered a Collegiate School to be Built at New Haven, without the Allowance or Knowledge of This Assembly."

Fortunately, the college's good friend Gurdon Saltonstall was now governor. He and the upper house replaced this angry blast with a more temperate request for the trustees to meet in town so the Assembly could "better contribute to the procuring of that Generall Satisfaction Relating to so good a work which is so much desired."

So again all the trustees, including even Woodbridge and Buckingham, met in New Haven to try to settle their differences. Again they failed. Each side then presented its case before a joint session of the General Assembly and, finally, after further bickering, politicking, and voting, the General Assembly—perhaps in exhaustion—on 31 October told the trustees to go ahead in New Haven.[1]

The victorious trustees reported to their active agent Jeremiah Dummer in London:

The affair of our School hath been in a Condition of Pregnancy. Painfull with a witness have been the Throwes thereof in this General Assembly. But we just now hear that after the Violent Pangs threatning the Very life of the Babe, Divine Providence as a kind Obstetrix hath mercifully brought the Babe into the World, and behold a Man-child is born, whereat We all Rejoyce.[2]

But their troubles were not yet over. Some of the students remained in Wethersfield, while the people of Saybrook insisted that the college could not legally move and, to force its return, refused to give up the college library. In the meantime, however, another event of more lasting importance occurred in England.

Jeremiah Dummer and the trustees still hoped that wealthy old Elihu Yale would do something for the college which had now moved to the town his grandmother, father, and uncle had helped to settle.* On 14 January 1718, at the behest of either Rector Andrew or Governor Saltonstall, Cotton Mather, who was ever a friend of the Collegiate School because of his feuds with Harvard, wrote to Yale to encourage him to give a large gift to the college. Mather held out the hope that they might name their new building after Yale and said that this would better commemorate him "than an Egyptian pyramid." Dummer was at work, too. Two months later he wrote to Governor Saltonstall, "I am endeavouring to get you a Present from Mr. Yale for the finishing your Colledge [building]." [3]

While this courting of Elihu Yale dragged on, Woodbridge and Buckingham continued to fight against New Haven as the location of the college. They refused to attend trustees meetings and appear to have persisted in their attempts to get the General Assembly to fix the site on the Connecticut River. But these endeavors were in part defeated by the events taking place in London. Mr. Yale, who had made a large fortune while in the employ of the East India Company and especially as governor of Madras, decided to make a sizable gift to the college. He packed up some possessions, shipped them off to Boston, and in late August there arrived at that port a large box of books, a portrait of King George I by Kneller (still in the possession of the University), and East India goods inventoried at £200 that the college sold in Boston for £562.12. [4]

Yale, a good Church of England man, had been doubtful about giving to an academy of dissenters. But Dummer finally convinced him "that the buisness of good men is to spread religion and learning among mankind without being too fondly attached to particular Tenets, about which the World never was, nor ever will be agreed." [5] The trustees would hardly have accepted that philosophy, but that did not dampen their happiness over the gift.

Their first step was to honor Elihu Yale. The new building, now practically finished, was to be used during the commencement exer-

* Jonathan Edwards College now stands on land that once belonged to David Yale, Elihu's father.

cises that September; Yale's beneficence and the completion of the hall were celebrated at the same time. But exactly what the trustees did, or thought they were doing, is now difficult to reconstruct. They seem to have decided rather hastily to call the Collegiate School Yale College, for they replaced the combined Theses and Catalogue that had already been printed for commencement with a new edition in which the name Yale College was used instead of Collegiate School.[6] Thus on first sight it appears that they named the college after Elihu Yale at this time; but like so much of early Yale history, this is uncertain. The only official vote of the trustees on the subject, taken at the annual meeting on commencement morning, says that "our College House . . . shall be named Yale-College," clearly designating only the building. But later in the meeting they referred to "our Collegiate School, which we have named Yale Colledge"; when they wrote to Governor Yale to thank him, they called the institution the Collegiate School; and they told Cotton Mather they had named the building Yale College.[7]

This confusing situation lasted for some time. As early as the October meeting of 1718, the General Assembly passed "An Act for the Encouragement of Yale College," but as late as 30 December 1719 the First Church in New Haven called it the Collegiate School. The trustees of the college rather avoided the subject, though they did mention in 1719 Rector Cutler's "service in Yale College." But not until 20 April 1720 did the trustees note at the head of their minutes that they were "the Trustees of Yale College." Probably the trustees intended to call only the structure Yale College, but it was almost inevitable when there was only one college building that its name should have become that of the institution.[8]

Commencement that summer of 1718 was a joyful occasion. The trustees, Governor Saltonstall, Honorable Colonel Tailer of Boston, who was representing Governor Yale, the whole Superior Court of the colony, and "a great number of Learned Men" gathered in the "Large and Splendid Hall" of the imposing new wooden edifice and proceeded, as the trustees informed Yale, to designate it "Yale-Colledge, and read off a Memorial of it in the Lattin Tongue, and also a Memorial of the Same in the English Tongue, answered with a Counterpart in Lattin, which Coll. Tayler was pleased to say was very agreeable to him representing your Honour."

The trustees and all the guests then marched in procession, with wigs and robes flowing in the breeze, to the meetinghouse on the Green where eight received Bachelor of Arts degrees and two, Master of Arts. Nothing could have been more fitting than that the namesake of that first of founders, James Pierpont, gave the salutatory oration and received his B.A.

After the addresses of Governor Saltonstall and the Reverend Mr. Davenport (a grandson of the founder of New Haven and by then a trustee of the college), the trustees and their honored guests returned to Yale College, where the "gentlemen . . . were Entertained with a Splendid Dinner [in the hall] and The Ladies . . . were also Entertained in the Library," except for that gay dog Colonel Tailer, who "was pleased to seat himself at the Table of the Ladies." The great day came to a close with the singing of Psalm 65, "Thy praise alone, O Lord, doth reign in Sion Thine own hill." [9]

On the same day a commencement was also held in Wethersfield, where the opposition still held out. Five young men received the B.A. degree from Timothy Woodbridge. They were, strange to say, a peculiarly unfortunate group. So many died young that their average age at death was thirty-four. The New Haven graduates of the same year had an average age at death of sixty-four—a statistic that would have provided a Puritan minister with material for a strong sermon.[10]

The General Assembly, meeting in New Haven in October 1718, tried again to resolve the dispute between the Woodbridge faction and the New Haven men. It passed "An Act for the Encouragement of Yale College," which attempted to end all opposition to the placing of the college in New Haven: among other things, it tried to assuage the anger of Hartford and Saybrook by voting money for the building of a new statehouse in Hartford and a school in Saybrook; it also guaranteed the right of every Wethersfield graduate to a Yale degree.[11]

This legislation did not immediately accomplish its purpose. When Governor Saltonstall heard that the students were still at Wethersfield, he ordered the act to be published in that town, for it contained the words, "it is ordered that the Scholars at Weathersfield come down to the School at Newhaven." Under this pressure, in the last week of November 1718, the Wethersfield students moved to New Haven.[12]

In the meantime, shortly after the passage of the act, the trustees tried to get the college's books from Saybrook—only to be refused.

Again Saltonstall moved to aid the college. He convened his council in Saybrook and arrested Daniel Buckingham, son of the founder, who was holding the library in his house. The council ordered Buckingham to hand over the books; he refused; and it was necessary to break down the door of his house and forcibly remove the volumes to carts that were waiting to carry them to New Haven. Unfortunately, Buckingham's actions were not based merely on personal anger. That he was supported by the townspeople of Saybrook was shown when, as a contemporary described it,

in the night the Carts were broken and confounded and [the] oxen turned away; nevertheless they made new provision and the next day under the Major of the County's Conduct they were transported out of Town, and some of the opposers that talked sausily were bound over to the next County Court. The books though they met with opposition by the way in that some of the bridges were broken up yet in 3 days they arrived at the Colledg at N. Haven . . . but we found about 260 wanting; however all we had being above 1000 vollums of choice books we fixed up in order in the Library.[13]

At last the books and all the students were in New Haven—but this happy circumstance was not to last long. The Wethersfield students disliked Tutor Samuel Johnson (B.A. 1714), later first president of King's College (Columbia). Perhaps encouraged in their dislike by the continuing opposition of those stubborn Hartford trustees, Timothy Woodbridge and Thomas Buckingham, early in January the Wethersfield group returned to that town and the more satisfactory teaching of Elisha Williams, leaving only seventeen scholars in the large new building in New Haven. Again the governor, who must have been fed up with the whole affair, intervened. He called his council to meet in New Haven and asked the college trustees to join them there. Woodbridge and Buckingham refused to attend, but most of the other trustees were present. The governor pointed out to the trustees that since the colonial government had founded the college (a point which would be much disputed by President Clap but was not now in question), it felt it should settle whatever difficulties prevented an end to the divisions in the college. The problem now seemed to center on Tutor Samuel Johnson, and the trustees admitted that though he had "sufficient learning," they were trying to get Reverend Timothy Cutler to come over from Stratford and serve as resident rector *pro tem*. The council approved this course and thought it would "prove a good means to put an end

to the contentions." Within two weeks Cutler had taken over and
the Wethersfield students had decided to return to New Haven.[14]

The last act in the long fight among the trustees over where the
college should be situated took place in May 1719. Because Governor Saltonstall had played—and continued to play—a leading role
in fixing the college in New Haven, "a powerful party to defeat his
re-election" was formed. They planned to elect Buckingham and
Woodbridge deputies for the town of Hartford and to replace Saltonstall with Deputy Governor Gold. But Saltonstall thwarted the
cabal, Buckingham refused to sit in the General Assembly (perhaps
out of fear), and formal charges were presented in the lower house
"against Mr. Woodbridge for defamation of the Governor and Council." The conquest of the plotters was complete when the Assembly
voted an extra grant of £40 a year to the college for the next seven
years.[15]

The rout of Woodbridge and Buckingham marked the end of the
schism. Soon afterward the Wethersfield students returned to New
Haven for good. Even more significantly, Woodbridge and Buckingham came to the annual meeting of the trustees on 9 September
1719. It was the first meeting they had attended since October
1717.* The new situation at the college was described by Jonathan
Edwards, who had been one of the Wethersfield students, in a letter
to his father written soon after the return to New Haven:

I take very great content under my present tuition, as all the rest of the
scholars seem to do under theirs. Mr. Cutler is extraordinarily courteous
to us, has a very good spirit of government, keeps the school in excellent
order, seems to increase in learning, is loved and respected by all who are
under him.

The troubles of the struggling college seemed to be over. It had a
rector who was respected by the students and who was made permanent in September 1719; its students and trustees were reunited; it
had the finest new building in Connecticut; its financial problems
seemed to be solved by the Yale gift and the increased colonial
grant.[16] But catastrophe was about to strike from a new and entirely
unexpected direction.

---

* It is ironic that of all the founding trustees (barring Pierson, who is memorialized
because he was rector), it is Woodbridge who is commemorated by a building at Yale.

Ichabod

Timothy Cutler, the new rector, was only thirty-five years old. He had been born in 1684 in Charlestown, Massachusetts, and was graduated from Harvard at the young age of seventeen in the same year that the Collegiate School was founded. Several years later some of the leading ministers of New England selected him to defend the faith in Stratford, Connecticut, where lived a group of Anglicans who had seduced his predecessor away from the orthodox faith. A determined, intelligent, persuasive young man was wanted to be the Congregational minister in the town, and Cutler seemed to fit that description. But Cutler also had great intellectual curiosity, especially in the field of theology, and this led him to the Anglican books in the Yale library, which either began or increased his secret doubts about Congregationalism. Thus when the trustees approached him to take over the college (probably at the suggestion of his father-in-law, Rector *pro tem* Samuel Andrew), Timothy Cutler may have been looking for a way out of his ministry or possibly even a position from which to undermine the established religion of the colony.

Despite his doubts about Congregationalism, Cutler was an immediate success in his new job. The college prospered under his direction. According to Clifford Shipton, he continued the teaching of Newton and Locke, begun under Tutor Samuel Johnson, which made Yale's "instruction in the new science and philosophy better than anything Mother Harvard could offer." [1] Not only were the students content, but so were the trustees and the General Assembly. The start of Cutler's first full school year in October 1719 (for the students now received a month's vacation after the September commencement) found thirty-five or forty students on hand.[2] And though there were intimations of that anti-intellectualism that has ever been an element of American life—as when the election sermon of 1721 noted that there was "too great a spirit of learning in the land; more are brought up to it than will be needed or find improvement" [3]—this does not seem to have been indicative of the true feeling of Connecticut. More representative was the General Assembly's exemption of Rector Cutler from taxation (it would take them eleven years to do the same for Elisha Williams), and the enactment of an impost on "rhum" for two years to pay for the building of a house for the rector. On top of that the parishes of the colony contributed £100 for the rector's house and in 1722 the colony added a further grant for the same purpose. The result of all these donations was a fine building on what is now called College Street, south of Chapel (about where the College Street Cinema now stands). This second Yale building was to serve as the domicile of the heads of the college from 1722 to 1799.[4]

Cutler's short term as rector was also marked by the receipt of another gift from Elihu Yale (worth about £100 sterling) and the death of that great benefactor of the college shortly afterward on 8 July 1721. Unfortunately, Yale had not yet sent "a present which he has bin long getting ready of Instruments, books, and pictures," so these were lost to the college. He had also said he would give the college £200 a year, but Dummer had warned in March 1721, "I am afraid lest being old he should dye and neglect it."

Jeremiah Dummer predicted correctly. Elihu Yale left only a rough draft of a will when he died, so that even the £500 he intended to leave to "Connecticote College" never reached it. Though Dummer attempted during the next few years to get the money for the college from the estate or the heirs, he failed.[5]

In the light of Elihu Yale's great wealth (his wedding gift to his daughter amounted to over £20,000) and the enormous benefactions the college received in other centuries, many have thought Yale bought his memorial rather cheaply. While the value of his gifts and the purchasing power of the money realized is hard to determine, it seems clear that he gave the college more at one time than any other private group or individual until well into the nineteenth century. Connecticut gave the college more in total during the entire century, and Dean Berkeley and his friends (whose generous donations will be discussed in the next chapter) perhaps gave more in value, but none gave cash—or its equivalent—to such an amount at one time. And to the struggling, impecunious college the propitious timing of Governor Yale's largest gift was most important.

Not only did the college's great benefactor die during Cutler's term, but Cutler presided at the commencement of one of Yale's greatest graduates, Jonathan Edwards (B.A. 1720), whom Perry Miller, excellent historian and biographer of Edwards, has called "one of America's five or six major artists," a "unique, an aboriginal and monolithic power." Edwards received the largest part of his college education in Wethersfield, but this does not qualify Yale's claim to him. The New Haven group always recognized the Wethersfield graduates as its own, and the "Act for the Encouragement of Yale College" of 1719 transformed their resolve into law. In addition, Edwards's teacher in Wethersfield, Elisha Williams, succeeded Cutler as rector of Yale College.[6]

While Timothy Cutler's term in office was marked by a welcome end to the divisions among the trustees, a short period of progress and stability, good relations with the colony, the graduation of Jonathan Edwards, and the death of Elihu Yale, his rectorate is best known for his departure from the college.

During the spring of 1722, as construction proceeded on the rector's new house, a disquieting rumor began to circulate. On 28 May Joseph Morgan (who had only recently received an honorary M.A. from the college and thus felt a bit guilty about relaying such gossip) informed Yale's old friend Cotton Mather, "I hear some in Conecticut complain that Arminian Books are cryed up in Yale Colledge for Eloquence and Learning and Calvinists despised for the contrary; and none have the courage to see it redressed." [7] In eighteenth-century New England, Arminianism was a favorite bogy that constantly frightened the orthodox. In its pure form, Arminians (followers of the Dutch theologian Jacob Arminius) believed that man could do something to effect his own salvation. To Puritans this idea was anathema. Only God by his predestined decree could bring about man's redemption. In fact, in this pure form few ministers of any sort in New England were Arminians. Instead, the term was usually used in an imprecise sense by New Englanders to mean any leaning toward Anglicanism (which, it is true, leaned in turn toward Arminianism).[8]

While it is doubtful that any at Yale College were true Arminians, that something was seriously wrong there soon became clear. On 12 September 1722 Rector Cutler closed the commencement proceedings—one of the colony's great public events of the year— with the customary prayer, but he repeated at the end of it words from the Anglican form: *and let all the people say, amen.* Consternation! Rumors. Meetings. The next day a dinner was held and the truth emerged. The rector, several ministers from nearby towns, and the tutor confessed that they either doubted "the validity of Presbyterial ordination in opposition to Episcopal ordination" or were convinced that presbyterial ordination was invalid.[9]

This was an earth-shaking pronouncement. No exact parallel can suggest the shock this statement must have given its auditors, but it was something like what might be expected if the current president and faculty of Yale and the leading citizens of several towns around New Haven were all to announce suddenly that some had decided and others were close to deciding that Russian communism was superior to the American economic and political system.

What the rector and his associates had done was even worse than introducing unorthodoxy in the form of Arminianism. Instead, by doubting that any of the New England ministers were legitimately ordained, they had struck at the very basis of the churches and thus at the very structure of society. They had raised the specter of all the area's ministers having to be ordained by Anglican bishops, hence introducing that hated system into their holy community. Two of the trustees reported their reaction in a letter written in graphic eighteenth-century prose replete with Biblical imagery:

How is the gold become dim! and the silk become dross. and the wine mixt with water! . . . But who could have conjectured, that its name being raised to Collegium Yalense from Gymnasium Saybrookense, it should groan out Ichabod in about three years and an half under its second rector, so unlike the first.[10]

The trustees were stunned by this incredible happening. So they temporized. They asked the seven—Rector Timothy Cutler and Tutor Daniel Browne (B.A. 1714) from Yale, and John Hart (B.A. 1702), Samuel Whittelsey (B.A. 1705), Jared Eliot (B.A. 1706), James Wetmore (B.A. 1714), and Samuel Johnson (B.A. 1714), all ministers from nearby towns—to repeat their declaration in writing and to meet with them again when the governor and his council were in New Haven for the convening of the General Assembly in October.[11]

In the interim, the trustees tried to prepare themselves to reply to the questioners. Joseph Webb wrote to Cotton Mather (who knew everything) to ask his advice on how best to meet their arguments.

Others probably rushed to their libraries to study the matter. The problem was that, while in the seventeenth century their forefathers had known and used various justifications for their form of ordination, there had been no real challenge to the New England ministers and these defenses had fallen into disrepair. Nor could they be reconstructed in a moment.[12]

When the trustees and the turncoats met on 16 October, Governor Saltonstall presided. The apostates continued in their course, and their recent studies in the new books in the Yale library—for that *was* the source of their challenge to New England orthodoxy—had prepared them far better than their opponents. As a result the meeting degenerated into name-calling by some of the trustees, and the excellent governor was soon forced to adjourn it.[13]

So it was that the following day, having failed to change Rector Cutler's mind, the trustees fired him and accepted the resignation of Tutor Browne. Ultimately Cutler and Browne, along with Samuel Johnson and James Wetmore, went to England to be ordained in the Church of England. The others, John Hart, Samuel Whittelsey, and Jared Eliot, having somehow brought themselves to accept their ordination as valid, were able to return to the fold and to respectability.[14] But Yale College, though the apostates had been turned out, was in a bad way. Public confidence in the institution had been badly shaken and, perhaps even worse, the college was again without a rector. Cutler had been a good one and the history of the college to this point clearly revealed that rectors of any kind were hard to come by.

Ezra Stiles, who may have known Timothy Cutler and whose father was a student of his and a graduate in the tumultuous year of 1722, wrote an excellent description of Yale's second full-time rector:

Rector Cutler was an excellent linguist—he was a great Hebrician and Orientalist. He had more knowledge of the Arabic than, I believe, any man ever in New England before him, except President Chauncy and his disciple the first Mr. Thatcher. Dr. Cutler was a good logician, geographer, and rhetorician. In the philosophy and metaphysics and ethics of his day or juvenile education he was great. He spoke Latin with fluency and dignity and with great propriety of pronunciation. He was a noble Latin orator. . . . He was of a commanding presence and dignity in government. He was a man of extensive reading in the academic sciences, divinity, and ecclesiastical history. He was of a high, lofty, and despotic mien. He made a grand figure as the head of a College.[15]

Now the trustees had to find a replacement for this imposing man. And they wanted to be particularly careful to find someone about whom there was no possible hint of heresy. They also tried to be sure that only the orthodox ever became officers of the college, voting that all persons elected to the office of rector or tutor must assent to the Saybrook Confession of Faith and "particularly give Satisfaction to them [the trustees] of the Soundness of their Faith in opposition to Armenian [*sic*] and prelaitical Corruptions or any other of Dangerous Consequence to the Purity and Peace of our Churches." In addition, they agreed to have "some meet Persons" fill the place of rector for a month at a time until their next meeting.[16]

But if they expected to replace Cutler in a short time, they were sadly mistaken. For the next several years the college failed in its pursuit of a rector. One trustee even approached Cotton Mather about the job, but apparently he had no interest in it. Fortunately, the college was firmly enough established that the absence of a permanent rector, though by no means a happy circumstance, was scarcely the problem it had been in earlier years. The college had some sixty students in residence each year and the graduating class of 1726, whose entire career in college was spent under temporary rectors, was the largest class to graduate from Yale up to that time.[17]

The year 1723 was marked by two events of widely varying significance for the college: a Yale graduate was scalped and killed near Rutland, Massachusetts—the first to die in such a manner—and "An Act in explanation of and Addition to the Act for erecting a Collegiate School" was passed by the colonial legislature. No doubt the scalping of Joseph Willard (B.A. 1714) went unnoticed by Yale at the time, but it serves as a useful reminder of the degree to which New England was still wild country.[18] On the other hand, the trustees were certainly aware of the passage of the explanatory act, but they chose not to adopt it.

The act seems to have been drafted by Governor Saltonstall in response to various questions asked by the trustees about their powers under the original charter. It provided that a trustee could resign and that a successor could be chosen for an incapacitated trustee

(Samuel Mather was still a trustee though he had been unable to attend a meeting in twenty-two years), indicated the number of trustees needed to make a quorum, lowered the age limit for trustees from forty to thirty, and made the rector a trustee *ex officio*. For some reason the trustees did not officially accept this act until 1728, though they did replace Samuel Mather in May 1724. It seems likely that the trustees were irritated that their request for information resulted in unasked-for legislation.[19]

The explanatory act was the last contribution of Gurdon Saltonstall to Yale College. The governor died in September 1724 after having done as much for the college during its difficult early years as all but a few others. He had helped to found it, assisted in raising money for it, been perhaps the chief agent in ending the divisions among the trustees over its location, secured the library from Saybrook, and clarified the original charter.[20]

When Saltonstall died the college still did not have a resident rector. In fact, not until 1726, after four formal elections and four rejections, either for personal reasons or because the candidates' congregations would not dismiss them, did Yale get a new rector. This was Elisha Williams, who had been the very successful head of the college Woodbridge and Buckingham promoted at Wethersfield. Williams was first approached in 1725 about the position, and he was willing to take it. Equally important, his congregation at Newington was willing to release him if they were reimbursed for the money they had spent on their pastor. After a good deal of dickering, the General Assembly voted to free the town of taxation for four years and to pay them £100 for their loss; the college also promised to pay them £100, and the town finally agreed to release Williams.[21]

The man who was inducted 13 September 1726 was at just thirty-two years the youngest man ever to lead Yale at any time in its history, but he brought to the college "an Active Genius" and experience as a teacher, minister, and representative in the General Assembly, where for four years he had served as clerk as well. Of even greater importance to the trustees, he was solidly orthodox. According to Clifford Shipton, biographer of Harvard graduates (Williams was class of 1711), the new rector was firmly attached to Calvinism because its logic appealed to the legal cast of his mind: "It was the grim God of unalterable law which he preached, not the God of

love of the older ministers and of his fathers." [22] Nothing could have
been more pleasing to the trustees—and to the many others who
feared that New England orthodoxy was on the decline—than the
election of such a man.

The Solid Accomplishments of Elisha Williams

The years from 1726 to 1739 saw the first extended period of progress in the history of the college. Free for a time from conflict and crisis, it grew steadily in strength, size, and stability under the wise direction of Rector Elisha Williams and the constant support of the colony. Williams made sure that the college provided a decent education to the young students, who came largely from Connecticut and western Massachusetts; the Connecticut General Assembly supplied generous infusions of cash to help make it all possible.[1]

The growth of Yale and the assistance provided by Connecticut may be seen by looking at the college finances. When Elisha Williams took over in 1726 he was paid a salary of £140 a year; the college had receipts of £263 (of which the colony provided £100); expenditures were £315.16.4. By 1739, when Williams resigned, his salary was £300, receipts had risen to £630.9.1 (of which the colony contributed £200) and expenditures were £594.13.5. If this growth was not quite so great as the figures make it appear (bills of credit were declining in value) still there was a very real increase. Another measure of growth was the size of the classes graduated during these years. Twenty-four men received degrees in 1735 and 1737—a number not surpassed until the new charter of 1745.[2]

Elisha Williams's greatest accomplishment was the steady, quiet development of the college. He was not an innovator, so few of the basic arrangements of Yale changed under his direction. Instead, he made things work. The jobs of the steward and butler were more carefully defined. The position of scholar of the house, recently established by the trustees, was continued and a new post, monitor, was created.[3]

The steward's job was to provide the food for commons and have rooms swept and beds made. The butler was to hand out the bread and beer in commons and for breakfast (which students probably ate in their rooms). Not until after Williams does there seem to have been a buttery where the butler sold "Cyder, Strong Bear, Loaf

Sugar, Pipes and Tobacco and Such Necessaries for the Scholars, not Sold by the Steward at the Kitchen." [4]

The scholar of the house was first appointed in May 1726 "to observe and note down all Detriment the College receives in its Windows Doors Studies Tables Locks . . . and to give an account Quarterly." And the other student functionary, the college monitor, was to keep track of absence or tardiness at prayers.[5]

All these positions were made active posts by Williams. As Richard Warch says,

> By 1730 . . . Williams supervised an active administrative hierarchy which ran the college: eleven trustees [of whom the rector was now one] dictated Yale policy, the Rector and two tutors did the teaching with one tutor acting as librarian, a steward provided the college commons, a treasurer handled all financial accounts, and the butler, scholar of the house, and monitor performed their assigned duties. Yale College had acquired a working insitutional framework.[6]

More lasting than any of Williams's earlier changes was the creation in 1737 of a standing committee of trustees to conduct certain college business between the regular annual meetings of the entire board. This committee ultimately became the Prudential Committee, which performs the same function today.[7]

Although Elisha Williams made few fundamental alterations in Yale, his years were still marked by one very important event: the gifts of land and books from George Berkeley, then Dean of Derry and later Bishop of Cloyne.[8] Berkeley had left Ireland intending to go to Bermuda to found a college. While awaiting a promised government grant, he settled on a farm near Newport, Rhode Island. After two and a half years there, he finally gave up hope of ever receiving the grant and decided to return home. During his period of waiting, Berkeley had gotten to know Samuel Johnson, sometime tutor and one of the recent converts to Episcopalianism, and Jared Eliot, one of the waverers and also the first graduate of the college to be made a trustee (1730). Through one or both of these men the dean had become interested in Yale, and in response to a question on the subject from Samuel Johnson, Berkeley on 7 September 1731 replied, "My endeavors shall not be wanting, some way or other, to be useful; and I should be very glad to be so in particular to the

College at New Haven, and the more as you were once a member of it, and have still an influence there." [9]

The dean was as good as his word. Almost a year later he wrote to Johnson, "Some part of the benefactions to the College of Bermuda, which I could not return, the benefactors being deceased, joined with the assistance of some living friends, has enabled me without any great loss to myself, to dispose of my farm in Rhoade Island in favor of the College in Connecticut." [10] And in his letter he enclosed the deed to Whitehall, his ninety-six acre farm. It was his intention that the income from this property should be used to support the first purely postgraduate fellowships in America. [11] They were doubtless founded in part because, though Berkeley saw Yale as an academy for dissenters, Samuel Johnson—his go-between—was a graduate who had become an Anglican minister. As Sir John Percival explained to Johnson, Berkeley's reasons for giving to Yale were that it "breeds the best clergymen and most learned of any college in America. That the clergymen who left the Presbyterian Church and came over to ours last year were educated there. That as this college, or rather academy, came nearest to his own plan, he was desirous to encourage it." [12]

The receipt of this gift was a matter of great pleasure to the rector and trustees. It gave them pause because of its Anglican source, but a careful reading of the deed of gift convinced them that this was not a subtle way of subverting the college. Others were not so sure. Benjamin Colman, minister of Boston's Brattle Street Church, wrote in alarm to the rector and two trustees, "I hope it comes to you without the Clog of any Condition that is inconsistent with or subversive of the known and true Intent of the Honourable Founders of your College." And he mentioned that there were rumors about "the prevalence of Arminianism in the College." [13]

Since the catastrophe of Timothy Cutler had taken place but ten years before, these fears were to be expected. But the rector and trustees were practical men who wanted the gift for the college despite its source. Elisha Williams replied to Colman, in the soothing manner often adopted by college presidents when dealing with large gifts from questionable sources, that the donation was not "clogged in the manner you hint" but was given in a "true Catholick Spirit." [14]

The rector and trustees were, in fact, sufficiently grateful and sufficiently unconcerned about the source that Berkeley was induced to make another and even greater donation to the college in 1733. This was his gift, with the assistance of "several gentlemen who had been liberal subscribers to his own intended colleges," of 880 books. The receipt of these volumes was not only, as a later Yale librarian called it, the greatest event in the history of the Yale library during its first one hundred years, but also "perhaps the outstanding library gift of the colonial period." It increased the Yale library by half, but, far more important, it added not only the usual theological books but volumes of English literature—works by Spenser, Shakespeare, Ben Jonson, Cowley, Milton, Butler, and Dryden, among others— natural history, medicine, and language. It gave Yale one of the finest libraries in the new world.[15]

The new books were placed in the Yale library, which was housed —like everything else—in the structure known as Yale College. Since that building remained, except for the rector's house, the only Yale edifice for over three decades and was for many graduates of the first seventy-five years the most imposing of Yale buildings, it deserves some description. The building achieved the look for which it was long remembered within a few years of the Berkeley gift when, despite the fact that it was not yet twenty years old, it received substantial repairs. New wood was substituted where necessary; new shingles were added; lead was placed around a chimney "to prevent rain coming in"; whitewash was liberally applied inside and new paint outside. All of this cost £180, which the Connecticut General Assembly paid.

The "refurbished" wooden structure was rather strange looking: very long (165 feet) and very narrow (21 feet), its "near 30 feet upright" contained three regular stories and a garret with dormer windows.* There were three entries running through the building with doors opening on both front and back. The roof was probably hipped and ten dormer windows protruded on each side. Six chimneys ran along the roof line, interrupted only by a belfry in the middle. The first bell, a gift from the wife of trustee Timothy Woodbridge, was installed in 1720.

The building seems to have been unpainted at first, but by 1736 it was "coulered" what was described at the time as "sky color."

* By comparison, Connecticut Hall is 105 feet long and 40 feet wide.

George Dudley Seymour explained later that the components listed in the bills, lamp black and white lead, produced the "bluish or lead color almost universally used in painting the better class of houses in the Colonial period." * Inside, on the ground floor at the south end, near what is now Chapel Street, was the dining room or Great Hall, probably about thirty-one feet by twenty-one. Above the dining room was the library, which was probably of a similar size. The rest of the building, including the attic, contained about twenty-five chambers in which some seventy or eighty persons lived. Around the periphery of each chamber were two or three tiny closetlike rooms where the students studied. There was, of course, no plumbing of any sort. As would be the case for long years to come, water for washing came from the college well and outhouses served as the only toilets.[16]

The library room, in addition to the books, housed the college's scientific instruments, a meager collection that was greatly augmented during the academic year 1734–35. By gift from Joseph Thompson of London the college received surveying instruments, and the trustees and "sundry other gentlemen" gave money with which the college purchased a reflecting telescope, a compound microscope (still at Yale), a barometer, and other "mathematical" instruments.[17]

The students who lived and studied in old Yale College had about as much freedom in both life and studies as there was room in the study closets. That was the way it had been in Killingworth and Saybrook; that was the way it would be until well into the nineteenth century. Entering students, who had prepared for college with a minister or in a local grammar school, were examined immediately after commencement to discover if they were "expert in both the Greek and lattin Grammer as also Grammatically resolving both lattin and Greek Authors and in making Good and true lattin." Then they were allowed to go home for one last fling, for the trustees now allowed a vacation after commencement. Classes began in October. When the boys returned they embarked on that long course of study of the tongues—Latin, Greek, and sometimes Hebrew as well—which was to last throughout their college careers.

* Since white paint was very expensive it was not used in New England until much later in the century. The 1748 Wadsworth map of New Haven shows all the houses as blue, red, or unpainted.

According to the laws, they were supposed to use Latin at all times while they were at college, even in private conversations, but the rule was probably not well enforced. In addition to the tongues, they studied logic, metaphysics, mathematics, and physics. "In all Classes the last Days of the week are allowed perpetually for Rhetorick, oratory and Divinity in teaching of both tongues, and Arts." And all classes studied disputation and declaimed throughout the college year. There would be no poor public speakers graduated from Yale if the college authorities could help it.

Religion was an integral part of the college course, just as it was an integral part of the life of every New Englander. The college rules were specific on that point: "Every student shall consider the main end of his study to wit to know God in Jesus Christ and answerably to lead a Godly sober life." And in addition to "secret prayer wherein every one is bound to ask wisdom for himself," they were required to be present "morning and evening at publick prayer in the Hall." But these were just the daily religious exercises. Much more serious was the Sabbath, the most important day in the week. Part of Friday and most of Saturday were spent preparing for that day. "All Students," the laws said,

> shall after they have Done resciting rhetorick and ethicks on fridays recite Wolebius theology and on saturday morning they shall Rescite Ames theologie thesis in his Medulla, and on saturday evening the Assemblies shorter Chatechism in lattin and on Sabbath Day attend the explication of Ames's Cases of Conscience.

On the Sabbath itself, most of the day was spent at prayers or at meeting. There were morning prayers at the college; then, hot or cold, rain or shine, there were two services at the meetinghouse on the Green; finally, there were evening prayers at the college. Since there was no heat in the meetinghouse, a lusty sermon of Calvinist theology was all that kept them warm in the cold New England winter.

The daily schedule was rigorous and restricted, too. Since their only light came from candles, they depended on the sun. Morning prayers were held at sunrise most of the year except from 10 March through the summer term, when they were at 6:00 A.M. On stomachs filled only by prayer they went to their first recitation and, when that was done, they finally had bread and beer for breakfast. After breakfast they were free for half an hour before going to their rooms to study until class just prior to dinner. Following that meal, the students were allowed an hour and a half to do what they wished before they had to return to their rooms for further study. A final class was held just before evening prayers, which came between four and five in the afternoon. At last, they had supper and liberty until nine, when they had to go to their chambers again. All candles were to be out by eleven and were not to be lit again until after four.

Even during their free time the students' activities were strictly limited. They were not to "intrude" into another student's chambers; they were not to go to a tavern or an eating house unless they went with a parent or someone acceptable to the rector or tutors; they were not to associate with dissolute persons or those of "unquiet life"; they were not to "go att Courts elections Keeping high Days or go a hunting or fowling without leave from the Rector or tutors." They were to

be slow to speak and avoid, and in as much as in them lies take Care that others also avoid profane swearing, lying, needless asseverations, foolish garrulings, Chidings, strifes, railings, gesting, uncomely noise, spreading ill rumors, Divulging secrets and all manner of troublesome and offensive behaviour.

And they were to

honour their naturall parents as also magistrates, elders, Rector, tutors, and all their superiors keeping Due silence in their presence and not Disorderly gaynsaing them, but shewing them always laudable expressions of honour and Reverence as uncovering the Head, etc.

Despite these strict regulations, student life did have its lighter moments. Though there were no organized games, the students did go hunting, fishing, sailing, and swimming in summer; in winter they went skating, sledding, and even, though more rarely, sleighing. Always, a major form of recreation was walking. Hikes through the woods, which began close to the college, across salt marshes at the base of East Rock, up to its top, and even all the way out to Judges' cave at West Rock, are often referred to in eighteenth- and nineteenth-century diaries.

Perhaps because of all the attempts to keep the students under strict control and away from temptation, college was seldom a peaceful place. One sophomore wrote in 1738 (coincidentally revealing the truth of a statement that composition was not much studied then):

Last night some of the freshmen got six quarts of Rhum and about two payls fool of Sydar and about eight pounds of suger and mad it in to Samson, and evited ever Scholer in Colege in to Churtis is [Peter Curtiss (B.A. 1740)] Room, and we mad such prodigius Rought that we Raised the tutor, and he ordred us all to our one rooms and some went and some taried and they geathered a gain and went up to old father Monsher [?] dore and drumed against the dore and yeled and screamed so that a bodey would have thought that they were killing dodgs there, and all this day they have bien a counsling to geather, and they sent for Woodward and Dyar and Worthenton, Briant and Styles.[18]

But college misbehavior seldom got much worse than a little "Rought" under Elisha Williams. In general the boys behaved well, the student body grew (the average graduating class under Williams was seventeen while in the previous thirteen years it had been ten), and the college prospered. Thus it was with genuine regret that the trustees heard at the fall meeting in 1739 that Williams was resigning. What caused him to come to this decision is not absolutely certain. Perhaps the little college world was just too small for a man with his restless talents. Or it may be that Samuel Johnson was correct when he informed George Berkeley that

Mr. Williams had been much out of health for some months, and last fall was persuaded it was owing to his sedantry life and the sea-side air, and accordingly took up a resolution, from which he could not be dissuaded, to retire up into the country, where he has lived ever since, and where, indeed, he seems to have enjoyed his health better.[19]

Berkeley took an interest not only because of his association with the college during Williams's term in office, but also because the rector's youngest son had just become a Berkeley scholar, thus following in the footsteps of his two brothers in the class of 1735.[20]

There was a rumor at the time, which Johnson also told Berkeley, that Williams resigned because he hoped to be elected governor of the colony.[21] Certainly his talents and character fitted him for the post, but though he did get a few votes, he never came close to election as far as we know. He did soon go to the Assembly, where he served off and on for the rest of his life. He was also elected a judge of the Superior Court, but was not re-elected in 1743, probably because he opposed the attempts of the dominant party in the colony to limit civil and religious liberty. It was this experience, no doubt, that led him to write the pamphlet entitled *The Essential Rights and Liberties of Protestants, a Seasonable Plea for Liberty of Conscience,* which has been called "probably the most effective and important piece of political writing New England produced between the time of Wise and that of Otis."

Soon after this venture in political journalism, Williams became involved in military affairs. The War of Jenkins' Ear, which became in the following year part of the War of the Austrian Succession (King George's War in America), broke out shortly after he lost his judgeship, and in 1745 Connecticut sent him to Boston to confer with the governor of Massachusetts about an expedition against Cape Breton. He accompanied as a chaplain the forces that captured Louisbourg. In 1746 he was made colonel and commander in chief of an expedition that was planned against Canada. Perhaps to his disappointment, it was never carried out. Some years later he was named one of three delegates from Connecticut to the Albany Congress, and it must have given him great pride to find there two of his former students who were representing Massachusetts: Oliver Partridge (B.A. 1730), who also attended the Stamp Act Congress in 1765, and John Worthington (B.A. 1740), a participant in the "Rought" incident. Williams must also have noted that a majority of the Massachusetts delegation were Yale men and that it was headed by Samuel Welles of the class of 1707. Also at the Congress was William Smith (B.A. 1719) of New York, who served on the committee that drafted the famous Plan of Union.

Elisha Williams died the following year, 1755, having served his colony and Yale College well. He had found Yale weak and sickly and during the thirteen years he served as rector it grew and prospered. He led it during the time when the last of the founding trustees passed from the scene: Woodbridge died in 1732 and Samuel Andrew in 1738. He gave it a more complete organizational structure. And, most important, his calm good sense allowed the college to avoid the acrimonious disputes that had for so long disrupted its life. Surely he was, as Ezra Stiles said, a "man of splendor." Yale College might have been a happier place if Elisha Williams had remained at its head until his death.[22]

Part Two

From Sectarian College

to the University Spirit

1740–1795

6

Tumultuous Years

Thomas Clap was elected rector a little over a month after Elisha Williams's resignation. He was inducted the following spring, on 2 April 1740. For the first time since the election of Abraham Pierson, the search had not taken years. The new rector, a graduate of Harvard in 1722, was nearly thirty-seven years old. He came to Yale from his ministry in Windham, Connecticut, where he had labored hard to build up church membership, establish morality (as he saw it), and uphold orthodoxy. In fact, it may have been Clap's far-flung activities in behalf of orthodoxy that brought about his election. In one case he had traveled all the way to Springfield to oppose the ordination of a young minister accused of Arminian tendencies. There he had met Elisha Williams, who had come up from Yale for the same purpose. Williams seems to have been so impressed by Clap that he suggested the young minister for the position at Yale.[1]

Clap may have been best known for his orthodoxy and harsh church discipline (it was said that his congregation "acted like boys let out of school" when he left for Yale), but he had other attributes. He possessed administrative ability and a sincere interest in learning, and he was skilled at mathematics. It seems likely, however, that he was chosen by the trustees of Yale College because of his conservative religious beliefs and his activities in support of them. Rumors of Arminianism at Yale continued to crop up and the board wanted to be sure they remained untrue.[2]

The trustees got more than they bargained for. Clap was not only a firm supporter of the established religion, he was authoritarian and pugnacious. Even in peaceful times he would have involved the college in conflict. But these were not to be peaceful times: his tenure began as the religious earthquake known as the Great Awakening began to shake all of New England, had its middle and final periods during the last and greatest of the French and Indian Wars, and ended as America began to move toward independence. Each of these events was bound to affect Yale, but under Clap the college was disturbed to a far greater degree than necessary. In fact, only by

49

understanding Clap's numerous battles is it possible to make sense of much of the history of Yale during the remainder of the eighteenth century.

The Great Awakening hit New Haven during Thomas Clap's first year in office. This religious revival, which was part of a movement sweeping the entire Western world, sought to reinvigorate with fervent evangelism what some felt to be a drily formal, declining religion. In New England, manifestations of the movement first appeared in the Connecticut Valley in 1734 and 1735 under the stimulus of Jonathan Edwards. After a period of calm it was revived and spread broadcast by the English minister George Whitefield. The message preached by Whitefield and those who came after him produced the Great Awakening and left deep and long-lasting scars on New England and especially on Connecticut and its college. To understand why their words had this effect, it is necessary to venture for a moment into the thicket of Puritan theology.

All Puritans agreed that only those selected by God would go to heaven. Those chosen were the elect, the "Visible Saints." Man, they agreed, could not affect his election; his fate had been predestined by God. The individual became aware of his status as one of the chosen through the conversion experience—a moment when he felt absolutely dependent on God and suddenly knew that God had saved him. The path to the conversion experience was long, hard, and lonely. A minister could do little to help: he could expound doctrine; he could assist men to lead outwardly godly lives; and he could help individuals to prepare themselves for the great moment. Beyond that, he was helpless.

In the first generation of Puritans in New England, the number of "Visible Saints" had been high. But in later generations, with the spur of persecution removed, the number of elect began to decline. Since church membership was open only to the "Visible Saints," the church itself seemed to be fading away (although all continued to go to meeting). Various methods were tried to keep the number of church members high, including the lowering of standards for membership, but these actions caused a good deal of complaint. Some ministers fell victim to a tendency to stress outward behavior (works) over inner experience (grace). Other ministers yearned for a way to enlarge their role in the conversion experience.

It was in these circumstances that some ministers began to preach vivid sermons that showed their congregations the fires of hell and the individual's complete dependence on God. George Whitefield and other itinerant ministers of the Great Awakening took this style, improved it, and produced turmoil in New England and the Middle Colonies. Meetinghouses were suddenly packed to overflowing, crowds filled fields, people sang, rolled on the ground, wept, and went into trances when they heard the evangelists depict the horrors of damnation.[3]

Whitefield and the other ministers who used these techniques thought that if they could convince their auditors of their sinfulness, of their need for God's merciful grace, they could put them in a state so open to God that they might have the conversion experience —that is, they might feel that God had saved them. As one student at Yale told another, "It [is] impossible for a person to be converted and to be a real christian without feeling his heart, at sometimes at least, sensibly and greatly affected with the character of Christ." [4]

At first, New England Puritan ministers were delighted with the Great Awakening. It was wonderful to have the people excited about religion, conscious of their sinfulness, actively seeking the conversion experience. But soon many ministers became aware of evils in the movement and began to turn against it.

One evil was that some New Lights, as supporters of the Great Awakening were called, began to suggest that certain ministers were unconverted and that this was a hindrance to the salvation of their congregations. In the past, while it was believed that most ministers had been converted, this was not a matter of great importance. A minister's personal state of grace—or lack of it—did not affect his teaching. Now the New Lights said it did, and some members of congregations chose to separate from their unconverted ministers and to form new churches. The Old Lights, who opposed the Awakening, felt that the attack on certain ministers and the disruption of some churches not only wrecked the unity of religion but undermined the very bases of society.

The New Lights also attacked the established order by questioning the value of education. They said that the only thing worth knowing was Christ, and that any other kind of knowledge might be a positive hindrance to knowing Him. Since the importance of edu-

cation and especially of an educated ministry had long been acknowledged in New England, the Old Lights considered this another very dangerous concept. Wherever they looked, in fact, the
Old Lights saw their society—and their positions in it—being challenged. So they moved to stop the revival. Rector Clap in his roles
as teacher, minister, and member of the standing order heartily
joined the fray. Yale College had been founded to train an educated
ministry and uphold the established religion; it would not be found
lacking when it was needed if Thomas Clap could help it.

Like most New England ministers, Clap had at first been delighted by the reawakening of religious interest produced by Whitefield. He too had been worried by the declining religiosity of the
people, so he welcomed Whitefield and brought him to the college
to preach to the students. Whitefield was soon followed by other
ministers with the ability to make an audience see their sinfulness
and the awfulness of God. One of the most effective was rough and
ready Gilbert Tennent, who was hailed at Yale and preached several
times to the students. But then a sizable number of undergraduates
disobeyed the college rules and trooped off to Milford to hear Tennent once more. The first seeds of doubt must have been planted in
Clap's mind. If authority and discipline at the college were undermined by this new movement, it might be the work of Satan instead
of God.[5]

Soon Clap's worst fears seemed confirmed. Itinerant ministers and
lay exhorters began to roam the land. One of the wildest was James
Davenport (B.A. 1732), a great-grandson of the founder of New
Haven, who stood in Joseph Noyes's own pulpit in New Haven and
damned his host as an unconverted man and a hypocrite.[6] Soon a
part of Noyes's congregation decided Davenport was right, that their
minister had never had the conversion experience and that they
could no longer remain in his congregation. They called for a division of the congregation's property.[7] And thus began the destruction
of church unity in New Haven that is now so clearly symbolized by
the presence of two Congregational churches on the Green.

The dangerous infection of judging another person's state of grace
even spread to the college. At about the time Davenport was pro-
nouncing Noyes unconverted the board of trustees found it necessary
to pass a rule that "if any Student . . . shall directly or indirectly
say, that the Rector, either of the Trustees or Tutors are hypocrites,

carnal or unconverted men, he shall for the first offence make a public confession in the Hall, and for the second offence be expelled."
And that same September 1741, according to Samuel Johnson, "two
of this year's [M.A.] candidates were denied their degrees for their
disorderly and restless endeavors to propagate" the Great Awakening.[8]

Clap soon found that it would take even firmer measures to stop
the infection. David Brainerd (later to become almost a Protestant
saint thanks to his diary and to a biography by Jonathan Edwards)
was one of the students most moved by Whitefield and Tennent. He
toured the college trying to prepare others for conversion. But he
alienated Thomas Clap when he said—or at least Clap thought he
said—that he wondered the rector "did not expect to drop down
dead for fining the scholars that followed Mr. Tennent to Milford."
Then in the fall of 1741 he broke the new college law by saying that
Tutor Whittelsey had no more grace than a chair. For this, he was
expelled.

Brainerd made a full confession and apology the following year
and offered to make a confession before the entire college, but the
trustees would have nothing to do with him. Despite the pleas of
Jonathan Edwards, Aaron Burr, and Jonathan Dickinson, the board
would not relent. It may be conjectured that they felt they could
not because the college was disrupted and the New Haven congregation split. The disintegration caused by the Great Awakening had
reached such a state that an example had to be made of Brainerd.

Aaron Burr (B.A. 1735), father of Jefferson's vice-president, was
reported to have said that "if it had not been for the treatment received by Mr. Brainerd at Yale College, New Jersey College [Prin-
ceton] never would have been erected." But as Thomas Jefferson
Wertenbaker noted, "It was not the Brainerd incident alone . . .
but the accumulated evidence of Clap's hostility to the Great Awakening which made Edwards, Burr, Dickinson, and others turn their
backs upon their alma mater." [9]

The founding of Princeton (1746) was still a few years off, however, as Clap tried to preserve the old order both inside the college
and out. He chaired a committee of the First Church of New Haven
that called the brilliant but unstable Reverend James Davenport to
task for his attacks on Noyes. Clap then headed another committee
which petitioned the General Assembly to summon a meeting of all

the Connecticut churches to deal with the turmoil caused by the Great Awakening. The Assembly complied with the petition, and in November a General Consociation was held in Guilford, which produced a number of resolutions aimed at stopping itinerant preachers and lay exhorters from touring the countryside and tried to prevent the disintegration of churches by separation. The General Assembly later supported these measures by enacting many of them into law.[10]

Still Clap faced problems. Noyes's congregation split despite the rector's attempts to prevent it. Clap even got the stable and responsible New Light Aaron Burr to share the pulpit with Noyes for a short time and tried to induce him to do so permanently to heal the schism. But Burr refused to continue and the church remained divided.[11] Meanwhile the rector faced serious problems at the college. The students refused to submit to discipline, avoided religious instruction from those they thought unconverted, and spent their time in lay exhortation and attending separatist meetings. Finally, in the spring of 1742 Clap closed the college and sent the students home. Perhaps he hoped that a little time away from college would damp down the fires of enthusiasm. He also looked to the General Assembly for assistance.[12]

The Assembly that met in May 1742 approved Clap's actions, supported the expulsion of those who were "Incorageable," and encouraged the college to hire "Grave Devins" to come to New Haven to preach orthodox religion to the students, but failed to vote any funds to help in that good cause. At this same session they enacted the laws that enforced the Guilford Resolves and showed that Connecticut would have no truck with disruptive New Lights. More important to the college, perhaps, than any of these actions by the General Assembly was the erection this same year by the New Lights of their own seminary for those who wanted to know only Christ. "The Shepherd's Tent" in New London drew off some of the more ardent undergraduates and by so doing assisted in improving order at Yale. The new school, under the direction of Timothy Allen (B.A. 1736), was soon driven to Rhode Island by a law that made it illegal to start a school without a license from the General Assembly. So not only were the most fiery students removed, but Yale's educational monopoly was preserved.[13]

The year 1743 was quieter for Clap and Yale as the Great Awakening slowly came to an end. Exhaustion had set in; no people could long remain at such a pitch of excitement. In addition, the

Old Lights were now alert, prepared, and aggressive. Orthodoxy, they felt, must prevail. Unless it did, "this would soon be an *Habitation of Dragons* and a *Court for Owls,*" as Isaac Stiles (B.A. 1722) put it in his election sermon of 1742.[14]

It took continuing vigilance and harsh discipline to put down all the symptoms of the disease. In 1744 Clap expelled the two Cleaveland boys, Ebenezer and John, for attending separatist meetings with their parents. When the Cleavelands protested that there was no college law against what they had done, Clap replied, "The laws of God and the College are one." [15]

Just as the college and the colony were becoming quiet—though things would never again be the same—George Whitefield returned to New England. Harvard denied him room to preach and, when he attacked that college "as a house of impiety and sin," the faculty replied with "The Testimony of the President, Professors, Tutors and Hebrew Instructor of Harvard College, Cambridge, against the Reverend Mr. George Whitefield, And his Conduct." Yale was not far behind. Like Harvard, Yale had been condemned as a place of darkness by Whitefield after his first visit. Early in 1745 appeared Yale's "Declaration" against Whitefield. Then, in April 1746, Clap expelled from the Corporation Samuel Cooke, who had assisted in setting up the separatist congregation in New Haven. This was his last flamboyant action against the New Lights.[16]

The reaction of Thomas Clap and Yale to the Great Awakening was, it is clear, far more harsh than was the reaction of Harvard. But Harvard was never forced to close because of the unrestrained enthusiasm of her students. Clap's activities against the revival left deep marks on the college. His actions moved Yale close to becoming a narrowly sectarian college with its principle aim being, as he and the tutors declared when they expelled the Cleaveland boys, "*To Train up a Succession of Learned and Orthodox Ministers.*" Certainly the provocation had been great. The college had been badly disrupted and the anti-intellectualism and attacks on authority of some New Lights did endanger the existing society. But both the rector and the college were to pay a high price for his activities, as Clap would ultimately discover.[17]

During the years of turmoil of the Great Awakening, Clap was doing more than just battling the heterodox. Upon his arrival at Yale, this restless, energetic man immediately found much that needed attention: the college laws were incomplete and in some cases outmoded; the library needed a real catalogue; the charter was insufficient for a growing college. Somehow, between his jousts with the New Lights, Clap found time to take care of everything.

The first task Clap completed was cataloguing the library. In 1743 he published one catalogue of the library by authors and completed two manuscript catalogues that listed the books by subject and shelf position. One librarian later said, "The three [catalogues] with all their imperfections may be considered 'perfect' in that they give the three approaches required by modern library science." [18]

At the same time, Clap worked on the reorganization of the college itself. The charter, the trustees had felt for some time, left much to be desired, "particularly," as Clap later wrote, "the Name, *Trustees,* by which the first Undertakers and Founders of the College and their Successors were usually called, was not so proper and usual a Title for the Governors of a College, in a more mature and perfect State." So he drew up a new charter which, after revision by Thomas Fitch (B.A. 1721), a member of the Upper House, was approved by the trustees and presented in May 1745 to the General Assembly.

The General Assembly had been quite as zealous as Clap in persecuting New Lights. And *The Declaration of the Rector and Tutors of Yale College against the Rev. Mr. George Whitefield, his Principles and Designs, in a Letter to him,* published in February 1745, signaled to the Assembly that the college had not wavered in its devotion to the Old Lights. Comfortable in the knowledge that all was right at the college, the General Assembly immediately passed Clap's charter unchanged.

The major contributions of the new charter were to alter the name of the governing board to "the President and Fellows of Yale College in New Haven," to make them an incorporated body, to clarify and add to certain other aspects of previous legislation for the college, and to bring everything together in one act. The most important aspect of this legislation was that it at last made Yale a corporation. Later commentators have often felt that the major change effected by the charter of 1745 was its conversion of a powerless rector into a dominant president. This does not seem to have been the case. The head of the college now became *ex officio* head of the board, it is true, but in fact Elisha Williams had often been chosen moderator of the board's meetings and, except for his first meeting, Clap always had been. Of course the rector had to be elected moderator each time, so he could be displaced; but for his new security as presiding officer, under the new charter the rector lost his right to vote except in the case of ties. It seems clear that while the title "President and Fellows" glorified the office of president, the power of the holder, like the power of the rector, depended more on his individual character—his ability to lead—than on anything granted by the new charter. Rector Clap, it seems, was just as predominant as President Clap. That the new charter was a good one, however, is shown by its survival to the present with few changes as the basic legislation for the university.[19]

Clap took the oath of office as president on 1 June 1745. Then he proceeded to complete another task he had been working on since 1740. At the annual meeting of the Corporation in September 1745 he presented his new college laws, which were approved by the fellows at that meeting and published in 1748. At the same time Clap had written down college customs that had grown up over the years, but these were kept in manuscript.

Thomas Clap had a very legalistic way of thinking. This went beyond the legalism inherent in Calvinism to a basic cast of mind which made him delight in writing laws, finding precedents, and, finally, even arguing the college's case before the General Assembly against two of the finest lawyers in the colony (see pp. 68–69). He was a man who, when establishing a new law, recorded, "N.B. This Resolve was founded on Sundry Rules of the Common Law in Jacob's Dictionary . . . Woods Institutes, p. 372. 408." [20] Clap believed that no society could exist without rules. He attempted to make his college laws cover every conceivable circumstance, from how often the tablecloths used in commons should be washed (once a week) to the penalty for one student's opening another's door "with a Pick-Lock or a False Key" (one shilling fine for the first offense, two shillings for the second, and anything from public admonition to expulsion for the third). Clap believed that it was possible to control students by drawing up a complete set of rules and precise punishments for infractions and making sure the students knew them. By this means, he thought, offenders against the law could be punished while the majority, who were merely weak, would be deterred by fear from following the "many temptations and evil examples" that were so often to be found "in such a company of giddy youth." [21]

The system reached its acme in the ceremony of public expulsion. When Asa Spalding was expelled for going on the rampage one night with some friends—yelling and jumping, knocking down the plaster in a tutor's room, insolent contempt to the tutors when told to stop, and worst of all in Spalding's case, saying he did not care if he was expelled—the following sentence, which is a typical example, was read by the president before all the students in the Great Hall as the offender stood before them.

Whereas You, Asa Spalding, have been guilty of sundry riotous and impudent Crimes, as particularly related in the Judgements of the President and Tutors now read which are scandalous to this College, and render you unfit to be a Member of it;

Wherefore to shew a due Detestation of such Evils, and to maintain the Honour and good Order of this College, and to prevent any of the Members of it from being affected or influenced by such evil Examples: I do, in pursuance to the Laws of this College, and with the Consent of the Tutors, utterly expel, reject, and cast out You the said Spalding from being a Member of this College; and from henceforth enjoying any of the Dignities, Privileges, and Immunities of it; and declare that your Relation to it shall henceforth intirely cease. And I do hereby command You immediately to depart out of this College, and the Limits thereof, and never to return to reside here any more. And I do command all the Schollars not to entertain any free or familiar Conversation with You any more. And I do hereby order the Butler and Monitor to erase and blot your name out of their Bills. And let all other hear and fear, and do no more presumptuously.

Then, as in all such cases where great crimes resulted in the major penalties of public admonition, rustication, or expulsion, Clap made "a solemn Address . . . to impress upon their Minds a Sense of the evil Nature and Consequence of such *Crimes,* and to persuade them to take Warning not to do the like." It should be noted, however, that the Puritans were not unbending. They realized that men would sin, and so a student like Spalding could return to the fold if he was truly sorry and confessed the error of his ways. Thus on 7 February 1752 Spalding made a public confession in the college hall and was restored. In his case the college may have made a mistake. He graduated in 1752 and went on to an undistinguished career marked by "intemperate habits." [22]

Timothy Dwight thought Clap's system mistakenly treated as men those who were really only boys. It was, he said, "the only serious defect in his [Clap's] presidential character." Still, it was a common failing; the Yale laws of 1745 influenced college laws throughout the country until well into the nineteenth century.[23]

Clap's activities seem to have found favor with most of the people of Connecticut, for Yale continued to grow. By 1747 only about half of the undergraduates were able to find room in the old college, while the remainder had to live with families about town. Since it was difficult to control the students who lived off campus and broke up the unity of the college, the president petitioned the General Assembly to be allowed to hold a lottery to raise funds for a new college building. The inspiration for using a lottery came from New York, where one had been authorized in December 1746 to raise money to found King's College. Clap feared Connecticut citizens might spend their money on New York tickets, so while he appears to have disapproved somewhat of the method, he told a fellow that it was "best to take Mankind in their own Humour and to set up a Lottery for building a College [hall] here." In May 1747, at Yale's request, the General Assembly granted the college the right to hold a lottery. Thus Yale became the first active American college to raise money by this relatively new method. The results were not, however, an unmitigated success. The sum of £500 sterling that was raised was insufficient to build the new hall. So the college turned again to the General Assembly, which thereupon voted to Yale the proceeds of the sale of a French boat recently captured by the colony's frigate (for King George's War had just ended). With this money in prospect, Clap gave the order to start construction, and the cornerstone was laid on 17 April 1750.[24]

Yale's second major structure was named Connecticut Hall in recognition of the colony's aid, but it was generally called New Hall or New College to distinguish it from Yale College. The building was made of bricks (about 230,000 according to Clap) and cost some £1,660 sterling. It was, apparently, largely designed by Clap, who also oversaw its construction. The model for it was Massachusetts Hall at Harvard. In interior arrangement, it followed the pattern of Yale College and medieval examples, with large chambers for sleeping containing small studies. Later John Trumbull was to be most critical of the way the rooms were laid out. He pointed out that the living space was "impaired by the studies which either lessen the light or incommode the size, while they are necessarily untenable a great part of the yare, those in front from the Heat of summer, the others from winter's cold." The floor plan shows why Trumbull was so critical.[25]

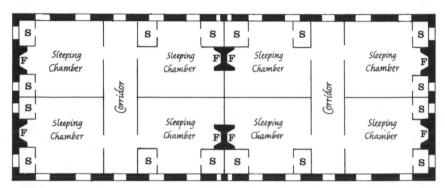

S = Study   F = Fireplace

Despite the shortcomings of its interior arrangement, the building was said to be the finest in the colony. Its site showed it off well:

It was set back in the yard, that there might be a large and handsome area before it, and toward the north side of the yard, with a view, that, when the old college should come down, another college or chapel, or both, should be set, on a line, to the south of it. Additional lands were also purchased on the north, and on the west, for its better accommodation.[26]

Connecticut Hall was completed and occupied in 1753, a year that saw President Clap again embroiled in controversy. The hard feeling engendered by the strife over the Great Awakening had never entirely disappeared; in fact, the differences that first arose then were to produce conflicts within the Yale Corporation and between Yale and the General Assembly for many years to come. The dispute that broke out in 1753 again involved Joseph Noyes, pastor of the First Church of New Haven and fellow of the Yale Corporation. Noyes has been called, perhaps with pardonable exaggeration, the dullest minister in all New England. He was, it will be recalled, an Old Light, and he appears to have been one of those who were gradually shifting away from Calvinism to a position that many thought smacked strongly of Arminianism. His enemies even suspected that "he did not hold the real divinity of the Saviour." Thomas Clap had, of course, defended Noyes during the Great Awakening. But as the years went by Clap's passions over the revival declined while his suspicions of Noyes's orthodoxy increased. He may, furthermore, have found his students becoming steadily less concerned about religion as they listened to the numbing sermons of Joseph Noyes.[27]

As his patience with Noyes reached its breaking point, Clap felt another spur. The Church of England began to hold services in New Haven. Clap had been able to get along with the Episcopalians as long as their nearest church was in West Haven, for that was too far away for students to attend services every Sunday. Now the church was on the college's doorstep and the minister wanted the Episcopalian students, including his two sons, to attend Anglican services rather than worship at the meetinghouse.

Clap reacted swiftly—so swiftly that it is probable he had been contemplating the move for some time. He called a meeting of the fellows on 21 November 1753 and, perhaps pleading the need to defend orthodoxy and guard against the possible loss of students to the College of New Jersey (Princeton), he persuaded the trustees to ask him, first, to serve as professor of divinity, and second, to hold separate worship for the students each Sunday in the Great Hall of Old College. Since 1746 the college had intended to appoint a professor of divinity, but the removal of the students from the First Church was a new and startling development.[28]

At the same meeting where these decisions were made, the Corporation erected a new bulwark against heterodoxy when they approved a far stricter religious oath to be taken henceforth by presidents, fellows, professors, and tutors. Since 1722 it had been necessary for rectors and tutors to declare their assent to the Saybrook Confession of Faith and show "the Soundness of their Faith in opposition to Armenian and prelaitical Corruptions." Now all officers had to subscribe to the Westminster Assembly's Catechism and the Saybrook Confession of Faith and rules of church discipline in a much fuller and more formal way. Clap may have strengthened the oath to indicate the college's orthodoxy while actually violating that orthodoxy by setting up separate worship at the college.[29]

The students began worshiping apart from Noyes's congregation at the end of the month, and criticism of the move began almost immediately.[30] For Clap had been far too clever. No doubt he thought he could use the presence of the Church of England as a pretext for setting up separate worship and thus blunt the criticism he knew would be forthcoming. But what he actually did was to lay himself open to attack by two parties instead of one. Sniped at by both Old Lights and Episcopalians, Clap published in April 1754 a pamphlet, *The Religious Constitution of Colleges,* wherein he attempted to defend himself from charges of both separatism and impingement on liberty of conscience. His key claim was that

Colleges are *Religious Societies* of a Superior nature to all others. For whereas Parishes, are Societies, for training up the *Common People;* Colleges are Societies of Ministers for training up persons for the work of the *Ministry* and therefore all their *Religious Instructions, Worship, and Ordinances, are carried on within their own jurisdiction, by their own Officers, and under their own Regulation.*

Unfortunately, he convinced none of his enemies. In May he found the General Assembly hesitating over its usual grant to the college. It finally voted the funds, but the warning was clear.[31]

The Episcopalians soon won their point—one of the few times Clap ever succumbed to anyone. Samuel Johnson, who was deeply involved in the argument, may have persuaded the stubborn president, for he presented a forceful case: he reminded Clap that only the king could "make a corporation," and that thus the charter of 1745 was illegal. If the Episcopalians complained, Johnson said, Yale might disappear completely. Under this threat, Clap allowed Anglican students to attend their own church. By late June 1754 Johnson's son reported to his father that he had heard that the president "seems to have yielded the point as to the Church scholars, that as many as ask leave to attend, have it, but the scholars are negligent and but few of them trouble their heads about it." [32]

The problems with the General Assembly did not pass away so easily. Clap had alienated his former allies, the Old Lights, while the New Lights had not forgotten his attacks on them. Still this opposition had not coalesced. In the fall the usual grant was voted and a supplementary grant equivalent to £250 sterling was given for the completion of Connecticut Hall. In fact, at that point it may have seemed to Clap that the storm would pass, so he continued on course. When Noyes offered to share his pulpit with the professor of divinity when he was appointed, the Corporation under Clap's direction laid down such harsh conditions that it seemed impossible the First Church would ever accept. Then, shortly afterward, Clap went so far as to allow his old *bête noir* George Whitefield to preach to the students and "treated him much like a Gentleman." This action was taken to mean, probably quite correctly, that Clap was trying to make his peace with the New Lights. Since they were gaining political power in the colony, he had decided to ally himself with his former enemies.[33]

Apparently Clap had miscalculated the remaining power of the Old Lights. Though the number of New Lights in the General Assembly had increased greatly, the Old Lights still had a majority and could attack effectively. They were aided by the fact that Clap's various moves had produced an opposition within the Corporation. Its members were Joseph Noyes, William Russell, Thomas Ruggles, and, most prestigious of all the fellows, Jared Eliot. In fact, it was Eliot's son-in-law, Benjamin Gale (B.A. 1733), who fired the first shot.[34]

Gale's pamphlet *The Present State of the Colony of Connecticut Considered,* which appeared anonymously in April 1755, largely shifted the battleground from religious to economic issues. Charging that the college had sufficient income to cover its expenses and no longer needed the colonial grant, Gale aimed to force Clap to retreat or resign by removing the annual grant to the college. The General Assembly, New Lights and Old coalescing, were delighted to accept this argument—especially as a major war with France was imminent. Using the excuse of wartime expenditures, the General Assembly refused to vote the annual grant in May of 1755.[35]

Though Clap must have been taken aback by the momentous loss of the colony grant (for the college was not as prosperous as Gale made out), he did not waver. He turned to the General Association of the Congregational Churches of Connecticut and persuaded them to urge the support of the ministers of the colony in the drive for an endowment for the professor of divinity. Clap had begun to think of establishing this professorship—Yale's first—in 1745 when the college received funds equivalent to £28 sterling from Philip Livingston, proprietor of Livingston Manor in New York, to be used for repairs on the old building or for a new one. Since this was the largest contribution from an individual that Yale had received since the Berkeley gift in 1732, Clap asked Livingston to allow the college to use it in any way it wished. Then he persuaded the Corporation to set it aside as endowment for a professorship of divinity.[36]

It is possible that Clap had wanted to make this appointment because of dissatisfaction even then with the teaching and preaching of Joseph Noyes, but very likely it was just another part of his drive to make Yale bigger and better. He had been at Harvard when its first professor, also a professor of divinity, was appointed in 1721, and he undoubtedly wanted to match that achievement. But whatever he had in mind when he first broached the subject of a professor of divinity, it should be noted that the appointment itself need not have led to separate worship. At Harvard the college church was not founded until almost a century after Edward Wigglesworth was made the first professor of divinity.[37]

The question of the professorship lay quiescent for almost a decade after the Livingston gift, until the Episcopalians gave Clap his excuse. As we have seen, he himself took the office of professor of divinity temporarily and began on 25 November 1753 to preach to the students on Sundays. Attempts to raise an adequate endowment had not yet been successful when the Corporation called Naphtali Daggett (B.A. 1748) in September 1755 to assist Clap in the college pulpit and to be inspected for the professorship. Though the General Assembly was displeased by all this, the people who sent their children to college appear to have been undisturbed. Both the freshman class entering that fall and the total number of undergraduates were the largest ever.[38]

Daggett was a success in his trial. But even though his views were probably well known after he had preached at the college for several months, he was subjected to a further search of his ideas. He was asked to write a long paper setting forth his religious beliefs and to submit to a day-long oral examination which, according to the historian of the Church of Christ at Yale, "makes the twentieth-century doctor's examination look by comparison but little better than a ten-minute paper." At last apparently satisfied, the Corporation inducted him as Yale's first professor—officially the Livingstonian Professor of Divinity—on 4 March 1756.[39]

Noyes now came forward again with the offer to share his pulpit with the new professor. He had seen his congregation split once, and he had no wish to preside over a further division. The Corporation continued to demand hard conditions, and Clap even urged the First Church to subscribe explicitly to the Assembly's Catechism and the Savoy Confession of Faith—something they had always refused to do. After resisting a bit, Noyes and his church yielded. Then the Yale students returned to the First Church's meetinghouse.

But it was soon clear that listening to Noyes even half the time was too much. Clap decided, come what may, to set up a separate church. The final division was accomplished with much further bitterness. Jared Eliot appears to have threatened to resign as a fellow if the separation took place, and it was even rumored that he intended to hand his resignation not to the Corporation but to the General Assembly, where Clap's opponents were still strong. One fellow wrote to Eliot to try to head off this attempt to involve the General Assembly in the affairs of the college. Whatever his intentions may have been, Eliot did not resign but remained on the Corporation to fight the president.

Undaunted by opposition within the Corporation, on 20 April 1757 a majority of the fellows decided that not only could Yale students worship separately, but they could become a real church and administer Communion. In response to this decision eight undergraduates, three tutors, and the college butler (a resident graduate) petitioned the Corporation for permission to form the college congregation into a church. The following day, 30 June 1757, the request was officially granted in a ceremony in the Great Hall where Professor Daggett preached and President Clap pronounced the Corporation's decision.[40]

The establishment of the first college church in America completely split the Yale Corporation. Jared Eliot, Joseph Noyes, and Thomas Ruggles (William Russell, also an opponent, was absent) presented a written protest against the move, which the other fellows answered by approving the church and attacking Noyes. The majority noted that "the Reverend Mr. Noyes, a Fellow of the Corporation, has been suspected by some of the members thereof of being unsound in the Doctrine of the Trinity, the Divinity and Satisfaction of Christ, Original Sin, Election, Regeneration, and the Doctrines thereon depending." He had been quizzed a bit at the April meeting and they had thought his answers unsatisfactory, so

now they voted to examine him formally in September. Their aim
was to drive him off the Corporation, just as he had assisted in forc-
ing out New Light Samuel Cooke a little over a decade before.[41]

In September, when Noyes refused to be examined or even consider resigning, the Corporation recognized defeat and did not pursue the matter. But that did not end the fight. The following May,
Eliot and Ruggles sent a memorial to the General Assembly in
which they described the setting up of a separate church at the college as

a direct violation of the Trust reposed in the President and Fellows, an
infringement on the order and rights of the regular Churches in this Colony, and a daring Affront to the Legislative power of this Colony, and
such a glaring Evidence of an undue aim at exorbitant power, as loudly
calls for the timely check of the Legislature.

They asked the Assembly to interfere in the affairs of the college
and overturn its illegal acts. But the opponents of the college lacked
sufficient votes, so the Assembly failed to act. After this defeat the
opposition to the college's course continued with diminished intensity. The church had been founded and it could not, it appeared, be
overturned. In 1759 Clap was so sure of its permanence that he decided to build a chapel for the college congregation (with room for
the library on the second floor), and though he found it very difficult to raise the funds, the new chapel was ready for use in 1763.[42]

As the dispute over separate worship began to lose heat, new
problems arose for the battling president. Discipline at the college
began to break down. The undergraduate of the eighteenth century
tended to be something of a roughneck in any case, but pranks
began to turn into riots as the decade of the fifties came to an end.
On the night of 10 April 1758, for example, the students went on
such a rampage of firing guns, ringing bells, and breaking windows,
"to the great Amazement and Terror of all that were near" that the
tutors called the sheriff "to quell the Mob." [43] This was only the beginning. In the sixties riot became rebellion.

Clap's method of discipline, as we have seen, was based on a very
complicated and precise set of laws, fines, and other punishments. It
depended on continuous enforcement and student cooperation—or
at least acquiescence. Both of these failed in the sixties. The reason

for the collapse is complex. Clap had greatly increased the size of
the college and mere numbers put a strain on the procedure. With
more students there was more misbehavior, which in turn produced
increased penalties and punishments. The students reacted against
these and then Clap, who seems to have grown increasingly bull-
headed as he grew older, became more authoritarian and erratic.
The entire situation was made worse—and the students were encouraged in their actions—by constant criticism of the president
and his system of government by people outside the college. Clap
became increasingly less predictable. He changed the date of commencement several times to try to avoid trouble; he was strict one
day, lenient the next. Overall there was less discipline, perhaps because Clap hoped that in this way he could avoid a confrontation
with the students. The monitor's bills for March of 1761 showed
how far control had slipped: several students had seventy and eighty
absences from morning and evening prayer, yet all the president
did was to reprimand them. In another instance William Nichols
(B.A. 1762) was caught hallooing, jumping, and screaming in another student's room. The Faculty Judgements speak of his "course
of Bad conduct, particularly being frequently absent from Prayers,
from his chamber in Studying time, frequent absence from meeting,
several times going to other meetings. Going away out of Town
without Leave, Speaking for an Entertainment at the Tavern for
the Junior Class etc." Despite all this the only punishment he received was to be "plainly told that for this Course of misdemeanor
he was in danger of being dismist." [44]

The collapse of discipline, which resulted even in attacks on the
president's house and the breaking of his windows "by throwing in
great Stones," strengthened Clap's opponents, who had never ceased
their opposition to him. In October 1761 three fathers of Yale students complained that "for the last half year little or no Study has
been done," and they called for the General Assembly to send visitors to the college. Nothing came of this petition, but on 10 March
1763 the call was repeated. This was to be the most dangerous attack
Clap had to face. Nine citizens, all but one graduates of the college,
complained to the General Assembly, as Dexter says, of "the arbi-
trariness and autocracy of the President, the multiplicity and injustice of the laws, the extravagance of the system of fines and of other
punishments, and the unrest of the students." The memorialists

called upon the Assembly to review the college laws (as it had a right to do under article 8 of the charter), reduce the fines, allow appeals to it from Clap's rulings, and most important of all, to "exercise its powers as the creator of the College Corporation by sending to it a Committee of Visitation." This last request was echoed in the election sermon when the Assembly met.[45]

The General Assembly decided to hear arguments on both sides of the issue. The memorialists were represented by Jared Ingersoll (B.A. 1742) and William Samuel Johnson (B.A. 1744), two of the finest lawyers in the colony, while Thomas Clap opposed their case. Matters had reached a head. The crux of the dispute was the right of visitation—the right to investigate and reform abuses in the running of the college. Ingersoll and Johnson argued that the General Assembly had founded the college and that to the founder went the right of visitation. Clap, who really should have been a lawyer, accepted the proposition that the founders had a right of visitation but "proved" (though he may have known that he was, at the very least, stretching the truth) that the college had been created not by the General Assembly but by the ministers with their donation of books. To bolster his case, Clap even moved the incident to 1700, thus helping to establish the belief that Yale was founded then.[46]

Clap based his argument on numerous legal precedents and the opposition failed to attack the weak point in his case. They neglected to note that as early as 1725, when a number of founders were still trustees, the college had stated that the "School had its being from [the] Honorable Assembly" and that the trustees had repeated this sentiment in various forms till as late as 1743, when they said the Assembly "were pleased to Found and Establish Yale College." [47]

Clap's argument, which may have been bolstered by a threat to appeal to the crown if he was defeated, convinced the legislature, which refused to act on the memorial. Franklin B. Dexter in the 1890s thought this victory marked "a distinct epoch in the history of the College, this defeat for all time of the attempt to subject its constitution and management to the varying will of a popular Assembly, takes rank with the new Charter of 1745" in importance in the history of the college. But Dexter may have been carried away by Clap's own view of his success and by a personal devotion to laissez faire. Edmund Morgan was closer to the truth when he called it "another of the pyrrhic victories" Clap had been winning since become-ing president. For the bitterness he engendered took years to abate, and the college returned to a closer relationship with the legislature only when it allowed—not visitors—but the governor of Connecti-cut, the lieutenant governor, and six members of the upper house to become full members of the Corporation.[48]

Clap's problems were by no means over after he stopped the visi-tation threat. Riot and rebellion continued at the college. Those who wished to rid the college of President Clap may have encouraged the students in these acts; but in part the disorders were due to the times. There was a rising spirit of independence in the air that showed itself when the scholars decided in 1764 to drink no "foreign spirituous Liquors any more" and especially when, in the following year, the year of the Stamp Act, Joseph Lyman (B.A. 1767) delivered a declamation in chapel which the conservative Corporation thought contained "unjustifiable Reflections on that August Body the British Parliament, and as appears by plain Implication on the Laws and Authority of this College." The president and fellows were discovering what others have often found since: when "respect-able" men resist what they feel are unjust laws, like the Stamp Act, the lesson is not lost on undergraduates and other "lower classes." [49]

A group of students and graduates (one of whom was an "old grad" of 1750), resorting to their own form of resistance, attacked the president's house during a fellows' meeting, broke "about thirty squares of glass" and injured the president by a flying fragment, "damaged the window sashes and clapboards and broke off and re-moved the gates." The Corporation decided that "unless the civil Authority in New-Haven will take Care to suppress the disorders that are frequently committed at the Commencement, and protect the President and Fellows from being insulted, the Commencement shall be holden in some other place, or some other Measures shall be taken." [50]

In February 1766 almost all the students signed a petition to the Corporation containing their "grievances" and the "intolerancies" of their situation. When the fellows failed to act on it and remove Clap, they stopped going to classes or prayers and made the lives of the new tutors such hell that they resigned. The Corporation was called into special session on 22 April in the face of this disaster and voted that spring vacation begin at once—two weeks early. When college reconvened after vacation, few undergraduates returned. Nonetheless, classes were held throughout the spring quarter. At the Corporation meeting in July President Clap faced reality and resigned. Enrollment had declined during the recent strife-torn years, discipline was gone, and the college had now almost ceased to function. The Corporation asked the weary man to continue at least until commencement. He agreed, but school was dismissed, the summer quarter was not held, and classes did not meet again until October. On 10 September 1766 President Clap presided over his last commencement, delivered his valedictory address, and then resigned. Broken and exhausted, he died four months later at the age of sixty-three.[51]

Thomas Clap's presidency is most often remembered for the strife which was a constant part of it, but there was much more to it than that. Educationally it was an excellent period. Clap described the curriculum in his introduction to the 1743 library catalogue:

I would advise you, my Pupils, to pursue a Regular Course of Academical Studies in some Measure according to the Order of this Catalogue. And in the First year to Study principally the Tongues, Arithmetic and Algebra; the Second, Logic, Rhetoric and Geometry; the Third, Mathematics and Natural Philosophy, and the Fourth, Ethics and Divinity. . . . Above all have an Eye to the great End of all your Studies, which is to obtain the Clearest Conceptions of Divine Things and to lead you to a Saving Knowledge of God in his Son Jesus Christ.[52]

Perhaps Clap's major educational contribution was in the greater stress he laid upon science and mathematics. He requested some knowledge of arithmetic for admission (making Yale the first college to do so) and added algebra and fluxions (differential calculus) to the mathematical studies. He purchased scientific instruments (which they called philosophical apparatus); and he built an orrery to show the movement of the planets. Nor did he neglect Greek and Latin. His success was such that Samuel Johnson had reported to Berkeley in 1741, "We have the satisfaction to see classical as well as mathematical learning improve among us."[53]

Instruction was bettered in 1745 by the addition of a third tutor, which allowed each tutor to care for one of the lower classes while the president taught the seniors. Standards were tightened as well. Oral quizzes had long been a part of daily classwork and the seniors were always examined in July of their final year. In 1761 public examinations once a quarter for all classes were added, and a new law was enacted that stipulated, "if upon Examination at any Time it shall be found that any Students are grossly defective in those Points of Knowledge which they might have been acquainted with according to their Standing, such Person or Person's shall be dismissed from being Members of College." Given the condition of the college in the sixties, it is perhaps not surprising that this rule was greeted by rebellion and riot. Some of the students objected to

the new Custom about to be introduced, viz; Examination, that we not having heard red or red any law for it, do unanimously agree Nemo Contradicente and without any Compulsion, that we the Subscribers will not be examined except it be for a Degree, untill we have heard red or red ourselves a Law enacted by and with the Advice of the Corporation, that we shall be examined, and think it hard that we must spend that Time being examined which we should spend in fitting for Examination, and we therefore unanimously agree that we will not be exammined by the President or Tutors untill such a Law shall be read etc. etc.

When the authors of this manifesto were punished, the students rioted, and only strict discipline brought a return to order.[54]

Clap taught much of the new curriculum himself. Ezra Stiles, who was both a student and a tutor under Clap, as well as being himself a man of incredibly wide-ranging intellectual curiosity, wrote of President Clap,

Many others, indeed, excelled him in the mechanic application of the lower branches of the mathematics: but he rose to sublimer heights, and became conversant in the application of this noble science to those extensive laws of Nature which regulate the most stupendous phenomena, and obtain throughout the stellary universe. I have known him to elucidate so many of the abstrusest theorems and ratiocinia of Newton, that, I doubt not, the whole *Principia* of that illustrious philosopher was comprehended by him.[55]

In addition, the president lectured on moral philosophy, many different legal and governmental systems, history, "the Nature and Form of obligatory Writings and Instruments, Agriculture, Commerce, Navigation, with some general Sketches upon Physick, Anatomy, Heraldry and Gunnery." [56] He was clearly the intellectual as well as the administrative head of the college.

Clap also made his mark on the physical Yale. The form of the campus ("the yard" as it was called then and would continue to be for more than a century)—the form it kept until Porter and Dwight changed it—was designed by Clap. He oversaw the building of Connecticut Hall, which still stands as the only representative of that earlier Yale. And he placed in line with it the first chapel, later called the Atheneum, which also housed the library.

He devoted more than just his time and effort to the college. He was also one of the largest contributors to the fund for the Livingstonian Professor of Divinity.* He bought the land for the professor's house and gave it to the college; he contributed to the fund for building the house. In fact, Clap was the largest single donor, except one, to the college during his presidency.[57]

While Thomas Clap gave more time, more effort, and almost more money to Yale than anyone else, he was filled with "natural Despotism and high notions of Dominion" which annoyed his friends and infuriated his enemies. Thus it was that one of his students could write of his resignation: "Tomme Clap you Fool do not think that I mind your Finis." [58]

But "Tomme Clap" deserves a better epitaph. He was the first leader of Yale to be an active organizer, administrator, and innovator. He gave the college its charter, designed its seal, codified its laws and recorded its customs, catalogued its library, increased its physical plant, created its first professorship, established its church, and improved it intellectually. Had this been all, we could easily say that he set it firmly on the road to greatness. Unfortunately, he undercut his achievement by alienating the General Assembly and thus, among other things, weakening the college financially. Furthermore, he made the college much more narrowly sectarian, split the fellows, and left Yale badly disrupted by the disputes he had so joyously entered. Still, he developed an institution which could become great. As the biographer of Harvard's graduates said of this complex man:

Thomas Clap was one of the three men who were chiefly responsible for shaping one of the great universities of the world. How much of what he did was for good and how much for ill, who are we to judge? [59]

* With a strange lack of historical feeling, President Woolsey allowed the name of Yale's first professorship to be changed in the 1860s.

7

The (Extended) Interregnum

Though Thomas Clap helped to establish the Yale that was later to become one of the world's great universities, he left it weakened within and under attack from without. Many students had departed —enrollment had dropped from around 170 to 100—and those who remained were in revolt. The General Assembly had largely withdrawn its financial support, and the dislike and distrust that this action indicated were echoed widely even beyond the borders of the colony.[1] The institution clearly needed peace and quiet to recover from Clap's reign, but the tumultuous period which saw Connecticut and her sister colonies in America hurtling toward independence from England was a difficult time in which to create that environment.

The seriousness of Yale's predicament was revealed immediately. James Lockwood (B.A. 1735), a fellow of the Corporation, was elected president on 10 September 1766, the day Clap resigned. He took a month to think the offer over and then declined the honor because of his age (fifty-one), feeble constitution (he died six years later), and the difficulty of leaving his ministry in Wethersfield. But Dexter says, "it was otherwise understood that a controling reason was the uncertain financial condition of the College."[2] The weakness of the institution was again discouraging interest in its presidency. Still, someone had to run the college, so the fellows turned to the one person handy, Professor of Divinity Naphtali Daggett, and elected him president *pro tempore*.[3] Daggett accepted and for a second time the college embarked on a period of extended temporary rule.

The first Yale graduate to hold the office of president was a steady, quiet, unprepossessing man of "middle height, strong framed, inclining to be corpulent, slow in his gait, and somewhat clumsy in his movements." There was nothing colorful or striking about him. He had been born in Attleboro, Massachusetts, in 1727, graduated from Yale in 1748, but had stayed on as a Berkeley scholar until called to a church on Long Island. He had returned to

Yale in 1756 as the first professor of divinity and he retained that office until his death in 1780. The most startling thing about Daggett was that some hot blood coursed through his veins. He was a fiery patriot. He was the first to attack Jared Ingersoll in public print for taking the post of stamp master in 1765. And when the British invaded New Haven, he grabbed his fowling piece and hastened off to fight. But in general, he was not an exciting man. Yale had had enough of that, though; it needed quiet steadiness now.[4]

As is usually the case, the beginning of a new presidency—even if only a temporary one—was greeted with delight by everyone. The Connecticut General Assembly received the announcement of Clap's retirement and Daggett's appointment with evident satisfaction. When the corporation requested a grant of funds (the annual grant had stopped in 1755), the Assembly immediately showed its new attitude by appointing a committee to study the situation at the college. Happily, the committee was favorably inclined: it recommended that the projected college deficit of £160 be covered by an impost on rum. (Yale, like New England generally, owes much to rum.) But the committee demanded a price for this assistance. It asked that the college laws be revised so that "the government of said college be as near like parental, and as few pecuniary mulcts as the circumstances thereof will admit; and that the steward in making up his quarter bills insert the punishments of each scholar with the offence for which the same was imposed, for the parents' information." In addition, it wanted the revised laws printed in English as well as Latin. Finally, it recommended that "in order for the continual support of College their accounts be annually laid before the General Assembly."[5]

The Assembly agreed with the committee and passed its report with little change. The college appears to have begun giving to the General Assembly information on the state of its treasury the following year (a practice it still continues), but in other matters it was less prompt. It did not translate the laws into English until 1774 (though a committee was appointed to revise the laws to this end in 1769); punishments were not put on the quarter bills; and discipline became more "parental" only very slowly.[6] Instead of changing the laws, Daggett merely enforced them in a different spirit. Indicative of the change was the comment in the Faculty Judgements in January 1767: the first punishment under Daggett was moderated because of "the orderly [behavior] of the Students in general this Year."[7]

The improved relationship with the General Assembly and the slow rebuilding of the size of the classes and the morale of the students that occurred during Daggett's eleven years of "temporary" rule are the most important aspects of his presidency; but probably most noticeable to the undergraduates of the day, in addition to the less severe discipline, was the decision no longer to rank students by their fathers' social positions but to list them alphabetically.

From the foundation of both Harvard and Yale, students were listed throughout their undergraduate years, at graduation, and in the catalogues of graduates, in a special order based in varying degrees at different times on appraisals of family position, intellectual promise, and parental relationship to the college. Once the class members were so ranked, a student took that place in everything he did: his seat in class, chapel, commons, and all else was fixed by it.[8] Thus a man's place in his class was far more important than just his position on a piece of paper. He had to act out his ranking every day of his college life. This fact helped to make the threat of "degradation" a strong one.

The punishment of degradation involved dropping a student lower in the class lists. It was not as often used at Yale as at Harvard, as far as can be ascertained, but there are several instances on record. For example, Isaac Burr of the class of 1753 was degraded from sixth to ninth place in his class for assaulting a senior when he was a junior (for there was also strict gradation of rank between classes). Jesse Denison (B.A. 1756) was expelled on a charge of stealing money from a classmate; he was given his degree a year after his class graduated, but where he had once stood in the middle of his class of thirty-three men, ever since he has been listed last.[9]

The system used to compute a student's position was never hard and fast, but a few elements in the rankings seem to be clear: a son of a governor or a president of Yale received the top spot; grandsons of governors, sons of lieutenant-governors, governors' assistants, and trustees also received this honored position. Certain families such as the Morrises and Livingstons of New York and the Winthrops and Saltonstalls of Connecticut always ranked in the first one or two places. For some reason the Gardiners of Gardiner's Island were not so highly esteemed. Fortunately, the son of a president of the college and the son of a governor never attended at the same time, but when the sons of different trustees were members of the same class, the date of the father's election to the board established precedence.

Next in importance after this group were the sons of ministers and the sons of alumni, often ranked by the father's date of graduation. These usually made up the middle of the class but sometimes held the top spots if no one more eminent was available. The bottom of the class was made up, as Shipton has said of Harvard, of the sons of "farmers, storekeepers, mariners, and artisans arranged in an order which cannot be explained by wealth or social position." The sons of merchants appeared in both the last and middle groups and wealth seems to have had little to do with their position. In the placement of ministers' sons, Dexter says, "there was never any disposition to exalt the ministerial order above laymen of distinction." But this is somewhat misleading: ministers had distinction by their office; very few laymen were felt to equal that rank.[10]

Most rules had their exceptions, and other considerations than those enumerated clearly came into play at times, but on the whole these guidelines were followed. A good example of the system is the class of 1751. First place was held by the son of the governor. He was followed by the grandson of a governor; this young student was no doubt assisted to his high position by being a Saltonstall. Then came the grandson of a deputy governor, whose position may also have been due to the fact that his father was a minister and a Harvard graduate of 1719. Next were the son of a minister who was also a Yale graduate of 1724, followed by the son of a minister from the class of 1725. The son of a successful civilian (who became a member of the governor's council in 1751) was followed by the son of a graduate of the class of 1727 who had never fulfilled his college promise and had died young: the father had been ranked second in his class, had served as a tutor, but then failed to enter the ministry and had become a sheriff instead. Clearly Clap thought the family had fallen thereby. Next below this student was the son of a family that had fallen even farther: Joseph Pierpont, a grandson of James Pierpont and Noadiah Russell, but whose father was not a graduate or a minister, only a merchant, came next. He was followed by the offspring of farmers, merchants, a goldsmith, and others of whom we know nothing.[11]

At Yale, placing registered only what a boy's father was, not what he himself was or would become. Berkeley scholars and college tutors were almost always chosen on the basis of talent, and they came from the very bottom as well as the very top of the class. In later life, a man could easily overcome his college rank. Daggett had ranked thirty-third in a class of thirty-six. Moses Dickinson (B.A. 1717) had been last in his class of five, but nonetheless he became a fellow in 1758. His son, who graduated in 1749 before his father achieved the exalted status of a member of the Corporation, still ranked second in a class of twenty-three, reflecting his father's rise.[12]

It was this system—if system it can be called—that the Yale Corporation decided to abolish in 1766 during a meeting dealing with the complete collapse of the college.[13] Samuel Eliot Morison, historian of Harvard, has written that it is untrue that "the system of placing at Harvard and Yale was given up before the Revolution because it was undemocratic, and that the abandonment of it marked the rise of democracy in the colonies." Instead, he declared categorically, "The records show that the old system was abandoned and students' names were arranged alphabetically simply because classes had become so big, and placing involved so much trouble, that the Corporations at both colleges decided to drop it."[14] One hesitates to argue with Professor Morison, but, at least as far as Yale is concerned, he is somewhat off the mark. Yale classes at this time had declined in size. President Clap, whose notes reveal that he did the ranking, probably rather liked placing the students and appreciated having another disciplinary weapon. His successor dropped the system because, as Dexter observed, "Professor Daggett's gifts were not in the line of strict discipline [though he could be very strict], and he cared comparatively little for the minutiae of ceremony and the dignity of office; . . . it was probably for him personally a welcome step, to discard the elaborate and perplexing system of class-arrangement."[15] No doubt, in addition, Daggett and the Corporation wished to avoid an area that could cause friction with the students. Clearly the change was not made to strike a blow for democracy. But it could not have been made had not democracy—at least in certain things—been on the rise. It could not have been made if everyone had thought like John Cotton, Harvard 1730, who wrote to Daggett when the change was announced:

I'm perswaded it will give great Dissatisfaction if the new Method takes place, it may perhaps save the Governours of the College Some Trouble, and prevent some Reflections from some few particular Gentlemen, who think their Sons have not their due Place; But the other way will disgust Gentlemen in general, whose Sons must perhaps Stand the lowest, and have one brot up by Charity or of the meanest Parentage often at their head.[16]

On the whole, people seem to have been willing to drop such gradations. Student reaction was excellent. David Avery, a junior when the change was made, wrote President Wheelock (B.A. 1733) of Dartmouth—where placing was never used—his impression of the change:

There appears [to be] a laudable ambition to excel in knowledge. It is not he that has got the finest coat or largest ruffles that is esteemed here at present. And as the class henceforward are to be placed alphabetically, the students may expect marks of distinction to be put upon the best scholars and speakers.[17]

Indicative of the parallel development of intellectual interest and democratic tendencies to which Avery refers was the opening of the Linonia Literary Society to freshmen (formerly the untouchables of the college community) in February 1767 and the founding the following year of a new literary society, Brothers in Unity, which was open to all classes from the first. These societies will be examined in more detail later, for now let us merely note that they added a welcome dimension to the intellectual lives of the students.[18]

Along with the abolition of placing, the rise of intellectual interest, better student morale, and improved relations with the General Assembly, another innovation was the addition of a second professor: in 1770 Nehemiah Strong (B.A. 1755) was appointed professor of mathematics and natural philosophy. His appointment was brought about because Clap was no longer present to teach these subjects. The new professorship did not indicate the addition of any new courses or any great alteration in mathematics or natural philosophy at Yale.

Change in any subjects taught at the college usually came, if it took place at all, within existing courses and rarely by the introduction of new course titles. This fact is best illustrated by the transformations in the natural philosophy course (an amalgam of biology, geology, astronomy, and physics). The first Yale students had used as a text Rector Abraham Pierson's college notes on John Magirus's

Physiologiae Peripateticae Libri Sex and the "Notes of Physicks" in the *Logicians School-Master* by Alexander Richardson. Unfortunately, this material had been out of date almost from the time Pierson wrote it down, for Harvard had stopped using Magirus and moved on to Descartes three years after Pierson left in 1668. Nonetheless, Yale students used Pierson's manuscript until at least 1722. Tutors Samuel Johnson and Daniel Browne between 1716 and 1722 did introduce some of Copernicus to the students, and Timothy Cutler reinforced the move to the Copernican system by using Gassendi's *Institutio Astronomica* as a text. In 1726 Elisha Williams supplanted Gassendi—and possibly the Pierson notes as well—with Samuel Clarke's edition of Jacques Rohault's *System of Natural Philosophy,* which contained sections on physics, astronomy, the earth and air, and anatomy and physiology. The physics section was the most significant, for it contained a Cartesian view of the universe; but Clarke had added footnotes which attempted to refute the text and show the Newtonian view. In 1734, with the purchase of additional scientific instruments the students were able even to see some physics problems solved. Thus, as Richard Warch says, between 1701 and 1739 Yale physics advanced "from an outmoded manuscript by Rector Abraham Pierson . . . to a relatively modern textbook which, in fact, was a disguised Newtonian treatise." [19]

Under Clap the natural philosophy course made further advances. For astronomy Clap introduced Isaac Watts's *The Knowledge of the Heavens and Earth Made Easy: or, The First Principles of Astronomy and Geography Explain'd by the Use of Globes and Maps* and illustrated it with two globes given by Watts and an orrery, the first to be built in the American colonies, that Clap had made himself. Clap also introduced as a text Willem Jacob van's Gravesande's *Mathematical Elements of Natural Philosophy,* which was pure Newtonian science. A step backward was taken around 1760 when Clap replaced Gravesande with Benjamin Martin's *Philosophical Grammar* and *Philosophia Brittanica,* which, as Edmund Morgan says, offered breadth at the expense of depth. Nonetheless, they were relatively "modern," so the student did not suffer from learning obsolete knowledge. After this substitution the natural philosophy course appears not to have changed, even internally, for more than twenty years.[20]

Even when the material presented in the courses was being

changed, the basic subjects of the curriculum remained much the same. The freshmen still spent most of their time studying Latin (Virgil and Cicero's Orations), a bit of New Testament Greek, and arithmetic. The sophomores continued the Greek Testament, got into Horace, and studied logic, geography, algebra, geometry, and rhetoric. Under Daggett sophomores also began to study English grammar (parts of speech, tenses, and other very basic material), which had never before been a part of the college curriculum.

The freshmen and sophomores recited their subjects at the customary time: seven in the morning (before breakfast), eleven, and four or five. The juniors had a less rigorous day, having only one morning class, at eleven, and the usual late afternoon session on such subjects as trigonometry, the Greek Testament, more of Cicero's Orations, English grammar, and an introduction to natural philosophy. According to Clap, by the time they were finished, many juniors understood surveying and the calculation of eclipses, and some were fairly proficient in conic sections and fluxions.

The seniors, having achieved almost the end of this "exhausting" curriculum, met only once a day at eleven (except when Daggett experimented with evening recitations in mathematics and natural philosophy). Despite this limited time in the classroom, they—like everyone else—were supposed to spend most of the rest of their time in their rooms studying. The seniors' main subjects were metaphysics and ethics, courses which, because they were supposed to represent the capstone of the student's undergraduate education, were taught by the president. As one historian has observed, these classes "embraced the tough problem of how to reconcile man's newly emancipated reason and natural law with the old theology and Christian law." Textbooks such as Locke's *Essay on Human Understanding* and William Wollaston's *The Religion of Nature Delineated* were used.[21]

The amount of time spent on the study of divinity was shrinking. In the 1726 college laws Friday afternoon and Saturday had been devoted to it. By 1745 only Saturday was used. And under Stiles even that amount would be lessened. Freshmen studied it through the Greek Testament while in Daggett's time sophomores and juniors read Thomas Vincent's very simple *Explicatory Catechism* and seniors grappled with the difficult *Abridgement of Christian Divinity* by Johannes Wollebius and William Ames's *Medulla Theologiae*.

At least of the last it could be said that "his Latin is of that kind so delightful to an American reader, where the English idiom and mode of arranging words are well preserved, and . . . would suit many a Freshman better than his Cicero." [22]

The juniors and seniors also had to dispute twice a week. Up to about 1750 this exercise had always been in Latin in the syllogistic form, but Clap then introduced forensic disputation in English along with the old method. Benjamin Franklin expressed his pleasure over the addition.[23] Disputes may have been the high point in the students' education. Recitation was often a boring exercise for student and teacher alike. Holding the textbook in his hands, the tutor would quiz each student in turn on part of the lesson for the day. If the student did not remember the passage or the right answer, he would reply *non paravi* and be judged accordingly; otherwise, he would struggle through as best he could. Basically all the student was asked to do was to memorize the text, while the tutor— unless he was an unusually ardent teacher—merely checked to make sure he had done the work.[24]

In disputations the format forced greater performance by both tutor and student. The tutor assigned a subject for two students to dispute (syllogistically or forensically). On the designated day they presented their oral arguments, one affirmative and the other negative, on the proposition. Since the forensic debates were in English, no doubt they led to a freer exchange of ideas. The sort of question discussed ranged from "Whether there are any such creatures as witches" and "Whether Samson was a self murtherer," to "Whether it is lawful to enslave the Africans" and "Whether it is lawful to resist the supream magistrate except in cases of conscience." The last was a very live issue when it was disputed in 1771.

A similar opportunity to use imagination and a certain amount of creativity was provided by declamations, which were presented by five or six students each week. These were written out in advance, corrected by the tutor, and then presented "memoriter from the oratorical Rostrum." Upon the completion of the address, according to Clap, "the President makes some Observations upon the Manner of Delivery and sometimes upon the Subject; and sometimes gives some small Laurel to him who best acts the Part of an Orator." [25]

The major curricular innovation that took place under Daggett was the introduction of English grammar and literature as subjects of study. As already noted, English grammar was begun as early as 1767, and belles-lettres was edged in later by two bright young tutors, Timothy Dwight (B.A. 1769) and John Trumbull (B.A. 1767). These young men, appointed in 1771, did much to encourage the desire for learning that swept the college prior to the Revolution. Because of their personal activities in belles-lettres (they were members of the group misnamed "the Hartford, or Connecticut, Wits") they made it a matter of interest in the college. In their delight over the subject, they may even have gone so far as to assist the students in the performance of as yet technically illegal plays.[26] In any case, their teaching was so inspiring that Timothy Dwight, at the request of the senior class, asked the Corporation in 1776 to allow him to instruct them in history, rhetoric, and belles-lettres. The Corporation grudgingly permitted these frills to be introduced as an extra course, but it could be taken only "with the approbation of the parents or guardians of said class." Despite the conservative Corporation's opposition to the turning of "solid learning into show," the English language and literature crept into the curriculum and would be expanded under President Stiles. But the slow movement of English into the college—beginning with Clap's introduction of forensic disputes in English in 1750 or 1751—is typical of the usually glacial rate of curricular change.[27]

There were many critics of the curriculum in the 1760s and 1770s, ranging from those who thought that the "fundamental defect" was "the slight Method of teaching the classics" to those who questioned the general content and agreed with Tutor Trumbull that the student was

> In the same round condemn'd each day,
> To study, read, recite and pray

only to emerge from college having gained ancient tongues and lost their own.[28] Most of the calls for change came from a growing anticlerical party and centered on a desire for a more practical education—by which they meant one that was oriented less toward the ministry and more toward other professions.[29] In fact, of course, the curriculum was not necessarily ministerial: it contained what the Western world had long felt an educated man should know. And the criticism tended to be of the strain that has produced cries for more "practical" or "relevant" college courses throughout American history.

This rising criticism was all a part of the turmoil of the years leading up to the Revolution—years which saw many accepted forms and institutions questioned. Not surprisingly, the college did not escape. What is surprising is that, despite the distractions, there was so much concern over education among students and critics alike. Students who could ask, after the war had already begun, for a course in history, rhetoric, and belles-lettres were capable of anything.

The undergraduates also showed their concern over the relations with the mother country. After the Townshend duties were passed in England, and nonimportation agreements entered into by merchants in America in response, the Yale class of 1769 published the following notice in the newspapers:

The Senior Class of Yale College have unanimously agreed to make their Appearance at the next public Commencement, when they are to take their first Degree, wholly dressed in the Manufactures of our own Country: And desire this public Notice may be given of their Resolution, that so their Parents and Friends may have sufficient Time to be providing Homespun Cloaths for them, that none of them may be obliged to the hard Necessity of unfashionable Singularity, by wearing imported Cloth.[30]

Despite the difficulty of getting enough homespun, the class seems to have accomplished its purpose and appeared in the clothes of the country. The class of 1770 was relieved of the problem by the repeal of the duties—except that on tea—and the collapse of nonimportation. Soon the period of improved relations between England and the colonies which followed the repeal was ended by the Tea Act and the Boston Tea Party. This and other disorders produced Parliamentary acts aimed at coercing better behavior in Boston and other legislation which irritated the colonies. Yale's reaction to all this was symbolized by the English dialogue of two M.A. candidates presented at commencement in 1774. Their subject was "The Rights of America and the Unconstitutional Measures of the British Parliament."[31] In less than ten years Yale had moved from chastising Joseph Lyman for his "unjustifiable Reflections on . . . Parliament" in a private college exercise to allowing such "reflections" at the greatest event of the college year. As the M.A.s debated, their subject was being discussed to more purpose at the First Continental Congress in Philadelphia.

The pace of student concern—as with their elders—was now increasing. In February of 1775 they formed a student military company and, with the aid of "two Regular Soldiers," began "practicing, marching, maneuvering" on the lower Green. Robert Sill reported to Nathan Hale in March that "the Military Art just begins to dawn in the generous breasts of the Sons of Yale. . . . College Yard constantly sounds with, *poise your firelock, cock your firelock &c*. These warlike noises are continually in College." Harvard, more in the center of things, had established a college military company as early as 1769 or 1770. In the greater world outside Yale, her graduates were less behindhand: perhaps one-half of the field officers in the Connecticut militia were Yale men, as were a majority of the Council of Safety.[32]

On 21 April 1775 New Haven was thrown into an uproar. One student noted in his diary, "Today tidings of the Battle of Lexington, which is the first engagement with the British troops, arrived at New Haven. This filled the country with alarm and rendered it impossible for us to pursue our studies to any profit." [33] The students no doubt watched with delight when—after the town voted in a special meeting not to send armed help to Boston—Captain Benedict Arnold formed his Second Company of the Governor's Guards on the Green, marched to Beers' tavern, catercorner across the street from Old College, demanded the keys to the powderhouse from the town fathers, marched out to that building (which was located about where the Yale Infirmary was for many years, at 276 Prospect Street), seized the ammunition, and soon thereafter departed for Boston. As these troops, dressed in their fur headdresses, scarlet coats, white breeches and vests, and black leggings, marched away, no doubt some Yale boys decided on the spot to go fight the British.[34]

In any case, with the future uncertain and classes disrupted by all the excitement, the students were dismissed the next day nearly two weeks before the beginning of regular spring vacation.[35] They reconvened on 30 May with the siege of Boston still in progress and were soon excited by the arrival of George Washington, the newly named commander-in-chief of the Continental Army, and Major General Charles Lee, who were on their way to join the troops outside Boston. The great lexicographer Noah Webster, who was a member of the class of 1778, later described the visit:

These gentlemen lodged in New Haven, at the house of the late Isaac Beers, and in the morning they were invited to see a military company of students of Yale College perform their manual exercises. They expressed their surprise and gratification at the precision with which the students performed the customary exercises then in use. This company then escorted the generals as far as Neck Bridge, and this was the first instance of that honor conferred on General Washington in New England. It fell to my humble lot to lead this company with music.[36]

Because of the war the regular public commencement in September was not held in 1775. Degrees were given privately to the seniors in July after their examinations. (The seniors had always had the period from exams in July until commencement in September for vacation. Only the poor undergraduates and faculty had to remain in New Haven during the humid summer months.) Public commencement would not be held again until 1781. Prior to this private commencement of 1775, David Bushnell of this class completed his invention of the submarine torpedo. And, shortly after returning home, he built the first submarine to be used in wartime.[37]

The Revolution affected the college in many ways. Immediately the Assembly discontinued the grants it had been making sporadically in response to annual requests from the college. Without this additional money the Corporation found it necessary to tear down its first building. Old College had been in bad shape for some years and repeated repairs had kept it just usable. But it could not last without major reconstruction, so in November 1775 two-thirds of wooden Yale College was torn down, leaving only the south end of the building, containing the kitchen, Great Hall, and former library room. Despite this loss, and despite the war, college persisted with some of its old flavor. The students began to assert themselves again. In April 1776 they declared their discontent with the existing administration by petitioning the Corporation to remove the president. Naturally, the Corporation refused, but it was a sign that the end was near for Daggett.[38]

In July the forming nation declared its independence, and when the signatures had been affixed, Yale could point with pride to the fact that four of her sons—Philip Livingston, Lewis Morris, Oliver Wolcott, and Lyman Hall—had put their names to the document. The college's representation was right for its age: older Harvard had eight signers and young Princeton, two.[39]

It was necessary to break up college twice during 1776: in August because of the prevalence of camp distemper and in December because of lack of food. But college reconvened early in January 1777 just after the nation had received some good news. One undergraduate recorded it in his diary:

We have most certain accounts which come in the New London paper that General Washington crossed the Delaware the night of the 25th of December and attacked a body of Hessians. . . . After an engagement of 35 minutes, he routed them and took upwards of 900 of them prisoner, besides killed and wounded.[40]

Despite the problem of getting enough wood for the fires that heated their rooms (Connecticut Hall was slightly damaged from a fire caused by students burning straw) and sufficient food to keep hunger away, college stayed in session throughout the winter. But on 13 March, Colonel Fitch, the steward, announced defeat. He could no longer keep commons open after the end of the quarter unless he was allowed to charge more for board. The quarter ended on 21 March, and the following day the president told the students to send for their horses as college would break up on the twenty-sixth. At the same time he announced that he was going to resign the presidency. One student noted that he gave "the scholars an affecting speech, so that their tune turned, for it used to be *old damned Tunker* but now *Bona Prefex.*" [41]

College was finally dismissed on the twenty-eighth. No date was set for the next meeting of classes. Tutor Timothy Dwight thought it likely the seniors might not gather again, but he approached the class to discover if they would come to him if he called them. The Corporation met on 1 April 1777 and concluded:

Whereas the Difficulties of subsisting the Students in this Town are so great,—the Price of Provisions and Board so high,—and the Avocations from Study, occasioned by the State of Public Affairs so many;—Difficulties which still increase and render it very inconvenient for the

Students to reside here at Present; and yet considering the great Importance; that they be under the best Advantages of Instruction and Learning, Circumstances will permit:—Voted that in the Opinion of this Board, it is necessary to provide some other convenient Place or Places, where the classes may reside under their respective Tutors; until God in his kind Providence shall open a Door for their Return to this fixed and ancient Seat of Learning; and that Messrs. Taylor and Goodrich be a Committee for that Purpose, and make a Report to the next Meeting of this Board.[42]

At this same meeting Daggett's resignation as president (but not as professor of divinity) was accepted and a committee was appointed to consult with the General Assembly about the college. The town of New Haven was asked to protect the deserted college buildings and especially to keep the destructive American troops out of them, while a third committee was appointed to care for the library. Many of the books were subsequently moved inland to safer places.[43]

At the end of the month the Corporation confirmed their belief that it would be better to have the students meet in quiet inland towns. New Haven, with an active fleet of privateers and British war vessels often lurking nearby, was far too vulnerable to attack. The fellows voted, therefore, to have the freshmen meet in Farmington, the sophomores and juniors in Glastonbury under Professor Strong, and the seniors under Tutor Dwight at whatever place he should select. Ultimately Dwight chose Wethersfield,* across the river from Glastonbury, so part of Yale returned for a second sojourn in that small town outside of Hartford.[44]

The vote to scatter the classes marked the beginning of about a year's exile from New Haven for most of the students, but it did not entirely solve their problems. In January 1778 the Corporation decided it was necessary to give the undergraduates even more freedom. It ruled that those who found it difficult to join their class in the place assigned might reside and study elsewhere. If examination showed they had kept up with their work, they could retain their standing in college.[45]

---

*Only the class of 1777 seems to have spent any time in Wethersfield. They were there for about a month during June and July. The class of 1778 appears to have met in New Haven, and an attempt to move them to Cheshire in November 1777 was probably unsuccessful.

Wherever the students were located, these were exciting and challenging years. Oliver Wolcott (B.A. 1778) went home after school was dismissed in March 1777. The British raided Danbury and Oliver was routed from bed to join the militia to oppose them. He took part in several skirmishes as a member of troops under the command of General Wooster (B.A. 1738). That old graduate had begun his military career in 1740 during King George's War and had taken an active part in the fighting during the Seven Years' War, so in 1775 he was made major general of the Connecticut forces. He ended his service during the Danbury engagements when he was mortally wounded.[46]

Another, more recent Yale graduate had lost his life the year before in one of the most famous incidents of the war. Nathan Hale (B.A. 1773) had been captured when on a spying mission and executed by the British on 22 September 1776. He died, by the most famous account, with the words "I only regret, that I have but one life to lose for my country" on his lips. Hale may have been the first hero of the Revolution.[47]

In the year of Hale's death, Joel Barlow received his first taste of military duty. Still an undergraduate, he took part in the great Battle of Long Island. Barlow was a member of the class of 1778, one of the greatest classes to graduate from Yale. Their education was so much disrupted by the war that it may be wondered if they got much more from college than their diplomas, but nonetheless this class of forty men must be singled out for special mention. The commencement program for their private wartime ceremony revealed the talent of the class:

A Cliosophic Oration in Latin, by Sir Meigs.
A Poetical Composition in English, by Sir Barlow.
A Dialogue in English, by Sir Chaplin, Sir Ely, and Sir Miller.
A Cliosophic Oration in English, by Sir Webster.
A Disputation in English, by Sir Swift, Sir Wolcott, and Sir Smith.
A Valedictory Oration in English, by Sir Tracy.

These young men entered many professions: Josiah Meigs, became a professor at Yale and president of the University of Georgia; Joel Barlow, in a most varied career, was poet, statesman, and radical; Asher Miller, became judge of the Supreme Court of Connecticut; Noah Webster, lexicographer and schoolmaster to America; Zephaniah Swift, chief justice of the Supreme Court of Connecticut; Oliver Wolcott, secretary of the treasury under Presidents Washington and Adams; Noah Smith, judge of the Supreme Court of Vermont; Uriah Tracy, United States senator from Connecticut. Not on the commencement program but also members of this class were men whose careers were to be equally distinguished: Congressman Ezekiel Gilbert; Stephen Jacob, judge of the Vermont Supreme Court; and Alexander Wolcott (cousin of Oliver Wolcott mentioned above), nominated for the U.S. Supreme Court but defeated by the Senate.[48]

Not all Yale men were heroes, just as not all were successful. Jared Mansfield (B.A. 1777) was "expelled from College in January of his Senior year, for complicity in a theft of books from the Library." In March he and some others were "taken . . . in a barn with about 300 counterfeit money." But from this low point he came back; by 1786 he was rector of Hopkins Grammar School in New Haven; in 1787 he was enrolled with his class and received his B.A. and M.A.; in 1793 he became surveyor general of the United States; and in 1808 the town of Mansfield, Ohio, was named after him. In 1825 Yale gave this once wayward youth an honorary degree.[49]

A small proportion of Yale men were Tories. One of these, Judge Thomas Jones (B.A. 1750) said that his alma mater was "a nursery of sedition, of faction, and republicanism." He thought it "a college remarkable for its persecuting spirit, its republican principles, its intolerance in religion and its utter aversion to Bishops and all Earthly Kings." Certainly the students were not friendly to loyalists in their midst. Abiathar Camp, Jr., an outspoken Tory, was treated as a pariah and ultimately withdrew from college.[50]

Faced by the problems of wartime and student opposition, Naphtali Daggett had resigned the presidency, as we have seen. He had been a good president. Though his term had begun in the cold of winter (in a year when it was reported that they were not without fires until June and that the leaves, on 12 June, "have yet but just got their growth"), and though it ended under the chill of war, it was marked by improved relations with the General Assembly, restored college discipline, and classes of respectable numbers. Daggett's greatest shortcoming, as far as the students were concerned, was that he was dull; since he was professor of divinity, pastor of the college church, and president all at the same time, this was difficult to bear. As one student residing in Wethersfield with Tutor Dwight reported in his diary, "Tunker is in town and I am afraid will preach tomorrow." [51]

For all that, he had brought the college back to what it had been in the best days of Clap. It was not a spectacular achievement—he was not a spectacular man—but it was a very important one. It meant that, though his successor would have to cope with the difficult problems of the war, at least he would not have to cope with the virulent anti-Yale feeling that had existed when Daggett took over from Thomas Clap.

The Rise of the University Spirit

The war, the resignation of Daggett, the scattered college classes, and the need for financial assistance made it clear to the Corporation that it would be diplomatic to seek the advice of the state government on who should fill the presidency. If a successor to Daggett acceptable to the General Assembly were chosen, the result might well be new grants from the state.

In consultations with a committee of the Assembly held in July 1777, the Corporation revealed its weakened financial condition. The committee recommended Ezra Stiles for the presidency and suggested that the General Assembly "should have a voice in concurrence with the Fellows in appointing professors supported by the State." If the Corporation followed this advice, they said, "the Assembly would do every Thing for the aggrandizement of Yale College otherwise they should not." [1]

While the Corporation was certain to balk at having to seek the state's agreement on certain appointments, especially with nothing but a general promise of help, the suggestion of Stiles for the presidency could not have been a surprise. He was a Yale graduate of the class of 1746, had been a tutor from 1749 to 1755, and since October 1755 pastor of the Second Congregational Church in Newport, Rhode Island. The war had forced him out of Newport, so he was temporarily preaching to the First Church in Portsmouth, New Hampshire. Stiles's fine mind, wide-ranging intellectual curiosity, and worldwide correspondence had brought him a reputation as one of the most learned men in America, while his residence in Newport had helped him to avoid the disputes between Old Lights and New and General Assembly and college. [2]

Despite his excellent credentials, Ezra Stiles was not the only candidate. When the vote was held at the annual meeting of the Corporation in September 1777, he was elected by a majority of the fellows, but some cast their ballots for one of their number, the Reverend Elizur Goodrich. [3] This lack of unanimity, along with all the other problems of the college itself, disturbed Stiles. How could he do all that needed to be done without the unanimous support of the Corporation? In November Stiles paid a visit to New Haven. He discussed the matter with the fellows and came away believing he had their support but still unsure that he wanted to accept an office he knew to be "a Crown of Thorns." As he mulled over the question, he sketched out a plan of what one might do to Yale. Viewing the needs of Connecticut, he decided that Yale should have a professor of physic (since the state needed doctors), a professor of law (to train men for government service), and also professors of ecclesiastical history, civil history, Hebrew and oriental languages, and oratory and belles-lettres. These were to be in addition to the two existing professorships in divinity and mathematics and natural philosophy. Stiles realized that to carry out this plan—the first that envisioned Yale as a university—would depend in part on the assistance of the state. And this necessity he welcomed: as Edmund Morgan says in his excellent biography of Stiles, he recognized that if the state provided the funds it would "give the public once more a sense of participation in the college." [4]

The realization of how difficult it would be to achieve the ends envisioned in his plans was brought home to Stiles while he was still debating whether to accept the election. When the Corporation and a committee of the Assembly met in January 1778 to pursue the subject of state aid, they found it impossible to agree on anything. The General Assembly wanted the college to do many things but failed to make any firm commitments in return, so the Corporation refused to make any agreements. Despite this disappointment, Stiles finally wrote the Corporation on 20 March 1778 to say that he had decided to accept the presidency.[5]

After Stiles and his family received smallpox inoculations and recovered from that dangerous ordeal, they embarked on a leisurely eleven-day journey from New Hampshire that brought them to New Haven on 20 June. The college had been ordered to reassemble there three days later, so the new president had to go right to work. His inauguration was held early in July in an elaborate ceremony that began his presidency with all the trappings he liked best: formality, elaborate processions, and much oratory. Stiles took an oath of allegiance to the state (instead of to the king as his predecessors had done) and made a simple affirmation of his beliefs—which was also indicative of the new reign. Clap's elaborate oath of assent to the Westminster Catechism and Confession of Faith did not fit Stiles's broader and more tolerant faith.[6]

Ezra Stiles began his presidency faced by many grave problems. Fortunately, the low point of the war for the Americans was past: Burgoyne had been defeated, the Franco–American alliance had been signed, the army had left Valley Forge, and the British had evacuated Philadelphia. Though the result of the conflict was still in doubt, American morale was definitely on the upswing. While the war continued, Stiles's major problem was to supply the Yale students with food. Summer was the easiest time, so commons was open for the new president's first quarter, in part because parents helped provide food in answer to an appeal from the college. The same thing was tried in the fall, but the plea did not work a second time. College was dismissed early, on 28 December, for a prolonged winter vacation.[7]

Stiles tried hard to open the college again. He got a promise from the governor for some flour. He appealed to the parents for aid and then threatened that without provisions college would not be held and no degrees would be given. Finally, a little flour was received, school was opened on 18 February 1779, and on the following day Stiles wrote the governor:

Encouraged by your Favor of the 3d inst., I have suffered the students to return and yesterday set up College orders, the Steward having got some flour for a beginning in setting up Commons. . . . This waits upon your Excellency praying that you would be pleased to favor us with an order or Permit . . . for supplying the Steward with flour to the amount of fifty barrels if necessary.[8]

By one means or another, Stiles kept college in session that year and commons remained open. Despite a fire in the library, which was quickly extinguished by an opportune rainstorm before any real damage was done, the year passed comparatively quietly.[9] Hardly had Stiles's first year in New Haven ended, however, when the British appeared on the scene.

The fourth of July 1779 fell on a Sunday, so the celebration was planned for Monday. Late Sunday night word arrived in New Haven that a large British fleet was approaching. Stiles was high in the steeple of the college chapel watching when the sun rose on the fifth. His telescope revealed to him the greatest fleet ever formed in Long Island Sound lying off the town: twenty square-rigged ships and about as many smaller vessels. Fearing the worst, President Stiles sent his "Children, the College Records and Papers, and my own MSS. and papers out of town."

The British had decided to attack the Connecticut shore in order to draw at least some of Washington's men away from the strong position he had resumed at White Plains. New Haven was to be the first target. As Stiles watched while day broke on that clear and very hot July morning, the British debarked some two to three thousand soldiers, one part to advance on the town through East Haven and the other by West Haven. The Americans were ill-prepared to oppose the raid. "Perhaps one Third of the Adult male Inhabitants flew to Arms, and went out to meet them," Stiles later wrote in his diary, "a quarter removed out of town doing nothing, the rest remained unmoved partly Tories partly timid Whigs."

College was dismissed immediately. Some students ran for home, but a volunteer company of around seventy (more than half of the entire student body) formed to fight the redcoats. Ezra Stiles, Jr., and George Welles led them first to the west to defend against the forces advancing from that direction. On the way they were passed by Professor Daggett "riding furiously . . . on his old black mare, with his fowling-piece in his hand ready for action."

The militia, students, and other town volunteers clashed with the British advancing from West Haven, retreated over West Bridge, destroyed it, and then defended the crossing. The enemy was forced by this maneuver to make a long detour to reach the next river crossing. As the redcoats made their way to the ford some distance away, the Reverend Dr. Daggett sniped at them until he was captured. Knocked about, poked with bayonets, and forced to walk long miles barefoot under the hot summer sun, the fifty-one year old professor of divinity barely survived the march. He never fully recovered from the experience, and his death in November 1780 was attributed to this ordeal. His son, Ebenezer (B.A. 1778), was also a victim of the war. He died of smallpox in 1781 as he returned from the Virginia campaigns.

A Yale classmate of Naphtali Daggett's, John Hotchkiss, was killed near the spot where Daggett was taken. He was with the town volunteers opposing the invaders. Since only about twenty-seven Americans died during the attack on New Haven, the Yale class of 1748 may be said to have done its share of the fighting.

After the battle at West Bridge, Ezra Stiles, Jr., led the college volunteers to East Haven to oppose that wing of the attack. On the way they fell into an ambush and, without assistance from a nearby force of militia, defeated their attackers and took many captives. But the students and townspeople could only delay the inevitable. The first enemy troops entered New Haven a little after noon, following a sharp fight at Ditch corner (where Whalley, Dixwell, and Goffe streets now meet).

As soon as the British troops were in the town, they began, as Stiles described it, "Plunder, Rape, Murder, Bayoneting, Indelicacies toward the Sex, Insolence and Abuse and Insult toward the Inhabitants in general." Fortunately, these horrors were not increased by severe physical damage to New Haven and Yale. The British had planned to burn the town, but, though they did fire the long wharf and the vessels moored there, they changed their minds about the town proper. Edmund Fanning (B.A. 1757), son-in-law and private secretary of the commanding general of the British forces, later said that he persuaded them not to burn the town (which helped to get him an honorary LL.D. from Yale). His claim may be true, but Yale sentiment was assisted by sound military reasoning. Major-General Tryon reported, "The collection of the enemy in force [outside of New Haven] and with heavier cannon than our own, diverted the General from that passage [burning the town]." Thus when they were allowed to depart without a fight, the British preserved New Haven. But it must have hurt to leave it standing. A comment in the diary of the commander of the fleet indicates British feeling about New Haven: "That place is a spacious and a very considerable town; it has the largest university in America, and might with propriety be styled the parent and nurse of rebellion." The raiding party made up for its kindness to New Haven by burning large sections of Fairfield and Norwalk a few days later.[10]

The raid on New Haven made Stiles decide not to call the college back into session that summer. He announced this conclusion in the newspapers on 5 August:

Such is the dangerous situation of the Town of New Haven that it is not judged expedient to call the Undergraduate Classes together again this quarter. It is, however, recommended to the scholars to apply themselves diligently to the studies of their respective Classes under the best Tuition they can find until God in his Providence may permit them to be peaceably reassembled at this seat of Learning.[11]

College did not reconvene until 22 October, the usual time for the school year to start. But the supply problem had not been solved, so winter vacation again began early. Most of the students left on 16 December, but about forty who were able to find board in town continued to study under Stiles until 10 January, the regular date for the beginning of vacation.[12]

After the last students departed, there was a real question whether college would reassemble that winter. It was clear that the steward would not be able to board the students in commons. He still faced the usual problems of wartime, even though the fighting had now moved to the southern colonies. To make matters more difficult for the steward, it was the worst winter in almost forty years. The temperature was often below zero and the roads were blocked by huge snowdrifts. Stiles decided the only thing to do was to put the students on their own. College, the students were informed, would open February first for students who could find their own board. Some fifty did, and with this greatly reduced attendance the college limped along until commons could open again late in May. Though the war was still far from over and much hard fighting lay ahead, the winter of 1780 marked the end of serious wartime difficulties for Yale.[13]

That there was a new confidence over the ultimate outcome of the conflict may have been indicated by the fact that, beginning this year, diplomas were no longer dated in the regular fashion: now they read "Annoque Independentiae Americanae" and the year, in this case "quinto." This practice continued well into the nineteenth century.[14]

One difficulty never encountered during the war was a lack of students. There were 132 when Stiles took over, even though the college had been scattered all over the state. In the history of the school this was a sizable number. Under Stiles during the war enrollment increased greatly from a low point of 124 in 1778 to a high of 265 in the fall of 1783. Many farmer fathers were prosperous during the war and sent their sons to college. Furthermore, while attending college a young man was exempt from service in the militia. Even those who had commenced B.A. and were waiting the necessary three years for their M.A. were considered students, though sometimes they had trouble convincing the militia officers of that fact. One recent B.A. wrote to ask Ezra Stiles for a certificate that he was still a "Student for the time being." He made much of the fact that for the militia officer to disallow his claim was to deprive Yale of its rights and, he said, he would not accept that any more than he would "tamely suffer my Country to be deprived of its rights by the Tyrant of Britain." [15]

Other students applied for early admission to escape service. One August, Stiles recorded in his diary that he had examined and admitted two young men for the college year beginning in October. "The reason of these applications for a premature Admission," he noted, "is to become free from Impress or Draughting into the military Service in the Time of War. But I am doubtful whether this would secure them, according to the true Intention of the College Charter or Acts of Assembly." [16]

Since so many came to college during the war—as the laws almost encouraged them to do—the question arises to what degree Yale men fought for their country. It admits, however, of no clear answer. In 1775 there were about 900 living Yale graduates; 163 more graduated through 1779. Of these 1,063 individuals at least one-third were ministers and many were probably too old for the armed forces. Nonetheless, some 234 (including chaplains) saw service for the Americans, or about one graduate in every five. How many served with the British we do not know. Considering only the more recent graduates, about 35 percent appear to have served on the American side for some period of time. Of those alumni who fought for independence, just under 9 percent died from service-contracted illnesses or injuries. Though many of the necessary figures are lacking, Howard Peckham has estimated that perhaps 40 to 50 percent of the men of military age saw service of some kind on the American side. Of these, a very conservatively estimated 10 to 12 percent died of illness or injury.[17]

In a day when all men were not expected to rush to the colors—

when avoidance of service was no blight on a man's future—the performance of Yale men in the Revolution becomes more impressive. While it may not be true, as Anson Phelps Stokes thought, that never has the university "played a more conspicuous or more admirable part in American history than it did at the time of the Revolution," it was still a contribution that merits admiration. Harvard's historian had to confess that his "College rendered her proper service to the country in council, through the constructive labors of such men as John Adams and James Bowdoin, rather than in the field or at sea." Yale men seem to have done both. Though none were of the caliber or importance of John Adams, there were five delegates to the Federal Convention, fourteen members of the Continental Congress, twelve generals and two aides to General Washington, as well as the four signers of the Declaration of Independence who have already been mentioned. It was an amazingly good record for a place that was still considered by some to be too much a school for ministers.[18]

The youth of the students (most entered at age sixteen) and the desire to avoid service meant that enrollment was not a problem for Ezra Stiles during the war; but he had plenty of other difficulties—some of which had little or nothing to do with the war. A major problem was that he was a minister and president of a Corporation entirely made up of ministers in a time of rising anticlericalism. On top of that, over the years the Corporation had seemed almost to go out of its way to annoy the General Assembly and the people of Connecticut.[19] Under Daggett and throughout most of the Revolution, the hostility to Yale and the Corporation which Clap had ignited lay dormant except for occasional flare-ups. The coals were always ready, however, to be blown into flame. The Corporation needed to be moderate, wise, and tolerant in a time not only of anticlericalism but of anti-intellectualism, egalitarianism, and vocationalism. Instead, Stiles discovered even before he took office that the Corporation had a talent for doing the wrong thing.

In 1777, before Stiles became president, there had been four excellent tutors in the college: Timothy Dwight, Joseph Buckminster, John Lewis, and Abraham Baldwin. By the time Stiles was inaugurated, only Baldwin was left. The Yale Corporation had forced out the others. Apparently because the tutors tried to change the curriculum by adding more English grammer and literature and even allowed theatrical performances ("turn'd College . . . into Drury Lane"), the conservative ruling body got rid of them.[20]

The first to go was Timothy Dwight, who had ambitions for the presidency that went to Stiles. In the face of a Corporation order that there should be no final exercises for the seniors in 1777, he held them in Wethersfield anyway. It appears that he was then called before the Corporation and forced to resign, ostensibly for this failure to obey orders. He was probably willing to leave, since he knew by then that he would not be the new president of Yale.

The next to depart was Joseph Buckminster. This may have been a bit of a shock to Stiles, because it is possible he had not heard of it when he accepted the presidency. To Buckminster the Corporation revealed its dissatisfaction that the tutors had "turned all solid learning into show." Faced with this ignorance, Buckminster resigned. That Stiles thought highly of him is revealed by his succeeding the president at the First Church of Portsmouth.

With Dwight and Buckminster the Corporation achieved its ends rather easily. Tutor Lewis was more stubborn. Nevertheless, the Corporation forced him out in an even more disgraceful manner. When he was informed that classes would soon return to New Haven and asked if he would return there from Farmington, where he was in charge of the freshmen, he requested time to consider. "I have a family," he is reported to have said, "am not, at this moment, certain of a house to accomodate them, and cannot resolve to remove them into the street." When the Corporation refused to give him more than half an hour to decide, he quit. Baldwin stayed for one more year. But he had had enough of the Yale Corporation. When he was elected professor of divinity two years later, in 1781, he refused the office. Stiles thought he did so because "he did not chuse to trust himself with our Corporation." [21]

As Edmund Morgan has noted, these dismissals "demonstrated not merely bad manners but a smallness of mind that substantiated the growing popular prejudice against clergymen." It must also have proved to Stiles that his path would not be an easy one. This impression was further confirmed before his presidency was three months old. Silas Deane (B.A. 1758), who had served the Continental Congress in France as a commercial and political agent and as one of the negotiators, with Benjamin Franklin (M.A. hon. 1753) and Arthur Lee, of the treaty of commerce and friendship with France, offered soon after his return to America to assist in raising money from "opulent friends" in France for a professorship of French. Immediately Stiles saw this as an opportunity to begin his planned expansion of the college. When he discussed the projected chair with influential men, he was heartened to discover no suspicion of "popery." Not, that is, until he got to the Yale Corporation. They feared this foreign influence and forced Stiles to inform Deane that they would not accept his offer. The following year, however, they did go so far as to confer an LL.D. on Conrad Gérard, the French minister to the American Congress.[22]

The Corporation soon returned to its policy of getting rid of those it disliked. They pushed Nehemiah Strong, professor of mathematics and natural philosophy, out of office in 1781 and left Stiles as the sole professor (he had been made professor of ecclesiastical history when he became president), assisted by a group of almost totally inexperienced tutors.[23] Clearly Stiles at this time still lacked the capacity to dominate the fellows of the Yale Corporation the way Thomas Clap had done. As a result, development was thwarted and the college was declining as an educational institution.

Even though the faculty was shrunken in size and possibly demoralized in spirit, students flocked to Yale. The freshman class that entered in 1781 was of exceptional size. It numbered seventy men at graduation, the largest class of the eighteenth century and a size not reached again until 1806. The total enrollment rose from 153 in 1780 to 224 in 1781, necessitating the hiring of a fourth tutor. This unprecedented number of students had recently arrived at college when the news of the victory at Yorktown reached New Haven. To celebrate the event Tutor Josiah Meigs gave "an animating, pathetic and ingenious oration" in the Brick Meeting House on the Green, and that night the college was "beautifully illuminated" with candles in every window. In December Yale conferred an honorary doctor of laws degree on General George Washington.[24]

The large enrollment increased the income from tuitions but led almost inevitably to student disorders, since it was difficult for a few young tutors to control the large mass of energetic boys. Student violence reached its peak in March 1782, when some twenty or twenty-five students went on a rampage after hearing the punishments for damages done to buildings during an earlier outbreak. They proceeded to demolish what remained of Old College. Stiles clamped down, expelling four students and rusticating twelve others, and even then he feared he had not been "severe eno'." Nevertheless, he hoped that the students now knew "we dare inflict the highest Punishments." [25]

The students' destruction of the Old College brought about the first new building in Stiles's presidency. A kitchen and dining hall were ready for use in December 1782 and were finished by the following May. This brick building stood in the yard behind the developing brick row, and after serving as commons for many years was used as the chemical laboratory from 1820 until its removal in 1888. [26]

In addition to the construction of a new building, 1782 saw the return of most of the library to the college. The books had been stored for safety during the war in inland towns along with some of the college's other prized possessions. Stiles recorded in his diary on 26 November the return of "the Kings (Geo. I) Picture by Kneller, and Mr. Davenports and also the Human Skeleton commonly called the Anatomy and the residue of the Apparatus." Not all the books got back safely. In 1785 the college advertised a number of times for the return of "sundry Books, which were scattered about the Country in the Removal from the College, during the War." From time to time, even into the present century, some of these volumes have found their way back to Yale. But the lack of books does not seem to have been much felt by the students, who seldom used the library. Only juniors and seniors were allowed to borrow books, in any case, though the president could "give Leave for the Sophimores to take out some particular Books upon the Rudiments of Language and Logic, rarely used by the upper Classes." [27]

The year 1783 was memorable to the nation as marking the official end of the Revolution. For Yale it also marked the renewal of attacks on the college—perhaps the most serious ever to be directed against it. First there were the brilliant and knowledgeable articles criticizing the Corporation by the never-identified individual, or group, writing under the pseudonym Parnassus. As Edmund Morgan relates, Parnassus clearly had inside information and he proceeded "week after week to cite chapter and verse of the corporation's insufferable stupidity." He revealed the treatment of the tutors and Silas Deane's offer and various other incompetent or arrogant actions. Then, in 1784, several memorials against the Corporation were presented to the General Assembly. Only one of these has survived, but apparently they all asked, in various ways, for the appointment of "civilians" to the still entirely clerical Corporation. At least one suggested that, if it was not done, the Assembly should found a new college.[28]

The Assembly never acted on these memorials, even though these were good times in which to attack the college. Democracy was the god of the day and special privilege of any kind was much hated. Fortunately for Yale, some of those who led the fight against special privilege were nonetheless friends of the college. But the best explanation for why the attack on the college failed, as it is the best treatment of everything about Stiles's presidency, is given by Edmund Morgan:

In the last analysis, the attack on Yale failed because Yale succeeded. In spite of shutdowns for lack of food, in spite of raids and fear of raids, in spite of a corporation that excelled in making enemies, Ezra Stiles by 1784 had made Yale the most popular and flourishing college in the United States. The surviving memorial speaks of Yale's "present depressed unpopular situation." But at the time the words were written, Yale had some 270 students, the largest enrollment there had ever been at one time in an American college, over a hundred more than the current number at Harvard. The large student body gave Yale an income (apart from charges for food) of £1,236 14s. 9d., a sum well above its annual liabilities.

In the face of such figures, it was no use talking about the depressed unpopular situation of the college. Stiles had made Yale a crashing success and everybody knew it.[29]

It is fortunate that this major attack on the college coincided with a time of such obvious prosperity, for the good times did not last long. With peace came economic depression, and the number of students at Yale began to decline. Enrollment, which had reached a peak of 283 in 1783, diminished to a low-point of 125 in 1788, and then leveled off in the 130s and 140s for the remainder of Stiles's presidency. With the decline in numbers came renewed dissatisfaction with Yale. Anticlericalism increased while at the same time New Divinity men (formerly New Lights) again turned against the

Corporation because of their candidates were no longer being elected to that body. Stiles feared a new attack.[30]

It came—or at least seemed to—when the General Assembly in May 1791 appointed a committee to inquire into the state of the college. A year later they reported. Expecting the worst, Stiles was relieved to discover that they had produced a statesmanlike document. The committee noted that while the college was in generally fine shape it could use financial assistance from the state. It recommended that the state turn over to the college certain arrears of taxes (which might amount to as much as £12,000) and in return the college should accept the addition of the governor, lieutenant-governor, and six senior councillors to the Corporation. Since this left the ministers still in a majority, and since only the ministerial members would select their own successors, Stiles and the fellows were willing to accept the change in the charter.[31]

The revision of the charter by the Act of Union of 1792 marked, as Stiles noted, the end of forty years of battling between the state and the college. It recognized the importance of the state to the college and of the college to the state. It confirmed what had long been true but not officially recognized: that the state was a partner in this great enterprise. It was certainly the most important single event in Stiles's presidency and one of the most important events in the entire history of Yale.

The first result of the new partnership was a new building. In 1792 the Corporation decided to build a long and very narrow four-story brick dormitory to be placed north of Connecticut Hall and at right angles to it. Public outcry against this proposal caused the Corporation to reconsider and accept a plan drawn up at the request of Treasurer James Hillhouse by the artist of the Revolution, John Trumbull. His plan put the new building in line with Connecticut Hall and the chapel, with the chapel in the middle. This decision marked the real beginning of the brick row and thus set the architectural tone and character of the college yard for the next three-quarters of a century. The cornerstone of the new building was laid during an elaborate ceremony on 15 April 1793. The building was named Union Hall in recognition of "the amicable union of Civilians in the Government of the College." [32]

The dedication of Union Hall was typical of one aspect of Stiles's administration. The five-foot four-inch president, with his shrunken face (he had lost all but two of his teeth by 1788), near-sighted eyes, great wig, and flowing robes, loved ceremonies. As a tutor, he had invented presentation day, when, after the seniors' final exams in July, the successful candidates were formally presented to the president. This occasion, and others like the cornerstone laying, commencements, and quarter days (which were like small commencements at the end of each quarter) were used by President Stiles to build up college and class spirit.[33]

Probably even more important in achieving that end—and also insisted upon by Stiles—was the strict subordination of each class to those above it, and of all classes to the faculty. The freshmen, being the newest in the college society, were the lowest in this special order. As one freshman in Clap's day put it, "I can't help laughing when I see the poor Freshmen creeping down stairs without the least noise, from the lash of their superiors. Freshmen have attained almost the happiness of negroes." [34] Upon their arrival at college the freshmen were taught their manners by the seniors. Benjamin Silliman (B.A. 1796) described the procedure:

They were . . . formed in line in the long gallery of the old chapel; the senior class being arranged parallel to and fronting them, when one of their number—a man selected for his gravity and weight of character explained to the novices the peculiar customs of the college, especially in regard to manners; the lesson was given with dignity and kindness, and received and regarded in a proper spirit.

But the seniors, being above all other undergraduates, could afford to be kind. The sophomores, having just risen from the lowly state of freshmen, took particular delight in treating them badly. "Trimming," disciplining the freshmen for infractions of the rules, was the sophomores' favorite sport. A poor frightened freshman would break a rule and be ordered before a group of sophomores in the attic or one of the college rooms. There the shophomores would chivvy him so that he would break other rules. Finally he would be forced through the "4 parts to a confession": to confess, be sorry, ask forgiveness, and promise reformation. If the freshman did not cooperate,

they put fists in his face, keep him constantly turning around to see those that are behind him—blow tobacco smoke in his face, make him hold a candle, toe a crack, bow to his shadow and when his back is turnd they are continually going in and out to trim him for not bowing.

In short a Soph is absolute and despotic as the great Mogul.[35]

And woe to the freshman who could not take it. One bolted when called in front of some sophomores and "went out of the room in Contempt of them, and said these Words, 'I sware I will not stay here any longer.'" This, the Faculty Judgements noted, was "contrary to the laws of God and this College" so the freshman was suspended until he made a full public confession.[36]

The freshmen were obliged to obey the most detailed rules, among which were the following:

When a Freshman is near a Gate or Door, belonging to College or College-yard, he shall look around, and observe whether any of his Superiors are coming to the same; and if any are coming within three rods, he shall not enter without a signal to proceed. In passing up or down stairs, or through an entry or any other narrow passage, if a Freshman meets a Superior, he shall stop and give way, leaving the most convenient side—if on the Stairs the Bannister side. Freshmen shall not run in College-Yard, or up or down stairs, or call to any one through a College window. When going into the Chamber of a Superior, they shall knock at the door, and shall leave it as they find it, whether open or shut. Upon entering the Chamber of a Superior, they shall not speak until spoken to; they shall reply modestly to all questions, and perform their messages decently and respectfully. They shall not tarry in a Superior's room, after they are dismissed, unless asked to sit. They shall always rise, whenever a superior enters or leaves the room, where they are, and not sit in his presence until permitted.

But the most odious rule of all was that freshmen were "obliged to perform all reasonable Errands for any superior, always returning an Account of the same to the Person who sent them." [37]

Not all the elaborate college rules applied only to freshmen. All undergraduates had to obey certain formalities. Among these were that they were "to be uncovered, and forbidden to wear their Hats (unless in stormy weather) in the front dooryard of the President's or Professor's House, or within Ten Rods of the Person of the President, Eight Rods of the Professor and Five Rods of a Tutor." (No doubt the students developed a fine eye for measuring distances.)

And all undergraduates had to "rise and stand, when the President or Professor is entering or going out of the Chapel; nor shall they take up their Hats, after Public Exercises, until all their superiors have gone out." The result of all these laws and customs was to make the college yard a fascinating and unusual sight. An excellent description by one who was soon to join the ranks of the lowly freshmen has come down to us:

I went up to college in the evening to observe the scene of my future exploits with emotions of awe and reverence. Men in black robes, white wigs and high cocked hats, young men dressed in camblet gowns, passed us in small groups. The men in robes and wigs I was told were professors; the young men in gowns were students. There were young men in black silk gowns, some with bands and others without. These were either tutors in the college or resident graduates to whom the title of "Sir" was accorded. When we entered the college yard a new scene was presented. There was a class who wore no gowns and who walked but never ran or jumped in the yard. They appeared much in awe or looked surlily after they passed by the young men habited in gowns and staves. Some of the young gownsmen treated those who wore neither hats or gowns in the yard with harshness and what I thought indignity. I give an instance: "Nevill, go to my room, middle story of old college, No.——, take from it a pitcher, fill it from the pump, place it in my room and stay there till my return." The domineering young men I was told were scholars or students of the sophomore class, and those without hats and gowns who walked in the yard were freshmen, who out of the hours of study were waiters or servants to the authority, the president, professors, tutors and undergraduates.[38]

College life was, in fact, much as it had always been. Pranks remained a constant: a freshman throwing a brick through the window of a sophomore who was giving him a difficult time; cutting the bell rope or ringing the bell at odd hours of the night; defacing books in the library—in fact any devilment they could think of. Athletics had changed only slightly. Hiking, swimming, sailing, hunting, skating, and sliding were still the major activities, but group sports had now begun to make an appearance. Charles Goodrich (B.A. 1797) left the first description of one of these at Yale:

The only sports or amusements which I remember, were foot races of ten rods and foot/ball. In these I freely engaged. . . . But Foot-ball was our common sport, amost every day in good weather and very often twice daily and I forget if more. We had three lines in front of the College buildings down to the road that crossed the Green by *two* meeting houses if I remember. Of the three lines the two outside were eight or ten rods apart. We would begin on the middle line and if the scholars were generally out on both sides, whenever the ball was driven over one of the outside lines, the party on that side were beaten, and the other party enjoyed the shouting. There was no delay of the game by choosing sides, the parties were divided by the buildings in which they severally roomed.[39]

The major new nonathletic activity that had become important since the first period of Yale history was the literary society. Of the first, Crotonia, which disappeared before the end of Clap's presidency, nothing is known. It was followed by Linonia, whose founding date is thought to be 1753, and, in the following decade, by Brothers in Unity. All undergraduates were members of either Linonia or Brothers, and though the clubs were highly intellectual they were much loved by the students. There they could debate, orate, and discuss to their hearts' content. And from the small society libraries they could borrow books of a lighter character than those owned by the college. Frederick Rudolph correctly says that these societies, which originated at Yale but soon appeared elsewhere, were "the first effective agency of intellect to make itself felt in the American college." [40]

In addition to public speaking and their libraries, the literary societies at Yale became the location of the thespian activities of the students. Though plays were still technically forbidden by the college laws, they were allowed as long as women were not permitted in the audience.* In fact, the students had long given plays. As early as 10 December 1754 the Faculty Judgements contained the ruling that "No Scholar is allowed to act any Comedies or Tragedies or any other plays or to be present at the acting of them," and on 2 July 1755 some students were heavily fined for publicly acting a play in Amity. This, the Faculty Judgements avowed, was not only contrary to the express order of the president, but "of very evil tendency" and "dishonorable" to the college. Worst of all, some of the students had even dressed as women.[41]

* As late as 1870 the college laws contained the provision that attending or taking part in a theatrical performance would cause a student to be admonished and, if he continued his misbehavior, to be expelled.

Despite rules and fines the practice would not down. Daggett, as we have seen, allowed it, and the number of plays may have increased under Stiles. Although Stiles would have liked them to be given in private, apparently he could not win that battle, for in 1790 the Brothers in Unity Society presented "Modern Knavery, Scholastic Pedantry, and Religious Hypocrisy" and a tragedy in a town theater. The society's minutes reported,

The Tutors, all the Literati of the City, and many respectable citizens of the place, together with the members of College composed our very respectable audience—No ladies were admitted, it being prohibited by the President and Tutors—Mr. Jones's Comedy was first performed; to which the audience discovered their approbation by repeated peals of laughter.[42]

The number of literary societies was increased during Stiles's time by the appearance of the first of the select secret societies, Phi Beta Kappa. It had begun at William and Mary, and the Yale chapter was started in 1781. Its program was much like those of the larger literary societies (which were also supposed to be secret) but its membership was limited to a select few.[43]

As the increase in play-giving indicated, there was a temporary slackening in the rigid Puritan morality enforced at the college and in the town. In 1782 a dancing teacher had been forced to leave New Haven by the citizens, but only two years later a teacher was advertising in the newspapers and a dancing assembly existed. Dances were held at the college on quarter days and a large ball at the State House followed the commencement ceremonies. The *New Haven Gazette* in 1784 reported on the commencement that year: "In the evening, an elegant Ball was attended in the State-House, to which almost 800 Ladies and Gentlemen were invited."[44]

All in all, college life was good. Men formed attachments to Yale and to their classmates that were strong and lasting. And this was true even during the war years when Harvard, according to her historian, had a "sorry student body" of whom few achieved distinction and many were "misfits and downright rascals."[45] Perhaps because of its location away from a large and tumultuous urban center, Yale seems to have escaped this problem. During the Revolution it was graduating men like James Kent, Noah Webster, Abiel Holmes, and Jedidiah Morse. In fact for Chancellor Kent, author of the *Com-*

mentaries on American Law, who graduated in 1781, the war may have been the best thing that could have happened. When college was broken up by the raid on New Haven, he "retired to a country village" and happened to begin to read Blackstone's *Commentaries.* He was so fascinated that he read right through the four heavy volumes and said of the experience, "Parts of the work struck my taste, and the work inspired me, at the age of 15, with awe, and I fondly determined to be a lawyer."

Kent had mixed feelings about the regular college course. At one point he said, "But even the collegiate terms, broken and interrupted as they were, proved sufficient to give the students a taste for classical learning and philosophical science, and to teach them how to cultivate their own resources in the various pursuits and duties of life." At another time, he was not so flattering. In his memoirs he wrote, "I stood as well as any of my class, but the test of scholarship at that day was contemptible." [46]

Stiles was able to alter the curriculum slightly and upgrade educational standards in the years after Kent's graduation. The Connecticut General Assembly's committee reported in 1792 "that the literary Exercises of the respective Classes have of late Years undergone considerable alterations, so as the better to accommodate the Education of the Undergraduates to the present State of Literature." Stiles returned Hebrew to the curriculum as a freshman requirement until 1789, when he made it an optional course. As professor of ecclesiastical history, the first professorship of history in the United States, he taught that subject on Thursdays. He also introduced into the college course some general history and political philosophy for juniors and seniors. He had the seniors study Montesquieu's *Spirit of the Laws* beginning in 1789 and in later years had them recite Vattel's *The Law of Nations* and Paley's *Principles of Moral and Political Philosophy.* Further, he encouraged and directed them in outside reading related to whatever professions they intended to enter. Stiles also moved English grammar down into the freshman year and had the sophomores study English literature. Beyond that, he changed textbooks for existing courses and, most important, judged the students' work more rigorously. [47]

The tightening of standards through stiffer examinations of the seniors began in 1784. Clap, it will be recalled, had first introduced examinations other than senior finals to Yale in 1762 (and got a riot for his trouble). But seldom, if ever, did anyone fail the old exams. Now Stiles began to make them count. He started to grade the exams, the first known use of grading at Yale (though it seems to have lapsed for a time under Timothy Dwight), and in 1785 he failed four seniors on their final exams. They were reexamined just before commencement and were still not up to par. Because the system was new, the tutors recommended and the Corporation voted that three of the four, Peter Bulkeley, Abraham Tomlinson, and David Hull, since they had spent four years at college but had been found not to know what they ought to, should receive their degrees "speciali gratia" (the fourth never came back). The Corporation noted that this was "the first time for many years that any such instance has happened." The degrees were given privately two days after commencement and Tomlinson and Hull then went on to become doctors of medicine. Hull, according to Dexter, "had a career of extensive usefulness, and was respected and beloved by a large circle of fellow-citizens." Of Bulkeley nothing is known after 1789.[48]

The succeeding class now saw that the policy was serious. They panicked. Special examinations held in January caused some seniors to leave in haste, and a few ended up at Harvard and Dartmouth. Exams were held again in April, and these produced rioting that went on for four days and resulted in three rustications and one expulsion. After this crisis, examinations were accepted.[49]

Under Stiles's leadership Yale grew not only in numbers and educational standards but also financially. Surprisingly, this most intellectual of Yale presidents also helped to lay a firm financial base for the future. When he took charge, the college had an income from student tuition and fees of about £500 and from endowment of some £236. By 1791 Stiles and his very able treasurer, James Hillhouse (B.A. 1773), had built Yale's total from all sources to £1,175. From the state the college received the 1792 grant that provided the funds for Union Hall and helped to endow the salary of a new professor of mathematics and natural philosophy who was appointed in 1794. The team of Stiles and Hillhouse also successfully raised £200 from private sources to purchase badly needed philosophical apparatus.[50]

Stiles continued to plan and work for the future. According to Morgan, the next items on his agenda were the "enlargement of the library [a list of books and priorities had already been drawn up, it appears], and then, as rapidly as the promised funds became available, the appointment of other professors." He was, furthermore, drafting a revised version of the college laws. Stiles realized that he might not complete all his work, but, as Morgan continues, "He faced the prospect with equanimity. After the great reconciliation of 1792 he knew that time would effect his purpose without further assistance from him." [51]

President Stiles died suddenly of a bilious fever as he neared the seventeenth anniversary of his induction to the presidency. At the time of his death the student body was only about 15 percent larger than when he began. His last graduating class, in fact, was only about one-half the size of his first.[52] But college enrollments were far more subject to outside influence then and temporary changes in the size of the student body tell little about Stiles's accomplishments. The college was stronger academically (which possibly helps explain its reduced size); it was, if not prosperous, at least on a stable financial basis; it was on good terms with the state government, which had recently become an actual partner in the enterprise; and, most important of all, Stiles had changed the college from a narrowly sectarian institution into one where knowledge could be pursued for itself.

Ezra Stiles's own far-flung intellectual enterprises were epitomized in a painting made of him in 1771:

He is drawn in a teaching attitude, with the right hand on the breast, and the left holding a Bible. Behind, and on his left side, is a part of a library; a folio shelf, with Eusebius, Livy, DuHalde's history of China, the Zohar, the Babylonian Talmud, Aben Ezra, Rabbi Selomo, Jarchi, Rabbi Moses Ben Maimon, and Moreh Nevochim. On another shelf are Newton's Principia, Plato, Watts, Doddridge, Cudworth's Intellectual System, and the New-England divines, Hooker, Chauncy, Davenport, Mather, Cotton.

At his right hand stands a pillar. On the other shaft is a circle, and one trajectory around a solar point, as an emblem of the Newtonian, or Pythagorean, system of the sun, planets, and comets. At the top of the visible part of the pillar, and on the side of the wall, is an emblem of the intellectual World.

Beyond the intellectual world he inhabited, he seems to have been without the bigotry so common to his age. He associated with all— Jews, Anglicans, and Catholics—and even worshiped in their temples and churches. He found "sincere good men" everywhere. His remark to President Clap in protest over Clap's removal of some deistical books from the Yale library exemplifies his approach: the only way to stop deistical ideas, he said, was "to come forth into the open Field and Dispute the matter on an even Footing." He brought that cast of mind, generalized, to Yale.[53]

While this liberal, broad-minded, tolerant gentleman was not able to make Yale the true university he had envisioned before he began his task, he was able to do something even more important: he left his successor an institution in which investigation and knowledge were valued no matter where they might lead; a place where, best of all, the university spirit prevailed.[54]

Part Three

The Development of a National Institution

1795–1871

9

College Becomes University

The fellows of the Yale Corporation quickly elected Timothy Dwight as president. Dwight was an obvious choice: at the age of forty-three, he was a well-known divine, an excellent teacher, a prominent poet, and perhaps the most famous living Yale alumnus. He had graduated from Yale in 1769 at the early age of seventeen, became a tutor at nineteen, and served for the unusually long period of six years. After being asked to resign by the Corporation (see p. 99), he had gone into the Revolutionary army as a chaplain and served for two years until called home upon the death of his father. Back in Northampton, Massachusetts, he had managed the family farm, supplied area pulpits, served in the legislature, and started a school that Ezra Stiles thought—with some reason—aimed at displacing Yale.

In 1783 Dwight had been called to the church at Greenfield Hill, Connecticut. There too he had established a school and, though it was technically only an academy, it carried some students all the way through college work. Like the school at Northampton, it was coeducational—an unusual feature at the time. While he was at Greenfield Hill Dwight made his reputation as a poet by publishing his epic poem *The Conquest of Canaan* (1785), a satire, *The Triumph of Infidelity, a Poem* (1788), and his most successful large poetical effort, *Greenfield Hill* (1794).[1]

On the basis of his numerous activities, but most of all due to his magnificent presence, Timothy Dwight was considered by many of his contemporaries to be one of the great men of the time. He was, as S. G. Goodrich said, "the most conspicuous man in New England, filling a larger space in the public eye, and exerting a greater influence than any other individual." Goodrich (better known as Peter Parley) left a striking portrait of the great man as he appeared in 1809. Dwight was, Goodrich reminisced in 1856, about six feet tall "and of a full, round, manly form" with the smoothest head he had ever seen. It had "no bumps" at all. "On the whole," Goodrich continued, his presence was singularly commanding, enforced by a manner somewhat authoritative and emphatic. This might have been offensive, had not his character and position prepared all around to tolerate, perhaps to admire it. His voice was one of the finest I ever heard from the pulpit— clear, hearty, sympathetic—and entering into the soul like the middle notes of an organ.

Goodrich considered Dwight

even more distinguished in conversation than in the pulpit . . . his knowledge was extensive and various and his language eloquent, rich, and flowing. His fine voice and noble person gave great effect to what he said. When he spoke, others were silent. This arose in part from the superiority of his powers, but in part also from his manner, which, as I have said, was somewhat authoritative. Thus he engrossed, not rudely, but with the willing assent of those around him, the lead in conversation. Nevertheless, I must remark, that in society the imposing grandeur of his personal appearance in the pulpit, was softened by a general blandness of expression and a sedulous courtesy of manner, which were always conciliating and sometimes really captivating. His smile was irresistible.

In later years men would say that only Daniel Webster had a similar impact on the region.[2]

It was this impressive man who was inducted as president on 8 September 1795 in the college chapel. That evening the college was brightly illuminated by the placing of eight candles in each window, and there were fireworks and music. The next morning Dwight was probably awakened by the discharge of the cannon on the Green— the traditional (though illegal) way the undergraduates welcomed the arrival of commencement day. A young Harvard graduate viewed the proceedings of that day and recorded his impressions in his journal:

The Exercises of the students . . . were performed to good acceptance. . . . The Meeting house was not crowded. The greatest decorum was observed. There was no clapping. The students were handsomely dressed. They had more gestures, than are common at Cambridge. Perhaps their compositions would have been more chaste, had they enjoyed the criticisms of Professor Pearson [of Harvard].

A prayer by the President; and an Anthem, "I beheld, and lo! a great multitude, etc." by Jacob French, an illiterate day-laborer, was performed in the most boisterous and tasteless manner imaginable by the students.

The President, in giving the Degrees, was obviously embarrassed; and, as he had not perfectly committed the Latin form to memory, he made frequent blunders in reciting it.[3]

Timothy Dwight had insisted he did not want to be president: "To build up a ruined college is a difficult task." But he deceived himself. He had probably always wanted the distinction of leading Yale, and the college, as we have seen, was in generally excellent shape within, while external conditions were once more favorable for further improvements. The country had entered a time of real prosperity after the depression of 1785–89. In New Haven the shipping industry had embarked upon its "glorious age," which would last until 1807. Local, state, and national good times meant increased enrollments and economic improvement at the college.[4]

Prosperity had not come soon enough to allow Ezra Stiles to pursue the development of the college that he had envisioned. Now Dwight had the good fortune to be able to take advantage of that circumstance. The only real problem—from Dwight's point of view —was the moral tone of the college and the country. Religion seemed to be on the decline and deism and skepticism rife. The spirit of the French Revolution was in the air. Lyman Beecher, a graduate of 1797, recalled as an old man that the students called each other Voltaire and Rousseau and made Tom Paine a college hero. And Roger Minott Sherman (B.A. 1792), who served as a tutor in 1795–96, remembered a similar tone in college and state.[5]

Beecher's and Sherman's recollections may have been exaggerated, but in the period after the Revolution, according to one historian, "many Americans imbibed deism, flirted with atheism, adopted a firm indifference to religion." Harvard students became atheists, Williams men mocked the Lord's Supper, and Princeton undergraduates burned the Bible. It was this situation, perhaps, that Dwight bemoaned when he referred to the state of the college. Stiles, who had remained "an unchanged Son of Liberty" until his death, did not fear the French Revolution the way the conservative Dwight did. Stiles was distressed by the rise of infidelity but, having flirted with a form of deism in his youth, he did not panic when students questioned religion. To Dwight, on the other hand, it appeared the most fearsome problem of the day.[6]

Dwight inveighed against deism, atheism, and the French Revolution in sermon and pamphlet. The great men of the state—laymen and lawyers—came to the college chapel, it was said, to hear President Dwight speak. The result, in college and out, it was later reported, was extraordinary:

The new philosophy lost its attractions. In Connecticut it ceased to be fashionable or even reputable; and the religion of the Pilgrims, which was fearfully threatened with extermination, regained its respectability and influence. The character of the College was restored; and its increasing numbers, gathered from all parts of the United States, extended an influence over the nation.[7]

This account, at any rate, is the one the college and historians generally have reiterated since Dwight's day: the college, morally ruined, was saved and restored by a great and good man. Yet as Stiles's best biographer has pointed out, the facts do not support the case. The college church, though very small, was not a wreck without members. Religious enthusiasm came and went in natural waves, and students who described great changes in atmosphere during Dwight's first year were soon complaining again. On 14 April 1796 Timothy Bishop noted to a friend that while the college was generally thriving,

there are some individuals in the class who are very negligent in their studies and likewise in their attendance upon the exercises of College more so I believe than they ever have hitherto been. Day after day and week after week will pass away when these persons will scarcely look into a book or attend once upon the exercises of the college.

Despite all Dwight's efforts, membership in the college church continued to decline (though all students had to attend). Prior to the turn of the century only the undergraduate Moral Society, founded as a secret society in 1797 with the aim of improving the religious life of its members, indicated that a change might be in the offing.[8]

One of Dwight's most influential positions for attempting to thwart what he considered bad opinions was in the classroom. He continued the old tradition of teaching the seniors metaphysics and ethics (as well as some treatment of other subjects) and overseeing their disputations. He used these opportunities to comment upon or discuss important subjects. Dwight was a persuasive teacher, and what he said moved many of his students deeply. As in Stiles's day, and perhaps the same may be said of all earlier heads of the college, these classes with the president were the freest period of discussion in their college lives, and the memory of them made a deep impression—particularly in the case of a man as personally awesome as Timothy Dwight. Years later members of his classes remembered these moments and recalled his remarks, and his son even published a book of Dwight's decisions.[9]

As Dwight lectured and preached, he moved on other fronts as well to improve the college. The college laws needed his attention immediately. The method of enforcing college discipline had been changing ever since the days of Clap. The committee of the General Assembly which recommended the Act of Union in 1792 had remarked, for example, that "the Severity of the antient Freshman Discipline is almost done away." But the college laws did not reflect the changes. Hence President Stiles and a committee of the Corporation had set to work in September 1793 to revise the laws. When Stiles died, they had almost completed the task. Immediately upon Dwight's election and prior to his induction the committee asked him to review and comment upon their work. Thus the final draft was part Stiles and part Dwight, but what changes reflect which man, we do not know.[10]

The most revolutionary suggestion of the committee was that the "fagging" system, the subordination of the freshmen and the right to send them on errands and to discipline them, be dropped entirely. The faculty was outraged. On 18 August 1795 Professor Meigs and the three tutors protested that the freshmen were "rude, from rude towns and families" and that the only way to tame them was by the fagging system. Without it, they complained, the freshmen would be haughty and learn vices and "subject the higher classes to constant scurrility . . . lessen their manhood and dignity, reduce all to an equal rudeness, [and] render College a meer great common school." Perhaps Stiles, with his years of experience, could have overcome this protest, but the president-elect could not. The plan to prevent fagging entirely was dropped and instead (as Meigs and the tutors suggested) the right was merely removed from the sophomores— thus they would have a year to mature and forget the treatment they had received before they in their turn could exercise this "civilizing" right. Though Harvard stopped the practice entirely in 1794, Yale did not finally do so until a decade later.[11]

Other changes in the written laws in this and later revisions during Dwight's presidency were minor. Symptomatic of the change in presidents, however, was a law which prohibited attendance at dancing assemblies or dancing school in New Haven during term time. A more strict view of moral behavior was to mark the tenure of Timothy Dwight.[12]

Historians have generally credited Dwight with a change in the manner and method of enforcing discipline. As with the sweeping away of infidelity, however, this is an exaggeration. Fines, which it is said were not collected under Dwight, remained on the books as possible penalties throughout his presidency, though their number diminished. Each successive president after Clap appears to have used them to a lesser degree, but they were still being collected for some offenses by President Day.[13]

Dwight is also supposed to have instituted a new approach to discipline, called the "parental system." But this, too, had begun long before. To President Clap, a written law and its vigorous enforcement were all that was necessary. Fines had, of course, been the penalty for numerous offenses. But in most cases fines hurt parent more than child and, furthermore, allowed one willing to pay to do what he wanted. It became evident, therefore, possibly to Daggett and certainly to Stiles and Dwight, that the college's written laws could not stand alone. So while Stiles enforced the rules with rigor, he also visited the students in their rooms to "admonish the negligent, or vicious; applaud the studious; assist and encourage all." This was the parental system that was intended, as Dwight said, "to prevent the commission of crimes by moral influences, rather than to punish them when committed." [14]

The parental mode was clearly a necessity considering the age of the students. During the presidencies of Stiles and Dwight entering students were about sixteen years old.[15] Thus it is not surprising that Dwight approved of a parental approach and perhaps carried it even farther than did Stiles. Dwight's disciplinary philosophy was based, like Clap's, on the idea that the breaking of small rules led inevitably to the breaking of greater. As he put it, "The progress toward the gallows is gradual; and so it is in ill conduct at this college." Thus there had to be laws (there were forty pages of them in 1817), and they had to be enforced. Nevertheless, he felt, "the laws of Yale College are very mild, and . . . every precaution has been used in framing them to prevent the necessity of severe punishment, though still sometimes it is found necessary." [16]

The supervision of the students was extended by Dwight to include the appointment of patrons in 1804 for all out-of-state undergraduates and in 1810 for all but New Haveners, to see that the young men made no debts without an adult's approval. And in 1810 a rule was placed on the books to prevent any student's being questioned by his fellows to discover if he had testified to the faculty about a violation of the college law. The penalty for trying to discover whether one of their number had turned informer was to be based on the "aggravation of the offense," but it could be dismissal.[17]

Dwight exercised his "parental" influence by lectures to the classes and private conversation with the wayward. In each case his personal impressiveness was probably the element that made the approach effective, for he was not given to strong language. In later years Professor Olmsted (B.A. 1813, tutor 1815–17) recalled that the severest reaction he had ever heard from Dwight was when, in reply to a student's impertinence, he took a pinch of snuff and "with a manner indicative of pain and displeasure, said, 'Young man, you are hasty.'" Nonetheless, Dwight was successful. Many a student left the private interviews tearful and shaken and prepared to live a better life in the future. One of his students later described Dwight's disciplinary approach:

> With the college students . . . [his] influence was wonderful. When, after public prayers, he said "Sedete omnes," we knew that we were to be reprimanded, and it was always done *ex animo,* and to the purpose. But after the *fortiter in re,* he knew how to put on the *suaviter in modo,* and there was a kindness and gentleness of manner and tone that restored good humor to all, as he concluded, "Juvenes, humanum est errare." Courtesy and dignity of manner were combined in a most remarkable degree in President Dwight and the students who were ready to call him "Pope" on being summoned to his study, generally left his presence with the exclamation, "He is a perfect gentleman!" "He is a wonderful man!"[18]

Not all escaped so easily, however. If a crime was sufficiently serious, a student might be suspended, rusticated, or expelled. And his chances of getting back into college were not as good as they had been in Clap's day. As the years passed, the old Puritan belief in forgiveness upon the expression of remorse appears to have declined, and under Dwight the old custom of public confession in the hall

seems to have disappeared completely. Now if the president expelled a boy he seldom returned. In part this may have been because the harshest discipline was reserved for freshmen. It was felt
that if "the chronically vicious and idle" could be rooted out early,
the tone of the college would be good and there would be no riots
and rebellions and no need for severe discipline later.[19]

Dwight felt he had to root out not only "vicious and idle" students but also bad ideas. To Dwight the decline of religion was a
product of the American and French Revolutions and the French
philosophers. While pushing for a spiritual reawakening he also attacked the dangerous philosophies of Voltaire, Rousseau, and other
"godless" men. One of his most famous sermons on the subject was
called "The Nature and Danger of Infidel Philosophy," wherein he
revealed the degraded morals of the philosophers themselves. Rousseau, he said, "is asserted to have been guilty of gross theft, perjury,
fornication, adultery, and of abjuring and assuming, alternately, the
Catholic and the Protestant religion; neither of which he believed.
Thus I have exhibited to you the nature, and the actual state of this
Philosophy." Clearly, no intelligent person could accept the beliefs
of such a man! And thus, by anti-intellectual means, Dwight attempted to defeat infidelity and return morality to the campus.[20]

It took some years for any real change to be felt in the college,
and when it came it was part of a great new religious revival that
swept the nation at the end of the eighteenth and beginning of the
nineteenth centuries. The Second Great Awakening marked the
start of what Perry Miller has called a "magnificent era of revivals"
that lasted right up to the Civil War. Under its influence, and with
Dwight preaching the cause, behavior within the college slowly improved and skepticism, rationalism, and infidelity were, at least temporarily, swept from the institution.[21]

The revival began quietly at Yale. First one student in March
1802 then another in April made public confessions of their saving
experience and were received into the college church. Then the
numbers began slowly to rise until by the end of the summer term,
"not less than fifty were numbered as serious inquirers, and several
daily and almost hourly, were found apparently submitting themselves unto God." As the Reverend Dr. Porter (B.A. 1803) of Farmington recalled,

Those were truly memorable days. Such triumphs of grace, none whose privilege it was to witness them, had ever before seen. So sudden and so great was the change in individuals, and in the general aspect of the college, that those who had been waiting for it, were filled with wonder as well as joy, and those who knew not "what it meant" were awestruck and amazed. Wherever students were found in their rooms, in the chapel, in the hall, in the college yard, in their walks about the city, the reigning impression was, "Surely, God is in this place." [22]

President Dwight encouraged and assisted the revival but kept it under strict control, for he wished to avoid the "enthusiasm" that had marked the first Great Awakening. He hoped to produce changes which were deeper and more lasting. He was successful, for in 1802 only one student came near to enthusiasm. Nor was college disrupted: regular classes were held and preaching remained the same. The most noticeable change from ordinary college life was in the greater number of private meetings of concerned students with the president, faculty members, or each other.[23]

For some, the results of this revival were lasting. Of those who were students at Yale in 1801–02 about one-third were converted, and of these about thirty-five entered the ministry—a number well above the average of previous years. In fact, whereas only about one-twelfth of the classes of 1800 and 1801 entered the ministry, almost one-third of the class of 1802 selected that career. Nonetheless, this did not last: the number of graduates entering the ministry soon resumed the decline that had long been under way. For the years 1701 through 1744, one-half of the graduates had entered the ministry. Between 1745 and 1778 this number had fallen to one-third; and then in the period 1778–92 it had dropped to about one-fourth and the law had emerged as the major occupation for Yale graduates, with almost a third entering that profession. Throughout Dwight's presidency—despite his great ministerial powers—the ministry as a professional choice continued to lose ground slowly. For the time span 1805 through 1815 (which was marked by revivals at the college in 1808, 1813, and 1815) not quite 18 percent entered the ministry, while almost 32 percent became lawyers.[24]

It is clear that Dwight's effect on religion could not reverse the long-term trend. Nor could his disciplinary procedures bring about a revolutionary change in behavior. As was usual with a new regime, the first few years were peaceful. But by 1798 the college was becoming somewhat turbulent. There were fights and firecrackers in commons. Thanksgiving of that year was marked by Dwight's fine sermon "Serve the Lord with fear, and rejoice with trembling" and a dinner at which so many goose bones were thrown that "they darkened the room almost." [25]

By the academic year 1802–03 college was almost "normally" violent. Moses Stuart (B.A. 1799), then a tutor and later a great biblical scholar, described the situation in letters to Benjamin Silliman. In December he reported that one student had been rusticated for two months "for rolling barrels down my stairs." Another "had received the darts of Dr. Dwight's quiver, until they were exhausted, for cutting bell-ropes and blasphemy, but without any harm." "In short," he wrote, "there appear to be more devils in college at present than were cast out of Mary Magdalene. I have been honored by a broadside at one of my windows, which popped off without ceremony six squares of glass. No matter; you were honored in the same way." In February Stuart informed Silliman, "As to College affairs, they go on much in the old way. We had many convulsions last quarter, many furious 'spasms of infuriated' Sophomores and Freshmen." One tutor's door was "almost split to pieces with stones," another's windows were broken; one freshman was publicly dismissed, a sophomore rusticated, and two sophomores and a freshman sent home. Nevertheless Stuart felt that after the "wars and rumors of wars" of the previous term, "this term there appears to be some disposition to enter into a treaty of peace; at least, a cessation of hostilities is agreed upon." [26]

This behavior indicates that not even Timothy Dwight could tame the barbarous undergraduates in a day when student youth, tight restrictions, hard study, and lack of organized athletics produced an excess of energy that had to emerge somehow. The particular wave of violence described by Stuart is striking, however, because it followed hard on the heels of the first religious revival of Dwight's presidency and indicates how slight were the long-term effects of those movements within the college walls.

What always happened, of course, was that graduation removed many who were converted from the college while vacation cooled the religious ardor of many of the rest. By the following fall, the students were inclined to be rambunctious and destructive again. Even so, Dwight's presidency when viewed as a whole does seem to have been more peaceful than the administrations of either his predecessor or his successor. Harvard appears to have been even quieter than Yale, but Princeton was racked by serious riots in 1800, 1807, and 1817 and suffered numerous other periods of great disorder.[27]

Yale students may have been calmer within the college yard than they had been in the past, but outside its walls they were entirely different. Dwight's presidency was the first to be marked by noticeable violence between town and gown. No doubt this was in part due to an increase in the number of undergraduates coinciding with New Haven's glorious age as a port. What could have been more delightful than for off-duty sailors and restless college boys to bait each other? [28]

The first recorded incident between students and sailors took place on 18 February 1799. As a student noted in his diary, "About 9 o'clock news came that sailors had come to pick a quarrel with the scholars; I went out with the rest to see the fray. They separated about 10 without many blows." The following month brought more action: "We began to play ball," the same observer recorded.

About 8 o'clock in the evening we were alarmed by the cry of sailors and the lower sort of town people, who came up to whip the scholars, under pretense of having been challenged by them. As they dared not come into the yard, and we would not condescend to go out, they dispersed about nine having wounded one scholar badly and one or two slightly. Five or six of the mob were put into jail by the authority of the city.[29]

This clash was only the beginning. By 1806 a full-scale riot took place and the office of College Bully came into existence. This position, which was finally banned by the faculty in 1840, was first bestowed by the people of the town on Guy Richards (B.A. 1807). In one fight, a student noted, Richards had "been very forward and I believe very imprudent, insomuch that the town-fellows have given him the epithet of College Bully." Naturally, the students quickly turned it into a title of distinction. Thereafter the undergraduates elected their own bully.[30]

After 1806 the next collision of note was the riot of 1812. A New Haven businessman described it in one of his letters:

We have had Considerable Bustle here two Sunday Evenings past between the Students in College and the Town Boys. Last Sunday Evening the number on each Side was Said to be nearly 400. They attacked with Clubs, Knives etc. The Sheriff and his Deputies and the Constables interfered Commanded the Peace etc. but to no effect. Mr. Morse was knocked down with a Club and Severely wounded. He was carried into Mr. Beers' and his wounds Dressed. Mr. Rosseter was knocked down but held onto the Scholar till he got assistance to carry him to jail. Severall were taken but procured Bonds. It has excited Considerable attention here and Serious Consequences are apprehended unless a Stop is put to the Business to which purpose exertions are making by the Mayor and the Magistrates.[31]

One young freshman of the day recalled long after the college bully who had led the students in this battle:

I stood in awe of no one so much as a certain Preston, from the South, who was at that time the College Bully, not because he was the best scholar and prospective valedictorian of his class, but because he was possessed, by right of physical superiority, of the Bully Club. This symbol of his power was carefully secreted by the holder, and only seen by any one when there seemed to be occasion at hand for him to wield it for the protection of his fellow students from outside enemies. I do not recollect getting a sight of it but once, and that during my Freshman year. For some cause a body of sailors and others, armed with bludgeons, were approaching, at night, the college yard. Not unwarned of their designs, there issued from the college halls a body of students with Preston at their head, the sight of whose terrible weapon and stalwart form checked the onset before the uplifted arm gave the signal of attack to his followers.

Bully Preston went on to be valedictorian of his class, study law, and become judge of the Supreme Court of Louisiana before his death in a steamboat explosion on Lake Pontchartrain. Another who held the office while Dwight was president was Asa Thurston of the class of 1816. Thurston was described by some who knew him as tremendously powerful and as "active as a cat." He is said to have once grabbed two sailors who attacked him, rapped their heads together, and knocked them cold. When not so violently engaged he was a college chorister, for he had "a tenor as soft as a flute" and was very pious. After college and study under Moses Stuart at Andover Theological Seminary, he went to the Hawaiian Islands to help establish mission work there.[32]

As Thurston's career indicates, violence and religiosity went hand-in-hand at Yale during these years. Dwight's presidency was marked by the awakening at the college and in the nation of the first hesitant interest in foreign missionary work. At Yale that interest seems to have been produced by the appearance at college in 1809 of Obookiah, a lad from Hawaii, who was probably the first foreign heathen ever seen by any of the college population. Obookiah was tutored by a Yale undergraduate who persuaded him to live with President Dwight for a time. And thus Obookiah may have influenced Dwight to help found the American Board of Commissioners of Foreign Missions, which was, as Ralph Gabriel notes, "the first American missionary society actually to carry its work beyond the boundaries of the nation." [33]

Riots, revivals, and missionary work did not prevent Dwight from pursuing his plans for the development of the college. He wanted to see it grow—in size of student body, number of buildings, area, and by the addition of whole new schools. To carry out these plans he needed money, so he petitioned the General Assembly for additional funds. According to the terms of the grant of 1792, half the money collected by the college was to be transferred to the state. In 1796 Dwight asked that the college be relieved of this restriction. The request was highly unpopular in the state because relief seemed just one more act of favoritism toward Yale and the established religion. Notwithstanding, the General Assembly agreed, and for the sum of perhaps $20,000 the people of Connecticut were again alienated from Yale. During Dwight's presidency no further funds would come from the state to the college until 1816.[34]

With the promise of these additional resources, the Corporation set out to buy more land in the block on which the college was situated. The college holding amounted to roughly a quarter of the present Old Campus (the block bounded by College, Chapel, High, and Elm Streets) and was located in the area where Bingham and Connecticut Halls now stand. Room for expansion was badly needed and, in addition, the land facing the Green that the college did not own was, according to Benjamin Silliman, "filled with a grotesque group—generally of most undesireable establishments, among which were a barn—a barber's shop—several coarse taverns or boarding houses—a poor house and house of correction—and the public jail with its prison yard—and used alike for criminals—for maniacs and debtors." The wild laughter of the insane resounded in the college yard.[35]

In August 1796 the college purchased most of the north half of the present Old Campus except for the two small plots of land on which stood the jail and the poorhouse. Naturally Dwight and the Corporation wanted to remove these nuisances. They succeeded in 1799 and 1800, and thus Yale finally owned the entire College Street front facing the Green.[36]

Also in 1796 the Corporation moved to fix up the college buildings: to refurbish Connecticut Hall, to replace the leaking roof of the chapel, and even to repaint the rooms of Union Hall and install new latches on its doors. The following year it was decided to add a fourth floor to Connecticut Hall (to make it similar to Union Hall). Later, the Corporation concluded that the president's house was in such bad condition that both it and the lot on which it stood should be sold.[37]

As these decisions were being carried out the college population began to grow at a rapid rate. When a tutor resigned at commencement in 1798, two were appointed in his place because of the large size of the entering class. The influx of students continued during the next few years, thus increasing the number unable to live on campus and hindering the college from protecting them from bad habits and bad companions. With a portion of the funds made available in 1796 a new dormitory was projected. New classrooms were also needed, and additional space for the library and laboratory apparatus, so it was voted to build one structure for library and classrooms and another for bedrooms and studies, and to remodel the library floor of the chapel into a philosophical room, apparatus room, and museum. The new buildings were to look just like the old. Aiming for balance and stylistic continuity, the Corporation voted that the new dormitory, named Berkeley Hall in honor of that great benefactor, should be just like Union Hall, while the classroom building—the first structure in the history of the college to be devoted solely to academic purposes—should be named the Connecticut Lyceum and should correspond "both as to the Site, and external appearance, essentially to the Chapel." The internal arrangement of Berkeley was to be similar to Union, except that the rooms were to contain studies "in lieu of bedrooms; with not less than two, and where it may be done with three Study rooms." The partition between the studies and the living room was to contain a large foldaway bed for the students, which would let down into the living room when needed.[38]

By 1804 Dwight had completed all the building that would be done during his administration: a president's house of wood and a classroom building and dormitory of brick. An attempt was also made to beautify the yard. On 14 September 1803 the Corporation voted to plant trees on both sides of the row of college buildings. No doubt the elderly treasurer, James Hillhouse, had much to do with this decision, for he was a prime mover in all the efforts to improve the looks of New Haven. At the end of the eighteenth century he had been active in the drive to plant trees that later made the town the "Elm City." He began the movement for a new cemetery to replace the crowded, messy burial ground on the Green. This activity led to the founding of the Grove Street Cemetery and to the beginning of improvements in the terrain of the public square. Thus college and town began to take on the look for which they would long be famous.[39]

As the physical Yale progressed, Dwight turned to building up the number of professorships and schools. As early as 1798 he got the Corporation to approve the appointment of a professor of chemistry and natural history if he could find the funds to pay for it. This did not occur until 1802, when he suddenly offered the post to young Benjamin Silliman (B.A. 1796).[40]

The selection of Silliman is of such importance to Yale's history and tells so much about Timothy Dwight and Yale, that it is necessary to describe it in some detail. Silliman had never studied chemistry and knew almost nothing about it. From 1799 to 1802 his time had been spent as a tutor at Yale and a student of law with Simeon Baldwin (B.A. 1781). He was just considering a move to Georgia when Dwight selected him for the new professorship. Dwight chose Silliman because he knew it would be difficult to find anyone in America with knowledge of chemistry and natural history and he was afraid to select a foreigner. He feared that "a foreigner, with his peculiar habits and prejudices, would not feel and act in unison with us, and that however able he might be in point of science, he would not understand our college system, and might therefore not act in harmony with his colleagues." Dwight's reasons for choosing Silliman did not stop there. Even more than foreigners he seems to have feared intellectuals. He made this clear in a baccalaureate sermon that he preached several times, describing the man whose only object was to be learned:

In his study he dwells: in his books he passes his life. *To think* appears to him the only proper end of human existence: while *to do* is not even entered upon the register of his duties. . . . He has not discovered that science is a means, and not an end. . . . He mistrusts not that the clown, who faithfully follows the plough, or wields the hoe and the spade, is a better member of society than himself: nor dreams, that the two mites of such a man will be accepted as a gift to God, while his own abundance will be slighted and forgotten.[41]

Such anti-intellectualism has not been uncommon among college presidents in America. Not many years later, in fact, the president of Dartmouth said, "The very cultivation of the mind has frequently a tendency to impair the moral sensibilities." [42] Dwight never went that far, but his fears of having an intellectual or a foreigner (and perhaps, heaven forfend, both in one individual!) on his faculty caused him to choose with care the men who taught in the college. It made him less concerned for what they knew than for what kind of men they were. Such a policy could, of course, lead to academic and educational disaster. But Dwight had a rare ability to judge men and his choices were nothing less than magnificent. In addition to Silliman, the most influential teacher and propagandist for science in America for half a century, his main appointments were Jeremiah Day (B.A. 1795), who became professor of mathematics and natural philosophy in 1801 and went on to become a great president of Yale, and James Luce Kingsley (B.A. 1799), who was made professor of the Hebrew, Greek, and Latin languages and of ecclesiastical history in 1805 (and as if that was not enough, he was to continue as a tutor and was also appointed librarian). Kingsley, the first professor of languages at Yale and an excellent critic and Latinist, was the most scholarly of the group. These three men, originally with Dwight, then largely alone, ran Yale for the first half of the nineteenth century. They were all impressive men; their influence on Yale was immeasurable; and they proved Dwight's acumen.[43]

Dwight's desire to place on the faculty men whose opinions he respected led him to drive out Day's predecessor as professor of mathematics and natural philosophy. Ezra Stiles had appointed Josiah Meigs to that post on a year-to-year basis because funds were lacking to make the appointment permanent. Meigs was a supporter of the French Revolution and the ideas of the Jeffersonians—and these things were anathema to Timothy Dwight. So Dwight got rid of him and conservative Yale graduates applauded. When he heard Meigs was off to Georgia, Jedidiah Morse wrote a classmate, "I am not sorry to hear of the removal of Prof. M. I wish him well for what he has been,—and for his present merits—but as his principles are contagious, it will be best for him I think to go where they can do no harm, as in Georgia he will find Jacobins formed to his hand—and who are past being polluted." [44]

Shortly after Meigs's departure, Dwight made his first move toward broadening the curriculum and making Yale a university. During 1801 Elizur Goodrich (B.A. 1779) resigned from Congress to take the post of collector of customs in New Haven—which was given him shortly before John Adams left the presidency. Thomas Jefferson decided not to allow this useful political post to remain in the hands of a Federalist, so Goodrich was dismissed. This made him available to do some teaching at Yale and, since his firing only reinforced the impression that his opinions were unimpeachable, he was appointed professor of law in the fall of 1801. As such, over a two-year period he was to give a series of thirty-six lectures on the law of nature, the American Constitution, and the jurisprudence of Connecticut. The idea was that the students needed this information to be good citizens and leaders in their communities. [45]

It may be that it was intended in time for the professorship to lead to a law school. Instead, Goodrich became increasingly busy with other matters. He was made mayor of New Haven in 1803 and was elected to the governor's council, while no doubt his own law practice increased continually. Thus in 1807 it was reported that he had given no lectures during the academic year 1806–07 and expected no pay. Finally in 1810 Goodrich, who by this time was a senior councillor and thus a fellow *ex officio,* resigned. For some reason this ended Dwight's attempt to teach law at Yale. The professorship was not filled again until 1826. [46]

President Dwight had more success with medicine. There were a few medical schools in the country, most notably at Pennsylvania (1765), Columbia (1768), and Harvard (1782), but the average young man still learned the profession from a practicing doctor. Connecticut, in fact, had only recently established a system of certification. As early as 1763 an attempt had been made to obtain legislation appointing a committee of doctors to examine and certify candidates, but the legislature refused to cooperate. In 1784 New Haven County organized its Medical Society and began examining candidates, but it was not until 1792 that the Connecticut Medical Society received a charter from the state. Because the college had many other problems, the Corporation did not formally move on the subject until 1806, when it asked that the Prudential Committee, assisted by the Reverend Dr. Nathan Strong and Benjamin Silliman, investigate the question of establishing a medical professorship. Apparently they decided that it would be best to plunge right in, for the following year the state Medical Society was induced to appoint a committee to consult with the gentlemen from Yale. The next few years were marked by various delays, but finally agreement was reached and in 1810 the matter was taken to the state legislature. The Assembly was asked to change the charter of the Medical Society so that its power to examine candidates and confer degrees would be exercised jointly with Yale. The legislature made the necessary change, but then there were further delays before the Medical Institution, as it was called, finally got going. The first man asked to be a full professor did not accept, and it was not until 31 August 1813 that the appointment of a faculty was completed. The school opened that fall and the first earned M.D. degree was given in 1814.[47]

One problem in selecting the faculty had been that, while Dartmouth's excellent Dr. Nathan Smith was willing to come to Yale, he was thought to be an infidel and thus not considered available by President Dwight. Fortunately Smith's views changed very suddenly and he "fully renounced his infidelity." As he wrote to a friend, "My earnest prayer now is to live to undo all the evil I have done by expressing my doubts as to the truth of Divine Revelation, and to render to Society all the good my talents and powers will permit me to do." He was as good as his word. For sixteen years he was the mainstay and major attraction of the medical school.[48]

Until 1860 the Medical Institution was situated in a hotel built by James Hillhouse at the corner of what are now Prospect and Grove Streets. This building, which Yale purchased for $12,500, later became Sheffield Hall and remained part of the Yale scene until it was removed in 1931 to make way for Sheffield-Sterling-Strathcona Hall. The location of the new school in this spot marked the beginning of the spread of the college to the north.[49]

The founding of the medical school was not delayed by exciting events in the country at large. In 1807, in response to the problem of neutral rights in the Napoleonic Wars, Jefferson clamped an embargo on all American shipping. This was followed by Madison's Non-Intercourse Act and ultimately by the War of 1812. These successive blows destroyed New Haven as a shipping center, and to absorb the financial disaster, the town turned to manufacturing. The industrial revolution had begun for New Haven when Eli Whitney (B.A. 1792), having returned from the southern sojourn during which he invented the cotton gin, in 1798 built a factory at the foot of the lake which now bears his name and began manufacturing arms by the revolutionary method of interchangeable parts. After the embargo went into effect, there followed a rise in other manufacturing, with the result that some years later New Haven area factories were pouring out woolens, cotton cloth, buttons, clocks, and numerous other products, as well as Whitney's muskets.[50]

That the wreck of its shipping industry was in large measure balanced by the new industries is indicated by the fact that two of the Congregational churches and the Episcopal church all voted in 1812 to build new houses of worship, and these three architecturally significant structures, which now grace the New Haven Green, were completed in 1814 and 1815. Ever since that time Yale men have gazed out upon a Green that has remained essentially unchanged and that holds, in Center Church, one of the most beautiful buildings in America.[51]

The War of 1812 affected Yale College very little. Thought was given to protecting the college property, but little needed to be done. The number of students increased—as it had during other wars—and eighty-two young men, the largest class until 1826, graduated in 1814. On the whole, for students and teachers alike, life remained much the same.[52]

The end of the war found Timothy Dwight in poor health. The Corporation made arrangements to relieve him of some of his duties, but though he sickened noticeably in February 1816, he continued all his tasks of preaching, teaching, and administering. Finally, in the late fall of that year, he was forced to give up these activities and remain at home. On 11 January 1817 he died of cancer. Moved as it had never been before, the Yale Corporation voted to go into public mourning for thirty days.[53]

Moses Coit Tyler said of Timothy Dwight, "He was himself greater than anything he ever said or did; and for those who came near him, all that he did or said had an added import and fascination as proceeding from one so overpoweringly competent and impressive." Since we cannot feel his personal magnetism, it is difficult to appraise Dwight fairly. Though the educational development of Yale was great during his presidency, his forte was administration, not curricular innovation. His greatest personal educational achievement was in helping to bring belles-lettres into the curriculum when he and John Trumbull were tutors. Beyond that, Dwight often seems to have been content with things as they were. Books such as Jedidiah Morse's *American Geography,* Hugh Blair's *Lectures on Rhetoric,* and William Enfield's *Natural Philosophy,* all of which Stiles had used, were studied under Dwight, too.[54]

Dwight's main contribution—and it was an important one—was administrative. He appointed the professors who were placed in charge of certain subjects: Kingsley for Hebrew, Greek, and Latin languages and for ecclesiastical history, Silliman for chemistry and natural history, and Day for mathematics and natural philosophy. But President Dwight often opposed curricular changes his officers wanted to make. The most innovative of these men was, surprisingly, James Luce Kingsley, who was later known as the most conservative man on the Yale faculty. Kingsley was continually trying to improve courses. Since Greek was one of his subjects, he did a great deal to try to develop it. When he was still only a tutor, Greek was taught by having the students translate the New Testament. Kingsley suggested to Dwight that they read Homer as well, but Dwight was opposed to the addition. Greek, the president pointed out, was recited on Mondays and thus students might be tempted to read a pagan book on Sunday. Kingsley protested that it was improper to study any book on the Sabbath, even the New Testament. Though Dwight recognized that Kingsley was theoretically correct, he felt that if a student *were* to work on Sunday, it was preferable to have him study the Bible. But Kingsley persisted. Dwight finally acquiesced and allowed him to use Homer—but only as an option, not as a requirement. Ultimately, Homer did become a requirement and Kingsley was able to add volumes containing selections of the best Greek authors to the Greek curriculum—*Graeca Minora* and *Graeca Majora.*[55]

Kingsley improved the Latin course as well—mainly by making it more exact and by demanding more "elegant scholarship." He also turned his attention to mathematics. While Day was busy lecturing to juniors and seniors and writing textbooks, Kingsley was listening to recitations, for he continued as a tutor after he became a professor. He decided that the students needed to study Euclid, though again Dwight had to be persuaded, since he "thought the short course of geometry contained in Ward's mathematics [was] sufficient." After 1812 Kingsley even gave lectures to the seniors on language and history.[56]

While Dwight may have hesitated over some of Kingsley's curricular changes, he was whole-hearted in his support and encouragement of Benjamin Silliman. He provided Silliman with money and time to learn his subject. The new professor spent most of the first two years of his appointment in Philadelphia studying chemistry and medicine (for even this early Dwight was planning for the medical school). Thus it was that Professor Silliman did not teach his subject until 1804. His first lecture—and it marks the birth of an era at Yale—was given on 4 April 1804 in a rented room in Mr. Tuttle's building on Chapel Street. Silliman "met the Senior class, and read to them an introductory lecture on the history and progress, nature and objects, of chemistry." He continued to lecture to this class until the completion of their course in July, and thus John C. Calhoun (B.A. 1804) had a chance to hear the young professor.[57]

President Dwight's desire to improve the library also worked to Silliman's advantage. He had taught for only a short time when he heard that the Corporation in their September 1804 meeting had authorized the expenditure of the enormous sum of $9,000 for library books and philosophical and chemical apparatus. Silliman rushed to Dwight and offered to go to Europe and do the purchasing if he could have the bookseller's percentage in addition to his regular salary. Then he could select everything personally and also study abroad. Dwight saw the benefit for everyone of this arrangement and with his blessing Silliman soon received the approval of the Prudential Committee.[58]

The need to go to England for equipment was indicated by Silliman's first experience with acquiring glass retorts in this country. The East Hartford glassmaker from whom he ordered them had never seen a retort but said he could copy one. Unwisely, Silliman sent him a model which was cleanly broken at the neck. The glass-maker duplicated the fractured original exactly and sent Silliman the product which, as the professor later recalled, looked "like decapitated kings in their coffins." [59]

Silliman sailed for Europe in March of 1805 and fortunately for Yale his ship did not sink—as one did later with another young teacher of whom great things were expected. He bought the books and equipment, met the great of England, and studied under the very best men at the University of Edinburgh.[60]

While working in Edinburgh Silliman became interested in geology, so some years later when he heard that Benjamin Perkins (B.A. 1794) had collected a "cabinet" of two thousand minerals, he immediately set out to persuade Perkins to let Yale buy it. He managed to obtain it for $1,000. Silliman's studies, trips, and purchases were beginning to mount up, and it is small wonder that old Treasurer Hillhouse called him, a bit gruffly no doubt, "the gentleman who can open the College Treasury." The Perkins Cabinet allowed Silliman to offer a course in mineralogy to any student willing to pay five dollars. Twenty to twenty-five immediately signed up, and thus began the study of mineralogy at Yale.[61]

The year of the acquisition of the Perkins Cabinet, 1807, also saw the spectacular event of the Weston meteor. On 14 December "a grand fireball passed over the town of Weston in the county of Fairfield." To observers it appeared "2/3 as large as the moon." It exploded, and pieces weighing up to thirty-six pounds fell to the earth. Silliman and Professor Kingsley dashed out to Weston, interviewed witnesses, collected specimens, and published an account in the newspapers which was, after Silliman made a chemical analysis of the specimens, revised and submitted to the American Philosophical Society. The paper created a tremendous stir of interest and ultimately was read before the Philosophical Society of London and the Academy of Sciences in Paris. Probably only dyed-in-the-wool Federalists believed the story that on reading the report Thomas Jefferson said, "It is easier to believe that two Yankee professors could lie than to admit that stones could fall from heaven." [62]

Silliman followed the purchase of the Perkins collection and the gathering of pieces of the Weston meteor with another and still more important acquisition, the great Gibbs Cabinet of minerals. Colonel George Gibbs had purchased the parts of this large collection (ten thousand specimens) in Europe, and Silliman had traveled to Newport to see it several times, thus getting to know the colonel. When Silliman finally asked Gibbs when he was going to open the collection to the public, Gibbs replied that he would allow it to be displayed at Yale if rooms were provided. Dwight saw the benefit to Yale of such a loan and he allowed Silliman to equip two rooms in Connecticut Hall. In June of 1812, despite the outbreak of war, the great new mineral gallery was formally opened.[63]

Benjamin Silliman did all these things while teaching, editing a chemistry textbook, getting the Medical Institution established, and even recovering from a serious accident. In 1811 an explosion in his laboratory caught him full in the face, and for a time it was feared he would never see again. Fortunately for Yale and for American science, a month in a darkened room and weeks of recuperation returned his sight to normal.[64]

All of Silliman's activities were very important in setting Yale on a course toward greater and greater achievement in science. To some this was a worrisome thing. Silliman recounted the story of how one of the fellows of the Corporation, the Reverend Dr. Ely, asked him, "Why, Domine, (his usual style in college matters) Domine, is there not danger that with these physical attractions you will overtop the Latin and the Greek?" Silliman apparently calmed Ely, but more dangerous were those who protested that science undercut religion. Silliman always tried to show that it did not and Dwight— despite his constant concern for the promotion of religion—agreed. It was quite clear to Dwight that scientific knowledge could only support the Scriptures and "disclose the ways and wonders of . . . God." [65]

Thus Yale under Timothy Dwight started on its way to becoming the chief center for the study of chemistry and geology in the United States. Though Dwight had no real understanding of the ways of the scholar, his organizational and inspirational qualities were such that while most other colleges in America stood still or went backward during this period, Yale, first under Dwight and then under Day, was "laying the foundation of its scientific eminence." [66]

In addition to the thrust Dwight gave to science, he doubled the size of the library (but cut its use to once a week from the twice a week Stiles had allowed). He also increased undergraduate enrollment: the average graduating class under Stiles had numbered 37.4 while under Dwight it was 50.4. At the same time, Yale became an increasingly national institution; became, in fact, perhaps the most national of American colleges.[67]

According to Samuel Eliot Morison, at Harvard "by 1810, eleven per cent of the entering class was from outside New England; after the war the proportion rose rapidly to eighteen per cent in 1816, and twenty-seven per cent in 1820, a proportion not again equalled until 1850 or surpassed until 1853." In contrast, at Yale an average of just over 25 percent of all graduates from 1805 to 1815 were from outside New England, and even for that early period 10 percent of all graduates came from the South: South Carolina (40), Georgia (10), North Carolina (9), and Virginia (6). As Morison notes, these additions of "students from afar were a very important factor in the social life of the College" for "they rubbed off the provinciality of the Yankee lads, [and] themselves learned to respect the solid qualities of New Englanders." Yale attracted Southerners because her reputation reached there early. In 1788 a graduate reported that throughout the southeast, they were calling Yale "the Athens of America," and when Benjamin Silliman visited Charleston in 1815 he found many Yale men, including members of the Gadsden, Grimké, and Legaré families.[68]

While Dwight was broadening the influence of Yale in the nation, making it a true university, and laying the foundation for its scientific eminence, he was also preaching good health (as a boy he had ruined his eyes studying), competitiveness, political and social conservatism, and, as we have seen, a message that was at heart anti-intellectual.[69] Because of his awesome presence and great abilities as a teacher, his support of these things in chapel and classroom must have carried great weight with his young listeners. The idea should not be pressed too far, but one wonders how much the conservatism of Noah Porter, senior, John C. Calhoun, and Augustus Baldwin Longstreet (to name a diverse few) was due to their mentor. And were the later muscular but unintellectual attributes of Yale in part a heritage of Dwight's opposition to learning per se? Still, a presidency that also saw the graduation of Thomas H. Gallaudet, Nathaniel W. Taylor, Roger Sherman Baldwin, and Josiah W. Gibbs cannot be easily stereotyped.

Though Timothy Dwight and Ezra Stiles were very different (and disliked each other intensely), they each made significant contributions to Yale. Stiles brought the tolerance, broadmindedness, and intellectual curiosity that gave Yale a university spirit, while Dwight, whose mind, as a later observer noted, "was closed as tight as his study windows in January," [70] brought an administrative talent to Yale that Stiles had always lacked. With it, and building on Stiles's groundwork, Dwight was able to create the beginnings of a university. Presidents Stiles and Dwight both brought with them their great personal prestige, and this reflected on the college and helped give it national status. On the whole, it can be safely said that Yale was fortunate to have two such remarkable men in succession lead it.

The Quiet Achievements of Jeremiah Day

If Timothy Dwight started Yale on the course it would follow throughout the nineteenth century, Jeremiah Day fixed it there. Day was Dwight's own choice for president. At a faculty meeting shortly before his death, Dwight abruptly turned and said, "Mr. Day, you must be my successor." The faculty approved this choice, but Day "utterly shrunk from it." It appears that the Corporation may have preferred "a man of some prominence as a preacher, and of strong qualities"; and when Day expressed his lack of enthusiasm for the job, they turned to another. The Reverend Henry Davis (B.A. 1801), president of Middlebury College and president-elect of Hamilton College, was offered the position in February 1817. On his decision to stay at Middlebury, the Corporation turned again to Day and convinced him that "the public interest" demanded his acceptance.[1]

So it was that on 22 April 1817 Jeremiah Day was elected president of Yale College.[2] It must have seemed to many observers at the time that the choice was not a good one. After the great intellectual, Stiles, and the teacher, preacher, and poet, Dwight, quiet and bookish Jeremiah Day probably appeared distinctly second-rate. There was certainly nothing in his life so far to make an outsider believe that he would be a successful president.

The new head of Yale was forty-three years old. The son of a minister, he had been born in New Preston, Connecticut. After graduating from Yale in 1795, he had first run Dwight's old school in Greenfield Hill, then served as a tutor at Williams College before returning to Yale as a tutor in 1798. In 1801 tuberculosis had forced him to take an extended vacation, but prior to his departure Dwight had nevertheless appointed him professor of mathematics and natural philosophy. For a time it had appeared that his illness might kill him, but to everyone's surprise a slow recovery had set in and in 1803 he had been well enough to take up the duties of his professorship. He had performed them without interruption until his election to the presidency. Though licensed to preach in 1800, he was not ordained until his inauguration as president on 23 July 1817.[3]

Despite these rather unpretentious credentials, Day proved to be a highly successful leader of Yale. Again Timothy Dwight's instincts about men (and he knew Day well after working with him for so long) were correct. For Jeremiah Day steadily and quietly promoted the interests of Yale College for twenty-nine years, the longest presidency of all, and during that time the institution was improved at every level.

While Yale's new president lacked the impressiveness of Dwight and the wide-ranging intellectual curiosity of Stiles, he had more real skill as a college president than either. Building on the accomplishments of his predecessor and snatching every opportunity that came his way, Day achieved so much that he should have earned himself a high place in the history of Yale and American education. Yet he has been overshadowed by the overrated Dwight in death as in life and has never received the credit that is clearly his due.

Jeremiah Day moved on several fronts to improve the state of the college. A new issue of its laws containing few major changes was brought out.[4] He checked on what was being taught and how. He attempted to cope with pressing financial problems. And he immediately expanded the corps of professors and worked to systematize the rule of the faculty.

It had been the custom at least since the time of Clap for presidents to consult the faculty on disciplinary matters. This practice had largely lapsed under Timothy Dwight, who was so confident of his personal influence with the students that he seldom felt it necessary to ask for the advice of the faculty. Under Day the practice of consultation was not only revived but greatly broadened. No doubt one reason for this was that Dwight, as a mature and famous man, was working with professors and tutors who had once been his students, while Day was dealing with Silliman and Kingsley, who had been on the faculty as long as he and with whom he had worked throughout his professional life. It was only natural for him to treat them as equals rather than as subordinates. In addition, Day's natural conservatism may have encouraged him to consult others before acting. But whatever the reasons, the faculty was granted an influential role in running the college, and this was one of Jeremiah Day's most significant contributions to American higher education.[5]

What the rule of the faculty meant was explained by Benjamin

Silliman in a speech to a convention of "Literary and Scientific Gentlemen" that met in New York City in 1830 to discuss the founding of the University of the City of New York. He explained that while legally the president and fellows had the only power of appointment of faculty members, the "opinions and wishes" of the faculty were usually accepted on such matters. He described how the president, "being the presiding officer both in the Corporation and in the faculty," carried the views of the faculty to the Corporation. And he explained that the Prudential Committee, made up of the president and three other members of the Corporation (one of whom was the governor or lieutenant-governor), took care of the accounts and devised plans and reports "in conjunction with the faculty," so that the Corporation could in one day a year take care of all its business. Thus, he noted, "although the Corporation is an independent body, it rarely acts in important cases, without the concurrence of both the faculty and the Prudential Committee—and as a great confidence always prevails between these respective bodies, the business of the institution proceeds harmoniously." [6]

No doubt the development of faculty rule was an almost automatic procedure for Day. This was not the case with his other problems.

The college Jeremiah Day took over in 1817 was, as we have seen, a national institution and the largest college in the country. In truth, by later standards it was a small, struggling college: the student body numbered around 275, of whom only three-fourths could be housed in the three college dormitories and the recitation rooms of the Lyceum, the sole classroom building. The library, which had grown to about 7,000 volumes, not including the 1,400 in the collections of the literary societies, was still so small that it could be kept in the Lyceum, which also contained seven recitation rooms, the chemical laboratory, and two professors' study rooms. [7]

Nor was the faculty impressive. Benjamin Silliman was professor of chemistry, mineralogy, pharmacy, and geology; James Luce Kingsley was able to drop ecclesiastical history from his title in 1817 and thus became plain professor of Greek and Latin languages; Day continued as professor of mathematics and natural history, but he was relieved of giving the "experimental lectures" by the appointment of an adjunct professor of natural history and philosophy in the person of Alexander Metcalf Fisher (B.A. 1813). In addition to Fisher, Day immediately added to the corps of instructors Eleazar Fitch (B.A. 1810) as Livingston Professor of Divinity and Chauncey Allen Goodrich (B.A. 1810) as professor of rhetoric and oratory. The increase in the number of professors allowed Day to drop one tutor, but still the faculty (including the president) grew from nine to ten.[8]

The growth of the faculty, especially in the upper ranks, pressed home Yale's major problem—finances. Though total annual income had been growing steadily (it reached about $10,000 for the first time in 1810) expenses had kept pace. Salaries had gone up rapidly. When Day began as a professor in 1803 he received $670 a year. He had expected to get a house, too, but this the Corporation found it impossible to furnish as the faculty grew under Dwight. Day complained at the time, "It seems, then, we have calculated too much upon the premium matrimonial. We must learn a little of Mr. Jefferson's republican economy to support families upon six hundred and seventy dollars a year." Fortunately, the Corporation relented slightly and the professors were granted $150 each in place of a house. In 1810 professors received a raise to a total (including house rent) of $1,000 and shortly before Day's accession their salaries were further increased to $1,100, where they remained throughout his presidency. Yale salaries compared well with the $600 professors were getting at the University of Georgia in 1815, or the $700 being paid at Williams in 1835, but they were far below salaries at South Carolina, Virginia, and Harvard. At Harvard some professors were receiving $1,700 in the 1820s, though they had to be cut back to $1,-500 in 1826 in the face of financial difficulties.

While Yale salaries were not up to some, they were among the best of the time. Richard Hofstadter has reported that while in the 1840s professors in New England earned from $600 to $1,200 per year, the low figure was the most common in the country as a whole. By the Civil War, the average had risen to $1,000. By comparison, at the outbreak of that conflict a skilled watchmaker or printer made about $600.[9]

To pay competitive salaries and all the other expenses of the college, the treasury depended mainly on tuition, for on 1 June 1817 it had only $54,440.06 in permanent funds (exclusive of land). From all sources other than tuition the college received less than $4,000 a year. To meet the growing needs of the college under Dwight, tuition had risen rapidly: from $16 a year in 1795 to $24 in 1807, and to $33 in 1815, where it remained until 1856.[10]

The higher salaries instituted by the Corporation and the enlarged faculty combined with the problems Day had inherited to create a serious situation. James L. Kingsley set forth the problem in a pamphlet entitled *Remarks on the Present Situation of Yale College; for its Friends and Patrons.* He explained that the college had very limited invested funds, insufficient dormitory space, only one partially endowed professorship, an inadequate number of instructors (and hence an inability on either their or the students' parts to specialize), and a library too small to allow the faculty to do advanced work. At the same time the last twenty-five years had seen Williams, Middlebury, Union, and Hamilton colleges founded in the area from which Yale had always drawn many students. Unless Yale improved quickly, Kingsley suggested, "Students may . . . be expected to resort to those seminaries, which possess the most abundant means of instruction: which will be, of course, those which are the best endowed." [11]

The response to this plea of 1818—the first general request for funds in the college's history—was not great. Nonetheless, Day pushed ahead with numerous improvements. In 1819 a new commons hall was built. It included a large room on the second floor for the mineralogical and geological cabinets. The following year the old commons was converted into a chemistry laboratory (where chemistry remained until 1888). The remodeling, as well as the new building, were probably paid for in part by a grant from the General Assembly in 1816 of $8,000 to $9,000.[12]

Because of the great need for sleeping and study rooms, and despite all the pressures on the college's limited endowment, a new dormitory, North College, was begun in 1821. At the same time, the legislature was approached in 1821 and 1822 for another grant, but to no effect. Despite these failures, Day moved ahead with the development of the institution. Belying his later reputation for extreme caution, in the face of an $11,000 debt for the new building and deficits averaging about $450 a year for the past four years, he now presided over the founding of the Divinity School.[13]

For as long as the college had existed, it had had an informal divinity school. It had always been the practice for a few graduates to remain to study divinity, and at least since 1795 one of the specific duties of the professor of divinity was to oversee the study of young men headed for the ministry. It was once usual to say, as Leonard Bacon did, that the colonial college was "essentially, in fact and in design, a theological seminary." But as many scholars have noted, that conclusion was false. The founders certainly had the provision of an educated ministry as their most important goal, but the road to that destination was through offering a good liberal education which. as the first charter said, prepared men "for Publick employment both in Church and Civil State." That education was, it must be stressed, merely preparatory. If a graduate wanted to be a minister, or in later years a lawyer or doctor, he had to continue his education under an established member of his chosen profession.[14]

The end of the eighteenth century and the beginning of the nineteenth saw a rising dissatisfaction with this rather informal system. When it worked well, few educations could be better, as Timothy Dwight's tutelage of Moses Stuart, Lyman Beecher, and Nathaniel W. Taylor revealed. But often the minister (or doctor or lawyer) was too busy, inadequately trained himself, or had a library insufficient for the task. As a result there was a move in all fields toward professional schools. Timothy Dwight, as we have seen, established the Medical Institution at Yale in conjunction with the state Medical Society, appointed a professor of law, and always hoped to start a divinity school.[15]

A new reason for founding a school came with the disestablishment of Congregationalism as the state religion in 1818.[16] But the immediate cause was probably the religious revival which began in the college in 1820. Fifteen members of the class of 1822 asked to remain at Yale to study divinity after their graduation. Eleazar Fitch, the professor of divinity, did not encourage them, but when they petitioned to be formed into a regular theological class, he supported their request. In a paper to the Prudential Committee he urged that the Corporation not allow Yale to be converted "into a mere school of science." [17]

Fitch had no reason to fear. An appeal was drawn up to the people of New Haven for funds for the new school, and the response was quick and positive. For the first time in the history of the college numerous individuals came forward with sizable gifts. Timothy Dwight, son of the former president, gave $5,000 to carry out his father's dream. William Leffingwell gave $2,000 and Titus Street,

$1,000. The college faculty was amazingly generous. Though none was wealthy, they gave in amounts ranging from Professor Fitch's $1,666.66 (more than a full year's salary) down to Silliman's offer of the interest on $500 for five years. By these means $15,000 was collected. When the Corporation insisted that they raise not less than $20,000, professors Fitch and Goodrich contracted to make up the additional $5,000 if the money was not found elsewhere. Fortunately it was not necessary to collect on this promise, for others soon came forward and the goal was achieved.[18]

On the strength of the pledge of Fitch and Goodrich, the Corporation voted to establish the Dwight Professorship of Didactic Theology and elected Nathaniel W. Taylor (B.A. 1807), minister of New Haven's Center Church, to the position. Professors Fitch and Kingsley were named to assist Taylor in the new school. Since the funds had been given strictly for the support of the new professorship, it was understood that the department was to be an entirely separate institution from the college. Thus began the economic separation of the various parts of the university—a policy which led to years of weakness for the professional schools.[19]

The successful fund drive for the new department did not, of course, do anything to solve the problems of Yale College. But it may have encouraged the Corporation to embark on another attempt to raise money. Kingsley revised his 1818 pamphlet and it was reissued in 1823. The college had some new needs, however, and these were now stressed. A new dormitory was desperately needed. With the construction of the new commons, enrollment had risen to 320 and the addition of a new dormitory, North College, had caused the number of students to jump again to 370. Once more many students were unable to live on campus. Kingsley noted, "Long experience has shown, that good order, industry, and morals, cannot be effectually secured . . . while a great portion of the students are dispersed, in different parts of the town." Even worse, the rise in enrollment meant that the chapel was overcrowded: "The evils proceeding from the want of a suitable *house of worship,* are still more alarming."

Kingsley thought that a dormitory and a chapel could be built with $20,000. To answer those who might say that Yale ought to raise its tuition to take care of such things, he replied with a philosophy that was to become a Yale creed. He wrote, "It is an object of high importance, to keep down the expenses, within the reach of persons in moderate circumstances. From these we are to expect the most vigorous and successful efforts while they are here; and the greatest amount of good to the community, when they enter upon the business of life." Kingsley regretted, in fact, that Yale was doing less for "indigent students" than almost any other college in the North.[20]

Supported by this plea, the college sent out agents to raise money for a new chapel. The need for that building was considered to be so great, however, that even before enough money had been raised, construction began in January 1824. The chapel was rushed to completion and dedicated on 17 November 1824. At the same time, the old chapel was remodeled to provide recitation rooms and space for the growing libraries of the literary societies. It was then renamed the Atheneum. The college library was moved to the fourth floor of the new chapel.[21]

Though Day's various campaigns for funds were not entirely successful, the attempts may have helped to interest men of wealth in the cause of the college.[22] Apparently without forewarning the Corporation heard that Sheldon Clark was interested in giving some money to the college for a professorship. Clark had been prevented by his tight-fisted grandfather from attending school for more than one year, let alone going to college. He had been forced instead to work hard on his grandfather's farm. When the old man died, Clark inherited his sizable estate and quickly went off to spend a year at Yale as a special student. He then returned to the farm, where aside from working the land and saving his money for philanthropic purposes he began to turn out philosophical essays in which, as Woodbridge Riley pointed out, there was "a surprisingly large stock of speculative questions." [23]

To discuss the projected gift, the Corporation met in Hartford. It was later thought that this meeting was held as a last attempt to prevent the chartering of Washington (later Trinity) College. As support for this conclusion, it was noted that the Corporation dropped the religious oath for officeholders at this time. That the Episcopalians intended to ask for a charter had long been known, however, whereas the decision of the Corporation to hold its meeting was sudden.[24] Just before the meeting, President Day explained to his brother, "Contrary to my late expectations, I have now a prospect of being with you, at the coming Election. The Corporation of the college is to meet at Hartford, for the purpose of taking into consideration, a proposition of a pecuniary nature, from a Mr. Clark of Oxford." [25]

The meeting, held on 7 May 1823, was largely devoted to Clark's desire to endow a professorship of moral philosophy and metaphysics. In the course of their discussions the old oath was dropped (only a brief paragraph in the records), marking the end—forever, we trust —of such tests at Yale. It is possible that the move to establish Washington, coupled with the critical attitude of the General Assembly and the people of the state, had something to do with the decision. But it seems very likely that the immediate cause was Sheldon Clark. Clark's essays indicate, according to Riley, "how pervasive were the influences both of materialism and of philosophic scepticism, how Hobbes and even Hume had penetrated not only to the freshwater college, but also to the farm." Surely one with such attitudes would have been rather uncomfortable with religious oaths and would have wanted his professorship to be unfettered. Since it had been possible to hold office without taking the oath throughout Day's presidency, and since religion was protected by the proviso in the deed of gift for the new professorship of didactic theology that the holder of that office must subscribe to the confession of faith, the Corporation was willing to drop the last vestiges of the old oath. Then Clark contributed $5,000 as a beginning of an endowment for the new professorship.[26]

Clark's contribution was soon followed by a gift of a similar amount for scholarships from David C. DeForest. The money was to accumulate until 1852, at which time DeForest calculated the principal would amount to $25,941.80 and 6 mills and the income $1,556.00. Yale was then to use $1,000 annually to educate the male descendants of DeForest's mother. If there were none, the scholarship could be given to anyone named DeForest; and if there were no DeForests, the recipient could be any indigent Yale student who was willing to change his name to DeForest. The records of the fund indicate that many students in the nineteenth century were willing to make the change.[27]

DeForest's gift further indicates the lessening interest in dogmatic religion. The donor insisted that "in the Selection of Candidates for the bounty herein provided the Religious or Political opinions of themselves or family shall not operate against or for them in any Case but a preference shall always be given to those who are of moral and virtuous conduct." [28]

Sheldon Clark, who soon became the college's greatest individual benefactor, offered another gift the following year. On 8 September 1824 the Corporation recorded the receipt of $1,000, which was to be put at interest for twenty-four years. At the end of that time the income was to be used for two-year scholarships to Yale graduates who were willing to remain in New Haven for at least nine months a year to study anything they wished except law, medicine, or divinity. This was Yale's first fellowship specifically for nonprofessional postgraduate studies.[29]

Clark's and DeForest's donations were, no doubt, pleasing to Day and the Corporation, but they did not solve the need for a general increase in income. Nor did circumstances combine to assist in solving the problem. Instead new difficulties arose. In May 1825 Colonel Gibbs suddenly announced to Benjamin Silliman that he had decided to sell his cabinet of minerals, which had been on deposit at the college since 1812. The collection was still the greatest in the country, and Gibbs wanted $20,000 for it. Though this must have been a frighteningly large sum (it was more than two-thirds of the college's entire income that year), the president, treasurer, and professors "were unanimous," Silliman later wrote, "in the feeling that the Gibbs Cabinet, so long our pride and ornament, must not be removed from Yale College." [30]

A door-to-door canvass was undertaken in New Haven and between nine and ten thousand dollars was collected. Silliman and Chauncey Goodrich tramped the city of New York "working on foot to save the expense of a conveyance," and raised another three or four thousand. A plea was mailed out "To the Friends of Yale College and of American Science." One who responded was Vice-President John C. Calhoun, who praised Yale as "one of the lights of the nation" and gave $100. Still the full amount was not immediately achieved. Fortunately, Gibbs was willing to take notes for $10,000, and this "pile of rocks" was saved for Yale.[31]

It would have been easier for Day and the faculty to let the Gibbs collection go. But Jeremiah Day never failed to grasp the main chance. This was proved many times, and it was further shown at this time when the college, as it was trying to raise the funds to save the cabinet, suffered its first great financial setback.

The Eagle Bank had been organized by the treasurer of Yale, James Hillhouse, and his friends Eli Whitney, William Woolsey, and Simeon Baldwin. With so stellar a list of sponsors, the bank had appeared to be such a wonderful investment that the college got special legislation passed to allow it to invest more than the statutory limit of $5,000 in one bank. Then it proceeded to pour money into the stock of the bank, even borrowing funds to do so. Unfortunately, the fine men who organized the Eagle Bank were too busy to oversee it carefully. Management was placed in the hands of George Hoadly (B.A. 1801), who proceeded to make loans, many on insufficient collateral, equal to the entire resources of the bank. The bubble burst in September 1825, and with it went some $21,000 of the funds of the college and the Dwight Professorship of Didactic Theology.[32]

The college finances had been weak for years; now the situation was critical. Total endowment income, exclusive of library funds, had fallen to only $1,800. Debts amounted to over $19,000. The Corporation naturally appealed to the General Assembly and pointed out that since the last request for funds in 1822, enrollment and hence expenses had increased. The legislature again turned a deaf ear to the pleas of the college.[33]

So Yale sought new solutions to its difficulties. First it tried a Society of Alumni of Yale College, which was formed in 1827. But memberships at two dollars each brought in very little. Possibly a change in the curriculum was the next suggestion. The college was now so dependent on student fees that the slightest drop in enrollment would have been a catastrophe. The famous Yale Report of 1828 (discussed at length below, pp. 162–63) rejected that solution. Then in 1830 another appeal was made to the state, and again the evils of raising tuition and making the college merely a school for the rich were painted. The General Assembly again voiced its sympathy but refused to help.[34]

Despite this failure, its debts and small annual deficits, the college officers were ready when a new opportunity beckoned. Colonel John Trumbull (Harvard A.B. 1773) was also in serious financial difficulties. When approached by his nephew, Benjamin Silliman, about his plans for the originals of his famous paintings of the Revolution, he instantly replied, "I will give them to Yale College to be exhibited forever for the benefit of poor students, provided the College will pay me a competent annuity for the remainder of my life." Since picture galleries were almost nonexistent in America, it is remarkable that the college officers so quickly grasped this opportunity. Yet Silliman later reported,

Our President, the Rev. Jeremiah Day, and my immediate colleagues among the older members of the College Faculty, as well as the officers of the fiscal department, were men of liberal minds, and I found no difficulty in exciting in them a lively interest and a strong desire to obtain the prize that was thus remarkably offered to us.[35]

Silliman went to Hartford to seek funds, and with his great persuasiveness got the legislature to vote Yale $7,000 in bank stock that the state had received for chartering a bank in Bridgeport.[36] With this support and the encouragement of the president and faculty the Corporation quickly approved the idea. By 29 October 1832 the first art museum connected with an educational institution in America, and one of the oldest in the English-speaking world (its chief chronological rival, according to Theodore Sizer, is the National Gallery in London) was opened. A special building, designed in the classical style by Trumbull, had been built just to house it.[37]

No matter how forward-looking it was to add an art gallery, that did not solve the college's financial problems. A suggestion had been received, however, from "some spirited friends of the College at the south" which pointed the way to a possible solution. Yale should make "one great and final effort on the broad scale of our whole country to raise $100,000 by subscription, and to place the entire institution *at once* on a safe and honorable foundation." [38]

Despite the magnitude of this suggestion—between 1701 and 1830 the college had received only about $145,000 in total gifts and grants—the college officers were delighted with the idea. They approached the campaign with great care. At least one agent began to raise money in advance, while circulars were sent out to announce the proposed plan and to invite attendance at a meeting on 13 September 1831 to discuss it.[39]

The preliminary response was excellent, and so everything was set to go forward when alumni and friends gathered in September. The discouraging financial situation was quickly outlined to them as well as the results: a deficiency of instructors (only one to twenty-three compared to one to thirteen as an average in the country); a deficiency of buildings (at least one and possibly two were needed), books (the college had only nine thousand and spent but $400 on acquisitions while Harvard had thirty-six thousand and spent $5,000 a year),* apparatus for the sciences, and "funds for the relief of necessitous students." [40]

After hearing the sad story, the patroon Stephen Van Rensselaer (LL.D. 1822) moved that the Society of Alumni approve both the object and the plan to raise $100,000. The resolution was quickly approved and the drive immediately got under way. By 1 December, when the college published "A Statement of Facts Pertaining to the Case of Yale College," it reported that $42,000 had been subscribed. But the college could not rest on its laurels, for under the terms of the drive no pledge was binding unless the full sum was subscribed by 1 December 1832. How difficult was their task was indicated a year later when Princeton failed to raise even $50,000 in a drive for $100,000.[41]

As with all fund-raising campaigns, activities at Yale caused misgivings among some of its graduates. The major source of trouble in the campaign for $100,000 (only later did it receive the name Centum Millia Fund) [42] was the Divinity School. There the New Haven theology, which Roland Bainton has called America's "one great contribution to the theological thinking of Christendom," was being developed and spread by Nathaniel W. Taylor.[43] To the Congregational old guard, the most distressing aspect of the New Haven theology was that it gave man a positive role in his own salvation. Though Taylor accepted the traditional belief in man's utter depravity, he thought the individual could actually choose good—could, in fact, act to bring about his salvation. Bennet Tyler (B.A. 1804), spokesman for the opposition to what was often called Taylorism, felt that this doctrine could only lead to the conclusion that God had failed. If man could choose to sin, then God must be "a disappointed and unhappy being, who is obliged to look with everlasting regret and sorrow upon the defeat of his designs, that he is forever engaged in fruitless efforts to render all his moral creatures holy and happy." [44]

* Actually, Harvard spent only $500 a year on the library, but in 1829 the Corporation had made a special appropriation for it of $5,000.

The effect of this dispute soon appeared. Wyllys Warner (B.A. 1826), the chief college agent in the drive, reported from New York City on 21 December 1831, "I have seen Dr. Spring [pastor of the Brick Presbyterian Church], find him more alarmed at the Theology of Yale than ever—he says he will not oppose me, but I fear his negative influence." Warner asked President Day's advice on how to proceed, for, he said, "I am at a loss to divine how matters will go here amid Theological difficulties, scarcity of money, Universities, tract, and home missionary operations." [45]

In addition to all the other difficulties Warner complained of, politics interfered—preventing donations from the South. The nullification controversy was in full swing. John C. Calhoun, who was soon to resign as vice-president, expressed "kind feelings" toward Yale but declined to give. Thomas S. Grimké (B.A. 1807), who opposed nullification, wrote from South Carolina to say that nullification seemed a certainty and no one could predict "what shock may be sustained by our institutions." Thus he could not give or ask others to do so. Despite these discouragements, an agent went South in November 1832 to try his luck. He got $50 from Grimké, but few others would give: in Louisiana only two came forward, one in North Carolina, and one or two in Georgia. President Day had predicted that even if the Georgians did contribute, they "would probably give little or nothing, unless it should be a lot of Cherokee land." Yale's sympathy with the Cherokees in their dispute with the state was too well known.[46]

In July 1832, with the campaign half over, a final push was made in New Haven. In a call for a meeting of citizens it was announced that about $70,000 had been raised, all but five or six thousand from outside New Haven, and it was suggested that if New Haven gave more, "old friends will rally, new friends will appear, and the effort will again go happily forward." A broadside was later released showing how much money Yale brought to New Haven. It warned that if the city did not support the college, the institution might decline and "it may go down to such a depth as will sink with it the value of all property, the prosperity of every branch of business, and, what is more, the honor and reputation of our city." [47]

Apparently the town did rally, for by commencement $87,000 had been pledged. But that left $13,000 to be raised in less than three months. A final plea announced, "In New Haven the subscriptions (including that of the President and six Professors, of 5,000 dolls.) amount to $25,000.—in Albany to 14,600.—in New York City to 15,000.—in the whole state of Conn.—about $50,000.—no more is expected from Conn.—and in no *one* place is a liberal subscription expected—the balance can only come from scattered individuals." [48]

Somehow the goal was achieved. On 27 November 1832 the presidents of three New York banks certified that more than $100,000 had been pledged and that all subscriptions were obligatory. A total of $107,341 had been subscribed, and though it took some years to collect (payments were to be in four equal installments) and some subscriptions had to be written off because of "misfortune and death," more than $100,000 was finally brought into the treasury. [49]

Yale's first large fund drive had succeeded, and it created an entirely new financial situation at the college. In 1832 and 1833 deficits totaling more than $3,000 each year had been incurred. By July 1834 the fund drive had added $2,000 to the income of the college (equal to the income from all funds prior to the drive), the deficit had been erased, and a small surplus achieved. From this time on, for the rest of Day's presidency, deficits were almost unknown and in most years a small amount was laid aside in anticipation of future needs. [50]

The large increase in endowment made Yale fear that at some point the state might decide to tax these funds. The charter of 1745 and other state laws had only exempted land and ratable estate up to a yearly value of £500 sterling. Under a new law, perhaps sought by Yale, the legislature in 1834 granted an exemption from taxation for all Yale property (and specifically its invested funds) except for real estate having an annual income of more than $6,000. Possibly to make this special treatment more palatable to the people of Connecticut, in the same act the Assembly withdrew the various exemptions from taxes of the president, faculty, students, and servants of the college. [51]

While solving Yale's day-to-day problems, the great fund drive of 1831–32 did not put an end to the college's needs. Money was raised in 1835 for a dormitory for theological students and in 1840 a fund drive was begun for a new library. The college collection now numbered somewhat over ten thousand volumes and the society libraries as many more. A new library building was badly needed. Fittingly, the Corporation decided to expend more money on this project than had ever been spent on a building at Yale. Henry Austin produced plans for the college's first stone structure, which was to be in the gothic style, resembling a small King's College chapel with wings added. Harvard's library, finished in 1841, had also copied that structure.[52]

Money came in slowly, but finally $34,000 was contributed and the library was completed in 1846. The college collection moved into one of the wings in 1844 and shifted to the main room in 1846. The society collections were then housed in the wings.[53]

The new building caused the Corporation to appoint in 1843 the college's first full-time librarian. Though Edward Claudius Herrick (M.A. hon. 1838) was not a graduate of any college, he had worked in a New Haven bookstore and publishing house for many years. Herrick's appointment allowed a startling liberalization of library hours: the collections were open four hours a day (except Sunday) in term time.[54]

Nor did the college stop with just a building and a librarian. Since 1837 the purchase of books had been kept to a minimum and funds accumulated for future use. At the same time Yale professors and experts elsewhere were consulted to ascertain what books the college needed. Then in 1845 Professor Kingsley, who had served as part-time librarian for many years, went to Europe at his own expense and personally selected the required books. He visited London, Paris, Leyden, Leipzig, Amsterdam, and Berlin, and, as he reported, "by an expenditure of nine to ten thousand dollars" he acquired 6,440 volumes at an average price of less than a dollar and a half, including "expenses for transportation, freight, insurance, and all charges of a similar nature." [55]

The library's purchases had been greatly assisted by a bequest in 1834 of $10,000 for a book-buying fund by Alfred E. Perkins (B.A. 1830). This was the largest single gift from an individual in the history of the college, and it indicates the generally small size of donations to the college during this period. At about the same time, Harvard received $100,000 from one individual—but this was most unusual. On the whole, colleges were not generously supported by private benefactors during these years. Though Bostonians seem to have given generously to the colleges of Massachusetts, they were unique. Yale and Princeton did not begin to receive large gifts until the 1850s and 1860s, and not until after the Civil War—when Darwinism and the laissez faire philosophy were rampant—did the old philosophy of the state as the major support of private education finally disappear. Only then, as Frederick Rudolph has pointed out, did "a partnership in public service, which had once been essential to the colleges and inherent in the responsibilities of government, . . . [become] insidious or . . . forgotten altogether." [56]

Because his was a time of small private gifts and declining interest on the part of the state, President Day was forced to devote a great deal of time to the finances of the college. But these were far from being his only concern. For not only was he the most aggressive financial director the college had yet had, but he was also its most influential educational leader.

Jeremiah Day is best known for his defense of the classical curriculum in the Yale Report of 1828. But before turning to that important document, let us look for a moment at the curriculum, the teaching, and the criticism that brought about its publication.

The entrance requirements and curriculum as they existed in Day's early years in office were most fully described in "A Statement of the Course of Instruction, Expenses, etc., in Yale College," first published for the academic year 1822–23. For admission to the freshman year, it stated, "Candidates . . . are examined in Cicero's Select Orations, Clark's Introduction to the making of Latin, Virgil, Salust [*sic*], the Greek Testament, Dalzel's Graeca Minora, Adam's Latin Grammar, Goodrich's Greek Grammar, Latin Prosody and Arithmetic." This was certainly more complicated and perhaps even more difficult than the entrance requirements of 1726, which had merely said that the candidate had to be "expert in both the Greek and lattin Grammar as also Grammatically Resolving both lattin and Greek Authors and in making Good and true lattin," but except for the arithmetic that Clap had added to the requirements in 1745, it was hardly different in kind.[57]

What the entrance examination was like in 1824 has been described by F. A. P. Barnard (B.A. 1828), later president of Columbia:

The applicants for admission were divided into squads of moderate numbers each. Mine consisted of eight victims besides myself. The examination was entirely oral, and was completed at a single session. One officer conducted the examination in all the subjects, while another sat by and looked on. My examiner was Professor Silliman, who, though Professor of Chemistry, took us up on Virgil, Cicero, the Greek Testament, Graeca Minora, Xenophon, Geography, and Arithmetic, all apparently with equal facility.[58]

If this short ordeal was successfully surmounted, the new student went home again and returned in six weeks (late October) to begin college. He was not immediately matriculated, however, so the college authorities could remove him easily if he seemed to be a troublemaker.[59]

The scheme of instruction the new student faced was almost entirely fixed for him. For the first three years he studied mainly Greek, Latin, and mathematics (algebra, geometry, and spherical trigonometry). In addition, he got a smattering of geography, history, science, astronomy, and English grammar and rhetoric. Senior year was devoted to metaphysics and ethics (very broadly interpreted) and a small amount of composition and belles-lettres.

Most of this material was covered by recitations. In addition, according to the "statement of the Course of Instruction" of 1822–23, all

classes receive lectures and occasional instruction from the Professor of Languages; the Junior class attends a course of experimental lectures on Natural Philosophy; and the Senior class, the courses on Chemistry, Mineralogy, Geology, and the principles of Natural Philosophy. The members of the several classes attend also the private exercises and lectures of the Professor of Rhetoric and Oratory. Specimens of English Composition are exhibited daily by one or more of each of the divisions of the Sophomore and Junior classes. Written translations from Latin authors, are presented by the Freshman class. The lower classes are also instructed in Latin Composition. The Senior and Junior classes have Forensic Disputations once or twice a week, before their instructors. There are very frequent exercises in Declamation, before the Tutors, before the Professor of Oratory, and before the Faculty and students in the chapel.[60]

We are fortunate that the very systematic Jeremiah Day, soon after becoming president, asked his professors to describe what they actually did in their courses. Since a few of these reports survive, this skeletal outline can be fleshed out a bit.

Professor Silliman described what he did in general terms. He said he gave his chemical lectures (with many experiments and illustrations) every day except Sunday during the first two terms to the seniors and medical students combined. These lectures were followed, for the seniors' short third term, with a course of about twenty or twenty-five mineralogy lectures "in which specimens of all mineral substances are exhibited and their uses and natural arrangements and situations in the earth are described." [61]

Chauncey Goodrich, professor of rhetoric and oratory, reported at length on the deficiencies of instruction in his two fields. What he noted shows the system under President Dwight, for Day soon made improvements and ultimately most of Goodrich's recommendations were accepted. When Goodrich reported in 1818, English grammar was studied at only one recitation a day for nine weeks in the sophomore year and rhetoric (in the literary sense of prose) for the same amount of time in the senior year. English compositions were required of a few sophomores and juniors every day, with the result that each member of those classes did seven or eight compositions a year. The juniors and seniors exhibited forensic disputations: juniors once a fortnight and seniors every six weeks. Freshmen, sophomores, and juniors declaimed "every day, in rotation, before their respective Tutors, at the close of the recitations at noon and evening." Unfortunately, Goodrich felt that the declamations at the end of the day were of little help, since the students were exhausted and "anxious only to be released from their confinement." A few members of each class also declaimed in the chapel before an audience of faculty and students each day of the week except Sunday. Goodrich considered the program not especially successful, since the students had no text on elocution, with the result that they did not understand "the *technical* terms," and "instruction, however clearly conveyed, must be chiefly unintelligible."

The course in rhetoric, Professor Goodrich thought, was just as bad: "The time allowed to the study of Rhetoric and the *Belles lettres,* during the whole Collegiate course, is equal only to two recitations a day, for *nine weeks*" (by 1822–23 this had been doubled) which was "hardly equal to that allotted to Geography." In addition, the timing of the course was unfortunate:

The admirable instruction on English Composition contained in Blair['s] Lectures, has been deferred till the Senior year; when the style of most Students has already been formed by the practice of two years in writing; and unfortunately, in many instances, formed in a manner so slovenly and incorrect, that all subsequent instruction is in vain.[62]

Some courses, such as chemistry, were taught by the lecture system, but most were taught by recitation. When a class arrived at the college it was divided into several divisions, a tutor was assigned to each division, and he taught the students almost every subject. Not until 1830 did the tutors begin to teach individual subjects according to their aptitudes or interests (or the needs of the college). Prior to that improvement each tutor met his division three times a day to teach the subject of the hour.[63] The way he taught has been well described by a graduate of the class of 1826:

> The tutors were . . . generally excellent drillmasters. They could hardly be said to teach at all, their duties being to subject every pupil three times a day to so searching a scrutiny before the whole division as to make it apparent to himself and all his fellows either that he did or did not understand his lessons. In the course of the recitation the tutor would furnish needed explanations and put those who were trying to improve in a way to do better next time. It was considered no part of his duty to assist his pupils in preparing for recitation. In that task the pupil was expected to be entirely self-reliant.[64]

Alexander Metcalf Fisher (B.A. 1813), the brilliant young adjunct professor of mathematics who was lost to the college when the *Albion* went down on its way to Europe in 1822, gave a faculty member's view of the recitation system as it worked in mathematics in his report to the president:

> The manner in which these text books are recited is the following. Lessons are given out varying from three to 6 or 8 pages, according to the difficulty of the subject. The propositions, rules, and general principles are required to be committed to memory. The proofs and illustrations are expected to be given in substance, by the student, in his own language. If the aid of a diagram is requisite, and those of the text book are not inserted by themselves at the end, copies of them are required to be drawn off and used in giving the demonstrations. In some instances however, when the demonstration is unusually complex, or is carried on in algebraic terms, the student is allowed to explain it from the book. Where demonstrations are omitted, or important steps left out, as is often the case in the latter part of the course, the class are expected to supply the deficiencies by their own ingenuity. To the few who succeed in it, this is regarded as a very useful exercise. In those branches which include numerical operations, examples differing from those of the text book are, to a greater or less extent required to be wrought; and in all

the branches such exercises are occasionally appointed by the instructor, as may contribute to inspire a taste for original investigation.

It seems unlikely that such teaching methods succeeded in inspiring such a taste in many students, but that it did succeed with some is indicated by the case of William Chauvenet (B.A. 1840), who did original work in mathematics even before he graduated and went on to achieve an international reputation in the field.

The course in natural philosophy, also Fisher's responsibility, was given in both junior and senior years. Juniors recited first, and then later in the year attended lectures where experiments were performed for them. For the seniors, Fisher reported,

A much more extensive course of written lectures is delivered . . . in which the principles taught in Enfield are reviewed, those deficiencies which are capable of being supplied with advantage independently of diagrams and demonstrations are made up, and the theory of every branch is pushed into its practical applications.[65]

The students were examined in all their courses twice a year, once in May and again in September, and if found seriously deficient they were liable to be degraded to the next lower class or even dismissed from college. In addition, on the third Wednesday of July, annually, the Senior Sophisters (as they were called for many years) were examined by the faculty "and other gentlemen of a liberal education, who may be present, as to their knowledge and proficiency in the learned Languages and liberal Arts and Sciences: And being found well skilled in them, and the whole course of academic literature, shall be advanced to the standing of candidates for the degree of Bachelor of Arts." [66] After this ordeal, most seniors went home until commencement in September.*

This curriculum and the way it was taught were subject to a great deal of adverse comment. Henry E. Dwight, one of President Dwight's sons, observed in 1830 during a period of particularly strong criticism that the teaching was often distinctly second-rate, since the men who did it as tutors were usually recent graduates pursuing professional studies, who taught for a few years and then moved on to another activity. Dwight's criticism was valid, but some saw then—as others see now—that the system had some good points.

* In 1832 commencement was moved to August, in 1851 to July, and not until 1873 was it held in June.

Julian M. Sturtevant, a graduate of 1826 who went on to be president of Illinois College for many years, observed in his *autobiography* that, though the course was "very faulty and inadequate" from the viewpoint of the late nineteenth century, it did help to develop the students' minds: "Its powers lay in its fixed and rigidly prescribed curriculum, and in its thorough drill." [67]

On the other hand, Sturtevant also realized the system's shortcomings. Like Henry Dwight he complained that the tutors were only drillmasters. Even Professor Kingsley failed to make Greek and Latin live. Kingsley once astonished Sturtevant's class by "closing a series of readings of Tacitus Agricola, by saying, 'Young gentlemen, you have been reading one of the noblest productions of the human mind without knowing it.' We might justly have retorted . . . 'Whose fault is it?' " [68]

These shortcomings in teaching were very real (though Sturtevant still thought "Yale was probably doing better work than any other college in our country" at the time), but strangely they do not seem to have been the real focus of concern. Instead the criticism of the 1820s, when the scattered voices of disapproval joined to form almost a movement, concentrated on the subject matter studied. Reflecting the egalitarian and practical temper of the times, it called for a wider diffusion of learning and courses that were "more meaningful and useful for contemporary life." [69]

Some reformers believed Latin and Greek should be dropped from the curriculum. At several colleges there were experiments with a course of studies parallel to those for the B.A. degree but without the classics. The University of Virginia even went so far as to allow complete freedom of choice to students in the selection of their courses.[70] The Yale Corporation, faced with financial problems in the 1820s, probably ever fearful that the slightest decline in the number of students would force a lowering of standards, and already subject to criticism for its traditional curriculum, was perhaps shocked when one of its own members, State Senator Noyes Darling (B.A. 1801), moved in the fall of 1827 that the "dead languages" be dropped from the curriculum and other studies substituted. This motion, coming as it did from a state legislator and perhaps reflecting the thought of many members of the General Assembly, caused the Corporation to appoint a committee made up of Governor Tomlinson, President Day, the Reverend Calvin Chapin, Noyes Darling, and the Reverend Abel McEwen to study the question. Their investigation resulted in the justly famous Yale Report of 1828 which was, probably for good and ill, the most influential educational statement ever to emanate from Yale.

The report had two parts, one by the faculty and one by the Corporation. The faculty report had two sections, one by President Day on the plan of education in the college and the other by Professor Kingsley on "the expediency of insisting on the study of the ancient languages." By far the most important, lasting, and quoted section was that by President Day. It is a profound and sensitive document with many facets, the most important of which was Day's declaration that the object of a college was "to LAY THE FOUNDATION OF A SUPERIOR EDUCATION." This was to be accomplished, he said, in the following manner:

The two great points to be gained in intellectual culture are the *discipline* and the *furniture* of the mind; expanding its powers, and storing it with knowledge. The former of these is, perhaps, the more important of the two. A commanding object, therefore, in a collegiate course, should be to call into daily and vigorous exercise the faculties of the student.

The report makes much of exercising the various "important faculties" of the mind, and while later educators and psychiatrists would probably disagree with the concept of the mind here envisioned, if one grants their end of producing well-educated men and not specialists, it is hard not to admire the completeness of the scheme they had constructed and the reasoning behind it:

In the course of instruction in this college, it has been an object to maintain such a proportion between the different branches of literature and science, as to form in the student a proper *balance* of character. From the pure mathematics, he learns the art of demonstrative reasoning. In attending to the physical sciences, he becomes familiar with facts, with the process of induction, and the varieties of probable evidence. In ancient literature, he finds some of the most finished models of taste. By English reading, he learns the powers of the language in which he is to speak and write. By logic and mental philosophy, he is taught the art of thinking; by rhetoric and oratory, the art of speaking. By frequent exercise on written composition, he acquires copiousness and accuracy of expression. By extemporaneous discussion, he becomes prompt, and fluent, and animated. It is a point of high importance, that eloquence and solid learning should go together; that he who has accumulated the richest treasures of thought, should possess the highest powers of oratory. To what purpose has man become deeply learned, if he has no faculty of communicating his knowledge? And of what use is a display of rhetorical elegance, from one who knows little or nothing which is worth communicating?

Nor did President Day stop with these excellent accomplishments. He stressed that classroom exercises were not enough. The student must be thrown "upon the *resources of his own mind*. Without this," he continued,

the whole apparatus of libraries, and instruments, and specimens, and lectures, and teachers, will be insufficient to secure distinguished excellence. The scholar must form himself, by his own exertions. The advantages furnished by a residence at college, can do little more than stimulate and aid his personal efforts. The *inventive* powers are especially to be called into vigorous exercise. However abundant may be the acquisitions of the student, if he has not talent at forming new combinations of thought, he will be dull and inefficient.

On top of this, Day hoped they might learn something. As he put it, in a somewhat elliptical fashion, "To the discipline of the mind . . . is to be added instruction. The analytic method must be combined with the synthetic."

President Day opposed shortening the course of instruction, making it more practical, dropping the dead languages, or modeling Yale on European universities. On this last point (a favorite reform of Harvard's George Ticknor), he made some observations that help to explain a good deal about why the American college curriculum took the form it did. He noted that the American college was more like a German gymnasium than a German university. He expected that most boys would graduate from college at eighteen (the age they finished the gymnasium), and, in fact, that as the lower schools improved this age would fall even lower. Day felt that to finish a graduate course three years later at twenty-one was hardly late in life. Even if the graduate were somewhat older, was that any reason, he asked, for giving him a limited education? Day stressed for those who thought the liberal arts prepared a man for nothing that a man at college was taught how to learn: the college graduate has merely begun his education, not completed it; he has laid a foundation, not finished the structure.[71]

In many ways, Day's message about the old classical education was timeless and of value to all men. Unfortunately, colleges all over the country patterned their courses of study after it and, neglecting its sympathy for curricular evolution, later used it to resist all change. Furthermore, those who knew only the older, conservative Day and who have never read his part of the report or felt its reasoned liberalism have used it to prove that Yale and Day were resistant to all change. This charge Day himself quite properly denied. He noted in the report the new subjects that had entered the curriculum: "Chemistry, mineralogy, geology, political economy, etc." He insisted Yale did not resist change but only the idea "that our colleges must be *new-modelled*." [72]

Yale, Day pointed out, only needed a *"School of Philosophy"* for the highest researches of literature and science" to be added to the theological, medical, and law schools * for it to become like a European university. It should not, however, sacrifice the college to achieve that end. The college should remain a separate department with the function of "teaching the branches preparatory to all others." This did, of course, become and, to a degree, remains the Yale philosophy. At Yale, as Richard Storr has pointed out, the philosophy was to emphasize the old arts course and use the graduate school to supplement it, while at Harvard graduate and undergraduate work sometimes became mixed and graduate education was used to transform the college.[73]

Day was even willing to add a short course of the type later identified with the Sheffield Scientific School, if money became available.[74] Despite the possibilities of new schools, of course, all this was conservative, in the sense that it kept the old liberal arts college course from revolutionary alteration and kept the college a distinct entity.

As Frederick Rudolph has pointed out,

The Yale Report was a magnificent assertion of the humanist tradition and therefore eventually of unquestionable importance in liberating the American college from an excessive religious orientation. In the meantime, however, the report gave a convincing defensive weapon to people who wanted the colleges to stay as they were. . . . Behind it the Ameri-

* In November 1824 the students of a local law school had begun to be listed in the Yale catalogue as members of the university. The slow movement of the Law School into Yale is discussed in chap. 11.

can college curriculum remained almost immovable until after the Civil War.[75]

But if Yale, with a good deal of logic, rejected the vague suggestions of the reformers, it did not stand still under President Day. The study of modern languages, for example, was much improved, though as usual the change took time. French was the first language to break the barrier. Students had been able to study the language with a private tutor for many years, but when, in 1820, the sophomore class asked that it be made an optional subject, the Corporation refused. Finally, in the summer of 1825, the president and fellows relented and allowed French to be studied as an option. German was even slower to appear. It was possible to take it, as well as Spanish, from a private tutor, too, but not until 1831 (by which time Spanish had become an option) was it officially recognized with the appointment of an instructor of French and German, and even then it did not become an optional study until 1841. By that point, even Anglo-Saxon was allowed as one of the choices for summer term of junior year. When that subject was admitted in 1839, President Day remarked, perhaps not entirely in jest, "that it might soon be necessary to appoint an instructor in *whittling*." [76]

It should also be noted that the absence of many subjects from the formal curriculum did not prevent students from learning them anyway. One undergraduate referred in his diary to Ebenezer Johnson as the best linguist in the class of 1833. Johnson, he wrote, knew, in addition to Latin and Greek, French, Spanish, modern Greek, and Italian, and had considerable knowledge of German, Portuguese, and Hebrew.[77]

More important than new courses or the courses taken outside the regular curriculum—and Day's main contribution to education at Yale—was a general improvement in the whole course of study by the provision of more professional teachers and stricter standards. Science, of course, had been a strong point of the college since the days of Dwight. Day encouraged its growth by allowing Silliman time for public lecturing, thus calling attention to Yale. And Silliman increased that attention by establishing the *American Journal of Science and Arts* in 1818 (it remained a family enterprise for nearly three generations). Benjamin Silliman's journal, his speaking, and his teaching attracted many bright would-be scientists to Yale. He was, in fact, so successful in promoting his field within the college that he caused the professor of didactic theology to mutter, "Money enough for breaking glass in the laboratory, but not a penny for theology." [78]

Silliman worked in chemistry, mineralogy, and geology, but good work was being done in astronomy as well. The field was not, of course, a new one, for it had been a personal favorite of Thomas Clap's, and Ezra Stiles had continued that interest. It was given a great boost, however, by Sheldon Clark's gift in 1830 of a five-inch reflecting telescope, the most powerful in America. The instrument was placed in the steeple of the Atheneum, and though the low windows prevented anyone's seeing anything higher than thirty degrees above the horizon, Denison Olmsted (B.A. 1813), who joined the faculty in 1825 as professor of mathematics and natural philosophy, and tutor Elias Loomis (B.A. 1830) were the first in America to report the return of Halley's comet in 1835, long before the news arrived from Europe.[79]

Nor was astronomy a subject only for the faculty. Student diaries reveal their use of the telescope, and Ebenezer Porter Mason and Hamilton Lanphere Smith, both of the class of 1839, spent most of their time outside the classroom constructing telescopes and observing the stars.[80]

Olmsted was able to concentrate on natural philosophy and astronomy after 1836 when, at his own urging, Anthony D. Stanley (B.A. 1830) was appointed professor of mathematics, for the first time making that subject a separate department.[81]

Specialization and professionalism came to the humanities with the appointment of Theodore Dwight Woolsey (B.A. 1820). He had been one of that initial small wave of Americans to pursue graduate study in Europe and the first to receive a thorough philological training there. He had spent the years from 1827 to 1830 mainly studying Greek in the great intellectual centers of the Continent. In 1831 he was designated professor of Greek language and literature, and he immediately started to improve the study of that subject. Because he found the textbooks in use inadequate, he soon began to bring out his excellent editions of Aeschylus, Sophocles, Euripides, and Plato.[82]

This was perhaps Yale's great age for the production of textbooks. The desire to improve the teaching of their subjects—and possibly make some money as well—impelled almost all Yale teachers to write texts. Denison Olmsted turned out books in various scientific areas which ultimately sold some 200,000 volumes. Day and Silliman had already done their work of this sort, and Woolsey was producing his Greek editions, while James Dwight Dana, an assistant to Silliman, was at work on the most famous of Yale texts, *A System of Mineralogy,* which appeared in 1837. Revised many times, it reached a seventh edition in 1944.[83]

The faculty was improved not only in the college. In 1841 Edward E. Salisbury (B.A. 1832) was appointed professor of Arabic and Sanskrit, opening the field of oriental studies in the United States. His was the first appointment in graduate education outside the fields of law, divinity, and medicine. In the Divinity School, the great philologian Josiah Willard Gibbs (B.A. 1809) was made professor of sacred literature. Gibbs was a scholar to such a degree that his more positive colleague Nathaniel W. Taylor observed, "I would rather have ten settled opinions, and nine of them wrong, than to be like my brother Gibbs with none of the ten settled." [84]

In addition to an improved faculty and better teaching, Day wanted more strict and advanced standards. In the 1828 report he had stated categorically, "The first and great improvement which we wish to see made, is an elevation in the standard of attainment for admission." In 1822, as we have noted, the entrance exam covered various aspects of Latin, Greek, and arithmetic. By 1828 English grammar and geography had been added. These remained the requirements until August 1845, when arithmetic was expanded to include algebra as far as quadratic equations.[85]

Recitations were made more rigorous after 1825. Denison Olmsted appears to have begun the change. Until he took office, according to Noah Porter,

each tutor sat upon the same floor with his pupils, comfortably or rather luxuriously seated in an elegant chair, the gift of the division, and, beginning the recitation with some person he might chance to select, followed the line in a regular succession, so that each student could very easily anticipate the passage or the problem which was awaiting him, and prepare himself accordingly. No record was made of the student's performance, only his absence from exercise. The innovation for which Professor Olmsted had the credit, or rather the very serious *dis*credit among the students, was the transfer of the tutor to an elevated post of observation behind a very ugly table, with a box before him, from which he drew the ballots which called up the students; and not long after a marking book in which was entered his estimate of their work. Till the year 1830 or 1831, the students were permitted to vote respecting the relative rank of their fellows as a basis for the action of the Faculty in assigning college honors.[86]

At about the same time that Olmsted tightened up recitations, attendance at exercises began to be much more strictly enforced. Precise records of class attendance began to be kept and a system of demerits was instituted whereby, as Porter described it, a letter home was written "for a certain number of marks; a second letter for an additional number; a reprimand in presence of the Faculty for a third increase; and dismission where the number exceeded the extremest limit." This disciplinary scheme prevailed for more than fifty years.[87]

The more demanding work and stricter discipline created pressures among the students that helped make the decade of the 1820s a time of violence at Yale, as it was at other colleges.[88] Matters came to a head in the great Conic Sections Rebellion of 1830.* Both faculty and students agreed on the cause: in the recitation of conic sections, the faculty explained, the students wanted "to recite from the *book,* and not from the *figure;* that is availing themselves of the printed page, instead of going through the demonstration with the aid of the diagram alone." The point of disagreement was the students' contention that most classes had done it by the book, while the faculty argued that doing it by the figure was the usual way at Yale. It is not necessary to follow all the twists and turns of petitions, answers, and misunderstandings, for the major point is that when recitations were held the members of the class of 1832 refused to do it the way the faculty wanted. In the face of what the faculty called "a combination to resist the government," classes were suspended and the students were asked to agree in writing to submit to the college laws. Ultimately, the faculty settled the matter by expelling forty-three of the ninety-six students in the class.[89]

The college then made sure this message was not misunderstood by the remaining students. The names of the expelled were circu-

* Conic Sections seems often to have caused trouble. The appearance of unexpected questions on the examination in the subject in 1825 caused a revolt by members of the class of 1827. For other riots and violence at Yale during these years, see chap. 12.

lated to other colleges to make sure they would never be admitted to another school. Only a few, William Kingsley reported with some pride, ever were admitted. Thus the college reacted to combinations of students as employers at the time reacted to combinations of workingmen. Both had to be crushed at all cost.[90]

The college did relent, finally. The great doctor Alfred Stillé, who graduated from the University of Pennsylvania in 1832, was given his degree in 1850. Most of the black-listed had to wait until 1879, however, and more than half never received their Yale degrees.[91]

It seems clear that the college reacted excessively harshly in this instance, but it must be admitted that for the institution as a whole the result was benign. After the blood-letting over the Conic Sections Rebellion, except for the usual pranks, peace generally prevailed on campus. Student energies were expended in riots in the town.[92]

Having improved standards, tightened discipline, and solved many of the financial problems of the college, Day sought to resign in 1843. "But," as he later wrote, "by the solicitation of gentlemen deeply interested in the prosperity of the college, and in whose judgment I have reason to repose special confidence," he was induced to remain in office.[93] There seems to have been no particular reason why Day should not resign just then, except that the library was not quite finished and perhaps his assistance was wanted to raise the money to complete the job.

By 1846, however, he could be persuaded to stay no longer. As he said to at least one member of the Corporation, "You had better let me resign now, when I have the intelligence to do so. The time may come when I shall not have it, but shall think that I am wiser than you all, and than I ever was myself before." In his resignation, with typical modesty, Day felt it necessary to apologize for the ill health that had plagued him throughout his life. He thought it had paralyzed his efforts and frustrated his purposes, and that now he ought to get out of the way and let a successor be chosen. Then this quiet man, who is supposed to have been the epitome of conservatism, remarked that one reason for changing was that an old man came to be satisfied with things as they are. "But our college must not remain stationary, surrounded as it is, by rival institutions, which are vigorously pushing forward their measures for securing the prize of literary eminence." [94]

After Day's resignation as president, the fellows, because of their great respect, trust, and dependence on the old man (he was now seventy-three), made a serious mistake. They elected him to the Corporation. What they did not realize was that despite his many ills he would live for another twenty-one years and serve on the Prudential Committee and the Corporation until slightly more than a month before his death at the age of ninety-five on 22 August 1867. He had worked for Yale for seventy years.[95]

The fact that Jeremiah Day remained in a powerful position throughout all but four years of Theodore Dwight Woolsey's presidency must have had some dampening effect on his successor's freedom of action. And it was perhaps during this period that Day's reputation for extreme conservatism took hold. That reputation is, in part, based on the remarks of the second President Timothy Dwight, who knew Day only at this time. Dwight wrote in his *Memories of Yale Life and Men* that Day was "too cautious, and too slow in his movements," and related stories to support that charge and deny the old man's reputation for wisdom.[96] But Dwight tended to overrate the excellencies of his grandfather and underrate Day's achievements. If, as Dwight says, the first President Dwight was an architect while Day was a builder, it must be granted that he was an incredibly aggressive, creative, and imaginative builder. The man who served Yale for seventy years, who put the college on a firm financial base, began the divinity and law schools and the Trumbull Gallery, started the move to a professional faculty, and gave the best and most influential definition of the old-time curriculum, deserves a place as one of Yale's great presidents.

President Woolsey and the Growth of the University

Early in the year 1846 it was known that Jeremiah Day would definitely retire in the fall. With so much warning there was much discussion of a successor. In May one group began to urge the candidacy of Benjamin Silliman. Though Silliman in his later years was often considered by intolerant students to be prolix, wandering, and excessively anecdotal in his lectures, he was, to the outside world, the voice of Yale. As President Woolsey later said, "He, in his prime, was our standing orator, the principal medium between those who dwelt in the academic shade and the great public."[1]

But Silliman had two heavy counts against him. As he informed those who favored him, the president was always a minister. Silliman had never even studied for that profession. Second, though he did not mention it, he was now sixty-seven years old. It seems probable that for these reasons the Corporation never considered Yale's great scientific leader; but as the day advanced for the expected resignation the fellows still had not reached a firm decision. As Silliman explained,

There has been much agitation of mind here and elsewhere this summer on account of the announced resignation of President Day. No one candidate has such commanding claims as was the case when Dr. Stiles died in May 1795. . . . Dr. Dwight was named almost by acclamation. When Dr. Dwight died January 11, 1817—then there was Professor Day. Professor Woolsey will, I think, be chosen if he will accept (which he does not favor).[2]

But the professor of Greek was not the only candidate. Leonard Bacon, pastor of the Center Church, was also considered for the job. He met the need for a minister, was the right age (forty-four) and seemed to have the intellectual credentials. But a number of the faculty and many graduates felt that he was too much of a controversialist (he was, for example, an outspoken opponent of slavery) and perhaps lacked the administrative ability necessary for the job.[3]

So the Corporation turned to the less public man, Theodore

Dwight Woolsey, the scholarly professor of Greek, and invited him to be president on 19 August 1846, the date on which Jeremiah Day's resignation was accepted. At the same time, they voted that if Woolsey accepted, he must be ordained. Theodore Dwight Woolsey was faced with two difficulties: while happy where he was, he felt a distinct "aversion to the Office" of president; in addition, he was very religious and, though licensed to preach, he feared he was not fit for the ministry. According to H. E. Starr, he was "extremely conscientious and subject to periods of acute consciousness of sin and moral responsibility that depressed him at intervals all his life." Because of these doubts Woolsey told the Corporation he would have to consider the subject. He promised that his personal feelings on the matter would not affect his judgment: "I mean to view the subject simply in the light of duty." [4]

Under the urging of President Day, the Prudential Committee, and his friends, he finally accepted, at the same time saying, "I earnestly wish that it had pleased God not to call me in his Providence to enquire whether the path of duty lay in this direction." And he made it clear that he still harbored such doubts about his religious character that if he found himself "burdened with a wounded conscience, or have and deliberately retain clear views of [his] want of qualifications as a Christian," he would resign.[5]

On 20 October 1846 Woolsey was examined on his fitness for the ministry, passed, and on the following day he was ordained in the morning and inaugurated in the afternoon. The new president, not yet forty-five, was in the prime of life. Five feet ten or eleven inches tall, with a slender, wiry frame and slightly stooped shoulders, he was the very picture of a gentleman and a scholar. His "slightly receding forehead" and clear and penetrating eyes, combined with his quick step, gave an impression of energy and intelligence. He is said to have had a very quick temper, which caused some to object to his consideration for the presidency, but in later years he apparently controlled this aspect of his character. It may have emerged, however, in the hasty actions and autocratic behavior that so impressed the younger men of the faculty. When this was combined with his tendency to speak bluntly and with an "excess of truthfulness," embarrassing situations could result. In one case, during a brief address at the grave of a fellow, Woolsey said, in substance, "Our deceased friend was well aware that his talents were but moderate and in-

dulged in no undue pretensions." In another instance, it was necessary to "smooth down" his remarks when his eulogy of another fellow of the Corporation was published. Fellows must have feared to
have the veridical president outlive them! [6]

Still, Franklin Bowditch Dexter, who was first a student under
Woolsey and then held numerous positions in the college during
the last quarter of the president's term, found much to admire in
him. As he pointed out, what Woolsey did openly, many others did
by underhanded means. Dexter afterward wrote that "he was the
most guileless and upright of men; humble and childlike in his religious faith, and obedient to the sway of that faith in the secret
springs as well as the open manifestations of his character." Woolsey's outspoken and authoritative ways were at first, it appears,
largely kept in check. In fact, at times he seemed somewhat hesitant.
In the discussion of biennial exams, a project he favored, Woolsey
endangered the whole idea by not assuming responsibility for it.
James Hadley thought the reason was "a desire not to bias the action of the Faculty." [7]

Woolsey—like so many other college presidents—was a descendant of Jonathan Edwards. The first President Dwight was his
uncle. Thus Yale was in his blood. And it was part of his life: he
had graduated in 1820, the valedictorian of his class, had been a
tutor from 1823 to 1825 (an experience that, he said, "made a man
of him"), and, after three years of study in Europe, had returned to
become professor of Greek language and literature.

While in Germany, Woolsey had written to his father, "I have en-
deavored to gain a minute and thorough knowledge of the Greek
language, and to lay a foundation for an acquaintance such as few in
America possess with classical literature, in order to teach it." The
belief in hard and careful work that he revealed in this letter became
the hallmark of his professorship. That it would also mark his presidency was shown soon after he took office, during a faculty discussion of whether a certain prize should be awarded for proficiency in
Latin or for rhetorical merit. James Hadley recorded in his diary,
"The President expressed himself quite strongly. He thinks that the
whole current, in College and out of College, sets toward rhetoric
and that sound scholarship is in danger of being swamped by writing and speaking." [8]

Enforcing "sound scholarship" in the college was the central theme of Woolsey's presidency. He promoted competitive scholarships, even giving the money for some himself. He published the names of winners of prizes and scholarships in the college catalogue. He began, in 1848, to list the rank of graduating seniors in the commencement program: there were two groups of colloquies (respectable students), three of disputes (for better performance), a group of orations (the top of the class), a very few philosophical orations, one salutatory oration, and, number one in the class, the valedictory oration. These appointments soon spread to the junior class and both were, for the first time, listed in the college catalogue of 1856–57 for all the world to see. When it was suggested in 1853 by a faculty committee on scholarship that behavior should affect one's standing as a student, the president revealed both his respect for academic achievement and a bit of his autocratic temper: he refused to consent to this part of the report, so it was dropped.[9]

Woolsey made senior year more demanding. Apparently he felt the seniors were not using their time to good advantage, for he added a second daily recitation for them. Thus, as Noah Porter so nicely put it, "it became their privilege . . . to attend recitations at 6 in the summer and at 7 in the winter." Life for all students was made even more trying by the institution of more thorough examinations. With the aid of assistant professor Thomas A. Thacher and despite opposition from some of the older men a new system of testing was instituted in 1851: oral examinations were given at the end of every term and two written biennial examinations were demanded, one on the studies of freshman and sophomore years and the other on the material covered during junior and senior years. In 1865 biennials were dropped and annual examinations were instituted of about three hours each on every subject studied during the year. In 1868, the faculty approved giving entrance examinations in writing.[10]

Within the college curriculum there were also evolutionary changes that are revealed by a comparison of the course of study at the end of Day's presidency and at the close of Woolsey's. By 1870–71 undergraduates had some choice about the amount of Latin they studied. If they wished, they could avoid about one-third of the work taken in 1844–45. In Greek the requirements remained much the same, although there was more concentration on Greek composition than there had been under Day. One term of either Greek or Latin could be dropped in junior year to take additional differential calculus for two terms. In rhetoric, logic, and mental and moral philosophy, the graduate of 1845 would have felt right at home in 1870–71. Some of the books read had changed and he would have had to write more English compositions, but on the whole the alterations were minor. On the other hand, in the areas of modern language, history, and science, there had been a revolution. The student in 1870–71 took more than twice as much history, including a full year of lectures on modern European history by the recently appointed (1865) professor of history, Arthur M. Wheeler. Whereas French, German, or Spanish could be taken as optionals for one term when Day resigned, the student of 1870–71 was required to take two terms of French and one of German, and could elect to take two more terms of German. At the same time, science courses had doubled in quantity and improved in quality, even including field trips in botany.[11]

In political philosophy (political science) and international law, under the stimulus of President Woolsey much was added. In 1844–45 students had read only Kent's *Commentaries,* volume 1, and Wayland's *Political Economy* and heard some lectures by the professor of law; now they had new texts and new fields. Woolsey was among the first to use Francis Lieber's books on political science in his classes, and in 1860 he produced his own *Introduction to the Study of International Law, Designed as an Aid in Teaching and in Historical Studies* to fill a need he felt while teaching international law to Yale seniors. His book played an important role in promoting the study of international law in American colleges. In this area the senior studies now included Roman law, political economy, international law, the Constitution of the United States, civil liberty, and natural rights. There was also a term of study in the history of philosophy and a year of modern European history.[12]

Yale's reputation for extreme educational conservatism has often prevented later commentators from realizing the significant changes taking place at the college. For example, one recent scholar has stated that "during the long Woolsey administration emphasis upon science, history, and economics had declined at New Haven" while the president stressed metaphysics. In fact, Woolsey never taught metaphysics, and during his term in office he was beginning to gain a reputation both in America and Europe as an authority on political science and international law.[13]

The changes in examinations and course of study described above do not take into account, of course, the fact that under Woolsey the scientific school was established. That development is discussed below. But it should be noted that there a whole new program devoted to science and modern languages was developed which led in three years to a Bachelor of Philosophy degree.

As far as the academic side of the college was concerned, Woolsey's administration seems to have been as willing to allow innovation at the end as the beginning. In 1868 the faculty permitted Hubert Anson Newton, the professor of mathematics, to divide his sophomore class on the basis of their academic standing in mathematics, thus for the first time officially separating the sheep from the goats so that each could be handled accordingly. The experiment was so successful that in the following year all classes except the seniors were so divided.[14]

The changes that produced the difference between the studies of 1844–45 and those of 1870–71 occurred slowly throughout Woolsey's term. Yale College remained a conservative place and Woolsey was a conservative man. As Timothy Dwight later remarked of Woolsey's first years, "There was . . . no action of a radical character, and no great overturning, as if the past should be neglected or forgotten. Neither was there undue haste in the movement for changes." Illustrative of this aspect of Woolsey's administration was the discussion over whether to institute a professorship of history. Harvard established a chair in ancient and modern history in 1838, and Woolsey suggested one in 1850, but when the Yale faculty discussed the matter in 1851 caution prevailed. It is true that the college had very limited means and was currently trying to raise money; nonetheless the discussion revealed a very limited outlook. An offer had been made of part of the endowment for a professor of history if the college would raise the rest. Hadley recorded that when the matter was brought up at a faculty meeting at the president's house, "the questions discussed were whether it is worth while to have a Professor of History, whether it is best to abridge so much the instruction given by the President, whether it is well to have a Professor of such limited range, whether it is desirable to give so much importance to the department of History." After a long discussion it was decided that history was sufficiently worthwhile "to accept a complete endowment if one were offered." It was not, so the chair was not established until 1865, when a partial endowment was again offered.[15]

This apparently excessive caution may have been caused by a feeling on Woolsey's part that he did not have a free hand. Until 1851 James Luce Kingsley remained active on the faculty (thus completing fifty years) and Benjamin Silliman was persuaded to stay until 1853 (he had started in 1799). Even more important, Jeremiah Day still had power. How many times Woolsey bowed to his wishes we shall never know.[16]

A revealing episode occurred in 1850. Fertile-minded Thomas Thacher, who was now considered the most influential member of the faculty in matters relating to the government and discipline of the students (no doubt it helped that he was Day's son-in-law), suggested a change in the college calendar. He proposed "an 8-weeks vacation from July to September, giving two weeks to each of the other vacations" and moving Christmas and New Year's Eve into the winter vacation. Since those two days had produced mischief and even riot during many of the years in which they were not recognized as holidays, and the idea of an extended summer vacation must have been most appealing to the faculty, it is surprising that the change had not been considered before.[17]

When the question was about to come before the faculty, Thacher discussed with Hadley its chances of passage and incidentally revealed the power of the old former president. Thacher remarked that "President Day has no objection [to the change] and . . . Woolsey will not make any if President Day does not." According to the second President Timothy Dwight, Day's influence was so great that "the suggestion of what he thought came to be considered, oftentimes, a sufficient settlement of questions in dispute." Even after his death, Day's opinion on some things was law. When Dwight had an argument with Treasurer Kingsley over the comparative value of two lots, the treasurer "abruptly closed the talk, as if nothing further could be urged by . . . any one, with the words: 'President Day regarded the corner lot as the less valuable of the two.' "

Apparently Day viewed schedule alterations with equanimity, for Thacher's plan for a more balanced calendar was accepted, as was another significant change. In 1859 a committee (the faculty was now large enough so that a great deal was done by ad hoc committees) was appointed to study the "routine of College exercises." They proposed "giving to the students one hour more for sleep in the morning,—having prayers and recitations after breakfast (instead of before as now).—having dinner one half hour later,—having the recitations at 11. and in the afternoon later than now. and the giving up of Evening prayers—." Harvard had given up evening prayers in 1855 to good effect—it cut out another obvious occasion for disorders—but what that college did in religious matters had never been a trustworthy guide. Nevertheless, the faculty approved the changes, though three dissented to having prayers and recitations after breakfast. The majority hoped that the new schedule would make the students more "serious and decorous" at prayers, and that there would be better attendance and fewer false excuses at prayers and recitations. The fellows also approved. The new schedule had the bell for breakfast at 7:00, for prayers beginning at 7:45 "and the tolling [to] be finished at five minutes before 8 o'clock." Recitations followed immediately after chapel. Second recitation was at 11:30, dinner bell at 1:00, evening recitation at 5:00, and supper bell at 6:00.[18]

This "revolutionary" experiment was a great success. Noah Porter —never a great one for new procedures—reported that there had been many arguments about altering the schedule: "Those for the change carried the day, with many misgivings and fears on the part of its opponents. After the experience of a week the change was unanimously accepted as an improvement to the health and comfort, as also to the manners and morals of the college commonwealth." [19]

If some things were made better in the college during Woolsey's presidency, the sad fact is that he was presiding over a dying system. At Yale and elsewhere the old required liberal arts curriculum was failing and student apathy rising. The new stress on examinations, prizes, rankings, and the like, which occurred everywhere during these years (though Yale was somewhat ahead in these matters, it seems) were symptomatic of the system's malaise.[20]

While the old-time curriculum had seldom been inspiring even during its best years, at least the classes had been small enough so that one tutor taught an entire class in all subjects throughout the first three years of their college course. In this milieu student and teacher got to know each other's good points and failings to a rare degree. Examinations and marks hardly seemed necessary. Furthermore, the amount of work required was never so much as to interfere with any other reading or activities a student might wish to pursue. As the world outside the college expanded and became more complex, as new subjects and new knowledge grew at an explosive rate, as classes became larger and were divided, as teachers began to specialize, the old homogeneity and purpose of the college began to break down. The attempts of the new European-trained teachers and their disciples to improve the old education and make the students really work were both a product of the system's decline and a factor that hastened that decline. Recitations, which could so easily turn the beauty of the classics into drudgery and boredom, were merely made more difficult, with no attempt to improve the teaching or to stimulate the student. Hence it is hardly surprising that all the external devices failed to turn the students away from their increasing attention to clubs, athletics, and other extracurricular activities.

Franklin B. Dexter, whose many services to his college over a long period of time vouch for his devotion to Yale, has left an absolutely damning picture of the college of his undergraduate years (1857–61). President Woolsey's classroom he recalled because of its "chilly atmosphere of repression." Professor, later president, Porter seemed "too tired or too bored to do himself full justice." Benjamin Silliman, Jr., following in his father's footsteps, lectured in such a flowery style that "his attainments" seemed "brilliant rather than solid." The language courses were no better. James Hadley "graded down" the instruction to the average ability of the class and then gave the "suspicion of being bored alike by the forward and the dull." William D. Whitney appeared uninterested in his German class and left Dexter with the impression that "he felt something akin to contempt of our shortcomings." Even in later life Dexter had "a covert dread of his sarcasm and of his disgust at poor scholarship." Hubert Anson Newton tried hard and was kind in sophomore mathematics, but he was still not a very successful teacher. Professor Larned, who taught rhetoric, was abrupt, frosty, and awkward, but withal personally helpful to Dexter. But most of Larned's students thought him "a dry and uninspiring instructor." [21]

Dexter's portraits are supported by many others. Years later Professor E. S. Dana wrote to Dr. William Henry Welch, "Certainly we lived through a strangely stagnant time in Yale's history." Still, men's reactions to their teachers varied. Andrew D. White (B.A. 1853), educational reformer and first president of Cornell, was no more pleased with his Yale education than Dexter, but he recalled James Hadley "as in some respects the most gifted instructor I have ever known." [22] Such memories were rare, however. Woolsey's attempts to improve and strengthen the Yale college education failed to get to the root of the problem: the simple fact that the teaching was atrocious.

Another aspect of Woolsey's drive to improve undergraduate education produced the Yale Graduate School. He hoped the example of graduate students would inspire the undergraduates, while at the same time the new institution would serve as a place to put new courses entering, or trying to enter, the undergraduate program of studies that were liable to make it "either archaic or superficial." Thus as Richard Storr, who traced the pre–Civil War development of graduate education, has said, "college authorities were forced to justify their old ways or to invent methods of adjusting the curriculum to the growth of learning. One result was experimentation with courses for graduates." [23]

Ever since at least the days of the Berkeley fellowships (1733), some young men had remained at Yale for further study after graduation. The desires of one group in this regard had led to the founding of the Divinity School. Also during Day's presidency, young men came to work under Benjamin Silliman, and in 1842 his son started a private school in his father's laboratory for those who wished to investigate chemistry and mineralogy. In the same years, others were remaining at Yale to learn advanced Greek with Woolsey, while still others were meeting with his brother-in-law, E. E. Salisbury, the professor of Arabic and Sanskrit.[24]

The whole situation was rather formless. So in 1843 the omnipresent Thacher urged that a regular program of graduate instruction should be organized. Matters were finally brought to a head by the arrival on the scene of John Pitkin Norton, a onetime special student of Silliman's, and an offer of $5,000, if Yale would raise $20,000 more, to begin the endowment of a chair in the fields of agricultural chemistry and animal and vegetable physiology. Norton, the son of

John T. Norton, a generous benefactor of the college, had studied agricultural chemistry not only in America but in Edinburgh as well. Silliman, who always recognized a good thing when he saw it, quickly recommended that Yale hire this talented and wealthy young man.

The Corporation resolved on 19 August 1846 that this professorship be established "for the purpose of giving instruction to graduates and others not members of the undergraduate classes," adding that "while efforts to complete the endowment are in progress he [Norton] may devote himself to study preparatory to his entering on the duties of that office."

At the same time, the fellows established "a professorship of practical chemistry for the purpose of giving instruction to others than the members of the undergraduate classes, in respect to the application of chemistry, and the kindred sciences to the manufacturing arts, to the exploration of the resources of the country and to other practical uses." Benjamin Silliman, Jr. (B.A. 1837), was elected to this post and was to be paid by his fees "till other provisions be made." [25]

Though the president, fellows, and faculty would continue to resist the introduction of "practical" courses into the regular undergraduate curriculum for many years to come, these votes show a certain sympathy for this side of the American character. They were not ready to admit, however, that direct practicality should be any concern of the liberal arts curriculum.

The addition of two new professors outside the regular departments of the college, along with the fact that the Clark Scholarships for graduate study in fields other than the professions were about to begin, indicated to the Corporation that some means must be found to organize these new areas. Thus at the same meeting at which the new professors were named, the Corporation appointed a committee made up of President Day, President-elect Woolsey, and Professors Silliman, Kingsley, Olmsted, and Salisbury to give "their opinion of arranging under distinct departments of the University the courses of instruction which are and ought to be given to others than members of the undergraduate classes," and if they favored setting up new departments, they were to recommend "arrangements and regulations" for them. [26]

One year later the committee presented its report. It gave the following reasons for beginning a new department: (1) the demand by graduates and others for instruction beyond that given in the college; (2) the existence of endowed scholarships for graduate instruction and the fact that they would be improved by providing regular instruction for their holders; (3) the desire to avoid crowding the undergraduate course and interfering with its training of the mind; (4) the good example graduate students would provide for the undergraduates; and (5) the presence at Yale of the materials for such a department. These reasons brought the committee to recommend the erection of a

fourth department of instruction for other than undergraduate students who are not in the Departments of Theology, Medicine, and Law, to be called the "Department of Philosophy and the Arts." The department is intended to embrace philosophy, literature, history, the moral sciences other than law and theology, the natural sciences excepting medicine, and their application to the arts.[27]

Acting on this recommendation, the president and fellows voted on 19 August 1847 to establish the Department of Philosophy and the Arts, out of which were later to grow the Graduate School and the Sheffield Scientific School. While Harvard, with a gift of $50,-000, started the Lawrence Scientific School this same year, that development killed the growth of the nonscientific fields. Yale, uninfluenced by a donors' wishes, was able to start in all fields,[28] and belying its reputation for conservatism, gained a twenty-five year head start on its longtime rival.

The new department began in the fall of 1847 with eleven students. The following courses were available:

1. School of applied chemistry.
2. President Woolsey, twice a week, on Thucydides or Pindar.
3. Benjamin Silliman [Sr.], lectures on chemistry, mineralogy, and geology.
4. James L. Kingsley, twice a week, instruction on a Latin author agreed upon with the student.
5. Josiah W. Gibbs, lectures on points of general philology.
6. Denison Olmsted, lectures on natural philosophy and astronomy; if desired private instruction in experimental philosophy and astronomical calculations.
7. Anthony D. Stanley, instruction in calculus or analytical mechanics.

8. Noah Porter, instruction in psychology, logic, and history of philosophy.

9. Edward E. Salisbury, instruction in Arabic grammar and points on relations of Arabic to other Shemitish dialects.

10. Benjamin Silliman, Jr., instruction in elementary and analytical chemistry, mineralogy, and metallurgy.

11. John P. Norton, instruction in application of science to agriculture and analytical chemistry.[29]

Clearly, the program favored science, but the nonscientific side continued and even grew during the succeeding years.

As with the other schools of the budding university, the new department was strictly on its own. The Corporation made that clear when it appointed Norton and specified, "The support of this professor is in no case chargeable to the existing funds or revenues of the college." [30]

So it was that the School of Applied Chemistry, forerunner of the Sheffield Scientific School, began with almost no money and only the expectation of a small return from fees. Benjamin Silliman, Jr. rented the president's house from the college (Woolsey had chosen to remain in his own house at the corner of Church and Wall), converted it into laboratories, and began training students. Silliman must have done almost all the conversion alone, for Norton went abroad for further study immediately after his appointment.

Students came, but not in great numbers. Then Silliman got a good offer from the medical department of the University of Louisville in 1849 and left Norton to carry on alone. Fortunately, the brilliant Norton turned down lucrative offers from other institutions to pursue his dream of founding a real field of agricultural chemistry at Yale, or this forerunner of the scientific school might have disappeared completely.[31]

Norton did everything. He managed the school. He did research. He paid to equip the laboratories himself. And, most important, he taught. One of his earliest students said of him, "I remember him as a model teacher, thorough in his methods, heartily detesting all shams, dignified but genial, with a lively humor, an easy, graceful, and persuasive speaker, an enthusiastic teacher who transmitted his earnestness to his pupils, by all of whom he was beloved."

As Norton struggled to keep the new school going, he helped to found the University of Albany, undertook a course of lectures there, and gave extension lectures on agriculture to farmers while continuing his own research and writing. But it was too much. His health broke down and he was forced to give up teaching. In July 1852, he was able to take part in the examinations of the first class for the new degree of Ph.B., which his action had brought the Corporation to establish for graduates of the Department of Philosophy and the Arts. On 5 September 1852, less than two months after his thirtieth birthday, John Pitkin Norton died. According to the *Dictionary of American Biography,* "in his brief span of life he had come to be regarded as 'the most practical agricultural writer and thinker of his time' . . . and had established a place for himself among the distinguished men of the age." [32]

Just before Norton died, another Norton entered the Yale scene. William Norton (USMA, 1831), a civil engineer who was no relation to John P. Norton, approached Yale about developing an engineering school. Supported by Benjamin Silliman, his proposal soon became a fact. In the fall of 1852 his School of Engineering opened on the fourth floor of the chapel (vacant because of the completion of the new library).[33]

Despite the new appointment in engineering, the death of John P. Norton created a crisis in the young life of the scientific school. He had founded it and, to a degree, endowed it with the personal apparatus and books that he bequeathed it, as well as the laboratory equipment he had purchased for it. The question was—could it exist without him? Fortunately, the college found at Brown a classmate of James Hadley, Professor John Addison Porter (B.A. 1842), who had studied chemistry in Germany and taught at the Lawrence Scientific School before going to Brown.[34]

Under William Norton and John Porter what John P. Norton began developed apace. Though still without adequate funds, and forced to promise not to interfere with a new fund-raising drive contemplated by the college, their germinal scientific school was thriving. Norton had brought his students with him from Brown, so the Department of Philosophy and the Arts had fifty-five students registered for the academic year 1852–53: twenty-five in applied chemistry, twenty-six in engineering, and just four in all other fields.[35]

In 1854 the School of Applied Chemistry and the School of Engineering were combined as the Yale Scientific School, which remained a division of the Department of Philosophy and the Arts.

The following year an even more important event occurred when Professor Porter married Josephine Sheffield, daughter of Joseph Earl Sheffield, a wealthy New Haven financier. Though Sheffield did not at once begin to pour money into his son-in-law's school, and though the curriculum and faculty continued to grow without his aid, his large-scale benefactions were the major factor in its great success. In 1858 Sheffield purchased the old Medical Department building at the head of College Street, added two wings to it, thoroughly remodeled the interior, and presented the whole to Yale for the scientific school the following year. At the same time he donated $50,000 to the school for "the maintenance of Professorships of Engineering, Metallurgy, and Chemistry." [36]

Sheffield's aid now made it seem that the school was no longer liable to "be crushed by ambitious rivals," as James Dwight Dana had feared it might be. Sheffield lived on Hillhouse Avenue just behind the school, which "was now virtually his child." To encourage this relationship and to show their gratitude to the man whose donations now amounted to over $100,000, the Corporation changed the name to the Sheffield Scientific School at commencement in 1861. At this same commencement—after the Civil War had begun—the degree of Doctor of Philosophy was first given in the United States. Three graduates received it in the fields of philosophy and psychology, classical languages and literature, and physics.[37]

When John P. Norton had requested in 1851 that a degree be given for study in the Department of Philosophy and the Arts, he had specifically referred to the Ph.D. The college professors had been "mostly favorable" to the idea of some degree, according to Hadley, while Woolsey was "rather adverse." The Corporation finally decided to award a Bachelor of Philosophy degree for work in the department.[38]

In 1856 a strong plea was made for endowment for the new school, and at that time James Dwight Dana called for Yale to become a true university. The plan drawn up for the school's development, he told the alumni at commencement,

bears its own evidence that in the will of her men and the breadth of her aims, Yale is determined to be up to the times. The desire is manifest that the College, as it now stands, shall not longer mark the limit of American training in literature or science, but that higher paths be laid out, and broader fields surveyed and occupied. . . . Why not have here,

The American University—where nature's laws shall be taught in all their fullness, and intellectual culture reach its highest limit.[39]

Dana's dream was not to be fulfilled for far too long, though Sheffield, former president Day, and other citizens of New Haven contributed generously to the cause. Yale men in general, however, remained more interested in the college than anything else. But an important step was taken in 1860 when the faculty of the scientific school asked the Corporation's permission to begin "a more complete course of scientific instruction extending through three years in the Chemical Section of the Scientific School" and requested that they be allowed to give the degree of Doctor of Philosophy for successful completion of the course. They recommended that it be granted as well for study in "such other branches [of learning] as may be taught in the Department of philosophy and the Arts."

The scientific school faculty made the request for the right to award the Ph.D. because, they said,

This degree has acquired a value by long usage which no new degree would possess. Its institution would remove a disadvantage under which our Department of Philosophy and the arts labors in comparison with similar departments of German Universities. The degree which they offer is an inducement which we do not present. Its establishment here would, in the opinion of the Faculty, enable us to retain in this country many young men, and especially students of Science who now resort to German Universities for advantages of study no greater than we are able to afford.[40]

The Corporation was convinced by this presentation and the degree was immediately instituted in the Department of Philosophy and the Arts with the requirements of at least two years of study, a final examination, and a thesis which gave "evidence of high attainment in the studies they have pursued." No prior degree was necessary to receive the Ph.D., but it was necessary for those who had not "previously received a degree furnishing evidence of acquaintance with the Latin and Greek languages" "to pass a satisfactory examination in these languages, or in such other studies (not included in their advanced course) as shall be accepted as an equivalent by the Faculty." Not until 1890 did anyone without a prior degree present himself, and then, strangely, the candidate was a German.[41]

The ability to award the Ph.D. degree was just one aspect of numerous changes taking place at the scientific school during these years. New faculty members were appointed; stricter entrance requirements were established; the course of study for the Ph.B. was more clearly delineated; in 1859 an advanced degree in civil engineering was instituted; and the group system emerged.[42]

The group system filled a middle position between the absolutely free selection of courses demanded by some educational reformers and the completely required course of studies which some defenders of the old liberal arts curriculum would have liked to retain. It was a scheme by which a student selected a certain field of instruction (chemistry, metallurgy, civil engineering, or whatever) and then took a set of required courses in his area. The system, as Daniel Coit Gilman's biographer has pointed out,

was not . . . the result of a deliberate plan, but was a gradual evolution from conditions existing at the Scientific School, where the men who gave the actual instruction were free to give out their ideas, step by step, without interference from higher authorities; and thus it was, to a certain extent, the result of the wholesome neglect with which the school was treated by the college proper, a neglect that proved to be conducive to freedom of growth and development.[43]

The "select course" was the most famous of the groups to emerge. The main reason for it, according to Russell Chittenden (Ph.B. 1875, Ph.D. 1880) longtime director of the school and its historian, was "to meet the demand of men who wanted a general knowledge of science, but did not desire to specialize in either chemistry or engineering." In addition, of course, it was a response to the desire for a more practical education than that offered by the traditional college curriculum. As such it served, as one historian of higher education has noted of scientific schools in general, to bring the American college "in the neighborhood of discovering some way of making a vital connection with American society." The scientific schools also formed an important stage on which to work out such new curricular ideas as the select course without disrupting the old college course of study.[44]

At Yale admission to the select course was open to any male student who was at least sixteen (the college by then required entering students to be fifteen), who could provide satisfactory testimonials of good behavior, and who could pass an examination in arithmetic, algebra, geometry, and plane trigonometry, natural philosophy, chemistry, English grammar, and geography. In mathematics and science, this test covered some material college students learned in their undergraduate course. In foreign languages, the scientific school demanded "the same preparation in Latin, which is required for admission to the . . . Academical Department [as the college was now called] . . . as facilitating the study of the sciences and of the English, French, and German languages pursued in the Scientific School." [45]

The course itself was of three years' duration. As outlined in the catalogue for 1861–62, it involved the following wide variety of subjects: In the first year the undergraduates studied mathematics, physics, English composition, rhetoric, elocution, chemistry, botany, mineralogy, and French. The second year was devoted to a full year of German and shorter courses on physical and political geography, logic, history, literature, astronomy, agriculture, chemistry, geology, mechanics and industrial mechanics, and drawing. The third and final year found the students getting bits and snatches of history, political science, economics, logic, mental and moral philosophy, theology, the history, structure, and relations of the English language, anatomy and physiology, civil engineering, and commercial law.[46]

Many of the younger faculty were distressed over the select course as introduced. The scientific school lacked the manpower to carry it out (having to supplement its own with instruction given in other departments) with the result, according to Thomas R. Lounsbury, that it "was necessarily an undigested system, which was satisfactory to no one, but was adopted for a while in consequence of the impossibility of procuring anything better." The main problem was senior year. Lounsbury (B.A. 1859), a famous teacher of English in the school and a member of its board of trustees from 1877 to 1910, observed in 1879 that "the subjects pursued in the last year, indeed, seemed to imply a doubt whether the institution was designed as a scientific school or a theological seminary." This sardonic observation may have been a bit strong, but the select course was always able to produce large reactions. Some hailed it early in its life as a great educational experiment, while others viewed it as nothing more than a slightly dishonest way to get a Yale degree.[47]

With its new degrees, new courses, and new building, "Sheff" was now on its way under the protective wing of Joseph Earl Sheffield.

It was given further momentum by the passage in 1862 of the Morrill Act, federal legislation allowing the states 30,000 acres of land for each representative and senator they sent to Congress. The money was to be used to support the establishment of agricultural and mechanical colleges. Connecticut sold the land scrip it received for $135,000 and gave the interest on the fund (under the law the state could not give the fund itself) to Sheff. Thus Yale for a time harbored Connecticut's agricultural and mechanical college. The state sent students to the scientific school and paid their tuition up to one-half the interest. The remainder was used to support the school. Thus, as Chittenden says, "the state was . . . enabled to profit from the gift of Congress without any expense whatever, while the Sheffield Scientific School gained added strength, which at that time was of inestimable value." In this way Yale, for the first time, even if only indirectly, received money from the federal government.[48]

While the Sheffield Scientific School was taking its great steps forward another entirely new department came into existence. Yale had had an art museum since 1832, it will be recalled, and the late 1850s saw an increased interest in art in New Haven, highlighted by a large loan exhibit at the college. Perhaps spurred by the evident interest this exhibit attracted (the railroad even offered half-fare rates to those who wished to attend) and urged on by Nathaniel Jocelyn, Augustus R. Street (B.A. 1812) suddenly came forward in March 1864 and offered to erect, entirely at his own cost, a building for a school of fine arts. The Corporation was not averse to accepting such a generous gift—though some people thought the whole idea absurd—and thus, despite the fact that the outcome of the Civil War was still in doubt, the cornerstone of the new structure was laid in November 1864. Though Street died before the building could be completed, he left the New Haven House (where the Taft Hotel now stands) to Yale, and the sale of this property provided the funds for the completion of the Venetian gothic structure as well as a partial endowment for the school. The building was finished in 1866, at which time the Yale School of Fine Arts was established. Thus Yale became the first major institution of higher education in the country to have an art school connected to it.[49]

Street Hall (which still stands at the corner of High and Chapel

Streets) cost the donor about $175,000. It was not, however, his only gift to Yale. This retiring man of wealth, who was born and raised in New Haven, also endowed the first chair in modern languages and by bequest established in memory of his father the Titus Street Professorship of Ecclesiastical History. His wife created at her death in 1878 the Leffingwell Professorship of Painting (named after her father) and the Street Professorship of Drawing. When Augustus Street died in June 1866 he was called "the most munificent benefactor of Yale College since its foundation." He was also one of the most generous in the long line of incredibly generous citizens of New Haven who have helped to build the university in their town.[50]

Shortly after the foundation of the Art School, the Trumbull paintings (and the bodies of Trumbull and his wife, who, at their wish, had been buried beneath the old gallery) were moved to the new building.[51] And soon after that, in one of its most startling financial deals, Yale acquired one of the greatest additions of all time to its art collection.

James Jackson Jarves had put together "a largely didactic collection" of 145 Italian paintings intended to show, as he wrote, "the chronological and historical sequence of Italian art from its revival in the thirteenth century to its decadence in the seventeenth." But Jarves's instincts as a collector had outrun the powers of his purse, and his debts had finally forced him to try to sell the paintings. His attempts to sell the collection as a unit (he could not bear to break it up) in New York and Boston had failed. Charles Eliot Norton had tried to interest Boston and Harvard in purchasing the paintings when they were exhibited there, but he was unable to do so. It was at this point that Yale became interested. At the urging of Lewis Richard Packard (B.A. 1856), Hillhouse Professor of Greek Language and Literature, Yale offered to lend $20,000 at 6 percent interest for three years to Jarves with the paintings as collateral. Jarves accepted, and the paintings came to Yale.

By the terms of the agreement, when Jarves paid off the loan Yale was to have the right to purchase the collection for $50,000. If, on the other hand, Jarves failed to pay either the principal or the interest of the loan, the collection was to become the property of Yale. This last condition was entered in the Corporation minutes, but somehow failed to be included in the written agreement made with Jarves.

Jarves in fact began to buy paintings again and thus could not pay Yale. He asked Treasurer Kingsley if he might sell the collection, and Kingsley agreed as long as Yale received $20,000.

The sale was advertised for 9 November 1871 and, according to the catalogue, the paintings were to be auctioned off individually. But when Yale heard this, it objected. No doubt the college feared that the proceeds would fail to reach $20,000, and it would be left with nothing but paintings no one wanted.

Yale's fears were well founded. There were many reports in circulation that the most valuable pictures had already been removed from the collection, that attributions were incorrect, that some pictures had been repainted, that there were defects in the titles to some. D. Cady Eaton (B.A. 1860), professor of the history and criticism of art, opposed Yale's bidding on them. As late as 1875 he still thought most of the paintings were fakes and declared that showing them was "an active fraud on the public." With this background, it is not strange that the most noticeable thing about the sale was the apathy it aroused. And this was true despite the fact that not until the auction began was it announced that the collection would only be sold as a unit. Yale made the sole bid, $22,000, and got the paintings.

Jarves was furious at his agent, Russell Sturgis, Jr. (M.A. hon. 1872), for allowing the sale, and he complained to the college about it, pleading for a chance to buy his paintings back. The Prudential Committee granted him less than a month. Not surprisingly, he failed to raise the money, and Yale kept the collection. Thus by methods which were strictly legal, and despite criticism from many persons who thought the college was wasting its money, Yale acquired one of its proudest possessions, Jarves's magnificent collection of early Italian masters. Sadly, Yale's gain was at the expense of a brilliant collector but impractical man.[52]

The gifts of Joseph Sheffield and Augustus Street mark a watershed in Yale's financial history. Suddenly large gifts from alumni and nonalumni alike began to be received. The change is even more striking when the story of the fund drive of the 1850s is reviewed.

That the financial position of the college was again weak was made clear by President Woolsey in the published version of his *Historical Discourse,* which added much to what he had said at the simple ceremony (mistakenly held in the summer of 1850) celebrating the 150th anniversary of the founding of Yale.* Woolsey pointed out that the total funds of the college were about $220,000 and income from all sources about $23,000. Professors' salaries were less than $1,150 and had scarcely changed in thirty-three years. The college also lacked enough teachers, and it needed professors "in the Romanic and in the Gothic languages" and separate chairs in astronomy and natural philosophy, while "a chair of history would not be undesireable." Furthermore, more scholarships and fellowships were wanted. On top of all that, "the present ugly row of colleges cannot remain for more than twenty-five years."

What was most needed, however, was increased faculty salaries. James Hadley noted in his diary what the current low professors' salaries could mean. He heard that Kingsley "during the forty years since his marriage" had spent "annually for living alone some 500 dollars more than his salary. Mr. Porter with all economy has exceeded his by $200 or $300, and has been obliged to use nearly half his available strength in eking out the deficiency. Apart from this, [he] would have been worth twice as much to the College." Because of this situation, as Woolsey noted, if salaries were not raised, young, unmarried men would have to be hired. This would alter the character of the faculty, which "would be highly disastrous; for it would bring instability into instruction and government, and would lower the reputation of the College by committing its entire interests to a younger and less permanent set of men." [53]

Unfortunately, Woolsey's moderate, forward-looking plea failed, as such general requests so often do, to stir the friends and alumni of the college. So about a year later, on 29 July 1851, the Corporation voted for another $100,000 fund drive. A broadside was printed containing many of Woolsey's points, but nothing seems to have happened, for a year later the faculty, led by Thacher, was still talking about raising money. [54]

After further discussion Thacher, in July 1852, took his usual intelligent lead. He suggested

---

* The reason for the confusion over the date of the founding is given on p. 68.

the expediency of combining the two measures which have been talked of. Raising tuition to $45.00 to provide for immediate increase of salaries, and making a call for money on the friends of the College as a means of permanent development and progress. He urged with much reason that we cannot in any way make out a case of distress, such as we had in 1830, and that most of those who will give anything to the College, will give if we only say the College needs money, a contribution is essential in our judgement to the prosperity of the institution.[55]

Since tuition was only $33—which was very low for the time—Thacher's case was persuasive.* But all feared raising it so high that it might turn away, as Woolsey said, "the children of the poor and of persons in moderate circumstances . . . —a class from which the best scholars and the most valuable members of society in after life are apt to come." Former president Day put his foot down. While acknowledging the need to raise the amount, he opposed any sum higher than $40 a year. Fellow Theophilus Smith "spoke clearly and strongly against any increase in tuition." But Jeremiah Day carried the field. Tuition was raised to $39. Thereupon salaries were raised as well: the president went to $1,500 from $1,340, the professors to $1,300 from $1,140, and tutors to $550 from $500.[56]

Finally, a printed appeal, *To the Friends of Yale College,* signed by Woolsey and Day for the Corporation and by Silliman, Goodrich, and Olmsted for the faculty and dated 25 January 1853, was brought out. The appeal reiterated Woolsey's arguments of 1850 and asked for $150,000 for the college. Fortunately, the point where pledges became mandatory was set at $100,000, for the goal was never reached. On 24 July 1855, however, the Corporation was able to announce that over $100,000 had been subscribed, and by 1859, according to the treasurer's report, $122,524 had been pledged. As with the Centum Millia Fund, death and disaster and depression reduced the amount actually collected to $106,390.92, of which $69,601.10 was for the college.[57]

While this drive was not a complete success it did enable the college to raise salaries at a rapid rate. They went up $200 in 1854 and reached $2,000 for the president and $1,800 for the professors in 1856. In that same year the Corporation noted that receipts for the pre-

---

* In 1973 tuition reached more than one hundred times that amount. If professors' salaries had increased to the same degree, they would have reached $110,000 in that year. Instead they averaged about a quarter of that amount.

vious year had been $55,583, while expenditures were only $52,324. The treasurer listed the assets of the Academical Department as real estate, $57,680.56; stocks, $48,735.14; bonds and notes (largely secured by real estate), $166,301.05; and bonds of railroads, $91,610.00; for a total of $364,326.75.[58]

Though Yale would again resort to the broad-gauge fund-raising drive in its ever-continuing search for increased endowment, its task would henceforward be made easier by the rapid increase of wealth in the nation, which first became apparent at Yale in Joseph Earl Sheffield's benefactions. That his was not an isolated philanthropy became apparent later in the year of his first gift, 1858, when Henry L. Ellsworth (B.A. 1810), known as the "father of the Department of Agriculture," bequeathed to the college all his numerous western lands. It took extended litigation to sell these lands, but by 1909 a little less than $100,000 had been realized. The income was to be used to assist undergraduates who intended to enter the ministry. Then in 1864 Henry Farnam (M.A. hon. 1871), a successful business-man who had worked closely with Sheffield on many projects, offered to pay for a new dormitory. Farnam thought one could be built of stone and still cost only $40,000 instead of the estimated $50,000. As it turned out, the finished structure, of brick, cost $126,-634.79, of which Farnam paid over $70,000. As a railroad builder he must have been appalled at the way the cost of Farnam Hall sky-rocketed; nonetheless, he and his family ultimately contributed some $400,000 to the college.[59]

During these years the college was receiving other large gifts, primarily that of Joseph Battell for a new chapel. And in 1864, the same year as the Street and Farnam donations, Bradford M. C. Durfee, apparently inspired by reading *Tom Brown's Schooldays* and seeing Rugby School in England, gave $80,000 for a new dormitory. He was an undergraduate when he made this gift. The following year, after leaving college because of ill health, he contributed a partial endowment (later increased) for a professorship of history, to be held by Arthur M. Wheeler, his former tutor. Durfee never finished college and died before he reached thirty. He surely ranks at the head of undergraduate donors to Yale, probably for all time.[60]

The Battell, Farnam, and Durfee gifts necessitated a decision on the future position and shape of the campus. In 1868 it was suggested that the college move out of the built-up part of town to the unpopulated area near the observatory where a fifty-acre site was available. The plan was given up, however, because of the expense of building Yale anew. So it was concluded to preserve space on the existing campus by building new structures cheek-by-jowl around the outer edge of the college yard, facing inward. Battell Chapel would be constructed on the corner of Elm and College Streets, with Farnam adjoining it on one side and Durfee on the other. With Graduates Hall already on one corner, Street Hall on another, and the library filling a large space between them, the completion of the new buildings would make the outlines of the new square clear. The long-range plan envisaged removing the brick row entirely and leaving the inside a large and beautiful court. Thus Yale, which had always been open to the town, began to look inward. In 1830 New Haven had been a pleasant small town, but by 1860 it had become the largest city in the state with 39,277 people. Yale began to withdraw from the growing hustle and bustle.[61]

Further large gifts followed close upon those of Farnam, Street, and Durfee. In 1866, George Peabody came forward with $150,000—the largest sum yet offered in a single gift—for the erection and upkeep of a museum of natural history. Peabody was interested in Yale by his nephew, Othniel C. Marsh, who had been appointed professor of paleontology, without salary, a few months before. And before the end of the decade Philip Marett, "an adopted citizen of New Haven, on whom the College had no other known claim," bequeathed it $150,000 for scholarships. At the same time, Joseph Earl Sheffield was continuing his donations. By the end of Woolsey's administration Sheffield had given approximately $250,000, of which $130,000 was for scholarships while most of the rest went for buildings and apparatus.* These liberal benefactions and others besides came during a period when the country was in its greatest crisis.[62]

The Civil War began while the college was on spring vacation. Unlike the Mexican War, which had had no apparent effect on Yale, the new conflict made itself felt immediately. Most of the few

---

* It is unfortunate that Sheffield's name seems to be disappearing at Yale. The school now exists only on paper. The one modern building with which his name is connected he shares with two others, and thus it is usually known as "S.S.S." Old Sheffield Laboratory is slated for removal. It would be fitting if the name of this great benefactor could be attached to at least one major professorship.

Southern students still in residence quickly left for home. The number of students from the South had already declined during the previous decade because of criticism from the people of their section and, no doubt, their own feeling of dislike for the North. Indicative of the attitude of many Southerners was John A. Englehard's letter to the North Carolina *Standard* in the fall of 1856. Englehard said that the catalogues of Yale and other Northern universities had but few Southern names, but "shame upon those few." "We are proud of such names as Harvard and Yale," he wrote, "and feel that such benefactors of the human race should be held in everlasting remembrance by a grateful country. But their laudable objects are being frustrated by . . . fanatics." Yale's crime was that it had assisted in sending rifles to the Northerners in Kansas. That Englehard's attitude was shared by others was indicated by the fact that at Yale in 1850 there had been seventy-two Southern students, while in 1860 there were only thirty-three.* The class that entered in 1853 had a total of thirty students from the Southern or border states at one time or another (twelve from the lower South, eight from the upper, and ten from the border), the class entering in 1856 dropped to eleven (seven lower, no upper, four border), the class entering in 1857 rose to twenty, but this was somewhat deceptive, for most were from the border states (five lower, no upper, fifteen border). Then an almost steady decline set in: 1858 had fifteen (five lower, no upper, ten border), 1859 had ten (one lower, five upper, four border), 1860 had fourteen (two lower, four upper, eight border), and the class that entered in 1861 had only three, all from the border states.[63]

At least one Southern student departed for home in November 1860, another followed in December, and many of the rest followed when the war broke out. In the class of 1861, however, two students from Mississippi, one from Texas, one from Kentucky, and one from Maryland, all of whom later fought for the Confederacy, remained at college to complete their course.[64]

The faculty held a special meeting shortly after the beginning of

* Harvard was less affected by this change. It had sixty-five Southern students in 1850 and sixty-three in 1860. As at Yale, the proportion from the border states had increased greatly between 1850 and 1860. Whereas in 1850 only 20 percent of all Southern students at Harvard were from the border, in 1860 this proportion had climbed to nearly 50 percent. At Yale the change was from 17 percent in 1850 to 45 percent in 1860.

the war. In the face of the fact that some students were departing for the wars, they decided that "those students who leave College to serve in the army can have a regular dismissal on the usual conditions, but cannot have a leave of absence." And they allowed Frank Bradley of the class of 1863 to be excused "for a time, from all college exercises except one a day, to enable him to drill volunteers for the army." Apparently this was a sufficient taste of military life for Bradley, for he did not serve during the war.[65]

Like Frank Bradley, many others at Yale were excited during 1861. Thirteen students (out of more than four hundred) left to enlist, and swords were presented to the Northerners who went—but both practices ended shortly. Drill companies were organized, but this did not last long, either. By 1863 the *Yale Literary Magazine* hardly mentioned the war. There was one story about an attempt to organize a unit to assist in suppressing the draft riots. Many students were willing to sign up for that duty when they thought the term would be thirty days, but the project collapsed upon their discovery that they would have to serve for ninety days. "In 1864," according to Ellsworth Eliot, the historian of Yale in the Civil War, "after the appalling losses of the Wilderness campaign, student patriotism reached its lowest ebb. No more swords were presented to men leaving the college to enlist, nor was any reference made by the *Yale Literary Magazine* either to those who had joined the colors or, in fact, to any event of the war." The attitude of the college officers was not dissimilar. On 22 July 1864 six undergraduates (including one who became the valedictorian of the class of 1865) received leaves of absence to join the hundred-days men. Woolsey sympathized with their motives but was distressed over their plan to travel on Sunday. He could not adjust to the fact that war would no longer wait for the Sabbath.[66]

But if some left college to go to war, others, like O. C. Marsh, J. W. Gibbs, and William Graham Sumner spent their days peacefully at Yale and upon completing their course continued to pursue their own interests. Sumner, who graduated in 1863, departed for Europe to study and did not return until the war was over. In later years a few men suffered certain pangs of conscience over their failure to serve and mentioned the fact in their class histories. Most, however, could refer to their activities during these critical years without mentioning the war at all. William Stocking of the class of '65, who served for six months, was bitter about the failure of his class to participate and wrote, "It would have been better for the reputation of Yale College, and better for the reputation of the young men, if all those who were prepared to enter '65 had enlisted in the Union Army, and if the ivy had trained its tendrils about the buttresses of the Library Building in memory of the class that never entered." [67]

Eleven percent of Stocking's class served during the war. While this is a very low figure, we must remember that they were under no obligation or public pressure to serve; that President Lincoln, as Samuel Eliot Morison observed, kept his own son at Harvard until 1864 and then gave him a safe staff position. Thus it becomes somewhat more impressive that 19 percent of all graduates of the classes of 1861 through 1868 did enter the military. For the classes from 1851 through 1863, slightly more than 35 percent of all graduates of Yale entered active service on one side or the other.[68]

In 1865 the university figured that there were 4,254 living graduates of the college, department of philosophy and the arts, medical and law schools. Of this total number, of whom quite a few were probably over-age, 932 or 22 percent fought in the war: 775 in blue, 157 in gray. The highest percentage of active participation was among graduates of the newest department: 60 percent of the few holders of the Ph.B. saw active service.[69]

Yale men from seventy-six year old John Pierpont of the class of 1804 to "Pop" Andrews of the class of 1876 in Sheff, who was the last veteran to graduate, fought on one side or the other. Yale produced twenty-five generals for the North and six for the South. As in the Revolutionary War, one of the first heroes of the Civil War was a Yale graduate. Brilliant young Major Theodore Winthrop (B.A. 1848), a descendant of John Winthrop on one side of his family and of Jonathan Edwards on the other, who told his uncle, President Woolsey, "I go down to the front for the purpose of lending my aid to the great work of attempting to get rid of slavery," was the first officer to die in the war. He was shot through the chest as he attempted to lead a charge on the Confederate battery emplaced at Big Bethel.

What Yale's record for service to the cause—North or South— would be if we could add all of those who served in a government post, sanitary commission, or in some way assisted the war effort, we will probably never know, but it must have been very impressive.

Even President Woolsey contributed to the full: three daughters served as nurses during the war.[70]

Despite the Civil War, Theodore Dwight Woolsey had to try to concentrate on the problems of Yale. One of the first serious issues to be dealt with after the war broke out was the condition of the Theological Department, which had fallen on bad times. Whereas it had had an average of eighty-seven students over the years 1838 to 1843, by 1858 there were only twenty-two. The excitement and fervor of its earlier days were gone. No longer was it producing such graduates as the Illinois Band, which went out from the school to found Illinois College. Julian M. Sturtevant, one of the band, became president of the college, and Asa Turner (B.A. 1827), another, became the father of Congregationalism in Iowa. Many others from the school went to the East, both Near and Far, as foreign missionaries.[71]

By the 1850s the great men of the faculty were "dead, dying, or decrepit." Nathaniel Taylor died in 1858, Chauncey Goodrich in 1860, Josiah Gibbs in 1861, and though Eleazar Fitch lived until 1871, he was generally inactive. At the same time, the dangers of the Yale policy of concentrating on the college and allowing the other departments to take care of themselves now began to be felt. The school was in financial difficulties. "Indeed," as Timothy Dwight said, "the limitation of its funds throughout the earlier period of its history was so extreme that one can scarcely understand . . . how the school was able to continue its existence and fulfill its work."

By 1861 young Dwight, who was promoted to professor of sacred literature that year, was the only full-time member of the department. During the course of the first summer of the Civil War, as the battle of Bull Run was lost and the seriousness of the war was revealed to the North, a decision had to be made at Yale about the Divinity School. Despite the difficulties of raising endowment—and even retaining students—in wartime, the Corporation agreed to attempt to save the school by hiring new men and endeavoring to raise additional funds. The task was not easy. After one year a new professor, Henry Hadley (B.A. 1847), was so pessimistic over the future of the school that he departed in 1862 to accept a professorship at Union Seminary. Things were so bad that some at Yale suggested that the school should be closed. But it remained open, and when peace came the small faculty attacked its problems with vigor. Immediate help came from Augustus Street's bequest in 1866 of funds to endow a professorship of ecclesiastical history. Dwight and Leonard Bacon walked New York City and, without receiving any really large gifts, raised enough to increase the endowment, by 1867, to $250,000 and then to pay for building East Divinity Hall, completed with steam heat, gas lights, fireplaces, and bathrooms, in 1870. Another improvement came with the decision to grant a Bachelor of Divinity degree for work in the school. The B.D. was first conferred in 1867. As with the other degrees given at Yale, no previous degree was required as a prerequisite for this one. When Timothy Dwight looked back at the decade 1861–71 he remarked that the school rose from a point where he was, for a short time, the only full-time teacher to where it had a strong group of students and a faculty equal in size and reputation to any divinity school in the country.[72]

The Theological Department was able to recover from neglect, but other departments of the university did not fare so well. "The attention of the College government," as Timothy Dwight noted,

at that period, was almost exclusively given to what is known as the Academical Department. All other departments were outside of the main institution—additions to it. They might live, if they could. Well, indeed, if they did survive and grow strong. But they were not the "Old College"; and their fate must be left to their own instructors, without the independent, or even actively co-operative forces of the central officials.

Lacking attention, the Law Department nearly failed completely.[73]

The Law School is the only part of Yale that began its existence entirely separate from the university. It was started in 1800, or shortly thereafter, in the home and office of Seth P. Staples (B.A. 1797). Staples owned one of the best law libraries in New England and this attracted young men to read law with him. He was also a great teacher, having, according to one of his students, "a magnetism over his students unsurpassed by any man I ever knew." After a time, Staples attracted so many students that he brought in a former pupil, Samuel J. Hitchcock (B.A. 1809), to help him.[74]

In 1824 Staples moved to New York City to practice law and Hitchcock took over the school. In November he got the prestigious David Daggett (B.A. 1783), who had served in both houses of the state legislature and been a U.S. Senator, to help him. And in the same month, Yale began to list in its catalogue the students enrolled in the school. This arrangement began, apparently, because most of the students reading law were graduates of the college and many resided there. But the connection between the Law School and the university was purely nominal.[75]

Two years later the ties between Yale and the school were tightened somewhat when President Day revivified the old professorship of law and appointed Daggett to the office. In the same year Daggett was named to the State Superior Court, and from 1828 to 1830 he also served as mayor of New Haven, so Hitchcock had to do most of the work of teaching in the law school. Nevertheless, Daggett's association with the school as well as its connection with Yale helped it to grow from ten students in 1826 to forty-four in 1831. In 1833 Daggett was appointed to the new professorship of law named for Chancellor James Kent, for which a partial endowment had been raised during the drive for $100,000.[76]

Hitchcock, with some assistance from Daggett (who was now nearly eighty), ran the school along the simple lines noted until 1843, when he wrote the Yale faculty and requested that the graduates of his school be granted a Bachelor of Laws degree. The faculty and Corporation agreed, and at commencement in August the Law School was formally placed under the control of the Corporation and the LL.B. was awarded to two students.[77]

The new relationship probably saved the Law School. Hitchcock died in 1845 and in 1847 Daggett resigned, as did Hitchcock's successor, and the remaining professor died. The Corporation, apparently guided by the principle that the school needed a "name" on its faculty, appointed Clark Bissell (B.A. 1806), the governor of Connecticut, to the Kent professorship. Henry Dutton (B.A. 1818), who later became governor and a judge of the Supreme Court of Errors, was also made a professor. But Woolsey and the university did nothing else for the school. It was supposed to make its own way, and it almost did not. After Bissell had retired there was even a period when Dutton struggled alone to carry on the school. In 1859 Dutton died and the school was left with no faculty at all. It weakly finished the Woolsey years in the temporary charge of three instructors—Simeon E. Baldwin, William C. Robinson, and Johnson T. Platt.[78]

The Medical School also faced difficulties during the administration of President Woolsey. Though the school erected a new building at 150 York Street (the former site of the professor of divinity's house) when Sheffield purchased its old hall for the scientific school, it continued a slow decline. The greatest enrollment had been in 1827 and the largest graduating class had been in 1829, when thirty six men received the M.D.; as with the Law School, 1870 marked the nadir—only two students took degrees.[79]

The decline coincided with an attempt to improve the school. In 1827 the delegates of medical schools and societies meeting in Northampton had decided that standards in the medical schools of the country should be raised. Yale tried to carry out this mandate. In 1829 it got the legislature to amend the school's charter to allow it to extend the period of medical education from three to four years for nongraduates of a college and from two to three years for graduates. A knowledge of Latin and natural philosophy was also demanded for admission to the medical institution. When no other medical school instituted similar requirements and enrollment continued to decline, the charter was again amended and the school returned to its former system.[80]

Still the school could not recapture its original popularity. This situation might have been acceptable if the caliber of the students had been better, but in 1850–51, a typical year, only 26 percent of the thirty-eight medical students had B.A. degrees. That same year, the Divinity School had an equal number of students, and 80 percent of them had the B.A., while of the twenty-six law students, 65 percent had degrees. At the same time, the area the students came from contracted in the years after 1830. In 1820, of sixty-two students, more than one-third came from outside Connecticut. By 1861, of twenty-eight students, only five were from other states.

One reason for the declining popularity and reach of the school was the development of additional competing schools in other states. Another was that Nathan Smith, the most prominent member of the faculty, had died in 1829. Though the professors of the school from 1830 to 1870 were generally competent local doctors, few had national prestige. In addition, the school was distinctly ingrown. As Whitfield Bell remarked, "At one period three of the six professors were brothers-in-law, who seemed to regard the school as a kind of family association—to the understandable irritation of their colleagues."[81]

In a sense, however, the quality of the faculty hardly mattered, for the students did not spend much time at Yale. Only two terms of sixteen weeks each were required for those who wished M.D. degrees, and only one term for students seeking licenses. The remainder of their period of study was spent working with practicing physicians—two years for college graduates and three years for nongraduates. Licenses and degrees, however, were granted only after an oral examination by a committee consisting of representatives of both the Medical School and the Connecticut Medical Society.[82]

The Yale professors did try to improve this education. A summer school was attempted for a short time in the 1830s. It was intended, according to the catalogue, "for those students who prefer the advantage of a regularly organized medical institution, to private tuition in the offices of physicians," but it seems to have been unsuccessful. In 1855 some of the professors of the department opened, as an addition to the regular school, their own private medical school. Here they held recitations that allowed them to communicate more than they could in their regular lectures, and here laboratory work for the students was first introduced. In 1867 this private school was absorbed into the parent institution and the hope was expressed that "eventually the study of medicine, like that of any other science, will be continued daily through the ordinary academic year." But that was not to come during Woolsey's administration; instead, the school continued its decline.[83]

The library did not thrive under President Woolsey, either. In 1849 the librarian reported that all holdings had been counted, and that they amounted to 20,515 volumes and about 3,000 pamphlets. The literary society libraries had more books than the college— 27,166 volumes. All of the books were housed in the new library building, where they were cared for by the first full-time librarian, Edward C. Herrick. Herrick further reported that during the academic year 1848–49 he had spent $1,412 for books, pamphlets, and binding, and had received as gifts $420. By comparison, Harvard in 1841 had owned 41,000 volumes, and by 1857 this had grown to 70,000, even though it had "but five hundred dollars a year for accessions." Yale seems to have passed 80,000 volumes by 1871. Princeton reached 14,000 volumes in 1868.[84]

Woolsey was content with the library. In 1850 he wrote, "The library although . . . small is a good one . . . and has a better fund devoted to its enlargement than is possessed by any other college interest. We do not therefore speak of any great deficiency here." But not everyone was so satisfied as the years passed. In 1858 Herrick, who had tried to be both librarian and treasurer of the university since 1852, resigned to devote himself fully to the financial affairs of the university. His place was taken by an activist, young Daniel Coit Gilman (B.A. 1852), who had been his assistant since 1856. Gilman struggled with the job for seven years and then resigned in disgust. He explained to Woolsey,

> Improvements and changes which have long been talked of as essential to the progress of the Library, the increase of the funds for the purchase of books, the employment of permanent assistance, the introduction of a heating apparatus, the opening of a quiet reading room, the consolidation of the society libraries, and other minor alterations, seem to be no nearer than when I entered on the office of Librarian. I am aware that the poverty of the college is a standing reason for the delay of improvements but this does not lessen my disappointment.

Gilman may have meant his resignation as a spur to force Woolsey to move. Franklin B. Dexter, then a young tutor, thought he was "chagrined" when it "was taken in earnest by President Woolsey." Though the library lost an excellent man, Gilman remained at Yale, for he had become professor of physical and political geography in the scientific school in 1863. He was succeeded as librarian by Addison Van Name (B.A. 1858).[85]

If Woolsey could not—or would not—do what Gilman thought absolutely essential, he was still deeply interested in the library. As a professor he had been one of the largest donors to the fund for the new building. In 1861 he gave it most of his Greek library, numbering nearly a thousand volumes. It was considered the most valuable gift the library had received since Berkeley's donation in 1733. Woolsey continued to donate books and money until his death.[86]

For some reason President Woolsey was not a subscriber for one of the library's great acquisitions of these years, but most of the rest of the faculty contributed to the fund for the purchase of George Catlin's drawings of North American Indians. Catlin had wanted these two volumes to remain in America, though he had had an excellent bid for them in Europe. He sent them to his daughter and instructed her to offer them to Harvard and, if they did not want them, to Yale. By some fortunate inadvertence the box was addressed to "Harvard College, New Haven, Conn." When they came to hand, Yale took advantage of the opportunity, kept them, and paid Catlin $564.44 for them, of which Van Name contributed nearly half.[87]

Perhaps the greatest acquisition of these years, however, was Professor Salisbury's contribution of his sizable collection of Oriental books and manuscripts, and $6,000 for enlarging it. At the bicentennial of Yale's move to New Haven this was mentioned first in the list of the library's "important special collections." [88]

In 1871 the decision was finally made to incorporate the private libraries of the literary societies into the main library. Thus the college added at one stroke some 27,000 volumes, largely of light literature, to its basic collection of about 44,000 volumes. The main advantage of this change was to make these books more accessible to all the students.[89]

Like the library, some other departments of the university improved during Woolsey's administration almost in spite of the president. In 1849 an unidentified graduate offered to try to raise $50,-000 for an astronomical observatory. The Corporation asked Woolsey and Professor Olmsted to look into the matter. Since the college needed money for salaries, they reported that it was not expedient to pursue the goal at the moment. It seems likely that Olmsted disagreed with this conclusion, for in 1851, in the midst of discussions about the need for a general fund drive, Hadley noted in his diary that Olmsted was pushing for an astronomical observatory:

But the President said, "We must rise from our extreme poverty before we can indulge in luxuries." [He] Thought an observatory was little needed for the immediate object of the College, instruction—a point on which all but Mr. Olmsted appeared to agree with him. As we were returning [from the faculty meeting], Mr. Olmsted remarked how much more had been given for chemistry than for [natural] philosophy. $500 recently allowed Mr. Silliman for buying apparatus, while his own demand for $500 to increase the apparatus of his department was refused. "Such," he said, "was the difference between one man and another." [90]

Woolsey and Olmsted were of course both right. The college could not afford it, but if there was to be astronomy there would have to be a decent observatory. The five-inch telescope presented by Sheldon Clark in 1828 had been the finest in the country for a time, but it had been far surpassed by such instruments as the fifteen-inch telescope that Harvard acquired in 1846. The top of the Atheneum, even with the spire replaced by an octagonal tower (1829) was never a satisfactory observatory. Yale astronomers concentrated on meteors because "important discoveries could be made without the aid of a well-mounted apparatus." [91]

Even if Woolsey did not wish to pursue the subject of an observatory, the need was known. In 1853 William Hillhouse gave a transit telescope and clock valued at $1,200 or more, and Mrs. C. L. Hillhouse and her daughters offered a site for an astronomical observatory. Apparently the gift was not accepted, for in 1858 they offered six acres on the top of the ridge between Prospect and Whitney to be used only for an astronomical observatory. This time the land was accepted, but nothing further happened until 1871, when Oliver F. Winchester, successful manufacturer of shirts and firearms, purchased thirty-two acres adjoining the Hillhouse donation for a cost of almost $100,000 and presented the land to Yale on the condition that the whole thirty-eight acres be constituted a foundation "for astronomical and physical researches." Thus though Olmsted died in 1859, his dream of an observatory at Yale finally appeared to be nearing fruition.[92]

The Winchester gift came at the very close of Woolsey's presidency. In the fall of 1870 he informed the Corporation that he intended to retire the following year, at the completion of twenty-five years in office.

Woolsey's presidency was marked by progress tinged with failure. Though the old college course (to which he had given most of his attention) had changed somewhat and had been made more difficult, it was near death. Eight buildings had been built; the funds of Yale had been increased by about a million dollars; the faculty had grown from 37 to 65 while the total student body had gone from 584 to 788. At the same time, the Sheffield Scientific School, the Art School, and the Graduate School had all been started.[93] On the other hand, the policy of concentrating on the college and ignoring the other departments had led to extreme weakness in the schools of medicine and law and had almost caused the expiration of the Theological Department. Important advances that might have taken

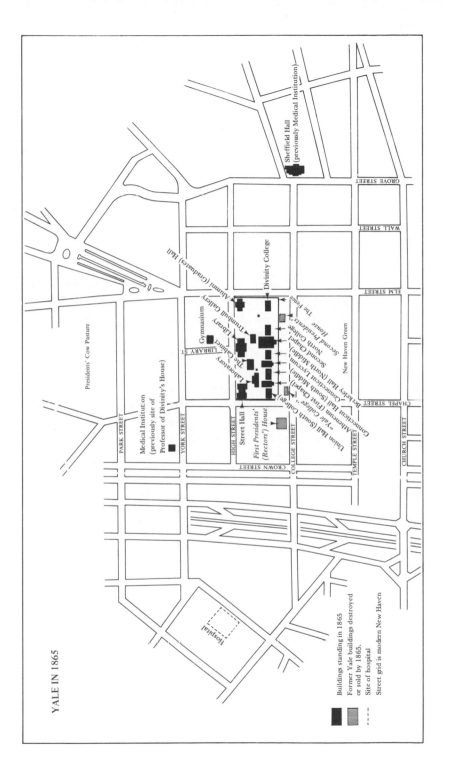

YALE IN 1865

Presidents' Cow Pasture

Medical Institution
(previously site of
Professor of Divinity's House)

Sheffield Hall
(previously Medical Institution)

Alumni (Graduates) Hall

Divinity College

Gymnasium

Trumbull Gallery

Library

LIBRARY ST

The Cabinet

Laboratory

The Fence

Second Presidents'
House

Second Chapel,
North College

New Haven Green

Connecticut Hall (North College)

Connecticut Hall (South Middle)

Lyceum

"Yale College,"
Second Chapel

Street Hall

First Presidents'
(Rectors') House

Union Hall (South Middle)

Athenæum (First Chapel)

"Yale College,"

Berkeley Hall

PARK STREET

YORK STREET

HIGH STREET

COLLEGE STREET

TEMPLE STREET

CHURCH STREET

CROWN STREET

CHAPEL STREET

ELM STREET

WALL STREET

GROVE STREET

Hospital

■ Buildings standing in 1865

▥ Former Yale buildings destroyed
or sold by 1865.

- - - Site of hospital

Street grid is modern New Haven

place did not because the central administration failed to act. Woolsey's intelligence often enabled him to recognize a problem; somehow his character prevented him from moving to solve it. In 1867 he clearly saw the condition of the Law School, yet he stated: "The college authorities have not been at fault in what they have done for the school, or rather what they have left undone. 'The destruction of the poor is their poverty.' We could have raised the school by funds and men, but to get the funds we must have the men, and to get the men we needed the funds. There was no leverage." [94] It was not good enough. There is no sign he had really tried to do much about either men or funds, and the school had not stayed the same but had actually declined.

Theodore Dwight Woolsey helped to create a university which had the promise of greatness. His failure to push forward to fulfill that promise, combined with the deeply conservative streak that caused him to favor an even more conservative man as his successor, lost Yale the great lead he had helped to give it and damaged the university for many years to come. Had he really promoted the new graduate department, to name perhaps the major missed opportunity, Yale could have become the center of advanced study in America decades before other institutions even began nonprofessional graduate education. His failure to do so was the first of a series of missed opportunities that was to mark Yale's history for many years to come.

College Life under Day and Woolsey

For more than half of the nineteenth century, daily life for a Yale student was little different from what it had been in the eighteenth century. A student of the earlier period could easily have written much of Donald Grant Mitchell's description of his days at Yale in the late 1830s and early 1840s. Mitchell, better known as "Ik Marvel" clearly recalled

the hardship of being routed from bed at half-past five, and of toiling in the winter season through snow drifts (before the days of Goodyear rubber boots) to college prayers at six; where the obscurity of the old chapel was lighted only by whale-oil lamps, flickering in the frosty atmosphere, and where the uneasy shuffling of benumbed feet was sure to come into the pauses of good Dominie Day's tremulous invocations. After this—we groped our way—still under night skies—to the Division Rooms—reeking with oily odors, and showing steaming pans of water upon the tops of the new "Olmsted's patent double cylinder stoves."

By lamp-light—which daybreak presently made dim—we had our drowsy recitation; then came the rush, not over eager, or with much Apician zest, to our "Commons" breakfast of half-past seven, under the benignant mastership of "Caleb Mix, Steward." If a boarder was ill and proper word came to this Benignity of the Commons, there was sent out a little brown pot, with white parallel stripes (capacity 3 gills) of coffee and milk, with two slices of bread atop it. And even such a breakfast I did sometimes devour with gusto—when the snows were too deep, or the way not clear, for a clandestine slip down Chapel Street to "Marm Dean's," (next above what is now Traeger's) for her better coffee and an unctuous bit of her buttered waffles.[1]

This hard schedule of chapel, recitation, and finally breakfast remained unchanged until 1859, when breakfast was finally put first in the day and chapel moved to the relatively late hour of 7:45. Though the afternoon service was dropped when the schedule was altered, morning chapel continued to be required until 1926 (See pp. 177–78).

But the morning meeting was hardly a religious service. President

Day's daughter, Olivia, and her friends Henrietta Whitney Blake and Louisa Torrey in their anonymous publication, *The Gallinipper,* gave the following picture of it, disguised as President Day's advice to the students:

Never think of starting until the second bell turns over. If in the morning do not stop to dress: it is generally expedient to put on a cloak and boots but no more is requisite; above all do not wash or comb your hair, or you might be thought foppish . . . rush up the aisles in a crowd and find your seats with the greatest possible noise . . . in your seat assume a horizontal position . . . go to sleep . . . whisper with your neighbors. If on a Sunday evening study the galleries to see what ladies are there. In short do anything rather than listen to the reading. That is designed to divert the faculty and give you a chance to enjoy yourselves. [At] the time of the prayers . . . your duty commences in earnest . . . crack jokes with your right and left hand neighbors . . . notify everyone of your presence who is within reach of your hands and feet . . . keep up a brisk circulation of peanuts. It is a very good plan to bring in a bat which can be let loose if things seem to be getting dull or if that cannot be obtained a dog will answer the purpose just as well. Whistle him from one seat to another and by pinching his ears, treading on his toes, and various other means which will suggest themselves with the occasion, extract as much noise from him as he . . . is capable of. Dogs were principally made for this purpose. . . . If these regulations are observed they cannot fail to make you patterns of dignified gentlemanly conduct and if adhered to through life, will ensure you the respect of all society.[2]

Even the faculty finally had to admit that the service did little more than bring the college together once a day. Nonetheless it continued despite its unreligious character. Perhaps what the students liked best of all was the old custom of bowing out the president. At the close of the ceremony, when the president went down the aisle the students would bow low to him and then, starting with the seniors, quickly fall in behind and follow him out. In later years it became almost a game to see how close one could come to the president without actually touching him.[3]

Sundays in the antebellum years were almost busier than weekdays. One student recorded in his diary how he spent one November Sunday in 1845.

Arose about 6: attended prayers at 6½ and then a prayer meeting: till 7½. thense to breakfast to Mrs. Ames' [?]. returned to my room to Mr.

Walkley's. read a portion of scripture and performed devotional exercises as usual; bathed in warm water, which I do every week, read a portion of the history of Lutheran reformation by Scott, which I find very interesting; at 10 attended church at the Chapel as usual listened to a discourse on the 7 chapter of Rev. [?] from the 9th verse through the chapter, delivered by Mr. Taylor D.D. full of life eloquence and instruction. Our usual preacher Mr. Fitch D.D. is now unwell. At 11½ returned to my room read an hour and went to dinner, return [ed] and read till 2 when I attended church and listened to a discourse from the same man on 16 chap. of Luke from the 19 verse through, which was equally as interesting and instructive as the former. I feel sorry that I am not in a mode [?] to enjoy and improve better the religious instruction with which we are favored here in college. Returned from church and read till dark, then conversed a few minutes with Mr. Winthrop in his room—till 5, when we went to prayers and thence to supper, thense to a meeting in the theological chamber 1 hour, thense to Mr. Nichols' room and conversed a short time with him and Mr. Noyse thense to Mr. Holliday's room and conversed a few minutes with him and Mr. Clark till 8 thense up stairs to my own room. read a portion of scripture and performed devotional duties as usual.[4]

Of course not everyone was so religious, and even those who were found it difficult to make it to chapel every morning. Sometimes the temptation to stay in bed was overpowering. One student reported how, one rainy weekday morning, he heard the school bell tolling and raised the covers to leap from bed when he was suddenly struck by "a keen puff of cold air." This "overcame every good intention" and he snuggled down again and only awakened after chapel and morning recitation were over.[5]

The faculty struggled constantly to retain the religious atmosphere of the college. One student felt it necessary to see the faculty to convince them that he was not an infidel. Such proof was sometimes necessary: in at least one case an expelled student was not allowed to return to college because he had, apparently, influenced about twenty others to be "free thinkers." [6]

The strict regulation of students went far beyond religion and classes, of course. By means of the so-called parental system of discipline, begun by Stiles and Dwight, an attempt was made to control every aspect of the students' behavior. The system worked rather well as long as Yale was small, but as Dwight's presidency drew to a close, he began to feel that "talking seemed to have lost most of its efficacy." Nonetheless the college tried to continue the system of treating the students in a "mild, affectionate, and winning" way— being "firm, never harsh or menacing," but never allowing the student to question authority.[7] Whereas, unlike the parent, the college had to cope with a large number of students, it had one advantage over parents: it could send away, for a short time or for good, boys who misbehaved.

Another device the college used to keep the students under control was to hold up matriculation for a time. Since a boy had not been officially enrolled in the college, he could be removed at any time even if he did not formally break any rules. At one point this term of limbo extended almost throughout a student's college career, but in 1847 the Corporation ruled that it must last not less than six months nor more than two years.[8]

The parental approach was supplemented under President Day by a system of marks which largely displaced the old fines. In its most highly developed form, one, two, or three marks were given for "various improprieties of conduct." Sixteen marks placed a student upon the "course of discipline" and meant a letter home; thirty-two points brought a second letter; and forty-eight usually led to suspension for a term. Twelve marks were dropped at the end of each of the first two terms and thirty-two at the end of the school year.[9]

All of these devices to control student behavior were used most rigorously during the first months of freshman year, when the tutors spent their time "weeding out the incorrigibles." Timothy Dwight (B.A. 1849) recalled clearly the warning President Day gave his class early in their college careers: "Doubtless not more than one-half of your number will graduate." And Day was right. Only 55 out of 110 made it, and 37 were dropped during the first year.[10]

Despite an appearance of monastic repression, life at Yale was probably not too different from life at home. Early rising, morning and evening prayers, long Sunday services, and strict rules of behavior were common throughout American society. On the other hand, at college there was much to do that was just plain fun.

One of the delights of student life was informal, unorganized recreation, for the paraphernalia of team sports and intercollegiate competition were largely absent during the years of Day and Woolsey. As in the eighteenth century, the main sports were walking, swimming, skating, hunting, and sailing. In the late fifties, skating enjoyed a particular boom. Daniel Coit Gilman reported to his brother in February 1859, "All New Haven is skate-crazy. Hundreds go to [Lake] Saltonstall, clergymen (Dutton, Fisher, Littlejohn, etc.); college professors (Salisbury, Whitney, etc.); tutors, lawyers, ladies, school boys, all join the fun." By 1864 it was even possible to skate at night, for Hamilton Park was lighted.[11]

President Dwight, especially, used to encourage the boys to exercise. Day provided a good example by chopping wood in his yard. But the college did not create a place for exercising until 1826, when $300 was appropriated to clear a spot behind the chapel and install apparatus for an outdoor gymnasium "with a view to the promotion of the health and improvement of the Students." Horace Bushnell (B.A. 1827) was soon showing his prowess on the turning bar and at throwing the discus.[12]

Though the outdoor gymnasium continued to be used after the first heat of the fad passed and private gyms soon appeared on the scene, these still promoted disorganized, individual activities.[13] Even so-called team sports like football were closer to free-for-alls than anything else.

The football game had changed little since the eighteenth century. It was always played on the Green, because no games were allowed in the college yard. At first the point of the game was to try to kick the ball over the goal line. Then it was possible to run with the ball laterally out of bounds, and by 1863 it had become a "rushing game" where the player carried the ball and tried to avoid being caught.[14]

The roughest event of the year was the annual freshman–sophomore game. It became so bad that the faculty banned it in 1857. At the same time the town began to oppose the wild melees on the Green. The college tried to uphold the old prerogative of the students to play on the Green, but when the town finally banned these activities in 1857 or 1858, the college authorities had to inform the students that they had no legal right to hold their games on the public square. Thus ended a tradition that may have existed since the college moved to New Haven in 1716.[15]

Fortunately, New Haven still had many open lots. Though the town had been growing rapidly since 1830, the country still came close to the college, so there were numerous places to play "two old cat ball," wicket (cricket), and other such ball games, and where, by

1859, regular baseball games were held. Cricket, or wicket as the American game was called, had been played in this country in colonial days and it may have been a sport at Yale then. The first clear reference to it, however, is in one stanza of a poem about Yale life in 1818 to 1822:

> And on the green and easy slope
>   where those proud columns stand,
> In Dorian mood, with academe and
>   temple on each hand,
> The football and the cricket-match
>   upon my vision rise,
> With all the clouds of classic dust
>   kicked in each other's eyes.

Wicket continued at Yale at least until 1857, but shortly it was completely displaced by the new rage for baseball.[16]

More significant, however, than any of these recreations in the life of the college was the appearance of another new sport—and intercollegiate competition—in the 1840s and 1850s. New Haven was a popular beach and resort area during much of the nineteenth century and Yale men had long used Long Island Sound for swimming and sailing. In 1843 William J. Weeks (B.A. 1844) organized a group, purchased a vessel in New York, and after spring vacation the seven-man boat, *Pioneer,* was launched. The idea rapidly caught on and two other rowboats and a canoe were quickly acquired by other groups.

The first boats were "ordinary and substantial" rowboats which could be taken on long excursions. Soon, however, "*shell boats* and intercollegiate races," both of which Weeks disliked, appeared. As early as 1824 a boat race in New York harbor had attracted 50,000 spectators and in the 1830s and 1840s there were many club races. Hence it was probably inevitable that the Yale club boats soon began to race each other and that then an intercollegiate race would take place.[17]

As an ominous sign for the future of American college sports, the first intercollegiate competition was a promotional stunt for the new Boston, Concord and Montreal Railroad. At the suggestion of the superintendent of the line, a race was held between Yale and Harvard on 3 August 1852 on Lake Winnipesaukee in New Hampshire, with the railroad paying the bills. Harvard's Oneida Club raced against Yale's Undine and Shawmut but refused to allow the small, fast boat that the Atalanta Club had hired to compete. Harvard won.[18]

Other rowing contests took place in the 1850s and 1860s—some with several colleges competing—but the great rage for intercollegiate sports did not arise until the last quarter of the nineteenth century. Until the Civil War most Yale sports remained individual or disorganized. Though some of these activities were brawls, like the popular class "rush" (football without a ball), they could not absorb all the students' excess energies. Sometimes the young men worked off their enthusiasm in the streets.[19]

Violence may not be as American as apple pie, but the United States has always been a rather tumultuous place and the college campus has experienced its share of this illogical strain in our national life. The first strong manifestation of it at Yale came under President Clap, and it has surfaced sporadically ever since. The 1840s and 1850s were decades of especially virulent outbreaks at Yale. The timing of classes, chapel, and study periods throughout the day so that extended periods of recreation were impossible; the lack of organized athletics; the tensions produced by the still strict Puritan morality; the emotions developed by rising sectional rivalry —all combined to make this a particularly difficult period at Yale. Viewed in the light of the college's experience in these decades, the outbreak of civil war becomes more easily understandable.

For a time under President Day the students reacted to repression by rebellion. Almost anything could produce a rebellion, and commons frequently did, even though the food was much more varied than the largely bread and meat diet of Clap's day. One of Dwight's students reported that they were getting

chocolate, coffee, and hashed meat every morning; at noon, various; roast beef twice a week, pudding three times, and turkeys and geese upon an average once a fortnight; baked beans occasionally; Christmas and other merry days, turkeys, pies, and puddings, many as we wish for; at night for supper we have chocolate and tea in general, pies once a week; I ought to have added that in future we are to have beefsteaks and toast twice a week; before this the cooks were too lazy to cook them.[20]

But this may have been one of the better times, for often the students complained. In 1818, two classes "left the hall . . . on account of the hardness of the fare." Recitations had to be called off for three days. And even the opening of a second, cheaper commons in 1827 could not prevent the great bread and butter rebellion of the following year, which was termed with hyperbole by a college historian of the 1870s "an uprising against the authorities of the college that for persistency and violence, and the numbers engaged in it, has, we believe, no parallel in the history of American colleges." The great event occurred in 1828 during the often troublesome summer session, when the seniors were no longer in town. The remaining students said they would not go to commons until the food improved. The faculty declined to discuss the matter unless the students fulfilled their "duty" of attending commons. When the students refused, the faculty expelled four they took to be ringleaders and could only end the rebellion by temporarily closing the college.[21]

But this did not solve the eternal problem. Commons was made voluntary in 1839 and then closed completely in 1842. For ninety years thereafter students made their own eating arrangements.[22]

The curriculum also created difficulties. Twice, in 1825 and in 1830, the students rebelled over conic sections. In the 1830 event, it will be recalled, almost half the class of 1832 was expelled. This action finally ended what President Woolsey called "the spirit of combination, for the purpose of redressing some grievance, or attempting to do away with some unpopular study, [which] threatened the safety of the institution." [23]

Probably even more dangerous to the institution, however, was the fact that a short time thereafter many students began to carry weapons. The hazards in this direction were first revealed when a freshman, Henry McCall, was suspended in 1837 for five months for "drawing his sword from cane in an affray down town." The college authorities might have reacted more harshly had they had any foreboding of what this type of behavior could mean in the future.[24]

Still the 1830s were comparatively quiet. Aside from students breaking up an abolition meeting, the decade was calm after the conic sections rebellion was put down. Shortly after the school year began in 1841, however, it became clear that a new era had started. A student battle one afternoon with the town firemen, who were competing to see which team could throw a stream of water highest on the spire of Center Church, led that night to a student attack on the High Street firehouse, just across from the campus. After the boys had destroyed the engine and hose, a crowd of townspeople quickly gathered and threatened to retaliate by burning the colleges. That mob was broken up, but the following night it was necessary to call out two military companies to keep the peace. And for about a week thereafter, one undergraduate reported to his father, the students were "obliged to keep thir rooms after dark to prevent any collision between them and the town people." A grand jury investigated this riot; each side started a newspaper to present its case and insult the other (and thus the *Yale Banner,* now the college yearbook, came into existence). Ultimately three students were fined for breach of the peace, but the college authorities took no action of their own.[25]

In fact, the judgments of the faculty at this time show an odd sense of values. In 1841 one undergraduate was suspended for a term for being involved in a duel. The following summer, however, the man selected valedictorian of the class of 1842 was expelled shortly before vacation for the crime of fornication.[26]

The faculty members should have taken the existence of weapons more seriously. If they had, perhaps several tragedies could have been averted. The first of these occurred on the night of 30 September 1843, when Tutor John B. Dwight (B.A. 1840), a grandson of the first president of that name and brother of the second, was stabbed three times when he tried to apprehend a drunken student who had probably been at "the wretched establishment . . . y clept 'The Shakespeare House.' " Dwight was not badly injured, but complications arose from which he died. Since his death came from a fever the doctor could not directly relate to his wounds, the attacker, Lewis Fassitt, might not have been punished for his crime. He avoided the possibility, however, by failing to return for trial and forfeiting his $5,000 bond.

Dwight's death forced the faculty to think seriously about weapons. They even considered checking students' rooms, but then decided "that nothing would be gained by returning to the old custom of espionage." More to the point, they felt, was the removal "from the vicinity of the College, [of] certain eating-shops, which are thought to be a cause of much dissipation and turbulence." [27]

There were no untoward incidents for a number of years, but then one night shortly before Christmas 1847 "the stillness was . . .

broken by the violent ringing of the Bells." Tutors Emerson and Goodrich rushed "to disperse the performers," only to be attacked with a sword cane and iron bar. Emerson was wounded on the arm and Goodrich was struck so hard on the head that at least one student feared for his life.[28] Goodrich survived but others outside the college were not so lucky.

Timothy Dwight's presidency, as we have seen, had been marred by a number of outbreaks between town and gown. Day's term was marked by the discovery in 1824 that a body had been removed from the West Haven cemetery and brought to the Medical School, an event that produced attacks on the school by townspeople of New Haven and West Haven for some five nights in succession. Nearly every window in the building was broken.[29] The firemen's riot of 1841 was Day's only other town–gown incident. But Woolsey was not so fortunate, for in the 1850s relations between Yale students and the citizens of New Haven reached their nadir.

The first great riot under Woolsey occurred in 1854. Students and townspeople had some differences in a theater two nights running, and on the second night a crowd gathered outside the place, Homan's Atheneum, to deal with the fifty or sixty students inside. With the help of a constable the boys got out of the theater, crossed Chapel Street, and began to march up it to the college. The mob followed on the other side of the street, hissing and jeering. As the undergraduates reached Trinity Church they began to sing "Gaudeamus Igitur." This bravado set off the mob, which was just passing a building site. Bricks began to fly, whereupon the students, clearly ready for a fight, pulled out pistols and began to fire. What happened next is disputed; some say the groups never physically clashed, others that they did, but in any case Patrick O'Neil, a leader of the mob, was stabbed through the chest and quickly died.

The students retreated to the yard and congregated with the faculty in South College where, without lights and with shutters pulled tight, they awaited attack. The mob brought up two cannons belonging to a local militia unit and aimed them at the building. Fortunately, Captain Bissell of the constabulary was able to spike the guns before the crowd figured out how to fire them.

The mob remained around the college most of the rest of the night before straggling away. During the next few days the students stayed on campus while constables patrolled the town.

A subsequent grand jury investigation failed to lead to any indictments in the killing. The students protected their own and either refused to testify or lied. The college officers confessed their inability to help. Professor Larned told the Grand Jury that the college authorities were completely unable to get the students to inform against one another. But the faculty was not quite candid. That they could find out something was revealed when the president replied to the charge that it was the Southern students who carried weapons and caused all the trouble. In a statement in the *New Haven Palladium,* he reported that only one in every ten or twelve students owned a weapon and only a single Southerner habitually carried one.

The New Haven *Register* thought the entire incident reflected the spirit of the times. Senator Douglas's recently introduced bill to organize the territories of Kansas and Nebraska without regard to slavery had created outrage throughout the North. New Haveners, including long-silent Yale professors, spoke out at mass meetings on 8 and 10 March. According to the *Register,* meetings such as these were the cause of the riot and the murder:

When men, whose mission is "peace on earth," grave professors, and ordinary sedate citizens, address words of wrath to public audiences, and countenance personal insult and outrage, by hanging honorable and upright Senators in effigy, perhaps it is not strange that the less thoughtful and responsible should forget to regard the peace and fair fame of our usually orderly city.[30]

The *Register* may have had a point. In 1856, in the same month that Yale students provided émigrés to Kansas with Sharp's rifles at the behest of Benjamin Silliman and Henry Ward Beecher, the unpopular tutor Fisk Brewer was attacked by students. Again there was a grand jury investigation, but this time the college authorities saw fit to expel several young men and suspend others.[31]

Two years later, town and gown violence recurred. Again the dispute was with the firemen of the High Street Station and this time, too, the tendency of the Yale men to carry weapons caused a death. Some students returning from their eating club had a run-in with the firemen, and an undergraduate shot and killed one of them. As with the stabbing, the killer was never found. Instead, the college contributed $100 to move the fire company and, in the fall of the year, President Woolsey informed the students that they were forbidden to carry any pistol, gun, club, or other deadly weapon.[32]

The firehouse conflict of 1858 marked the end of the deadly riots, though there have been many less lethal encounters ever since. It was not the final killing, however. In 1860 a medical student killed a townsman with whom he had been drinking. This seems to have been the last such occurrence. Perhaps the Civil War and then the subsequent organized violence of football helped to get the Yale students through the next decades without any such tragedies.[33]

Riots, classes, and unorganized sports were far from the only activities of Yale men in the antebellum period. They had debating clubs, secret societies, proms, and a myriad of customs to complicate their days.

The office of college bully, which has been described, evolved over time into a major bully and a minor bully (the smallest man) for each class. The major bully of the senior class was *the* college bully. The transfer of "the great black club" from the senior to the junior bully in June of each year became a major college affair, with the usual speeches, music, and parades. In the late 1830s, however, some students began to feel that having the leader of the class called a bully was unrefined. One undergraduate explained to his father, "All the college classes are divided in to two parties the Bullymen and Martialmen. The bullies are for keepeing up long and well established costoms to which all gentlemen belong. . . . The martialmen are a codfish set of folks." The split came to a head in 1840 with a battle between bullies and marshals over who should lead the commencement procession. Thereupon the faculty ruled that there would be no class leaders of any sort and the bully disappeared forever.[34]

The faculty was not always so successful with its rulings. The Burial of Euclid persisted despite numerous unfavorable decisions. This enjoyable (and highly anti-intellectual) event belonged to the sophomore class. It was their habit, when they completed the study of Euclid, to dispose of the book in a wild ceremony complete with poems, tragedies, marches, and the burning or burying (or both) of the volume. By the late 1840s the faculty tried to prohibit the practice. Despite an express prohibition—and the presence of numerous tutors—in 1848 the ceremony went off "like a perfect brick," according to one student. A furious faculty immediately dismissed three participants, but to no avail. The custom continued, even becoming more elaborate, until the students themselves let it die in 1861.[35]

As the completion of the study of Euclid produced the burial ceremony, so Junior Exhibition fostered the more important Wooden Spoon. Junior Exhibition seems to have evolved out of Stiles's and Dwight's quarter days. The juniors who received good appointments (grades) used the exhibition in April to show what they could do in speeches before the president, faculty, and friends. Between speeches a band played. And thus an entire day was spent. The Junior Promenade, either the day before or the day of the exhibition, was first held in 1851; prior to that there had been a junior ball in August.[36]

Junior Exhibition and prom were followed in the annual calendar of events by the Wooden Spoon Presentation and Promenade. The Spoon presentation began in 1847 as a lampoon of the Junior Exhibition. But soon the Spoon event and its prom overshadowed the older exhibition and dance.

The first wooden spoon was presented to one of the lowest on the list of junior appointments. Soon this original purpose changed, and before long the whole ceremony had become a popularity contest. In its mature form, during the 1860s, the junior class elected a spoon committee called the "Society of Cochleaureati," and they elected from their own number the spoon man. The committee, it was said, was made up of the nine "best fellows" in the class, and the spoon man was supposed to be the best of all. Because "the position of Spoon Man grew to be the highest elective honor of college, and that of Coch was but little inferior to it," the Spoon Exhibition became the greatest event of the year and drew the largest and most brilliant audience of any event in New Haven. The Spoon Promenade the night before the exhibition was equally dazzling.

The Wooden Spoon ceremonies usually took place on the Monday and Tuesday in July preceding Presentation Day. In 1871 Presentation Day was moved to Tuesday, and the two-week vacation which had always followed it was done away with. This alteration in the calendar, along with the extreme political machinations over the election of the Cochs (always pronounced with a hard "ch" and many visual puns), brought the end of the Wooden Spoon ceremonies.[37]

Presentation Day was a more formal event. Ezra Stiles had started it when he was a tutor under President Clap, as an occasion for the presentation to the president of the seniors who had passed their exams. Over the years it developed into an elaborate ceremony that included a dinner, a class poem, an oration, a class history (begun in 1853), the smoking of clay pipes, the planting of class ivy (1851), and the serenading of buildings and professors. Ultimately it evolved into the current Class Day.[38]

For many years Presentation Day marked the end of the seniors' college careers, for they went on vacation until commencement. Until 1870, when the college calendar was changed to omit the summer session, the day after Presentation Day was an exciting occasion. On arriving at chapel, each class moved up to the seats of the class above them. To celebrate their accession to the sophomore seats, the freshmen began (about 1850) to hold a pow-wow on the steps of the state house on Presentation evening. As usual, there were speeches, songs, poems, and music. In this case, all were supposed to be funny or at least entertaining. As with all things collegiate, the Freshman Pow-wow became increasingly elaborate and expensive. Perhaps for this reason, the faculty was successful when they banned it in 1862.[39]

With their speeches, poems, and plays, these and other occasions too numerous to list all had a certain intellectual character. In addition, the literary societies of Linonia and Brothers in Unity provided, at regular weekly meetings, serious occasions for speeches and debates. For almost a century, in fact, these institutions of the students' own devising were perhaps the major stimulus to things intellectual.

For a time, from 1819 to 1853, Linonia and Brothers were joined by a third society, Calliope, formed by Southerners and a few Northerners. Throughout its history it was small and retained its Southern character, but not until 1851 did all Southerners withdraw from the other societies to join Calliope. The *Yale Literary Magazine* reported, "By this change, Calliope . . . has drawn more definitely the sectional differences of the students." For some reason this separation did not last. Perhaps in a momentary flush of good feeling, or because they could not afford to pay their share of the cost of Alumni Hall (where the societies were to have rooms), Calliope disbanded in February 1853.[40]

The great age of the literary societies was probably the fifty years from about 1780 to 1830. In these years they performed two very

worthwhile functions. First, at a time when there was almost no freedom in the curriculum, they gave the undergraduates a chance to
discuss the questions that seemed important to them. Second,
through their libraries they provided many of the books the students wanted to read at a time when the college library was seldom
open and, in any case, contained little light literature.[41]

Both Henry Barnard (B.A. 1830) and F. A. P. Barnard (B.A.
1828) felt that these societies were the best part of their education.
F. A. P. Barnard, toward the close of his term as president of Columbia, wrote in his memoirs, "No part of my training at Yale College seems to me to have been more beneficial than that which I derived from the practice of writing and speaking in the literary
society to which I belonged." He viewed their fading away in the
seventies with sadness: "It seems to me that, with the loss of her literary societies, half the glory of Yale has departed from her." [42]

The slow decline began in the 1830s. It may have been due in
part to the banning of the literary society exhibitions, probably because they became too elaborate and difficult for the faculty to control. There may also have been a lessening of interest in speaking;
but probably most important, the growth of the college began to undermine the closeness that had once existed among the members. As
the size of classes grew, new societies in which the undergraduate
felt a more personal interest emerged. As early as 1819 Theodore
Dwight Woolsey and some of his friends formed a club called Hex-
ahedron in order to read poetry together. In 1821 Professor Kingsley and some undergraduates started Chi Delta Theta to encourage
an interest in literature. Others found their fun in Phi Beta Kappa,
which had as its object the "promotion of literature and friendly intercourse among scholars." It too held orations and debates periodically during the academic year. That it was sometimes less than serious is revealed in the faculty records for 9 December 1822, when it
was noted that the faculty should attend the meetings of the society
and use their influence "to prevent excess and disorder" and see that
everyone went home at a "seasonable hour." [43]

Membership in Phi Beta Kappa was from the beginning usually
—but not always—based on academic excellence. This did not,
however, make the society any stronger than Linonia and Brothers.
Phi Beta Kappa began to decline in the 1840s and became defunct
in the 1870s. The last oration was given in 1870 and the last poem

in 1871, and in 1879 it was reported that "since that time the annual election of undergraduate members has also been given up, and . . . the Society has been extinct at Yale." It seems probable that Phi Beta Kappa had the same problems as the great literary societies. Not only was the college growing and becoming more heterogeneous, but college work was becoming more demanding and extracurricular activities more varied. In addition, Phi Beta Kappa's reputation suffered because, it was charged, it began to elect socialites.[44]

Phi Beta Kappa was the direct cause of the appearance of Yale's first senior secret society, Skull and Bones. No doubt the growth in the size of the college would have caused the appearance of smaller societies in any case, but in 1832 the Anti-Masonic movement produced attacks on secrecy which involved Phi Beta Kappa. According to Charles Tracy (B.A. 1832),

a grave question of consience [*sic*] arose about the promise of secrecy exacted on initiation to the Phi Beta Kappa Society. Harvard was for dissolving the secrecy, and it sent Edward Everett to the private meeting at Yale. He used a tender tone, stood half drooping as he spoke, and touchingly set forth that the students at Harvard had such conscientious scruples as to keep them from taking the vow of secrecy, and the society's life was thus endangered. There was stout opposition, but the motion prevailed, and the missionary returned to gladden the tender consiences of the Harvard boys.

In protest, apparently, William H. Russell, valedictorian of 1833, got Alphonso Taft and thirteen other members of '33 to form what is now perhaps the most famous secret society in the United States.[45]

Skull and Bones was, and remains, a strictly secret society. Its purpose and programs were not revealed when it was founded and have never since been known. But that like most Yale societies it pretends to some intellectual and educational purpose can probably be assumed.

"The Scull and Bones," as it was known at first, was almost immediately unpopular with the professors. On Christmas Day 1833 the faculty met to deal with "a convivial meeting" of the society the night before. Some nine members of the group, including boys who were to become a future associate justice of the Supreme Court of Louisiana, a member of Congress, and a treasurer of Yale, received warnings and letters were sent to their parents. Two members who had not yet been matriculated were told they would not be, and hence could not receive their degrees (later the faculty relented and they graduated with their class).[46] But though the faculty did not like Skull and Bones they did not suppress it, and soon the other classes created their own secret societies. By July 1840 every class had at least one, and the system continued to grow.

These were all class societies. A student was a member for only one year. The societies were, in addition, supposed to be secret, but only the senior societies, Skull and Bones and Scroll and Key (1842), were able to keep their mysteries from becoming common knowledge. Since the members of the other societies all remained at college and tended to talk about their former activities, their secrets were soon well known. In addition, only the senior societies made a fetish of their secrecy—at the same time that they advertised their existence. The senior society men wore their pins openly, often affixed to the tie knot or shirt front, but became ostentatiously insulted if the name of any society was mentioned in their presence.[47]

The senior societies, as the final step in the chain, had the greatest prestige, but the junior societies were in some ways more important to the life of the college, for there most of the heated political machinations took place. Coalitions between the junior societies tended to decide the elections to the most important places in the college: the cochleaureati of the Wooden Spoon, and editors of the *Yale Literary Magazine*.[48]

Strangely, the senior class had fewer society members than any other. For many years only thirty members of the class belonged to societies. Some seniors continued to play a role in their junior organizations; some formed their own temporary groups; others tried— and failed—to start new, permanent societies; still others became openly antagonistic to the existing system. But on the whole the senior societies were admired because it was felt they chose, in their then private, unostentatious elections, the very best men in the class. This general respect allowed the senior societies to sink their roots deep into Yale. Hence where all the other old class societies have died or changed their form, the senior societies remain— anachronisms which oddly continue to thrive.[49]

The faculty of Woolsey's day disapproved of these organizations. In 1844 they voted to advise students who requested guidance not to join the societies. Five years later, they decided to give no financial aid to students who became members without first asking permission—and permission was not always granted. In 1857, it was noted that non–society-members would be given preference in receiving financial support from the college. Five years later it was concluded that members of secret societies "whose membership costs them nothing are to have only one-half of the usual abatement [in tuition] and the others to have nothing." It was all to no avail. The societies boomed and early members ultimately rose to become important college officers.[50]

While the secret societies were undermining the old literary groups from the social side, other new endeavors undermined their intellectual aspect. Most important in this regard was the appearance in February 1836 of the *Yale Literary Magazine.* This was far from the first Yale magazine. That honor seems to belong to the *Literary Cabinet,* which was first published in the fall of 1806 and expired a year later. Other attempts were made periodically thereafter, but none was really successful until William T. Bacon, Horace Colton, and William Maxwell Evarts, all of the class of 1837, and Henry C. Deming of 1836, brought out the *Lit.,* which has been called "the most successful periodical in American college literature." It has now fallen on difficult days, but for many years it was the favorite college vehicle for Yale undergraduates with literary pretensions.[51]

The next decade saw the emergence of another publication that is still in existence. The *Yale Banner,* founded to present the student side of the firehouse riot of 1841, reappeared the following year with lists of the members of the college and the secret societies. It has performed a somewhat similar function ever since. A competitor, the *Pot-Pourri* appeared in 1865, and later the two publications were merged. In the same year as the *Pot-Pourri,* the first successful newspaper appeared, the *College Courant.*[52]

Many of these new activities, though undermining the old literary societies, did reinforce the concept of the class as the center of Yale life. The importance of the class dated back at least to the days of fagging and the stress upon the carefully demarked rights and privileges of each class. Secret societies, junior elections of "Cochs" and *Lit.* editors, and even sports reinforced this old system. For many years, what team sports there were, were played by classes. In 1879 Lyman Bagg criticized an attempt of the sixties to replace class boats with clubs made up from all classes. "The class is the real unit of organization at Yale," he said. "As a substitute for 'class feeling,' which supplies a natural motive power for exertion, they attempted to introduce a purely factitious sentiment of 'club feeling,' or pride in the success of permanent rowing clubs merely as such." In the end, of course, Bagg lost this argument, and ultimately class feeling would decline; but for most Yale men of the nineteenth century, their class came before everything else.[53]

Despite the rising complexity of college life in the years prior to the Civil War, Yale remained—as did most of American life— basically simple: a place of arching elms that lessened the heat of the summer sun, where the grass in the college yard was cut by scythe, so that the smell of newly mown hay drifted in at the college windows; where dress and dates, and dancing and singing, and just sitting on the fence remained important.[54]

The Yale fence—that was something old grads never forgot. Though students had sat on it for years, it only began to become important as the Civil War approached. The first reference I have been able to find in the college records to "sitting upon the fence" is a faculty decision of 22 September 1858: "The Students shall be told that they are liable to be marked for sitting upon the College fences and for making noises of any kind upon the College grounds." This warning began a long, and losing, attempt to keep the boys off the fence. In 1862 the faculty gave notice to the students that they were prohibited from gathering in groups on or about the fence and from disorderly singing. This rule was passed again in 1866, and in 1867 seats were provided around the trees in hopes that these might provide an alternative to the fence. But it was no use. By the summer of 1867 the fence had won and thereafter it reigned supreme. Each class—except the freshmen, who were not allowed on until after Presentation Day—had a specific place upon the fence at the corner of Chapel and College Streets where, as Bagg described it, "on pleasant days, for an hour or two after dinner and supper, crowds of undergraduates perch themselves, and smoke, chat, laugh and sing together." [55]

The fence was particularly a place for singing, and singing had a long history at Yale. It began with a music society in 1812, an organization that later became the Beethoven Society. For many years it provided orchestral music and singing at the college religious exer-

cises, for it was not until 1851 that Yale broke the old Puritan tradition and installed an organ. Fence singing, society singing, class singing groups, and college singing clubs gave such impetus to this
activity that a book of Yale songs (the first songbook of any college)
was published in 1853. New editions followed every few years in the
fifties and sixties.[56]

Formal singing was given impetus when Gustave Stoeckel was authorized to teach that subject in 1855. By the late sixties class glee
clubs (usually about a dozen men) were common, and these groups
would come together with others (including graduates) of good
voice to form the Beethoven Society and also the University Glee
Club, which first appeared during this decade.[57]

Clothes were seldom as important as song in the lives of Yale
men, but periodically they became a subject of great interest. One
such period was in the teens and twenties of the nineteenth century,
when there was a passion for dress. One undergraduate of the class
of 1821 recalled a student of his day who wore "an entire suit of
light changeable silk." The college officers opposed such wasteful
luxury and the students themselves reacted against it. Showing that
at least a little classical training had rubbed off on them, they
formed a Lycurgan Society to encourage plainness and simplicity in
life, manners, and apparel. But again they went too far. An outfit
was developed, "namely, a close coatee, with stand-up collar, and
very short skirts, *skirtees,* they might be called; the color gray; pantaloons and vest the same." Not surprisingly, this did not last, and
when President Day received a request from his son for a plaid
cloak, he replied, "I am willing you should get a plaid cloak, if you
find it necessary. They are as common in college now, as the Lycurgan suit was a year ago."

Finally, to put a stop to fads in dress the students petitioned the
Corporation in the fall of 1824 for "a uniform dress." The Corporation first disapproved, then reconsidered, and finally allowed the faculty to lay down rules. In November the professors noted the following uniform for undergraduates:

The coat to be a plain frock-coat, with standing cape. The classes to be
distinguished by marks of braid on the cape of the coat; the Freshmen
wearing one, the Sophomores two, Juniors three, and Seniors four. The
color of the broadcloth or cassimere coat and pantaloons to be blue; the

vest either black or blue. The thin coat for summer to be a black frock-coat; the vest and pantaloons either black or white. The cravats to be black or white.

The college uniform was about as successful as the Philencration Society of the 1820s and early 1830s, which was first devoted to temperance and then to abstinence from alcoholic beverages. Neither could change the Yale man. By early 1826 the faculty noted that it was "inexpedient" to try to enforce the wearing of the uniform, and thus ended that aberrant experiment.[58]

Clothes, drink, and song—what would they be without women? The Yale students of the nineteenth century found theirs in the town—both good girls and bad. Fortunately, New Haven had numerous dancehalls and girls schools, while professors and townspeople had daughters upon whom it was customary to call. In fact, on a Sunday, by carefully timed visits, it was possible to pick up all one's meals that way.[59]

A much gayer time could be had by taking a night boat to New York. In commemoration of the delightful trips on the ship *Richard Peck* the following song was later sung:

Invitation from the Right

I will tell you of a little scheme I've got,
And I hope, sirs, that you will refuse it not,
To go down upon the Richard Peck tonight,
And have fun aplenty in the moo-oon light.

Acceptance from the Left

We accept your generous invitation,
Since having pleasure is our occupation.
We will meet you on the dock at twelve o'clock,
And to get the dough we'll put our watch and chain.
    in hock.

Chorus. Both Sides

Oh, we will have the hell of a time, I'll tell you
    what,
Loving, lushing, stowing wine into our faces.
And we'll sit up till the morning and enjoy the
    light of dawning,

> Hully Gee!, by God, we'll raise hell on the Peck!
> > Diddly Dum.
> > Take my advice,
> > Diddly Dum,
> > On the Peck.

But of course it was not necessary to go to New York City for "loving" and "lushing." In 1849 Garrick Mallery recorded with delight how two undergraduates

> kept a female in man's clothes who frequently a nights paid visits to them of long duration. Landlady smelt a rat and one day chucked the woman under the chin—saying—"You're too pretty for a man." Rich! Whole thing exploded they ditto. Wilcox also ran off with Grace Goodyear—Mischief to pay about that.[60]

The most interesting female on the college scene, however, was the college widow. The first description of her I have found is in John W. De Forest's *Miss Ravenel's Conversion from Secession to Loyalty*. De Forest entered Yale life when he married in 1856 the brilliant daughter of Professor Shepard. The female he described is "of a certain age" and makes a career of flirting with students: she "can't relish a man who hasn't a flavor of Greek and Latin." A more flattering and affectionate portrait is in Henry Seidel Canby's *Alma Mater* which, though written much later, describes the same interesting woman:

> Still another institution the college gave to the society of the town, the college widow. I knew two of them in their old age and profited greatly from my friendship with them. For the college widow had a depth and richness of emotional experience never developed in American life of that day outside of the few metropolises, and seldom there. She began at sixteen or eighteen [in De Forest's day, it was fifteen], as a ravishing beauty, the darling of freshmen; she passed on in the years of her first blooming from class to class of ardent youngsters, until, as her experience ripened, she acquired a taste, never to be satisfied by matrimony, for male admiration, abstracted from its consequences; and more subtly, for the heady stimulant of intimacy with men in their fresh and vigorous youth. By her thirties she had learned the art of eternal spring, and had become a connoisseur in the dangerous excitement of passion controlled at the breaking point, a mistress of every emotion, and an adept in the difficult task of sublimating love into friendship. The students lived out their brief college life and went on; she endured, and tradition with her,

an enchantress in illusion and a specialist in the heart. Twenty, even thirty years might be her tether; when suddenly on a midnight, a shock of reality, or perhaps only boredom, ended it all, she was old—but still charming and infinitely wise. To smoke a cigarette with her when cigarettes were still taboo for women, and drink her coffee and liqueur, was a lesson in civilization.[61]

As Woolsey's presidency drew to a close this simple, bucolic Yale was beginning to disappear. The appearance of more and more activities, the beginnings of more and more intercollegiate sports—these things signified that an important change was taking place at Yale. The extracurriculum was on the rise and would soon displace the curriculum from its previously unchallenged position. Where a student in 1853 could report to his brother that the main subject of conversation was marks! marks! marks!,[62] by the end of Woolsey's era Phi Beta Kappa was dying, and the extracurriculum was conquering all. But that was a problem to be handled by Woolsey's successors.

Part Four

Age of Uncertainty

1871–1921

13

Stagnation

Theodore Dwight Woolsey had changed and improved Yale. But as his term was drawing to a close, discussion and argument broke out over the course the university should take in the future. American higher education was reaching a turning point in its development and many men in and around Yale recognized instinctively that the institution was at a critical point in its history. From some alumni —the group called Young Yale—came criticism of existing conditions; from faculty came serious proposals for building a true university. The response of the fellows to these suggestions, especially in the selection of a new president, would do much to fix the development of Yale for years to come.

The first sign of serious unrest was the Young Yale movement, based in New York and led by talented graduates like William Graham Sumner (B.A. 1863) and William Maxwell Evarts (B.A. 1837), who called for alumni representation on the Yale Corporation. This was not a new idea. President Woolsey had suggested it in 1866, but the Corporation had failed to see the value of the change. Alumni frustrations were rising, however, and the continued failure of the Corporation to act brought some of the reasons for their unhappiness into the open. At the alumni dinner during commencement in July 1870, the usually saccharine sentimentality of the speeches was broken by outspoken criticism of Mother Yale. C. G. Child (B.A. 1855) set the mood by criticizing the faculty for being aloof from the student body. Then, W. W. Phelps (B.A. 1860), son-in-law of Joseph Earl Sheffield and a wealthy man himself, created a sensation. He bluntly stated, "The younger alumni are not satisfied with the management of the college. They do not think that in anything, except scholarship, does it keep progress with the age. They find no fault with the *men;* they find much fault with the spirit of the management. It is too conservative and narrow." Yale, he said, was out of touch with the world; it needed an addition of active intelligent alumni to its governing board so that it could have "a knowledge of what is wanted in the scenes for which Yale educates her children."

No longer should the college be ruled by "Rev. Mr. Pickering of Squashville, who is exhausted with keeping a few sheep in the wilderness, or Hon. Mr. Domuch, of Oldport, who seeks to annul the charter on the only railway that benefits his constituency." [1]

Needless to say, Phelps's description of the fellows was hardly appreciated by the Corporation, and his speech touched off a running battle. Many hard words were said about both ministers and young alumni. Nonetheless, the alumni finally got their way. The six senior state senators were replaced as fellows by alumni through an act of the Connecticut legislature passed 6 July 1871 and accepted by the Corporation a few days later.[2]

At the same time as the argument over the makeup of the Corporation, there was a serious discussion of the direction Yale should take under the next president. It was started by Professor Noah Porter, who published his articles "The American Colleges and the American Public" in the *New Englander and Yale Review* in 1869. In these articles, which later emerged as a book, Porter took the most conservative line. He concentrated on the college and strongly defended the traditional curriculum and the mental and moral discipline it was supposed to produce. It was, one modern scholar has said, "the outstanding defense of mental discipline and the nineteenth-century college written after the Civil War." [3]

Porter was answered by James Dwight Dana and Timothy Dwight. Dana, the great scientist who had called for a university in New Haven in the 1850s, now pounded hard on the fact that Yale already was a university and that every effort should be bent to further its development.[4] Timothy Dwight directed his essays to the question of what the new president must do. He too stressed the fact that Yale was no longer just a college. It was a university—and the president must actively support the development of all its parts. It was no longer right to have the schools "hanging on the verge of the government." The president must lose his attachment to the college, let a dean do that work, and connect himself to all the faculties. He must work from now on for the whole university.

Dwight suggested meetings of all the faculties in one body so that each could hear the views and problems of the others. He was quickly supported by the faculties, who called on the Corporation to create a University Council of all the professors plus the president, treasurer, librarian, and registrar. Dwight and Dana both pointed to numerous physical and monetary needs of the university, and these too were echoed by a published report of a committee of the faculties that outlined clearly the needs of the various departments for professorships, scholarships, books, buildings, and all the other myriad requirements of a great university. Dana estimated that the university needed an additional three and a half million dollars. Since the entire permanent funds of Yale amounted to only a little over a million dollars, this was a staggering figure.[5]

The faculty, clearly, dreamed of great things. It also knew the moment was critical. Dana called it "the best University scheme in the land" but noted that it could only be achieved with "just the right man in the Presidential chair." The committee of the faculties agreed: "The present time seems to be regarded as critical in relation to the future of Yale College." [6]

There were three definite candidates for the presidency on the Yale campus: Noah Porter (B.A. 1831), Clark Professor of Moral Philosophy and Metaphysics; Daniel Coit Gilman (B.A. 1852), professor of physical and political geography in the Sheffield Scientific School and secretary and trustee of that school; and Timothy Dwight (B.A. 1849), professor of sacred literature in the Divinity School and grandson of the great president.

There is no evidence that Dwight was considered for the position at this time, but surely he nourished some hope as he wrote his articles entitled "Yale College—Some Thoughts Respecting Its Future." Since his grandfather was always much on his mind, it seems unlikely that he would have missed the significance of the fact that he was almost exactly the same age as the first Timothy Dwight when he became president.[7]

Daniel Coit Gilman was a more powerful candidate. As one of the chief architects of Sheff he had been invited to become president of the University of Wisconsin in 1867 and of the University of California in 1870. He rejected both offers, no doubt with his eye on the Yale post. Gilman was not, like Dwight and Porter, an ordained minister, but that was not a problem, for he had studied divinity under Porter and had been licensed to preach. He could have been ordained before he took office in the same way Day and Woolsey had been. Gilman's candidacy was encouraged in the newspapers, especially by Young Yale, but it seems doubtful that he was ever considered seriously by the Corporation. Not only was he a Sheffield

Scientific School man, but he was also an outspoken exponent of the "new education," far removed in his thinking from Noah Porter or the Yale Report of 1828.[8]

It was evident quite early that Gilman did not have much of a chance. Woolsey favored his good friend Porter, and Gilman stood for the wrong things. Gilman must have known the cause was lost when he supported the addition of alumni to the Corporation in an article in *The Nation* toward the end of May 1871. There he blasted the fellows:

In all the efforts which have been made to secure new endowments for the different departments of Yale College, the efforts of the Corporation have, to say the least, not been conspicuous; nor can those who are most familiar with college publications recall any recent statement in respect to the college emanating from the Trustees more comprehensive and satisfactory than the annual catalogue.

He went even farther, remarking that the trustees were not merely "non-interfering," but actually "non-cooperative." They had lost, he thought, the moral support of a large number of graduates.[9]

With this blunt criticism ringing in their ears, a month and a half later the fellows made their choice: a group of old men, presided over by an old man, they chose the old way and an old professor, Noah Porter, to lead Yale along it.

Certainly Yale knew what it had done. In the bulky two-volume history of Yale compiled by William Kingsley and published in 1879, it was candidly stated that Porter's "election was a guarantee that the college was still to maintain its conservative attitude in respect to all the educational questions which were attracting attention; that it was still to maintain its character as a bulwark of the Christian religion and of all sound learning."[10]

The newly elected president was within six months of his sixtieth birthday when chosen, the oldest man ever selected for the post. His ties to Yale were strong. His father had been a member of the Corporation from 1823 to 1862 and had served on the Prudential Committee much of that time. His wife was the daughter of Professor Nathaniel Taylor. He himself had graduated from Yale in 1831, had served as a tutor there, and then, after ten years as a minister, had returned as Clark Professor of Moral Philosophy and Metaphysics in

1846. He had remained there ever since, except for one year spent studying at the University of Berlin.[11]

Perhaps even more than his predecessor, Porter was the scholarly type. Action was not his forte. Though more enthusiastic and optimistic than Woolsey, even this tended to work against him, for he was confident, according to Timothy Dwight, "that results will prove better than the present circumstances may seem to indicate, and will prove thus even if we do not ourselves intervene to direct the progress of events toward them." So during his presidency he spent much of his time writing, producing three books and numerous articles. His books were widely read and through them, as Ralph Gabriel has said, he "influenced importantly the ethical and religious thought of the students not only at Yale but throughout the nation." Unfortunately, at this point in its history Yale did not need a scholar at its head. It needed an administrator—and that Porter was not. The second President Dwight concluded that Porter's "executive ability . . . did not equal that of Dr. Woolsey, whose gifts in this respect were, indeed, quite remarkable." He failed to take command when it was needed and "was accordingly not so strong as a leader, and not so efficient a helper in matters which required instant energy and a general's activity." [12]

Beyond being a scholar, Porter was a teacher. And, ignoring Dwight's recent advice that the president should not teach, he continued to do so after taking office. Under Porter, the president again taught mental and moral philosophy, the traditional capstone of the classical curriculum. The seniors loved it. As Patton said, "Year after year the senior class voted him the most popular teacher of the faculty, until the thing became so assured that he was ruled out of consideration." In class he was warm, kindly, and considerate. He helped to break down the formidable barrier between student and teacher. He was, however, gentle to the point of laxness, so many students did not learn their lessons very well. On the other hand, Theodore Munger remarked, they did learn the lessons of the human heart, and Munger felt that was more important.[13]

Noah Porter—this kind, gentle, conservative man—was inaugurated on 11 October 1871. Even nature seemed to support those who were distressed over Yale's choice. A severe rainstorm prevented many from attending the ceremony. Those who did heard the new president give his inaugural address on the theme of the higher education in America. First he called for increased intellectual activity in the colleges. While he admitted that "our universities and colleges are not primarily designed to be academies for learned acquisition and research, yet they must be made such in fact, in order that they may be schools of the highest culture." This could be done through the addition of graduate and other schools to the colleges, "encouraging college professors to enter upon higher teaching," and by establishing scholarships and fellowships to assist young men to do research and to write. He pointed out that "a well-furnished and well-endowed library" was needed for research, but that Yale's library was very inadequate in both regards. Museums and collections —especially in modern science and art—were also necessary to make the college such an institution as he envisaged.

But in addition to being seats of learning, the colleges, Porter said, had *the duty of training to the highest intellectual power and achievement.*" Then Porter's real conservatism began to be revealed, for to accomplish their duty, he said, "Two principles must be regarded as unquestioned: *The higher education should aim at intellectual culture and training rather than at the acquisition of knowledge, and it should respect remote rather than immediate results.*" The chief object of education should be intellectual training, and this was achieved by studying subjects which gave good discipline— and not all subjects did that equally well.

Porter recognized that different students had different needs, but Yale already provided for this situation by having two undergraduate schools: Sheffield, which prepared for the modern and active life, and the Academical Department (Yale College), which was "classical, historical, and speculative." Both, however, had a fixed curriculum, and the "spirit of both is disciplinary." For while the two schools each allowed some freedom of election, both held to "the same theory, that severe and enforced attention and patient labor open the way to intellectual power and thorough acquisition."

After thus defending the old ways, Porter faced directly the major educational question of the day: "the plan of *elective studies*" by which some educators hoped to make college studies more palatable. He rejected it outright, saying that it contained very serious evils. Most students were not mature enough to choose their own studies. It had "the certain evil of breaking into the common life of the class and the college." Lastly, it was productive of "unprofitable expenditures" and "insuperable complexity."

Then Porter turned to another important issue—the desire to shorten the time it took to earn a B.A. This too he rejected. In fact, he wanted a longer course to produce educated men who were "elevated and refined by a culture which is truly liberal." Such men the country badly needed. "Instead, then," Porter continued, "of providing university studies for undergraduate students, *we desire to make our undergraduate departments preparatory for university classes and schools.*" [14]

Though basically in agreement with the ideas of the Yale Report of 1828, when Porter took this approach to the function of the college he fell into an error common to its critics. He forgot that Jeremiah Day had been talking about very young men in college, that in the forty-odd years since, the average age at entrance had risen to over eighteen, whereas Day had referred to men who graduated at that age or even younger. Thus to keep the college disciplinary and preparatory, in the belief that this was continuing the old Yale tradition, missed the mark. These were no longer schoolboys but young men, and some adjustment to this fact needed to be made.[15]

Porter had much more to say about other aspects of the college and about some of Yale's specific needs, but some members of his audience must have been unhappily comparing the man before them with young, dynamic Charles William Eliot and his great inaugural address at Harvard two years earlier. In one of his more powerful moments Eliot had said, "This University recognizes no real antagonism between literature and science, and consents to no such narrow alternatives as mathematics or classics, science or metaphysics. We would have them all, and at their best." Few expressed such catholic fervor for greatness at Yale.[16]

The institution that Porter was to lead had its weaknesses, especially in the graduate and professional schools, but it was still one of the greatest educational institutions in the country. In 1870, Timothy Dwight had called for the recognition of that fact by changing its name from Yale College to Yale University. President Porter and other conservatives who cherished the idea of old Yale rejected so extreme an action. Instead, the Corporation voted on 13 March 1872 that Yale had "attained to the form of a University." Yale College, they declared, should be "recognized as comprising the four departments of which a University is commonly understood to consist, viz: the departments of Theology, of Law, of Medicine, of Philosophy and the Arts." George W. Pierson has assessed the significance of this act:

By this vote the Corporation recognized the existence of the University so far as to enlarge the Department of Philosophy and Arts, which was now made to include the Academical Department and the Art School as well as the graduate courses and the Scientific School. Yet the several faculties of Arts, Science, and Fine Arts were not merged. The Department of Philosophy and the Arts was given no Inter-Faculty council, no head, and no funds. The graduate Faculty remained almost entirely a borrowed faculty, with only two graduate professorships, no full-time men, and no formal administration. The Art School was not used for the instruction of students generally and came to be attended almost exclusively by women. And the struggling Scientific School . . . was not any more warmly embraced or supported.

So while all the ingredients for a great university were there in plenty, they were not used to make the declaration of fact into a greater reality.[17]

The major and irreplaceable ingredient was the first-rate faculty that Woolsey had brought together. With Newton, Dana, Thacher, James Hadley, and young Willard Gibbs (appointed professor without salary the day Porter was elected) in the Academical Department, Benjamin Silliman, Jr., in medicine, John Ferguson Weir in art, Simeon Baldwin in law, Addison Van Name as librarian, Othniel C. Marsh in the Graduate School, and the great group at the Sheffield Scientific School of Gilman, George J. Brush, William Dwight Whitney, William H. Brewer, Daniel Cady Eaton, Addison Verrill, and Thomas Lounsbury, President Porter commanded a stellar corps. He immediately improved it, in 1872, with the appointment of William Graham Sumner to the Academical faculty.

In fact, at a time when there was still no real academic profession in America, when Yale professorial salaries were only $3,000 (a figure they reached in 1871), the university had some of the greatest men in its history.[18] First in importance was the greatest scholar Yale has ever produced or harbored, Josiah Willard Gibbs (B.A. 1858, Ph.D. 1863), who was appointed professor of mathematical physics without salary in 1871.[19] The failure to provide a salary did not indicate any lack of esteem for Gibbs but rather the poverty of Yale.

During the years from 1871 to 1878 Gibbs was doing his greatest work. In 1876 he published the first part of his great paper "On the Equilibrium of Heterogeneous Substances," in the *Transactions of the Connecticut Academy of Arts and Sciences;* he completed it in 1878 in the same journal. As Gibbs's biographer in the *Dictionary of American Biography* notes, "It was this work on the equilibrium of heterogeneous substances which provided the basic theory for that great new branch of science, more recently developed, known as physical chemistry." The repercussions of this seminal work are still being felt.[20]

At Yale, on the other hand, Gibbs's influence was small. He taught only a few seniors (vector analysis) and even fewer graduate students. It has been estimated that in thirty-two years of teaching, a total of less than one hundred graduate students attended his courses. Despite this, Yale held on to Gibbs. When Gilman (who had left Yale shortly after failing to become president) tried to hire him away to Johns Hopkins in 1880, with an offer of $3,000 a year, Dana wrote to Gibbs:

I have only just now learned that there is a danger of your leaving us. —Your departure would be a very bad move for Yale. I have felt, of late, great anxiety for our University (using a name we are striving to deserve) because there seemed to be so little appreciation among our Graduates as to what we need, and so few benefactions in our favor; and now the idea of losing the leading man in one of our departments is really disheartening. I do not wonder that Johns Hopkins wants your name and services, or that you feel inclined to consider favorably their proposition, for nothing has been done toward endowing your professorship, and there are not here the means or signs of progress which tend to incite courage in Professors and multiply earnest students. But I hope nevertheless that you will stand by us, and that something will speedily be done by way of endowment to show you that your services are really valued.

Johns Hopkins can get on vastly better without you than we can. *We can not.*

With this plea and others, a promise of $2,000 a year immediately and an increase as soon as possible, Gibbs agreed to stay and Yale kept its greatest scientist. As still happens, however, it had taken an outside offer to make Yale really recognize its own.[21]

James Dwight Dana, who helped to keep Gibbs at Yale when Gilman tried to lure him to Hopkins, was another great Yale scientist of the day. Silliman Professor of Geology and Mineralogy, Dana had graduated from Yale in 1833 and then, like so many other famous scientists of the nineteenth century, served as an assistant to the first Professor Benjamin Silliman. His work with Silliman took little time, however, so he was able to write what George W. Pierson has called "perhaps the most famous of Yale texts," *A System of Mineralogy*. Dana's development as a scientist was probably helped by his membership in a sort of forerunner of the seminar, the Institute of Natural Science, later known as the Yale Natural History Society. This group had been formed by a young Brazilian, J. Francisco Lima, who was studying medicine at Yale (M.D. 1839). Its purpose was to promote the study of nature, and its membership included Edward C. Herrick, the librarian, who was "an excellent early economic ethnologist," the two Sillimans, Dennison Olmsted, as well as two other Yale professors and several students. The opportunity the society provided to hear and present papers and to talk with other scientists must have been very beneficial to young Dana.[22]

Dana's great opportunity came with his appointment as mineralogist and geologist of the United States Exploring Expedition to the South Pacific under Captain Charles Wilkes. After four years (and one shipwreck), Dana returned to New Haven, married one of the senior Silliman's daughters, and began to write his reports based on his work on the expedition. He could not, however, get a job. There seemed no place in America, just then, for a natural scientist. After his first report, *Zoophytes,* appeared in 1846, Harvard offered him a position. Dana wanted to stay in New Haven. "But," as he wrote Asa Gray, "I have felt it very doubtful whether anything towards a professorship here could be accomplished, as there are no funds here, and no source to look for funds, as far as now appears." So Dana told his friends in New Haven that he would have to accept the position at Harvard. This produced the wanted reaction. Professor Edward E. Salisbury, President Woolsey, and two others endowed a Silliman Professorship, and Dana was appointed to it.[23]

By 1859 Dana was teaching, serving as an editor of the *American Journal of Science,* writing articles and his *Manual of Geology,* as well as working on the scientific parts of a new edition of Webster's dictionary. Not surprisingly, he suffered what one biographer describes as a serious "nervous breakdown" (as Charles Darwin had warned him he might). Though thereafter husbanding his strength more carefully, Dana continued his work and in 1862 brought out his *Manual of Geology,* which, according to a historian of American geology, gave "for the first time an authoritative summary of the geology of North America and held its own through all the years following down to the fourth and last edition, that of 1895." This was followed in 1864 by his briefer *Textbook of Geology,* an enlarged version of the *Mineralogy,* and a second breakdown. From that time on his health was poor. He continued his teaching and writing, but at a greatly reduced rate. Dana was ever a loyal Yale man, and a forward-looking one as well. As early as 1856 he began to call publicly for a real university in New Haven, and though it took much too long to happen, by his death in 1893 his dream was finally beginning to be fulfilled.[24]

Another great scientist on the faculty was the professor of paleontology, Othniel Charles Marsh—the first to hold such a chair in America and probably the second in the world. His rapacious collecting and haste to publish his findings, along with his battles with the Philadelphia paleontologist Edward D. Cope, have earned him a reputation as one of the robber barons of late nineteenth-century science. Since he was paid no salary he seldom did any teaching, but graduates and undergraduates visited his home and accompanied him on his western expeditions, thus gaining a special education. Marsh's great fossil collecting expeditions provided, as William Goetzmann has said, "the nucleus of exotic creatures around which one of the world's great museums [Peabody Museum at Yale] would be constructed." And his work with the evolution of the horse and the *Odontonithes,* the great toothed birds, gave, as Darwin wrote him, "the best support to the theory of evolution that has appeared within the last twenty years." [25]

First, last, and always, Marsh was a collector. Not only did he form one of the most complete osteological collections, but as George P. Merrill observed in the *Dictionary of American Biography* "Minerals, invertebrate fossils, archeological and ethnological materials also came within his domain. 'He not only had the means and the inclination, but entered every field of acquisition with the dominating ambition to obtain everything there was in it.' " Between 1868 and 1882 he spent about $200,000 of his own money collecting vertebrate fossils. In 1898 he deeded these and all his other collections to Yale, and upon his death he bequeathed to the university his house and surrounding property and left the museum $30,000, the remainder to an estate depleted by depression and his many purchases.[26]

Benjamin Silliman, Jr., was also on the faculty in Porter's day. He had graduated from the college in 1837 and then assisted his father in the laboratory and as an editor of the *American Journal of Science*. He was appointed to the faculty as professor of applied chemistry, without salary, in 1846 and helped Norton to found the Sheffield Scientific School. In 1849 he resigned to become professor of chemistry and toxicology in the medical department of the University of Louisville. He returned in 1854 as professor of general and applied chemistry in the college and medical school, teaching some in the scientific school, and later serving on its governing board.[27]

Shortly after his return to Yale, Silliman made his most famous scientific contribution, his *Report on the Rock Oil, or Petroleum, from Venango County, Pennsylvania,* which, by indicating the commercial uses to which oil could be put, was the basis of the entire oil industry for fifty years, until the development of the internal combustion engine.[28]

Oil both helped and hurt Silliman. He, like Marsh, shared the robber baron psychology of the late nineteenth century. He was a born optimist: at heart an entrepreneur and a speculator. As perhaps the first member of the Yale faculty to serve as a consultant to business (from which, in his best year, he made almost $55,000), he helped to trigger silver and gold rushes and an oil boom in California. He was also an active promoter of the New Haven Gas Company, and his was the first house in New Haven to have gas lighting (1848).[29]

The Great California Oil Bubble of 1865 was caused by Silliman's ecstatic reports of oil in such quantities in Southern California that it was floating on the water off Santa Barbara and making great pools on the land. Silliman's opinions were used to help promote at least three companies for the area. Then, when the oil companies failed because the oil was not as easily accessible as Silliman had thought, or as pure as he had believed, and when the Bodie gold strike (which he helped to bring about) also ran into technical problems, Silliman's reputation began to suffer. It received a near fatal blow when it was revealed that the California oil he and two other scientists had analyzed, and on which he had based some of his reports, was not pure but had been altered by the addition of Pennsylvania oil. Many Yale faculty members, led by W. D. Whitney and William Brewer, had been critical of Silliman's consulting activities. Now it appeared he might be a swindler as well. So the worst fight in the history of the Yale faculty was set off. Finally Silliman found his position so uncomfortable that he resigned from both the faculty of Yale College and the governing board of the Sheffield Scientific School. He held on at Yale, however, as a member of the faculty of the Medical School, and he retained his appointment in the scientific school, though he was given no teaching assignment. He also kept his place on the board of the Peabody Museum. He successfully resisted the attempts to have him ejected from the National Academy of Sciences. And finally, as a recent chronicler of these battles has said, his reputation was "undoubtedly rehabilitated to a considerable extent" by later successful oil strikes in Southern California and by gold strikes at Bodie, California, which occurred toward the end of his life.[30]

There were other notable scientists on the Yale faculty when Porter took office, among them Elias Loomis, Chester Smith Lyman, Hubert Anson Newton, and Addison Emery Verrill. Of this group Verrill was by far the most important. He came to Yale in 1864 on the recommendation of Louis Agassiz and was made professor of zoology, but he had so few students that he taught physical and historical geology from 1870 to 1894. As Wesley Coe later remarked—and he could have said the same of other Yale professors—it was unfortunate that "so able an investigator" was burdened with so much routine teaching. Nonetheless he was, according to the *Dictionary of American Biography,* "one of the greatest systematic zoologists of America." [31]

Professors Elias Loomis, H. A. Newton, and Chester Smith Lyman might have been important investigators in astronomy, but the lack of adequate equipment prevented them from doing much. Loomis spent most of his time teaching and writing his incredibly successful textbooks on a wide range of subjects. His texts brought him wealth, and on his death he bequeathed his estate of $300,000 to Yale to be used solely for the support of the observatory. Never before had Yale received such a sum at one time.[32]

In addition to Verrill, the scientific school had several other fine scientists. Daniel Cady Eaton (B.A. 1857), a grandson of the great botanist Amos Eaton (who had studied under Silliman and Dr. Eli Ives early in the century) was appointed professor of botany in Sheff in 1864. Friends first offered to endow a professorship for him in Yale College, but according to the historian of the scientific school, it was intimated that the college had no use for botany. Fortunately, the scientific school needed such a professor for the agricultural courses it was to give under the Morrill Act, and that need was explained to Woolsey. Thus the $20,000 already raised was accepted, and Yale agreed to complete the endowment "when circumstances are favorable for so doing." Apparently, they never were. Eaton was immediately elected to the governing board of the scientific school, where he did most of his teaching. His most important scholarly work was *The Ferns of North America,* which appeared in two volumes in 1877 and 1880.[33]

Also working in agriculture, but far more influential in that particular field than Eaton, was Samuel William Johnson, who had studied under Norton in the School of Chemistry, the forerunner of Sheff, and then in Germany. He was appointed in 1856 professor of analytic chemistry in the scientific school and chemist to the State Agricultural Society. Johnson was a prolific author (7 books and 172 articles) as well as the founder of the first state agricultural experiment station. His two most famous books, *How Crops Grow* and *How Crops Feed* were translated into many foreign languages and gave him worldwide renown. According to the *Dictionary of American Biography,* "Although a man of modest and retiring disposition, he exerted a greater influence upon scientific agriculture in America than any one else of his generation." [34]

Other scientists of lesser note were also active at Yale when Porter took office—or were appointed during his presidency—but enough have been mentioned to make it clear that Yale's place as one of the leaders—if not *the* leader—of American science was still secure. It is, in fact, an oddity of Yale's history that at a time when Porter and many of the faculty of Yale College were striving with all their might to defend the old classical curriculum and the old college values, Yale's strength was greatest in science. Had the president and his followers chosen to develop that strength, Yale would no doubt have remained at the forefront in these important areas. Instead, Porter and others failed to pursue this great opportunity.

Yale was not nearly so strong outside mathematics and science despite the predilections of its officers, but it did have some notable men. By far the greatest of these was William D. Whitney, a graduate of Williams in 1845, who was appointed professor of Sanskrit language and literature in 1854. Whitney first came to Yale because E. E. Salisbury was the only professor of Sanskrit in the country. After studying with him, and then in Germany, he returned to America but was unable to find a position. In 1854 his old teacher endowed a chair of Sanskrit at Yale for Whitney. Salisbury retained the professorship of Arabic language and literature for two more years and then retired to continue his private studies (and to do his most important work). And when President Eliot as one of his first acts tried to attract Whitney to Harvard, Salisbury increased the endowment. This, it should be noted, was just one more of Salisbury's contributions to Yale. Not only did his own efforts make it great in oriental languages, but he brought Dana and Whitney to it and gave generously of his money, books, and manuscripts.

The importance of W. D. Whitney's work in Sanskrit, linguistic science, modern languages, and lexicography is unquestionable. His industry was staggering. In just over thirty years he produced 360 titles in the form of articles, translations, books, and edited works. He served the American Oriental Society from 1855 to 1890 variously as librarian, secretary, editor of publications, and president. At Yale he formed and headed the department of modern languages in Sheff, where he taught French and German to undergraduates.

Whitney, working with Thomas R. Lounsbury and later with William Rainey Harper, made the Yale Graduate School a center for the study of comparative philology and scientific linguistics. In the mid-1930s it could still be said that few American Sanskritists had not been trained under Whitney or one of his students.[35]

Thomas R. Lounsbury (B.A. 1859) was hired by the Sheffield Scientific School in 1870 to teach English, and the following year he was made professor of that subject. In that position the burly veteran of the Civil War was to work a revolution in the teaching of English in America. Lounsbury recalled that in his day in Yale College he had never studied or even heard the names of the authors of the great books of English or American letters. Nor had the situation changed by 1870. The major stress in English at Yale and elsewhere was on rhetoric, which has been described as "a science of

which the fertile sections are narrow and the deserts extensive."
Lounsbury and Whitney, later assisted by H. A. Beers in the college,
changed all that. When hired by the scientific school, Lounsbury insisted on the right to teach English literature and soon he had his
students reading Chaucer, Shakespeare, Milton, Dryden, Pope, and
the like for the beauty of what they wrote, not merely for its gram-
matical construction. The change was so successful, in fact, that for
the next twenty years college professors came to see Lounsbury to
find out about the course. Under Beers, whose great scholarly promise was never fulfilled, it even spread to Yale College, though there
Professor Northrop continued the old teaching method until he left
to become president of the University of Minnesota in 1884.

Lounsbury not only revolutionized the teaching of English, he
also made a significant scholarly contribution as well. The best of
his numerous books was his three-volume *Studies in Chaucer*. But in
scholarship as in teaching, Lounsbury felt thwarted. According to
Henry Seidel Canby, who experienced the disdain with which
Lounsbury treated his generally lackadaisical students, Lounsbury
would have earned national renown at another period in American
history, but at that time he "was just a professor of English, who, except among his fellow scholars, had only a local reputation." So he
turned upon his students and other scholars with anger and scorn.
Here Canby found the "pure thwarting, and warping, of a fine
mind." [36]

This impressive faculty—and there were others of lesser note who
might be included, but the list is already too long—was immediately improved by the addition of William Graham Sumner to the
faculty of the Academical Department. The selection of this outspoken leader of Young Yale so soon after the battles over the makeup
of the Corporation and the presidency speaks well for the strength
of the institution. That his election was opposed by some of the faculty is not surprising; that it did not prevent it completely, is.[37]

Sumner had been a tutor at Yale in the late 1860s, teaching math
one year and Greek in two others. Even then the difference between
his classroom technique and that of other faculty members was profound. Sumner did not just hear recitations, he taught. His class on
Plato, as his biographer noted, "opened up to his students the whole
world of Greek thought, and was as much an introduction to philosophy as it was practice in translation and drill in syntax." [38]

Wilbur Cross, a graduate in 1885, has left one of the best pictures of Sumner as a teacher:

To step from traditional courses of study into the large room of the Old Chapel for a recitation, half lecture, half quiz, by William Graham Sumner . . . was to step into a new and enlarged world. It took but three minutes to make the transition to this wide realm where land and population, capital, currency, banking, taxation, economic history, and political science were explored.

Sumner enlivened his course by the force of his powerful character, by using editorials and news stories from the day's papers to illustrate his points, never shutting down free discussion, and giving his students the feeling they were getting hard facts about important matters. Sumner did not know how to be diplomatic. He saw life as tough and hard, so he was tough and hard. His abrasive directness often must have infuriated his colleagues, but he did much to make Yale a better place.[39]

Retaining this great faculty during Porter's years became a problem. And though some excellent men joined the group, there were certain difficulties in attracting the best young teachers and scholars to Yale with Porter at its head. Charles R. Lanman, who had studied in Germany a further three years after taking his Ph.D. at Yale in 1873, rejected a tutorship at his alma mater and went to Johns Hopkins at a lower salary because, as he wrote, "I should very likely have to teach Algebra or something else that I don't know enough to put in your eye, and that 16 hours a week to immense classes. The result would be plainly just ruinous to my prospects." In 1880 Eliot hired this "scholar of unusual depth, precision, and imagination" to be professor of Sanskrit at Harvard.[40]

Minton Warren, who studied at Yale under Whitney, James Hadley, and Lounsbury, and then for three years in Germany, also declined an offer from Yale to go to Hopkins as associate in Latin at a lower salary. Late in life, he too would end up at Harvard.[41]

Why a young man might avoid coming to Yale to teach may be illustrated by the early career of Arthur Hadley (B.A. 1876) the son of James Hadley, whose death in 1872 was a severe loss to the boy and to the university as well. Young Hadley was a tutor in Greek in 1879–80, tutor in Latin the following year, and tutor in German in 1881–83. During these years he was also called upon to teach some

Roman law and also logic. Nothing he taught was in the field of his real interest, political economy. The life of a tutor, teaching what was needed, could hardly have been a happy one. Hadley finally resigned because he loathed teaching German, could not teach what he wanted, and could not find time to do any research. Only then did he get part of what he desired: he was appointed instructor in political science, without salary, in the Graduate School. He taught a course on "Railroads and Their Industrial Effects" the popularity of which caught the attention of the press because, as the *New York Sun* noted, "Into the banks, the manufactories, and the railway offices the young men are now going who formerly would have looked for a career only at the bar and in politics." This appointment also gave Hadley time to write *Railroad Transportation, Its History and Its Laws,* which helped to get him his professorship in 1886.[42]

Though the situation at Yale may have prevented several men from coming on the faculty, there were some good appointments. S. Wells Williams was made professor of Chinese language and literature in the Graduate School in 1877. Williams had spent most of his adult life in China and had helped Perry open Japan. Though an expert in his field, he seems to have attracted few students. Instead his time was spent revising *The Middle Kingdom,* which had first appeared in 1848 and which remained for many years the best book in English on China. Williams died in 1884. His subject was not again taught at Yale until his son was appointed to the faculty in 1893.[43]

Another important appointment was of difficult George Trumbull Ladd, who became professor of moral philosophy in 1881. William Adams Brown (B.A. 1886) recalled Ladd as "a man not only of considerable learning but real philosophical eminence. Unfortunately his method as a teacher was so dull that he repelled instead of attracting his students. He had, moreover, a very high opinion of his own attainments." Ladd's attainments, in fact, were great. He was a highly productive scholar who did much to acquaint Americans with the thought of post-Kantian German idealists. More importantly, his *Elements of Physiological Psychology* introduced Americans to "the study of psychology as an experimental science grounded on physiology." [44]

Brown found, however, that he learned much more about philosophy from a logic course given by Frank Bigelow Tarbell (B.A. 1873,

Ph.D. 1879) than he ever did from Ladd or President Porter. Tarbell taught Greek from 1876 to 1887 and logic from 1885–87. He was very popular with the students—even finding it necessary to give extra lectures to satisfy them. Tarbell held somewhat unorthodox views on religion, and it must be said in President Porter's favor that Tarbell remained on the faculty while he was in office. The more rigid Timothy Dwight dropped him despite his eleven years of service as tutor and assistant professor. Academic freedom was still so unheard of that there was not a murmur of anger over Dwight's act. Fortunately Tarbell was able to go on to a highly successful career as a classical archaeologist at the University of Chicago.[45]

Other faculty members—their tragedies and triumphs—could be described; but what seems obvious is that with such a faculty Porter could have easily made Yale a great modern university. And the failure to move forward at this time was doubly tragic. It hurt not only Porter's Yale, but prejudiced the institution's future for years.

In American educational history, the two great movements of the period from 1865 to 1900 were the elective principle for undergraduates and the rise of the university. Because of Porter—and no doubt he properly represented the beliefs of most Yale men: Corporation, faculty, and alumni alike—Yale was late to join both. Because of Porter the university got a belated and unbalanced development; because of him Yale was very slow to appreciate the real force of the elective movement—that serious, if somewhat misguided, attempt to adjust the curriculum to a new era. Yet it is unjust to blame him too much. Other roads were open to the Corporation and they, consciously and knowingly, chose to follow conservative Noah Porter. That Yale could have done otherwise is clear, for in this great age of the rise of universities the major names were Andrew White of Cornell, William Watts Folwell of Minnesota, Charles W. Eliot of Harvard, Daniel Coit Gilman of Johns Hopkins, and Frederick A. P. Barnard of Columbia—probably the most influential group of college presidents ever seen in America.[46] And three of the five were Yale graduates!

As the universities began to bloom under the ardent cultivation of their active presidents, Porter continued the traditional Yale policy of concentrating on the college. The other schools of the university were dependent on the personal activity of their individual faculties. This procedure, as George W. Pierson pointed out, produced an unbalanced development of the university.[47] In some cases, schools did well.

It will be recalled that the Divinity School was in desperate straits just as the Civil War began. But the arduous walking of the streets of New York and pounding on the doors of the wealthy which Timothy Dwight and others performed during the 1860s ultimately produced the buildings and money necessary to save the school from an early demise. When Dwight thanked Woolsey for helping to bring about this change, Woolsey replied, "With respect to helpfulness, I do not know that I have done anything for the Theological professors, except to allow them to raise their own salaries." As Dwight remarked, this was not only typical of Woolsey but of the general attitude toward the schools.[48]

In the 1870s two new dormitories, a chapel, and library were built for the Divinity School. New professorships and fellowships were added as well. In 1879 a year of graduate work was first offered. During Porter's years endowment rose from $295,882.19 to $413,-585.49. A small part of this increase was the gift of Mary A. Goodman, "of African descent," who left her life's earnings to educate men of her own color for the ministry. In recognition of her bequest, Mary Goodman was buried in the Yale lot in Grove Street Cemetery.[49]

Under the indifferent eye of the administration, other parts of the university fared less well than the Divinity School. The Medical School found the going very difficult. Since the faculty members received their only pay from fees and private practice, they had little time for fund-raising. And even when they tried, they were unsuccessful. Usually they found that representatives of the college had preceded them. Finally, in 1873, the faculty complained to the Corporation, "How long, on the present plan, can the Medical Department be continued?" In response, the fellows voted a few hundred dollars—but that was all.

Still progress was made. While no buildings were added, a chemical laboratory was constructed in their building on York Street. In curricular matters, the faculty was more successful. Despite the school's small enrollment, they began in 1871 to work, tentatively and incompletely to be sure, toward a graded course. In 1875, they began to insist on written exams and instituted a year-long course. In 1879, they finally completed the conversion to a three-year graded course. No longer would students receive degrees for little more than listening to lectures—all of the same level of difficulty—for a few terms. From that point on, after a written entrance exam the student was forced to pass through a three-year course of increasing difficulty, combining lecture, laboratory, and recitation, and ending in a written final examination. This move made Yale much more difficult than many of its competitors and caused an immediate drop in enrollment. The first class to go through after the change numbered only two, whereas none of the preceding four classes had graduated fewer than ten. As one historian of the school observed, "One of the constant features of the school's history in the nineteenth century is the almost unvarying support the faculty gave high standards, and there is not a little foundation for the claim that the Yale Medical Institution did poorly because it insisted on doing well."

Of perhaps even greater long-term significance, however, than the new graded course, was the beginning of active involvement by the Corporation in the affairs of the Medical School. By 1875, economic conditions in the school had become so bad that the fellows put the college treasurer in charge of the school's finances. And in 1877 the Yale Corporation increased its commitment by purchasing property near the Medical School so that the New Haven Dispensary could move there. The building was rented to the dispensary at a low cost with the proviso "that the Medical Faculty shall have the right to nominate the medical attendants, and the medical Students of the Institution shall have the privilege of viewing the medical and surgical practice." Thus at one blow the Corporation began to show greater concern for the future of the school and to improve the education the school could provide its students.

Another step forward came in 1885 with the severance, by mutual agreement, of the tie between the Medical School and the Connecticut Medical Society that had existed since the school was founded. Though the partnership had been beneficial in the early days of the school, it was necessary—if Yale was ever to achieve excellence—for the faculty alone to choose its own members, establish the curriculum, and examine candidates for degrees.

These steps only pointed toward the future. Throughout the

1880s the number graduating averaged only seven. Whereas the faculties in 1871 in *The Needs of the University* had said that the Medical School needed $200,000 to extend the period of study, give partial support to the existing professors and add a new one, increase the museum, and enlarge and repair the building, or at least $100,000 even to begin this pressing work, the school's endowment only went from $21,332.57 in 1871 to $37,236.91 in 1886 (of which over $9,500 represented a loan from the college).[50]

In the Law School the period of real trial began in 1869 with the death of Judge Dutton. He had been a professor in the school ever since 1847 and he had recognized, as his life came to a close, the dangerous position it was in. It existed in a single room in the Leffingwell Building, "which served," as the *College Courant* said in 1873, "at once for library, recitations, moot courts, debating societies and lounging place." With "its dingy walls, its ill-furnished shelves, . . . its inadequate accommodations," it was hardly a pleasant place. On top of this physical debility, Dutton had been the only professor since 1865.

After Dutton's death, the school was placed in the temporary charge of three young New Haven lawyers, William C. Robinson, Simeon E. Baldwin (B.A. 1861), and Johnson T. Platt. Though Woolsey expressed concern for its future, he seems to have lacked the energy to help the school. A solution to its problem could only come through his successor. Fortunately, even Porter was unwilling to see the Law School die, and he included in his inaugural address a reference to its importance to the university.[51]

One answer to the school's problems came without any action on the part of Yale. The need for a new courthouse suggested to members of the New Haven bar the desirability of locating the Law School library in the building, where they could use it. Hence it was decided, in 1871, to construct the third floor for the Yale Law School. The building was completed in 1872, and the school moved into its luxurious new quarters early in 1873. In 1872 the organization of the school was made more permanent by the appointment of Robinson, Baldwin, Platt, and Francis Wayland as professors of law. The following year Wayland, the oldest of the four by many years and by far the most distinguished (he was lieutenant governor in 1869–70), was made dean. He was, as Frederick Hicks has pointed out, "the first person to accept a Yale law professorship with the intention of devoting himself wholly to it, and he remained unique in this respect for many years thereafter." [52]

The new law professors had their problems. They had only twenty-one students in 1871 and their library amounted to a mere two thousand volumes. Fortunately, the pleas of the new group for support, backed by Woolsey, who was now teaching in the Law School, and by other members of the Corporation who finally bestirred themselves on behalf of the school, brought in money that saved the situation.

The enthusiastic new faculty rapidly increased the library to over seven thousand volumes. They even persuaded the Corporation, in 1873, to pay a librarian. This was the first salary ever provided in the Law School by Yale. It amounted to $400.[53]

Progress was made on other fronts as well. In 1876, two years after the celebration of the Law School's semicentennial, advanced courses in law and political science leading to the degrees of Master of Laws and Doctor of Civil Laws were offered. These were perhaps the first studies for a legal doctorate to be offered by an American law school.[54]

The promise of the new and aggressive Law School faculty was not, it must be admitted, entirely fulfilled. By rejecting the case method which Langdell was developing at Harvard and generally holding to the conservative textbook approach, the school did not move ahead in later years as fast as it might have. Nonetheless, it was in generally good shape at the end of Porter's presidency.[55]

When Woolsey's term in office came to a close, Yale still had the largest and the best graduate school in the country. But that is not saying very much. In 1870 there were only forty-four graduate students in the nation. Twenty-four of these were at Yale, eight at Harvard, six at Michigan, and three at Princeton. In 1871, the University of Pennsylvania became the second institution in the United States to grant the Ph.D. degree.[56]

Yale soon frittered away its ten-year lead. Little was done under Porter to build up the department. It was administratively reorganized in 1872, when an executive committee was set up to take care of admissions and programs of study. And for the first time, all students in the arts and sciences were listed together in the university catalogue. But that was all.[57]

The department controlled only the Ph.D. degree. The degrees in

civil engineering and mechanical engineering (added in 1872) were
granted by the Sheffield Scientific School, even though they were
graduate degrees. The Master of Arts degree remained in the hands
of the college, but the requirements for the degree were finally
raised in 1874. It will be recalled that by the nineteenth century the
M.A. had become something of a joke. James Hadley wrote of it in
1850,

The M.A. is no honor at all. It certifies indeed that a man has been B.A.
3 years earlier, but the first diploma certifies that. It proves also that a
man has paid 5 dollars to the College, but that only shows him 5 dollars
poorer than he was before. . . . It is notoriously no certificate either of
application or attainment. If it had been from the first what it now is, it
could not have come into use, and being what it now is, must ere long go
out of use or change its form to something significant.

It took, in fact, twenty-five more years to change. Harvard granted
the old degree in 1872 for the last time and Yale voted in March of
that year not to give the degree after 1874 "unless satisfactory evidence has been given that the candidate has been pursuing professional, literary, or scientific studies since receiving his first degree."
It was further provided that the degree would only be given after
one year's study and only if the candidate was a graduate of two
years' standing.[58]

   In 1874 another anachronism came to an end. On 24 June the
Corporation voted to cease granting degrees *ad eundem gradum* to
graduates of other colleges, of good moral character, who chose to
apply and pay a fee. From at least 1724 on, giving the same degree
to graduates of other colleges was a rather common practice at Yale.
The original procedure was, according to Martha Wright, "a kind of
intercollege courtesy, a relic of medieval tradition particularly prac-
ticed at Oxford, Cambridge, and Trinity College in Dublin." In
America it was especially useful because distances were so great that
a Yale man who lived in Boston might seldom be able to get to New
Haven, but would enjoy holding a degree from Harvard and being
associated with its alumni. To some, however, it appears to have
been merely one more diploma pelt to hang at their belt.[59]

   While Yale was improving its handling of degrees, others began to
grant the Ph.D. Harvard gave it in 1872, when its Graduate Department was formed, and even more significantly, Johns Hopkins first

did so in 1876. With Daniel Coit Gilman at its head, Hopkins was intended to advance scholarship and train graduate students. There, for the first time in America, the Ph.D. began to have real meaning.[60]

The existence of Hopkins and the weak Harvard school had an immediate effect on the Yale graduate department. Enrollment fell rapidly. From the academic year 1873–74 to 1876–77, the number of graduate students was sixty or above in every year but one. In 1877–78 it dropped to fifty, and the next year to forty-five. In Porter's last year only forty-two students were registered in the department. Though fellowships and scholarships increased from seven to seventeen during Porter's years in office, the number receiving Ph.D.s fell. From 1871 through 1879, Yale granted an average of just above five; from 1880 through 1886, the average was 2.7. A few men like Thorstein Veblen (Ph.D. 1884), who left Hopkins, or Edward Bouchet (B.A. 1874, Ph.D. 1876), probably the first Negro to receive the degree, came to Yale for what it could offer, but the promise that surely could have been fulfilled by a faculty that contained Sumner, Marsh, Gibbs, Whitney, Dana, and Lounsbury was not pursued with any interest by the college-oriented Porter. In 1871 in *The Needs of the University,* the committee of the faculties had said that everything remained to be done in the graduate area. It still remained to be done when Porter retired.[61]

Despite Porter, important things were happening at Yale in some fields. In 1876 the Peabody Museum of Natural History was completed, at last giving Yale a place to house its important and rapidly growing collections. Not to speak of Marsh's tremendous activity gathering bones, the mineralogical collection alone was the largest in America. The donor of the museum, financier and philanthropist George Peabody, was the uncle of Othniel Charles Marsh. Because of the persuasiveness of his nephew and his admiration for Benjamin Silliman, Sr., Peabody had decided in 1863 to bequeath $100,-000 to Yale to promote the natural sciences. In 1866, the year his nephew was made professor of paleontology, Peabody decided to increase the amount to $150,000 and give the money immediately, for a museum. Part of the amount was to be invested to provide for additions to the building and another segment was to be used for its care and for increasing its collections.[62]

An elaborate building was planned and in 1874–76 the north

wing was erected at the corner of Elm and High, opposite Alumni Hall. The new museum allowed the university's scattered collections to be brought together in one place for the first time. It also released President Porter and Treasurer Kingsley from the discomfort of sharing the old art gallery (then called the Treasury Building) with Marsh. From time to time, when the smell of chemical solutions used in cleaning specimens became too strong, Porter wondered if science could not advance with less odor.[63]

Soon after the completion of the museum, activity began for the erection of a first-rate observatory. Though the college and Sheff each had telescopes for teaching purposes (Sheff used "a model of the *Monitor's* gun turret" for its observatory), Yale had long lacked anything adequate for research purposes. It will be recalled that the Hillhouses and Oliver F. Winchester had donated land for an observatory. Winchester, with typical nineteenth-century optimism, hoped that by land speculation alone $500,000 could be raised for the purpose. With this in mind, an elaborate plan for an observatory was drawn up by R. G. Russell, and Winchester purchased the glass for the very large telescope it was expected to house. Unfortunately, the severe depression of 1873–78 wrecked these dreams and the plan remained on paper. With the return of more favorable economic conditions, activity began again. In 1879, the trustees turned all the land over to Yale, a Board of Managers was appointed by the university, and though land prices were still insufficient to complete the entire project, the sale was made and in 1882 it was voted to build a truncated and disjointed version of the plan. The managers had the institution verify thermometers and sell time to the state. Since standard time did not yet exist, there were many time zones in Connecticut, so the state was willing to pay $2,000 a year for the correct time according to astronomical observation. Soon these activities began to dominate the observatory and only after a fight in 1884 between those who favored research and those supporting the applied scientific endeavors, combined with a recession and the withdrawal of the contract with the state, did the observatory return to the primary research function for which it had been intended. The loss of income meant that William L. Elkin, who was appointed astronomer in charge of the heliometer in 1884, had to be paid by subscriptions from interested alumni.[64]

Despite the financial problems, a new heliometer built by the

Repsolds of Hamburg was provided, the "most improved instrument of its kind that had up to that time been produced." Using this instrument, Elkin made new and more exact measurements of stellar distances.[65]

If things were improving at the observatory toward the end of Porter's administration, such was not the case at the Art School. There, too, Yale was frittering away a great lead. With little money except what Mr. and Mrs. Street had provided, not much could be done to develop the school. Only by bringing in special exhibitions and charging admission was the director, John F. Weir, able to equip the classrooms of the building. Three professors gave all the instruction to the largely female student body (for Street's donation had come with the explicit proviso that the school was to be open to "pupils of both sexes"). No degrees were given.[66]

The most important school at Yale, next to Yale College, was the Sheffield Scientific School. Yet the college tended to look down on what happened in "darkest Sheff." That school, in fact, served the useful function of giving the college an excuse for not changing. Educational experiments could be tried at Harvard or Sheff—not in Yale College! The scientific school in its turn developed a complex about the college, and its jealous protection of its areas of interest was later to play a part in the decline of Yale as a scientific center. But that was still to come, for when Porter took office the school's patron saint, Joseph Earl Sheffield, was still alive; Eliot at Harvard was lauding Sheff as "at once an epitome of the past history of scientific institutions and a prophecy of the future"; and Sheff seemed to be dynamic, growing, and forward-looking.[67]

Like every part of the university, the scientific school needed money. In 1865–66 its entire income amounted to only $18,552.02. In 1868 the officers embarked on a campaign to raise an endowment fund of $250,000. It was hard going. Businessmen still felt college of any sort was a waste of time for those going into business, and most others who could afford to give were opposed to the new education. Thus it took several years to complete the drive. By 1872–73 income had risen to $50,236.19, of which some 16 percent came from the state land grant fund.[68]

These years mark the progressive legal separation of the Sheffield Scientific School from Yale. In February 1871, perhaps in doubt about the direction Yale would take under its new president, Joseph

E. Sheffield requested that the property of the school be vested in a board of trustees incorporated under Connecticut law. This was immediately done. Then, because of changes in the laws and the suggestion of Mr. Sheffield, who wanted to make sure his beneficiary was safe from unsympathetic Yale officers, a specific charter for the school was obtained from the state legislature in 1882.[69]

James Earl Sheffield remained the school's largest benefactor throughout Porter's presidency. In 1872–73 he had built North Sheffield Hall for Yale, thus allowing Verrill to come back from the Treasury Building and the professor of botany from his home. The department of dynamic engineering, holed up in the basement of the School of Fine Arts, also escaped to the fresh air of Prospect Street.[70]

The Sheffield Scientific School again faced a period of economic stringency during the depression of 1873–78, which forced it to turn to the university for money to cover its deficits (one of the first times the university came to the aid of a department) and, in 1876, to cut professors' salaries from $3,000 to $2,600.[71]

The school's economic problems were ended, for a time at least, by the death at the age of eighty-nine of Joseph Earl Sheffield. He left to each of his children one-seventh of his estate, and he treated his school in the same way, except that he also willed it his home and the surrounding land after the death of his wife and son. From the estate, the scientific school received in 1882 property valued at $591,463. This brought Sheffield's total contributions to the school to an estimated $1,100,000. No other donor would give Yale so much until the twentieth century.[72]

Sheffield was the perfect benefactor. Except for the general condition that the gifts were to be used "to promote the study of physical, natural, and mathematical sciences in . . . the 'Sheffield Scientific School,'" they came without strings. Furthermore, he did not interfere once money was given. He never concerned himself, the school's historian said, with the management of the institution. Seldom has a school been so fortunate in its benefactor.[73]

The Sheffield Scientific School was also fortunate in its faculty. With men like Whitney, Eaton, and Lounsbury, it was an exciting place. What interested most people, however, was its curriculum. The leaders of Sheff rejected both the old curriculum and the idea of absolutely free elections. Instead they prescribed specialization through the selection of a particular group of courses. Thus election was between groups rather than individual courses. The degree of Bachelor of Philosophy was given after three years.

The group option system—copied by White at Cornell (where its success was so great that his third freshman class, in 1871, was the largest in the history of American education up to that time), carried by Gilman to Johns Hopkins, and desired by Sumner for Yale College—seemed to many a perfect solution to the problems of the curriculum, for it allowed a certain amount of freedom to the student without sacrificing mastery of a subject. By 1870–71 the "most distinctly marked out" groups were (1) chemistry and metallurgy, (2) civil engineering, (3) dynamical (mechanical) engineering, (4) agriculture, (5) natural history, (6) pre-medical, (7) pre-mining, and (8) "select studies preparatory to other higher pursuits, to business, etc." The pre-medical group first offered in 1869–70 was the original course of this kind in the country. It was created by the responsive faculty when two students who intended to study medicine, T. Mitchell Prudden (Ph.B. 1872, M.D. 1875, LL.D. 1897) and Thomas H. Russell (Ph.B. 1872, M.D. 1875) found that there was no course combining zoology, botany, and organic and physiological chemistry. The course in dynamical engineering was also the first, according to Professor Trowbridge, who taught it, to have "for its object *exclusively* the preparation and training of young men for the pursuit of this comparatively new profession." [74]

Of greatest interest to the educational world, however, continued to be the course in select studies, or select course, for in some ways it was a standing rebuke to the old curriculum. The course had changed somewhat by 1870–71. Like his fellows in other groups, in the first year the select student studied German, English, math (descriptive and analytical geometry, spherical trigonometry, surveying and plotting), physics, chemistry, drawing, and one term of botany and "laws of health." After this introduction the students branched into their various specialties. The select student went on to study in his junior or second year mechanics (one term), modern European history (two terms), English literature (two terms), German (two terms), French (three terms), astronomy (one term), agricultural chemistry (one term), physical geography (one term), zoology (two terms), botany (two terms), mineralogy (one term), and drawing (one term). Senior year the select students studied the history of language for a full year ("Whitney's Language and the study of Language. Hadley's Brief History of the English Language"), French, botany and zoology, agriculture, agricultural chemistry and physiology, geology, human anatomy and physiology, and astronomy, and heard lectures in *"Military Science, History, Political Philosophy, International Law, Political Economy,* etc." After this full course, with its concentration on language and science (including laboratory work), the students were prepared, it was felt, for work in the modern world.[75]

Not only was the curriculum different but, unlike the college, the Sheff students had no dorms, no required chapel, no disciplinary marks, and no proctors. It was a whole new world.[76]

Things were very different at the college. There the old ways seemed to go on forever. Nonetheless an explosion was brewing that gentle, kindly, Noah Porter could not keep down. With men like Sumner and Dana on the faculty, the college could not be a stagnant backwater. While Porter might wish to avoid change, he must fail.

The Yale theory of education, as we have seen, was based on the idea that the old time curriculum was the best foundation for a young man's future life. It stressed discipline and training more than content. It "operated on the assumption," as George W. Pierson has well said, "that the better part of a college education was a training in good habits: habits of worship and devotion; habits of industry and exact study; good moral and physical habits; habits of square and manly dealing." Discipline was the key to the whole and unity a very important aspect. The cohesiveness created within a college class by the challenge of facing together all the same hard subjects, all in the same hard way, was highly valued.[77]

The old curriculum, at Yale and elsewhere, stood up well for hundreds of years—though there were some loud dissenting voices. It took the explosion of knowledge to kill it. As early as 1818, in fact, Professor Goodrich reported to President Day that the course of study was "so crowded" that time for the study of composition had to be stolen from other courses.[78] Modern languages and sciences scuffled for room in the crowded curriculum just as the traditional courses became less and less tied to the vocational demands of the students. The old program was becoming obsolete before most Americans really knew it. Porter was, in fact, defending a system that was largely dead. The senior year was no longer capped by the president's course on philosophy; instead it was a confusing hodge-podge of everything with too little time for anything.

One solution to the problem of the over-crowded curriculum was the erection of scientific schools like Sheff, where modern studies could be offered in an attempt to preserve the old curriculum else-where. But still room had to be found in the liberal arts for the ex-panded body of knowledge, and as a result crowding and condensa-tion of material continued. Another approach that grew out of this necessity was constantly to tamper with the curriculum: courses were shoved down into earlier years, even into secondary school, the amount of work was increased, exams were stiffened, entirely new courses were given junior and senior years. Still the problem re-mained. Under President Eliot, Harvard chose to reject the idea that one course was better than another and to allow students a free election of anything they wanted. Still another alternative was to allow the election of one of several lines of study, as the Sheffield Scientific School, Cornell, and Johns Hopkins were doing.

Yale College tried to preserve the old curriculum by tampering with it and by allowing those who wanted something else to go to Sheff for it. Nor were Porter and Yale the only ones who hoped to preserve the tried and true oldtime curriculum. Probably the major-ity of college presidents wished to do the same. Yet at a critical point in the history of American higher education, Yale was on the wrong side.[79]

At first this may not have seemed true. During the 1870s students continued to flock to Yale and the other conservative institutions. As Morison noted, "During the 1870's, Harvard enrolment had in-creased only 3.7 per cent, as against 37.3 per cent for Yale, 34 per cent for Princeton, and 61 per cent for Williams. Parents still pre-ferred to send their sons, and schools their pupils, to colleges with the traditional prescribed curriculum." Yet at Yale the gain was de-ceptive, for most of the increase occurred in the scientific school. The last class (1870) from the Academical Department to graduate under Woolsey numbered 120, while the class of 1880 was only 122. The number of Ph.B. degrees granted, however, rose from 27 in 1870 to 43 in 1880. Total freshman enrollment at Yale and Har-vard was almost exactly the same throughout the 1870s, but while Harvard's small growth came in the college, Yale's was all in the sci-entific school.[80]

Of course, Yale and the other conservative colleges did not stand still. At Princeton, President McCosh allowed a wide variety of electives in junior and senior years. Yale took a similar course. At the urging of James Dwight Dana, Hubert Anson Newton, and William Graham Sumner, in 1876 classics and mathematics were dropped as requirements in junior year and more science was added with some laboratory work included. Senior year was rearranged and the afternoons opened up for optional study. The only options available during three-fourths of the junior year were Greek, Latin, math, or French, but in Senior year a wide variety of choices was available. Still, as Professor Pierson notes in his excellent history of this period,

in the main the optionals [for they carefully avoided the use of the word electives] were in addition to, rather than in place of, any element of the old curriculum. They were placed in the afternoons, so as not to disturb the morning calendar of required studies. Mark also that more optionals were offered in the ancient languages than in any other discipline, even in Senior year—a year from which the classics had long since disappeared. This leads to the discovery that the new freedom of Junior year had been so safeguarded that the only optionals available until the very end of the year were Greek, Latin, mathematics, and French: that is precisely those studies which were no longer supposed to be required. Yet instead of spending a fraction of the year on each of three disciplinary subjects, a Junior *might* now study a single one throughout the year. And in certain fields he could carry his chosen subject still further in Senior year. By twentieth-century standards this would scarcely qualify as specialization. Yet for the first time it was possible to hope that it wouldn't be long before instructors could become pioneers and students begin to concentrate in really modern studies.

So to these provisions for slightly greater freedom, slightly greater variety, and slightly greater attention to science was added the whispered suggestion that the College should not rest content with elementary work. In such limited and indirect ways began the disintegration of the old Course of Instruction, the promise of a better day.[81]

Once the system was altered by the modest reforms of 1876, it became increasingly easy to question what remained. The result was the elective battle of 1883–84.

The forces pushing Yale to change were many. The new world being created in the latter part of the nineteenth century produced altered attitudes, as we have noted. Criticism of Yale College was voiced by some alumni and, more important, freshman enrollment began to decline in the eighties. Had Porter had his way, Yale would not have changed; but his faculty was not united behind him. Some of its ablest members, in fact, were against him. No university can resist the popular will without a largely united faculty.

The faculty discussed changes in the curriculum during 1883–84. Committees were appointed to plan the studies of the different years and finally a committee was delegated the task of harmonizing the various proposals and presenting the finished plan to the Corporation. The members of this final committee were Edward S. Dana (son of J. D. Dana), Sumner, George T. Ladd, and Tracy Peck. Dana and Sumner represented the physical and social sciences while Peck and Ladd upheld the classics and philosophy. Their differences forced them to compromise, but still they produced a report which freed more than half the junior year and 80 percent of the senior year from requirements. Sumner's hope for group options of the Sheff type was defeated by keeping the requirements of logic, psychology, physics, astronomy, and geology in junior year and psychology, ethics, and natural theology in senior year. A bow was made to the group principle by presenting the options as group subjects, but nothing prevented the student from browsing as he wished.[82]

The whole plan was hashed out in faculty meetings and with President Porter throughout the winter of 1883–84. Sumner added his public thoughts in his usual hard-hitting style in the *Princeton Review* for March 1884. It could hardly have helped his cause when he proclaimed in his article "Our Colleges Before the Country"

that college officers are, for many reasons, unfit for college management. They are exposed to all the pitfalls of every pedagogue. They have to guard themselves against the vices of dogmatism, pedantry, hatred of contradiction, conceit, and love of authority. They, of course, come each to love his own pursuit beyond anything else on earth. Each thinks that a man who is ignorant of *his* specialty is a barbarian. As a man goes on in life under this discipline he becomes more self-satisfied and egotistical. He has little contact with active life; gets few knocks; is rarely forced into a fight or into a problem of diplomacy; gets to hate care or interruption, and loves routine. Men of this type, of course, are timid, and even those traits which are most admirable in the teacher become vices in the executive officer. Such men are always over-fond of *a priori* reasoning and fall helpless the moment they have to face a practical undertaking. They have the whole philosophy of heaven and earth reduced, measured out, and done up in powders, to be prescribed at need. They know just what ,ought to be studied, in what amount and succession of doses. That is to say, they are prepared to do any amount of mischief at a juncture when the broadest statesmanship is needed to guide the development of a great institution. Certainly the notion that any body of men can now regulate the studies of youth by what was good for themselves twenty, forty, or sixty years ago is one which is calculated to ruin any institution which they control. It is always a hard test of the stuff men are made of when they are asked to admit that a subject of which they have had control would profit by being taken out of their control and intrusted to liberty.[83]

As he wrote these words, Sumner may well have been thinking of Ladd and President Porter. Ladd was willing to experiment as long as his subject of philosophy remained a requirement, and the president was not willing to change at all.

In any case, on 14 May 1884 the faculty approved the memorial drawn up by the committee only to be suddenly informed by the president that he disapproved of the whole scheme and would vote against it at the meeting of the Corporation. The committee was shocked. According to Sumner's biographer, "They had conferred with the president throughout the year on every detail, and apparently he had given his approval." The Corporation appointed a committee to confer with the faculty committee, only to be reminded that curricular matters were vested, by the Corporation's own rules, in the hands of the faculty. The faculty committee then took the only course that seemed open. They cornered Porter in his office and after two or three hours of pressure, they broke him down. E. S. Dana said, "It was a brutal procedure, but it was effective." [84]

The result was that the new curriculum was tried for one year, 1884–85, as an experiment and then, in 1885, after voting that Porter's course on "the Evidences of Christianity" must remain a required course, the Corporation approved the change. That Porter had not altered his ideas at all but merely succumbed to the pressure was revealed in his article "Greek and a Liberal Education," which appeared in the September 1884 *Princeton Review*. He strongly attacked Harvard's plan to drop Greek as a required subject and took direct issue with the idea that one subject might be as good as another in a liberal education. His concern was even greater when he discovered, after the article was written, that Harvard had gone, as he put it in a footnote, "even farther than we had supposed, inasmuch as not only Greek but Latin and Mathematics are remanded to the Electives, while, with a singularly pointed defiance of the old traditions, the only studies which are prescribed are Rhetoric and English Composition, German and French, Physics and Chemistry." [85]

Despite the relatively minor changes in the curriculum, the picture of Yale College education remained depressing. The faculty, except for a few, were aloof disciplinarians. The students, as Veysey has noted, "betrayed many of the symptoms of a deeply disloyal subject population." They used "ponies" most of the time. They stole exams whenever they could and cribbed on them when they could not. Some later remembered their days at Yale with hot anger. The strongest public blast came from Harlow Gale (B.A. 1885) of the psychological laboratory of the University of Minnesota. In 1902 he still felt indignation over the way he had been taught classics. The sciences were little better. In the main they were still taught by the old lecture and demonstration method. Gale concluded, "In none of these sciences was any apparent effort made to reveal the real stuffs, forces, and laws of nature to us and therewith to arouse a wonder and admiration of nature which should enlarge our petty intellectual Ptolemaic horizon to the modern gigantic Copernican scale." Mathematics "were made unadulterated discipline in self-denial," English language and literature "was considered the greatest snap in college," French and German were studied too late "to get beyond the grammar and reader," and in philosophy they "were stuffed with the dry bones of dates, attenuated verbal abstractions, and dictated distinctions which were as indigestible to us as an ostrich diet." Not all was completely dark: Sumner gave them an "abiding and growing interest in economic, political, and sociological subjects"; E. J. Phelps, Kent Professor of Law, was a great teacher who broadened them through his undergraduate course in elementary law; and Frank Tarbell's elective course on Mill was so stimulating that he had to continue the course without credit so the students could hear and discuss more. But the broadening influence that should have

been provided by Peabody Museum and the Art Gallery was nonexistent. So too was the broadening influence of teachers doing research,

for we never saw nor heard of any of our instructors doing any original
work. . . . Consequently we had no idea of the sifting of evidence, the
patience and labor necessary thereto, no example or practice in the use of
the inductive methods of disentangling this knotty world into its causal
relationships and laws, and no cultivation of the critical spirit and caution which is so decidedly essential to any man's taking a place in this
complicated civilization.

They knew of O. C. Marsh and his bone collection but thought him
an "eccentric creature." Apparently they had never even heard of
Willard Gibbs. The main virtues Gale found in his Yale career were
in the democracy and competitiveness of its student life.[86]

Though some students may have criticized the system, most were
like Wilbur Cross, who did not question it but merely "sawed
wood." [87] It is clearly a damning critique of Yale—and perhaps of
American society as well—that with a senior faculty as good as
Yale's, the teaching was as bad as it was.

Shortly after the elective battle of 1883–84 Porter announced his
intention to resign. This marked the end of an era, for he was the
last representative of the old Yale. His presidency was marked by
battles: it had been preceded by Young Yale and reached a climax
with the elective struggle of 1883–84. In 1879–80 Porter had
clashed with William Graham Sumner over Sumner's use of Spencer's *Study of Sociology* in his undergraduate class. Porter, who
thought the book attacked "every Theistic Philosophy" and would
"bring intellectual and moral harm to the students," formally objected to it, "As I am presumed to authorize the use of every textbook." Sumner was outraged. He went to Porter and explained that
"with Mr. Spencer's individual opinions on the matter of religion I
have nothing to do, but this work on sociology is the only book of
the kind in the English language." He threatened to resign if he
could not use it. There the matter rested until Sumner discovered
late in 1880 that Porter had assured the Corporation in June that
Sumner would no longer use the book. Nor did he do so, for he decided that the excitement had destroyed its usefulness. But in the

winter and spring of 1880–81, in anger over Porter's act Sumner withdrew from administrative duties and began to look for another position. In June 1881 he wrote the Corporation and permanent officers of the college a long letter in which he defended his position. He said explicitly, "I have no controversy with the question whether the President has a veto on textbooks. I do not admit that he has it, and I do not know of any college officer who admits it." The question, he said, "involves rights and interests which no honest teacher ever ought to concede." Later scholars have judged Sumner's letter to be "an important document of academic freedom." As far as Yale was concerned, Sumner neither resigned nor used the book. But Sumner felt he had upheld the point and won a moral victory. He was probably right, for censorship of textbooks never occurred again at Yale.[88]

Porter's presidency was not all unpleasant clashes. In fact, as Timothy Dwight looked back on it after his own term had ended, he felt it was a time of noticeable forward movement. Physically, there were great changes: Marquand Chapel, North Sheff, West and East Divinity, the Trowbridge Library, Peabody Museum, Battell Chapel, the Yale Boat House, Sloane Physical Laboratory, the observatory and offices for it, Lawrance and Dwight Halls, and Henry Farnam's gift of his house for a president's residence all came during these years. It was true that the college had grown little, but the number of students in the entire university had increased from 755 in 1871 to 1,076 in 1886. In finances as well there had been growth. While the drive for a general university fund, the Woolsey Fund, amounting to $500,000, was a failure and only brought in $168,000, large donations were received at other times. It has been estimated that the buildings alone represented $800,000 and the endowment had been doubled by the addition of nearly a million dollars. Almost half of this had been in the new category of university funds—funds to be used for all and not just for one school.[89]

Despite these material achievements, which were to a great extent due to the efforts of Thomas A. Thacher, the chief fund-raiser of the administration, Porter's presidency cannot be viewed without a feeling of sadness: sadness that for fifteen years of a period of enormous change in America's colleges and universities, Yale was run by a man who was opposed to change; sadness for Porter, who was the wrong man at the wrong time.[90]

Franklin B. Dexter, who was secretary of the Corporation, registrar of the college, and assistant librarian throughout Porter's presidency, and who became Larned Professor of American History during it, gives a touching picture of Porter's last years:

When he reluctantly laid down the presidential duties in 1886, in his 75th year, he had retained them to a greater age than any one of his predecessors, although no doubt to himself he seemed quite as capable as when ten years younger. I do not know what suggestion led to his resignation; but when the spur to effort was withdrawn, his powers speedily failed. There was something inexpressibly melancholy in the sudden relapse into old age; but this was no justification for the unfeeling manner in which he was treated as no longer a person of influence or consideration.[91]

The truth is that Noah Porter was a good man who was bad for Yale. It would have been better, perhaps, if the Corporation had accepted Woolsey's suggestion in his *Historical Discourse* at the sesquicentennial that the presidency should be rotated among the professors. James Dwight Dana had crowed, just after news of Peabody's gift to Yale, "The fact is that Yale is going to be largely rebuilt, and all at once! The time of her renaissance has come." Yale was largely rebuilt, but there was no renaissance because of Porter. Thus it is better to recall Porter not as a president but as a man of whom a graduate could write,

> Alike all loved him: careful student, drone,
> Scapegrace or steady man. . . .[92]

14

Beginnings of Change

The Yale Corporation hardly hesitated in its choice of a successor to Noah Porter. Though several laymen were considered, Timothy Dwight, an ordained minister and grandson of the first president of that name, was selected on 20 May 1886.[1]

This quick election did not indicate that the alumni were satisfied by the reforms of 1872. For perhaps a decade thereafter they had been quiet, but the whole question of the makeup of the Corporation was reopened when Simeon Eben Baldwin (B.A. 1861), professor of Constitutional law, corporations, and wills in the Law School, devoted a paper delivered at the New Haven Colony Historical Society to the right of the Corporation to select laymen for its board. This set off another dispute over the nature of the charter and the right of the fellows to choose not only lay board members but also a lay president. When Porter in 1885 announced his decision to resign, the point ceased being academic. *The Nation* again turned its attention to Yale and opined that while Yale had changed in recent years, it continued to cling

pretty stoutly to the original theory of its establishment. It is still an institution practically governed by a few clergymen of a single denomination in a single State. It is still insisted by the believers in the old theory that the first requisite for a President is that he shall be a clergyman of the "orthodox" church. The conservative party may carry their point in the election of a new President, but they will only postpone the inevitable. A great modern college cannot be permanently conducted upon the same lines as a colonial divinity school.[2]

But Yale was not yet ready to change. Despite the presence on the board of alumni representatives who had replaced the state senators in 1872, the clerical successor trustees still held control, and their conservative bent was revealed by the selection of Dwight as president. Had Dwight been chosen in 1871 it would have represented a significant step forward. But the world had changed in fifteen years and Dwight had not. His election meant that Yale would only slightly alter its course.

Timothy Dwight was a delightful man. Born to a wealthy family, raised in Norwich, and graduated from Yale in 1849, he had done graduate study in the university for two years and then served as a tutor for four more years before going to Germany for further study. Dwight always took pride in the fact that as a tutor he had begun to break down the suspicion and opposition between faculty and students. His attitude toward the undergraduates is best exemplified by one small incident. While chasing two students for some prank, he called out to them, "Gentlemen, if you do not run a little faster, I shall be obliged to overtake you." As Roland Bainton so charmingly put it, "His youth was marked by a rollicking gaiety and his age by a genial drollerie, which beguiled alike his pupils and his colleagues." [3]

Dwight's main concern, as revealed in his 1870–71 articles on the future of Yale, was the university: "The first and most important work to be done in the years immediately before us is, as we believe, a work of unification." The president must actively promote the growth of all departments. Though the college would remain an important part of the whole, it would no longer dominate the entire university. Dwight's career since 1858 had been spent in the Divinity School, so his sympathy for the departments hanging on the fringes of the college was based on personal experience.

To accomplish the end of unifying the university, Dwight thought first that greater aid should be given to those departments that needed it and that every officer should labor for every department. Second, the various faculties should meet together to consider matters that concerned them all. Third, a large endowment fund was needed for general university purposes. And finally, the president must be president of all and not, as formerly, of just the college.[4]

Dwight's ideas about the importance of the university derived not only from his own experience but also from his heritage. Ever conscious of his grandfather, the first President Dwight, Timothy Dwight the younger always advanced while looking backward: his thoughts constantly turned to what his grandfather had done to begin the university, and he considered his task to be the completion of that work.[5]

The second Timothy Dwight was inaugurated on 1 July 1886. He immediately began to convert his fifteen-year-old ideas into reality. His first step was to convince the Corporation to change the name of the place to Yale University. Though there were some, like ex-President Porter, who opposed the move, the Corporation approved at its meeting in October 1886. By the end of May 1887, the alteration was a legal fact. Henceforward Yale College was only the undergraduate liberal arts department of Yale University. Even more important was the fact that Dwight, right from the start, acted as president of the whole university. He refused to teach in Yale College so that he would have time to devote himself to all the parts of the university. He attended the meetings of all the faculties. Where Porter had appeared only a few times at the Sheffield Scientific School, and then on minor matters like trying to make the Sheff students attend chapel, Dwight was constant in his attendance at meetings there and worked actively to promote the development of all parts of the university.[6]

Dwight put a dean at the head of each school that did not yet have one. He had called for the appointment of a dean for the college in 1870–71 and Porter had finally (and most informally) picked Henry Parks Wright (B.A. 1868) for that post in 1884. According to Arthur Hadley, it was Wright who allowed Dwight to act as president of all. Dwight liked to deal with students and parents and he continued to act as dean of the Divinity School for nine years after he became president. But Wright at least forced him to stop dealing personally with college disciplinary matters and other minor concerns that the Yale president had once wasted his time upon. Without these duties, he was able to find "the time for the work of administrative organization which brought honor to him and Yale." [7]

Dwight brought a quickening in the whole institution. Enrollment began to move upward again. In his first six years in office, for the university as a whole it rose from 1,076 to 1,969. Money began to flow in and new buildings to go up. That Yale had not entirely changed, however, was indicated by the removal from the faculty of Frank B. Tarbell, Alfred Lawrence Ripley (later to return as a fellow), and Ambrose Tighe. It was whispered that their departures were brought about by the president because he was dissatisfied with their religious views. Here, too, Dwight followed his grandfather.[8]

The new president was assisted in bringing some change to old Yale by the fact that, unlike Woolsey and Porter, his predecessor was not elected to the Corporation. He was also freed by the deaths of Thomas A. Thacher and Treasurer Kingsley. Naturally the loss of these two men in 1886 just as his presidency was beginning seemed serious to Dwight. In fact, however, their absence gave him a greater chance to institute his own ideas. The death of Kingsley allowed Dwight to become acting treasurer and thus learn more about the college finances than any recent president. Since Dwight felt that so many of the needs of the university could be tied to the lack of money, this information must have been most useful. He had been critical at least since 1870 of the failure of the leaders of Yale to search more aggressively for funds. Now he attempted to remedy that shortcoming.[9]

Dwight's presidency got off to a successful financial start with the donations of $100,000 by Simeon B. Chittenden for an addition to the library and $125,000 by Mrs. Miriam Osborn for a new building containing lecture and recitation rooms. In the first three years alone income increased by over 25 percent and by 1899 it had more than doubled. In 1886 it had amounted to $305,918.64, and by 1899 it had reached $776,767.28. The rise in the funds of the various departments was equally spectacular: [10]

Permanent Funds	31 July 1886	31 July 1899
University	$489,683.31	$1,636,975.79
Academic	941,246.53	1,568,278.07
Theological	413,585.49	646,810.16
Sheffield	152,223.01	405,907.53
Medical	27,651.57	105,794.13
Law	11,600.00	82,813.77
Art	75,200.00	103,250.00
Music	———	5,000.00
TOTAL	$2,111,189.91	$4,554,829.45

Clearly the university had come a long way since 1886, though it was still very poor compared with Harvard. Yale had, in fact, increased its funds at a greater rate than Harvard, rising some 300 percent from 1876 to 1900. Harvard gained something more than 250 percent, but since Harvard started the period with $5 million, the result was that it had $13 million in 1900 compared to Yale's $5 million. Anson Phelps Stokes, who became secretary in 1899, explained the discrepancy to John D. Rockefeller by saying it was "Noah Porter writ large." Of course he oversimplified. One cause of the difference would seem to have been the fact that Harvard was located in one of the country's great financial centers while Yale was in the small town of New Haven. Its citizens, while generous to an amazing degree, could not match the Boston philanthropists. Nor were there yet enough wealthy alumni, though the number was growing rapidly, to overcome that lack. Hence while Yale's finances increased noticeably under Dwight, the gap between Yale and Harvard in dollars widened. And this comparative poverty continued to hinder the drive for a great university in New Haven.[11]

Nonetheless, Yale did come up with the most original of fundraising schemes during Dwight's presidency. On 23 June 1890, in response to "a widespread sentiment among Yale graduates in favor of some systematic endeavor to increase the resources of the University," the Corporation voted "to establish a fund to be known as the Alumni University Fund." This was, as Merle Curti has pointed out, the beginning of "the organized effort to institutionalize philanthropic support" for colleges. The first year, 1890–91, 385 alumni gave just over eleven thousand dollars. It took fifteen years to reach an annual sum of $100,000, and not until 1915–16 did the fund collect that amount or more consistently. Amazingly, despite this success other colleges and universities took years to adopt the idea.[12]

In addition to increasing the endowment funds and beginning the Alumni Fund, Dwight rebuilt the campus. Of the twenty-nine buildings Yale owned when he took office, he tore down six and added twenty-one (more than Porter and Woolsey combined), fifteen by construction and six by purchase. Two chemistry laboratories, a library, several dormitories, an elaborate gymnasium, two classroom buildings, and a new Law School were among the most important structures built during his presidency. On top of that, Battell Chapel was enlarged and the Medical School entirely repaired and improved.[13]

The most controversial building Dwight put up was Osborn Hall. The gift of Mrs. Miriam A. Osborn, initiated by her lawyer, John W. Sterling (B.A. 1864), who would himself later become the university's greatest benefactor, Osborn Hall was announced for the important College and Chapel Street corner of the developing Old Campus. The problem was less the incredible architecture (it was once described as "that fantastic dream in stone perched like a squatting toad with open lip") than that it would necessitate removing the fence, the favorite gathering place of the students. Even Timothy Dwight did not want to tear the fence down, but he feared to alienate a donor from whom more might be expected. Also, it was the first big gift of his administration. So he agreed to the removal of the fence. The students, joined by twenty-one hundred alumni, petitioned against the destruction of the sacred fence. As Welch and Camp remarked, "Land was valuable, but land could be bought. Not all the money in the world could buy the Yale Fence." [14]

But the fence went and in its place rose Osborn Hall. It was the first building constructed following Dwight's architectural prescription as outlined in his articles of 1870–71: that not only should buildings be of stone, "the glory of architecture," but those on the old campus should have a double frontage, facing both the street and the quadrangle. Thus Osborn faced the corner, Welch Hall (1891) had a door opening on College Street, and Vanderbilt Hall (1894) had its court on Chapel Street. Dwight had also suggested that the college should consult the citizens of New Haven on its building plans, but it is not recorded that they approved of the plans for the "toad."

Dwight's scheme for the Old Campus, as outlined in 1870–71, was for a quadrangle of buildings surrounding a chapel which would stand, symbolically, in the middle of the square. All other buildings within the quadrangle would be removed. The construction of Battell Chapel in 1874–76 at one corner destroyed part of the plan, but Dwight still dreamed of his great, open square. The only building he hesitated over was Connecticut Hall. Fortunately, before he got to it there was organized resistance from officers, faculty, and alumni, or that oldest Yale building would have fallen to the wrecker's ball. Dwight later confessed that "his greatest regret was that he had not torn" it down.[15]

Like his grandfather, Timothy Dwight added by purchase much land to the Yale campus. But the expansion of Yale alarmed the city. As Henry Seidel Canby remarked, the relationship between the town and the college was difficult "since there was always some doubt in the minds of the town folk whether the college was an asset or a parasite. The town with its college was like a woman's club committee with a celebrity in tow, a credit to them but also an embarrassment and sometimes a nuisance." In the 1890s the city tried to tax all university buildings used partially or wholly as dormitories, dining halls, or gymnasiums, since they were not used for education. The university replied that a college had always been considered a place to live and therefore these buildings were tax exempt. The case went all the way to the state supreme court, where the court agreed with Yale.[16]

Yale grew under Dwight not only in funds, buildings, and property, but in students and faculty. Whether it was all Dwight's doing or not, or whether Yale was just sharing in the general rise in college attendance that began after 1885, we cannot know. What is clear is that there was an immediate change. The freshman class that entered in September 1886 had some 30 more members than that of September 1885, and thereafter freshman enrollment increased steadily, as it did throughout the university, so that in 1893–94 there were 1,000 students registered in the college for the first time, and over 2,000 in the university. By 1898 the largest college graduating class in history departed from the university 301 strong, and in Dwight's last year over 2,500 were enrolled in the university with 1,224 in Ac and 567 in Sheff. Dwight pointed with pride to these figures, noting that one-third of all the graduates of Yale had received their degrees during his presidency. What he did not or could not recognize, however, was that the college enrollment stopped growing in 1896. All was not right at Yale.

The students, though they continued to come from all over the United States, were different from their predecessors. For the first time, business as a career had become a significant goal for the undergraduates. Whereas in Dwight's own class of 1849 only 9 of 94 had gone into business, 71 of 182 members of the class of 1891 chose that field. And while the learned professions still garnered almost two-thirds of all the graduates of 1891–93, a swing that had first become evident during the Civil War was now clearly under way. Businessmen themselves protested against it. One study gives some reasons for their opposition:

One element of it was the belief that higher learning undermined the rugged personal qualities necessary for success. Success demanded a strong will, diligence, persistence, ambition, good health, and self-discipline, qualities which colleges allegedly crippled and dwarfed in their concentration on the development of mental faculties. Some observers argued that few young men left college with their health unimpaired, while others expressed concern over the morals of those who spent four years in the fleshpots of college. There was a widespread feeling that no college man could qualify as a paragon of moral virtue, so, consequently, no prospective creditor or employer would trust him. He was also thought to be deficient in determination, drive, and backbone.[17]

Though it was still true in 1900 that 84 percent of the eminent businessmen listed in *Who's Who in America* had no college education, a change had already set in. As Charles Eliot noted, successful businessmen, despite what they said, sent their sons to college for the prestige involved. In addition, the economic system was losing some of its free-wheeling aspects, the organization man was beginning to appear, and apparently colleges did an adequate job of training organization men. But the presence of young men attending college as a road to business put additional pressures on the curriculum, while those coming to Yale only because of their families' wishes further promoted the rise of the extracurriculum.[18]

As the student body grew and changed, so did the faculty. In 1871, when Porter had taken over, the faculty numbered 71 men. Under him it had grown to 114. When Dwight was inaugurated it had reached 120, and he added 140. Of the total faculty of 260 when he retired, there were 120 professors and assistant professors and 140 instructors on term appointments.[19]

In 1870–71 Dwight had noted that one of the most urgent needs was for either the abolition or the modification of the tutorial system. Dwight basically approved of having young men teach the undergraduates part of the time, but he suggested that graduate students, or at least men intending to go into teaching, might be selected for the position rather than almost automatically choosing the college salutatorian or valedictorian, which often led to mistakes. Porter followed this suggestion in part and Dwight pursued it further. Many of his tutors were graduate students and, he remarked with satisfaction in his *Memories,* all but one of his appointees had gone into teaching.[20]

Dwight's presidency saw the appearance on the faculty of some famous names. Prior to his inauguration, Arthur T. Hadley, who had been serving as an instructor in political science in the Graduate School and receiving fees for his salary, was appointed Yale's first professor of political science. The Corporation noted that it was not "at present able to make themselves responsible for any permanent salary in connection with this chair," but Henry Farnam, donor of Farnam Hall, came forward and provided a part-time salary of $1,600 for five years. Since Hadley was still teaching only part-time, this appears to have been satisfactory. At the end of five years, Hadley became a full-time member of the faculty, was appointed to a professorship of political economy, and received a full salary. From this point Hadley began to teach undergraduates as well as continuing his graduate courses. At the same time he coached the tennis team and debating, edited the *Yale Review* founded in 1892 and often wrote for it, and the same year became the first dean of the Graduate School.[21]

One of Dwight's finest appointments was of William Rainey Harper (Ph.D. 1875) as professor of Semitic languages. Harper, whom a great teacher, William Lyon Phelps, thought was never surpassed as a teacher, attracted students to the study of Hebrew in the Divinity School, and when he was appointed Woolsey Professor of Biblical Literature in 1891 (while still retaining his other chair) undergraduates and graduates alike flocked to his course on prophetic literature. Harper, it might be noted, was already being approached by Rockefeller and those working to found the University of Chicago, and this is probably why he was given "an extraordinary appointment, including two chairs held at a salary and a half, an assistant, leave for travel in Europe at full salary, and a cash advance." Despite all that Harper left for Chicago in 1891. Dwight, who believed it was disloyal of any instructor to think of going elsewhere, must have considered Harper as something of a traitor. No doubt his opinion did not improve when Harper took five faculty members from Yale for his new university, although only one, William I. Knapp, was at the professorial level. Knapp, who taught Romance languages, left because he was disturbed over the continuing preponderance of appointments in the classical languages at Yale. But Dwight could still take some satisfaction in the fact that more of Harper's new faculty had been trained at Yale than at any other institution.[22]

On the whole, excellent faculty appointments were made during these years, but Dwight's freedom of action was severely limited by the rule of the faculty—a rule that was made a formal part of the Corporation by-laws during his presidency. For the Yale faculty was incredibly conservative. William Lyon Phelps's troubles were most revealing. In the 1890s, when Phelps began to teach, the old line between faculty and students still remained. As Phelps explained, "In the traditional teaching at Yale, formality was the rule. Nearly all the members of the Faculty wore dark clothes, frock coats, high collars; in the class room their manners had an icy formality; humor was usually absent, except occasional irony at the expense of a dull student." Phelps thought there was "a blight, a curse on the teaching," and with his great enthusiasm and easy manner he tried to exorcise it. The result was that he became popular. Nothing could have been worse for his future, for popularity led the faculty to "feel that the candidate must have stooped to conquer." Soon he was warned to look elsewhere for a job. As he recalled, "I do not believe any member of the Faculty ever received so many invitations to leave Yale that came *from the inside.*" Finally, after a bitter fight within the faculty, Phelps was appointed an assistant professor of English literature, only to be turned down three years later for a professorship and passed over for a younger man. President Dwight and the fellows approved that selection but then proceeded to elect Phelps as well. The faculty rejected his appointment. It took two years more before he was finally made a full professor.[23]

While the appointment of men like Phelps was a significant step in breaking down the barrier between faculty and students, even more important may have been the existence of Dean Wright, whose selection has been referred to. Under Dwight, Wright took over disciplinary duties from the president and faculty and thus relieved them of that onerous task. No longer would they have to be, in quite the same way, both teachers and rulers.[24]

The lot of the faculty members was also improved by the institution of a pension plan in 1897. No longer were they forced to continue teaching until death, or incapacity, intervened. The effects of the plan were not immediately felt, but under Hadley it helped, along with death, to remove one-third of the entire body of professors in a four-year period.[25]

When Timothy Dwight viewed the future of Yale in 1870–71, the first specific department that he turned his attention to was the Graduate School. The presence of graduate students residing at the college, Dwight felt, "is an honor to their instructors, as well as a continual inspiration to the undergraduates who are following them." The Graduate School formed "one of *the essential parts* of the university, without which its life cannot, by any means, be complete." Yet this segment of the university was the last to be provided for. "A quarter of a century has . . . passed away and we still see only the small beginnings—two or three young men entering this section of the Department from year to year, and no instruction except from professors who are overburdened with other work." No one, he felt, could "fail to see that the work of this part of the institution is, mainly, a work of the coming era." At the time Dwight wrote, instruction in the school largely entailed a student consulting a professor. There were few regular courses. By the time Dwight became president progress had been made. Where twenty-three courses had been listed in the school in 1871, sixty-one were given when Dwight took over, and the existence of university funds gave the school some financial backing.[26]

Dwight did much to improve the school. Funds were raised. Scholarships and fellowships were established. The Department of Philosophy and the Arts had been reorganized in 1872, and at that time the Graduate School was established to take charge of all advanced instruction in the liberal arts. A dean of the school, Arthur Hadley, was appointed in 1892. Hadley claimed that he was only dean of the courses of instruction, and he may have been right since the school did not even have an office. In 1894 an administrative committee of twelve men was set up and a dean's office was opened in a house near where Harkness Tower now stands. Though it shared a floor with the university paint shop, the existence of an office did mark a step forward. In 1895 Andrew Phillips, professor of mathematics, was made dean. To stress the importance of the appointment the university found it necessary to state clearly that the position was "equal in authority and dignity to the deanships in law and medicine."[27]

The year 1892, which saw the appointment of a dean of the Graduate School, also marked its opening to women who wished to study for the Ph.D. Twenty-three immediately enrolled. In fact, women had long been attending courses with the permission of the instructor, but this was their first official entrance into the program. The first women graduate students were a most impressive group. Of the 110 women who received the Ph.D. from 1892 through 1916 the greatest number (40) came from Smith, Vassar, and Wellesley, but there were others from universities and colleges in such states as California, Washington, Idaho, Illinois, Kansas, Nebraska, Iowa, Ohio, Missouri, Mississippi, and Texas. They took their degrees in sixteen different fields ranging from astronomy and botany through Semitic and biblical language and literature and zoology, but most (37) studied English language and literature. After graduation 90 percent (99) went on to careers and 76 went into education: 64 were in higher education and over a third (35) became full professors.[28]

The size of the graduate body increased significantly under Timothy Dwight. Whereas only 42 students had been enrolled in 1885–86, there were 283 (including 40 women) in the department by 1898–99. The number of courses had risen to over two hundred. Accompanying this growth was an attempt on Dwight's part to make it easier for faculty members to teach in the school. For the first time college professors were relieved of some undergraduate teaching when they offered graduate courses and some professors were appointed with the specific understanding that they would instruct graduate students. The growth of the department did have some drawbacks, however, for the increase in students forced a concomitant growth in the number of courses. As a result many graduate courses differed little from undergraduate offerings, and in 1892 more than 45 percent were college courses merely open to graduate students.[29]

Even in the Graduate School the conservatism of the Yale faculty was a problem. Wilbur Cross, following the example of William Lyon Phelps in the college, decided to give a graduate course on the English novel from Defoe to Scott. He was unaware when he announced this decision that Phelps had been forced to drop the course because of the opposition of older faculty members. Cross soon received a message from President Dwight asking him not to give the course. Since Cross felt this was, in effect, a demand, he "acceded immediately." Only the insistence of Thomas Lounsbury, who saw the dean, the president, and various powerful professors, finally brought permission to teach the course in 1897–98. The following year Phelps gave a course in the college on the American novel. Thereafter the bars came tumbling down.[30]

An important part of the education in the Graduate School took place in the numerous clubs, where faculty and students presented papers on the results of their own investigations. By the 1890s there were eleven of these in classics, mathematics, political science, philosophy, Semitic languages, Bible, comparative religion, modern language, English, physics, and engineering. In 1886–87 Gibbs, H. A. Newton, and others gave papers in the Mathematics Club. The Political Science Club, which was founded in the fall of 1886, was organized like a German seminar and was specifically designed to supplement the lectures and recitations of the graduate students in that field. The Classical and Political Science Clubs had private rooms and special libraries, while the Philosophical Club had a laboratory.[31]

The problems of the Graduate School had not by any means been solved when Dwight left, but much progress had been made.

Other schools had gone even farther. The Law and Medical Schools had continued to improve from their low points of 1871, despite the persistent handicap of their location in a small city. For many years, in fact, the presence of Yale in a comparatively rural area probably had operated in the college's favor. Parents may have chosen Yale over Harvard out of dislike for the more urban atmosphere of Cambridge. To the development of a great university, however, a city like New Haven, with a population in 1900 of just over 100,000, had little to contribute. As Arthur T. Hadley noted in 1895, the attractions of great cities, their courts and hospitals especially, hurt the rise of Yale as a university. President Dwight could proclaim that a great city was not necessary to a university, that an atmosphere of study was the most important thing—but that did not persuade everyone.[32]

Nonetheless, the Law School made great progress. The endowment rose 700 percent under Dwight, reaching $82,813.77, a far cry from the $200,000 called for in the *Needs of the University* in 1871, but a great advance over the $11,600.00 it had in 1886. The student body grew so rapidly after 1886 that a new building was needed. Hendrie Hall, fronting on the Green, was partly completed and occupied in 1895, but difficulties in raising money kept it from being finished until September 1900.[33]

In 1888, Simeon E. Baldwin suggested that Yale's law course should be lengthened to three years. As usual, a conservative faculty first opposed and then, perhaps emboldened by the Law School's growth in numbers and endowment, voted the change in 1894 to

take effect in 1896–97. The result was an immediate drop in enrollment. Since Yale College graduates tended to go to New York, Columbia, and Harvard for their law training, the Law School asked
the college in 1898 to help find ways to keep them at Yale. The
problem was not really faced, however, until Hadley became president.[34]

Part of the Law School's problem may have been due to its failure
to hop on the case system bandwagon. Yale continued to insist "that
definite and permanent impressions concerning the principles and
rules of any abstract science are best acquired by the study of standard text-books in private, followed by the examinations and expla-
nations of the recitation room." In fact, the case system was slowly
making its way into the curriculum on the upper-class level. By
1895, the Yale System was explained as a combination of "the case
system and the textbook system in a way which appeals to reason
and common sense. It teaches and believes in the logic of the law,
and it illustrates the theories taught and believed in by cases which
contain the recent utterances of the best judges and that emanate
from the highest courts in America and England." The Yale approach was, however, only a holding action.[35]

These years of Dwight's presidency were even more prosperous
for the Medical School. One historian noted that "when President
Dwight became head of the university, he at once espoused the cause
of the Medical School, and has continued its most steadfast friend."
Enrollment increased by 400 percent in the first eight years of his
presidency, and while it dropped again when the course was extended from three years to four (1896), the gain was still from 27
students in his first year to 110 in his last. Despite the cost of increased laboratory work, a new building for chemistry and physiology was constructed and new courses added. A building was purchased and remodeled and the dispensary moved next door to the
school. In its first year of operations at the new location (1889–90)
5,400 consultations took place in this small forerunner of the great
out-patient clinics now operating at Yale–New Haven Hospital.
This number more than tripled by 1899–1900. All of these endeavors cost money, and by 1894 debts were greater by $6,000 than
endowment. By 1899, though, the debts were being paid off and endowment had risen to over $100,000. It was still only a beginning;
much remained to be done and the school's future was by no means
secure.[36]

Timothy Dwight wanted to bring the Art School into connection with the whole university so that its broadening cultural influence could be felt by all. While his efforts were not as successful as they were for law and medicine, there was advancement: endowment increased, collections grew, standards were improved by the institution of a bachelor's degree in 1891, and enrollment rose. While Sheff had long used the school for training its students in drawing, now academic students also began to attend.[37]

The artistic interests of the university were also fostered by the founding of a school of music. Suggested in 1888 by the alumni of Fairfield County, it was approved by the Corporation in 1890 with the proviso that it would be begun when $300,000 had been raised. The school did not wait for this difficult goal to be reached, however, for Robbins Battell and Mrs. Ellen Battell Eldridge contributed funds for the salary of a professor of music in 1890, and Gustave Jacob Stoeckel, who had been teaching the science of music on a Battell fund since 1854, was appointed to a chair in the new department of music. Stoeckel began teaching at once courses open to undergraduates, graduates, and special students, but no degrees were given for this work. When Stoeckel retired in 1894, Horatio W. Parker was appointed to the chair. That same year the department was ranked as a school and the degree of Bachelor of Music was first conferred. Under Parker the school flourished. Additional faculty members were appointed, the College Street Church (near the location of the first president's house) was purchased for it, and the New Haven Symphony Orchestra under the direction and training of Professor Parker was organized in connection with the department. The orchestra provided a place for the students to play and also to perform some of their own works. Thus while the endowment of the school was only $5,000 when Dwight retired, the Music School had made substantial progress in only nine years.[38]

While art and music were advancing under Dwight, the sciences were not neglected. For the observatory the most exciting event was the gift of $300,000 from Professor Loomis for the promotion of pure research. While it was subject to certain life interests which prevented the observatory from using the whole for many years, the income of one-third immediately became available.[39]

At Peabody Museum, the major problem was lack of space. Even after the mass of material Marsh had collected for the federal government was sent off in five freight cars, the building was too small.

When a valuable discovery was made in the basement of the museum, the *Yale Alumni Weekly* observed, "There are many other things of world interest in this great Marsh collection which must remain undiscovered because there is no room to show them." [40]

President Dwight's catholic approach was best seen and most appreciated in the Sheffield Scientific School. Sheff, as Arthur T. Hadley pointed out,

with its independent character and freer methods, attracted the progressive elements, and left the academic department in constant danger of over-conservatism; the monopoly by the academic department of traditions, of religious influences, and of many of the things that did so much to characterize college life, made the course in the scientific school seem somewhat imperfect by contrast; while Harvard, with its fuller elective course and more progressive, not to say destructive, spirit, was combining the freedom of a scientific school with the traditions of a college. The two things seemed to be drifting further apart.

They began to come back together, Hadley felt, under Porter, when alumni were added to the Corporation. It helped that Porter "was a man of less intensity of purpose" than Woolsey, "and though conservative himself, did not keep the work of the college from broadening." Dwight further closed the gap, for under him "the scientific school obtained its due recognition as a co-ordinate department of the university, and the way was paved for greater co-operation between the different parts than had previously been possible." [41]

Unlike Porter, Dwight was usually present at board meetings of the scientific school. When the school desperately needed a new building in the 1890s, Dwight allowed construction to go ahead using university funds. His hope that gifts would be forthcoming to pay the expense was fulfilled when Mrs. Oliver F. Winchester came forward with a promise of $100,000 for the building if it was named after her husband. This was done and she later gave $30,000 more, thus paying the entire cost of Winchester Hall. The new building was turned over to the departments of physics and civil, mechanical, and electrical engineering. The scheme of raising money for a building after construction had begun did not always work, however. Almost the entire $100,000 cost of the Sheff chemical laboratory, built in 1894–95, had to come out of income balances on hand and permanent funds. It was, as Chittenden said, "one of the penalties of growth." The entering class in 1886 had been the largest ever, and the years 1888–94 saw rapid increases in enrollment.[42]

The growth in the number of students was due in part to the additional funds provided by the new Land Grant Act of 1890. The first payment was to be $15,000, and it was to grow by $1,000 a year for the next ten years until it reached $25,000 a year. The money was "to be applied only to instruction in agriculture, the mechanic arts, the English language, and the various branches of physical, natural, and economic science, with special reference to their applications in the industries of life, and to the facilities for such instruction." At Yale the $31,000 (the first two payments) that became available in 1891 was used for apparatus and machinery for the courses, to increase the faculty by nine to a total of forty-nine, and to provide more scholarships. From the twenty-five available prior to the act, fifty or sixty were now offered to the citizens of the state. These new students caused some of the crowding that necessitated new buildings.[43]

Though the income from the land grant fund of 1890 came to the scientific school, not all was happy in the relationship between Yale and the state. The Sheffield Scientific School was trying to tread the difficult ground between becoming either a trade school or an old-time college. It attempted to teach "principles rather than details." The school, in fact, wanted to succeed "not so much by offering peculiar attractions to farmers as a class or to mechanics as a class, as by inviting students who wish to become scholars in science, well-trained in the higher departments of investigation, able to stand unabashed by the side of scholars in letters." But the high entrance requirements and the rigorous course of study with its stress on theory rather than practice tended to alienate many of the farmers of Connecticut.[44]

A favorite story of the time was that only six or seven students had been educated in agriculture over a period of twenty-four years, while $180,000 had been turned over to Sheff. Thus it appeared to have cost the state over $25,000 to educate each one. Of course the farmers who made this point were ignoring mechanical training. During the period prior to 1887, 241 state scholarship students came to the school and 152 received the Ph.B. Most of these were trained not in farming but in the "mechanic arts." [45]

The State Board of Visitors found no fault with the school. They pointed out that "here original research is instituted and carried to its practical application. In the broadest and best sense, scientific training is furnished and at the same time a basis for technical skill is laid." They also noted that "to every dollar given [by the state] are added seven [by the school]—immeasurably increasing the utility and power of the sum contributed." But neither this nor the school's leadership through Professor Samuel William Johnson in the agricultural experimental station movement satisfied the farmers. The state Grange was particularly vocal in its criticism.[46]

The first crisis came in 1887, when an attempt was made to cut off the grants to Sheff. But the legislature finally voted unanimously that the contract between the state and Yale was binding so long as Yale continued to live up to its side of the contract. Though this seemed to settle the matter, it continued to be agitated, and after the passage of the Land Grant Act of 1890 the attack on the school increased. Finally in 1893 the General Assembly voted to make the Storrs Agricultural School the state's land grant college.[47]

Yale protested that it had lived up to the contract with Connecticut and brought suit against the state treasurer. The courts agreed with Yale and ultimately damages in the amount of $154,604.45 were awarded to the college, "this being equivalent to the entire land grant fund of 1862, assigned by the Congress to the state of Connecticut, i.e. $135,000 plus the interest on this amount, from the time of the legislative act of 1893 to the date of the decision of the commission." While Sheff disliked the loss of the annual land grant donations, the addition to its permanent funds by the court's decision and the freedom from fear of attempts at increased state control helped to offset the financial distress. Now they were at liberty to go their own way. Nonetheless, the removal of the state scholarships combined with an increase in entrance requirements to cause a sudden and precipitate drop in enrollment in the freshman class from a high of 250 in 1894–95 to 150 the following year.[48]

The question of increasing the length of the Sheffield course for the Ph.B. from three to four years was seriously discussed at the very beginning of Timothy Dwight's presidency. He noted in his first presidential report that the school wanted to make the change but could do so only if $250,000 were raised. Charles Eliot wrote from Harvard, warning against lengthening the course: "Hadn't you better go mighty slow towards that four years' course? I am inclined to think that the comparative shortness—and therefore cheapness—of the S.S.S. course has been a factor in its success." Despite Eliot's advice, the Sheffield board went on record in 1888 as desiring a fourth year, perhaps in the hope that this would help to put the Ph.B. on a par with the B.A. But the money could not be raised. Though the school's endowment did increase from $152,223.01 to $405,907.53 during Dwight's presidency, much of the addition came toward the end of his term from the court-awarded land grant fund. By that time opinions had changed. Many educators were wondering if the European system of a three-year college course should not be accepted, and Eliot was actively promoting the change.[49]

As Dwight came to the close of his presidency, the improved relationship between Sheff and the college that he had helped to bring about was once more signalized by his farewell gift of $1,000 to the school. As he wrote to the new director, Russell Chittenden, "It is not a large gift but it will serve at least as a testimonial to my interest in the work and welfare of your Department of the University and of my most kindly regard for yourself and your associates on the Board." [50]

Dwight was also able to assist the library. He understood as well as anyone that the university could not exist without a great library. He had noted in 1871 that the Yale library was inadequate for scholarly work. Under Porter and Dwight the library grew rapidly. In 1870 it had had only 55,000 volumes, but by 1880 it had reached 120,000 and by 1890, 180,000. This rapid increase put a great strain on the old library, and fortunately one of the first gifts of Dwight's presidency was the offer of a new building by Simeon Baldwin Chittenden. Chittenden had never had a college education himself but had instead been an apprentice in a New Haven store at the time he might have been in college. His success in a mercantile business in New York later enabled him to assist the university more than most of its sons.[51]

Chittenden's gift of $100,000, which was equal to nearly all the library had received in its entire history, enabled the university to build and open for use in 1890 the first wing of a new library building. Symbolic of a certain conservatism on the part of the administration was the failure to install any lighting in the structure. The *Yale Daily News* complained bitterly over this fact and noted that Harvard was now putting lights in its building. By April of 1891 it was reported that both gas and electric lights were being installed and gas lights were beginning to be used. But as late as 11 October 1895 there was still no electricity. In December it was announced that work was going forward on the electric lights and by January of 1896 the reading room was open every evening until 9:00 P.M. At least the library had done better than the Law School, which lacked electric lighting in its classrooms until 1916.[52]

The situation of the library was made more difficult in 1894 by the death of W. W. Phelps. Ever since 1874 Phelps had contributed annually one-half of the entire funds used for the purchase of books. On his death, however, the fund from which this income came was donated to the university to build Phelps Hall, the gateway to the Old Campus and the home of recitation rooms and the Classical Club and its library. Fortunately, at this time there became available to the university a $200,000 bequest from Thomas C. Sloane (B.A. 1868), one of the donors to the Sloane Physics Laboratory. The Corporation decided, no doubt at the behest of Dwight, to give the entire sum to the endowment of the library. Though Dwight was delighted over his ability to do this and noted that it placed the library "in a condition of hopefulness and promise, in view of the needs of the times," he still realized that the library needed twice its existing endowment of $300,000 to be in really good shape.[53]

Despite Dwight's interest in seeing the whole university develop, Yale College remained preeminent. Though the university's funds at last began to amount to more than the college's, the college remained far and away the richest part of the university, the one with the greatest number of students, faculty, and buildings. Even under Dwight, more construction was undertaken for the college than for any other department. The most important developments in the college during Dwight's presidency, however, were curricular. Dwight made it clear that the old standards would not be allowed to decline while he was president. Harvard dropped Greek as an entrance requirement in 1887, but Dwight said in his presidential report of that year that the amount of Greek and Latin required for admission, "which was diminished somewhat a few years since," would be brought back up to the old level. Yale continued to believe that it rejected a higher number of applicants than any other college and that, once admitted, it was harder to stay in than any other college in the land. In 1895 Arthur Hadley claimed that both [undergraduate] departments are alike in requiring from their students a higher degree of regularity as to attendance and continuous study. The constant pressure to work is not only much stricter than in the graduate or professional schools, but stricter than in the undergraduate department of Harvard or Princeton or almost any American college. Harvard is strict about her degrees and lax about the previous course of her students. If a man has been idle for four years he will lose his degree. Yale, on the other hand, has no room for idlers in her elective halls.[54]

The curriculum studied under these strict rules was a compromise, being entirely required in the first two years but allowing a good deal of freedom in the last. At first the principle that freshman and sophomore years were prescribed for the purpose of laying the foundation for a liberal education was strictly adhered to. The old recitations in the dead languages, mathematics, and a bit of modern languages were continued. But very early in Dwight's years it became difficult to hold the line. The number of course offerings kept increasing and demanding a better place in the curriculum. This produced a constant shuffling around and condensation of courses. In 1887 the junior required course in geology was dropped. Logic and psychology were made a term course the following year. In 1890 the old stand-bys of senior year—moral philosophy, natural theology, and evidences of Christianity—were made part of the junior course in logic and psychology. Astronomy was added to sophomore mathematics and then was made an elective. Only physics remained of the old junior-year science courses. But even it could not hold out for long. In 1893, physics was moved to sophomore year and made an alternative course. As George Pierson observed, "for the first time since 1701 it could be avoided." The sophomores were now allowed a certain amount of freedom. They could choose any five out of the following courses, or groups of courses: Latin, Greek, mathematics, French or German, English, and physics. In addition, by 1886 the two lower classes were allowed to anticipate any required course by passing an examination in it, and in 1894 this right was specifically stated in the catalogue.

Then, with the juniors down to three required courses (logic, psychology, and ethics), the seniors to two (selected from four courses offered in psychology, ethics, and philosophy), and even the first two years broached, Yale called a halt in the spread of electives. It was not, as George Pierson pointed out, a logical place to stop: "Probably it was the human element which was responsible. The leaders of the Faculty were men of slow-moving conviction, not logicians. The undergraduates were afraid of what the opening up of Freshman and Sophomore years would do. And the influence of Timothy Dwight must not be underestimated." Dwight refused to go further.[55] Nonetheless, the results of these rather moderate changes were, in reality, highly revolutionary. The logic of the old curriculum, even of the 1883–84 compromise, had been destroyed.

The elective principle that had now made such headway at Yale created problems of its own, students did not necessarily select their courses wisely nor pursue subjects in depth but often sought what was easy or entertaining. Furthermore, electives undermined the old system of appointments at commencement. With all the changes, it no longer seemed fair to name the first and second scholar, so after 1886 the valedictorian and salutatorian were no longer chosen. Dwight even suggested in 1896 that it was no longer possible to really compare scholars at all (since they did not take the same subjects), and that while appointments might still be given, the whole idea of ranking should be dropped and men should henceforward just be put in general groups. In 1885–86 an attempt had been made to solve both problems: special honors were awarded for more directed study pursued with distinction and including the preparation of a "meritorious thesis." Still, no matter how one tampered with the curriculum, interest in scholarship continued to decline.[56] The increasing importance of the extracurriculum, which had become noticeable under Woolsey and accelerated under Porter, continued under Dwight.

Even a move toward vocationalism did not help. Undergraduates were allowed to take many Divinity School courses. Seniors were permitted to take a nontechnical course in law, and the Law School, in hopes of getting them to stay in New Haven, authorized them to complete the new three-year course in two years if they could. At the same time, the holder of a Yale B.A. could enter the second year of the Medical School "with conditions." Thus, Yale College, slowly, jerkily, and incompletely, was beginning to follow the vocational route taken so many years before in the sciences by Sheff. Of course, no one would admit it.[57]

As Dwight approached the close of his presidency, the Spanish American War broke out. The jingoism that produced it had already appeared at Yale, it seems. In 1895 an elective course in military science had been started in the college. In the Scientific School, where, under the original Land Grant Act, the presentation of a course on military science had been demanded, at the request of the students the subject remained a requirement after the severing of that tie. The Sheff students even asked for drill, and despite the fact that the only time available for it was Saturday afternoon, two or three companies of Sheff juniors and seniors and a company or two of Yale College students turned out to do "drill in the School of the Soldier and School of the Company." [58]

There were, of course, voices raised against the move toward war. On 4 April 1898 Professor Arthur M. Wheeler spoke out strongly against going to war with Cuba or extending our territory in any way. What we needed, he said, was to concern ourselves with internal affairs—especially purifying our politics of corruption. On the same day President Dwight wired President McKinley to say that the faculties of Yale University supported his attempt to find a peaceful solution to the problems between Spain and America. Meanwhile, the students marched. Despite Spanish agreement to American demands, McKinley turned to a war policy and on 11 April asked Congress to authorize the forcible intervention of the United States into Cuba. On 20 April Congress adopted a war resolution and the president signed it. Only the day before, Yale had been pleased to discover through an announcement in the *Yale Daily News* that an auxiliary cruiser, the *Paris,* had been renamed the *Yale*. Immediately a drive was undertaken to make a gift to the university's namesake.[59]

The announcement of war apparently silenced opposition at Yale to America's pugnacious policy. At first it was hoped that a Yale battery could go to the war, and 150 undergraduates immediately volunteered. But then the governor decided to fill up an existing battery first. He allowed the students to form a platoon of 40 men within it. This was immediately done and the Yale men were soon shipped off to Niantic (where they remained until the armistice was declared). Thirty-five other undergraduates rushed off to enlist in other units.[60]

Yale's feelings about the war were best shown in a great mass meeting held in College Street Hall on the night of 20 May 1898. Here all the aspects of patriotism were displayed: the hall, decorated with a huge flag and covered with red, white, and blue bunting, was jammed with undergraduates, faculty, and alumni who had come to hear the report of the committee raising funds for the two maxim rapid-fire guns and complete stand of color (51 flags) that they wished to give to the cruiser *Yale*. The pitch of the meeting was indicated by the Reverend Dr. Lines, who, according to Welch and Camp,

made his most effective point in emphasizing the righteousness of the cause of the war, and made his most effective appeal to the University audience present in asking them to use all their means and influence, whether they were at home or afield, to hold the country throughout the war, and after its close, true to the consecrated cause of the struggle.

Professor Bernadotte Perrin even went so far as to say that the university should be closed if the necessity arose. Perrin admitted that he and others at Yale had felt that the war should have been averted, but now that time was past: "When a government of the people, by the people, and for the people, after much longsuffering and under great provocation, deliberately, with full legislative process, and with a certain majesty, appeals to war to right the wrongs of others, all voices of criticism and dissent must cease." So, closing with a hearty rendering of "For God, For Country, and For Yale," Yale went to war. The students returned to the campus that night marching behind the second regiment band and singing patriotic songs. Later, men like Sumner, in his "The Conquest of the U.S. by Spain" and "War," would oppose American expansion and the irrationality of the war; but in 1898, after the conflict began, they were silent.[61]

The Spanish-American war hardly disturbed Yale. College life went on as usual. There was more marching, more patriotic singing, but no real change. And when commencement came, those who had gone off to war received their degrees as if they were there—unlike during the Civil War.[62] The martial spirit of the college officers was rising.

But the war did not last long, and Timothy Dwight's final year was spent in peace. He announced to the Corporation that he was going to resign at the end of the 1898–99 academic year, for he was now seventy, and he refused to allow them to change his mind. After they had accepted the idea, he went over to the newspaper office and told the manager, as George Pierson related it,

"I came down to give you a little piece of news. I have just resigned as President of Yale University. Thought you might like to put it in the paper." Then he went downstairs. A moment or two later he came all the way up again, put his face in the office: "If there is anything to pay for this service, please let me know." [63]

Like Yale itself, Timothy Dwight was conservative. He was, nonetheless, optimistic. And as he ended his presidency he viewed the developments in the university with satisfaction. All of the departments had grown. The permanent funds of the university had doubled—though there was still not nearly enough. In the college a proper limit to the elective system had been found, or so Timothy Dwight thought, while the various schools had been kept from commingling too much. Yet Yale was not as ready for the twentieth century—its third century—as he thought. It was still "a one-sided republic," still excessively dominated by the college, which gave the whole place a somewhat nineteenth-century tone. It had lost, under Porter, its educational leadership, and Dwight had not been able to reverse this trend. Though even some of the most critical commentators thought Yale still at least one of the greatest institutions of higher education in the country, Dwight had not really been able to halt the quiet decline. Especially in the sciences Yale's greatness was going into an eclipse from which it is still trying to emerge.[64]

Uneasily, Yale men faced the future.

15

The Rise of the Extracurriculum

There was good reason for the uneasiness with which Yale men faced the twentieth century. Interest in scholarly things was just reaching its lowest point in the history of the college. Years later the classes that entered in 1900 and 1901 would argue over which had the honor to be the worst class to go through Yale.[1]

The faculty wondered what had happened. Why had the old, simple, sometimes uncouth Yale of Day and Woolsey disappeared? Professor H. A. Beers noted in 1895 that the old individuality, the "accidental, spontaneous charm" which had existed when he was a student (1865–69) "had gone out of college life." Now it was "as if everyone were enrolled in some organization or other, was in training for something, and carried on his amusements strenuously and in a corporate way." [2]

Owen Johnson (B.A. 1900) in his classic *Stover at Yale* explained the new atmosphere better than anyone else. Speaking through one of his characters, he said,

Our colleges to-day are business colleges—Yale more so, perhaps, because it is more sensitively American. Let's take up any side of our life here. Begin with athletics. What has become of the natural, spontaneous joy of contest? Instead you have one of the most perfectly organized business systems for achieving a required result—success. Football is driving, slavish work; there isn't one man in twenty who gets any real pleasure out of it. Professional baseball is not more rigorously disciplined and driven than our "amateur" teams. Add the crew and the track. Play, the fun of the thing itself, doesn't exist; and why? Because we have made a business out of it all, and the college is scoured for material, just as drummers are sent out to bring in business.

Take another case. A man has a knack at the banjo or guitar, or has a good voice. What is the spontaneous thing? To meet with other kindred spirits in informal gatherings in one another's rooms or at the fence, according to the whim of the moment. Instead what happens? You have our university musical clubs, thoroughly professional organizations. If you are material, you must get out and begin to work for them—coach with a professional coach, make the Apollo clubs, and, working on, some

298

day in junior year reach the varsity organization or go out on a professional tour. Again an organization conceived on business lines.

The same is true with competition for our papers: the struggle for existence outside in a business world is not one whit more intense than the
struggle to win out in the *News* or *Lit* competition. We are like a beef
trust, with every by-product organized, down to the last possibility. You
come to Yale—what is said to you? "Be natural, be spontaneous, revel in
a certain freedom, enjoy a leisure you'll never get again, browse around,
give your imagination a chance, see every one, rub wits with every one,
get to know yourself."

Is that what's said? No. What are you told instead? "Here are twenty
great machines that need new bolts and wheels. Get out and work. Work
harder than the next man, who is going to try to outwork you. And, in
order to succeed, work at only one thing. You don't count—everything
for the college." [3]

The situation Johnson described was the product of many causes,
but perhaps the root of it all was the rise of a new, pragmatic, materialistic American culture. Many students now came to Yale seeking
social prestige or a route to a business career. The new culture and
these different students made even Dwight's revised curriculum
seem out of date. So the students turned their attention elsewhere. [4]

The first and most obvious product of the change in attitude was
the rise of organized sports. The tentative beginnings took place before the Civil War, but the great athletic age at Yale was the period
between 1870 and 1910. Then it was that Yale became *the* power in
college sports.

The first sport to benefit from the new conditions was baseball,
which had been played informally at Yale before the war but did
not blossom until later. The troops on both sides had played baseball during the war; when they brought it home, the game swept the
country. The first regular baseball nine at Yale seems to have been
formed in 1865. It played its first intercollegiate game against Wes-
leyan that same year, and, as a prefiguring of things to come, Yale
won 39 to 13. [5]

The score was typical of those days when a "lively, elastic ball" was
pitched underhand without curves and strikes were called only
when the umpire "thought a cowardly or too fastidious batsman was
letting too many good balls go by." Bats were "big, long, semi-'pudding sticks.'" Fielders were allowed to catch flies on the first bounce

for an out until sometime in the mid-sixties and fouls caught on first bounce were outs until early in the next decade. But while fielders generally avoided catching the ball on the fly, the batter was still favored because "the uncertainties of the first bound, due to the vagaries of the ground, made it an exciting gamble for player and spectator alike." Many times a missed bounce meant a home run.[6]

The first official Harvard-Yale baseball game took place in 1868 at Worcester, Massachusetts, during the boat races. Yale lost 25 to 17. Every year thereafter until 1874 Yale met Harvard at least once, only to lose each time. Not until 1880 did Yale begin to win consistently in that and other sports.[7]

Blue as Yale's color became more fixed as athletic contests increased in number. School colors were not too common before the early days of baseball and they did not become universal until the football craze swept the nation. In the early 1850s Yale men seem to have thought of green as the college color. Each of the great literary societies then had its own color: Linonia was pink, Brothers in Unity was blue, and Calliope was gold. The college, according to an orator at the Linonia centennial celebration, was green—"*Ever green may she be!*" But at the same time blue began to appear at boat races, and by 1854, the Yale crew "were wearing blue flannel shirts as a kind of uniform." The blue flag that had flown on the first Yale boat in 1843 was given to the Yale Navy in 1858 to be competed for by the various boat clubs. By the late sixties blue had clearly become Yale's color—even the spectators at the regatta who were rooting for Yale carried or wore blue. By that time, baseball as well had picked up the color. But it was football that spread blue across the land.[8]

The fever for baseball was swept aside and buried by football. The old class football games, it will be recalled, had been outlawed by the faculty in the fifties. Though the game was played periodically thereafter, it was always stopped as soon as the faculty discovered it. Football did not return for good until 16 November 1870, when the classes of 1872 and 1873 played a match at Hamilton Park. Yale's first intercollegiate game was played against Columbia two years later.[9]

The football Yale played in the beginning was more nearly what we now call soccer, as was the so-called first intercollegiate football game between Princeton and Rutgers. Yale's first rules specifically prohibit pitching, throwing, or carrying the ball on any part of the field, though it could be batted with the hand. While Yale, Princeton, Columbia, and Rutgers were playing this game, Harvard was developing the Rugby-type game. In November 1875 Yale met Harvard in New Haven in a special game under Rugby rules but with some changes requested by Yale. Harvard won that first "concessionary game," as it was called, but Yale so liked the Harvard game that it took up the new sport. In 1876 Yale, Harvard, Columbia, and Princeton met at the call of Princeton to form the Intercollegiate Football Association. They adopted, in modified form, the Rugby Union rules. So ended what Walter Camp called "the American game" and began the evolution from Rugby to American football.[10]

That same year, 1876, Yale defeated Harvard at its own game. The event was further noteworthy since it marked the first appearance on the field of Walter Camp. Camp (B.A. 1880) played for Yale from 1876 to 1882, when he was injured. Since for many years any student in the university could compete, Camp played while he was studying medicine. Thereafter, until 1910, he was the graduate adviser to Yale football. From 1877 to 1925, on the national scene, he was a member of every football rules committee. American football is indebted to Camp for its eleven men, scrimmage, four downs, gridiron, tackling below the waist—and for making the "All-American Team" famous.[11]

Camp was the Yale coach only in a very informal way. In those days there were no coaches in the modern sense of the word. Students, aided by alumni, ran sports. Each team captain was chiefly responsible for what happened his year. At first (from about 1872 to 1888) each football captain directed affairs with whatever graduate help he chose to call on. Camp began to assist around 1885, and from 1888 to 1906 he was the advisory head coach. The teams were actually handled on the field by either the former captain or a leading player from the previous year. On the occasion of big games, some of the greats of earlier years would return to help out. Because Camp had a regular job, he seldom attended practice. Instead, his wife Alice, William Graham Sumner's sister, observed the players in action and reported back to Camp. He then coached the coaches, and sometimes the players, in his home at night.[12]

Walter Camp *was* Yale football until around 1905. Under his tutelage Yale had a success which can only be called phenomenal.

From 1883 through 1898, Yale produced nine undefeated teams. Of these, three were not even scored upon. From the last game of 1890 to the ninth game of 1893, Yale scored 1,265 points to none for its opponents. During the last two decades of the nineteenth century, some of the giants of the old game played for Yale: Camp, A. A. Stagg, '88 (who played as a graduate and was even better known as a baseball pitcher), W. W. "Pudge" Hefflefinger, '91 Sheff, Charles Gill, '89, W. H. "Pa" Corbin, '89, Frank S. Butterworth, '95, Lee "Bum" McClung, '91 (who scored 500 points in four seasons), and little Frank Hinkey, '95 (whom Pop Warner called the greatest football player of all time). Though the great Yale power began to fade slowly during the first decade after 1900, these years saw other memorable players: Henry Holt, '03, James J. Hogan, '05, Tom Shevlin, '06, Tad Jones, '08 Sheff, Ted Coy and Stephen Philbin, '10, and John L. "Dutch" Le Vine, who played only in 1905 while attending, in turn, Yale College, Law School, and Art School. (No doubt exhausted with the effort, he left Yale after that one year.)[13]

From 1872 through 1909 in all games of soccer, Rugby, and American football, the fantastic Yale teams ran up a record of 324 victories, 17 losses, and 18 ties. Yale's success against Harvard was so great that Cambridge men began to think of Yalies as nothing but muckers, while Yale men had serious doubts about the manliness of the Harvards. When the end came, it was marked by Ted Coy's 1909 team, which went undefeated, untied, and unscored upon. Walter Camp wrote of them that the question used to be whether Gordon Brown's eleven (1900) could beat Lee McClung's (1891); now it was, could Coy's team beat either or both. When Camp picked an all-time all-star team in 1911, he put Coy at fullback and said he had "the most remarkable combination of qualities that have been gathered together in any player on the gridiron." [14]

Through the days of the flying wedge, running drop kick, tackles back formation, and the development of the forward pass, Yale conquered all. It was only with the rise of the professional coach (epitomized by Percy Haughton at Harvard and his string of victories over Yale) that the great blue squads lost their dominance. It was clear that the wonderful days were over when, in November 1914, Yale opened its enormous new Bowl—the largest stadium built till then in America—and with 70,000 in attendance proceeded to be beaten 36-0, the worst defeat it had ever suffered. And though Yale men complained, called for the return of Camp, and criticized the rising professionalism, nothing could bring back Yale's old glory. Perhaps the only thing that soothed some Yale men was that where in 1897 football and baseball had brought in a little over $37,000, in 1914–15 the revenue from sports (mostly football) amounted to $151,812.07.[15]

During the great football era, Yale was competing in many other sports and doing almost as well as on the gridiron. From 1880 through 1895, the crew won 12 of 16 races against Harvard. In baseball, between 1880 and 1898 Yale won 247 games, lost 95, and tied 3. Other sports were proliferating: track began in a small way in 1872; a tennis club was organized in 1881; in 1893 a gymnastic association and the Corinthian Yacht Club arrived; basketball and hockey teams were formed in 1895; golf came in 1896, a bicycle association in 1898, and swimming in 1901.[16]

Walter Camp and others noted with satisfaction that the rise of all these organized athletic activities paralleled the fall of town-gown riots and numerous other disciplinary problems. Unfortunately, it also paralleled the fall of scholarship from importance. As late as 1870, success in athletics brought no special distinction at Yale. That a change was taking place, however, was signalized by the disappearance of Phi Beta Kappa in 1871. The transition was complete by the mid-1890s. Whereas between 1861 and 1894 only eight out of thirty-four valedictorians were not tapped for a senior society, from 1894 through 1902 none of the eight valedictorians was selected. A faculty committee on numbers and scholarships reported in 1903 that "an impression is very strong and prevalent that the athlete is working for Yale, the student for himself. To be a high-stand man is now a disadvantage rather than otherwise. . . . In fact, hard study has become unfashionable at Yale." [17]

Yale College has always been a competitive place, but where once competition had been in the class and the literary society, now it was on the playing field or in the newspapers, magazines, managerships, or for some position in one of the many other organizations that had sprung up.

The organization, energy, ambition, and drive that all who observed Yale commented upon even extended to religion. Though religious feeling was not nearly so widespread as it had been before the Civil War (one graduate of the seventies recalled that he was not even interested enough in religion to be a skeptic), there was an amazing amount of religious activity. Under the influence of Dwight L. Moody, the Christian Social Union was formed in 1879. It became the Young Men's Christian Association in 1881 and in 1886 it received money for a building which was named Dwight Hall. Later the organization, which still exists, became known by the name of the building.[18]

The period in which Dwight Hall flourished was nearly the same as the era of successful athletic endeavor. Between 1887 and 1914 under such graduate secretaries as A. A. Stagg, W. L. Phelps, and Henry Wright, Dwight Hall played an important role in college life. Even Sheff, which did not share in many college activities or sentiments because it had no compulsory chapel or dormitories, had a YMCA, later called Byers Hall after its building. In 1901 the YMCAs at Yale had a thousand members. Together they were the largest college Christian association in the country.[19]

The most effective of all graduate secretaries of the Yale College YMCA was Henry B. Wright (B.A. 1898). Wright strongly influenced Sherwood Eddy (Ph.B. 1891), despite the difference in their ages, and through Eddy many of Wright's ideas reached Frank Buchman. According to Ralph Gabriel,

In course of time Buchman, promoter extraordinary of religion, took over from Henry Wright the four absolutes, the technique of the group confessional, the idea of guidance, and the emphasis on personal evangelism, but not Wright's self-forgetfulness. Eventually a movement emerged called first the Oxford Group and later Moral Rearmament.[20]

Out of Dwight Hall, under the influence of A. A. Stagg, came the Yale Mission for social and religious work in a poor section of New Haven, and in 1907 another secretary of the organization founded the Yale Hope Mission, serving homeless men. Yale students were involved, too, in New Haven's Bethany Sunday School and the city's numerous boys' clubs.[21]

As with all such student activity at Yale, altruism was not the only stimulus to doing good works. The president of Dwight Hall was almost certain to be tapped by one of the prestigious senior societies. And the religious organization was often criticized for the involvement of its members in college politics. Still, the concern of some of these young men was deep and lasting. Under the influence of the missionary movement that swept the colleges of the country in the late nineties and especially the beheading of Horace Tracy Pitkin (B.A. 1892) during the Boxer Rebellion, A. C. Williams (B.A. 1898) led a movement to establish a Yale Mission in the Far East. Williams was not able to go to China, but John L. Thurston (B.A. 1897) found a perfect site in Changsha, which was considered "probably the most inaccessible of the main cities" of China, and in 1906 Dr. Edward H. Hume (B.A. 1897), Brownell Gage (B.A. 1898), and Warren Seabury (B.A. 1900) opened what was to become Yale-in-China there. In time, this endeavor came to consist of a middle school, liberal arts college, hospital, nursing school, and medical school. Forced to leave by the Communists in 1951, Yale-in-China now exists in Hong Kong, but the old schools are still running under new names.[22]

Behind all the hurly-burly of organized college activity lay something called the Yale spirit—usually called "sand" by the undergraduates. Sand was placed under the wheels of locomotives to make them go and sand—grit, determination, "persistence, reliability, self-reliance, and willingness to face the consequences of one's actions"—was what made Yale undergraduate life go, for they ran it all with little interference from the faculty, administration, or alumni. The idea of a special Yale spirit seems to have appeared just before the Civil War. Joseph C. Jackson (B.A. 1857) said he had never heard the term before he used it in 1859, when Professor Felton of Harvard said there was something about Yale he did not understand. Jackson replied, "Yes, Professor, it is College Spirit—or Individuality—as developed at Yale." When Felton asked what Yale Spirit was, Jackson explained, "It is a combination of various elements—Inspiration, or faith with enthusiasm, sacrifice, or self-denial, fidelity and loyalty, cooperation and patriotism." Felton confessed, "We have not got that here." [23]

A prime element of Yale and the Yale spirit was the belief in Yale's democracy. It did not matter, they said, who you were or knew or how much money you had. "These, in fact, are matters concerning which no one ever thinks or enquires, or cares to know." Each man had to prove himself to his class and the college. To preserve this vaunted democracy, Yale had long tried to hold its tuitions low so that all could attend; whenever costs went up, fears were voiced for Yale's democracy.[24]

Even the senior society system was meant to reinforce Yale's democracy. Though bitterly attacked in the eighties, at most times the societies were criticized only when they elected "worthless men." Since the selection process had become public in the 1870s with the institution of Tap Day (due to the insistence of the juniors who wanted to see who went where), the community now knew immediately what judgments the societies had made. In a history of Yale written in 1898, the Yale view of the societies was clearly revealed: the societies elected on the basis of merit, and "taps" were generally greeted with "hearty applause" unless the prize had not been earned. The class society system, Arthur Hadley said in 1895, "is a characteristic product of Yale life, with its intensity of effort, its high valuation of college judgements and college successes, and its constant tension, which will allow no one to rest within himself, but makes him a part of the community in which he dwells." [25]

Fortunately, there were a few places around Yale where the constant strain of competition for "success" might be partly forgotten. The favorite was probably Mory's. This famous place had been discovered by members of the class of 1863 who were walking back from boat races on the New Haven harbor. Spotting a pleasant alehouse on Wooster Street, they wandered in for refreshment and discovered the delights of Mr. and Mrs. Moriarity's hospitality. Later in the sixties the Moriaritys moved to Court Street and opened "The Quiet House." The students flocked to the new, more convenient location. In 1874, no doubt to the great regret of the undergraduates, the Moriaritys sold "The Quiet House" and retired. Happily for Yale tradition, Scranton's private bank failed, the Moriaritys lost nearly everything, and they were forced to go back into business. In 1875, Frank and Jane Moriarity opened the Temple Bar, even closer to the college. Frank died the following year, but aided by Eddie Oakley, Mrs. Moriarity carried on. When she died in 1885 Oakley took over, and soon a new custom, the velvet cup and the cup men, was born. Unfortunately, Eddie was not a very good businessman and in 1897 the place was closed. But the following year it was leased by another popular New Haven bar man, A. G. Traeger. Traeger died that same year and Louis Linder took over. Under Linder, "the place where Louis dwells" thrived, and when he decided to retire in 1912 a storm of protest from Yale men, and their financial aid given through the Mory's Association, helped him to relocate at 306 York Street, the present location of Mory's.[26]

There were, in fact, still many delightful things to do at Yale. Calcium Light Night was always fun to watch: the junior societies, dressed in their robes and carrying burning red and green lights, marched on campus to inform new members of their elections. There was also the Omega Lambda Chi, which commemorated the freshman societies abolished by the faculty in 1880. On this occasion sophomores, juniors, and seniors marched by classes around the college cheering the buildings. Then they went to the narrow space between Dwight and Alumni Halls and, in what came to be known as the Pass of Thermopylae, the freshmen ran the gauntlet between the massed upperclassmen. With luck, the new men emerged not too badly bruised. In 1899 the *Yale Alumni Weekly* reported, "The whole proceeding was business-like and orderly and in half an hour the campus had assumed its ordinary aspect." But the following year the faculty banned the rough ceremony.[27]

There were many other things to do: glee clubs and singing groups, dances (Germans were very popular) and the great junior prom, debating, eating clubs, class games, and a myriad of other activities. One strange aspect of it all was a certain childishness that adhered to it. An Englishman who visited the college in 1869 remarked on "the addiction of the students to lollipops and the honour in which 'Candy Sam,' their vendor, is held." And G. Stanley Hall was amazed to find Yale seniors playing with marbles and hoops. A Columbia sociologist thought American college students generally seemed to be living in "a play world." Perhaps it was, at least at Yale, an attempt to escape the strain of college competition.[28]

While Sheff did not share in most of the odd customs of the college, it did share in the society movement and in sports. Yale football greats like W. T. Bull, "Pudge" Heffelfinger, and Vance McCormick, to name only a few, were Sheff men.

The society system appeared early at Sheff, the first being the Berzelius Society founded in 1848. In 1860 the L. and S. (Literary and Scientific) Society was established. In 1863 this became Book and Snake. At first these societies were for literary and academic discussions and debates, but in 1874 Book and Snake members of the class of 1876 rented a house and established the first society dormitory. John Hays Hammond (Ph.B. 1876) called it Cloister, and from that time until the house was given to Yale in 1933 the name of the building and the society were interchangeable.

Other societies in the Sheffield Scientific School soon followed Cloister's lead, building dormitories and even windowless "tombs" for their meetings. Soon the students of Sheff were divided between small select groups living in private dormitories and the rest, who found what living quarters they could around the town. By 1910 there were eight societies or fraternities in the school.[29]

In 1892, before the strange Yale College life began to disintegrate, the philosopher George Santayana visited Yale. He found it delightful. "What is more," as he later said, he *"believed"* in it." The Yale Spirit impressed him, and he found it was produced not only by the kinds of students and their isolation from the outside world but also by the college discipline of early morning chapel and recitation, prescribed freshman and sophomore courses, and the old disciplinary marking system. All of these helped to unify the students, and upon them the Yale educational ideal did its work. "The essential object of the institution," Santayana correctly observed, "is still to educate rather than to instruct, to be a mother of men rather than a school for doctors." As a result, he wrote,

Yale is in many respects what Harvard used to be. It has maintained the traditions of a New England college more faithfully. Anyone visiting the two colleges would think Yale by far the older institution. The past of America makes itself felt there in many subtle ways: there is a kind of colonial self-reliance, and simplicity of aim, a touch of non-conformist separation from the great ideas and movements of the world. One is reminded, as one no longer is at Harvard of Burke's phrase about the dissidence of dissent and the Protestantism of the Protestant religion. Nor is it only the past of America that is enshrined at Yale; the present is vividly portrayed there also. Nothing could be more American—not to say *Amurrcan*—than Yale College. The place is sacred to the national ideal. Here is sound, healthy principle, but no overscrupulousness, love of life, trust in success, a ready jocoseness, a democratic amiability, and a radiant conviction that there is nothing better than one's self. It is a boyish type of character, earnest and quick in things practical, hasty and frivolous in things intellectual. But the boyish ideal is a healthy one, and in a young man, as in a young nation, it is perfection to have only the faults of youth. There is sometimes a beautiful simplicity and completeness in the type which this ideal produces.

Santayana did not despair of Harvard, however, but noted that

some universities have greater beauty and a richer past, some have maturer scholars and more famous teachers, Yale herself has more unity, more energy, and greater fitness to our present condition. Harvard, instead of all these advantages, has freedom, both from external trammels and from the pleasant torpor of too fixed tradition. She has freedom and a single eye for the truth, and these are enough to secure for her, if the world goes well, an incomparable future.[30]

So Santayana, in effect, saw the dangers as well as the benefits of the Yale system. For Yale was, it is clear, *too* traditional, *too* conforming, *too* much a creature of the age. Very soon these weaknesses and others became apparent. The elaborate structure grew decadent and began to disintegrate.

Its destruction came about because the whole thing went too far. The extracurriculum became more important than anything else. The high point in this dominance was reached, ironically, sometime around Yale's bicentennial. The growth of the student body may have helped to produce this condition. The great influx of students under Timothy Dwight meant that many could not be housed in the college, and while numerous students had lived off campus for many years, the problem only became serious as New Haven grew, wealth increased, the student body changed, and private dormitories for the wealthier undergraduates began to appear. The most famous of these was Hutchinson, "The Hutch," where the rich and the socially ambitious prep-school boys congregated in order to improve their chances of getting into the lower class societies. In 1905 the *Yale Alumni Weekly* reported with alarm that 41 percent of Ac could not live in the college. Sixty-one percent of the freshmen and 58 percent of the sophomores resided off campus. The *Weekly* worried about Yale's democracy, reporting that in the recent fraternity elections, the three older organizations took three-fourths of the men they selected "from the 'swell' dormitories of College Street, and that about two-thirds of these men as Freshmen had roomed in the high-priced dormitories of York Street." Increasingly criticized as a rich man's college, a place where it was becoming difficult for the poor man to work his way through, Yale tried to prove it was not so, but the stories would not down.[31]

All of the shortcomings of Yale were glaringly revealed in *Stover at Yale:*

On Yale democracy:

"You came from a school that doesn't send many fellows here. You haven't the fellows ahead pulling for you the way the other crowds have. I don't want you to make any mistakes. Remember you're going to be watched from now on."

On choosing friends:

"You may think the world begins outside of college. It doesn't; it begins right here. You want to make the friends that will help you along here and outside. Don't lose sight of your opportunities and be careful how you choose."

On study:

"Now, you've got to do a certain amount of studying here. Better do it the first year and get in with the faculty."

On conformity:

Directly, clearly visualized, he perceived for the first time, what he was to perceive in every side of his college career, that a standard had been fashioned to which irresistibly, subtly, he would have to conform.

On Yale and the American spirit:

For the first time, a little appalled, he felt the weight of the seriousness, the deadly seriousness of the American spirit, which seizes on everything that is competition and transforms it, with the savage fanaticism of its race, for success.

On college life:

And yet, what completely surprised him was the lack of careless, indolent camaraderie which he had known at school and had expected in larger scope at college. Every one was busy, working with a dogged persistence along some line of ambition.

On the effect of a year at Yale:

by the perfect averaging system of college, he had lost in one short year all the originality and imagination he had brought with him.[32]

When Johnson wrote his fascinating book (which first appeared in *McClure's Magazine* in 1911) with its harsh description of Yale, the situation was already changing. Faculty, students, and alumni alike had become concerned about what had happened. President

Dwight felt called upon in his *Memories* to deny that fancy new dormitories and the presence of wealthy young men undermined Yale democracy. He insisted, "If the democratic spirit animating our University is now, or ever becomes, so weak and unmanly that it cannot endure inequalities of expenditures—in the means of satisfying the desire for special comforts or even luxuries, or gratifying the artistic taste—it will be unworthy of its origin; it will have contradicted its earlier self." Yale democracy, he thought, meant equality of opportunity, not equality of possessions.[33] But others felt it necessary to act. More dormitories were added; a "Bureau of Self-Help" was set up in 1900 to assist those working their way through (though its efforts may have been undermined a bit by Hadley's belief that no aid should be given that was not earned). It remained possible to work one's way through Yale and still "succeed." A student who was doing it observed in 1910:

It will not do to throw glamor about the opportunities at Yale for the boy who must work his way, yet it must be acknowledged . . . that Yale offers a remarkable variety of jobs and schemes worth while. New Haven itself supplies work to non-capitalized students at the same time that certain of the cold grasping business world capitalize their more fortunate sons.

As for the more democratic spirit of the University in regard to men who work their way, no one should throw up his sweaty nightcap and cry Caesar King; but to give Caesar his credit for the virtues he possesses, Yale does not discriminate against the poor. Poverty is a handicap here only in so far as it limits a young man in his ability and capacity to do those things which count in college life. Quite recently Yale has had a football captain whose own efforts put him through Yale, and a chairman of a Junior Prom, the highest social honor of Yale, has run a club table at an eating joint for his board.[34]

On the curricular front, there were many changes under Hadley (see pp. 342–46) and also a reaction among some undergraduates to the excessive interest in organizations and athletics; things intellectual began to make a comeback early in the first decade of the twentieth century. Phi Beta Kappa was revived, instruction improved, course offerings were opened in some directions but limited in others, the college calendar was made more balanced, and there was an attempt to make course elections more rational. Cheating, which had always been considered by the students a perfectly legitimate way to stay in college but an improper means of attaining a high stand, began to be frowned upon by the students, and the faculty began to clamp down on it. Somehow all of this worked. Scholarship began to improve and the students began to recognize academic achievement again. Six of the fifteen men tapped for Skull and Bones in 1910 were members of Phi Beta Kappa.[35]

The most significant indication that a shift was taking place was Yale's "Literary Renaissance." Yale had never been a literary place —except for a brief period with the Connecticut Wits. This failure had always rankled. At the bicentennial celebrations of the founding of the college and the move to New Haven, orators were able to point with pride to Yale's college presidents, ministers, doctors, lawyers, and even foresters and lexicographers, but it was very difficult to say much about Yale's literary men. Anson Phelps Stokes confessed in *Memorials of Eminent Yale Men* that "our Alma Mater has been more conspicuous for *fortiter in re* than *suaviter in modo.*" [36]

For some reason, this situation suddenly began to change. As George W. Pierson described it,

Even as the great football machines ground out their last great seasons, however, Yale's literary philistinism was being left behind. Then in the years 1909–1920, for the first time since the days of the Connecticut Wits, the College could laugh at its literary detractors. The change could be measured in a wide variety of activities. Instructors of all ages were publishing more voluminously and in better style than ever before. In 1908 the Yale University Press had been started. Three years later the *Yale Review* was reorganized as a literary quarterly. Simultaneously the new Elizabethan Club began bringing students and faculty together for companionship and discussion of their literary enthusiasms. Most gratifying and astonishing of all, the undergraduates were scribbling as never before, scribbling and play-acting and composing and reviewing and—best of all —being published. First an occasional poet, then whole shoals of poets. Where once the undergraduate had fleetingly dabbled, had heeled the *Lit.* and *Record* more for the fun of it and prestige than in strict service of art, now these minnow authors were serious enough to grow up in their element: to plan on literature as a career.[37]

The first indication of this new interest was the appearance at Yale of Clarence Day (B.A. 1896), Henry Seidel Canby (Ph.B. 1899), Sinclair Lewis (B.A. 1907), and William Rose Benét (Ph.B. 1907). Then in the next decade men interested in music, drama, literature, and publishing began to graduate in numbers: Edgar Montillion Woolley and Thomas Beer in 1911; Cole Porter in 1913; C. A. Merz and Archibald MacLeish in 1915; Bruce Simonds in 1917; Philip Barry and John C. Farrar in 1918; Quincy Porter and Stephen Vincent Benét in 1919; and Thornton Wilder, Briton Hadden, and Henry R. Luce, all in 1920. There were many others as well, but the major point is that an enormous wealth of talent emerged from Yale during these years.

The organizational impulse did not die at Yale (it never has). During these years there emerged the Yale Dramatic Association in 1900, the Whiffenpoofs, organized by some members of the classes of '09 and '10, the Pundits, 1903, and (from outside) the Elizabethan Club, 1911. The organizational impulse was still strong enough that Stephen Vincent Benét and his roommate J. F. Carter composed a poem which advised,

> Do you want to be successful?
> Form a club!
> Are your chances quite distressful?
> Form a club!

and concluded,

> you'll get your heart's desiring—
> and the rest will get the raz!
> *Form a club!* [38]

Nor was Yale democracy fully recovered. Wilmarth Lewis (B.A. 1918), who was later to serve many years as a fellow of the Corporation, said in his autobiography that when he came to Yale in 1914 clothes were of great importance, but

More important than clothes was the air of "belonging." The swift appraising eye of adepts in the art of social intercourse recognized a fellow initiate on sight, the rest might as well not exist, but acquirement of an acceptable appearance was not in itself enough to ensure success. You had to prove your worth, a fact subsumed in the concept of "Yale Democracy." To the Western boys who came to Yale from Thacher without a year or two in a good Eastern prep school, the talk about Yale Democracy was ironical. Although it made no difference whether you had money or not (few knew who were rich unless they had famous names) and there was no Harvard Gold Coast into which the *jeunesse dorée* withdrew, by Western standards Yale was anything but "democratic." The word at Yale had a special meaning. When in 1902 [*sic*] the Public Orator presented Theodore Roosevelt for an honorary degree he explained that the President "is a Harvard man by nature; but in his democratic spirit, his breadth of national feeling, and his earnest pursuit of what is true and right, he possesses those qualities which represent the distinctive ideals of Yale." This was received not with gales of laughter, but with prolonged applause. By "democratic spirit" the Public Orator meant that Yale was a place where the highest undergraduate social honors were attainable by boys without money or "family," a refinement lost on some of the Western Thacher boys who found Yale so chilling that they clung together in obscurity, longing for the smell of wet sage on mountain sides and fishing in the Sespe.[39]

Nonetheless, as athletic prowess and the admiration of it declined, as managers and editors climbed to prominence on the eve of World War I, intellectual activities had risen to a position of importance they had seldom enjoyed before at Yale. While the majority of each class may have been untouched by the deeper currents of the movement—still cheated, competed, played, and slipped their way through Yale—an important shift had taken place, which it could only be hoped would continue and grow in the decades to come.[40]

16

Revival

Hardly had the Yale Corporation received the news of President Dwight's forthcoming retirement at the close of the academic year 1898–99 than they were presented with a candidate for the presidency who was supported by many of the faculty and alumni. The man they wanted was Arthur Twining Hadley, Yale's charming and brilliant professor of political economy. The Corporation was not so sure. There were several problems: Hadley was not a minister; he was young; and he did not seem very conservative. So the Corporation looked elsewhere. They sounded out several ministers, but none wanted the job. They even tried to interest William Howard Taft (B.A. 1878) in the place, but he firmly took himself out of contention. In a letter to his brother, he wrote

I venture to think . . . that in our enthusiasm over the material advancement of our University and the pride we may feel in a President who worthily represents our Alma Mater to the world and is a power in the nation that makes for righteousness, we may become unmindful of the fact that the prime object of a University is to maintain the highest educational standards and that the first duty of the head of a University is to see to it that the educational opportunities it affords are progressively higher from year to year.

Taft felt his education and training did not prepare him to fulfill the duty he described. So he explicitly refused to accept the position if he were offered it. Many universities have been less fortunate when they approached famous men.[1]

As others refused to be considered, Hadley's candidacy was strengthened. Still some of the fellows hesitated. The Reverend Edwin P. Parker decided to sound out Hadley on some important points for the unconvinced Corporation members. Referring to Hadley in the third person, Parker asked him about

(1) His Christian faith and standing. Is he, broadly speaking, a Christian believer? Is he, for instance, a member of the Christian Church? It is not a question of "orthodoxy," old or new, but rather a question of per-

sonal and (I may add) vital relation to the essential and the historic Christ.

For instance (again) do you think he would accept or does accept, substantially, that symbol known as *The Apostle's Creed?*

Parker also questioned Hadley concerning

(II) His attitude towards what I may generalize as *classical studies* in the Academic Department. This is not a question of improvements or changes to be made; but rather a question whether or no, in your opinion, Prof. Hadley would be inclined or disposed to *revolutionize* and 'rip up' things in that department, and to act the part of a *radical reformer* in the *College,* to the undoing of its distinctive character?

This was a matter of some concern to the good reverend, or perhaps to his colleagues, for he asked again, "Is it not a question of development by *evolution* or *revolution?*" [2]

Hadley replied directly to most of these questions, though he expressed reluctance to have his words quoted, preferring that the Corporation learn about him from others. Nonetheless, he answered, "I am a member of the Church of Christ in Yale College, and . . . I believe it to be of fundamental importance for Yale to keep its essentially Christian character; also . . . I am conservative on the question of classical study and am emphatic in the belief that in this as in other matters our progress must be through evolution rather than revolution." Though he dodged the question about his acceptance of the Apostle's Creed, Hadley's reply seems to have quieted outright opposition, and on 25 May 1899 the Yale Corporation broke the precedent of nearly two hundred years and elected a lay president. Perhaps even more significant was the fact that his election marked a return to the leadership of young men for the first time since 1846. Thus Hadley's election appeared to signalize a revolution in Yale's history. In fact, it was not.[3]

The new president was the brilliant Yale son of a brilliant Yale father. James Hadley, professor of Greek in the college from 1851 until his death in 1872, had been salutatorian of his class and was considered to have one of the best minds of his generation. Arthur had an equally fine college record and was valedictorian of the class of 1876. He had then done graduate work at Yale and in Germany in political science and history. He took no degrees for these studies. He had then returned to New Haven and the difficult life of tutor, researcher, and free-lance that has been described above (pp. 251–53). He was not made a full-time professor on regular salary until 1891.[4]

Arthur Twining Hadley was well known outside of Yale for his scholarly achievements. Inside the institution he was famous as a teacher—not less because of what his son, Morris Hadley (B.A. 1916), referred to as "his extreme eccentricities of manner." To attend a lecture by Hadley was a memorable experience: he twirled; he teetered on the edge of the platform; he twined about any object handy. Meanwhile, one arm slashed in his famous pump-handle motion, while the other swung about his head. He had even been known to step into a wastebasket and then struggle to extricate himself, all without interrupting the flow of his lecture. Fortunately, the intellectual content of his material was so absorbing that it never got lost in all his gyrations or in the peculiar drawl, singsong, and deliberate calm that marked his speech.[5]

His eccentricities extended beyond the classroom. The Hadley stories were legion: How he had introduced his sons to their uncle. How he had boarded a trolley car, greeted the conductor, and given his fare to a friend. How when visiting the kaiser he had identified by taste alone the source of a wine he could never have drunk before. How he arranged his books by their color, yet still found each volume with ease. He was, as his son said, "nervous, brilliant, and impulsive." Fortunately, his charming wife was calm and orderly, so she helped to tone down some of his oddity.[6]

This strange man was loved and admired by all who knew him. It was hoped he would make a great Yale president and that he would —without any revolutionizing, of course—bring the changes to Yale that would remove the lurking unease that filled the place. Under Hadley, perhaps Yale could become first again.[7]

Arthur Hadley did not really want to be president of Yale. He liked research and writing and did not want to become an administrator. But he felt that Yale was out of touch with the times and he believed he might be able to change that; at the same time, Helen Hadley pointed out to her husband how he could broaden his influence by taking the position. Thus inclination and urging persuaded him to accept the difficult job of president of conservative old Yale in a time of transition.[8]

Clearly, the problems were great. Despite Timothy Dwight's at-

tempts to create a more balanced university, the college was still predominant. Dwight's plea to his successor was to build up the university. Money was not only in short supply but too much centered in
the college. Dwight had greatly increased the university funds,
which were unconnected to any school, but much more was wanted.
The graduate and professional schools had made important progress
from their low points, but all needed money and much attention.
Even the college, the keystone in the university arch, was in trouble.
Enrollment had not increased since 1896.[9]

Timothy Dwight outlined the needs of the university in his report for the year 1896–97. As he looked forward to Yale's bicentennial, he thought the institution needed an auditorium and a dining hall which would be specifically university buildings. These
seemed terribly important symbolically to Dwight, since the university had no buildings of its own at the time; everything belonged to
one department or another. Then Dwight pointed out the numerous wants of the various schools for buildings, professorships, and
general endowment. All in all, Dwight computed, Yale ought to
raise three to four million dollars in the next six or seven years. The
first goal was set at one and a half to two million dollars for university buildings for the bicentennial. Thus when Hadley took office he
found himself committed to a bicentennial fund-raising campaign
and building program. Whether he would have chosen these particular priorities, we do not know, but certainly the bicentennial, the
need to present himself and his ideas to alumni groups around the
country, and the normal hesitancy of a new president to push ahead
too fast, meant that the first years of his administration were not
marked by great achievement.[10]

Yale's two hundredth anniversary was celebrated with pomp and
circumstance in October 1901. None of her problems—the heritage
of at least a generation of conservative rule—had been solved, but
for a few days Yale could stop worrying about its current position
and reflect in pride on its long and distinguished history and the
achievements of its graduates.

The celebration was, in the main, a serious one, for Hadley
wanted to stress the intellectual side of the university; but enough
pageantry was included to keep those happy who came for entertainment. The celebration began on Sunday, 20 October, with special

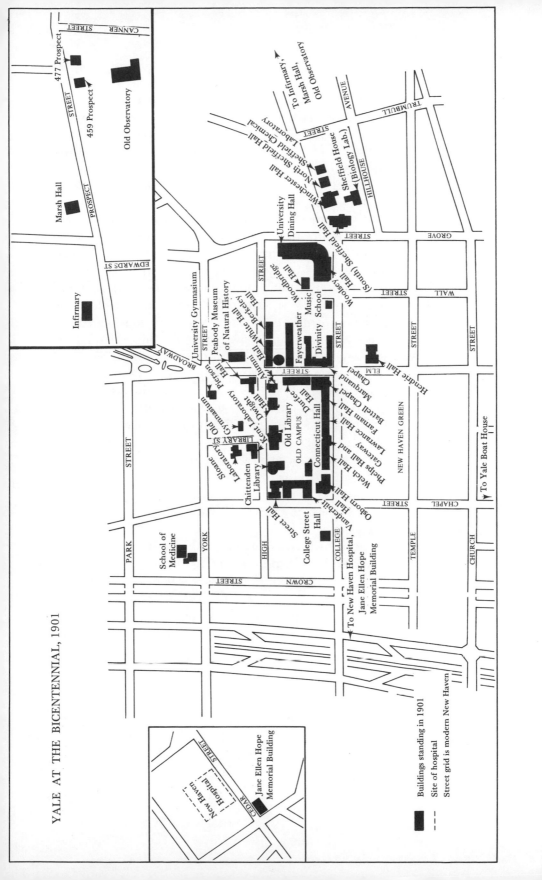

YALE AT THE BICENTENNIAL, 1901

CANNER STREET

477 Prospect
459 Prospect
Old Observatory
STREET
PROSPECT
Marsh Hall
Infirmary
EDWARDS ST

To Infirmary,
Marsh Hall,
Old Observatory

AVENUE
TRUMBULL
STREET

Winchester Hall
North Sheffield Hall
Sheffield Chemical
Laboratory
Sheffield House
(Biology Lab.)
HILLHOUSE

University
Dining Hall

STREET
Woodbridge Hall
Music
School
Wolsey
(South) Sheffield Hall
Hall

GROVE

STREET
WALL
STREET

University Gymnasium
Peabody Museum
of Natural History
Berkeley
Hall
White Hall
Fayerweather
Divinity

STREET
Battell Chapel
Marquand Chapel
Durfee Hall
Farnam Hall
Lawrance Hall
Gateway
Welch Hall
Phelps Hall and
Gateway
Osborn Hall
Vanderbilt

Alumni
Hall
Dwight
Hall
Kent Laboratory
Peirson
Hall

Hendrie Hall
ELM

NEW HAVEN GREEN

To Yale Boat House
CHAPEL
STREET
TEMPLE
CHURCH

Chittenden
Library
Sloane
Laboratory
Old
Gymnasium
LIBRARY ST
Old Library
OLD CAMPUS
Connecticut Hall
Street Hall

College Street
Hall

BROADWAY
STREET
PARK
School of
Medicine
YORK
STREET
CROWN
HIGH
COLLEGE

To New Haven Hospital,
Jane Ellen Hope
Memorial Building

Jane Ellen Hope
Memorial Building
CEDAR STREET
New Haven
Hospital

Buildings standing in 1901
Site of hospital
Street grid is modern New Haven

services in Battell Chapel and the churches of the city, and it continued through Wednesday with many speeches on Yale in its relation
to everything from Christian Theology and Missions (success) to
Literature (failure). These were broken by a great torchlight parade
of five thousand graduates and students in costumes illustrating
Yale's history, two short football games, in one of which the university team defeated Bates and in the other a team made up of many
of the greats of yesteryear defeated a college team, and a pageant in
the great central square of the campus. This space, on what is now
known as the Old Campus, had been cleared of North College, the
Lyceum, and the Treasury Building (Trumbull Gallery) just in
time for the ceremony. Now only Connecticut Hall remained to
break the openness of the square and remind men of old Yale.

On Wednesday morning the commemoration exercises, the major
event of the celebration, took place. Since the bicentennial auditorium, Woolsey Hall, was not finished, the ceremonies were held in
the Hyperion Theater. There Justice Brewer (B.A. 1856) of the United
States Supreme Court gave the commemorative address on Yale in its
relation to public service, and then honorary degrees were given to
sixty-two worthies including Mark Twain and Theodore Roosevelt.
Roosevelt, the only recipient to speak, said of Yale what it most
liked to hear: "I have never yet worked at a task worth doing that I
did not find myself working shoulder to shoulder with some son of
Yale. I have never yet been in any struggle for righteousness or decency, that there were not men of Yale to aid me and give me
strength and courage." [11]

The bicentennial was marked not only by speeches, theatricals,
and games, but also by exhibitions, the dedication of buildings, and
the publication of a large group of scholarly books. The most important of these volumes was prepared by Josiah Willard Gibbs, whose
life was nearly run. His greatness was recognized at Yale, and it was
fortunate that he was able to produce for this occasion *Elementary
Principles in Statistical Mechanics*. It was, according to one biographer, a fitting capstone to his career—though "it took about as long
to be appreciated as his first great work." [12]

After all the joy and celebration, after the five thousand graduates
and all the dignitaries who attended had gone home, Yale was left to
face its problems. These were largely financial, organizational, and

attitudinal. On the financial side, large endowments were needed; on the organizational, much needed to be done to make Yale a real university instead of merely a collection of schools surrounding a dominant college; on the attitudinal, all Yale men had to begin to support the entire university.

As universities grew larger in the late nineteenth century they were all forced, at one time or another, to create some sort of more detailed administrative structure. In time, as Laurence Veysey has pointed out, these structures all began to look very much alike. Yale resisted this movement longer than most institutions, but it did so to its own damage. A large university could not be run like the Yale of the first Timothy Dwight, or even the second. If Yale was to be a great university with strong departments throughout, then it could no longer follow a policy of drift. The president and fellows must actively assist all parts of the university to improve. No longer could they concentrate on the college and allow the other schools to go their own ways—to live or die by their own acts. As new, powerful, private universities like the Johns Hopkins, Leland Stanford, and the University of Chicago rose, and as the large public institutions began to make their mark, Yale's lack of organization began to threaten its position as a great national institution. If Yale was to hold its relative position—or ever rise to the top again—it had to have a more balanced development. The president could do something, as Timothy Dwight had shown, merely by becoming president of the entire institution and by making the Corporation as well university rather than college oriented. But this was not enough to solve Yale's problem.[13]

Yale would, of course, ultimately emerge with an organization similar to other American institutions, but the difficulty of achieving that form was a typically Yale experience. Nowhere else, perhaps, was faculty rule so strong; nowhere else, certainly, did it have such a strong tradition. Hadley mentioned the problem in his inaugural address. Yale, he noted, "is a group of colleges whose property is held in the name of a single corporation, but whose management is, by tradition and in some slight degree by legal authority, located in the hands of the separate Faculties." There was no point in discussing whether this was good or not: "It is here, and we cannot for the present change it." [14]

The new president had, in fact, just been warned not to tamper with it. In the address of greeting from the faculties that immediately preceded Hadley's inaugural address, the Reverend G. P. Fisher, who had been a professor at Yale since 1854, explained the way Yale worked and said, "We know that you appreciate a polity in which not a spirit of dictation, but a spirit of cooperation, is a marked characteristic, and that you are conscious to what extent the prosperity of this institution has been owing to it." [15]

Hadley did recognize that there were advantages to the system, but that there were serious shortcomings, he was also well aware. Under the Yale system, he noted in his inaugural, "there is sometimes difficulty carrying the whole university sharply forward into any definite line of policy, however strongly it may be demanded." And beyond that,

> There is yet more frequently a lack of coordination in the courses; the work of each of the separate parts or schools having been originally devised with reference to the needs of members of that school, rather than to those of the university as a whole. And finally, there is a certain amount of duplication of appliances, which involves some actual loss of economy and makes the impression on the public of causing even more loss than really exists.

Any attempt to solve these problems, Hadley said, must come through discussion and negotiation. If he tried to form a policy and push it through, the result would only be disaster. "The president who would succeed in establishing real harmony must occupy himself with providing the means to lead men to a mutual understanding, rather than with predicting the results which should follow." As one way to achieve the harmony he sought, Hadley suggested a university council made up of representatives from the several faculties to discuss problems important to all.[16]

With this old proposal of a university council (first suggested by Timothy Dwight in 1871), and his analysis of Yale's organizational problem, Hadley revealed a good deal about his approach to leading the university. In later years many Yale men indicted Hadley for his failure to direct affairs forcefully. Despite his brilliant mind and his cogent analyses of problems, "he was most cautious in dealing with new ideas." He often failed to give the faculties needed direction; he would analyze the problem from many sides for them but then suggest no course of action. And often when a policy he had wanted was passed by the faculty and Corporation, he failed to see that it was carried out.[17]

These criticisms of Hadley as an administrator are no doubt fair, but they do not take into account that his method of leading was not only characteristic but philosophical. He had said at the beginning that he would not try to force policies through. His course was, as Wilbur Cross said, to be an opportunist: "If he did not try hard to mould circumstance to educational ideas which he elaborated in eloquent speeches . . . he would be quick to seize circumstance for some far-reaching purpose he had in mind." [18]

Caution in the face of the Yale College faculty was probably wise. Yale was a conservative place, and in part this was because of its vaunted faculty control. While teachers individually may often have had liberal political leanings, when gathered as a faculty they tended to be conservative on educational and institutional matters. They disliked change, and they were supported in this characteristic by a certain institutional pride in being conservative. As the Reverend J. H. Twichell said in his induction address at Hadley's inaugural,

This Yale of ours has in all her history been marked by a certain somewhat decided conservative habit, by a tendency to cling with considerable tenacity to means and methods that are traditional. . . . We conceive it intrinsically becoming the scholastic community and a permanent condition of genuinely sound learning and broad culture to give an attentive ear to the great teachers and teaching of former times.

Hadley was faced with a conservative tradition, his own conservative character and philosophy, and a system of government that inherently made change difficult. At the same time, however, he knew that on the "proper treatment" of the problem of university organization depended the future of the institution.[19]

If Hadley had faced the problem alone, his presidency might have been a complete failure. Fortunately, he believed that an efficient executive appointed good assistants and gave them freedom to act. Since the university treasurer and secretary under Dwight decided to leave office when he did, Hadley was able to appoint his own men to these positions. He selected Anson Phelps Stokes, only three years out of Yale College, to be his secretary, and induced Morris Tyler, president of the Southern New England Telephone Company, to become his treasurer. They were strong men, and if Hadley frequently tended, as the *Yale Alumni Weekly* later said, to allow "others to take the lead in new matters," they were able to do it, and he gave them full support when it was needed.[20]

Anson Phelps Stokes brought to his office youth, energy, ability, intelligence, vision, loyalty, and strength. When Hadley vacillated, he was firm. He was a perfect teammate for the eccentric president. And the remaking of Yale during the Hadley years was due as much to Stokes as to anyone. When he took office, he later related, he inherited two half-time assistants and a single letter file of correspondence. During the previous administration, Yale had made its first experiment with using a stenographer, who was shared by the secretary, college dean's office, and treasurer. The president refused to use her, however, because "so many of his letters are of a formal and private character, he perhaps shrinks from giving their contents to a third person." Under Stokes, the secretary's office became "the great central clearing house and executive organ of the University" with a staff of forty. Hadley used to "wonder how any university keeps running without Mr. Anson Phelps Stokes." [21]

Morris Tyler and his successors, Lee McClung and George Day, transformed the treasurer's office as well into a modern business organization. New bookkeeping procedures were instituted, better methods of purchasing and maintaining university equipment were installed, new officers were added, and more informative treasurer's reports were issued.[22]

The new administrative efficiency instituted by Stokes and the treasurers was symbolized by one of the bicentennial buildings. In Woodbridge Hall, named without conscious irony for that most disruptive of Yale's founding trustees, the university had for the first time decent administrative offices. Here, also, the Corporation and Prudential Committee could meet on specifically university ground.[23]

At the same time that the viewpoint of these Corporation bodies was, perhaps, broadened by their environment, they were also changed in their makeup and had their work increasingly systematized. The Prudential Committee began functioning as a true executive committee and thus the full board, relieved of details and emergency business, was, as Hadley said, "enabled to discuss with due deliberation those general questions of policy which necessarily come before it." At the same time, its work was increased. When Hadley took office the Corporation and the Prudential Committee each met about four times a year. By 1915 the Corporation was meeting eight times a year and the Prudential Committee every two weeks when the university was in session.[24]

The Corporation was also, perhaps, made more effective by changing the qualifications of the successor trustees. This group, it will be recalled, was made up solely of Connecticut Congregational ministers. Many questioned whether the charter allowed it to be anything else. After years of argument, the first hesitant step toward change was made in 1902, with the selection of a minister from outside Connecticut to the board. Then in 1905 the great alteration was finally made: Payson Merrill (B.A. 1865), who was not a minister, was made a fellow. The Connecticut ministers, recognizing the need for men with other qualifications, had begun the transfer of power. By 1917 half the successor trustees were laymen. Despite this fact, as one of the fellows observed, the Corporation continued to many years to be dominated by the ministers "by the sheer weight of their knowledge and ability." [25]

In 1905 the Corporation also began the job of revising its nebulous rules. The *Alumni Weekly* thought there was "no better evidence of the new spirit in Yale administration." The new laws, completed in 1907, clarified and made explicit much that had long been unwritten university procedure. They also established even more firmly the power of the faculties. While the new rules made deans and directors the executive officers of their faculties and organizations (instead of merely presiding officers at meetings) they also gave the faculties the right to select their own deans. As a result, the university historian observed, "under Hadley was the republic. Now, after two hundred years, the democratic custom of the constitution had again come to bloom. Between 1899 and 1914, Yale's habits of autonomy were rationalized, organized, and made solid." [26]

Other reforms during these years were also mixed blessings. The organization of the alumni to advise Yale and support it was probably wise, but it too produced its own problems. In 1904 Secretary Stokes suggested that an Alumni Advisory Board made up of men elected by the various Yale Clubs scattered around the country would help to bring into Yale a wider viewpoint than could be encompassed in the small and necessarily eastern-oriented Corporation. Since that body was meeting with increasing frequency, it was impossible for men from far away to be members of it. Hadley supported the idea of the Alumni Advisory Board in his report for 1904. The board was officially authorized by the Corporation in February 1906. It was intended to "meet the desire of Yale graduates in different parts of the country for representation on the councils of the University." Unfortunately, like so many groups at Yale, it tended to be dominated by men from the college, for they were most active in the local Yale clubs.[27]

At the same time the Alumni Board was being organized, Stokes was working on other alumni questions. He brought into his office the records of the class secretaries (who were in charge of the meetings, records, and news of each class) and of the class alumni fund agents (who canvassed members of their class for needed money). The loyalty and support of the alumni was further promoted by the institution of a special day for them to return to Yale to find out what was going on there. The first Alumni University Day was held on Washington's Birthday in 1914. The university also began, in 1905, to send the alumni the report of the president and also, for a time, the reports of the deans to the president.[28]

The organization of the alumni—and the loyalty that made that organization possible—had only one shortcoming: it allowed them to concentrate their dissatisfactions. The result was, as Woolsey had warned years before, that the alumni finally were able to move together. And if it was not to govern Yale, it was to reorganize it radically.[29]

Before that traumatic experience, however, many other organizational and financial changes (the two were often only opposite sides of the same coin) were made. One important transformation was in the approach to the faculty. Hadley was by no means convinced that all research carried on at universities was worthwhile, but unlike Timothy Dwight he did feel that it was necessary to do research to be a good teacher. He did not want to create a special group of research professors, by any means, but he wanted to encourage investigation, to assist junior instructors to publish their work, and to make sure that only productive men were appointed to full professorships. Research as a specific function of university teachers was a relatively new phenomenon. It did not appear on the American scene until around 1880. Then it swept all before it. Yale resisted this movement to a degree, but it did not ignore it, as was revealed when E. G. Bourne published an article in 1886 entitled "Intellectual Activity in Yale College," which contained "an informal listing of all writings by Yale faculty members since January 1, 1880." Nonetheless, Dwight had remained firm in his belief that Yale should continue to appoint teachers, as well as researchers, to its faculty. Yale was criticized for its failure to become research-oriented. Yet, surprisingly, it was a place where researchers, those "true monastics of the new university," could live and work. Men like Marsh, Gibbs, and (off and on) the biochemist Thomas B. Osborne by their example helped to further the concept of solid scholarship in America.[30]

Still, Yale resisted. Though a scholar himself, Hadley was never quite comfortable with the ideal the new scholars represented. To the president, the best kind of research was publicly useful; it was work that advanced "things worthwhile." The publications that resulted from this kind of investigation were good for the university. On the other hand, Hadley felt that specialized research should be undertaken elsewhere:

The studies which are to be essentially the privilege of the few seem to me to belong in the research laboratory rather than in the university. That provision is being made for specialized work by munificent gifts of capital, I rejoice to see; but I should deem it a misfortune if the rise of these endowments and the distinction of those who were entrusted with their use led our professors to believe that such research was a function superior in dignity or public importance to the plain everyday work of teaching men to do their work as men.[31]

Despite this attitude, Hadley did try in a number of ways to develop a faculty of greater scholarly distinction. For one thing, he moved out the old men. Mandatory retirement at age sixty-eight was passed by the Corporation in 1903. This rule, combined with Dwight's pensions and natural losses, changed the faculty radically. Then Hadley resisted the automatic promotion of men to fill these openings. No one, he felt, should be made a professor just because a subject needed to be taught. In addition, by letting assistant professors fill these slots, the number of full professors could be decreased and salaries for the remainder raised.[32]

Hadley did not intend by this to make assistant professors only teachers. They, too, were to do research. While the president recognized that they were underpaid and worked very hard, he thought that if their surroundings could be made pleasant and publication of their work made easier, they would be happy at Yale. But he did not want them to be too happy. It was in Hadley's years that the now familiar policy of promotion or departure ("up or out") came to Yale. Men were no longer to be encouraged to remain contentedly teaching on the lowest rung of the academic ladder for their entire lives. From now on young men were to be asked not only to teach well but also to profit themselves and Yale by earning national reputations with their research and publications. The assistant professor's appointment was shortened from five years to three, which was sufficient, Hadley thought, to find out if a man was any good. If extra time were needed, he could be appointed for another three-year term. But only a few especially useful individuals were to be allowed to remain at Yale as assistant professors thereafter.[33]

Salary was also used to encourage advancement or departure. A major salary revision was begun in 1905 and completed in 1910, raising salaries at all levels. Instructors were started at $1,000 and advanced every year until the fourth, when they reached $1,600, where they remained. First-term assistant professors received $2,000, second-term, $2,500, and thereafter they received $3,000. Professors' salaries ranged from a minimum of $3,500 to $5,000. In 1915 Hadley explained how these salaries worked, beyond just the amount paid, to achieve a better faculty:

The rapid increase in instructors' salaries from one thousand to sixteen hundred dollars enables us to keep men here when they are proving useful. The comparatively small margin between the highest instructor's salary and the lowest assistant professor's salary prevents heads of departments from retarding the promotion of the better men for economy's sake, and prevents men who do not quite deserve promotion from complaining of pecuniary hardship when it is withheld. The shortening of the term of an assistant professor's appointment has proved one of the best features in the system. In the old days assistant professors were kept for five years on the lowest scale of salary. Now the question of their promotion comes up at the end of three years instead of five.

And the same consideration applied to second-term assistant professors:

One of the greatest evils of our old system was that the decision [on promotion to professor] was made too late. It is far easier for a man to change his location when he has served only six years as an assistant professor than when he has served ten years. Under the old system we were often urged, and perhaps sometimes led, to keep people here permanently because we had already kept them here so long that it seemed unfair to compel them to go. Under the new system we decide at an early period whether we want to keep an assistant professor for an indefinite term or not. The effect of this is to reduce the number of cases to a minimum. We have a few assistant professors of the third grade and they are among the most useful men in the faculty; but as a rule it is not wise, either for the man or the institution, for him to stay here unless he has a combination of qualities which warrant us in promoting him to a full professorship.[34]

Hadley also attempted to improve the faculty by varying the amount paid to professors within the same faculty. There were already differences between faculties, since it was clear that there was a greater demand for doctors and lawyers than for ministers, classicists, historians, and the like. But Hadley also pushed for variations within a faculty, and in 1910 he persuaded the Corporation to accept the idea that there should be a distinction between professors, "with length of service, University responsibility, and individual distinction as a scholar or teacher forming the criteria on which the President and Dean of a department base their recommendations for advance to the Corporation." [35]

In addition to improved salaries and changes in terms, Yale also improved the working conditions of its faculty by defining precisely in its new rules its previously informal sabbaticals. Every full professor was allowed a year's leave at half salary every seven years, and second-term assistant professors were allowed leave at full salary if the governing board of their department recommended it *and* if they paid their own replacement.[36]

Yale also began to look harder outside its own ranks for new professors at this time. President Porter had been the first to appoint a non–Yale-College graduate to a college professorship. Timothy Dwight had followed his lead and increased the number. But most of these men had done their graduate work at Yale, so they were not complete barbarians. Hadley's aim was to get the best, no matter where they had done undergraduate or graduate work. As a result, even in the junior appointments in the college, which had always been almost entirely made up of Yale graduates, one-third of those hired between 1900 and 1908 were graduates of other colleges.[37]

Hadley actively involved himself in the pursuit of eminent men for professorships. He once wrote, "Don't refuse to suggest a man's name because he probably won't take it. The best men I have got were men who probably wouldn't take the places they hold." So with the advice of the faculty, who had the right to nominate professors under Yale procedure, Hadley approached, directly or indirectly, numerous men. He failed to get Ernest Rutherford, James Rowland Angell, G. Lowes Dickinson, and several others, but he was successful with Ernest William Brown in mathematics, Ross Granville Harrison in zoology, George Lincoln Hendrickson in classics, Charles C. Torrey in Semitics, Ernest Carroll Moore in education, Charles McLean Andrews in history, and Julius Petersen in German. How carefully Hadley considered the men on his faculties is revealed in a story about two appointees from within Yale to the new Sloane Physics Laboratory, B. B. Boltwood (Ph.B. 1892) and Henry A. Bumstead (Ph.D. 1897). Hadley said of them, "Boltwood is a man of great mechanical ingenuity, and an untiring experimenter. His vivacity will counteract the effects of Bumstead's seriousness, and Bumstead's concentration will prevent Boltwood from scattering his brains loose around the table. . . . I predict great things for them." [38]

These various approaches undoubtedly helped to improve the faculty, but such changes do not occur overnight. Toward the end of Hadley's first decade in office, one study found that while Yale had educated ninety-three of the finest one thousand scientists in the country, third best of the universities, it ranked behind Harvard, Columbia, Chicago, Cornell, Johns Hopkins, and California in terms of the distinction of the scientists on its faculty. Some departments were excellent: "Yale stands second in geology, fourth in mathematics, fifth in astronomy, second in chemistry and sixth in zoology, her standing in geology being only exceeded by the Geological Survey." But Yale was not good enough even to appear in the tables for physics, botany, anatomy, pathology, and psychology.[39]

Edwin E. Slosson in *Great American Universities,* which appeared in 1910, was highly critical of the Yale faculty. He found among other things that they were not as productive in scholarship as their ability should have made them. They were, he thought, too comfortable and too interested in teaching. He felt that "the professional spirit prevails in Yale athletics, and the amateur spirit prevails in Yale scholarship." One problem was revealed by the fact that at other institutions Slosson visited, professors were eager to show him what was going on in various departments of the university. At Yale, on the other hand, the departments seemed isolated from each other. "I fear," Slosson wrote, "that at Yale it indicates rather a lack of coordination and cooperation." [40]

Slosson was right on this point, and Hadley knew it. It was one of the problems the president worked hardest to overcome. His first attempt was through a university council made up of representatives of the various departments. It was never very successful in breaking down the divisions, however, for it had no real power. It could only discuss problems, not act on them.[41]

Much more successful was the building of university laboratories. These emerged out of the private purchase by Anson Phelps Stokes and some associates of the Hillhouse estate, Sachem's Wood, for the university in 1905 in order to provide a large piece of property for future development. During the years it took Yale to repay the purchasers and take control of the property, a decision was reached to use the land to try to break down some of the separation and competition between the Sheffield Scientific School and Yale College and to end a certain amount of duplication of laboratories. It was thought that these changes could be accomplished by building laboratories to be owned by the university and shared by all university scientists. The opportunity to begin this process came with a gift in 1909 of $425,000 from William D. and Henry T. Sloane for a university physics laboratory. At the same time the president said the Hillhouse site should be used for a zoology laboratory, followed by others for botany, physiological chemistry, and physical chemistry, and the Corporation voted "that the policy inaugurated in the Sloane Physical Laboratory demands the immediate erection of a laboratory or laboratories of Biology on the Hillhouse property so maintained that the students of the different departments in the University shall have all requisite facilities for work and instruction." [42]

The reaction of the Sheffield Scientific School to these proposals revealed how badly divided Yale was. Sheff was not too upset about the physics laboratory, since they were not well equipped in that field, but biology was something else. Director Chittenden later wrote:

> The biological courses at Yale had become a success through the efforts of the Sheffield Scientific School. The Sheffield Trustees had expended considerable money on laboratory building and equipment, while a number of professors had given all their energies for thirty or forty years to making the Sheffield Biological Laboratory a worthy center for instruction and research. Both the Governing Board of the School and the Sheffield Trustees had a feeling of pride in the position the School had attained, and they were deeply concerned in any movement that threatened to result in the transfer of courses of study that had become an integral part of the school structure to general university control. If such a line of action was adopted as a general principle what was applied in biological studies might well be expected to follow with other studies later on, and the Scientific School be reduced to a mere skeleton. No one believed that the Corporation deliberately planned to undermine the position of the Scientific School. Doubtless they looked on the movement as a direct help to the School, as well as to the University in general. The president had stated in one of his reports that 'the Corporation should not curtail in any way the privileges and independence of the Scientific School' and probably there was no intention of doing so, yet there was a serious menace, both to the privileges of the Scientific School and its independence, in the proposed plan.

Chittenden recalled that he was deeply worried: "What would it all lead to? University control, university management, were vague terms, wholly undefined, and the very indefiniteness tended to magnify the possible ultimate dangers to the Sheffield Scientific School." [43]

Director Chittenden was, of course, correct in seeing a danger to Sheff's independence, but from the point of view of university development—of the destruction of just such an attitude as he revealed—the idea of university buildings with faculty members in separate schools though in the same field working together rather than separately offered a chance to strike a blow for unity and to achieve some important financial economies at the same time.

The director of the scientific school was a doughty opponent. Nor was he alone. His cause was assisted by the college faculty and alumni who did not want the buildings placed so far away. Fortunately for Hadley and Anson Phelps Stokes, who was the driving force behind the plan, these opponents did not unite. Instead, the basic principle was allowed by Chittenden when he accepted the physics laboratory, and with his support the college faculty was overriden. With this achieved the Corporation voted to agree to Chittenden's strong terms for the way the proposed laboratory of zoology and comparative anatomy was to be run: Sheff was given great control over the operation and conduct of the new laboratories. More importantly, however, the goal of university laboratories was achieved, and thus began the unification of the university which was ultimately to result in the Sheffield Scientific School's becoming only a name. Hadley, it must be said, did not have that end in view, but others did. The Alumni Advisory Board had asked the Corporation in June 1909 for information on the "legal and other obstacles which interfere with a closer correlation of Yale College and Sheffield Scientific School." They did not press the question after an agreement was worked out on the university laboratory issue, but the threat was in the air.[44]

The independence of Sheff, the college, and other schools was also undermined by financial policies. When salaries were raised, for example, a part of the new cost was met from university funds. But Sheff still found itself with new expenses that were difficult to carry. Even worse, from the scientific school's point of view, was the decision to charge each school its fair share of university administrative costs. Sheff already paid fees to the college for the use of the gymnasium and the library, and as the new university laboratories were opened, it paid its share of those. Then came the university charge for administration instituted in 1913–14, amounting to $25,000 or more for the school. This was a serious burden for Sheff, which suddenly found itself when seemingly most successful—in equipment, buildings, numbers of students, and so on—faced with large deficits. Since these losses were to continue, the school's independence was rapidly undermined.[45]

From the point of view of the university, these changes in salaries and administrative and financial procedures were an important element in converting Yale from a collection of schools into a university. If each department had been allowed to go its own way financially and administratively, they would never have been able to see the overall university viewpoint. Sheff would have remained jealous, guarded, and independent, aware of only its own problems. And the college—which was the most self-centered of all—would have continued to think that it was Yale. The scientific school was hit first by the changes outlined above, but the college was to have its turn. The administration followed a policy of raising endowment for the university as a whole and for its weaker parts. This procedure meant that the endowment of the college increased very little under Hadley. Then when the college's enrollment began to grow again during Hadley's second decade as president, and this was followed by rising costs during the war, the Academical Department soon found it no longer had the funds to continue without substantial university help.[46]

All these policies that undermined the independence of the college and Sheffield Scientific School promoted the interests of other parts of the university. The Medical School especially benefited from the change. When Hadley took over, the school was still a small, semiproprietary institution that asked only a high school education for admission. It possessed two old buildings and almost no endowment and was, in fact, in debt to the university. The largest salary paid a full-time teacher (and there were few of those) was $2,000.[47]

Despite this weak condition, the school was making progress. The number of students enrolled had been increasing steadily since 1888 and even the lengthening of the course from three to four years in 1896 had not stopped that growth. This development meant that the school had to consider its future expansion. It decided that it must move near the New Haven Hospital, and in 1899–1900 a large tract opposite that institution was purchased. In 1901 a new clinical building was erected there. In 1902 the first combined course with the college to shorten the time to a medical degree was instituted. And in 1905 the university began to make payments to the school "so to improve the work and increase the reputation of the School that it will be possible five years hence to appeal for special gifts and special endowments on such a scale as to make this subvention no longer necessary." [48]

The real forward movement began, however, in 1906. The first stimulus was Dr. Harvey Cushing's (B.A. 1891) rejection of a position in the medical school. Cushing, the great neurological surgeon, was especially critical of two aspects of the school. The first was its failure to have "clinical and teaching privileges *the year around*" in the hospital, and the second, its lack of mature students "who in their fourth year could safely have the freedom of hospital wards and benefit by the opportunities of working there." But "the crux of the situation" was the hospital. Perhaps as a result of this letter, a committee of the Corporation began conferences with a committee of the hospital looking toward a closer relationship between the two institutions. At the same time, the executive board of the school called the attention of the Corporation to the financial needs of the Medical Department.[49]

But here too, improvement took time, perhaps in part because the president and the Corporation were not yet convinced that it was possible to develop a first-rate Medical School in a city the size of New Haven. In 1909 entrance requirements were raised to a minimum of two years of college—causing an immediate drop in enrollment. Since the school was largely dependent on tuition fees for its income, a desperate situation resulted. At this point, however, it received assistance from outside. A study of medical education in the United States by Abraham Flexner for the Carnegie Foundation for the Advancement of Teaching reported in 1910 that Harvard and Yale had the only medical schools in New England worth developing. But of the Yale Medical School, the study said,

As the School now stands it would, in point of facilities still have to be classed with the better type of those on the high school basis; for though it has advanced to a two year college basis [for entrance], there has been as yet no corresponding improvement of facilities. To deserve the high-grade student body it invites, a more liberal policy ought to be pursued. The laboratory branches ought to be better manned, so that instructors may create within them a more active spirit. A University department of medicine cannot largely confine itself to routine instruction—certainly not after requiring two years of college work for admission to its opportunities. For the same reason the clinical faculties should be extended, probably through a more intimate connection with the present hospital. Its wards should be more generously used; more beds should be made accessible in them; and the missing pavilion for contagious diseases provided. Enough money ought to be spent on the dispensary to ensure in every department systematic and thorough discipline in examining patients, keeping records, etc.[50]

Abraham Flexner had put his finger on the same shortcoming noted by Cushing. The relationship of the school and the hospital was not satisfactory. The General Hospital Society, Inc., had been founded in 1826 to raise funds for a hospital in New Haven "auxiliary to the Medical Institution." But for some reason the hospital never achieved the promised close relationship with the school. By the time of the Flexner report, however, each institution realized that it needed the other. An agreement was finally reached in May 1912, whereby if Yale built and equipped for the hospital a modern pathological laboratory for $100,000 and endowed it with $500,000, by 4 July 1914 the hospital would then place itself at the disposal of the Medical School for teaching purposes and allow the Medical School to nominate the hospital's attending physicians. Since the university estimated that it would cost two to three million dollars to duplicate these facilities, it was delighted with this offer.[51]

Still Hadley hesitated. When the Medical School's centennial dawned in 1913, nothing had been done. Finally, faced with a proposal that it either "kill or cure" the school, the Corporation appointed a committee of doctors, graduates of Yale College but not of the Medical School, to study the situation. They concluded unequivocally that there was a place for medicine at Yale.[52]

With this encouragement and a first-class rating from the American Medical Association, Yale decided not only to carry out its agreement with the hospital but also to raise the two million dollars in endowment that the dean and faculty of the school had been calling for since at least 1907. A whirlwind campaign by perhaps the school's strongest supporter in the administration, Anson Phelps Stokes, enabled the Corporation to announce one year later that the Anthony N. Brady family had pledged $125,000 for the pathology laboratory and $500,000 for its endowment, on condition that the university raise two million dollars in endowment for the school within ten years. At the same time it was revealed that over one million dollars in gifts and pledges had been received toward that goal during the centennial year, 1913–14.[53]

The remainder of the needed endowment was harder to get. Not till 1918 was the *Alumni Weekly* able to announce, "The Yale Medical School now has not only the amount it started out to get, but it has increased that amount to over $2,500,000 and its future is assured." Little did the magazine realize that World War I and inflation would place the school in nearly as critical a position as it had occupied in 1913, but a commitment had been made that would be increasingly hard to deny.[54]

Despite excessive hesitation, the Medical School was helped perhaps more than any other department by the university-wide approach of Hadley's administration. But other departments received important aid as well. The Graduate School finally came into its own under Hadley. The greatest problem for that school, and for the administration, was that the Graduate School did not exist as a budgetary unit. It had no endowment and it borrowed most of its teachers from other schools. As Hadley said, when donors were approached to give to the Graduate School, they hesitated to do so. They could hardly believe there was such a place since so little money appeared to be spent on it. In fact, teachers in Sheff and the college gave substantial amounts of time to teaching in the school, but the salaries of these men were donated by their parent departments. To be fair to all, the Graduate School was set up as a separate unit on the books of the treasurer, and the shares of overhead were distributed to the various departments on 17 February 1913. This move, Hadley said, marked the beginning of a system of cost accounting at Yale. Charging the Graduate School for what it really cost to run it "will enable the Treasurer in his reports to come much nearer telling the truth about the financial relations between the departments than he has ever been able to do before." It was hoped, as well, that this would help to create a real faculty for the school, which would have some loyalty to it. It would also enable the dean to do some real planning:

As long as the Graduate School was regarded as a cooperative enterprise, it was impossible for the Dean and administrative committee of the department to arrange the course of instruction systematically and economically, or to perfect plans for their most efficient development. Each professor was at liberty to announce such graduate courses as he pleased, subject only to the control or advice of his colleagues in the undergraduate Faculty of which he was a member.[55]

This was a promising beginning, but further development ceased when Dean Oertel chose to remain in Germany upon the outbreak of war in 1914. The school continued under acting deans until 1916, when it was finally realized that Oertel would not be back and Wil-

bur Cross was persuaded to take the post. Cross was already professor of English in the Sheffield Scientific School and editor of the
Yale Review, but one more task seems not to have daunted him.[56]

That the Graduate School, despite its successful graduates, had a
long way to go before it could take its proper place at Yale was revealed by the comments of the new dean's friends: "There is no Yale
Graduate School," they said, and "Why did you accept an empty
title?" Cross did not intend to hold an empty title for a nonexistent
school. He immediately set about developing the powers of the dean
and raising the status of the school. Possessed of a "personality com-
pounded of salty humor, shrewd insight, and massive self-confi-
dence," and soon revealing an "exceptional ability to outguess and
outmaneuver those who opposed his designs," Uncle Toby Cross
rapidly achieved these goals. Professing his fear of fire in the old
dean's office (still next to the paint shop), he got a new office for the
school in a small brick building he called Gibbs Hall in memory of
the school's greatest graduate, J. Willard Gibbs. Then he reorganized the graduate faculty, splitting it into three divisions: language
and literature, mathematics and natural sciences, and social science,
history, philosophy, and education. And he created an executive
board to run the school. All this was approved by the faculty on 28
October 1916.[57]

Cross's most brilliant maneuver was the executive board. Because
the Graduate School faculty was made up of professors from all over
the campus, it tended to be large, diffuse, and unable to agree on
anything. The new executive board by-passed this ungainly body.
The board had the power to set admissions requirements, appoint
all committees, pass on departmental recommendations for fellowships and scholarships, and nominate to the Corporation professors
and other officers of instruction. The divisions handled what little
was left.[58]

The eight-member executive board was made up of the president
of the university, the dean, a representative elected by each division,
the chairmen of the committees on the degrees of M.A. and Ph.D.,
and the chairman of the admissions committee. It was created so
that Cross could move quickly and do what he thought necessary,
and it fulfilled these requirements. "Of all the boards and committees with which I have been connected," Cross wrote, "no other has
equaled this Executive Board in efficiency and mature wisdom." It

was this board which enabled the Graduate School to take its rightful place in the university after the war.[59]

Another old school which desperately needed help in Hadley's early years was the Divinity School. Most of its endowment was tied up in scholarship funds and a significant part of the faculty was aged. As a first attempt to revivify the school, Hadley appointed Frank K. Sanders as dean when George P. Fisher finally resigned after forty-six years in the department. Hadley wanted Sanders to be an active administrative head of the school and to raise money for it. Sanders seems instead to have accepted the place to promote his own field of study, though as the historian of the school pointed out, "what the school needed at that juncture was not a shot of Semitics." When Sanders failed to raise the endowment needed, it was suggested that the school break tradition and charge tuition. The Reverend Theodore Munger, an influential member of the Corporation, asked, "Why should divinity students be coddled? Are they poor? Then let them go and earn." But the Divinity School faculty was not swayed by this or other arguments. They voted down the tuition proposal, whereupon Sanders resigned.[60]

At this point in 1905 the Divinity School reached another low point. The failure to exercise retirement control brought about the loss of several faculty members in the space of a few years. After Sanders left, only Edward L. Curtis, Frank C. Porter, Benjamin Bacon, Williston Walker, and Lewis O. Brastow remained, and Brastow was on the verge of retirement himself. To carry on the school while a new dean was sought, Hadley appointed Edward L. Curtis acting dean. Curtis and his colleagues faced a depressing situation: attendance was declining, deficits were mounting, and the faculty was almost nonexistent. As its share in the effort to save the school, the Corporation agreed to assume half the school's $30,000 debt to the university if the school could raise the rest. So the dean and his young colleagues went forth during the summer of 1905 and collected the needed cash. This successful sacrifice of their own time and energy by the faculty for the sake of the school marked the turning point. New faculty appointments were made, the school's old buildings were renovated, the curriculum was revised, and, with all this, enrollment began to rise. The school had long been effectively nonsectarian, but to make sure there was no doubt on this point, the Corporation explicitly affirmed it in 1907.[61]

Finally, during 1911 a new dean was appointed. But it was too late to save Edward Curtis, who had "carried on despite a failing heart and eyesight half gone." He died just a week before Charles R. Brown took over. Curtis, with the help of Porter, Bacon, and Walker, had saved the school. Now Brown had the challenge of relating it "to the wider Church constituency, interdenominational and national in scope." [62]

The Corporation had appointed the right man. Brown was a gripping speaker, a diplomat, and an excellent administrator. Under him between 1911 and 1928 enrollment rose from 114 to 162 and the students came from an ever-widening area and an ever-increasing number of Protestant denominations. The faculty was increased from nine to fifteen, and the school's endowment rose from $900,000 to $1,500,000. At the same time, the curriculum that had been first worked out under Curtis was implemented and enlarged by Brown. Made up of several groups of studies, it allowed a student to prepare for one of several fields of work: pastoral service, missions, religious education, or social service. To indicate the widened goals of the school, the name was changed to the Yale School of Religion in 1914. It resumed its old name in 1920, when a department of religion was created in the Graduate School.[63]

While the Medical, Graduate, and Divinity Schools profited most from Hadley's attention, others also forged ahead. The Law School improved steadily during these years. Dean Wayland, who had saved the school from complete collapse in the 1870s and then developed it so carefully in the ensuing years, resigned in 1903. There were then 15 faculty members (though only the dean was full-time), 18 special lecturers, 348 students, a "stately" building, a library of 20,000 volumes, and an endowment of $150,000. On this small, firm base, a new dean might build. Henry Wade Rogers, a graduate of the University of Michigan, dean of its law school (1886–90), and president of Northwestern University (1890–1900), was just the man for the job. Under him the school continued its rise toward greatness. Quietly, by a process of constantly bettering the faculty, the student body, and the curriculum, the school improved. In 1904 its semiproprietary status was ended and it became an integral part of the university. The old relationship, whereby the Governing Board was paid out of whatever tuition was collected, was clearly not in the best interests of the university or the school. The faculty was gradually converted to a full-time basis. The case method was extended, despite the opposition of some of the old guard. In 1909 two years of college work were demanded for entrance, and in 1911 this was raised to four years. While the dean was allowed to waive this requirement, and did so when necessary, enrollment still dropped precipitately. In 1912 there were only 107 students. But from this low point, except for the disruptions of war, the school soon recovered.[64]

Rogers brought the Law School to a place among the very best law schools in the country before he was appointed to the United States Circuit Court bench. His successor, Thomas W. Swan from Harvard, continued Rogers's stress on full-time faculty members, a better student body, and the use of the case method. He also changed the slant of the education away from legal logic and toward a greater emphasis on social utility, definite and accurate terminology, and legal analysis. He was especially successful in bringing in excellent teachers. Under him, as well, it was decided in 1918 to admit women as regular students. But the first woman had already graduated from the Law School in 1886. Courageous Alice Rufie Jordan had caught Yale by surprise. When she arrived to enroll, she was told women were not allowed. She pointed out that there was no rule on the books prohibiting women, and thereupon registered. As soon as she graduated, the Corporation passed a rule restricting the Law School to men.[65]

It was not only the old schools that improved during these years. One new school, Forestry, appeared on the scene, and it immediately moved to a position of great influence in the land. The Forestry School was the gift of the Pinchot family in 1900. Since Hadley believed that public service in a worthwhile cause was one of the highest forms of activity, he was delighted with the gift. He also hoped to get money for a school of irrigation and a school of colonial administration, but with these (perhaps fortunately) he failed.[66]

The Forestry School was an immediate success. When New York State ceased providing Cornell's school with funds, it collapsed, and Yale inherited its students and the title of oldest forestry school in the country. The presence of Henry Solon Graves (B.A. 1892) and James W. Toumey during the early years and the active support of Gifford Pinchot (B.A. 1889) and his family brought the school quick prosperity. Its graduates within a very few years were dominating federal and state forestry and forestry education. After only fifteen years of existence, it had 153 men in the United States Forest Service.[67]

But no matter how the university and its schools grew, no president of Yale could ignore Yale College. Nor did Hadley want to. In addition, Yale College during the years of Hadley's presidency had many problems: problems of admissions, honors, the ordinary curriculum, vocationalism, teaching, student interest, and academic standards. As usual, Yale did not face these difficulties alone. They were questions at every college and university in America. But also as usual, Yale's history and traditions helped to give the college its own attitudes toward these issues.

Yale had been particularly fond of the old prescribed curriculum. Echoes of the famous Report of 1828 were still heard bouncing out of odd corners of the land. But by Hadley's time the old curriculum with its stress on mental discipline—on the functioning and not the furniture of the mind—was long gone. It was missed at Yale because it had articulated values that were hard to replace. The old Yale had enjoyed a marvelous closeness, familiarity, and competitiveness bred of each class's spending four years together, taking most of its courses from the same teacher. The intellectual leaders who emerged in this milieu were acclaimed by the entire class. Now, with the increasingly diverse curriculum and a much larger student body, all that seemed to be gone.

Yale did not, of course, ever accept the elective system in all its freedom and eclecticism the way Harvard did. Even when the elective system had taken over a large part of the curriculum (as it had by 1903), it tried to hold on in some small way to of the idea that there really were some things the educated man should know, and that there was some value in discipline—in just plain hard work. Yale College also leaned toward the idea that education should stress liberal culture, but whereas to Hiram Corson of Cornell, Barrett Wendell of Harvard, and many others the stress in that belief was on beauty, at Yale it remained moral.[68]

Beauty had never been Yale's strong point and it did not become so under Hadley. Though there were some teachers at Yale, like William Lyon Phelps, who were emotional "culture" men, most of Yale was akin to Phelps's other side—his love of athletics and activity for their own sake. Very few at Yale rejected the hustling, bustling world of the early twentieth century. Yale liked competition; it admired success; and even in a ruthless business culture, it thought the curriculum should promote these values.[69]

Yale was able to pursue the values of liberal culture not only because of its long-time traditions against the useful and scientific but also because it continued to have the Sheffield Scientific School as a safety valve. Those who wanted useful or scientific knowledge could always go to Sheff, the college said. In the same way, Yale was able to resist the pressure for a three-year B.A. course that threatened to sweep the academic world. Why, Yale men asked, change the college to three years, when anyone who wanted that could go to Sheff?[70]

President Hadley was a leader in Yale's endeavors to recapture the old values of hard work and competition. He worked out his ideas and expressed them, of course, over a period of time, but there was enough unity to what he said to treat it as a whole. In 1915 Hadley gave his criteria for the B.A. in what the university historian has called "Yale's most important official restatement of the liberal arts since 1886." Hadley said,

1. It must contribute to the intellectual training of the student. Rightly or wrongly, we exclude those studies which involve manual or physical ability alone. We do not count the ability to play an instrument . . . unless it is accompanied by a knowledge of musical theory and musical composition. . . .
2. The subject should be one where it is possible to test the attainments of the students. How are we to test the appreciation of pictures? . . .
3. The subject must be one in which we can obtain proper teachers. . . .
4. . . . The course should be such as to invite a certain degree of emulation. . . . If a study is of such a nature that each man works in isolation and does not derive much help and stimulus from others about him engaged in the same pursuit, his place is in the graduate school or in the research laboratory. . . .
5. . . . It must make him a profounder thinker and a better citizen. A public motive rather than a private one must constitute the dominant note in its appeal. . . .[71]

Hadley also stressed, on numerous occasions, competition: the idea of the curriculum being "a race course." It was an axiom with Hadley, the *Alumni Weekly* said, that the elective system destroyed competition and that competition was the breath of life to scholarship. The "prime necessity" of the course of study, Hadley thought, was character-building, and after this character was formed it was to be used in public service. College study, like university research, should be directed toward worthwhile public goals, not toward selfish purpose.[72]

Hadley's beliefs were more or less shared by most of the college faculty and by many of the alumni. While they often disagreed among themselves on the means of achieving the primary goals of intellectual power, character, and service, they tended to agree that the goals themselves were worthwhile. Thus the academic history of Yale College during this period can be viewed as a search for a way to recapture the perhaps idealized values of the old curriculum in this new, freer, age. The search was by no means consistent and it was often marked by division and conflict.

At first the drift was toward more freedom in elections, though an attempt was made to retain some continuity and progression in courses. At the same time that some were proclaiming the value of the breadth achieved by this program, however, an amazing number of vocational courses were creeping into the curriculum. Studies in professional subjects had been allowed since 1886, but under Hadley they grew at such a rate that law, medicine, divinity, and architecture had all worked themselves into the college curriculum prior to World War I. By 1907 Hadley was even saying that professional specialization could begin in the sophomore year.[73]

While Hadley thus supported hard work at the expense of breadth, he also worried about the top men. Yale, he thought, did a better job than anyone (even including the British universities) with the regular students. But Oxford certainly and Harvard probably did a better job "in developing independent intellectual activity." To help the superior student, Hadley suggested a pass–honors system for the college. The course of study committee approved the idea, but when it came to a vote of the entire Yale College faculty, it was rejected. As usual, the junior faculty wanted more attention paid to freshmen and sophomores, so they opposed the scheme. They were supported by the alumni. The Alumni Advisory Board made their position clear: "While opportunities for the minority who are keen for study should be constantly improved, the main purpose of Yale—as to undergraduates at least—is to fit the majority for useful work in the world. No scheme out of line with this thought would, we are satisfied, be approved by the alumni." [74]

The Yale College faculty seems to have been somewhat of the same mind as the alumni. The honors scheme finally developed in 1914, which continued with only minor changes through 1939, hardly favored the development of the better students. The program was based on the interests and capacity for work of the general student. It even lacked much in the way of honor, since general honors for high marks in regular work were still allowed. So the college faculty's interest in the regular student left the more intelligent with little reason to pursue honors work.[75]

Then the faculty turned back to the apparently more congenial job of deciding how to improve the lot of the ordinary undergraduate. In 1911 an attempt had been made to group freshmen and sophomores into those interested in languages, science, or social studies, though each was to take certain core studies in a modern foreign language, history or English literature (or both), mathematics or a modern science, and Greek and Latin (unless a student took both math and a science). The groups were formed to make sure these courses were taken in proper combination.[76]

At the same time as this reform was worked out the faculty voted an even more important change for upperclassmen—though with far less attention. It was prescribed that they should take a major in one subject and a minor in another related subject, for a total of twelve to fifteen hours. The remaining fifteen hours were open for free election. The significant element in this reform was, as George Pierson has pointed out in his thorough study of the educational developments of this period, that "after years of searching, the principle of coordinated, concentrated work was to form the backbone of upper class studies, even for the below average student." [77]

To certain members of the faculty, the reforms in the freshmen and sophomore studies seemed just too much "temporizing with vocationalism." Professor Edward P. Morris and a special committee "On the Policy of Yale College" found the old Yale curriculum so congenial that they even included in their 1915 report a section of the catalogue of 1846–47 that was little different from the 1828 report. Then with Morris putting the alternatives in such a way as to make the faculty uncomfortable, he steered them away from "vocationalism." The group system was dropped and certain minimal requirements instituted. So Yale College backed away from the 1911

movement toward what the students might find interesting and useful and returned to stressing certain basic liberal subjects and the
idea of discipline.[78]

The movement toward greater prescription was carried even farther in 1917. Under the leadership of Chauncey Brewster Tinker,
the faculty (acting with extraordinary speed because of the outbreak
of war) voted on 10 May that freshmen and sophomores were required to take ten specific subjects. Though anticipation through
examination was allowed, the Yale faculty had returned to the old
idea that certain things should be known by every educated man.[79]

The 1917 program was, in part, an attempt to answer certain
bothersome admissions questions. The whole problem of entrance
procedures was a sensitive one, affecting not only the undergraduate
schools but the alumni as well. From 1906 to 1910, of three thousand freshmen admitted to the college, only seventy-five came directly from midwestern high schools. This disturbed Yale, but it angered the western alumni, who called for Yale to accept high school
certificates for admission instead of demanding numerous entrance
exams in very specific subjects—many of which a typical western
high school boy had never had. Yale refused. In 1911 Dean Jones
told the aggressive western alumni, "We are not going to have any
certificate system, even if the Western Association of Yale Clubs tells
us to. That is flat." And he repeated that refusal time after time in
the same speech. At the least, his language was injudicious, for he
infuriated the westerners when, in fact, he was very interested in
getting more high school boys into Yale. For an institution that
prided itself on its national character and democracy, Yale was embarrassed that it took a higher percentage of its students from the
private preparatory schools than any place except Princeton.[80]

So Yale worked to solve the problem. And over the years, especially from 1911 to 1916, it worked out, as Pierson has said, "a substantial accommodation" without ever accepting high school certificates for admission. It not only became a full-fledged member,
jointly with Sheff, of the College Entrance Examination Board, but
it set up an alternative entrance procedure whereby a student's
school record was taken into account and he was only examined in
four subjects. To retain its ties with the preparatory schools, the old
system of fifteen examinations in various subjects was also continued. In addition, the scientific school and the college adopted the

same admissions requirements and the same examination papers. By these means, the Yale education was made more available to students the country over. All of this had been done so slowly and so seemingly grudgingly, however, that the western alumni were still not happy.[81]

But the admission of students under this new plan meant that Yale might be getting boys who were not as well prepared as they had been under the old fifteen-subject system. The required courses approved in 1917 were intended to ensure that every Yale graduate would have taken certain subjects: Greek or Latin, French or German, English, European and American history, economics, philosophy or psychology, chemistry or geology, and two of the following: mathematics, physics, biology.[82]

All the juggling with the curriculum had been an attempt not only to recapture old values but also to deal with the fact that Yale students were more interested in their games, newspapers, sports, and societies than they were in the curriculum. And in one way or another a change did come to the college that produced a new rise in enrollment, the slow retreat of the extracurriculum, and an increased interest in the things of the mind.

Thus as war clouds loomed over the Atlantic, Yale College was enjoying its literary renaissance and Yale University was a more balanced place than it had been when Hadley came to the presidency. Of course, much still needed to be done; no problem had been completely solved; but progress had been made on all fronts. Nonetheless, there was still much dissatisfaction over the condition of Yale —especially among certain alumni of the college. The war would give them a chance to transform the institution.

War and Reorganization

Yale men were not of one mind about the Great War. Professor G. B. Adams wrote from England that Germany must be defeated, while Dean Oertel of the Graduate School reported from Munich on the thrill of mobilization in defense of the fatherland. Other Yale men prepared to fight. The university was well represented at the summer military training camps in 1913 and 1914.[1]

By 1915 a number of graduates were calling for the university to be more active in preparing for war. Never questioning whether it was proper for a college dedicated to training men for service in church and civil state to prepare its students for military duty, the Alumni Advisory Board recommended instituting military training at Yale. Secretary Stokes, an *ex officio* member of the board, dissented from its report and, quoting William Graham Sumner, warned "What we prepare for is what we shall get." Few listened.[2]

Yale was again well represented at Plattsburgh and other training camps during the summer of 1915. And President Hadley was enthralled and excited by the preparedness movement. He praised military training for students during their long summer vacations and even suggested that such training could count toward a degree if associated with one or more courses during the academic year. To those who protested that military training was scarcely a proper part of a liberal education, Hadley argued that the content of a liberal education was now so uncertain that the change would make no difference.[3]

When Hadley visited the camp at Plattsburgh during the summer of 1915, he asked General Leonard Wood what Yale could do institutionally to aid preparedness. Wood suggested training men for service in the field artillery. So Hadley began to work with some students to create a Yale battery as part of the Connecticut National Guard. In the fall they called for volunteers and over a thousand students tried to enroll. Since there was a statutory limit on the size of the state Guard, only four batteries, 486 men, could be accepted. Hadley persuaded the army to assign an officer, Lieutenant Danford, to Yale. The faculty somewhat grudgingly allowed him to give a course in military history for college credit.[4]

It was easier to get men than equipment, Yale found. But finally in March 1916 artillery pieces arrived and training began in earnest. When the summer vacation of 1916 arrived, the units had had little opportunity to develop their skills. Nonetheless, they were called up when President Wilson mobilized the National Guard for the Mexican incident. Fortunately, instead of going to the border, the Yale batteries were sent to Camp Tobyhanna in Pennsylvania for training. Their adventures there, including the antics of Major Hiram Bingham (B.A. 1898), Yale's flamboyant discoverer of Machu Picchu, have been most entertainingly described by Dean Acheson (B.A. 1915).[5]

The first half of 1916 had also seen the formation, by F. Trubee Davison (B.A. 1920) and some of his college friends, of the Yale Volunteer Coast Patrol—a naval air unit—and the Yale Naval Training Unit (YNTU). But there were still some members of the university who opposed America's increasing militarism. Professor William Lyon Phelps, though beloved by many Yale graduates, alienated most of them during the spring of 1916. He made a speech at Hartford in which he said, according to newspaper reports, that "to spit on the flag was not so bad as to fight for it." The *Yale Alumni Weekly* explained that Phelps had actually said, "If a foreigner should spit on our flag that would not disgrace us so much as if we dyed our flag with American blood to avenge the insult." But many graduates seem to have felt that this statement was equally distasteful. President Hadley had to resist strong pressures to fire Phelps.[6]

The summer of 1916 was marked not only by the mobilization of the Yale batteries but also by the passage of the National Defense Act. This legislation provided for enlarging the army and for instituting Reserve Officers' Training Corps at universities, colleges, and military camps. Yale immediately became involved and, because of its previous experience, it became the sole college to give field artillery training. There were a number of hurdles to be surmounted, however, before the program could get under way. After the Yale batteries were demobilized, they had to be removed from state control. This was finally done by the device of cutting off federal recognition of them. Then officers had to be detailed to Yale by Washington, and the faculty had to vote credit for the new program. But the professors were not enthusiastic. President Hadley explained to them that while the army determined the amount of time students must spend on the program, the faculty had the right to decide what amount of credit they would receive. Finally in December 1916 the faculty affixed a preamble to the proposal stating that "the policy had been set by the President and the Prudential Committee," and then voted thirty-eight to nothing to give credit for ROTC training, though twenty-four professors abstained and some made their opposition clear.[7]

The Yale ROTC officially got under way in February 1917. Under the law only 220 students were allowed to enroll.[8] By that time, however, the pace of international events was rapidly quickening: on the first of the month, Germany had resumed unrestricted submarine warfare; on the third, diplomatic relations between the United States and Germany were severed. Two months later, war was declared.

Yale tried to keep up with this headlong progression, but some graduates complained that the university was not doing enough. On 9 March the *Yale Alumni Weekly* replied to the critics:

The feeling in some jingoistic quarters that the University "has done nothing" at a critical period in the nation's history doesn't hold water in the face of facts. Instead of talking, Yale has acted. Secondly, what Yale has done has been to take a pioneer stand among American universities for the new movement in this country for rational preparedness all along the line. Working first of all for permanency in such a programme, the University has organized its units of the Reserve Officers' Training Corps, of the Coast Patrol Aviation Corps, of the Motor Boat Patrol, and admitted students to them to the limit of the equipment. It has organized its section of the National Research Council, and of the Intercollegiate Intelligence Bureau.[9]

The university was proud of what it had accomplished. It should, perhaps, have been even more proud that it did not close off debate on the issue of peace or war. When David Starr Jordan asked to speak at Yale and was sponsored by William Lyon Phelps, Hadley was not happy; but under the urging of Secretary Stokes, he allowed Jordan to come. To a large and polite audience the pacifist made his address, and though he probably converted no one, he had at least been allowed to speak.[10]

Just as in the domestic conflict half a century earlier, war came while the students were on spring vacation. One Yale unit had already been called to arms. On 28 March, Aerial Coast Patrol number 1 had departed for active duty in Palm Beach, Florida. This unit and the Yale Aerial Coast Patrol number 2 (which was called up on 16 April) played a primary role in establishing the naval air force as an important fighting group, for the foresight of these young men enabled the navy to expand its tiny air wing with rapidity when the war broke out. In April 1917 the navy had only thirty-eight qualified aviators, and the Yale units were almost the only source of additional pilots. It was for this reason that Admiral Sims, who commanded the U.S. Naval forces in Europe, wrote after the conflict was over that "the great [naval] aircraft force which was ultimately assembled in Europe had its beginning in a small group of undergraduates at Yale University." [11]

Except for the Aerial Coast Patrol, most of the students returned to Yale after spring vacation. Soon they found themselves in a "voluntary" military camp. Nearly the entire student body was enrolled in an informal artillery training course. Physical exercises were held every morning, chapel was shortened, and classes were speeded up. Even many faculty members began to do military drill. [12]

At the request of the government, Hadley and numerous professors urged the students to stay in college. But there was a steady stream of departures. In May the *Alumni Weekly* estimated that 108 had left the college with 125 soon to follow, and 103 had left Sheff. Only a week later the magazine thought some 700 had already gone. No one really knew because the situation changed daily, but it was clear that it was going to be hard to keep the boys at their books. Uncertainty was one cause of the exodus. Even those officially enrolled in ROTC had no guarantee that they would receive a commission, so some undergraduates rushed to the army training camps where they were assured of becoming officers. Others entered ambulance units that the government asked Yale to provide. And a third group just went off and enlisted. [13]

In April the Corporation authorized the Medical School to form a mobile hospital after a pattern originated by the Italians. Though the U.S. Army table of organization provided for no such unit, the Yale hospital was accepted by the government and sailed for France in August. In its tents near the front lines in France at least one Yale medical student received his degree. [14]

The months after the outbreak of war were difficult ones for the Yale administration. The government's uncertainties and inabilities kept everything in confusion. Yale was prevented from having a summer camp for its ROTC. Lieutenant Danford and his assistants were called away for more important duty in May. But Yale had invested too much time, money, and effort in the program to let it die. Not only had it built Artillery Hall behind the gymnasium, but it had erected one of the finest armories in the country out near the Yale Bowl. So the Yale administration sought new officers for the corps and finally found some (including a disabled young Canadian officer named Raymond Massey), located guns, signed up 674 members of the depleted student body, and kept the Yale ROTC going.[15]

It continued to be difficult to keep the students in college. Not only were there still no assurances that their work in the ROTC would be of any use, but there was a definite environmental pressure to leave. On 5 October the *Yale Alumni Weekly* proudly announced that no member of Scroll and Key Society had returned to Yale, only two of Skull and Bones, one of Wolf's Head, and three of Elihu. Then in November Professor E. B. Reed pointed out that all the high stand men were gone: the *Yale Daily News* chairman and fourteen members of its board; the *Lit.* chairman and three of its four board members. Reed commented, "The intellectual leaders among the students are just where they ought to be—in France or making ready to go there." With these warlike tones ringing in their ears, more students left.[16]

The college tried to stem the flow. In January 1918 a new program was instituted. The ROTC and YNTU programs were revised as fifteen-hour, three-year curricula of straight military instruction. The courses would count toward a Yale degree, but it was expected that most college students would enter the service after they finished their program. They would have to return for one more year to graduate. In Sheff, however, by taking a few more hours during the military course, it would be possible to receive a Ph.B. based almost entirely on military studies.[17]

Yale's revised program did not last long. In May the army announced that for the next academic year new voluntary units would be established in many colleges and the ROTC would be coordinated with these units. This plan never went into effect, however, for late in the summer of 1918 the draft age was lowered to eighteen. If carried through, the new age meant the colleges would lose almost all their students and face at the least financial crisis and possibly bankruptcy. To prevent this denouement and at the same time train men, the government created the Students' Army Training Corps (SATC). Yale agreed to become one of the training camps, and under university urging, 1,300 students, including 800 freshmen, returned to Sheff and the college in the fall of 1918. By spring this number had grown to 2,400.[18]

Now Yale was an army camp. According to the *Yale Alumni Weekly,*

The graduate, dropping off at New Haven just now for a glance around the old University of his youth, walks reminiscently up Chapel Street and then steps over to the College Campus only to find himself suddenly translated into a foreign country. He is directed out of Osborn Hall, now a Red Cross workers' quarters, visits a nearly empty Dean's Office, glances into Connecticut and Lawrance rooms that are bare of all furniture except army beds, leaps out of the path of a student column quickly rounding through Phelps Gateway to a recitation, wanders into the basement of Wright Hall to be asked in one room whether he wants a physical examination by the local draft board lining up Class A 1 candidates for the Army and to find in another a former professor of German teaching mathematics, sees in various directions batteries of artillerymen "hep-hepping" it in foot-drill or to Artillery Hall, and crosses Elm Street only to be stopped at the gates of Berkeley Oval by very spruce young men in blue uniforms and white hats who hold him up with a gun for his admittance pass. Or, if he is a Sheff man, he finds that he cannot enter Sheff Vanderbilt Campus, now being utilized as barracks, and that his old society clubhouse is either empty or occupied by enlisted scientific students or is an emergency hospital. On his now bewildered way back to Elm Street such a graduate runs into the columns of artillerymen or sailors marching to a mess in the University Dining Hall, and will then wind up at the Graduates Club to find out at lunch from such old friends on a decimated Faculty as are not yet on war duty at Washington or in active service in Europe, what it is all about.[19]

Outside undergraduate Yale there was much going on as well. The university donated buildings and laboratories for the use of the Army Laboratory School which, between 1 August 1918 and 1 January 1919, trained at Yale 1,016 officers and men in the bacteriological and chemical techniques needed to combat epidemics in the field. Another important but smaller activity was the Yale Chemical Warfare Unit. It was the nation's center for the study of the medical

aspects of chemical warfare. Two Yale professors, Frank P. Underhill (Ph.B. 1900) and Milton C. Winternitz, accepted commissions
and ran the operation. Their group worked particularly on discovering the principles of gas poisoning and how to treat it. Some studies
were also undertaken on the development of new gases, particularly
of the mustard oil type. After the war the major general in charge of
the Chemical Warfare Service wrote Hadley to commend Yale especially for its study of the therapy of lung oedema, shock, and the pathology of toxic war gases. The work of this Yale unit later bore
fruit in an unexpected way. When the Dionne quintuplets were
born, it was revealed that the combination of gases used in their in-
cubators had been developed at Yale and had evolved from the wartime work done on the treatment of gassed soldiers.[20]

Another army activity at Yale, and one somewhat more under the
control of the university, was the Yale Signal Corps School for Officers and Officer Candidates. It was established in September 1918
under Yale faculty members supplemented by teachers hired from
other places. A radio communications course was given that, at its
maximum, had five hundred men in attendance. One hundred to
110 signal corps officers were being produced each month when the
program ended. Research was also done in this school on magnetic
methods of detecting and destroying submarines and on developing
a new explosive.[21]

On top of all these training units, Hadley found when he reported on Yale's wartime contributions in March 1918 that Professor Charles S. Hastings (Ph.B. 1870) was helping the navy to improve periscopes, telescopes, and other optical instruments;
Professor James F. McClelland was in charge of developing and
judging aircraft metal; Theodore S. Woolsey (B.A. 1901) from the
Forestry School was supervising the purchase of timber for housing
in France; Assistant Professor Charles Seymour (B.A. 1908) had left
to work for the Inquiry, the group helping the government to prepare for the peacemaking; Professor Henry A. Bumstead (Ph.D.
1897) as scientific attaché of the American Embassy in London was
an important link in the transmission of scientific knowledge between the allies; Andrew Keogh, the university librarian, was spending four days a week indexing and classifying things so the government could locate information it needed. Chittenden was serving as
chairman of the International Food Commission. There were many

others as well serving the government in a wide variety of activities.[22]

Thus when the war ended Yale felt great pride in its contribution. Almost 9,500 graduates and students had served in the armed forces (including 1,400 in SATC and YNTU when the war ended), while 384 more had served abroad in the Red Cross, YMCA, and other service organizations. Yale men had been awarded 594 orders, decorations, and insignia by countries as disparate as the United States and Montenegro. One graduate may have had problems with his Princeton friends after China awarded him the Order of the Striped Tiger. Some 227 Yale men lost their lives in the conflict.[23]

But Yale played its institutional role in the conflict at a great price. The idea of the university as a place of objective research and scholarship was undercut. On another level the institution's independence was reduced. Throughout the war the university faced the prospect of mammoth deficits, which were avoided only by the great generosity of the alumni. In 1917–18 the university would have had a $250,000 deficit had not the alumni contributed $500,000. Just two years before, for the twenty-fifth anniversary of the alumni fund, only $90,000 had been donated. In 1918–19, when the university would have had a deficit of $300,000, the alumni gave over $655,000. By these lavish gifts, however, the university's graduates became, more than ever before, shareholders in the enterprise. For even after the war ended, Yale continued to need their financial aid—and it could only be had at a price.[24]

The university emerged from the war with serious financial problems. As Hadley reported, "from the standpoint of Yale finance, the war came at exactly the wrong time." A generous gift caused part of the problem. In March 1917 the Corporation had revealed that Mrs. Stephen V. Harkness had offered to erect, on the block bordered by High, Library, York, and Elm Streets, dormitories for the college in memory of her son Charles W. Harkness (B.A. 1883). Work on the great new quadrangle had begun when the war struck, and Yale had already torn down one dormitory (Pierson Hall) and removed the heating plant and Peabody Museum. Then it had to stop construction on the new buildings. Since at this time Yale still viewed dormitories as productive investments, the loss of room rents was seriously missed. Hadley also reported that, on top of the losses caused by Harkness Memorial Quadrangle, the war came when we had committed ourselves to a large increase in salaries in the Law School. It deferred for two or three years the growth in numbers which will make that loss good. It created new problems for the Medical School and the Hospital. It deferred the time when endowments could be secured to solve these problems. And besides these three special difficulties, which are of a temporary character, the war has compelled us to deal with a more permanent one: the problem of salary increase.

Inflation had cut professors' salaries in half. In addition, according to Professor Irving Fisher, inflation had robbed the university of half of its endowment because that money was largely invested in bonds instead of common stocks.[25]

All of these financial problems made the university more than ever dependent on alumni contributions. But the alumni were not happy with the way Yale was being run.

When the war began, Yale had made great strides toward more centralized organization, control, and planning. The money power had begun to shift from the college to the university. The process of centralization was assisted by the war, as men in different schools but similar fields began to work together. But Hadley was opposed to systematizing everything. He thought the ill-effects of duplication between Sheff and Ac were greatly overdrawn and that the division was in many ways beneficial. Thus, though Hadley wanted a certain amount of additional reform, it would not have gone as far if he had had his way. But he did not. Aggressive, powerful alumni took control out of his hands and forced a radical reorganization of Yale.[26]

The great reorganization—revolution, in fact—was a result of a variety of influences. In the first place, Hadley's two able aides, Secretary Stokes and Treasurer Day, wanted to continue reforming the institution after the war. As George Pierson has written in his excellent chapters on the reorganization,

Stokes, in particular, had been impatient of Chittenden's intransigence [at Sheff], more interested than Hadley in building up the Medical School, more bold in looking toward growth along many lines. One of his pet schemes was the establishment of an active and forward-looking Department or School of Education. Another was an aggressive drive to increase the University's endowment and improve faculty salaries. Between them, in 1916–1917, Stokes and Day had persuaded the Corporation to recognize the necessity of long-range planning for the future needs and expansion of the University. At their suggestion the Corporation had created an Alumni Committee on a Plan for University Development and asked a number of prominent graduates—men of influence and large affairs—to look into the situation and help advise.

Stokes and Day opened Pandora's box. Discontent was rife among the alumni. They were disturbed by the continuing duplication between Sheff (especially its select course) and Ac. As noted earlier, many in the Middle West had been outraged by the handling of the admissions question. The curriculum still seemed out of touch with the realities of the day, as well as increasingly aimless and easy. Where were the hard work, competition, and camaraderie of the old required curriculum? Gone, they thought, into a pallid reflection of the Harvard elective mess. The Yale administration seemed distant, disdainful, and difficult. The whole place must be changed.[27]

These were the emotions prevalent, largely among western alumni but among easterners as well, when the alumni committee proposed by Stokes and Day went to work. In the fall of 1917 the new committee reported that it would investigate (1) university accounting and finance, including the salary question; (2) the administrative organization of the university and its departments; (3) the entrance examinations and the results of the current system; (4) the purpose and character of the undergraduate courses.[28]

As these subjects were being explored, America went to war. Then, in the summer of 1918, John W. Sterling (B.A. 1864) died and left Yale fifteen million dollars for new buildings, new professorships, and other worthwhile causes. These two events made the alumni committee more certain than ever of the importance of what it was doing. After the war and the Sterling bequest, Yale would face a whole new world. It must do so wisely and well.[29]

When the armistice came, Yale was deeply involved in the discussion of various educational and organizational questions. The pot was being stirred as well by Edwin Oviatt, pugnacious editor of the *Yale Alumni Weekly,* who was filling his columns with demands for reform. In one article in the form of a letter signed "Pater Studentis," which appeared on 22 November 1918, Oviatt voiced many of the dissatisfactions of the alumni. First, he was concerned about the university's organization: he wanted everything pulled together into a single interlocking whole, with consolidated departments and a unified plan. Second, he felt the Graduate School, the keystone in Yale's intellectual arch, had been neglected: it needed professor-

ships, fellowships, dormitories, and a faculty of its own composed of
the very best men in the country. Showing a continuing opposition
to all things German, he urged that it be the first graduate school in
America to drop the Ph.D. fetish. Third, Yale must improve its relationship with the public schools: "You have made progress along
these lines," he wrote, "but the last Dean's report of a normal Freshman Class showed that only twenty per cent of the boys came from
high schools, and those almost entirely from neighboring public
school systems that had the Yale requirements in mind. So long as
Yale demands Latin as a necessary requirement for entrance, just so
long will it fall short of being the 'national institution' we hear so
much about at Yale alumni dinners." Fourth, he stressed good teaching. This, Pater Studentis said, concerned graduates more than anything else. They did not care if a man was a celebrated scholar; they
only wanted to know if he could teach. Fifth, what was taught
should be harder and college life should become more competitive.
Sixth, the elective system should be dropped, and a group system
adopted, for Oviatt feared the students were slipping into taking
"gut" courses. Seventh, on the subject of the Sheffield Scientific
School, he did not like to see it ranked as second class by the U.S.
Commissioner of Education because it crowded four years' work
into three. If the course was lengthened, Sheff could become a technical scientific school at the same time that it allowed the students
greater opportunity to study the liberal arts. And eighth, Pater Studentis wanted the scientific school to become part of the university:

So far as I can see, Sheff is tending to become a university itself, with its
engineering and natural science courses in one school, its business administration and Select Course in another, and its postgraduate course in a
third. Sheff finances ought to come into the general University pool, as
also should its educational policies.[30]

The day after the appearance of Pater Studentis' letter the alumni
committee, which had held most of its meetings in New York, came
to New Haven, interviewed Stokes, Day, and one professor, and then
voted some startling recommendations:

1. That steps be immediately taken to provide that all undergraduate instruction shall be under a common control while the teaching force
   may be subdivided into such separate departments of instruction as
   may be deemed necessary.

2. That a definite course of instruction, or that a curriculum consisting of a consistent and largely prescribed character be provided in such undergraduate school leading to each of the several professional schools, or towards the life work of various students.

3. That emphasis among the instructors in such undergraduate school be laid on teaching rather than on research work.

4. That steps be taken as soon as practicable to consolidate, if possible, the Corporation known as the Trustees of the Sheffield Scientific School with Yale University.[31]

These sweeping proposals galvanized the president and fellows into action. They voted on 16 December 1918 to lengthen the Sheffield Scientific School's undergraduate course to four years (a recommendation Sheff had made itself) and to abolish the select course. They decided to improve the joint admissions policies of the undergraduate schools. And they approved a recommendation of the executive board of the Graduate School to place the administration of all advanced degrees and certificates in science under the jurisdiction of that department. The president and fellows failed to act on a recommendation that a joint freshman year for both the college and scientific school be instituted, but they went on record as making no promise to keep the freshman classes separate.[32]

The Corporation at this point feared that university reform was slipping out of its control. Fellow William Adams Brown later reported that while they felt the alumni committee's suggestions deserved respectful consideration, "it hardly seemed consistent with the dignity of the Board or conducive to sound educational procedure to make the alumni report, as such, the basis of academic discussion. It seemed to the Corporation that if changes were needed, it was they who must suggest them." [33] So at this meeting on 16 December they appointed a Conference Committee of the Corporation consisting of Hadley, Brown, and Henry B. Sargent.

The pressure for reform continued to build during the following month. By 20 January 1919, however, the fellows were taking control. When President Hadley seemed somewhat unenthusiastic about the various proposals, the fellows circumvented him by abolishing the Conference Committee and creating the Committee on Educational Policy made up of Brown, Sargent, and Alfred Ripley. And at the same meeting the Corporation voted to reduce the residence requirement for M.A. and M.S. degrees from two years to one, to recommend the grouping of faculties of the university into departments of study, and to send this last proposal to the University Council for its consideration. The fellows also at this time asked representatives of Sheff to meet with the Prudential Committee to discuss various proposals looking to a closer integration of the scientific school with the university. The most important of these suggestions asked

that the Trustees, as elective vacancies occur in their Board, follow the procedure of the Peabody Trustees by submitting nominations "to the approval and confirmation by the Corporation of Yale University," and that as far as possible such vacancies should be filled by electing members of the Yale Corporation with a view to securing complete harmony between the boards.

It was also proposed that the Sheffield trustees consider the advisability of changing their act of incorporation to assist in making their board ultimately the same as the Yale Corporation. As Sheff learned of this bold attack on its independence, the Corporation Committee on Educational Policy was organizing, mapping a brisk campaign, and inviting any permanent officer who so desired to get in touch with the committee either in writing or in person.[34]

When the Corporation met on 17 February 1919, they heard from the scientific school trustees that, while they would be willing to make a few gestures in the direction of a closer connection with the university, they had received legal advice informing them that they would be recreant in their trust if they allowed themselves to become merely a carbon copy of the Yale Corporation.[35]

At this meeting the board also received the printed proposal of the Alumni Committee on a Plan for University Development, which had been rushed to completion upon the Corporation's hasty conversion to reform. These recommendations were first discussed publicly before a large crowd on Alumni University Day, 22 February 1919. In its major points, the committee recommended that

1. A chancellor be appointed to serve as something of a president for education (thus stripping the titular president of most of his powers in this important area)

2. Sheffield Scientific School be made part of the university

3. All faculty members be appointed for a term of years and to the university rather than to a particular school

4. Faculty members be organized in departments of study

5. Yale College become the undergraduate school for the humanities while Sheffield Scientific School serve for the sciences

6. A combined freshman year with its own dean and faculty be formed to serve as a sort of junior college for Sheff and the college

7. Executive boards be formed for Sheff, the college, and the combined freshman year

8. Higher salaries be paid, but teaching be more efficient and no limit set on the amount of teaching a faculty member could do

9. Undergraduates take prescribed courses in preparation for their ultimate careers

10. A dean of students be appointed to deal with disciplinary and other undergraduate problems

11. The University Council be enlarged and invigorated

12. New Corporation committees be created

13. Common entrance requirements be adopted for Sheff and the college and Latin dropped as a requirement for admission

These were revolutionary proposals. But the university was warned, in effect, to accept them. In an Alumni Day address, Samuel C. Bushnell told the university administration that "nothing could do more to keep the stream of alumni generosity flowing than hearty support by the university authorities of such policies as seem after mutual conference worthy of adoption." [36]

When President Hadley spoke to the massed alumni on this important day, he immediately alienated them. If Hadley had been at his best during the war, as some thought, he was at his very worst now. He was, his son felt, tired after the strain of seeing Yale through the conflict, so he reacted badly and even misrepresented his attitude toward the proposals. Since his greatest concern at this point was to raise faculty salaries, which had been badly depleted by inflation, he seemed opposed to everything else. He told the alumni that "nearly everything that has been proposed this morning has merit—if we had money enough to carry it out. But no reform is worth carrying out if it is going to tie our hands in such a way as to drive good men from Yale to other colleges, or from college service into business and professional life." He favored the organization of the faculties into departments of study, but suggested that plans for more administrators should be postponed until Harkness Memorial Quadrangle was finished and university attendance had returned to normal. As to the faculty, what Yale could do right now was to select men who were capable of earning money outside the university and help them to do so. Hadley thought an assistant professor getting $2,500 from Yale should be able to earn $1,000 to $1,500 more during the summer. That, in fact, was what the long summer vacations were for.[37]

Hadley's financially conservative policy angered the alumni and his proposals on summer work even caused Dean Jones of the college to publicly split with him in a speech to the alumni that afternoon. The *Yale Alumni Weekly* was appalled by the president's remarks. In an editorial published 28 February it confessed to "an entire inability to understand or to accept the point of view regarding Yale reorganization which the President of the University gave to the graduates on Alumni University Day." The outraged reaction to his speech was so great that Hadley had difficulty sleeping for weeks afterward. And very soon after the address, he caved in. He restated his position in a letter to the *Alumni Weekly* published 7 March. The editor was delighted:

That letter is precisely the right word at the right time. . . . The President supports completely and enthusiastically the findings of the Alumni Committee on University Development. The cordial and candid manner in which he accepts those proposals can make only the best impression and leaves no doubt as to the success of the principles recommended by the Alumni Committee, when, incorporated in the Corporation's Committee Report, and herewith endorsed by the President, they will come before the Corporation to-morrow.[38]

The Committee on Educational Policy submitted its own somewhat similar reorganization report to the president and fellows on 8 March 1919. The Corporation approved the draft and ordered Secretary Stokes to circulate it to faculty and alumni and informed them that the Corporation would act in just nine days. They would, however, consider "minor modifications" in the proposal. The pace was now headlong.[39]

Stokes mailed out the draft on 11 March and asked for replies by the fifteenth. The copy sent to the alumni noted the differences between the alumni proposal and the committee's suggestions and explained the reasons for the changes. The most significant alteration was in the position of chancellor (ultimately called the provost). While this officer would be appointed, he would be responsible to the president. The committee commented, "Any plan to divide the final executive authority now placed by the Corporation in the President would be unwise." On the matter of additional Corporation committees, while accepting the need for them the fellows felt that except for the financial committee they should only be advisory, making their recommendations to the Corporation or its Prudential Committee. The Committee on Educational Policy also rejected the suggestion of term appointments for all faculty members. It noted that such a change would be interpreted outside Yale as an attack on academic freedom and that it would probably prevent the university from getting or keeping the services of independent thinkers. In any case, the committee pointed out, the Corporation had the right to remove professors. Whereas the alumni had recommended that chairmen of the departments should be appointed by the chancellor, the Corporation felt they should be nominated by the professors of all grades, subject to the approval of the president. The Committee on Educational Policy accepted the idea that Ac should be the school for the humanities and Sheff the school for science. It pointed out, however, that this difference could not be made absolute because of existing endowments. Furthermore, it was thought wise to keep a few men from other fields on each faculty to assist in developing curricula. The idea of having executive boards for the college and Sheff was rejected. The committee believed that "the interest of the individual Professors in the institution will be, at least in the near future, more surely maintained if he continues to be a member of a Governing Board." [40]

Even in the short time allowed, the Corporation received numerous responses to its report. The most forceful came from the Yale College faculty. The professors felt Hadley had made an implied promise that they would be consulted about these changes, yet they had not been. So they called a meeting without informing either President Hadley or Dean Jones, and on the fifteenth they voted their disapproval of the common freshman year. They also asked to be allowed to consider the whole question of Latin and what degree should be given in the college for those who had not studied it. Further, they forcefully resolved

that the General Faculty of Yale College learns with concern of the intention of the Corporation to establish a common Freshman year for the

College and the Scientific School, and hope that the Corporation will cooperate with the Faculty to prevent the change from exerting any deleterious influence upon the life of the institution.

As George W. Pierson commented, "This was . . . strong language.
The Corporation can hardly have relished the hint that their own
action might be deleterious to the institution." So without more
ado, the Corporation at their meeting of 17 March 1919 accepted
the reorganization plan with only minor changes. They also chas-
tised the Yale College faculty for meeting without notifying the
president and dean.[41]

The new plan accomplished the following: The university was divided into four main divisions, all under the president. There was
to be a division of instruction and research, directed by the provost;
a division of records, publications, and public relations, subject to
the secretary; a division of business administration, under the treasurer; and a division of student welfare, conducted by a dean of students. For the Corporation, the Prudential Committee was to continue as the executive committee, but rotation in membership was
provided for. In addition, there were to be five standing committees
of the Corporation: educational policy, finance, honorary degrees,
architectural plan, and buildings and grounds. The president was to
be *ex officio* member of all committees.

To improve the coordination of the work of the university, the
University Council was expanded and given the right in all matters
where two or more schools were concerned to determine questions
of educational policy—subject only to the approval of the Corporation. The schools of the university were to be ruled by governing
boards made up of all their full professors, except in the Graduate
School where the executive board was retained, although with somewhat diminished powers. Deans of schools were to be elected for a
term of years by the governing boards, subject to the approval of the
Corporation. In a reaffirmation of an earlier vote, the old division
between individuals in the same fields but different schools was broken down by the creation of departments of study. Chairmen of departments were to be nominated by the president, after consultation
with the professors, and elected by the Corporation.

For the undergraduate schools, the select course was transferred to
the college and a common freshman year was set up. The college,
the plan said, was to be for nonprofessional study of the arts and sci-

ences, while Sheff was to be for professional study of science and engineering. In any case, however,

the Schools of the University [were] to be so coordinated and interrelated that "the principle of interchange of course and facilities" [would] be applied to all the Schools to the fullest extent, so as to prevent unnecessary duplication of similar courses and to make it possible for any well-qualified student of one School to take any course approved by his Faculty in another School.

The Corporation also approved the alumni's suggestion of group courses "designed to meet the needs of men planning to enter various professions and callings." [42]

There were many other less important aspects of the total plan, but what it came to in sum was that the graduate and professional schools and the central administration were all strengthened at the expense of the undergraduate departments. Both the scientific school and the college were stunned. Director Chittenden clearly saw that the Sheffield Scientific School was finished. How could anyone decide what was professional and what nonprofessional study of science? The faculty of Yale College were upset because, as the university historian said,

Apart from the virtues or demerits of particular provisions there was no blinking the unpleasant fact that Reorganization had been initiated, shaped, and finally put through without adequate consultation, and in some matters in almost casual or scornful defiance of Faculty wishes. More accurately it had been rushed through, largely by outsiders, in disregard alike of their constitutional powers, their experience, and their most cherished beliefs.[43]

But how could this radical reform have ever happened at conservative old Yale? In part, it came about because fellows like W. A. Brown, chairman of the Corporation's Committee on Educational Policy, thought Yale was "conservative, democratic, self-centered, self-satisfied." It seemed to him that nothing ever changed at the university because some venerable figure always prevented it by protesting that "such a thing has never been done before." In addition, the undergraduate schools had been disorganized by the war. When the reorganization movement began, many of the schools' leaders were away, so the momentum increased to the point where it could not be stemmed when they returned to the scene. Further-

more, despite the affection of the alumni for President Hadley, certain of his actions over the years had alienated them enough so they
were willing to override his wishes. All of these factors combined
with the old desire for a more efficient university to produce the
great reorganization.[44]

Despite the fact that reorganization was, at least in part, aimed at
him, Hadley accepted it cheerfully and worked to make it a success.
Then, in the spring of 1920, feeling that good progress was being
made, Hadley announced that he was going to retire on 30 June
1921, by which time he would be sixty-five. His long presidency
had been marked by great achievements. All the schools of the university had been improved. Over forty buildings had been purchased or erected, running from the huge bicentennial buildings,
Harkness Memorial Quadrangle, and Yale Bowl, through laboratories and classrooms, down to power plants and a baseball cage. In
addition to this great physical development, the endowment grew
from $4.5 million to over $25.5 million. And this sum did not even
include the great Sterling bequest, whose promise still lay in the future. Even more important than these physical and financial
achievements, however, or the development of the various schools,
was the shift in administrative and monetary power away from the
constituent parts, especially the college, and to the university. Yale
was still not a balanced institution, but now it could become one.[45]

Part Five

Action and Inaction

1921–1950

James Rowland Angell and the
Triumph of the University

The announcement of Arthur T. Hadley's impending retirement set off perhaps the widest and most intense search for a successor in Yale's history. Everyone recognized that the university had reached another crossroad in its history. If the advances made under Hadley —and especially the important progress looked for from the trauma of reorganization—were to be realized, no mistake could be made in the choice of the next president.[1]

A Corporation committee, chaired by Samuel H. Fisher and made up of men with a wide variety of interests from many geographical areas, was appointed to undertake the search. The members were immediately forced to face the fact that there was one leading candidate for the post: Anson Phelps Stokes. His important contributions to Yale during his long tenure as secretary of the university were unquestioned. On the other hand, despite support from Hadley and several Corporation members, his candidacy had some severe shortcomings. He was a minister at a time when many Yale men wanted to escape from that old tradition for good. As perhaps the most influential and dynamic member of Hadley's administration, he had made numerous enemies as he pushed through various programs. In addition, his early outspoken resistance to military preparedness, his "YMCA spirit," and his tendency to sometimes appear to treat people with condescension combined to bring many others into the camp of those who opposed him.[2]

Confronted with this clear-cut resistance to Stokes, the committee decided to spread its net wide. Ultimately, nearly eighty men were considered for the presidency and ten months were consumed before a conclusion could be reached. After the first few months, Stokes was still in the lead, followed by Henry Sloane Coffin (B.A. 1897), well-known Presbyterian minister and fellow of the Yale Corporation, Herbert E. Hawkes (B.A. 1896) dean of the college at Columbia, and George E. Vincent (B.A. 1885), president of the Rockefeller Foundation. A string of others trailed behind: Henry Solon Graves

(B.A. 1892), chief of the U.S. Forest Service, Henry P. Davison and Dwight Morrow, partners at J. P. Morgan, and even William Howard Taft (again) and Herbert Hoover.

As the committee struggled with its difficult job, it learned that the impression Yale made on the outside world might make it difficult to get someone to accept the presidency. Some possible candidates had heard too much about the independence of Yale College faculty to be eager for the post. The chairman of the Corporation committee, and perhaps other members, began to wonder if that independence was the cause of Yale's failure "to grow in numbers and public estimation."

Sometime in the fall of 1920 the name of James Rowland Angell was introduced for consideration. Soon he joined Dwight Morrow at the head of Fisher's list of possible contenders from outside Yale. By November the Stokes supporters began to realize the hopelessness of their cause and to move to other candidates. At the Corporation meeting in January 1921, Coffin still seemed to be in the lead, closely followed by Vincent, Angell, and Morrow. But Coffin, like Stokes, suffered from the bar sinister of the ministerial collar, so he soon fell by the wayside. Morrow was then informally sounded out, but he felt that he had a dual disability: he lacked educational experience and he was not a Yale graduate. So he withdrew himself from consideration. By this time Angell was drawing increasing support. When he was questioned about his interest in the position, he was not enthusiastic, but he did not say no. Finally, after a campaign to encourage and convince him, he agreed to come to Yale. Thereupon, on 19 February 1921, the first nongraduate since Thomas Clap was unanimously elected president.[3]

James Rowland Angell had impressive credentials. Son of a great president of the University of Michigan, he had had a distinguished career as a professor of psychology, dean of the Faculty of Arts, Literature, and Science, and, for a time, acting president, at the University of Chicago. He had served as chairman of the National Research Council and, most recently, as president of the Carnegie Foundation. He was now in his early fifties, "a brisk middle-sized man with a generous nose, shrewd, reticent grey eyes, hair bordering on the carroty, and a quizzical way of talking out of the side of his mouth." Good-humored, quick-witted, and with great speaking ability and rare analytical power, he made an ideal presiding officer. His most serious fault was an unwillingness to insist on the course he favored, which sometimes misled his critics into believing that he lacked convictions. But Angell's philosophy was quite clear and very different from his predecessor's. Where Hadley had spoken of the moral value of Yale life, Angell stressed things intellectual. He had four basic beliefs from which all else stemmed: in intellectual quality, flexibility (in habit and organization), diversity (in men, values, and approaches), and integration (of parts and studies).[4]

In his inaugural address, Angell devoted a major section to the importance of research and the need for strong graduate and professional schools. They were the most "bracing influence" to which the college could be exposed. He said, "It will always be true that where the great investigators and scholars are gathered, thither will come the intellectual *elite* from all the world." His words for the college were few and none too comforting to the college faculty, for he spoke of the need for change, of the failure of the liberal arts to secure either culture or discipline, and of the necessity of thinking anew about the problems of motivation and the boundaries of the liberal arts.[5]

Angell's inaugural was welcomed by men in the graduate and professional schools and sciences, for they all felt their fields would prosper. The college faculty was not encouraged. Some had been disturbed by even the suggestion of a non-Yale man for president. Professor Phelps reacted to the idea by saying he would feel "exactly as a Catholic would feel if a Mohammedan were elected Pope." Phelps had come around to support of Angell, but others greeted his election and his inaugural with suspicion and even, in some cases, hostility.[6]

But while the college attitude was serious, it was not Angell's only difficulty. The university he took over faced many real problems. Angell felt that "the most menacing was . . . financial." For many years Yale had made ends meet only because of large alumni fund donations. Since no university had ever done this before, it seemed unsafe—even unnatural. In 1919–20, the alumni fund had taken in over $640,000, thus saving the university from a $475,000 deficit. In 1920–21, it had taken an appropriation of $50,000 from special income and over $40,000 from the contingency reserve fund, in addition to the alumni fund gift, to balance the books. Two more problems with financial ramifications were how to use the great Sterling bequest and how to keep it from stopping other gifts. Since it was to be used largely for entirely new buildings and projects, the university had to make clear that it still needed large donations to support existing programs.[7]

Beyond the financial difficulties, there were other matters of major concern. There was the need to carry out the reorganization plan and at the same time deal with the morale problems it had left in its wake. As George Pierson noted, because of reorganization, Angell would find "the Professors of Yale College sometimes suspicious and hypercritical, sometimes indifferent to the point of stupor." In addition, the university was still too college-oriented: far too much of all the money available was spent on the college; the college faculty still had inordinate power, and the alumni continued to be most interested in that department.[8]

As if these problems were not enough, the rush of students after the war put numerous strains on Yale—on its teaching and housing as well as its finances. To top it all off, these students came from a new postwar world—a place of different attitudes and changed behavior—and this created additional pressures for the old institution.[9]

Despite all these concerns, Angell's reign began with what must have seemed to some observers an auspicious sign: the Yale crew, which had been defeated by Pennsylvania, Columbia, Princeton, and Cornell, and then labeled "gutless" by its coach, reversed form and defeated Harvard two days after Angell's inauguration. It was one of the great upsets of all time.[10]

Perhaps buoyed by this omen, Angell turned to the complicated task of running diffuse, difficult old Yale. And the sixteen-year presidency that followed was to be marked by extraordinary achievement. The most obvious development, though not the most important, was the rebuilding of Yale.

Angell inherited, it will be recalled, the promise of the Sterling bequest. Based on plans begun while Hadley was president, a great building program was undertaken, and over the years from 1922 to 1932 so many buildings were constructed and named after Sterling —Sterling Chemistry Laboratory, Sterling Hall of Medicine, Sterling Power House, Sterling Memorial Library, Sterling Law Buildings, Sterling Divinity Quadrangle, Sterling Tower, Sterling Quadrangle, and (by some strange oversight *not* called Sterling) the Hall of Graduate Studies—that some observers thought Yale should change its name to Sterling University. Through all the building, Yale just kept drawing on the Sterling trustees, never knowing when the money would give out. In the end, $22,773,648 was spent on buildings, $12,539,799 had gone to endow professorships, fellowships, and scholarships, and $3,665,621 had been put aside for maintenance and the residential quadrangle. Over the years, the $15 million estate had grown to such an extent that a total of $38,970,068 came to Yale.[11]

As this tremendous program was beginning to draw to a close, Yale heard the news that Harvard had received a gift of $3 million for a residential house plan (soon $11 million was promised). This "bolt from the blue," as President Lowell called it, came from Edward S. Harkness, a graduate of the Yale College class of 1897. But why, Yale men wanted to know, had it gone to Harvard rather than to Yale? The story that finally emerged was a highly complicated one that revealed much about both Yale and President Angell.

Ever since the end of World War I, Yale had faced a housing shortage. Some new dormitories had been built, but they were, as George Pierson put it, "mere city barracks." In 1923 a limit of 850 had been put on the size of the entering freshman class, but there was some doubt that this line could be held. There was also a lack of decent places to eat. All-in-all, the old closeness of the class and the college were being lost.

The first change away from the old-fashioned Yale dormitory had come with the Harkness Memorial Quadrangle. Its existence, along with the pressure of numbers, helped President Angell to reach the conclusion that perhaps the way to build in order to allow for future expansion and also solve the problem of the increasing diffusion of college life was to construct residential quadrangles of the Oxford–Cambridge type. He first suggested the possibility to the Educational Policy Committee of the Corporation in January 1925.[12]

There were problems in the way of such a radical restructuring of college life. The class had long been the most important unit at Yale, and no one wished to lose the loyalty engendered by that unit. When Woodrow Wilson had proposed residential quadrangles at Princeton in 1906 the *Yale Alumni Weekly* had disapproved. At

Yale all such a plan could do, the *Weekly* thought, was to hurt class spirit by breaking up the group. That sentiment still existed in the 1920s. But there were some members of the university who were definitely interested in Angell's suggestion. Samuel H. Fisher got the president to write down his ideas during the summer of 1926, and in September he took them to Edward S. Harkness.[13]

The Harkness family had already done much for Yale. From their fortune, which was based on Stephen V. Harkness's ventures with John D. Rockefeller in Standard Oil, Edward's mother had given the memorial quadrangle and $3 million for faculty salaries. His brother had made a donation for a new classroom building. Edward had already provided the funds for a drama department and theater, to fix up Weir Hall for the architecture department, and to build a new tomb for Wolf's Head senior society. In April of 1926 he gave the money for a new art gallery, and during 1926–27 he subscribed $3.5 million for Yale's endowment drive.[14]

Clearly Edward S. Harkness was devoted to Yale. And Fisher was quickly able to interest him in Angell's idea. Harkness had personal reasons for liking the proposal. While he had enjoyed his years as an undergraduate, "it had troubled him," as George Pierson explained,

and it continued to trouble his thoughts in later years, that some of the men he knew and liked—"average men" like himself—had not been chosen [for fraternities and societies], and so had been excluded from experiences that would have been rewarding and constructive. The system of the college seemed to him in some part defective as an environment for individual development and growth.

Harkness asked Fisher why Yale did not begin construction. Fisher explained that it was considered best to start with several quadrangles, not just one, and that would cost $10–12 million. After mulling the question over for several hours, Harkness said, "Sam, I'll do it." [15]

But from donor's wish to Yale's deed turned out to be a long and tortuous way. Fisher told Angell of the offer but informed him he must keep it secret. On top of that, Yale was in the midst of a great endowment campaign for "a better, not a bigger, Yale" so it was felt that little could be done about Harkness's offer until the drive was over. In March 1927 Angell went to England on what appeared to be a spring vacation but was really an exploration, with Fisher and architect James Gamble Rogers, of the English universities. Then in May Angell asked the undergraduate Faculty of Arts and Sciences to study the whole question of housing the college. A strong faculty committee was appointed with Angell as chairman, but unfortunately the president felt he could not even hint that money might actually be available for solving Yale's problems. Perhaps for that reason the committee never even discussed his suggestion of many small colleges. In March of the following year the committee finally produced a report in which it recommended building four quadrangles for freshmen, completing the Vanderbilt–Sheffield quadrangle, and further study of the question of what to do about Yale College.[16]

Even before this report emerged, Harkness was becoming impatient. He informed Angell that the deadline on his offer was 1 July 1928. But he still insisted on secrecy. Then when the committee reported, he was not especially interested in their proposals. So the mills turned. A Corporation committee studied the idea of freshman colleges, but the freshman faculty was opposed to the concept. Angell tried to get the Corporation to do more, but they were busy and still did not know of Harkness's offer, so nothing happened. Finally, Angell gave up and left for Europe for a summer vacation without even writing to Harkness. The deadline came and went without any word from Yale.

Furious, Harkness began to think of promoting the plan elsewhere. In the fall he turned to Harvard. President Lowell, who had somehow heard of the offer to Yale, was all ready for him. Harvard's certainty of what it wanted convinced Harkness. In December 1928 he agreed to support the house plan, and by April 1929 he had promised over $11 million for it.

Before it was revealed that Harkness was Harvard's benefactor, Yale continued to investigate the housing question. A high-powered group made up of Treasurer Day, Provost Seymour, Fisher, and Rogers drew up a quadrangle plan. Then, with Angell pressing for small residential units, on 8 December 1928 the Corporation (which still knew nothing of Harkness's original offer) approved the concept of building for the undergraduates "small units housing from 150 to 250 students each, with Common Rooms and other facilities designed to foster a spirit of social intimacy and companionship."

News of this proposal was rushed to Harkness, and despite his recent anger at Angell and Yale, he said he would probably support the plan. Though the revelation that Harkness was Harvard's benefactor came out shortly thereafter and produced much embarrassment and many recriminations at Yale, ultimately all the problems and misunderstandings were overcome. The main difficulties throughout, as George Pierson has observed, had been the secrecy that Harkness insisted on and the fact that he and Angell could not get along:

Temperamentally they were poles apart: the one simple and slow of thought, but unshakeable in his convictions, the other with a mind like quicksilver but a sensitivity approaching indecision. Angell feared he was confronted with a man of wealth, too literal in his agreements and too sure of his own judgements. Harkness came to think the Yale President a poor administrator and personally weak and unreliable.

Nevertheless, on 3 January 1930 Harkness came through with a promise of $15,725,884.96 to build, equip, and endow eight new quadrangles. With these funds, the Sterling bequest, and other important gifts besides, Yale was largely rebuilt under Angell. He found it in brownstone and he left it in granite.[17]

In commenting on all Yale's new physical grandeur, Angell might have paraphrased a remark made about the new Sterling Memorial Library building and said, "This is not the university, that is inside." For he was probably most proud of the rise of the graduate and professional schools during his presidency. And that was his greatest achievement.[18]

When he came to Yale, Angell said in his last annual report, the graduate and professional schools

were in peculiar need of help. They had been too often cold-shouldered because there were not enough funds to go around and the undergraduate tradition was firmly in the saddle. It was essential at the outset to try and build up these integral parts of the University before there could be any advance on a wide front.[19]

One of his primary concerns was the development of a first-class graduate school. With Wilbur Cross still at the helm and with Angell strongly supporting him, the school moved during the twenties "to become the queen and empress of all advanced education at Yale save such as led to a specific professional degree." The Graduate

School took over all nonprofessional advanced degrees and even some of the master's degrees with designations, such as the Master of Fine Arts. It even tried to set up its own programs for its own degrees in the professional schools. By this means, in medicine for example, it was expected a student would be able to transfer from studying for the M.D. to a Ph.D. in scientific biological work without difficulty. Cross's successor noted that while such shifts were a good thing, there was no doubt that in certain places the Graduate School under Cross invaded "the areas of education that are the proper territory of the professional schools." Programs were created within the Graduate School that were well beyond the realm of the liberal arts: the M.F.A., M.S. in Engineering, Doctorate in Public Health, and a course in political science which allowed the student to qualify for the LL.B.[20]

Cross was able to develop the school in this way in part because he had an almost magical ability to get what he wanted. The clearest example of this side of the dean's character is given by Edgar Furniss (Ph.D. 1918). One day a friend met the dean of Yale College looking disconsolate. Asked what was the trouble, he replied, " 'Oh, I've been overreached by Uncle Toby (Dean Cross).' 'In what way?' 'I don't know exactly and that's what bothers me. I have just finished a luncheon conference with Uncle Toby about a matter in dispute between the College and the Graduate School; he agreed to everything I proposed; so it stands to reason that I've been overreached.' " [21]

Cross was also helped in his drive for dominance for the Graduate School by the fact that his ideas generally coincided with Angell's. One of the president's basic beliefs, it will be recalled, was in integration. He believed strongly in interdisciplinary studies and expected much from the cross-fertilization which should result. In the past, he felt, the intellectual resources of the university had been "too often scattered and uncoordinated." Furthermore, he believed the movement of the ideals and methods of the Graduate School into the professional schools would bring more research and scholarship into those departments.[22]

Perhaps it did have this effect (though later Dean Furniss led the school back from its incursions into the professional schools), but even more significant in the rise of the Graduate School was the addition of first-rate men to the faculty. Despite the opposition of certain recalcitrant departments, by constant prodding and finding money when needed, first Cross and then Furniss forestalled bad appointments and encouraged the selection of men with proven scholarly ability. The kind of opposition they sometimes received was exemplified by one professor in the English department who objected to the appointment of anyone not a communicant in the Christian religion (because of the many biblical references in English literature). The sociology department was a constant problem. Yale sociologists lived with the ghost of William Graham Sumner and damned all other approaches to the field as heresy. Once when Furniss suggested the possibility of getting a certain prestigious scholar for the department, the chairman replied, "I can't be expected to whistle just anybody in from the street and set him to teaching this all-important subject." [23]

Despite such difficulties, fine appointments were made: Tucker Brooke, Robert Menner, Frederick Pottle, and Karl Young, all in English; Winthrop Daniels in transportation; Francis W. Coker and Charles P. Howland in government; James Harvey Rogers in economics; Clark Hull and Raymond Dodge in psychology; Franklin Edgerton and Edgar Sturtevant in linguistics and Edward Sapir in linguistics and anthropology; Eduard Prokosch, Albert Feuillerat, and Hermann Weigand in modern literature; Arnold Wolfers and F. S. Dunn in international relations; Marcel Aubert and Henri Focillon in the history of art; Michael Ivanovich Rostovtzeff in ancient history and classical archaeology; George Vernadsky, Wallace Notestein, Ulrich B. Phillips, Samuel Flagg Bemis, and Hajo Holborn in history; and, in mathematics and the sciences, Oystein Ore, Rudolph Anderson, Louis McKeehan, and Herbert Harned.[24]

With a better faculty that insisted on (and attracted) better students, and the new Hall of Graduates Studies providing, for the first time, adequate dormitory space, classrooms, and offices, the school prospered. The result in research in the humanities alone showed the change. Grants from the General Education Board and the Rockefeller Foundation supported the great Dura-Europos excavations under Rostovtzeff which brought forth, among other things, the earliest known church paintings. The same funds supported other accomplishments which, as the university historian recorded,

ranged from the catalogue of the great Goethe collection, to Judaic mysticism, from the elephant lore of the Hindus to *De arte illuminandi* and a bibliography of Hellenism in nineteenth-century France, from the useful beginnings of the *Yale Classical Studies* through a still wider series of investigations in the Romance languages and literatures, from Italy to Latin America. A striking cluster of books was that which dealt with the eighteenth century in England and France: with Rousseau and Voltaire, John Locke and Samuel Richardson.[25]

These years, in fact, saw another leap forward in the Yale library's holdings in eighteenth-century materials. The Goethe collection of 1913 was followed in 1936 by the great addition of the William Smith Mason (B.A. 1888) collection of Benjamin Franklin papers. By the end of the Angell years, the Graduate School had risen from a position where it was looked down on even at Yale, to a place as one of the great schools in the country.[26]

One department of the school that made especially significant progress in the Angell years was education. That department had traveled a rocky road ever since the first specific course had been given in the field by E. Hershey Sneath in the fall of 1891. Despite its constantly reiterated claims to train for public service, in this field Yale let opportunity after opportunity slip away because most Yale professors believed that the place to learn to teach a subject was in a class on that subject, not in an education class. Thus Charles H. Judd was lost to the University of Chicago and Ernest Carroll Moore to Harvard. Finally in 1920 a new department of education was formed with Frank Edward Spaulding at its head. Spaulding brought with him George Sylvester Counts from the University of Washington and J. Crosby Chapman from Western Reserve. Catherine Turner Bryce was also appointed assistant professor of elementary education—the first woman ever appointed at such a high level in Yale's history.

Under Spaulding and, after he fell ill, Clyde M. Hill, the department developed a novel plan of instruction by which it was felt Yale could make a significant contribution to educational training. It concentrated on producing leaders in the field—superintendents, principals, supervisors, and college teachers of education—by having a few excellent faculty members instruct a carefully selected group of top students in wide-ranging seminars.[27]

As progress was being made all along the line in the Graduate School, important efforts were under way to improve the professional schools. One particularly difficult area, as usual, was medicine.

At the start of World War I the Medical School had seemed on the verge of better times. Then inflation wiped out the economic gains that had been made and deficits again became an annual event. The university treasurer made it clear that the school would not be allowed to remain a drain on general university funds for long. So it was that in 1919 another in the long line of studies of Yale medicine was made, and again it was decided to save, and develop, the school.[28]

Before any action could be taken, however, the Medical School nearly succumbed. Dean Blumer, who had done a great deal to hold the school together and improve it during a critical period, decided he had done all he could and resigned. He was followed by other professors. The faculty fell in 1920 to seven full professors, of whom one had submitted his resignation, to take effect the following year, and two others, Harrison and Mendel, worked mainly in other departments of the university.[29]

At this point fiery, dynamic Milton C. Winternitz was appointed dean and the General Education Board came forward with a pledge of $1 million if the university could raise an additional $2 million. Still the situation Winternitz faced was, as Angell later wrote, "as unpromising and depressing as could well be conceived": the hospital was inadequate; many of the alumni still opposed the school; and "the University community was anything but sympathetic." [30]

The departments of the school were spread all over: anatomy was in the old Medical School building on York Street; chemical physiology had space in the Sheffield mansion on Hillhouse Avenue; pharmacology was divided between the York Street building and Brady Laboratory; applied and physical physiology as well as public health were located in a converted brick house a quarter mile from the hospital; everything else was jammed into the badly overcrowded Brady Laboratory. Fortunately, the Sterling bequest soon solved the space problem with the erection of the Sterling Hall of Medicine. In addition, Brady Lab was doubled in size and three other buildings were constructed for bacteriology, pathology, and public health, for surgery and obstetrics, and for medicine and pediatrics. By 1935, when Winternitz retired, the amount of floor space available for all activities had increased from 78,000 square feet to over 423,000. At the same time, endowment went from under $2

million to over $8 million and the budget rose from $253,000 in
1919–20 to over $900,000 in 1933–34. By 1935 the board of perma-
nent officers had 27 members, of whom 17 were primarily concerned
with teaching, and the total number of full-time faculty members
had risen from 45 to 150. Between 1929 and 1935 Winternitz added
to the faculty Edgar Allen from Missouri in anatomy, Stanhope
Bayne-Jones from Rochester in bacteriology, Harvey Cushing from
Harvard in neurology, Johannes Gregorius Dusser de Barenne from
Utrecht and John Fulton from Oxford in physiology, Eugen Kahn
from Munich in psychiatry and mental hygiene, and Walter Richard
Miles from California in psychology. As Charles-Edward Winslow
wrote, "How many of us in 1920 could have dreamed that the Yale
School of Medicine might attract new recruits like these?"[31]

Also during the 1920s and 1930s, the hospital was rebuilt: a new
private pavilion, two new wards, and a clinic building were all constructed. For the first time, clinical offices, laboratories, and ward
service were all adjoining, forming what Professor Winslow considered "one of the most conveniently planned systems to be found
in any teaching hospital in the world."[32]

Along with the improved faculty and buildings went efforts to
strengthen the student body and curriculum. Rising enrollments
brought a restriction in numbers in 1922, and increased applications
thereafter allowed the school to select its students much more carefully. The curriculum they studied was gradually changed throughout the period. Required courses and examinations were done away
with slowly until by 1932 the only requirements that remained were
an examination when the student wished to move on to clinical
training and another at the end of the entire course that tested the
student's mastery of the principles of medicine as a whole.[33]

The focus of the curriculum, as well as the attention of the faculty
and the hospital staff, were first shifted from the medical techniques
of treating disease to the concept of preventive medicine as more
than just "a pious catchword." And then Winternitz tried to push
beyond this point to consideration of "the patient . . . not only [as]
an individual with a mind as well as a body, but [as] an individual
living, and acted upon by, a social environment." When Winternitz
developed these ideas, he moved beyond the bounds of the Medical
School to the university as a whole. And it happened that at the

Law School there was a young man thinking along similar lines, Dean Robert M. Hutchins (B.A. 1921). Winslow later described the meeting of the minds:

Just as we were dreaming of medicine as a means of promoting the welfare of man in society, and not as a picture puzzle in chemical or bacteriological diagnosis, so our colleagues across town were thinking of law as a means to promoting the welfare of man in society, and not as a dialectic exercise in correlating formulae set down in the musty tomes of the law library.[34]

Hutchins and Winternitz were, of course, strongly supported by Angell, for not only was he a psychologist, but their concepts fit well with his desire for the interrelation of departments and the cross-fertilization of ideas. Cross at the Graduate School was hardly enthusiastic, but if the grandiose schemes of his younger compatriots came off, he wanted to be able to control the result. So he joined the other two in a committee to draw up a plan. Between Winternitz and Hutchins, Cross said that as advisory chairman he felt "as if I were a snowball between two balls of fire which in an instant would consume me." [35]

Winternitz and Hutchins dreamed of a great complex of buildings that would contain the Divinity, Medical, Law, and Graduate Schools—all of which needed new homes. But Dean Weigle of the Divinity School rejected the idea and then the Corporation, over Hutchins's objections, decided to put the Law School in the middle of the campus. Thereupon Cross selected a site across the street from the Law School and the library.[36]

Despite this defeat, money for a building and endowment was raised from several sources and in 1929–30 the Institute of Human Relations was built onto the Sterling Hall of Medicine. At the same time the Human Welfare Group was formed, made up of various departments concerned with research, teaching, and treatment in the field of human conduct from the sociological and biological viewpoints: the Institute, the New Haven Hospital and dispensary, the schools of Medicine, Nursing, Law, and Divinity, as well as the Graduate School and the university departments of sociology, government, economics and psychology, were all involved. Though many were skeptical of the institute (Abraham Flexner said, "As far as I can make out, the Institute is just another name for Yale University"), some felt that at least for a time "the fundamental concept of the Institute of Human Relations . . . [worked] in a thousand subtle ways to leaven and liberalize the spirit of every member of the Human Welfare Group." [37]

The rise of the Medical School was helped not only by the Institute and the Human Welfare Group, but also by the development of the Nursing School. Despite the existence of two nursing schools in New Haven, both loosely affiliated with Yale, the hospital did not have adequate nursing services. Professor Winslow had chaired a committee, supported by the Rockefeller Foundation, which in 1918 had investigated the whole question of nursing education. Spurred by their report, the Board of Permanent Officers of the Medical School recommended the creation of a Yale School of Nursing bearing the same relationship to the university as the other schools. No such institution existed anywhere in America at the time. Nonetheless, the idea was approved, and with support from the Rockefeller Foundation, the school began in 1923. Though Yale thought it was first with this idea, Western Reserve started a school on similar lines the same year.[38]

The Yale school was different from previous nursing training organizations in that it had a shorter course (twenty-six months compared to the usual three years) and was an entirely separate school. "This implies," the first dean said, "that it has its own budget, its own Faculty, and that it is in a position to base its curriculum on the content of education required for the practice of the profession of nursing in the community, not on the nursing care required by patients in a given institution or organization—one of the weaknesses of the schools under the apprenticeship system." [39]

The school was a rapid success. In 1929 it received $1 million for endowment from the Rockefeller Foundation and in 1934–35 it was able to raise its entrance requirements and demand a B.A. for admission. It was the only nursing school in the country with such a requirement. Like the Medical School, it tried to give a broad training not only in clinical and physical matters but also in social and psychological subjects.[40]

Developments in the other professional schools of the university paralleled those in the Graduate, Medical, and Nursing Schools. To relate them all in similar detail would be to create an interminable list of new buildings, excellent faculty appointments, and curricular reforms. Certain events must be mentioned, however.

In law, especially, the Angell years were marked by exciting progress. Dynamic figures came to stay for long or short periods on the faculty: in the twenties there were William O. Douglas, Karl Llewelyn, Underhill Moore, W. W. Cook, Walton Hamilton, and Wesley Sturges, in the thirties, Thurman Arnold, Jerome Frank, Fred Rodell, young Abe Fortas, Harold Laski as a visiting professor, and Rexford Tugwell as a research associate and visiting professor. Under a succession of able deans (Swan, Robert Hutchins, and Charles E. Clark), the talented iconoclasts of the law faculty went from one success to another.[41]

In curricular matters, Yale followed Columbia's pioneering lead and carried those ideas forward when that school faltered. Yale shifted its study away from constant dependence on printed precedents and instituted a program in which study of the social forces behind the legal precedents became important in the school's educational system. To assist the program, men were appointed who were specialists in fields such as government, trade regulation, and criminology but who also had a reasonable knowledge of law.[42]

The atmosphere may not have been quite as heady at the School of Fine Arts as it was at the Law School, but there too important events were transpiring. Not only were new faculty and buildings added, but also an entirely new department. In 1924 Edward S. Harkness contributed $1 million for a building and faculty for a drama department—the first in the country. George Pierce Baker of the famous English 47 "Workshop" was lured away from Harvard to head it in what that university's historian described as "Yale's greatest victory over Harvard in the present century." The only unfortunate side effect was that it meant, ultimately, the departure of the undergraduate drama coach, Edgar Montillion Woolley. Baker and Woolley could not get along and Baker refused to put Woolley on the drama faculty. After much sound and fury marked by numerous student protests between 1925 and 1927, Woolley left for the Boston Repertory Theater.[43]

But while Yale drama lost something when Woolley left, the School of Fine Arts gained much more when, in December 1928, the Garvans loaned their great collection of early American furniture to the gallery and then followed it with their wonderful collection of American silver. Soon Francis Garvan gave both to the university. He hoped to be able to endow them as an institute of American arts and crafts, but he was not able to carry out that part of his program. Nonetheless, the concept was important and should be recalled, for as President Angell said, the Garvan collections were important not only to Yale but to the whole country: the objects were "not to be hoarded in Yale's own halls, but are rather to become mobile units and thus made available through Yale for the enjoyment and inspiration of men, women and children in all sections of our country." Some day, it is to be hoped, Yale will be able to carry out this part of the project.[44]

A final significant development in professional education during Angell's years was the setting off of engineering as a separate school. Prior to the reorganization of 1919–20, engineering was part of the Sheffield Scientific School; but in one of the reorganization's less logical moves, the field was divided: undergraduate engineering remained in Sheff, while graduate engineering programs moved to the Graduate School. Dual control was difficult, however, and the engineers felt their field was neglected, in part because of their continuing connection with Sheff. The programs were reunited as a distinct school in 1932.[45]

While the graduate and professional schools prospered from Angell's attention, the college sulked. The faculty had been demoralized and angered by reorganization, and now many distrusted the new, "foreign" president. Throughout the twenties Angell found the college faculty a fractious and difficult body. In the "seven irreconcilables," as they were called, Angell met them at their most perverse. They were "a group of brilliant humanists, intensely devoted to the old College and suspicious of strangers," and they did not like Angell. There were not, in fact, just seven of them, nor were they entirely unreasonable, but they knew Angell wanted to influence the college and they recognized that his wishes were different from their own.[46]

Angell wanted to improve the faculty, do away with certain childish aspects of the college, and gain some control of that school. But he faced great problems. While reorganization had provided some of the instruments by which the college might be ruled—especially in the provost and departments—these had to be defined and used. Meanwhile the president could not initiate college legislation, preside at faculty meetings, or even choose his own dean. Nonetheless, under Angell a significant shift in power took place from the college to the central administration. The power of the provost slowly grew —especially because he presided over all budgets. The departments destroyed the unity and the loyalty of the college faculty. An ungainly Faculty of Arts and Sciences was formed, made up of the faculties of the Graduate School and the undergraduate schools, and an executive committee was appointed. In 1930 the Corporation gave this committee, which consisted of the president, provost, and deans of the Graduate School, Sheff, College, and Freshman Year, the authority to decide all questions affecting more than one school, to pass on all appointments at the upper levels, and (with the treasurer and comptroller) to revise departmental budgets. Since the Faculty of Arts and Sciences could not reverse the decisions of the executive committee, the faculty ceased to meet.[47]

At the same time, the president was given the concurrent power to nominate men for the faculty. This was followed, over the next five years, by a series of Corporation votes that gave the president the power to nominate his own departmental chairmen and deans. When, at the end of his presidency, Angell and Seymour selected William C. DeVane to be dean of Yale College and persuaded the faculty to support him, as George Pierson observed, "the new order had been made firm. Now the most critical appointments, as well as policies and budgets, could be centrally initiated or reviewed." By the end of Angell's term, the president had somewhat more control of Yale College—though a wise president still recognized that the college faculty retained sufficient power to make life very difficult.[48]

The college changed socially and intellectually during Angell's years. Perhaps the most striking alteration was revealed in 1922, when Heywood Broun complained that Harvard was becoming too successful in football while "literature thrives at Yale and, more than that, is fashionable. Our magazines are filled with poems from New Haven and essays. Within a year we have seen with our own eyes a Yale football captain listening to a reading of lyric poetry." Things had come to a pretty pass![49]

The influences producing this change were numerous, but of importance were certainly the boisterous, questioning 1920s, the lingering of the literary renaissance, the limitation on the number of entering students, and undergraduate leaders who criticized the curriculum and their fellow students and called for improvements in both. When these elements were combined with the president's desire for a more intellectually oriented college, the result, over the entire term of Angell's presidency, was the emergence of a much more mature and sophisticated curriculum and the conversion of Yale into a university college—a place where the existence of art, music, graduate, and other schools added immeasurably to the undergraduate experience.[50]

In the process of attaining a more mature college course there were many false starts, many failures, and even trouble with the Corporation. But over a period of time, the first definite distributional requirements for freshman and sophomore years were set up, the Latin requirement and the Ph.B. degree were done away with, the major was slowly enlarged and placed in the charge of the departments, reading periods were established, comprehensive examinations were instituted (first taken by the class of 1937), and finally, in 1940 a senior essay was required. In typical Yale fashion, this program was for all. As usual the attempts to differentiate between the top of the class and the rest by means of real honors work were defeated. Though such a course was established, it was soon undermined and merged with the regular departmental programs. Yale still could not bring itself to separate the sheep from the goats.[51]

College life changed markedly during these years. The first significant action was the ending of daily chapel. Though it had been supported by generations of college seniors long after its religious purpose had disappeared, the attitudinal changes of the 1920s and the growth in numbers of the college finally killed it. In 1925 it was necessary to divide the three upper classes into two separate groups, each attending chapel on alternate days. Then a *Yale Daily News* poll revealed that the undergraduates had swung seven to one against compulsory chapel. Though a faculty committee recommended the continuance of chapel with certain revisions, the faculty overruled its committee and voted to end it completely. In May 1926 the Corporation approved, and so ended a tradition over two centuries old.[52]

The greatest alteration in college life, however, was produced by the residential colleges, the first seven of which opened officially on 25 September 1933. While the colleges were not as important educationally as some had hoped, socially and in an informal educational way they were very successful. Immediately they began to break down some of the old wall between faculty and students. The mixing of students from the college, Sheff, and engineering helped to destroy the old line between the undergraduates. Participation of a much greater number of students in a wide variety of sports was encouraged by the formation of college teams. College newspapers, interest clubs, special classes, song and drama groups all appeared. Through the residential colleges Yale recaptured some of the closeness of the old, smaller college, while at the same time enjoying the privileges of a great university.[53]

Sheffield Scientific School was aided, in one sense, by having its students in the new colleges, but that did not solve its long-term problems. The faculty was furious over the removal of the select course to the college and the concomitant loss of students. As Angell once said, to express their sentiments over the loss of the course, "would involve unparliamentary expressions." A further point of dispute was the existence of science majors in the college. Even a rule prescribing that a student must do three-fifths of his work in his own school, though easing the friction somewhat, did not entirely mollify Sheff, because it still remained possible to major in science and be enrolled in Yale College. But the real problem was that after reorganization Sheff never got enough students. The reasons for this situation were multiple. There was a nationwide trend away from science in the 1920s, and this explanation comforted the Yale scientists somewhat. As usual, however, there were inherent problems at Yale—problems that still have not been entirely solved.[54]

First, Yale College had always looked down on the Sheffield Scientific School, and this attitude continued after reorganization. While the new residential colleges solved Sheff's lack of dormitories, it also placed the science students where they would be influenced by all the humanists. In addition, the faculty of the common freshman year tended to promote the values of the college and thus influenced freshmen against the sciences. On top of all that, work in Yale College was usually easier than that in the scientific school, so many science students, failing to see why they should work so hard, dropped out of the program. Another element was the location of the laboratories out on Prospect Street, far from the college classrooms and residences. It is clear that Stokes and the others who urged the placing of the university science buildings on Pierson-Sage Square underestimated the seriousness of the decision to move the sciences even farther from the college.[55]

Some of the difficulties of the Sheffield Scientific School were the fault of the scientists themselves. While they complained about their lack of students, they were unwilling to proselytize by giving courses for nonprofessionals. When, for example, the departments of physics and chemistry were urged to give a combined introductory course to the physical sciences, they replied that it was not "feasible at present." President Angell noted,

There is, in my judgement, much reason to believe that at Yale, as in many other institutions, the sciences have suffered somewhat from their natural disposition to stress the training of professional scientists and the advancement of the investigating frontier of science itself, as against the larger and more cultural aspects of scientific studies and the educational needs and opportunities of college students who are not themselves to become specialists.

What the Yale scientists did do was to push through a requirement that every student had to take two sciences, of which at least one had to be a laboratory course. Most students escaped from this experience "resolved never, under any circumstances to get caught in a science course again." Finally in 1933 the science requirement was lowered to a single course without laboratory work. So Yale students in the 1920s and 1930s were graduating with either an active distaste for or lack of knowledge of fields and forces that were transforming their world.[56]

Yale had had many financial problems when Angell took over, but during the 1920s there was a dramatic upswing on all fronts. At the end of Angell's first decade in office twenty-seven new buildings had been built and eight were under construction (and many were endowed as well), the university budget had increased from $3,098,549.29 to $4,720,829.06 and the endowment had soared from $25,677,010.70 to $93,975,551.61. At the same time, the total faculty went from 587 to 939 and salary levels rose dramatically. Professors were now receiving a minimum of $6,500 and a normal maximum of

$9,000, with a limited group getting $10,000. The number of students had gone up from 3,820 to 5,914, and nearly every school in the university had placed a limit on its numbers. Though Yale could have grown much larger in the 1920s, it decided to seek quality in its students, not quantity. In 1926, Angell wrote, "So far as I am aware this is the first time that a great university has adopted the policy of a selective limitation of its students for all schools." [57]

Prosperity was short-lived. Even as the first decade's achievements were reviewed, the depression was closing in and the future was in doubt. In January 1932 it was necessary to announce that the size of the faculty would be reduced by curtailing certain reappointments. Then in February Angell revealed that it appeared Yale's income would fall $500,000 short of its expenses. He asked for budget reductions of 10 percent. Even so, Yale ended 1931–32 with its first real deficit in twenty-five years. There was a gap of $278,066.23 that could not be covered and had to be carried on the books as a debit balance. The Yale alumni had tried to help, for the alumni fund provided $422,081.26. [58]

Unfortunately, the alumni fund was one area where Angell made a serious error. He seems to have feared that dependence on it would limit Yale's freedom, and therefore he lowered Yale's requests for donations to the fund during the 1920s. Angell did have one sound point when he said he wanted to decrease Yale's need for alumni support so that "we should not, on occasion, be obliged to exert greater pressure on alumni generosity than is compatible with the maintenance of the finest relations between the University and its graduates." It might have been better to keep slowly building the habit of alumni giving; in any case, during most of the 1930s the fund provided less than $200,000 a year. [59]

Despite constant deficits during the depression and the need to spend a small amount of principal (while fighting off New Haven's attempts to tax the university), and the further necessity of cutting back all along the line, Yale continued to do well educationally during these years. In the main, programs were unhurt, while much "fat" was undoubtedly removed. Unavoidably, however, there was damage. Good young faculty members had to be cut off. Students were forced to leave despite increased financial aid. Just at the point that the quality of undergraduate applicants was declining because of the economic situation, the Corporation insisted the admissions office should accept more students to keep the college full, with obvious effects on the excellence of the student body.[60]

Fortunately for undergraduates who needed financial aid, the new bursary system began with the new colleges. The basic idea of the plan endowed by Harkness was that there should be "employment useful to the University and related to the life of the college or to the student's intellectual interests." No student was allowed to work more than eighteen hours a week and the pay ranged from $200 to $1,000 a year depending on the amount of responsibility involved. Jobs ranged from the prestigious posts of aides to the college masters through college librarians and college athletic secretaries to the often fascinating work of assisting some of the great research projects at the university. In the first year some 287 students got bursary jobs. These positions became so sought after in some cases that one wealthy father whose son wanted to be senior aide to a college master "even complained that Yale was discriminating against the rich." [61]

In some ways the depression was not bad for college education. As George Pierson observed,

The depression benefited American education in unexpected ways. It broke the spell of Wall Street and big business. It recalled many an innocent from the worship of success. Continued unemployment led the New Deal into cultural projects and the first substantial national encouragement of the arts. The same lack of jobs kept many young people in school, and sent others back to graduate or professional study. In colleges the country over a more serious tone soon became manifest. Not infrequently this transfer of attention from college frivolities to classroom study paid such handsome dividends that observers were tempted to bless the depression for revivals of learning that it had apparently generated.

At New Haven, the intellectual revival that had begun in the 1920s continued in the 1930s. But the blossoming of the university that Angell had started now ceased. World War II would prevent any further forward movement and Yale's development as a university was halted for many years.[62]

In 1937 President Angell reached the age of sixty-five and retired. His had been a great presidency. Physically, the university had been largely rebuilt. Financially, despite the depression, endowment reached over $104 million in 1937 and the university's own expenditures had doubled since 1921.[63] Even more important, nearly every department (excluding the sciences) had risen to a position among the best in the land. The college, which had been aided enormously by the new residential system, had become a true university college, benefiting from all the schools of the university while they in turn benefited from it. The locus of power in the university had shifted to the central administration. The faculty had been improved all along the line. Intellectually, Yale was a far better place than when Angell had come to it.

Yet strangely, Yale had never really accepted James Rowland Angell. He arrived an outsider and he remained one. Nonetheless, he did what none of his predecessors had been able to do. He made Yale a great university.[64]

19

"Holding at the Three-Yard Line"

On 13 February 1937 the Yale Corporation elected Charles Seymour president of the university. He had, according to the *Yale Alumni Weekly*, spontaneous support throughout the entire institution. As in the case of Stokes, he was the most obvious candidate, but this time there was little opposition.[1]

A graduate of King's College, Cambridge, in 1904 and of Yale College in 1908, Seymour had received his Ph.D. from Yale in 1911. He had then worked his way up the Yale ladder, taking time out to serve in Paris as chief of the Austro-Hungarian division of the American Commission to Negotiate Peace and as U.S. delegate on the Rumanian, Yugoslavian, and Czechoslovakian territorial commissions. From 1922 to 1937 he had held a prestigious Sterling professorship at Yale. Since 1927 he had been a most effective provost. His successor in that position, Edgar Furniss, said, "It was Mr. Seymour whose work placed the provostship at the head of the faculty structure, and who won for it recognition throughout all the faculties as possessing an authority outranking that of the deans." Not least in his favor was his ability to get along with Yale's great benefactor, Edward S. Harkness.[2]

Charles Seymour was every inch a Yale man. His family was Yale: his great, great, great grandfather, Joseph Coit, had received an M.A. at Yale's first commencement in 1702; his great, great grandfather was Thomas Clap; his great uncle was Jeremiah Day; and his father was Hillhouse Professor of Greek Language and Literature from 1880 to 1907. Charles Seymour was the quintessential Yale man in other ways as well: he was a member of Skull and Bones, loved football and crew, and was conservative in his outlook. He always regretted, for example, the end of compulsory chapel—not for religion's sake, but because of the loss of its social values. Seymour clearly represented tradition and sentiment for old Yale. On top of that, with his silver hair, neat mustache, and even features, especially the fine straight nose, he was an idealized version of a college president. He was also the diplomat par excellence. He possessed, in fact, "a rather formal suavity of person" under which he seems to have hidden "essentially a warm, responsive personality." At times, however, he was so diplomatic, even secretive, that he was not able to communicate with his colleagues. He had a fine, subtle mind, but his failure to give direct answers and his tendency always to leave himself a way to change his mind were annoying to many who dealt with him.[3]

The new president was, as has been noted, a conservative man, and his selection revealed and strengthened, as Professor Pierson has pointed out, "a conservative trend." In an astute analysis, Robert D. Heinl, Jr. (B.A. 1937) wrote in the April 1937 *Yale Literary Magazine* of Seymour,

His is the job of "mopping up," behind the wide front lines of Yale's academic advance. We know in outline what we want our University to be, but the task of balancing every factor and evaluating every force which will affect the precise structure of 1954's Yale remains to be done. It has been entrusted to efficient and meticulous Charles Seymour. After his seventeen years of consolidation, it will again be time to storm new positions.

Seymour saw his role in the same light. And even his skillful new dean in Yale College agreed: William C. DeVane told an Alumni Day audience in 1940 that it was time for Yale to pause, digest, and take stock.[4]

One of Seymour's first acts as president, in fact, had been to get DeVane to come to Yale. DeVane had firmly refused the offer of the deanship made at the end of Angell's presidency and he again refused when first approached by Seymour. Somewhat later Seymour asked DeVane to define the function of the dean, and DeVane explained that he thought that officer should make educational policy rather than just dealing with the mechanics of running Yale College. Seymour then asked DeVane to take the position as he had defined it, and DeVane finally agreed.[5] It was an important moment, for in DeVane, Seymour got a man who was to become perhaps the most successful dean Yale College ever had. Like the president, DeVane was a diplomatic man and not a fighter, but by persistence, careful planning, and compromise, he often got what he wanted. With the aid and support of Seymour, DeVane, acting as he had said the dean should, made Yale College in the image he desired.

Seymour saw Yale's most pressing need as a larger faculty. A member of his Committee on Educational Planning concluded, after talking with departmental chairmen, "that Yale's prestige as a teaching institution has been achieved and is being maintained at the expense of her reputation as a body of productive scholars." The cutbacks of the depression years were hurting Yale. The whole concept of small classes and individual attention was in danger. So in October 1937 Seymour persuaded the Corporation to approve, even if only in principle, "a plan calling for a large faculty increase over the next ten years." Even more importantly, he induced the Corporation to vote funds for some additional instructors and then persuaded Edward S. Harkness to add to this amount by the gift of a Fund for Educational Supervision. By these means sixteen new instructors were added to the faculty for 1938–39.[6]

But the continuance of the depression made it difficult for Seymour to accomplish very much in his early years. He had to concentrate on finding ways to economize in the operation of the university. Nevertheless, there were certain things he would not sacrifice:

As a privately endowed institution we must keep alive various aspects of learning which without protection run the danger of death. They may attract merely a handful of students and to the general public they may appear quite without value. Classical philology and archaeology, linguistics, Semitic languages, paleontology, aspects of the higher mathematics, and specialized scientific investigation without any apparent relation to any so-called "useful" application—these and other activities represent scholarly effort which it is the University's duty to foster simply for their own sake, and because without them the heritage of human experience is impoverished.[7]

Charles Seymour's overall approach to the presidency was quiet, broadly concerned, but always careful. Often he would recognize a need, but only appoint a committee to study it. Intelligent plans were made but little was done to carry them out. With this kind of approach there was what one fellow later described as a "controlled state of progress" which caused, at least in retrospect, increasing frustration in the younger men on the Corporation, especially Robert A. Taft, Dean Acheson, and Wilmarth Lewis.[8]

Seymour's quiet efforts to develop "the normal functions of the university, especially the course of study and the strengthening of the faculty," were cut short by the outbreak of war in Europe. The academic year 1939–40 opened with Germany about to finish its conquest of Poland and ended with France suing for peace. Since Seymour believed that "the justification of a university is to be found in the service which it gives to the nation," university planning shifted to how Yale could help the government. "For the immediate future and, in my opinion, for years to come," Seymour said, "we must all of us, students and professors, recognize that whatever demands the necessities of national defense lay upon us, they are paramount." [9]

Not all Yale students agreed with him. As early as 1936 there was a "Peace Week" at Yale (somewhat sparsely attended), and the following year part of the university supported a nationwide antiwar demonstration. The *Yale Alumni Weekly* observed that war was "distinctly unpopular with the present college generation." In 1939 R. Douglas Stuart, Jr., and some of his fellow students at the Law School began the discussions which led in 1940 to the founding, through Stuart's efforts, of the Committee to Defend America First. Kingman Brewster, Jr., in the Yale College class of 1941, joined with Richard Bissell (B.A. 1932, Ph.D. 1939), an assistant professor of economics, to make the preliminary speeches and introduce Charles Lindbergh when an America First unit was formed at Yale. Some students petitioned against intervention, to the annoyance of some graduates, while others, including McGeorge Bundy (B.A. 1940), petitioned for it.[10]

Yale could not, however, avoid the repercussions of the war even in 1940. That summer Yale faculty members assisted wives and children from Oxford University to find homes in America away from the war. The Yale School of Medicine affiliated with the army's 39th General Hospital in preparation for war. By 1941 more than a hundred faculty members had been called into government service. The School of Nursing was giving refresher courses to inactive professional nurses. On 1 July 1941 students lost their blanket deferment and by November the *Yale Alumni Magazine* reported that the seniors were "gaunt, unshaven, and hollow-eyed" over the draft.[11]

When 7 December 1941 converted worry into reality, Yale was at least partially ready for wartime, for plans for the university had begun to be drawn up as early as May 1941. On 15 December President Seymour announced that Yale would operate on a year-around basis and give undergraduates their degrees at the end of three years. This decision for the college was soon followed by most of the graduate and professional schools. As plans, proposals, and projections were announced during 1941–42, the university made one of its least excusable moves: it fired the tennis coach of twenty-nine years' service, the baseball coach of twenty, and the golf coach of ten years, as a wartime economy measure. Henceforward, the administration said, the university must stress sports on a group basis (so Howard Odell was hired as football coach). In that same year more than a hundred undergraduates left for active service while more than a thousand became involved in one or another of the many training programs: ROTC, NROTC, V-1, V-5, V-7, EV-G, quartermaster corps of the army, navy supply, navy cryptography, and civilian pilot training.[12]

On 1 July 1942 the year-around program for undergraduates began, and 98 percent of the students returned. Seymour reported with pride that a higher percentage had enrolled than at any other large university. Still the uncertainties were great. Washington seemed to have no plan. Seymour complained, "Ill-advised and conflicting announcements on the matter of enlistments and Selective Service, emanating from various Washington offices, have done great harm." [13]

Developments were not dissimilar to those during World War I. First, Yale became a "voluntary" military camp. In the summer of 1942, army, navy, and marine enlisted reserve units were set up. The programs provided for "enlistment in the armed forces with leave of absence to pursue studies which will make the man a better officer when he enters active officer training and service." New special war courses were started (in explosives, aeronautical problems, map-making, etc.) and new programs (in Latin American Affairs and Oriental Studies). Much work was done on developing intensive language courses. Students were guided into courses in physics, math, or chemistry that would better prepare them for service. They were also very much involved in the Red Cross, New Haven Hospital, air raid warning centers, USO, and working on farms in the area. All of these extracurricular activities were overseen by the Undergraduate War Council.[14]

Even as these programs were being established, however, it became clear that they would not be enough. During the spring and summer the government substantially altered its policies. "Long range values," according to Seymour, "were subordinated to the immediate demand from the battle front." It seemed clear the student reserve groups would soon be called into service.[15]

At the same time the university was losing its faculty. The most severe damage was done to the sciences, but literally every department was hurt. Seymour reported, "In the departmental reports the story is always the same—able men of the younger group called to service, with no adequate replacements available." On top of that the president feared the effect of the year-around educational program on those faculty members who were left behind. If they taught constantly, there would be no time for research. "To deprive the faculty of this opportunity [for research] is to dry up the lifeblood of creative scholarship." So he suggested allowing each faculty member time off periodically for research. "The loss of our students during wartime is an inevitable sacrifice," Seymour wrote, "but it still remains possible for us through our faculty to maintain our scholarly tradition. If this should die, Yale would cease to be a university." [16]

In the fall of 1942, the army began to terminate its program of enlisted reserves. It was immediately clear that undergraduate enrollment would fall, and this did not bode well economically for Yale. President Seymour pursued the military for replacements. When a black member of Yale's junior class was rejected by the navy for V-1 and fellow Henry Sloane Coffin protested to the president, Seymour replied,

I am trying to get from the Navy a statement with regard to their intentions with regard to the use of our facilities for the training college which was agreed upon some two years back, and I do not want to get into any controversy with regard to their acceptance of Negroes recommended by us until that matter is cleared.

He said he would see what he could do personally, but he was not willing to do more at that time.[17]

After receiving Yale's reports of its extra room, the army in December requested Yale to lease it housing, mess, and laboratory facilities for training aviators in a technical training school. Yale agreed and soon appeared well on its way to becoming little more than a military base. So, at least, some of the faculty feared. Despite statements by Seymour supporting the need to preserve the liberal arts, his actions seemed to belie his words. A group of young humanists worried about the future and worked to preserve the liberal arts. George W. Pierson wrote an article entitled "Democratic War and Our Higher Learning" for the *Yale Alumni Magazine*. Pierson's concerns were many, but the key one was this: can the American university president, "unaided, somehow convert the university to the all-out service of the nation *without,* by that very act, destroying its usefulness for future generations?" [18]

Soothing words were issued by the president and the Corporation supporting the humanities and the faculty. The president, in his annual report for 1941–42, had said they must be defended, "otherwise it will not profit us to win the war, for we shall have lost the values essential to the national soul." The Corporation supported the president in a moving declaration that helped, somewhat, to calm fears. But both statements seem to have been intended mainly to quiet the liberal arts faculty. Henry Sloane Coffin, who is said to have written the Corporation's declaration, reported to Seymour that he had met with Pierson and his colleagues and had tried to be sympathetic, but had not learned much. He concluded that if the group were able to tell the Committee on Educational Policy what troubled them, all would be well. "It is largely a matter of maintaining morale in that branch of our Faculty," Coffin wrote.[19]

So Yale converted to war. In January 1943 the Army Air Force Technical Training School (AAFTS) was established. By February three thousand cadets, officers, and instructors had taken over most of the Old Campus, Silliman College, and the Law School. Six- to twenty-week courses were given in photography, airplane armament, communications, and airplane maintenance. The Old Campus looked again as it had in World War I, but the military pace was even more frenetic: there were two shifts, one with reveille at 4:50 and taps at 8:50 and the other with reveille at 7:00 and taps at 11:00. The students attended classes eight hours a day, six days a week.[20]

The rest of the college was in a state of flux as the army continued to call up the enlisted reserves. One student remarked, "People keep moving in and out so fast that you're liable to find a complete stranger moving in on you one day . . . and the next find everyone, including your roommate, evacuated from the entry." Elsewhere in the university enrollments were falling fast. The Forestry School had dropped from an average of thirty-seven students to just six, Law was reduced from four hundred to seventy, and all the other schools, except Medicine, Divinity, and Nursing, were down to a lesser degree.[21]

Slowly, most of the numerous training groups that had sprung up began to be liquidated and largely replaced by single units for the army and the navy. The Army program was the Army Specialized Training Program (ASTP), the navy had V-12. The only difference between the two was that the navy course led to a commission, while graduates of the army course went on to Officers Candidate School.[22]

The Army Special Training group arrived on 14 June 1943 and was soon followed by V-12. There were five main areas of army training: (1) the basic engineering course made up of math, physics, English, history, geography, chemistry, and engineering drawing), (2) area and language, (3) advanced officers schools (military intelligence and civil affairs training schools), (4) pre-medical, and (5) advanced medical. The navy asked Yale to give medical training, basic V-12, V-1 (intelligence), and V-7 engineers. About half of the first V-12 trainees were originally civilian Yale students who were assigned to continue at Yale, but most other students were ordered to Yale by their service. Nonetheless, Yale considered them its own undergraduates and eligible for its bachelor's degree if they completed the regular academic requirements. If they left the university in good standing, they could return after demobilization to complete the necessary work for a degree.[23]

The most interesting of these military programs from an educational point of view were those in area and language studies. The idea for them had come from Arnold Wolfers, who had been associated with the School of Military Government in Charlottesville, Virginia, and recognized the rare advantage Yale possessed in fields where language was a significant element. Leonard Bloomfield, Sterling Professor of Linguistics, had developed new, specialized techniques of intensive language instruction using native instructors. With Sturtevant and Edgerton, he had trained a very able group of young instructors in the European and Oriental languages. Yale could draw upon its anthropologists and historians for the nucleus of the area work. These men were then supplemented by the addition to the staff of native speakers as well as businessmen, journalists, and diplomats who had lived in Europe and the Far East. A. Whitney Griswold (B.A. 1929), a young associate professor of government and international relations, was put in charge of the language programs and also of the academic program of the Civil Affairs Training Specialists who were preparing for service in countries occupied by the United States during the war.[24]

In a special unit, the Military Intelligence School, Professor George Kennedy taught a group of officers who were studying Chinese in order to train Chinese troops in modern warfare. It was reported that at the end of their intensive four months' course, the graduates were able to speak the Mandarin dialect fluently.[25]

The army and navy took over the residential colleges. Army men filled Calhoun and Berkeley, while the navy and marines (1,500 strong) occupied Branford, Saybrook, Davenport, and Pierson. Jonathan Edwards, Timothy Dwight, and Trumbull remained, at least for a time, to house the approximately 700 civilian undergraduates left on campus. The armed forces dealt with the discipline of the troops, but the Yale faculty did the teaching. The instructors had their teaching burden increased by 30 percent. Despite Seymour's wishes, most research projects went by the board. A special salary bonus only partially made up for the service and sacrifice of the faculty.[26]

By August of 1943 Yale was largely a military camp containing 7,000 men—nearly 2,000 more than its average prewar enrollment. Some 3,000 of these were in the AAFTS program, which still continued. The Air Force Band, in fact, helped add a little color to military Yale. The *Alumni Magazine* reported that "Mr. Tinker was forced to end his first lecture of the term early because it came down College Street at 9:50 one morning playing a deafening arrangement of *The Jersey Bounce*." [27]

Despite the war, the university tried to give its military students some feeling that they were part of Yale College. One member of the ASTP reported his reaction to being a wartime member of Berkeley College:

Things have changed at Berkeley College since June, 1943. Built originally for only two men, the spacious three room suites have found themselves crowding six within their doors. The hardwood floors have been shorn of their carpets and left bare, to be dusted each morning by the occupants. Comfortable single beds have been replaced by the well-known GI double decker. In the dining hall, instead of eating from china dishes, the soldier finds himself consuming his meal from the standard Army trays, so familiar to reception center camps. And we find that even the insignificant butt can, familiarly lining the walls at numerous bases, has found its way to Berkeley College, Yale.

Long after we leave Yale we shall remember everything Berkeley College has given us, its foster members. We will remember the luxurious living quarters, the library, and the common room, in which we spent so many pleasant hours reading, talking, or listening to the radio or piano. We can never forget the meals in the college dining hall, reputed by the New York *Sun* to serve some of the best food offered to the Army. And we can never forget Professor Hemingway, the ever-patient Master, with always a smile for each of his hundreds of foster charges. We can never forget the Friday evening receptions and Sunday afternoon teas in the Master's House which helped to make us feel that we are really a part of Berkeley. As is true with the hundreds of graduates since the college was opened in 1934, and with the thousands who will graduate in years to come, the memories of Berkeley which we take with us when we leave at the end of this month will always linger on.[28]

The year 1943–44 marked the peak of Yale's war effort. By May 1944 the undergraduate civilian population had fallen to 565 and the total university civilian student population was only 1,720. During that spring, however, the military cutback began. First, the army closed down its basic ASTP course. This program, Yale had to confess, was not a great success. Though the men had good natural ability, many either lacked or had forgotten their high school training. Tutoring classes were given, but even these failed, either because such a large number of students were weak or because the faculty was unable to adjust to teaching facts at the high school level.[29]

The second stage of demilitarization began in the fall of 1944 with navy cutbacks and the phasing out of AAFTS. The air force school was slated to close 31 January 1945. Perhaps more important to many at Yale, however, was the fact that this fall saw the first undefeated Yale football team in twenty years. Though the army did not allow its men to play and Harvard was not on the schedule (they had dropped football after 1942), the largely navy- and marine-dominated team of 1944 went undefeated.[30]

During the course of 1944–45 the military programs wound down rapidly. Also in that year the first veterans returned to the various schools of the university. Yale was ready, for it had begun planning for the postwar years during 1942. For the year 1945–46, Yale put its plan in operation in the form of Yale Studies for Returning Service Men, under the direction of Professor Ralph Gabriel. In this program veterans could graduate in six or seven terms.[31]

Though important research was done at the university during the war—especially on the atomic bomb and radar—Yale's major contribution came through the faculty members it furnished for active service and the courses it gave to over 20,000 soldiers, sailors, and marines. Yale also trained thousands of workers in its Engineering, Science, and Management War Training Program in New Haven and Fairfield counties. From the doctors and nurses it provided for the 39th General Hospital (which treated 30,000 men in the South Pacific between 22 November 1942 and 14 November 1945) to the Yale men who made up 20 percent of the personnel of the Monuments, Fine Arts, and Archives Section of Military Government, Yale faculty members worked all over the world in the war effort.[32]

The effects on Yale of the war were many. At the beginning of the conflict rare books and manuscripts had been squirreled away for safety in the library basement; the most precious paintings had been sent to galleries away from the East coast. Library service had had to be seriously limited. But Seymour had said early in the conflict that the library must continue to collect—it must be the last part of the university to suffer any curtailment in that sort of activity. And collect it had. In 1942–43 the president reported that the rare book collection was growing at the rate of 2,500 volumes a year. In that same year Yale received not only the papers of Frank L. Polk (B.A. 1894) and Gordon Auchincloss (B.A. 1908), which supplemented the valuable Edward M. House Collection of papers dealing with World War I and the Paris Peace Conference; its own Professor Asakawa; and the Hillhouse family; but also William Robertson Coe's great collection of Western Americana.[33]

The war enabled the university to solve the lingering problem of the Sheffield Scientific School. As early as 1928, when it was suggested that engineering should become a separate school, Angell had said the reason for undergraduate Sheff would then cease to exist. Even Charles Warren, the school's long-time dean (1922–45), came

to the conclusion the scientific school should stop teaching undergraduates. But the Sheffield trustees resisted, convinced that they
must use their funds to support the faculty and students of the
school. Finally, the war gave Yale the opportunity. As Seymour said,
"Our former procedures have been necessarily altered and our future policy will have to be recast." Working together, Provost Furniss and Dean Warren drew up a plan whereby the undergraduate
courses moved to the college and the "faculty and students" of Sheff
were preserved as a legal fiction. Since 1945, graduate students studying science and the men teaching them have been considered the
faculty and students of the Sheffield Scientific School.[34]

World War II had a strange effect, economically, on Yale. At first
the administration found, perhaps contrary to expectations, that
even with the faculty taking no additional compensation for teaching in the summer, the cost of running Yale went up. One reason
for this was that normal summer earnings by students largely disappeared. So university scholarships had to be increased and new types
of employment found in New Haven. Seymour feared that financial
difficulties lay ahead.[35]

Soon, however, the economic situation changed dramatically. Yale
became a crowded military post with 8,000 instead of 5,000 students.
The total faculty salary bill was held at or below its prewar level.[36]
So Treasurer Laurence Tighe found himself in 1943 with what he
described to fellow Reeve Schley as an embarrassing surplus that
needed careful handling. To avoid publicizing this and later surpluses that might discourage wanted donations, various devices were
used. In 1942–43, for example, when it appeared the university
would have a surplus of over $800,000, the opportunity was taken to
write down various mortgages, real estate, and other investments by
$709,745.49 while the rest was credited to a contingency reserve and
reserve for rehabilitation. The following year a further reduction of
$283,000 was made, and $650,000 was put aside for rehabilitation
and reconversion. By these means the treasurer was enabled to report only very small surpluses or deficits during the war years and
the university was able to set aside some funds for the reconversion
period.[37]

As Seymour looked back on Yale's wartime experience at the end
of his term, he found it not all bad. The university, he thought, had
justified itself by its service in the national defense. The humanities

had been kept alive. Yale's morale had been heightened by the way its war effort had revealed the university's fundamental strength. Furthermore,

the Yale experience of the students assigned to us by army and navy has broadened our reputation and our contacts with distant parts of the country. Our own experience with new methods of teaching and fresh fields of study has enriched our curriculum and stimulated our scholarship. War conditions forced us into administrative reorganization much to be desired but which would have been difficult to impose in normal times.

On the other hand, he confessed that war and the postwar period did seriously threaten Yale's "magnificent teaching tradition." [38]

Yale thought it was well prepared for the war's end and the return to peacetime operations. It had been told by the government that troops would be demobilized very slowly. Instead, the university was suddenly faced with a flood of returning servicemen supported by the GI Bill. Edward Noyes, dean of admissions, complained, "The American people wanted a speedy demobilization. They got it. From the point of view of the colleges, it is tragic to have what might have been a steady stream turned into a rip-roaring flood, with its inevitable accompaniment of waste." The very idea of the number that might possibly arrive as freshmen in September 1946 was frightening. Nine hundred men who had left freshman year during the war were entitled to return. Fifteen hundred more had been admitted, but had never matriculated. And Yale did not want to sever its contacts with the schools by cutting off those who would normally enroll in the fall. Even though it was recognized that not all these men could or would arrive at the same time, the college administrators were worried.[39]

By September 1946, as feared, the flood had hit. The university had decided it could handle an increase of 60 percent in enrollment (to about the wartime level of eight thousand). Soon nearly nine thousand were in attendance. As school opened, students were jammed into the residential colleges: four were housed in what was formerly a two-man suite, three in a one-man suite, and two in a single room. Others were living in the Ray Tompkins House and old Winchester Hospital in Allingtown; two hundred were housed with faculty and alumni about town; some three hundred were temporarily located in the gymnasium until former navy barracks were thrown up on Pierson-Sage Square. In the college dining halls, where once there had been printed menus at each table, white tablecloths, and meals served by waitresses, there were now cafeteria style lines and metal trays.[40]

Complicating the housing problem was the influx of married students. One hundred quonset huts were rapidly erected on Pierson-Sage Square and near the Yale Bowl. Each of the forty-eight by twenty foot metal structures was divided into two three-room apartments. Further space for families was created in converted dormitories, fraternity buildings, and private homes.[41]

The faculty housing problem was even worse. The faculty had increased from nine hundred to thirteen hundred, and they had to find homes in a community that had a severe housing shortage. In addition, the professors, overworked and underpaid, were even subsidizing the university to a sizable degree. Between 1940–41 and 1953–54, the real purchasing power of their salaries declined by 36 percent for professors, 32 percent for associate professors, and 30 percent for assistant professors. Despite all these difficulties, with varying degrees of discomfort, most faculty members and students made it through the trying years of postwar adjustment. The only alternative was to depart, and this choice some made.[42]

The press of numbers did bring an improvement in the student body. Yale did not raise its requirements, perhaps because it could not without cutting itself off from much of America. It did try to be more selective, but even this was difficult because many of the entrance examinations tested aptitude, not attainment. Often the students admitted were able but untrained.[43]

Yale did not achieve its goal of a sizable increase in the number of high school students enrolled. It did not decrease the number of alumni sons, either, but in this case it did not want to. The number of Yale sons had, in fact, steadily increased over the past generation. In 1924 they had made up only 13.2 percent of a class. Throughout the 1930s the number remained in the twentieth percentile, until in 1939 the class of 1943 reached 31.4 percent. In 1947 Edward S. Noyes, the chairman of the Board of Admissions, while reporting on how Yale was benefiting from the increased applications, noted that this increased the problem of alumni sons. He wrote,

The Board of Admissions recognize fully the debt of the university to the alumni and is eager to maintain Yale traditions in a family. It is also, however, pledged to select for the University the best possible freshman class. Sometimes these two aims conflict. I do not, however, recall a case where a Yale son whose record showed him to be qualified for Yale work and whose school recommended him fully failed to secure admission. The fact that thirty per cent of the normal freshman class are alumni sons would seem to indicate not only that the boys want to follow in their fathers' footsteps, but also that the Board of Admissions has not been ungenerous.[44]

In fact, the generosity of the board at this time may have helped to promote the belief among the alumni that the admission of their sons was a right. This misconception would cause difficult problems when Yale tried to change its admissions policies in the 1960s.

As Yale struggled with the problem of numbers in all its manifestations, the college instituted a revised curriculum which was to be followed with only minor changes for nearly twenty-five years. Even before the war began, the Course of Study Committee had begun to worry about the loss of breadth in the curriculum. As the committee reported later,

A feeling was prevalent among the Undergraduates just before the War that the Major was all that mattered, and that when they had completed successfully the requirements in the Major they were entitled to their degrees, no matter what other requirements remained unfulfilled. In this the students merely reflected the preoccupations of the faculty.

Acting on this dissatisfaction, the faculty moved to reintroduce some breadth into the curriculum. In 1941 they established a six-group requirement, three of which were considered "basic" (classical languages or civilization, modern language, and a science), and three distributional (social science, arts and letters, and systematic thinking: math, philosophy, or an advanced natural science, and a course on the history of language).[45]

During the war the Course of Study Committee continued to study the baffling conundrum, "Who is the educated man and how is he to be produced?" Their answer was given to the Yale College faculty in the fall of 1945 and was reported in front-page stories in the *New York Times* and *Tribune*. What the committee tried to produce was a program that would equip the student "to live magnanimously and intellectually in the modern world." To do this they recommended a standard program and two special ones. The standard program was an attempt to build on the beginnings made in 1941. As the committee explained,

In the proposed Standard Program provision is made for three Basic requirements and for six distributional requirements. Among the nine requirements, choice of specific subject is allowed in six of the groups; a controlled choice in two; and a single subject is required in one. Even this is not strictly accurate, for an intelligible system of anticipation allows greater liberty than is at first apparent. Approximately one-third of the student's time, if he anticipates none of his requirements, is given to free electives; one-third of his total time is given to his Major subject; and the remainder is given to required groups of studies, some of them Basic, and some for purposes of Breadth.

Since it was assumed certain abilities were needed in order to pursue learning, the basic subjects demanded were English, formal thinking (math, philosophy, or linguistics), and a modern language. Then it was necessary for the educated man to have "a broad view of the world he lives in and to equip him with the means of understanding it." For this end, there was the program of distribution. Each student was to take one course from each of the following groups:

1. *Inorganic Science* (freshman year): Science I (chemistry–physics) or, if qualified, Science II (geology–astronomy)
2. *Organic Science* (sophomore year): Science III (botany, zoology, psychology) or, if qualified, Science II
3. *The Ancient World:* Greek or Latin (at a high level), classical civilization, philosophy, or religion
4. *Studies of Society:* anthropology, economics, history, political science, psychology, or sociology
5. *Literature and the Arts:* literature, ancient, biblical, or modern (above the elementary level), the fine arts, music
6. *Interrelationships of Knowledge* (junior or senior year): certain specified courses in history, political science, philosophy, or the history of art.

Those studying for the B.S. followed a similar but slightly different program.[46]

Beyond the standard program, the Course of Study Committee suggested two additional paths. One, the Scholar of the House program, allowed "the exceptionally able man" to pursue his own project in his final year, "under the guidance of a supervisor, ignoring if he chooses all formal course work." The second special program, a pet project of Dean DeVane's, was called Directed Studies but was known more informally to many undergraduates as Guided Missiles. This plan was open to a limited number of students and consisted of completely required work in the first two years. It was an attempt to recapture "the signal virtue of the old classical curriculum—a community of intellectual experience." The courses were specially designed for the program: "In the first year the emphasis is upon the laws and principles which operate in our natural world. In the second year the emphasis is upon the social and moral laws which bind together the individual and society." But the real feature of Directed Studies, the committee explained,

is the pair of philosophical courses, one taken in each of the first two years, which attempt to bind up and unify the studies of that year. The philosopher teaching the key course stands by, so to speak, like the Commentator in Wilder's play, "Our Town," and informs his students upon the educational experience which they are passing through.[47]

These programs were all adopted by the faculty in 1945 and went into effect upon Yale's return to a peacetime schedule in 1946. Under the new plan the old requirements for the major remained much the same as in the late 1930s, with most students writing senior essays in their final year. The tremendous influx of undergraduates with the end of the war, especially the mammoth size of the class of 1950, forced the Course of Study Committee to rethink the major as well—how could the faculty supervise, read, and grade all those essays? So the committee offered, at the end of 1947, a program that was not "merely a temporary solution," but one that would "make a more thrifty and profitable use of the resources available to the College." The committee reported that it had two "major motives":

first, to break across departmental lines and make more meaningful combinations of studies for the general student than single departments can usually supply; and, second, to devote a greater share of the attention and care of the Faculty than is given at present to the superior student. The first motive is responsible for the proposed "Concentration in General Studies" in Junior and Senior years. The second motive is responsible for the design of the Intensive Major.

From these recommendations, three programs emerged: the divisional majors, cutting across several fields and having no senior essay or comprehensive examination; the standard program, which was a regular major in a field with comprehensive examination and no senior essay, for which one could receive general honors for excellent work; and the intensive major, which reduced the student's course load to four in junior and senior years and required a seminar each year and a senior essay and departmental examination. Departmental honors were given for satisfactory completion of this work.[48]

With these programs and a highly motivated student body (which extended even to the nonveterans, it was said), the college was a dynamic, exciting place in the 1940s. Not until the 1950s was there a reversion "to the less heroic mold of pre-war generations." In 1947 Seymour reported that the students were the best motivated and had the highest grades ever. The freshman class of that year, as well, he said, was the finest to enter Yale. As one observer later wrote, "After the war . . . the Yale classes filled with student veterans whose industry, motivation and maturity virtually created an academic golden age on the campus, and only their excessively large numbers and brief stay prevented them from fully doing so." [49]

Overcrowding not only made life difficult for all and prevented the golden age from fully flowering, it also affected the development of the faculty. Seymour reported, "In more than one case we have lost a new faculty appointee to a sister institution because there was lacking a suitable home for him and his family in the New Haven area." On top of that, the caliber of some of the teachers "at the lower levels" was not the best. Yale had been forced by the influx of students to increase the number of teachers just at the time when there were not many capable young instructors around.[50]

The pressure of numbers produced one change that was to become the norm in years to follow: commencement was held outside. The class of 1950, with 1,500 members and their families, was just too large for Woolsey Hall. Thus in that year commencement moved to the Old Campus and, for the first time in many years, higher degrees were conferred at the same ceremony where the B.A.s were given.[51]

Many of the problems of the postwar years could be solved without too much difficulty or, in some cases, would just pass away with the graduation of the veterans. More serious, however, and far less publicized by the central administration, the masses of students helped to conceal serious financial difficulties.

University buildings needed rehabilitation after the war, inflation was causing prices to rise and salaries to deteriorate, and the endowment was scarcely growing to meet the demands. The endowment problem was caused by several factors. The uncertainties of wartime cut into donations. There was a failure aggressively to pursue financial support. Finally, an investment formula that had been worked out by Treasurer Laurence Tighe was being used. By Tighe's formula, in a rising stock market Yale would keep its money invested 65 percent in fixed income securities and 35 percent in equities. If the market continued rising so that equities became a larger percentage, part of all holdings would be sold (preventing arguments over what to get rid of) to bring the ratio back to 65–35. When this formula was tried out on a hypothetical fund of $1 million over the years 1 January 1926 to 5 August 1938, it had outperformed the market and thus seemed foolproof. But by using it Yale missed the early stages of the change in the market that began in 1942 (with the Dow-Jones Industrials at 92.7) and really got under way in 1949 (when the Dow-Jones Industrials stood at 160.6). In 1950, out of a total endowment of $127 million, the university had only $39 million invested in common stocks. In addition, perhaps to increase income, Yale had sold off much valuable real estate in New Haven, which would later be sorely missed. Between 1941 and 1950 the university's New Haven property (excluding land used for educational purposes) declined from a book value of a little over $3.75 million to about $2 million. This was not, it might be noted, the first time Yale had disposed of real estate in New Haven. Under President Hadley property not needed for university development was sold in order to avoid conflicts over taxes with the city.[52]

The financial problem was particularly bad in the Faculty of Arts and Sciences. Seymour informed Bishop Sherrill, "The fact is that while actual expenditures of the University over the past fifteen years have increased, the expenditures in the Faculty of Arts and Sciences have actually shown a decrease." The professional schools, especially medicine, and certain research centers had increased expenditures, and while Seymour considered them important, he did not think "that the central Faculty of Arts and Sciences ought to be starved in order to feed them." [53]

Yale began to think seriously about its plight in 1946, but Seymour found it hard to get action. A Corporation committee was appointed by the president in the spring of 1946 to consider ways to raise money. But the committee moved slowly. Seymour informed Sherrill of his discouragement in August 1946 and Sherrill replied, "I am sorry but not surprised that the general plans for securing money have moved slowly. Perhaps the summer is partly responsible but I feel sure that there must be greater drive, faith and enthusiasm on the part of certain members of the Corporation, etc." Unfortunately, Seymour could not dominate the fellows and make them move. Meanwhile the faculty was getting worried. On 12 December 1946, in an unprecedented move, the Law School professors sent a message to the Corporation which said, "We most earnestly petition that the raising of capital funds be made the first order of the University's financial policy. The time is late, but not too late—And the stakes, in our judgment, are nothing less than the freedom, the vitality and the capacity for growth of Yale itself." [54]

But if there was one thing, above all others, that this administration was not good at, it was answering clarion calls and acting with haste. In his report on the academic year 1946–47, Seymour said that instead of a great fund-raising campaign, Yale needed a permanent fund-raising organization. And as late as 1948, with the university about to enter a period of unprecedented deficits, Tighe announced that the university was in good financial shape.[55]

Finally, in June 1947, the Corporation committee on university development came forth with a report that recommended still more committees. First there was to be a small alumni university council, "better adapted [than the Alumni Board] to the purpose of bringing the alumni into close contact with the University, or drawing upon their advice, and of enlisting their active support in conducting its business and developing its resources." It was to study the major parts of the university through other committees made up of individuals from outside Yale as well as members of the council. In addition, there was to be a council committe on university development, which was to consider Yale's various needs and "draft a program for the combined development of new financial resources." [56]

So with everyone studying everything, the university entered a period of financial crisis. In the fall of 1948 it was decided to bend "every effort" to raising funds. Seymour said, "Unless we embark upon a vigorous campaign . . . we must run the risk that our excellence may slip into mediocrity." [57]

As usual, one of the most serious problems was in medicine. The Medical School was running what were, at that time, enormous deficits—nearly $700,000 for 1946–47 alone. On 18 December 1946 Seymour forcefully informed the school's Board of Permanent Officers, "*The question as to whether the University can actually afford a four-year medical school must frankly be faced.* Any increase in contributions to the Medical School budget from general University sources is out of the question." The situation at the Medical School was, in fact, destroying that institution. George B. Darling, who was appointed head of the new division of medical affairs in 1946 reported that upon taking office he found

relations between the Medical School and the rest of the University were poor. A large segment of the University and an important fraction of the Corporation questioned the advisability or, indeed, even the possibility of continuing a four-year medical school. While the reasons for this were clearly related to the heavy financial burden of the Medical School, this was further aggravated both by a general lack of appreciation of the real contributions of the School and, as far as alumni and colleges were concerned, by awkward handling of School admissions. The School's own inadvertently poor relations with the medical profession in the community of New Haven and of Connecticut reflected a lack of understanding of the need for an integrated community program, particularly in post-graduate education, but also in intra-hospital relations.

The morale of the School was at a low ebb.

Perhaps because of the state of morale, the school lacked unity. According to Darling,

there was little real professional cooperation. Departments, and even individuals at times, acted as completely isolated units. Personal animosities, both suppressed and expressed, reached extraordinary potentials. This was true not only within the School but between units of the School and other sections of the University.[58]

When the University Council was formed in February 1948, its committee on medical affairs immediately began to look into the

Medical School, Nursing School, and hospital. The situation, they found, had not improved, and strong action was needed. Within three months they brought in a preliminary report that tried to focus the attention of the university on the need for immediate action. As usual, the demand for haste produced no response. In October 1948 the committee passed a resolution calling on the University Council and the Corporation to announce their intent to support the schools. The council did so in November and the Corporation soon followed suit, but wild rumors over the future of the Medical School would not die—rumors that were "highly destructive of the morale at the School." [59]

Finally, the chairman of the council's committee on medical affairs wrote to President Seymour and asked him to publicize the council's and the Corporation's resolutions on Alumni Day and announce them personally to the faculty of the Medical School. His letter concluded,

If these two things are done, I am sure there will be an immediate and electrifying response and the unwholesome atmosphere now surrounding the School will be completely dispelled. That in itself will set the stage for a confident and aggressive effort to establish a widespread public relations program; to secure funds, and to attract new manpower which the School must acquire if it is to maintain its high standing.

Fortunately, the president followed this advice and the morale of the school began to improve.[60]

Still, as late as April 1949 the committee had to proclaim its faith in the quality of the school and its belief that it should be supported. Furthermore, it felt impelled to ask that if any budgetary cuts were made, they be made across the board, "and not by eliminating any one *major* function or unit of the University, except as a last resort." [61]

Despite all the hesitation, the situation slowly began to improve. New contracts were worked out with the hospital, by which the university's contribution to the hospital could decline and, ultimately, be phased out. The hospital did not succeed, however, in shifting the cost of community care from the university to the community (which made, and still makes, no general contributions to the hospital). Attempts were made then (which also continue) to explain to the community the relationship between the hospital and the Medical School, and to make people in the New Haven area appreciate the value to the community of the talented men in the Medical School. At the same time Yale was working to become a regional medical center with postgraduate courses for area physicians, courses in various community hospitals, and the assignment of interns and residents to a number of area hospitals.[62]

While Seymour's administration struggled with finances and medicine, overcrowding and plans for the future, it found itself faced by many other problems. Though salaries had been increased somewhat between 1947 and 1949, Yale was still behind its competitors at the graduate and professional school level. In addition, certain fields badly needed new appointments. In economics and sociology especially there were serious difficulties. Sociology still suffered from the dead hand of Sumner. Between 1935 and 1945 economics lost six outstanding professors through death, retirement, or absorption into the administration. To help solve the problems in these particular fields, the divisional organization that Seymour had begun creating after the war was carried further by setting up a separate division of social sciences with Arnold Wolfers at its head.[63]

The sciences were, if anything, in even worse shape. Despite President Angell's good intentions, little progress had been made in this area during his presidency. The most recent science laboratory had been finished in 1923 and the physics building had been put up in 1912. At that time it was one of the best in the country, with "ample space for fifteen professors, seven graduate students, and a relatively small number of undergraduates." This building served well until the 1920s, but for the great period of development of knowledge in that field that began then, it was clearly inadequate.[64]

When Lyman Spitzer, Jr. (B.A. 1935), reported as chairman of the University Council committee on the division of the sciences, he had to confess that until recently the area had been in the doldrums. When he reviewed the number of National Research Fellows in various fields who had elected to work at Yale between 1923 and 1938, he found that

the figures indicate that with the one exception of the psychology department, Yale's standing in science during this period was about that of some of the smaller Eastern colleges and the Middle-western state universities; this relatively unimpressive showing is in marked contrast to the high standing of Harvard in all fields.

Though Spitzer felt that Director Sinnott had done a great deal to improve science since 1945, much more remained to be done.[65]

The old Sheffield–Yale College rivalry probably continued to hurt Yale science in Angell's day, as did the failure to build new laboratories. But perhaps even more damaging was the fact that the university science departments did not take advantage of the great influx of talented Jews fleeing Hitler's Germany. The same attitude prevailed in most parts of the university until after World War II. In only a few fields was there any willingness to tolerate Jews on even a temporary basis. The always excellent history of art department, while perhaps slow to make permanent appointments, "had such a long trail of visiting émigrés, including Ettlinger, Krautheimer, Panofsky, Sterling, Wind, and Wittkower, that one of them jested about the 'rabbinical succession' at Old Eli." Most other departments were less open to Jews. And of course, Yale was not alone. As Charles Weiner observed some years later,

American scholars and European visitors were aware of anti-Semitic attitudes and unwritten policies within the science departments of many American universities. They recalled that even under ordinary circumstances in the 1920's and early 1930's it was often especially difficult to find faculty positions for well qualified Jewish graduates.

Where this attitude was not present—as at Princeton and Columbia —science blossomed. At Yale, unfortunately, it prevented the university from seizing a great opportunity.[66]

Even when Yale attracted a top scientist, as it did with the appointment of Gregory Breit, a crisis might be generated. Breit came with seven research assistants and it was difficult to find room in the offices and laboratories for them. The lack of laboratories at a time when the government was beginning extensively to support research hurt Yale badly. Yale was willing to accept funds for what it called "objective" research, but it could not get grants because it lacked space to house equipment. At this point the government would not pay for buildings, so at a critical moment, Yale was unable to participate.[67]

Seymour clearly saw what was wanted: "There is urgent need of fulfilling the plans which have been long considered to provide adequate quarters for the life sciences, chemical engineering, geology, and anthropology." Nor were these the only new buildings Yale desired. Seymour pointed out that the art gallery needed to be enlarged (plans for an addition had been made before the war), Peabody Museum had always been too small, more library facilities were necessary, an administration building was wanted, and adequate living quarters ought to be provided for the schools of medicine, nursing, fine arts, and music. "Yale," Seymour confessed, "is the only important university in the country that has not embarked upon a great building campaign." [68]

But the administration seemed paralyzed by its problems. Studies continued, organizations prepared, letters were written. In 1949 the deficit amounted to $525,029 and for 1949–50 it was predicted that it would reach $1 million. Still it was not until January 1950 that the *Yale Alumni Magazine* could list Yale's capital needs, and even then the university hesitated to place a price tag on most of them. Later the total figure was put at $80 million, and even this was below the needs seen by the president's committee on projects, which had arrived at a total of over $97 million.[69]

Before Yale's capital needs were revealed, Seymour announced on 9 April 1949 his decision to retire on 1 July 1950. In his statement, he said that the internal organization of the university was "well-nigh complete." By this he meant the transformation of the Sheffield Scientific School into a division of science and the creation in 1946 and 1947 of the divisions of medical affairs, humanities, arts, and (in 1949) social sciences, each with its own director. These directors not only oversaw the affairs of their groups but also sat with the central university officers and representatives of the Law School, library, and Office of University Development on a committee on projects which surveyed the needs of Yale as a whole. The second reason Seymour gave for being willing to resign then was that

the development of alumni and public relations under the leadership of the University Council is proceeding successfully. Plans for active and permanent methods of increasing University resources are in progress and will be crystallized by the end of the next academic year. It is with the conviction that fresh leadership of the most vigorous sort will best serve Yale's interest that I avail myself of the privilege of retirement at that time.[70]

So Seymour left the university at a critical point. Endowment had scarcely grown. Deficits and spending of principal appeared necessary in the future. Still, the picture was not all black. In the period 1938–49, the university's total income and expenses had more than doubled. The faculty had increased from 958 to 1,396. The number of full professors, 196 in 1949, was 21 percent above what it had been when Seymour took over.[71]

Some excellent appointments and promotions had also been made. To name just some of those from the postwar years, Lars Onsager was promoted to full professor and given the J. Willard Gibbs chair in 1945; 1946 saw the appointment of Ralph Linton, Harold Lasswell, Quincy Porter, Paul Weiss, and René Wellek and the promotion of Carl Hovland, Henry Margenau, Harry Rudin, George Vernadsky, and Leonard Doob. The following year brought Gregory Breit, Cleanth Brooks, Fowler Harper, and the promotion of Werner Bergmann, Cecil Driver, Raymond Kennedy, Sherman Kent, and David Potter. And in the next two years there came Milton Senn, T. G. Bergin, Gustav Hedlund, V. O. Key, and Josef Albers. Thus Yale remained a great university in school after school despite extreme problems.[72]

The library was also improving during these years. Especially under the direction of James Babb, who became acting librarian in 1943 and was confirmed in his post in 1945, the special collections increased enormously. Of Babb one man observed, "Other librarians collect books; Jim Babb collects collectors." And under Babb in the Seymour years arrived the great Coe Collection of Western Americana, Carl Van Vechten's James Weldon Johnson Memorial Collection of Negro Arts and Letters, the Boswell papers collected by Ralph Isham and purchased for Yale by Paul Mellon's Old Dominion Foundation, and one of only three perfect copies of the Bay Psalm Book, purchased for $151,000, at that time the highest price ever paid for a book at public sale. At the same time Babb pursued incunabula. In 1940, the university had fewer than 300 volumes. By 1946 it owned 1,000, and this number was growing rapidly.[73]

The college, although still over-crowded and suffering from some poor teaching, was in surprisingly good shape, in large measure because of Dean Devane. There was only one trouble, in fact, with DeVane. Because he was capable and efficient, and perhaps because there was often a need for someone to act, he took on too many jobs. In 1948 a faculty committee on the Yale College deanship recommended he be offered another five-year term, but they requested that he appoint others to chair the two executive committees of the division of humanities, retaining oversight as director, and that he resign from the following positions: chairman of the committee on foreign area studies, chairman of the department of Slavic languages and literature, the governing board of the Yale University Press, the board of editors of the *Yale Review,* and the executive committee and board of trustees of Yale-in-China. Clearly, there was hardly an area of Yale life that Dean DeVane did not touch in some way. Young men on the faculty knew that DeVane was the man to see when they wanted anything. And they also knew that they would always get a hearing from him. So Seymour knew the college was in good hands.[74]

As the president reviewed his administration at its close, he saw, quite correctly, many other areas of strength. In the Divinity School, the quality of the students was higher than ever and the faculty continued to be distinguished. The president believed its influence at Yale, in the nation, and even internationally, was large "in the fields of Biblical revision, of ecumenical conference, of New Testament scholarship, of religious history and religious education." [75]

In art, the progress made under Dean Everett Meeks, who retired in 1947 after twenty-five years, had been great. In Angell's day, his vision and action had been important factors in founding the drama department, getting George Pierce Baker to head it, and setting up the fine theater and drama workshop. Meeks also had hired Henri Focillon and Marcel Aubert from France as visiting professors. They gave the Yale school a noticeable Gallic orientation and, under Seymour, brought about the establishment of the history of art department. The committee of the University Council on architecture, painting, and sculpture reported, "Yale is unique among the major American universities in the possession of full-fledged professional schools of all the major visual arts, and the opportunity thus afforded for stimulating collaboration must be kept robustly alive." [76]

Seymour was especially satisfied with the situation in music. The department of music was having an ever larger influence on undergraduate and graduate students, while the School of Music had been greatly strengthened by the appointment of Paul Hindemith, Quincy Porter (B.A. 1919), Ralph Kirkpatrick, and Leo Schrade. The school, according to another University Council committee, was "capable of attracting to Yale the most talented students of the country," and had done so despite crowded and inadequate conditions and heavy teaching burdens for the faculty. Seymour said, "it is imperative that steps be taken to remedy this situation and to capitalize the opportunity that is open to us." [77]

In medicine, Seymour felt the "serious crisis" that has been described had been met and the worst difficulties overcome. In the Graduate School, the faculty had increased in size and the entire Faculty of the Arts and Sciences had steadily risen in scholarly prestige and teaching quality, thus also helping the school. Some areas, Seymour confessed, were not as good as they might be, but in others, "such as Philosophy, Psychology, Linguistics, [and] Geology, we are unsurpassed." For this he gave credit to Edgar S. Furniss, provost and dean of the Graduate School. The Law School, though with a larger enrollment than in prewar days, retained the atmosphere of a small school and enormous intellectual vigor. The Forestry School, whose enrollment had nearly disappeared during the war, was now, as it had been since 1945, overcrowded. "The distinctive quality of the school," Seymour felt, "lies in its strength at advanced levels of study as well as in the published research of its faculty." The school had begun to offer the doctorate in 1946, the second school in the country to do so. In addition, in February 1950 it had been announced that the first graduate program of research and instruction in the conservation of natural resources was being established.[78]

Despite the feeling of satisfaction and hope contained in his final report, Seymour knew that all was not well at Yale. At the end of his presidency, he observed of his entire term, "I like to think that perhaps I have been holding on the three-yard line, while the college has been passing through a world war and its confusing aftermath." [79] To a degree, he was right. Certainly the times had been difficult—depression, war, and its strenuous, overcrowded aftermath. The university had held and it was, in the main, still a great institution. But, like a football team on its own three-yard line, it was in trouble. And part of that trouble was because Seymour was a gracious gentleman, well-equipped to handle a time of consolidation but not to handle war and postwar confusion. While he often saw what needed doing, somehow he could never quite get the action needed to solve the problem. There was always a certain hesitancy, timidity, and conservatism in the policies pursued. Committees, organization, plans, respect for the past, and wise glimpses into the future were really not enough. One problem, of course, loomed above all others. It had been visible since 1945; it had been studied by committee after committee; but it was not even near solution. So it would be left to his successor. Unless the next president could raise money—lots of it—Yale's future as one of the world's great universities would be in serious trouble.

Part Six

The Modern Era

1950–1963

20

March toward Greatness

When Charles Seymour decided to follow the example of Arthur Hadley and retire at the age of sixty-five, there was no clear-cut candidate for the presidency of Yale. At President Seymour's suggestion, the Corporation appointed a survey committee to "act as a clearing-house for candidates and report them to the corporation." The committee's members, Wilmarth Lewis, Irving Olds, and Bishop Henry Knox Sherrill, spent ten months studying the field. In an unprecedented move they even sought the advice of fifty carefully chosen members of the Yale faculty. As Lewis put it, "The faculty was pleased to be consulted, after 250 years, on the choice of a new president." [1]

During the search for a successor to Seymour, Wilmarth Lewis gave the classic description of the qualifications of the man Yale was seeking:

The Yale President must be a Yale man. He must be a person of character with religious convictions. He must be a scholar of international reputation with deep respect for science if he is a humanist and who loves the arts if he is a scientist. He must be a man of the present with knowledge of the past and a clear vision of the future. He must not be too far to the right, too far to the left, or a middle-of-the-roader. Poised, clear-eyed, informed, he must be ready to give the ultimate word on every subject under the sun from how to handle the Russians to why undergraduates riot in the spring. As a speaker he must be profound with a wit that bubbles up and brims over in a cascade of brilliance; his writing must be lucid and cogent, his style both Augustan and contemporary. He must be young enough to have "dynamic ideas," but old enough to be sensible about them; courageous, but not foolhardy. He must be "a great personality," by which is meant one who commands respect, who soothes the ruffled and charms the sentimental, an Olympian who is one of the boys without affectation or jocularity. He must have intimate knowledge of all the University's colleges, schools, departments, institutes, libraries, museums, and special projects, and know how to administer them efficiently and economically, delegating authority while keeping his finger on every pulse and in every pie. He must be a man with a heart who will share the private joys and sorrows of his faculty. Above all, he must be a leader, leading of course in the right direction, which is to money. Morning, noon, and night he must get money; money for salaries, money for buildings, money for scholarships, money for new projects that will prove he is dynamic. Since his job takes eighteen hours a day seven days a week eleven months a year, his health must be good— no colds, no ulcers, no slipped discs. Finally, his wife must be a combination of Queen Victoria, Florence Nightingale, and the Best-Dressed Woman of the Year. As I have been talking you have guessed who the leading candidate is, but there is a question about Him: *Is* God a Yale Man? [2]

When the Corporation announced its choice, many observers could not have been more surprised if Yale *had* chosen God. The faculty, according to Lewis, had been convinced the new president would not be found within the university. Yet surely someone must have suggested the most obvious candidate at Yale, Dean William C. DeVane. Much of the excellence of Yale College at this time, especially the pressure for small classes, was due to that diplomatic gentleman. But for some reason DeVane was passed over. Instead, the Corporation singled out A. Whitney Griswold, a forty-three-year-old professor of history.[3]

Griswold had long been a friend of Wilmarth Lewis. More important, he had impressed Lewis and Ted Blair when, after rejecting an administrative post dealing largely with alumni affairs and public relations, he came up with a report that revealed a broad concern for the university as a whole and led to the formation of the alumni University Council. He had shown the same broad concern, and eloquence in expressing it, when he helped to write the introduction to *Yale Plans for the Future,* the Seymour administration's statement of Yale's needs.[4]

Thus when it came time for Yale to select a new president, four fellows, according to Dean Acheson, wanted Griswold. But he had handicaps: "They were serious—youth, little reputation (he was not in *Who's Who*), gaiety and the gift of mimicry, fierce intolerance of the shoddy and second-rate. His virtues were unfashionable and not so well known: excellent historical writing and teaching and a passion for education." To get Griswold elected would take "discretion, some managerial skill, and, on occasion, guile." It was necessary, for example, to hide Acheson's support of Griswold from Robert Taft. Acheson gave the following account of how it was done:

A committee narrowed the list of all those put forward. Our candidate remained on it; so did an able non-Yale man who was president of an eminent smaller college. We concentrated on him, talked of the need for new blood, the danger of inbreeding, the great contributions of President James Rowland Angell, Yale's only non-Yale president. Support for the outsider grew to two short of a majority. Two or three others split the true-blues. They became alarmed (so, incidentally, did we, since the ballots were secret). In the interval between the January and the February meetings our manager [Blair], a classmate [*sic*] of Griswold's, former football captain, New York lawyer, and a sound Yale man, was approached to wean away some of those who had fallen for a foreign importation. He thought he might have some chance if he could report growing sentiment for Griswold. He was told that he could. The new president was elected on February 11.[5]

Though Acheson does not mention it, Griswold may have had President Seymour's support as well. After the election, Henry Sloane Coffin wrote to Seymour to congratulate him on his successor: "I recall with amusement your telling me over the phone that you could not lead the Corporation in this choice. I think the issue reveals quite the contrary."[6]

Most people were surprised at the selection of Griswold. Even his friends were startled, while some faculty members and officers were aghast. Many faculty members knew nothing about the new president and would not have recognized him if they had seen him on the street. Alistair Cooke explained the situation nicely:

The fitness of "Whit" Griswold to preside with conspicuous courage and humour over a great university in the McCarthy era was a very well kept secret until the moment he was appointed.

His wildest admirers would have bet on a life-time professorship agreeably relieved by a gift for dialect stories.

Griswold himself was amazed at his selection. He had never been approached by the Corporation to see whether he wanted or would accept the position. On the day of his election he was not even in New Haven. He had gone to New York to the theater and, after lunch with Roswell Horne, president of Mount Holyoke, had observed to his wife, "Thank God we're not in *that* racket." When he was finally found and informed of his election, he hesitated to accept. Dean Acheson overrode his protestations and advised, "Pull up your socks, boy, and get on with it!"[7]

Though born in New Jersey, Griswold was a descendant of many

New England Yale men and he looked, and sometimes acted, like a flinty New Englander. This side of the new president was captured in the story that "upon the advent of Griswold and the Puritan reformation" chairs of "enduring oak" were placed in the Corporation room. It was not for this, however, that Griswold was known when he was elected. Instead, it was for his wit, gaiety, and gift for mimicry, for his teaching ability, and for the rubber stamp with which, in the 1930s, he had left the message "Raise Faculty Salaries" on his letters and the menus at Mory's. He was, in all ways, a sprightly man.[8]

His ability to write well and wittily had been revealed as an undergraduate when he produced a column, under the name of Sancho Panza, for the *Yale Daily News*. As president this capacity often surfaced. When Dean of Admissions Arthur Howe suggested admitting women to Yale, and President Griswold was twitted about it by McGeorge Bundy during a meeting, Griswold then and there penned the following lines for the Harvard dean:

> By keeping in step with the male,
> We proceed at the pace of a snail,
> Said the Dean of Admissions,
> Let's shift our positions
> And get some fast women at Yale.[9]

The Griswold stories are almost as legion as the Hadley tales: standing on a Timothy Dwight College balcony, pretending he was Il Duce and making a long speech in a thick Italian-American accent to a friend standing in the street below; finishing a class before Derby Day * and having the whole lecture, even the outline on the board, suddenly, at the very end, deliver the message, "Happy Derby Day," and then departing with cane and straw hat, doing a soft-shoe routine; describing his first football experience at Hotchkiss as leaving him looking like a "soft-shell crab" or a "fried footprint"; playing cowboys and Indians around his office desk with a former student who had decided to write his dissertation on a western subject. His friend Thomas Mendenhall, president of Smith, said of Griswold, "His common sense went to the heart of the mat-

* Derby Day was a day in the spring when a large part of student Yale went to the banks of the Housatonic near Derby, got terribly drunk and behaved accordingly, and pretended to watch the crew compete. It was banned early in Griswold's administration.

ter, but his imagination set it afire while his wit danced like a bad boy around the flames." [10]

Griswold was hot-tempered (one observer called him "a sudden man"), opinionated, and independent. He was, as Wilmarth Lewis said, a "Do-It-Yourself, Don't-Fence-Me-In president." He was also something of a loner. Though he had good friends—many from the history department—they did not (contrary to rumor) form a kitchen cabinet. Griswold was perfectly willing to seek advice and often called people he hardly knew on the telephone to get their opinions, but he made his own decisions—sometimes contrary to the advice. He liked to withdraw to his house, think, read, and establish principles for a decision. He probably read more (Jefferson, Whitehead, and the like) than any Yale president in modern times.[11]

All presidencies are, to a greater or lesser degree, personal ones. Even in a university as large as Yale had become, the president was able to set the tone of the entire place. Especially was this so when the president was one of whom it could be said, "he did not like administration or routine, but when he made a decision it was thoughtful, clear, backed with lawyerlike reasoning, and defended unswervingly." [12] As a result, Griswold's administration was even more personal than most. It is this fact as well that makes his term controversial. There are some who loathed Griswold, just as there are some who loved him. Since we are still too close to these events for the dust to have settled entirely, for all the papers to have been opened, and for numerous recollections and studies to have been written, what follows on the Griswold years must perforce be a somewhat subjective and tentative appraisal of Yale during these years. No attempt will be made to cover everything that happened, but perhaps I can suggest where the university was when he took over, where he tried to lead it, and how successful he was in his task.

One thing is certain: Yale had chosen a great "voice" for the university. In a time of trial, this was an important asset. For if the problems bequeathed him by Seymour were not enough, the Korean War began just five days before Griswold took office. Again it was necessary to allow faculty to leave, to volunteer the university's resources, and to fear that Yale might lose a large percentage of its students. Griswold began his presidency worrying not about the future

of Yale but about its very existence. Yet by the time of his inauguration in October he was able to issue a stirring call "to renew the life
of an old and honorable institution." Though another war made the
times inauspicious, that did not matter: "If the scholars of the past
had waited for auspicious times to do their work, I doubt that we
should be assembled here today. If they should now wait for total
war to produce total peace, I doubt that our successors will be assembled here to mark Yale's 300th anniversary." There were certain
things, however, that allowed Yale to be hopeful for the future:
"The briefest glance into history shows us that we are supported by
powerful traditions—not symbols or legends, but vital forces with
remarkable capacity for survival. I would cite three of these traditions this afternoon: the tradition of higher learning, the university
tradition, and the tradition of American democracy." From his definition of these traditions emerged what were to be the guidelines of
his administration: stress on the university's continuing role in expanding basic knowledge but rejection of the idea that a university
should "attempt to cover every field of learning," and belief in
higher education—especially the liberal arts—as a preparation for
citizenship and life. The new president concluded, "These traditions give us courage for the future no matter how black it may look
from day to day. These are the things Yale lives and works for, in
war and peace. They are things to cherish and defend in times of
war; to fight for, when there is fighting; and to return to when the
fighting is over." [13]

Almost immediately after Griswold took office, he had to face the
celebration of Yale's 250th year—which makes an excellent point to
pause and consider how far Yale had come since its birth.

When *Newsweek* looked at Yale, it saw a great Graduate School,
except in science where the university seemed "to have been caught
by the Atomic Age with its moleskins in the locker room." The
magazine also admired the Forestry School for its "top-notch" graduates and the Law School, which had "a world reputation for excellence." It praised the library, not just because it was fourth largest in
the nation but also for the greatness of its collections—especially the
"monumental" Boswell and Walpole papers. But what *Newsweek*
gave Yale the greatest accolade for—and this would have pleased
many Yale men most of all—was that "over a quarter of a millen-

nium no American institution has better served the nation than Yale." [14]

Time magazine noted many of the same good points about Yale: "top-flight schools of law, medicine, divinity; the nation's oldest forestry school; the world's second largest university library." But it was especially enthusiastic about "Yale's whole interlocking curriculum, where psychiatrists teach in the law school, physicists rub elbows with philosophers, engineers teach in the medical school. At 250 years, Yale is more than ever what it has always taken pride in being—a teaching institution." *Newsweek* pointed to the special "atmosphere" of Yale and *Time* noted its great *esprit,* which it thought came "partly from the fact that Yale is a dynasty, perhaps the most inbred of all ivy-league colleges. Since 1766 only one President, James Rowland Angell, has been an outsider, and today 55% of its faculty are Yale men. It also springs from a carefully nurtured sense of responsibility and community service." *Time* also pointed to Yale's famous conservatism:

Consciously or unconsciously, Yale has traditionally waited for others to lead, observed their course, then picked the middle road to follow.

Thus if its progress has not been speedy, it has been selective and generally sound. If it has opened few new frontiers, it has at least held fast to old and solid principles. In the best and truest sense of the word, Yale has stood from its earliest beginnings for conservatism triumphant.[15]

While *Time* ignored Yale's many important firsts: the first art gallery connected with a university, the first university art school, the first American Ph.D., the first university drama school and nursing school—to name only the most important—there was, of course, a strong element of truth in its statement. The Yale attitude toward change had been most blatantly voiced by James L. Kingsley when he wrote to Benjamin Silliman, "Let them at Cambridge try experiments, and we will try to profit by them. They are better able to experiment than we are." [16] Less openly, many Yale men viewed change in the same way.

Despite the conservative philosophy that still marked it, Yale had grown by age 250 to be a relatively large institution. One indication of how far Yale had come was the receipt in June 1951 of the Carl Bosch collection of minerals—236 cases weighing forty tons and filling two and a half railway box cars. Not quite 150 years earlier Benjamin Silliman had carried Yale's entire mineral collection to Philadelphia in a candle box. By other more standard measurements as well, Yale had grown. Out of a total of 1,505 teaching personnel, there were 760 full-time faculty members, of whom 219 were full professors. At the undergraduate level, 4,197 were enrolled, and there were 3,073 degree-seeking students in the graduate and professional schools. The library contained over four million volumes. The university's endowment was more than $134 million. Since the beginning, Yale had awarded 84,624 degrees.[17]

The graduates of Yale tended, like the institution itself, to be conservative. They were generally not intellectual leaders but avoided scholarly pursuits for the professions and business. A committee of the University Council reporting in 1949 found among students and alumni alike a "deplorable ignorance of the extraordinary intellectual resources at Yale." The committee observed that "the average undergraduate and alumnus has an indifference to the treasures of the place; the magnificent libraries, collections, exhibits, and lectureships, that approaches the sublime." Still, the alumni of Yale were good men, men who did things for their communities. One observer was impressed by the fact that a surprisingly large number of graduates went into public service for some period of their lives. Dean DeVane of the college thought, however, that it would be better if there could be added to their other accomplishments a somewhat greater concern for intellectual things.[18]

Some of the students felt that the university continued its old tradition of discouraging individualism. A graduate at the 250th commencement later wrote, "one often felt at Yale that leadership was said and conformity meant." While they may have been conformists, Yale had produced many men who were currently leaders. A recent study by George W. Pierson, the university historian, has shown that in law, business, banking, philanthropy (foundations), architecture, learned societies, on Broadway (directors), and in *Who's Who,* Yale ranked far higher than its size could account for —and this is to take only fields in which Yale men were active around the time of the 250th.[19]

By the anniversary year, the Yale College student was reverting from the exciting creature of the immediate postwar years to his more normal mold. Though written during the war, D. H. Marshman's lampoon of the "white shoe" boy reveals a great deal about one type of student who was much in evidence in the 1950s:

To find out what sort of a person a man is at Yale, you look at his shoes. Now as far as shoes at Yale are concerned, there are only two primary colors: black and white. Everybody has brown shoes, so they count for nothing, but a real index is obtained by noticing whether a man happens to be wearing shoes that are black or white.

Suppose they are black. Dismiss the man. Forget him. He will never get you anywhere and with him your only destination is oblivion. The facts are hard and cruel, but they are true: *Men who wear black shoes at Yale University will never be worth a tinker's dam, here or anywhere else.* This University has been going for 241 years and it has found this to be true, and when Yale takes a stand on the matter of shoes as an indication of eligibility, Yale is right—there can be nothing more important.

On the other hand, suppose the shoes are white. Suppose they are white buckskin with plain toes and thick red rubber soles. Ah, my friends, that man will go far. "Look at the shoes and you can tell the man," is an old saying. If the shoes are as described above, chances are that the man hails from New York or out on the Island (the only *chic* island in the western hemisphere is Long Island), from Greenwich, Connecticut, or from such isolated outposts of culture as Grosse Point, Lake Forest, or Pasadena, with an occasional interloper from Dixie.

Now as a last possibility, suppose the shoes are white all right, but not the same as those described above. Suppose they have hard soles and perforations. Cross to the other side of York Street. This man, God help him, has neither the background for "right whites" (as the term is) nor (realizing this) the common decency to wear blacks. In the Eli caste system, he is something akin to untouchable.[20]

Clare Mendell said of this white-shoed, khaki-panted, button-down-shirted, tweed-jacketed student that he was harder to teach than the completely nonintellectual Yale undergraduate of the turn of the century. Then the student knew he was not prepared for life, so "the Faculty could begin at a fairly elementary stage to inform and discipline a reasonably receptive subject, to provide him with a somewhat simple set of tools. Today it is a longer operation, and not the least difficult part is a process of preliminary deflation."[21]

Though perhaps unreceptive to learning, these undergraduates had a veritable cornucopia of some 930 different term courses to choose from. To support such a selection—and all the graduate and professional programs, too—took sums of money undreamed of in

Yale's earlier days. Income during the 250th year totaled $16,-253,466, of which less than $1 million was provided by the federal government. Expenses that year were greater than income by a little over $100,000.[22]

The continuing deficit—even though it appeared to be getting smaller—was a burdensome problem. Nor did the future look any brighter. The president of Brown warned that American institutions of higher learning were about to be hit by "a financial hurricane." And President Griswold did not conceal the problem during the year of quiet celebration. On Alumni Day, 22 February 1952, he told Yale's graduates,

> Since I assumed the office of President of Yale, not yet two years ago, I have been at pains to alert all members of the Yale community—students, Faculty, and alumni—to the extraordinary dangers that stand in our path. It would be more appropriate to this festival year to celebrate the solid accomplishments and the going concerns that make Yale what she undoubtedly is, one of the greatest universities in the modern world. But this world is too much with us for celebration, and although I have some good news for you, I must again preface it with a warning. Yale still faces three major tests set for her by circumstances beyond her control, all three of which she must pass before her future as a private institution of higher learning will be secure. The first and most obvious of these is the test of war. The second is a test compounded of economic factors, the worst of which are inflation and an indifferent public policy that gives lip service to the survival of the private universities but makes inadequate provision for its accomplishment. The third is a cultural test, a proof of our ability as a people to understand the fundamental aims and principles of a university and, having understood them, of our willingness to give them support.[23]

The cultural test that Griswold warned of had been complicated by Senator Joseph McCarthy and his followers. For Yale individually, it was raised by William F. Buckley, Jr. (B.A. 1950), whose *God and Man at Yale* charged that the Yale faculty was teaching agnosticism and atheism instead of Christianity and collectivism instead of individualism. Buckley thought that since the trustees and alumni "are committed to the desirability of fostering both a belief in God, and a recognition of the merits of our economic system," the Corporation should see that those values were taught.[24]

In replying to those who attacked not only Yale but all universities, Griswold strongly defended the cause of academic freedom. In one speech to the Yale alumni he gave them a concise and lucid explanation of the purposes of the university:

These purposes are to carry on the quest for the ultimate truths concerning man and his place in the universe that began with the ancient Greeks and Hebrews—man's age-old effort to rise above his passions and put his powers of reason and conscience to the service of his fellow men —and to prepare our students not just for intellectual or vocational pursuits but for the whole of life as free men in a free society. This is the responsibility Yale shares with her sister universities. This is the mission of higher education in a troubled world.[25]

Of course Griswold did not convince all the alumni, or the nation, with this or any other speech. But he kept his voice raised against the philistines and was a leading defender of the freedom of individuals and universities. At the 250th commencement on 11 June 1951, one of those who received an honorary degree was Dr. Edward C. Tolman, who had been forced to leave the University of California because he refused to sign a loyalty oath. Yale saluted him not only for his work in psychology but also as a "valiant defender of the freedom of the mind." And in 1958 Yale withdrew from the federal student loan program because it contained not only a loyalty oath but also a negative affidavit by which the student, who had already proclaimed his loyalty, said that he did not believe in and was not a member of any organization seeking to overthrow the United States government. Griswold likened this affidavit to the test oaths used through the ages to persecute Catholics, Protestants, Quakers, and Puritans. After Griswold died, the *New York Times* said his loss was greater to the nation than it was to Yale because of "the vigor and articulateness he marshaled against the suppressors of freedom." [26]

Griswold was a doughty battler for everything he believed in. He spoke and wrote about what mattered to him. Since he presented his ideas with lucidity, concision, and persuasiveness, he was a very great teacher. The combination served Yale and his nation well. It is a revelation to sit down and read, all together, the annual reports, baccalaureate addresses, articles, and speeches that Griswold prepared when he was president. They were of such high caliber that three years after he took office he could publish some of them in a little book entitled *Essays on Education* and follow it, four years

later, with a similar volume called *In the University Tradition*. By
his writings A. Whitney Griswold taught at least some of the alumni
of Yale the meaning of the liberal arts, the purposes of the university, and the need to support them generously.

The first great task facing Griswold when he took office was to
raise money. Yale had once done this most successfully. In the 1920s
it had led all other universities with total gifts for all purposes
(buildings, endowment, current operations, etc.) of $91 million.
Again it had been first in the 1930s, receiving $77 million. During
the 1940s, however, it had fallen to a distant second with only $46
million. When these lowered donations were combined with a conservative investment policy, the effects on Yale's competitive position were unfortunate. In the 1920s and 1930s Yale raised enough
money to bring its total assets (at book value) from 56 percent of
Harvard's in 1927 to 72 percent in 1937. By the end of the Seymour
years Yale's assets had fallen back to about 56 percent of Harvard's.
The income figures were even more distressing. In 1937 Yale's total
income was 76 percent of Harvard's. By 1950 it had dropped to just
below 50 percent and deficits were growing. Despite these facts and
all the groundwork done in the Seymour years, Yale did not immediately rush into a great money-raising campaign.[27]

Yet the need was great, especially for faculty salary increases. Between 1940 and 1951, while the cost of living went up 86 percent,
Yale faculty salaries had only increased 32 percent. Though it took
time to correct this imbalance, it was finally done. First, however, in
1953 it was necessary to institute a freeze on nearly all faculty promotions and especially on the number of full professors, since most
of these positions were not endowed at all. Fortunately, Griswold
was able to raise the money, and beginning in 1955 salaries started
to go up. By 1960 professors were receiving $12,000 to $20,000, and
Yale's average salaries in all ranks were rated in the top group of colleges and universities by the American Association of University
Professors.[28]

Griswold also attacked another area where Yale was sadly
deficient—the sciences. Wasting no time after he took office, he announced on 15 December 1950 that a new physics laboratory was an
immediate and primary need. And one month later, the president
and fellows resolved that "as part of its responsibility in the national

emergency this University must promptly make available adequate facilities for research and teaching in the science of physics." So preliminary designs were drawn up for the building, and Yale tried to find $5 million.[29]

Unfortunately, the money was not forthcoming. In 1952 Griswold confessed that the new laboratory was as far beyond Yale's resources as ever. As he informed the alumni

I shall say once more that until we build this laboratory, the opportunities for study and research in the sciences at Yale (not physics alone, but all the sciences) must remain out of balance with the arts, out of joint with the times, and out of keeping with our fundamental responsibilities as a university. This is an all-too-conspicuous educational deficit that might be compared in kind to the operation of a modern hospital with inadequate supplies of penicillin.

Griswold insisted, "Our scientists deserve better. So does the university of Silliman, Dana, and Gibbs. And so, for that matter, do the security and welfare of the United States." But despite his pleading and persuasiveness, it was hard to overcome the indifference of college alumni and the suspicions of Sheff graduates about Yale's motives toward science. Finally, the university had to put up over $1 million of its own funds to build the new physics laboratory.[30]

Though large gifts came to Yale throughout the 1950s (Griswold raised $101.5 million in his first seven years and even larger sums thereafter), they were not great enough to solve the university's problems. These problems, Griswold explained to his largely businessman audience, were caused in part by the competitiveness of universities. They were constantly fighting each other for faculty and students and trying to prevent other activities from taking their teachers away from them. Yale and its competitors had all had enormous increases in expenditures over the years. Yale's alone had gone from $784,906 in 1900 to $22,191,297 in 1955. Harvard, Michigan, and others had increased even more. At the same time, Yale, like everyone else, had been hit by the inflationary spiral that "raised the national index of consumer prices from 100 in 1904 to 311 in 1955." Griswold made it clear, however, that Yale's need for money was a natural state of affairs,

something normal and healthy rather than a symptom of illness. It is not the result of extravagance or of an unexpected crisis in our affairs; nor would our long run needs be met if every penny of it were presented to us tomorrow. It is no more and no less than what the Chairman of the Alumni Fund called it in 1891. It is "proof of our progress and life." [31]

In spite of Griswold's success in raising money and balancing the university budget, he was probably mistaken to wait until 1960 before embarking on a major fund drive. And he was undoubtedly wrong to make the goal so small. The Program for the Arts and Sciences was announced as being for $69.5 million, but it was actually for only $47 million and an increase in the alumni fund over three years of $1 million (representing, they figured, $22.5 million in principal).[32]

The $1 million increase in the alumni fund was to be combined with the income of a $22.5 million endowed development fund to give the president $2 million a year. This was a pet project of Griswold's. The idea seems to have grown out of the difficulty of raising money for the new physics building. In addition, matching grants were now common, and unless Yale had the funds, it could not get the grants. So the president of Yale was to be given this special fund "to be available for capital grants for essential teaching and research for the Arts and Sciences." [33]

After setting aside the development fund, Yale was thus asking for only $24.5 million for immediate needs. And of this amount, $10 million was to go for buildings and only $14.5 million for endowment. Development officers wanted to ask for more, but Griswold refused. He did not, it is true, expect this campaign to solve Yale's problems. Drives for the various schools were to follow immediately. But Yale probably missed a good opportunity to raise a much larger amount for the endowment fund.[34]

Though Yale's endowment did jump from $121 million to $375 million under Griswold, and twenty-six buildings worth over $75 million were in process or completed when he died, it is still possible to regret that he did not raise more. The clearest way to see this is again to compare Yale with its old rival Harvard. During the Griswold years Yale's total income in relation to Harvard's rose slightly to 54 percent of the older university's, while her total assets (at market) slipped to less than half of Harvard's. While Yale under Seymour and Griswold was fighting deficits or putting only small amounts aside, Treasurer Cabot at Harvard was tucking away "odd millions" so that "by the time he retired [in 1967] Harvard had a rainy day cache of more than $60 million of undistributed income —which itself now generates an extra 2.5 million or so in income annually." Thus Harvard under Cabot began to run on the conservative principle of paying out only last year's income. In fact, in twenty-five years Harvard, by almost always having a surplus after paying all the bills, had been able to leave Yale far behind in terms of the size of its assets and the income received from those assets.[35]

While the growth of Yale's endowment thus was not as large as it might have been, total income did rise from $15.2 million in 1949–50 to $48.6 million in 1962–63. The change was partly due to federal aid. Though Griswold distrusted money from the government (he once said of it, "We must be sure each time that we can ride the horse and that it bears no trace of Trojan ancestry"), the amount received by Yale grew enormously during his years. As late as 1954, Yale got only one percent of its income from the federal government. By the time of Griswold's death in 1963, federal support made up approximately 20 percent of the university's income, and within a short time thereafter, it had reached 30 percent. In the fifteen years from 1949–50 to 1964–65, gifts and grants from the government rose from $596,000 to $19,037,000.[36]

The rise in Yale's income meant a bigger faculty and higher salaries. When Griswold took office, the total faculty (full-time, part-time, research associates and assistants) amounted to 1,505 individuals. When he died in 1963, the total faculty was 2,300. The full-time faculty had increased from 760 in 1951 to 1,103 in 1962. As has been noted, their salaries increased substantially as well.[37]

The great fund-raising campaign of 1960—the Program for the Arts and Sciences—was especially directed at helping the sciences, where Yale continued to face "a serious deficit." Griswold constantly wondered how Yale could have neglected the sciences in "a period of history in which the advancement of scientific knowledge has been more rapid than at any other time since the scientific revolution of the seventeenth century." Fortunately, a $10 million gift from C. Mahlon Klinc (Ph.B. 1901) allowed Yale to begin construction of new buildings for chemistry, biology, and geology. Griswold said with pride that

when all three are completed, they will represent, together with Gibbs Laboratories completed in 1955, the first major construction for these sciences at Yale since 1922 in the case of chemistry, 1914 in the case of biology, 1912 in the case of physics, and 1902 in the case of geology. In retrospect it is hard to understand how, especially in the sciences, where both the premium on equipment and its rate of obsolescence are exceptionally high, such a deficit could have been permitted to develop. It is unthinkable that Yale should ever allow it to happen again.[38]

The beginning of work on the new science buildings did much to revivify Yale science departments. With the university's obvious commitment to improvements in the field, it became somewhat easier to attract scientists to Yale. But the new buildings could not solve all the difficulties. Yale scientists continued to feel neglected. (Griswold is criticized by some scientists for not moving soon enough or ardently enough to improve their field despite his early statements about their needs.) Undergraduates still failed to study science in anything like the numbers that might have been expected. Whereas over 20 percent of the undergraduates at Michigan and Harvard majored in a science, only 11.5 percent did so at Yale. The science faculty's feeling of neglect was in part paranoiac—a heritage of long years of being looked down on by the college—but like the shortage of students, it was also based in part on the old decision to put the sciences on Pierson-Sage Square. Out there, away from the rest of the campus, the scientists felt separated from university life—isolated—while students begrudged the long walk to class and laboratory. This problem not even magnificent buildings could solve.[39]

The Kline Science Center buildings were not the only buildings put up under Griswold. As previously noted, when he died twenty-six new buildings were under way or completed at a cost of $75 million. They included Morse and Stiles residential colleges, the Art and Architecture Building, Ingalls Rink, and Beinecke Rare Book and Manuscript Library, to name just a few. And they were distinguished structures. Architects loved Griswold. In one of his most famous remarks, the president had said,

Could *Hamlet* have been written by a committee, or the "Mona Lisa" painted by a club? Could the New Testament have been composed as a conference report? Creative ideas do not spring from groups. They spring from individuals. The divine spark leaps from the finger of God to the finger of Adam, whether it takes ultimate shape in a law of physics or a law of the land, a poem or a policy, a sonata or a mechanical computer.

Following this philosophy, Griswold chose good architects and left them alone. The result, according to the *Architectural Forum* in a eulogy of Griswold, was that "of the twenty-six buildings commissioned under Griswold at old Yale, an amazingly high proportion are really proud attempts to put up structures with new intellectual content." [40]

If Griswold left his mark on physical Yale, he also left it on intellectual Yale. The president had a basic philosophy about the function of the university that strongly affected the development of the entire institution. He made his most important statement about the intellectual aims of Yale in 1955, when in his presidential report he wrote:

In the light of our own ideals and first principles it seems to me we should be able to agree on the following seven aims:

1. To strengthen and support liberal education as the *fons et origo* of higher education.

2. To strive for a balance between the arts and sciences in which each becomes instructive and useful to the other, as an object lesson to the country that such a thing is possible.

3. To have the best of two worlds, the college world with its emphasis upon the communication of knowledge and the university world with its emphasis upon the discovery.

4. To preserve the residential principle in the fullness of its strength as the most powerful ally of formal education.

5. To maintain the highest possible ratio of teachers to students in order that education, which is fundamentally a two-way process, may continue to flourish as such at Yale and never descend to mass production.

6. To maintain for our Faculty the greatest possible opportunities for original research side by side with the most favorable possible conditions of teaching.

7. To support an extracurricular life for students and faculty in which both may find inspiration as well as recreation from their labors.[41]

Of these aims, the first is the key to understanding Griswold's presidency. The reason the liberal arts were important was stated most concisely by the president when he said,

If I had to reduce that purpose [of a liberal education] into a phrase I should say it was to expand to the limit the individual's capacity—and desire—for self-education, for seeking and finding meaning, truth, and enjoyment in everything he does. I believe that purpose should inform and enlighten everything we do, in our graduate and professional schools as in Yale College and in the School of Engineering. When we combine this ideal with the ideal of excellence we have the true university, we have Yale.

Further sharpening these principles was Griswold's belief that Yale should continue to be an educational leader by doing the things it could do best and letting others do what they could do. Corollary to these ideas were his dislike of the "service station" concept of the university and his distrust of cooperative research.[42]

Griswold's main effect in certain areas was to push for a greater infusion of his favored liberal arts and to strike at those schools or departments which did not seem to live up to his concept of Yale excellence. One of the very first areas to receive his attention was the training of teachers. He believed strongly that the liberal arts would be lost beneath "vocational and other substitutes" unless they were enlivened in the primary and secondary schools just as much as in the colleges. Teachers in the lower schools were too much steeped in pedagogy, however, to solve the problem. Yale could help by creating a new teacher training program. In the fall of his first year in office Griswold raised money from the Carnegie Foundation "for a small, essentially experimental program whose purpose was to inject as much as possible of the actual substance of the liberal arts into the training of secondary school teachers while at the same time giving them the essentials of pedagogy that would enable them to meet their professional requirements." Ominously, this program was created outside the department of education.[43]

Possibly even at this point Griswold had decided to end that department, for he was uncertain it lived up to Yale standards. As 1954 approached, a decision had to be made, for three professors, including the chairman, were leaving the department. When the experimental Master of Arts in Teaching program received a new large grant, registration in the department of education was halted, no new faculty appointments were made, and a committee was established to consider the entire question. Griswold said he wanted "a new map of the terrain" so he could "decide how best to develop our M.A. in Teaching, and what, if anything, we should do in addition to this program." [44]

In January 1956 the committee presented Griswold with a preliminary report recommending that Yale establish a Ph.D. program "to prepare carefully selected teachers of experience and outstanding promise for leadership in either of two professional areas: administration and supervision or instruction and research in colleges and universities having programs of teacher preparation." Griswold gave the committee the impression "that it was not now a matter of *whether* the Department of Education was to be rehabilitated, but rather a question of *when* and *how*." But Griswold did nothing. Slowly, quietly, the department was allowed to expire. Apparently like many Yale men, Griswold just did not believe that the art of teaching could be passed along scientifically. Under his successor, Yale's M.A.T. program would in turn be cut off because it too did not seem to meet Yale's wished-for standard of excellence, and the university would embark on another "new" program in education.[45]

It would seem that among the things for which Yale can be faulted during its long history is its failure to play a significant role in the field of educational training. For all its talk of service, in this area it has done little. Experiment follows experiment, but commitment is always lacking. For much of the university's history, Yale men have played an important part in education. Yale's proud title of "mother of colleges" is not an empty one—as the forty-one representatives of its offspring who came to the 250th anniversary attest. In recent years, however, Yale seemed to be lagging. When George W. Pierson checked the educational backgrounds of presidents of 150 prominent colleges and universities in 1961–62, he found that Yale was in fourth place behind Harvard, Columbia, and Chicago. But Yale had only nine presidents, compared to Harvard's thirty and Columbia's eighteen. Yale's role in higher education seemed to be on the decline.[46]

Griswold's interest in the liberal arts affected other areas of Yale. The number of liberal arts courses required in the engineering program was increased. The president's committee on general education concluded that the B.A. should generally be required for admission to the schools of Music, Fine Arts, and Drama,* and soon the

---

* Fine Arts was renamed Architecture and Design in 1955 and then Art and Architecture in 1958. Drama was set off from Fine Arts as a separate school in 1955.

schools followed this advice. At the end of the academic year 1956–57 Griswold announced that with the adoption that year of the bachelor's degree requirement by the schools of Music and Architecture and Design, "all Yale's constituent schools now recognize the liberal arts as the foundation of their several disciplines and mean to ensure that educational standard through their standards of admission." [47]

Even when schools required the B.A. they were not safe from the president's interference. Since the Nursing School had been admitting students with four years of undergraduate training ever since 1934, little change could be made in that requirement. But practicality in university work was not a virtue to Griswold: Yale University existed for exploration, not application. So in 1958 Griswold had the school cease training people to be nurses. Instead, the School of Nursing instituted a Master of Science in Nursing program for those who were *already* nurses and had earned the degrees of B.A., B.S., or B.S.N.

Not everyone agreed with Griswold's approach. A later dean of the school, Donna Diers, said that pockets of bitterness over the president's action still existed fifteen years later. Nonetheless, the nursing program instituted in 1955 was important. As Dean Diers explained,

> Just as the basic program was unique [because of the bachelor's degree requirement], the graduate nursing program which replaced it was also unusual. The tradition of scholarship is not strong in nursing, but the Yale School of Nursing began in 1958 to offer and then to require a curriculum in clinical nursing research. At that time Yale was one of the very few graduate schools of nursing to have a research concentration, and among the first to define the proper field of inquiry for nursing: the problems in patient care.[48]

Griswold's sword could cut even more ruthlessly than it did in nursing. Since he believed creative ideas did not spring from groups, opposed the "service station" concept of the university, and thought everything that went on at Yale should strengthen the liberal arts, he moved to drive out or close down some of the various institutes or centers that had grown up. Before his first year was over, the Institute of International Relations had decided to debark for Princeton, and by the end of his presidency the Laboratory of Applied Biodynamics was gone, the Alcohol Study Center had moved to Rut-

gers, and the Institute of Human Relations was little more than a
shell. Many never forgave Griswold for these moves.[49]

International and nonwestern studies were not really encouraged
until much later, 1961, when a solid program finally got under way.
At that time there were created "six interdepartmental councils and
committees on East Asian Studies, Russian and East European Studies, Southeast Asian Studies, International Relations, African Studies, and Latin American Studies . . . presided over by a Concilium."
Funding was sought aggressively and the program got under way
with a $3 million grant from the Ford Foundation.[50]

Under Dean Eugene Rostow, especially during his first term
(1955–60), the Law School forged ahead. The size of the faculty rose
from an abnormally low eighteen (the average was twenty-seven) to
forty. More importantly, the caliber of the appointments was the
highest. The curriculum was revised. While it continued to follow
the traditional Yale approach of "studying and teaching law as a living part of the social process," even greater emphasis was placed on
"small classes, individual research by the students, and sustained
contact between students and faculty." This school too was helped
to carry out these changes by a $1.6 million grant from the Ford
Foundation.[51]

The Medical School finally came into its own during these years.
Under Dean Vernon Lippard (1952–67) the school grew enormously. The opening of the Veterans Administration Hospital in
West Haven in 1953 added 880 beds to Grace–New Haven's 667.
This enabled the school to increase its enrollment substantially, for
the new hospital was used for teaching and training purposes. Not
including the Veterans Hospital, $15 million was spent for buildings
for the Medical School and Grace–New Haven Hospital between
1950 and 1960. In 1962 the Rockefeller Foundation Virus Laboratories decided to move to New Haven (where they became the Yale
Arbovirus Research Unit) and a new nine-story laboratory was constructed for them and the department of epidemiology and public
health (completed in 1964). The rise of the school was probably
most clearly shown, however, by such things as the development of
the first heart-lung apparatus (now at the Smithsonian) or by the
rapid increase in research gifts and grants from $337,776 in 1946 to
a little over a million dollars in 1952, to over $7.6 million in
1962–63.[52]

In school after school the story was much the same: new buildings, greater funds for research, enlarged enrollment, bigger and better faculty. But not everyone shared in this progress to the same degree. Drama stagnated, despite the president's personal interest in the theater.[53] Forestry and Art and Architecture, though they added new buildings, suffered some uncertainties over where they were going. Despite a few such weak spots, however, the significant thing was that the graduate and professional schools were becoming increasingly important at Yale.

There are few objective standards by which to measure what happened during these years. One of the few was a ranking of graduate education made in the spring of 1964 and published in 1966. Since such assessments always measure what was true at some earlier time, we may take this as an appraisal of what others thought about Yale in the early 1960s. By this ranking, "if one were to arrange the scores of each department, Yale would emerge either third (behind Harvard and Berkeley) or eighth . . . depending upon whether engineering was excluded or included." On the other hand, when surveys of 1924 and 1957 were compared with the 1964 report, it was shown that while Yale for the first time had three departments ranked first in the country, the number of departments in the first five had increased by only one since 1924. In addition, the number of departments ranked below tenth had risen since 1957. What it all seemed to prove to the author of the report was that Yale had done well to keep its place, because competition in graduate education was so fierce. The author was most complimentary over the fact that Yale had kept its position while still retaining "the tradition of a *teaching* faculty." Another study had shown that "Yale was one of only three major universities in the country where less than 3 percent of the teaching was performed by graduate students and teaching assistants." By comparison Stanford had more than 10 percent done by those groups and Harvard over 11 percent. In addition, it later became clear that Yale was gaining momentum during these years. A 1969 survey that probably reflected conditions around 1967 or 1968, if not earlier, showed that Yale had remained in third place but had moved up on Berkeley (now first) and Harvard. The best news for Yale, perhaps, was that it had the largest number of departments with higher scores (15) of all the universities rated.[54]

Since even such "objective" ratings are somewhat subjective, a completely subjective report might better catch the flavor of Yale at this time. McGeorge Bundy commented, upon visiting Yale shortly before Griswold's death, "I was struck by the restless energy of the place." [55]

An area of particular difficulty for Griswold was engineering, which was clearly one of the university's major weak spots. In department after department—especially electrical and chemical engineering—the school suffered from lack of space and outmoded laboratories. In 1958 the problem was somewhat mitigated by the construction of an architecturally undistinguished (one of Griswold's few) addition to Dunham Laboratory. Strangely for a historian, Griswold allowed the addition to be built where it caused the destruction of the old Sheffield mansion—a unique structure built by Ithiel Town for himself and remodeled by Henry Austin for Sheffield. It was an irreparable loss. [56]

Griswold had been worrying at least since 1955 about finding the "true place of engineering at Yale." In 1960 the president appointed a committee to study the whole question. He wondered if engineering was "taking full advantage of the University's total resources or producing as generally fruitful results as it might." The committee agreed it was not. They pointed to the connection between engineering, applied science, and pure science as well as between engineering, the humanities, and the social sciences and concluded that the engineer must know both science and society. In addition, they felt that the speed of technological change was so great that old-fashioned engineering courses would soon be useless to a student who took them. So the committee recommended that the four-year undergraduate curriculum as well as the program leading to a Ph.D. should be placed in a department of engineering and applied science, while the professional degrees of M.E. and D.E. were to remain in the School of Engineering. The school and department were to be tied together by making the same person both dean and chairman. "By these means," Griswold reported,

it was felt that all three phases of engineering education at Yale would be strengthened, the undergraduate foundations and the graduate training for academic careers by becoming truly integral parts of the arts and sciences curriculum and as such direct beneficiaries of its resources; and the more specialized training of professional engineers by making itself the responsibility of a truly professional school. [57]

While by these arrangements, for the first time in a century, Yale College again became responsible for all undergraduate education, the engineering course allowed its accreditation to lapse in 1966 and then was not able to regain it. Though the committee had recognized that Yale might lose its accreditation, the fact did not bother them. It did bother Yale's engineering alumni, who were further annoyed by the disappearance of the old standard engineering programs. But most of this outraged reaction had to be faced by Kingman Brewster, Griswold's successor.[58]

While Griswold was concerned about all aspects of the university, he was more interested in Yale College than anything else. In 1954 he said, "We may wonder whether 'How the University Strengthened its Liberal Arts College' will prove as appropriate a title for the next fifty years of Yale's history as 'How the Liberal Arts College Became a University' is for the past hundred and fifty." So under Griswold a great deal of effort was spent on strengthening all aspects of college life. The residential colleges received much attention: seminars for sophomores and juniors were endowed in the colleges; two new colleges were constructed to relieve the pressure of numbers (for though enrollment declined after the veterans left, it never returned to the prewar level), and the college libraries were enlarged and developed to serve as a scattered undergraduate library. For these programs Griswold's old friend and classmate Paul Mellon contributed $20 million through the Old Dominion Foundation.[59]

On the social side in the colleges, one important change had to be made during the Griswold years. By the personal selections of the students—sometimes helped by an over-eager master—the colleges were taking on distinct characters. Calhoun and Davenport were strongly athletic and "white shoe," only engineers (it was whispered) congregated in Silliman and Timothy Dwight, and no one knew *who* lived in Trumbull. One unidentified master complained to the *Yale Alumni Magazine,* "As long as these present social distinctions are permitted to exist . . . I'm afraid that the intended re-creation of the atmosphere of the small class will not be fully achieved." To obviate this problem, starting in 1954–55 with the class of 1958, students were no longer allowed to express a preference for a college. A new system was instituted whereby each residential college was to have a cross section of each class. Partly as a result of this change, Thomas Bergin would say that the colleges were formed on "two administratively sanctioned prescriptions. The first is that all colleges must be exactly alike; the second is that all the colleges must be different." [60] Strangely enough, they achieved that implausible goal.

Because of his interest in Yale College, one of Griswold's first acts was to appoint a committee on general education with himself as chairman. The committee produced a report which criticized the maturity of Yale students and their failure to commit themselves to what Yale offered. The committee was especially disillusioned about the distributional system: "We find the present course offerings 'minced into such infinite numbers of little quillets' that the student sees no more purpose to his labors than the vaulting of eight hurdles before reaching the straightaway of his major." Nor was it producing an educated man. The committee reported harshly, "As several graduate Deans told the committee, Yale is still not fulfilling the need for men with power to make judgments about complex subjects and to present those judgments coherently and precisely."

To remedy these shortcomings the committee suggested two possible alternatives. The first and least controversial indicated a way to bring a certain amount of concentration and progression to distribution. The second tried to accomplish even more by abolishing all the usual freshman and sophomore courses and instituting entirely new programs such as "the Arts in America," "Democracy in America: Past and Present," "Government and Economic Life in Contemporary America." To carry out these programs the faculty concerned with the first two years would be divided into four parts, "each part corresponding to one of the areas of instruction or to the category of training subjects." The divisions would have the right to suggest appointments and, together, would constitute the Faculty in General Education. With this faculty, the committee hoped to do something about "the gradual disappearance of a more corporate faculty life at Yale" that had been brought about by the departments. The committee found that the departments tended to have "too limited a horizon" and "too hierarchical" an organization to allow the young teacher "much chance to try his wings." [61]

If Griswold did not already know the limitations on the power of the president, he discovered them now. The Yale College course of study committee, despite its being headed by the president's friend Thomas C. Mendenhall, studied Griswold's report for over a year and a half and then revealed that it did not agree entirely with any part of it—neither its premises nor its conclusions. The course of study committee was especially eager to protect the distributional offerings, one of Dean DeVane's favorite reforms. As a result, only minor modifications were made in the existing curricular arrangements. Admitting that the problems of excessive interest in extracurricular affairs and the rise of the departments had not been dealt with, however, the course of study committee asked,

First, how far can any manipulation of the curriculum make intellectual achievement more attractive than these outside activities in the context in which the educational process now operates? Second, how far does the faculty wish to go beyond the curriculum to explore the conditions that foster or impede the achievement of the educational goals which it sets?

But to these questions the faculty gave no answers.[62]

Griswold certainly had not received what he wanted from the course of study committee and the Yale College faculty, but he set his seal of approval on what they had done.[63] The undergraduate educational problems Griswold had seen when he began his presidency continued to bother him, however, so in 1960 he appointed a committee to study the Freshman Year.

The Freshman Year, it will be recalled, had been set up in the 1919 reorganization for two main reasons: first, to prevent a boy from having to make a choice between Sheff and the college before he even arrived at Yale; and second, to give more specific attention to freshman needs and problems. The Freshman Year did achieve its first end. It only partly accomplished its second, for control of its curriculum was always difficult because of the requirements laid down by the college for its programs. When the new college course of study went into effect in 1945, Dean Buck of the Freshman Year had complained that the requirements severely limited a freshman's freedom of choice. Dean DeVane, according to George Pierson, "replied that 'a parochial institution,' convenient for handling Freshmen's problems, had a very dubious place in College policy-making." [64]

In 1954 the Freshman Year had lost its status as a separate school, becoming only the administrative unit responsible for "housing, discipline, counseling, and social life." Still Griswold, and no doubt Dean DeVane as well, were not entirely happy with it. So the president asked his new committee two questions:

1. Can our students be given a more lively sense of the purpose of the educational process in which they are engaged at the beginning of that process, i.e., in the Freshman Year?

2. Can the Freshman Year, both in its curricular and in its institutional arrangements, be brought into a more integral and more profitable relationship to the upper-class undergraduate and post-graduate years?

In short, can the beginning of the educational process at Yale be made more significant to its conclusion? [65]

The committee, chaired by Leonard Doob, did much more than answer those questions. Its wide-ranging reply was a blueprint (soon followed) not only for an end to the separate Freshman Year, but for a new admissions procedure, a new student body, and a new attitude toward what Yale College should do.

The committee felt that Yale was now a twentieth-century university and that, as such, it should emphasize the advancement of knowledge and the training of future scholars. To this end, it must make more scholarly demands on its students: they should "exemplify and radiate the power and grace of learning. More of the graduates of Yale College, we think, must become professional scholars and teachers."

For Yale College this marked a major and revolutionary shift in approach. From that assumption there naturally stemmed recommendations for changes in admissions procedures. Yale must now emphasize intellectual distinction in its applicants:

1. Candidates whose records show exceptionally high promise of continuing intellectual achievement should be sought out and admitted without regard for any other criteria save those indicative of emotional maturity and good character.

2. All other applicants for admission should be considered in the light of the fact that Yale is first and foremost an intellectual enterprise and that, consequently, those being educated here must be equipped with intellectual powers equal to the demands of the educational process at every stage. These students should show evidence of possessing intellectual curiosity, imagination, creative ability, inventiveness, and other qualities of mind and person that are less readily revealed and less accurately measured by formal academic tests than is the capacity for purely formal scholastic achievement.

To see that Yale got such candidates and that their entrance was not prevented by an admissions office of which the faculty was increasingly suspicious, the committee recommended that faculty members play an active role in the admissions procedure. Henceforward, professors should visit schools to seek out talent and sit on the admissions committee as well.

The committee went even farther. It suggested that Yale College admit women. Yale, the committee said, had a national duty to "provide the rigorous training for women that we supply for men." The number of women admitted, it recommended, should be more than just a token, but at the same time, the number of men enrolled should not be lowered.

The freshmen, the committee said, should not be placed in a separate Freshman Year. The improvement in secondary school education and in Yale's selection of students, as well as the consolidation of the undergraduate schools, all eliminated the reasons for delaying the student's choice of his ultimate program. From an educational point of view, the reasons for the Freshman Year had ceased to exist. Socially and intellectually, as well, the program had no rationale, for it merely delayed student development in these areas. For these reasons, the committee recommended that ultimately all freshmen should be taken directly into the residential colleges.

The study also concluded that Yale's manner of handling financial aid was unfortunate. It deplored

the fact that some students of the highest intellectual potential decide not to come to Yale because of our present policy of demanding that all students on scholarship shall earn part of their expenses by a job, or in some cases take a loan. The system of mandatory bursary work, moreover, brings hardship to some students, especially those who are promising but at the outset less well prepared, in that it prevents them from making the most of their educational experience at Yale.

So the report recommended that the entering student "be offered one of our scholarships or loans, or both, and no other demands . . . be placed upon him." If he wanted more money, he could take a bursary position. This work would now be entirely voluntary.

In addition, the report suggested that the Dean's Office should be dispersed by appointing deans in the residential colleges, responsible to the dean of Yale College, to handle student records, disciplinary problems, and other student matters within each college.[66]

The Freshman Year Report was to have a major effect on Yale

College. Ultimately, all of its recommendations were accepted. One might have expected the alumni to have some comments to make about a proposal to change not only the nature of the student body but the sort of training they would receive. But the alumni were distracted from the other important parts of the report first by the suggestion to admit women and then by the award of an honorary degree to President John F. Kennedy. While they were fulminating over these things, Yale moved to carry out the report's recommendations. Here again, however, Griswold's successor would bear the brunt of the criticism when the alumni discovered what was happening.[67]

In addition to all the other myriad activities at Yale during these years there were certain significant organizational changes. The first thing Griswold did, even before taking office, was to insist that Edgar S. Furniss resign one of his jobs—dean of the Graduate School or provost. Furniss chose to become provost and the Corporation then finally wrote into its by-laws what had become practice under President Seymour: the provost was chief educational officer of the university, the supervisor of all the internal operations of the university concerned with education and research.[68]

Upon taking office, Griswold had hired a firm of management engineers to study the university. According to one probably apocryphal story, after investigating Yale for six months they reported to the Corporation that the university had all the organization of a candy store. Perhaps because of the firm's report, a business manager was appointed. Balancing the provost, he was to be the chief university administrative officer in charge of nonacademic operations.[69]

Griswold also dismantled some of the internal organization created by President Seymour. The divisions of Medical Affairs and Art were both brought to an end. On the other hand, an attempt was finally made in the late fifties to make the divisions of Science, Humanities, and Social Sciences more meaningful. The directors of the divisions were given greater responsibility in appointments, and it was hoped they might become more active in shaping educational policy for their fields. Following that, during the summer of 1961, the powerful new team of Provost Kingman Brewster, Jr., and Dean of the Graduate School John Perry Miller, together with Dean DeVane, reinvigorated the executive committee of the Faculty of Arts

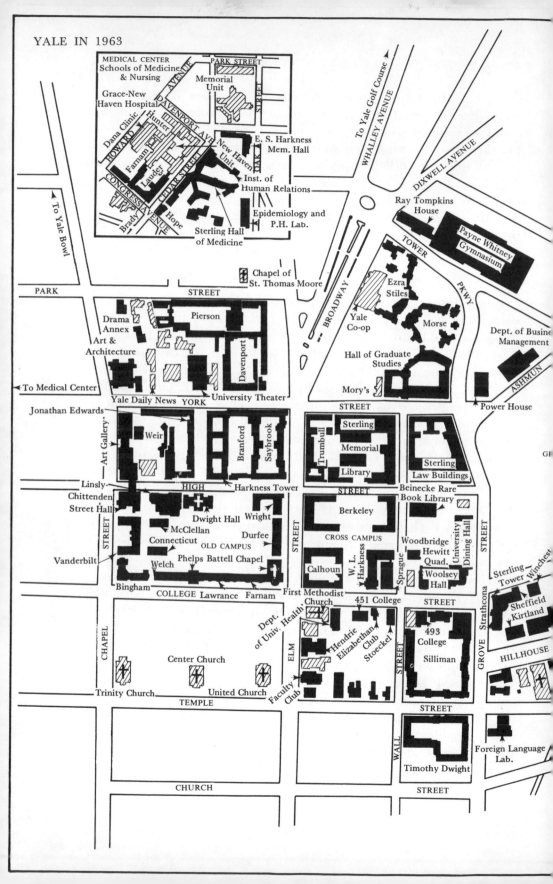

YALE IN 1963

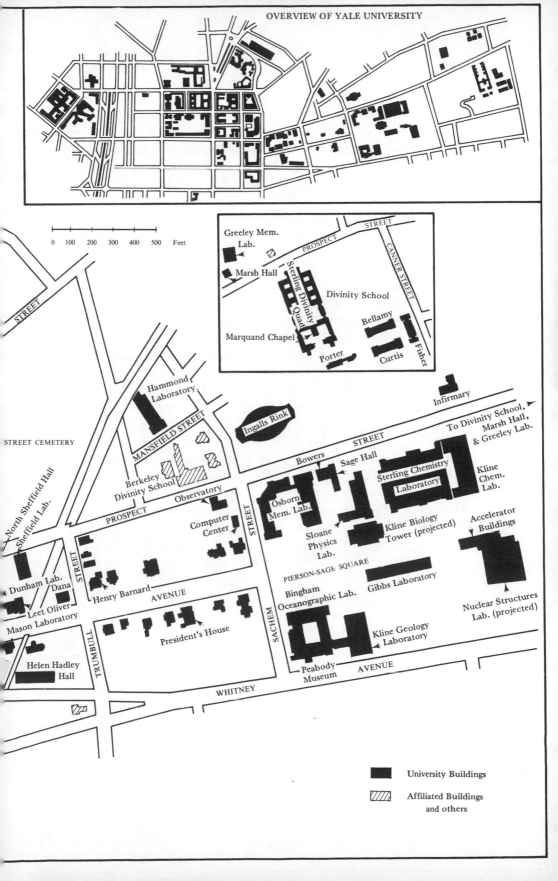

OVERVIEW OF YALE UNIVERSITY

0 100 200 300 400 500 Feet

Greeley Mem. Lab.

Marsh Hall

STREET

PROSPECT STREET

CANNER STREET

Sterling Divinity Quad

Divinity School

Marquand Chapel

Bellamy

Porter

Curtis

Fisher

Hammond Laboratory

Ingalls Rink

Infirmary

To Divinity School, Marsh Hall, & Greeley Lab.

STREET

MANSFIELD STREET

STREET CEMETERY

Bowers

STREET

Sage Hall

Sterling Chemistry

Laboratory

Kline Chem. Lab.

Berkeley Divinity School

Observatory

PROSPECT

Osborn Mem. Lab.

Sloane Physics Lab.

Kline Biology Tower (projected)

Accelerator Buildings

North Sheffield Hall

Sheffield Lab.

Computer Center

STREET

PIERSON-SAGE SQUARE

STREET

Dunham Lab.

Dana

Henry Barnard

AVENUE

Bingham Oceanographic Lab.

Gibbs Laboratory

Nuclear Structures Lab. (projected)

Leet Oliver

Mason Laboratory

President's House

SACHEM

Kline Geology Laboratory

TRUMBULL

Helen Hadley Hall

Peabody Museum

AVENUE

WHITNEY

and Sciences, adding to it the divisional chairmen, changing its agenda to include broad problems of educational policy and resource allocation, and instituting weekly meetings. The deans of Yale College and the Graduate School were thus finally encouraged to interact on a wider range of issues. In addition the appointments procedures were reorganized. Three joint appointments committees were established; these committees included members of the divisional advisory committees and the two deans. A joint committee to review junior appointments was also established, and it was provided that recommendations of these committees were to be acted upon by the joint meeting of the Boards of Permanent Officers of Yale College and the Graduate School, a further step in melding the activities of the college and the Graduate School in a matter where there was a strong joint interest. At the same time the deans and the faculties of the college and Graduate School remained separate powers to deliberate upon educational policies which were unique to the respective schools. The revitalization of the divisions and the executive committee came about largely because of President Griswold's feeling that he needed better advice on appointments.[70]

These significant changes took place as President Griswold's life neared its end. Whether they represented a real shift of his vision outward from the college to a greater concern for the Graduate School or whether they were only another aspect of his insistence on excellence is uncertain. It seems clear, however, that in his new Graduate School dean and new provost, Griswold for the first time had strong men in those positions. It has been conjectured that Griswold lacked full confidence in Provost Furniss and Dean DeVane and that therefore he tried to do too much himself. As a result, and perhaps because of a lack of interest, certain schools did not develop as well as they might have.

Because Griswold was active and often went outside proper administrative channels, certain faculty members felt that power moved significantly toward the central administration during these years. This feeling, it should be noted, is hardly a new one. In 1942 Dean DeVane had observed,

It seems clear to me that the Faculty feels that many of the affairs of the College which were formerly in their control have passed from their control . . . that the trend toward the concentration of the power in the University began long before [the war]. . . . It feels that a number of its powers have been usurped, and that too often special commissions and agencies have been set up to do work for which there are already constituted committees and offices.[71]

Yet this situation existed under a far less active president than Griswold. When that tough, opinionated, decisive man came in, it was bound to seem that power was flowing to the center, for there was real decision-making taking place at Woodbridge Hall. It is true, as well, that some weak deans were appointed by Griswold. But it does not seem possible that a man who could appoint men like Rostow, Miller, Buck, and Brewster to office was looking for a way to shift all power to the president.

In 1962 Griswold reported to the alumni that all was well at Yale. Using the "acid test of any university . . . its ability to attract and hold a faculty of outstanding distinction," Yale was an enormous success. During the past two years, he said, the university had made some of the most distinguished appointments in its history "in fields as varied as physics, geophysics, history, anthropology, and Slavic languages and literature; and . . . the Program for the Arts and Sciences has provided the means of making others, especially in the sciences and Russian history, of like distinction." At the same time, Yale had been able to hold most of the excellent faculty members it already had.

With a first-rate faculty, new programs for engineering, the freshman year, and international and nonwestern studies, numerous buildings under way, and the fund drive for the arts and sciences successfully completed, Griswold wrote,

I conclude this Report in the conviction that Yale's educational collateral is sound and that, while maintaining the university tradition of which she is part and the educational standards to which that tradition commits her, she is building for the future in ways that will justify the faith of all who have contributed to her welfare during the past two years and reflect credit upon their benefactions.

Within a few months A. Whitney Griswold was dead of cancer at the age of fifty-six.[72]

The shock of Griswold's loss was greeted with editorials, letters, and comments that mentioned his well-known qualities of wit, strength, and courage. Eugene Rostow, dean of the Law School, called him "the strongest President Yale has had in modern times." The *New York Times* pointed particularly to his championship of freedom. The best appraisal, however, was made by another man of wit, strength, and courage—Dean William C. DeVane, ruler (as Whit Griswold well knew) of Yale College. DeVane wrote,

He became a very great president of Yale, and the foremost spokesman for liberal education in America. For Yale, too, his assumption of the presidency was equally fortunate. After the decade of the Second World War and its aftermath Mr. Griswold's qualities were those exactly which the University most needed to resume her march to greatness. The man, the cause and the time made his presidency a stirring and happy time.[73]

No part of Yale had been left unchanged by President Griswold's very personal, philosophical view of what a university should be. It had been a dynamic, challenging, and exciting time. To some, Yale College, with its stress on small classes, seminars, and a teaching faculty, at this time offered the best undergraduate education in the United States. Though the graduate and professional schools had not received nearly the same amount of personal attention from the president, in most cases they too were forging ahead to greater and greater achievements. Griswold's successor, Kingman Brewster, wrote that "Yale was in sound shape, and moving with steady speed in a direction of high promise when President Griswold had to let go the wheel." Under Brewster the pace of that progress would be even quicker for a time. But soon Yale, like all American universities, would be struggling first with a new, irate student generation and then with financial problems of a magnitude that seemed to bring into question the very survival of the university. Only the passage of time would allow the historian of the future to appraise what happened during the tumultuous sixties and the financially troubled seventies and how well Yale coped with its problems. But as one viewed the history of Yale, such crises seemed an integral and yet not terribly important part of its past. What seemed more significant was the long and complex life of the institution. President Griswold, as he so often did, put it best:

Yale, like Ulysses, is part of all that she has met, part of all the scholars and students who have trod paths of learning across her campus, of their ideals and accomplishments, and of their lives and times, for over two and a half centuries drawing strength and inspiration and character from them all yet transcending them all in her importance to society. Such things, the environment they create and the time it takes to produce them, are irreplaceable. They must live or perish. They cannot be duplicated. They have no substitutes.[74]

Notes

CHAPTER 1

1   Franklin Bowditch Dexter, "The Founding of Yale College," *A Selection from the Miscellaneous Historical Papers of Fifty Years* (New Haven, 1918), p. 59; Samuel Eliot Morison, *Three Centuries of Harvard* (Cambridge, Mass., 1965), p. 49; Rollin G. Osterweis, *Three Centuries of New Haven* (New Haven, 1953), p. 39. See also Edwin Oviatt, *The Beginnings of Yale (1701–1726)* (New Haven, 1916), pp. 55–57, whose sometimes fictionalized and often overly romanticized account is far from trustworthy.

2   Samuel Eliot Morison most clearly indicates the Puritan educational desires: "The two cardinal principles of English puritanism which most profoundly affected the social development of New England and the United States were not religious tenets, but educational ideals: a learned clergy and a lettered people" (*The Founding of Harvard College* [Cambridge, Mass., 1935], p. 4). Both Richard Warch, who kindly allowed me to see in manuscript his study of the period, *School of the Prophets: Yale College, 1701–1740* (New Haven, 1973), and Dexter, "Founding," p. 61, stress the point that the length and expense of the journey were primary spurs to the founding of the Collegiate School.

3   Oviatt, *Beginnings of Yale,* pp. 83–85; Osterweis, *New Haven,* pp. 40–41; Samuel Eliot Morison, *Harvard College in the Seventeenth Century* (Cambridge, Mass., 1936), 2 : 362, 389; Dexter, "Founding," p. 60; Morison, *Three Centuries,* pp. 56–57.

4   The history of the New Haven Colony is given in full in Isabel Calder, *The New Haven Colony* (New Haven, 1934); though it concentrates on what became the city of New Haven, Osterweis, *New Haven,* is also useful; Davenport's bitter disappointment is revealed in Franklin B. Dexter, "Sketch of the Life and Writings of John Davenport," *A Selection from the Miscellaneous Historical Papers of Fifty Years,* pp. 31–58.

5   Almost all that remains in the way of primary source material on the founding of Yale is published in Franklin B. Dexter, ed., *Documentary History of Yale University under the Original Charter of the Collegiate School of Connecticut* (New Haven, 1916). Since there is very little, historians have had to depend, to a great extent, on carefully weighing the importance of every existing word.

6   Morison, *Three Centuries,* pp. 49–50; Dexter, "Founding," pp.

60–61; Roland H. Bainton, *Yale and the Ministry, A History of Education for the Christian Ministry at Yale from the Founding in 1701* (New York, 1957), p. 1.

7 On charters and incorporation in general and the Yale charter in particular, see Richard Hofstadter, *Academic Freedom in the Age of the College* (New York, 1955), pp. 134–44; Simeon Eben Baldwin, "The Ecclesiastical Constitution of Yale College," *Three Historical Papers Read before the New Haven Colony Historical Society* (from the Advance Sheets of vol. 3 of the Transactions of the Society, New Haven, 1882), pp. 405–42; the most astute comments are in Daniel J. Boorstin, *The Americans: The Colonial Experience* (New York, 1958), pp. 172–76; for Harvard's charter problems, see Morison, *Founding of Harvard,* and *Harvard in the Seventeenth Century.*

8 No copy of the letter of the ministers has been discovered. Its date and contents must be deduced from the replies received, which are published in Dexter, *Documentary History,* pp. 6–15.

9 Ibid.; Thomas Clap, *The Annals or History of Yale College . . .* (New Haven, 1766), p. 3.

10 The whole "story of the books" is thoroughly destroyed by Dexter in "Founding," pp. 67–68, 74–76. But that the tale will not down can be seen in Reuben A. Holden, *Profiles and Portraits of Yale University Presidents* (Freeport, Maine, 1968), p. 9, and his *Yale, A Pictorial History* (New Haven, 1967), opposite picture 1. It is constantly reiterated in university publications. The only evidence that there even was a Branford meeting is the fact that John Eliot addressed his reply to the ministers to Abraham Pierson "at Bramford." The possibility that a pledge of books was made or discussed in Branford is revealed by James Noyes's letter, 28 October 1701, to James Pierpont (published in Dexter, *Documentary History,* pp. 24–25), informing Pierpont that he cannot attend the trustees meeting in Saybrook and continuing, "Probably my brother will be with you. I doe hereby desire and impower him to give out of my books at his house my full proportion." Noyes adds in a postscript, "I intend at night to write more fully to my deare brother at Lime with order about books that I will send as soone as I can." Since it is doubtful that Noyes was present at the meeting at Branford (if he could not ride from Stonington to Saybrook a month after going to New Haven, it seems even more improbable that he would have gone all the way to the New Haven area twice in early October), it appears most likely that the question of books for the new college was discussed by the trustees in New Haven at the time of the chartering.

11 The Sewall and Addington draft charter, with Pierpont's corrections,

is in the Beinecke Library at Yale. It is published, with Pierpont's changes as footnotes, in Dexter, *Documentary History,* pp. 16–19.

12 Dexter concluded that the institution was chartered 16 October (see Franklin B. Dexter, *Biographical Sketches of the Graduates of Yale College with Annals of the College History* [New York, 1885], 1 : 3, and "Founding," p. 71). The fifteenth seems more likely to me, since Sewall to Pierpont, 29 October 1701 (in Dexter, *Documentary History,* p. 26), refers to Pierpont's letters of 15 and 16 October bearing the good news of the founding. (All dates before 1752 are Old Style.) Sewall's and Addington's remarks are in their letter of 6 October 1701 to Thomas Buckingham, ibid., pp. 15–16. The charter as passed is in ibid., pp. 20–23.

13 Frederick Rudolph, *The American College and University: A History* (New York, 1965), p. 167; Richard Hofstadter and C. DeWitt Hardy, *The Development and Scope of Higher Education in the United States* (New York, 1952), p. 129.

14 Dexter's explanation for the change in the title of the act is in "Founding," p. 70. Oviatt says, incorrectly, that Pierpont made the change *(Beginnings of Yale,* p. 180).

15 The usual form of title for undertakings of various sorts may be seen in *The Public Records of the Colony of Connecticut* (Hartford, 1850–89), vol. 4. When a ferry, for example, was to be established at a point on the Connecticut River, the undertaker was given "liberty to erect" a ferry (ibid., January 1697/8, p. 241). In another case, the court granted "liberty to erect a troup" to a New Haven group (October 1702, p. 401).

16 Dexter, *Documentary History,* p. 27; the description of Mather is in Oviatt, *Beginnings of Yale,* p. 149, and Dexter, *Documentary History,* p. 23; Sewall's report to Pierpont on Woodbridge's health, 29 October 1701, and Noyes's letter are published in ibid., pp. 26, 24–25.

17 My appraisal of the relative importance of the trustees is based on the frequency with which their names appear in, or on, the remaining manuscripts. From this evidence it seems clear that Pierpont was the leader of the venture.

18 For information on the founders, see John L. Sibley, *Biographical Sketches of Graduates of Harvard University in Cambridge, Massachusetts* (Cambridge, Mass., 1873–85), vols. 2 and 3 (hereafter cited as *Harvard Graduates*); William L. Kingsley, ed., *Yale College, A Sketch of Its History* (New York, 1879); Oviatt, *Beginnings of Yale;* and Dexter, "Founding." For Pierpont, Pierson, Saltonstall, and Andrew, see also the *Dictionary of American Biography* (New York,

1935), hereafter cited as *DAB*. The complex relationship of the trustees to each other is detailed in Charles F. Thwing, *History of Higher Education in America* (New York, 1906), p. 72; and in Dexter's "Founding." The story about Noyes is in Sibley, *Harvard Graduates*, 2 : 45–50.

19 The most active promoters of the college plan lived along the seacoast, as Oviatt has observed. The addition of trustees from the Hartford area, he believed, was due to the long-time jealousy between Connecticut and the former New Haven Colony (*Beginnings of Yale*, pp. 181, 182). This is possible, as is Dexter's statement that the trustees were "in general, the ten oldest settled clergymen in the colony," and represented, on the whole, the most important towns ("Founding," p. 69). My conjecture as to the inclusion of up-river trustees is based on the further fact that a clear concern for the entire colony was revealed by the selection of Saybrook for the site of the college. The term *Up-river Trustees* is used in "Remarks on the Remonstrance Against Settling the Collegiate School in New Haven," in Dexter, *Documentary History*, p. 85.

20 Dexter, *Documentary History*, pp. 27–34.

21 When William and Mary really became a college is unknown. A commencement of some sort was held in 1700, but Hofstadter (*Academic Freedom*, p. 132) states that "Yale was graduating students long before William and Mary" and believes that no real college curriculum was offered there until 1729. Herbert B. Adams, *The College of William and Mary* (Washington, D.C., 1887) briefly records that college's history but does not say when degrees were first granted.

22 For the use of the title "rector," see Thwing, *Higher Education*, p. 15, and Morison, *Founding of Harvard*, p. 13. After Massachusetts lost its charter in 1686, Increase Mather was asked to continue as "rector" of Harvard (Morison, *Harvard in the Seventeenth Century*, 2 : 477; Dexter, *Documentary History*, p. 14.

CHAPTER 2

1 The estimate of population is from Virginia D. Harrington and Evarts B. Greene, *American Population before the Federal Census of 1790* (New York, 1932), p. 4. Dexter says there were only 15,000 in the thirty-four incorporated towns ("Founding," p. 65). For the activities of the early settlers, see Osterweis, *New Haven*, p. 33, and Dexter, "The New Haven of Two Hundred Years Ago," *Selected Papers*, pp. 318–34. On the college corn, see Morison, *Founding of Harvard*, p. 318.

2 The first recorded private gifts to the college were from James Fitch

on 16 October 1701 (Dexter, *Documentary History*, pp. 19–20), Nathaniel Lynde and "three or four others" also in 1701 (ibid., pp. 36–37), and Major John Clark, Jr., early in 1702 (Dexter, *Biographical Sketches*, 1 : 6). In addition, as already noted, the trustees appear to have pledged books at an early date. President Clap in *Annals*, pp. 94–103, gives a list of benefactions from the founding to 1766 of a value of above £40 sterling. In that time span the colony's gifts were more than twice those of private individuals. In *A Statement of Facts Pertaining to the Case of Yale College* ([New Haven], 1831) the college reported that between 1701 and 1831 it had received about $75,000 from the colony and state and "not far from $70,000" from individuals. According to the *Report of the Treasurer for the Fiscal Year 1966–1967* (New Haven, 1968), p. 18, "as much as about 30% of the Operating Budget came . . . from the Federal Government."

3   Dexter, *Documentary History*, p. 31.

4   There are biographical sketches of Pierson in Sibley, *Harvard Graduates*, 2 : 253–58; Kingsley, *Yale College*, 1 : 17–18; Oviatt, *Beginnings of Yale*, pp. 205 ff.; Dexter, "Founding," pp. 80–81; *DAB;* and Dexter, *Biographical Sketches*, 1 : 59–64. The quotations from Stiles and Clap are in ibid., p. 62.

5   The pulling and hauling among the town, Pierson, and the trustees may be followed in Dexter, *Documentary History*, pp. 36 ff. That Pierson did consider moving, however, is revealed by the fact that in November 1703 he purchased land in Saybrook, and when he died his "house and barn, lands and meadow at Saybrook" were valued at £200. His property in Killingworth was worth £358.10.0 (Dexter, *Biographical Sketches*, 1 : 18, 63).

6   On Heminway and Chauncy, see Dexter, *Biographical Sketches*, 1 : 9–11, 22–26.

7   Most of the little that is known about the first school year is in ibid., pp. 1–8. There is some uncertainty about the date of the first commencement. Dexter wavered between 13 September and 16 September (ibid., pp. 8, 9) and once even said 16 October ("Founding," p. 71). Clap says the first commencement was on 13 September, but that seems doubtful since it was a Sunday—a difficult day for ministers to be away from home. The rules for commencements were passed at the first meeting of the trustees. For Harvard commencements, see Morison, *Three Centuries*, pp. 33–34, 119–32.

8   The graduates of 1701 are listed in Dexter, *Biographical Sketches*, 1 : 8. But only Chauncy, as the presumed sole recipient of the B.A. degree, has a biographical sketch.

9   There is some question whether there were vacations at this time or

not. Dexter implies (ibid., p. 13) that there were not, saying that the school year began in September. The same conclusion can be drawn from the minutes of the trustees meeting of 30 September 1702 (Dexter, *Documentary History,* p. 41), where it was ordered that all students should be at the school and remain there unless given liberty to leave. Also, at the meeting of 15 September 1703 (ibid., p. 44) the number of students at the school was said to be so large that a tutor must "be speedily supply'd." The lack of a vacation would have been similar to the procedure at Harvard early in the seventeenth century and in the English colleges (Morison, *Three Centuries,* p. 27), but by 1685 Harvard did have a vacation after commencement (idem, *Harvard in the Seventeenth Century,* 2 : 454–55), so if Yale was following the existing Harvard College rules, it would have had a vacation after commencement. Abraham Pierson may have been following the rules of Harvard in his day, 1664–68, and at that time there do not seem to have been vacations (ibid., 1 : 110). There was a month's vacation after commencement at Yale at least by 1718 (Samuel Johnson, "Some Historical Remarks Concerning the Collegiate School of Connecticut in New Haven," in Dexter, *Documentary History,* p. 158), and perhaps even earlier. The rules for the Collegiate School signed by Jonathan Ashley in 1726 (Dexter, *Biographical Sketches,* 1 : 349) refer to a one-month vacation after commencement. Since the school is referred to in these rules as the Collegiate School, it is assumed they much predate 1726. On 8 June 1720 the trustees specifically ruled: "For Explanation of the Law referring to Schollars Absence from College we agree that at the Commencement there be a Months Vacation allowed and as to any other Time of particular Schollars Absence there is no claim of Liberty by the Law but as the Rector or Tutor shall see Reason to give them Leave notwithstanding any Custom to the contrary" (Dexter, *Documentary History,* p. 203).

10 There is no firm evidence on how many students were in residence the second year. The appointment of a tutor is recorded in the trustees' minutes for 30 September 1702 (Dexter, *Documentary History,* p. 41).

11 The three-year rule for getting the B.A. was, like the lack of vacations, a return to early Harvard practice (see Morison, *Harvard in the Seventeenth Century,* 1 : 301; and idem, *Three Centuries,* p. 11). The saving of expense is referred to in the minutes of the first trustees' meeting (Dexter, *Documentary History,* p. 33).

12 Dexter, *Documentary History,* p. 44.

13 Ibid., p. 45; Morison, *Harvard in the Seventeenth Century,* 1 : 23–25.

14 There is little information on the college's existence in Killingworth. That life was generally quiet, I gather from the minutes of the trustees' meetings; that it was not perfect is clear from the minutes of 22 February 1703/4, when the trustees voted their thanks and support to Tutor Hart and ordered a system of fines "for the preventing of irreligion idleness and other immoralities In the Students," and a statement of the trustees to the students, 23 February 1703/4, concerning "some discontents" of the undergraduates (Dexter, *Documentary History,* pp. 46–48). The requirement of morning and evening prayers was established in the first trustees' meeting. That the students attended meeting twice on Sunday may be assumed, since that was the regular practice for everyone for many years.

15 President Clap's description of Pierson is in *Annals,* p. 14. The tombstone inscription is printed in Oviatt, *Beginnings of Yale,* p. 245, but I recorded it from the tombstone.

16 Clap, *Annals,* p. 14; Morison, *Harvard in the Seventeenth Century,* 2 : 439–40. We have little knowledge of this move. Clap is not entirely trustworthy, but his account is confirmed by Samuel Johnson in "Some Historical Remarks," p. 150, although Clap says the seniors went to Milford, while Johnson says "part" of the students went there.

17 The trustees' minutes for the years 1704 through 1715 are missing and the *Documentary History* contains nothing at all for the period 8 October 1707 to 22 May 1711. Samuel Johnson, who was a student from 1710–1714, says little in "Some Historical Remarks" beyond listing the tutors chosen. His "Autobiography" in Herbert and Carol Schneider, eds., *Samuel Johnson, President of King's College: His Career and Writings* (New York, 1929), 1 : 1–50 contains some information on the curriculum and the library, as does the letter of his classmate, Benjamin Lord, to Ezra Stiles (in Dexter, *Biographical Sketches,* 1 : 115–16).

18 Clap says, "The Tutors and Students being now about twenty in Number resided and boarded in private Houses" (*Annals,* p. 14). Dexter says the deed of gift for the Lynde house was executed the same day as the Saybrook Synod, 9 September 1708. As he notes, we do not know if the house was ever used by the college (*Biographical Sketches,* 1 : 79).

19 Dexter, *Biographical Sketches,* 1 : 33.

20 Ibid., pp. 19–21, *Catalogue of the Officers and Graduates of Yale University, 1701–1924* (New Haven, 1924), pp. 115–16.

21 On Dummer and the books he collected for the college, see Dexter, *Biographical Sketches,* 1 : 141–43; Clap, *Annals,* p. 15; Johnson, "Some Historical Remarks," p. 151; and, for the most complete ac-

count, Anne Pratt, "The Books Sent by Jeremiah Dummer to Yale
College," *Papers in Honor of Andrew Keogh* (New Haven, 1938),
pp. 7–44. Also see Morison, *Three Centuries,* pp. 56–57; and Louis
Shores, *Origins of the American College Library, 1638–1800* (New
York, 1935), pp. 52, 76–78, 127–33. Samuel Johnson in his "Autobiography" (p. 7) notes how poor the library was before the Dummer
gift. The observation on the Dummer collection in the text is from
Thomas G. Wright, *Literary Culture in New England, 1620–1730*
(New Haven, 1920), pp. 180–87, as quoted in Shores, *American College Library,* p. 76. Morison says Yale was "easily superior" to Harvard in modern literature and belles lettres (*Harvard in the Seventeenth Century,* 1 : 295–96), and Clifford K. Shipton believes Yale's
library was "unequalled in New England" (*Biographical Sketches of
Those Who Attended Harvard College . . .* [Cambridge, Mass.,
1933–   , 5 : 49], hereafter cited as *Harvard Graduates*).

22 For Dexter's appraisal of Pierpont, see *Biographical Sketches,* 1 : 1,
143. Pierpont's continued importance may be followed in the *Documentary History,* pp. 1 ff. Much of Jeremiah Dummer's early correspondence, for example, is directed to Pierpont.

23 The actions of the General Assembly are recorded in Dexter, *Documentary History,* pp. 60–63. The proceeds and appraisal of the sale
are in Dexter, *Biographical Sketches,* 1 : 148.

24 The dissatisfaction and unruliness of the students are mentioned by
Johnson, "Some Historical Remarks," p. 151.

25 Dexter, *Documentary History,* pp. 64–65. Johnson says that "many
of the Scholars" left, but the vote of the trustees only applied to the
"Senior Sophisters" ("Some Historical Remarks," p. 152). Johnson is
supported by a "Memorial to the Connecticut General Assembly" in
Dexter, *Documentary History,* p. 96. Less than a month later the
"Representation from Hartford" referred to "the present declining
and unhappy circumstances" of the school (ibid., p. 65).

26 Dexter, *Documentary History,* pp. 65–67.

27 The right of the General Assembly to decide on a site for the college
is uncertain in this case, but since the charter granted the trustees
the right to erect the school "in such convenient place or Places . . .
as to them shall seem meet" it seems to me that the trustees who opposed the Assembly had a strong case.

28 There is no record of the trustees' meeting in Hartford, but Johnson,
writing soon after the event, says six trustees came to the town
("Some Historical Remarks," p. 152). Dexter (*Biographical Sketches,*
1 : 150) says the three senior members thought the call illegal and
thus did not attend. I cannot find the source for his statement. The

decisions made at the Hartford meeting are given in Johnson, "Some Historical Remarks," p. 152, and "Memorial to the Connecticut General Assembly," May 1717, *Documentary History,* p. 96.

29 *Catalogue of the Officers and Graduates of Yale University, 1701–1924,* p. 116; Dexter, *Documentary History,* p. 72.

30 The complicated and bitter fight over the site is best followed in Dexter, *Documentary History,* pp. 64 ff. Johnson, who was teaching the East Guilford group at this time, describes the division ("Some Historical Remarks," pp. 153–54); Clap gives the numbers (*Annals,* p. 20).

31 My description of New Haven and the Green in 1717 is from Henry T. Blake, *Chronicles of New Haven Green from 1638 to 1862* (New Haven, 1898); Osterweis, *New Haven* (where the Wadsworth 1748 map is reprinted); Oviatt, *Beginnings of Yale;* and Dexter, "New Haven Two Hundred Years Ago," pp. 318–34.

32 Benjamin Lord, B.A. 1714, described many years later commencements as they were in the Saybrook days. Since Samuel Andrew presided in both cases, I believe Lord's description (in Dexter, *Biographical Sketches,* 1 : 115–16) is generally accurate.

33 Ibid., p. 163. The manuscript of Griswold's oration is in the University Archives.

34 *Mundus non est infinitus, sed indefinite extensus.* This was actually one of the theses at the commencement of 1718. No theses for 1717 were printed, as far as we know. The theses for 1718 are listed in ibid., p. 179.

35 On the use of "Sir" for B.A.s see Morison, *The Founding of Harvard,* p. 32; for examples at Yale, see Dexter, *Documentary History,* pp. 44, 46. The requirements for the M.A. are listed in the "Orders and Appointments to be Observed in the Collegiate School in Connecticut." The earliest copy of these is dated 1726, but the reference to the "Collegiate School" implies that they date from an earlier time. The 1726 copy is printed in Dexter, *Biographical Sketches,* 1 : 347–51. By 1766, Clap observed: "The Law obliges all the Candidates for the Degree of Master of Arts to attend before the Commencement, and give some Specimen of their Proficiency in Knowledge: but this has been two [sic] generally dispensed with" (*Annals,* p. 87). This change must have been due to the trustees' ruling of 1740 that with special permission a man could receive the degree without attending commencement (Dexter, *Documentary History,* pp. 344–45).

Not all the Theses or Quaestiones listed were spoken at the commencement. Those commencing B.A. or M.A. usually spoke "set-pieces" that were identified by a symbol in the text. The candidates were, however, supposed to be able to reply on the published subjects if any spectator raised the question. Richard Warch pointed out to me the significance of the symbols in the lists of Theses and Quaestiones. James J. Walsh, *Education of the Founding Fathers of the Republic* (New York, 1935), contains much information on Theses and Quaestiones.

36 Andrew's question to the trustees and their answer is from Lord's description, in Dexter, *Biographical Sketches,* 1 : 115–16. The wording for the presentation and the handing of the book is from Morison, *Three Centuries,* p. 34, but I have omitted the section "according to the custom of the universities in England," since Lord says there was "no *pro modo Anglice* then." Lord also says that no diplomas were given at the commencement. The observation about the presentation of diplomas is quoted in Warch, *School of the Prophets,* p. 249.

37 The description of the valediction is from Clap, *Annals,* p. 87, and refers to examination day. I believe the words apply equally well to commencement. For the parallel between this ceremony and those of the Middle Ages, see Morison, *Founding of Harvard,* p. 12.

38 Dexter, *Biographical Sketches,* 1 : 163–64.

39 George Dudley Seymour, "Henry Caner, 1680–1731, Master Carpenter, Builder of the First Yale College Building, 1718, and of the Rector's House, 1722," *Old Time New England (Bulletin of the Society for the Preservation of New England Antiquities)* 15, no. 3 (January 1925): 100; Dexter, *Biographical Sketches,* 1 : 162. 8 October 1717 is the date usually given for the beginning of the structure and that is confirmed by the trustees' letter to Jeremiah Dummer, 31 October 1717, printed in Dexter, *Documentary History,* p. 146. Samuel Johnson says, however, that the raising was in the first week in October ("Some Historical Remarks," p. 155).

CHAPTER 3

1 Dexter, *Biographical Sketches,* 1 : 173; idem, *Documentary History,* pp. 109 ff.

2 Dexter, *Documentary History,* pp. 146–48.

3 Ibid, p. 164; Dexter, *Biographical Sketches,* 1 : 176.

4 On Elihu Yale, see Hiram Bingham, *Elihu Yale, The American Nabob of Queen Square* (New York, 1939), and the sketch in *DAB;* Dexter, *Biographical Sketches,* 1 : 177, gives the value of what Yale sent.

5 Dexter, *Documentary History,* pp. 192–93.

6   The change of name on the Theses and Catalogue is reported, with photographs of the documents, in the *Yale Alumni Weekly,* 4 December 1931; see also Anne S. Pratt and others, "The Name Yale College," *Yale University Library Gazette* 6 (July 1931): 15–16.

7   Clap, *Annals,* pp. 25–26, gives in Latin and English the formal vote of the trustees on naming the building. The minutes are in Dexter, *Documentary History,* pp. 171–74. The letter to Yale is in ibid., pp. 176–77.

8   Dexter, *Documentary History,* pp. 179, 196, 199, 200; Johnson, "Some Historical Remarks," pp. 157–58.

9   Dexter, *Documentary History,* pp. 176–77; idem, *Biographical Sketches,* 1 : 177–97; Johnson, "Some Historical Remarks," p. 158. I assume two took M.A. degrees at this time, since this class contained thirteen members, five of whom took degrees at Wethersfield. Psalm 65, in the same Sternhold and Hopkins version, is now sung at every commencement.

10 The age at death of the graduates of the class of 1718 may be computed from Dexter's *Biographical Sketches,* 1 : 180–97. Dexter identifies Buck, Buckingham, Lord, and Steel as the Wethersfield graduates (ibid., p. 181). I believe that Newell was the fifth, since he came from Farmington, outside of Hartford. The other Wethersfield graduates all came from Hartford or Wethersfield.

11 Dexter, *Documentary History,* pp. 179–80.

12 Ibid., pp. 182–83; Johnson, "Some Historical Remarks," p. 159.

13 Johnson, "Some Historical Remarks," p. 160; Dexter, *Documentary History,* pp. 183 ff.

14 Johnson, "Some Historical Remarks," pp. 160–61; Dexter, *Documentary History,* pp. 187–92.

15 Johnson, "Some Historical Remarks," p. 162; Dexter, *Biographical Sketches,* 1 : 202; "Saltonstall," *DAB.*

16 Johnson, "Some Historical Remarks," pp. 162–63; Dexter, *Documentary History,* pp. 195–96.

Chapter 4

1   For an excellent biographical sketch of Cutler, see Shipton, *Harvard Graduates,* 5 : 45–66.

2   On vacations, see chap. 2 n. 9; Dexter, *Biographical Sketches,* 1 : 203.

3   Ibid., p. 237.

4   Dexter, *Documentary History,* pp. 199, 214–16, 220–21. Dexter, *Biographical Sketches,* 1 : 237, says the "brief" to the parishes was ordered by the General Assembly "reluctantly." On the rector's new house, see Seymour, "Henry Caner," pp. 115–19.

5   Elihu Yale and his gifts are discussed in Bingham, *Elihu Yale*, pp.
    326–35. Bingham put Yale's total donation at £1,162 or about $28,-
    000 in the currency of the 1930s. Yale's gifts may be followed in Dex-
    ter, *Documentary History*, pp. 192–93, 209, 212. Some of the letters
    dealing with Yale are published more fully in Henry H. Edes, ed.,
    "Early History of Yale University," *Publications of the Colonial So-
    ciety of Massachusetts* 6 (April 1899): 177–210. On 25 February
    1724/5 Dummer wrote Woodbridge concerning the legacy, "We lost
    our Cause in the Commons by the vile decree of the Dean of the
    Arches, who, I verily beleive [*sic*] was corrupted" (Dexter, *Docu-
    mentary History*, p. 257).
6   Perry Miller, *Jonathan Edwards* (Cleveland, 1964), foreword; Dexter,
    Documentary History, pp. 179–80.
7   Dexter, *Documentary History*, p. 225.
8   On Arminianism, see Edmund S. Morgan, *The Gentle Puritan: A
    Life of Ezra Stiles, 1727–1795* (New Haven, 1962), pp. 15–19; Perry
    Miller, *The New England Mind: the Seventeenth Century* (Boston,
    1961), pp. 367–69; and Richard Warch, *School of the Prophets*, pp.
    99–100.
9   Dexter, *Documentary History*, pp. 226–30.
10 Ibid., pp. 226–29.
11 The temporizing of the trustees can be seen in their failure to con-
    duct *any* business at their meeting the day after commencement.
    Their only action was to decide to meet in October at the time of
    the session of the General Assembly. The request for the declaration
    to be put in writing is mentioned in ibid.
12 Francis L. Hawks and Williams S. Perry, eds., *Documentary History
    of the Protestant Episcopal Church* . . . (New York, 1863), 1 : 62–64.
    Webb referred to the scriptural basis for presbyterial ordination but
    said, "I should be glad of the help of some good arguments used by
    those who are skilled in the controversy." There is also in ibid., pp.
    75–78, a manuscript attributed to Cotton Mather on the subject of
    episcopal and presbyterial ordination. Shipton refers to the rustiness
    of their defenses in *Harvard Graduates*, 5 : 52.
13 The important books in the Yale library on the subject are men-
    tioned in Bainton, *Yale and The Ministry*, p. 10. Samuel Johnson
    said he "read several of the earliest and best of the Fathers in their
    originals. The result was, that from the facts in scripture, compared
    with the facts of the primitive church immediately after, and so
    downward it appeared very plain that the episcopal government of
    the church was universally established by the Apostles wherever they
    propagated Christianity" (Johnson, "Autobiography," pp. 13–16).

The meeting itself is also described by Johnson, who said that to the ministers opposed to them "the subject was in great measure new" (ibid.).

14 Dexter, *Documentary History*, pp. 231–34; idem, *Biographical Sketches*, 1 : 271.

15 Dexter, *Biographical Sketches*, 1 : 272.

16 Dexter, *Documentary History*, pp. 233, 235. Timothy Woodbridge was asked to serve as resident rector for the first month.

17 Ibid., pp. 238 ff.; Dexter, *Biographical Sketches*, 1 : 273 ff. The approach to Cotton Mather is recorded in Warch, *School of the Prophets*, pp. 110, 127. There were about sixty students in 1724 according to Dexter (*Biographical Sketches*, 1 : 291). Based on the size of the graduating classes there were an average of about sixty present each year. Twenty-three graduated in 1726 (ibid., p. 323).

18 The death of Willard is mentioned in Dexter, *Biographical Sketches*, p. 139. He was a classmate of Samuel Johnson, Benjamin Lord, Daniel Browne, and James Wetmore.

19 Ibid., p. 284; Dexter, *Documentary History*, pp. 247–250. Boards seem to have been touchy about such matters. Of Dartmouth's rejection of an 1816 act, John Whitehead has commented, "Like the Harvard Corporation in 1812, they were distressed that their assent to the act had not been necessary to implement the bill" (John S. Whitehead, *The Separation of College and State: The Transformation of Columbia, Dartmouth, Harvard, and Yale, 1776–1876* [New Haven, 1973], p. 64). Mr. Whitehead kindly allowed me to see his book in manuscript.

20 A trustee, Rev. Eliphalet Adams, said in the funeral sermon that the college had lost "its best friend under God" (Dexter, *Biographical Sketches*, 1 : 312).

21 Dexter, *Documentary History*, pp. 238 ff., 261–64; idem, *Biographical Sketches*, 1 : 321–22.

22 On Elisha Williams, see the sketch in Shipton, *Harvard Graduates*, 5 : 588–98; Holden, *Profiles and Portraits of Yale University Presidents*, pp. 25–29; and "Williams," *DAB*.

CHAPTER 5

1 Dexter says there was an influx of students from western Massachusetts as soon as Williams took office, with at least ten of the eighteen graduates of the class that entered in 1726 coming from that area (*Biographical Sketches*, 1 : 322).

2 Dexter, *Documentary History*, pp. 335–36; idem, *Biographical*

Sketches, 1 : 421; *Catalogue of the Officers and Graduates of Yale University, 1701–1924,* pp. 118–20.

3 Warch, *School of the Prophets,* pp. 134–35.

4 Dexter, *Documentary History,* pp. 268, 304; idem, *Biographical Sketches,* 2 : 13. I can find no evidence of afternoon sizings at Yale, although they had them at Harvard, as Morison notes (*Harvard in the Seventeenth Century,* p. 90). Even supper may not always have been served in commons at Yale, since the 1745 rules concerning "Order" in the hall only applied when "hot Victuals" were served. At Harvard breakfast was not served in the hall until 1764 according to Morison (*Three Centuries,* p. 117).

5 Dexter, *Documentary History,* p. 265. Later the Berkeley scholars were also called scholars of the house (ibid., p. 309). Prior to the appointment of the scholar of the house to note damages, the butler did that job, too (ibid., p. 246). The first mention of the monitor is in 1727 (ibid., p. 273), and though the first reference to his duties is in the college laws of 1745, there is no reason to believe that this represented a change, since the monitor had the same duties at Harvard (Dexter, *Biographical Sketches,* 2 : 13; Morison, *Harvard in the Seventeenth Century,* 1 : 108).

6 Warch, *School of the Prophets,* p. 135.

7 Dexter, *Biographical Sketches,* 1 : 570.

8 The Berkeley gifts have been much written about: see Daniel Coit Gilman, "Bishop Berkeley's Gifts to Yale College," *Papers of the New Haven Colony Historical Society* (1865), 1 : 147–70; Andrew Keogh, "Bishop Berkeley's Gift of Books in 1732," *Yale University Library Gazette* 8 (July 1933): 1–26; Louis Shores, *Origins of the American College Library,* pp. 79–82, 136–38, 244–62, which contains a complete list of the books; Samuel Johnson, "Autobiography," pp. 26–27.

9 Schneider, *Johnson,* 1 : 81–82.

10 Ibid.; the deed is published in Gilman, "Berkeley's Gifts," pp. 154–56; Yale University still owns the Whitehall farm. President Clap began to lease properties that were difficult to reach and control for terms of 999 years, and Whitehall was let for this period in 1762. The Colonial Dames have acquired title to the house and a half acre of land and preserve the building as a historical landmark. The university now receives $140 a year as rent on the remaining land in place of £18 sterling and 40 rods of stone wall that the Clap lease called for. In another such long-term lease, the college was to receive cash and a single peppercorn. Unfortunately, the college no longer receives the peppercorn. The information on the current state of these lease payments was given me by Spencer Miller, asso-

ciate treasurer of the university. See *Yale Alumni Weekly* (hereafter cited as *YAW*), 20 October 1907, for the rents on Whitehall.

11   The fellowship has been held by some of Yale's most famous graduates, including the first award—to the first president of Dartmouth —and later to Eugene Schuyler, the first Ph.D., and, greatest of all, Josiah Willard Gibbs. Unfortunately, the fund is now valued at only $28,751.22, so the award has declined in prestige (*Historical Register of Yale University, 1701–1937* [New Haven, 1939], pp. 118–24). The Mowlson scholarships at Harvard were intended to carry a student through his undergraduate career and on to his M.A., according to Merle Curti and Roderick Nash, *Philanthropy in the Shaping of American Higher Education* (New Brunswick, N.J., 1965), p. 7.

12   Warch, *School of the Prophets,* p. 174.

13   Dexter, *Documentary History,* p. 298.

14   Dexter, *Biographical Sketches,* 1 : 470–71.

15   Johnson, "Autobiography," pp. 26–27; Shores, *Origins of American College Libraries,* pp. 79–82, 136; Kingsley, *Yale College,* 1 : 185.

16   For the Yale College building, see Seymour, "Henry Caner," pp. 99–124. *YAW*, 20 October 1916, has drawings and a floor plan; the dimensions are mentioned in Dexter, *Documentary History,* p. 146. A kitchen and dining room were added to the building in 1761 idem, *Biographical Sketches,* 2 : 683). On a visit to New Haven in 1787, Mannaseh Cutler (B.A. 1765) wrote of the absence of the building, "But the most affecting change to me is the loss of Mother Yale. Yale College was by far the most sightly building of any one that belonged to the University and most advantageously situated. It gave an air of grandeur to the others" (Seymour, "Henry Caner," p. 106).

There is some conflict over how many lived in Yale College. Dexter (*Biographical Sketches,* I : 198) says sixty-five in all could live there, but Philip George Van Reck, who visited Yale on 20 June 1734, said it contained eighty-three people including the teachers. The classes of 1734–37 did, in fact, graduate eighty-one students. Reck's observations are in Dorothy Bridgewater, "An Early Description of Yale College," *Yale University Library Gazette* 9 (January 1935): 62. In 1740 the Reverend Mr. Noyes and Rector Clap informed a committee of the General Assembly that in the previous year there had been eighty-five students at Yale but room for only forty-five in the building. They hoped, however, to persuade the Assembly to provide money for a new building (Dexter, *Documentary History,* p. 347). The arrangement of the rooms was similar to that of university dwellings in medieval England (see Morison, *Founding of Harvard,* pp. 280–81).

17   Dexter, *Biographical Sketches,* 1 : 521; Clap, *Annals,* p. 97. For an

account of the microscope, see Lorande Woodruff, "The Advent of the Microscope at Yale College," *American Scientist* 31 (1943): 241–45. Woodruff says that this was the first compound microscope to have been acquired by an American college.

18   On preparation for college, see Morison, *Three Centuries,* p. 26; and Robert Middlekauf, *Ancients and Axioms: Secondary Education in Eighteenth-Century New England* (New Haven, 1963). The description of life in the college is based on the "Orders and Appointments to be Observed in the Collegiate School in Connecticut," printed in Dexter, *Biographical Sketches,* 1 : 347–51. Warch offers detailed information on the curriculum and points out that only those authors who agreed best with the Scriptures were to be studied, though, as he notes, the version of the laws printed by Dexter happens to lack that proviso (*School of the Prophets,* p. 192). On Ames and Wollebius, see Bainton, *Yale and the Ministry,* pp. 9, 39. Bainton calls Ames the "Puritan most influential in New England." The best way to discover the students' recreations is to read Anson Phelps Stokes, *Memorials of Eminent Yale Men: A Biographical Study of Student Life and University Influences during the Eighteenth and Nineteenth Centuries,* 2 vols. (New Haven, 1914), and the student diaries in the Yale University Archives. The account of the "Rought" is in Dexter, *Biographical Sketches,* 1 : 598. Benjamin Lord said there was little interest in composition in his day, and this seems to have remained the case (see ibid., p. 116).

19   Schneider, *Johnson,* 1 : 101; see also Grace Pierpont Fuller, "Papers of Rector Williams," *Yale University Library Gazette* 1 (October 1926): 44; Dexter says Williams had headaches from the sedentary life (*Biographical Sketches,* 1 : 620).

20   The appointment of Williams's son as a Berkeley scholar was in this case, and perhaps in all, perfectly justified. Samuel Johnson informed Berkeley that the boy "had manifestly the advantage of the rest" (Dexter, *Documentary History,* p. 332).

21   Schneider, *Johnson,* 1 : 101; Dexter, *Biographical Sketches,* 1 : 632.

22   For the remainder of Williams' life, see the biographical sketches mentioned in chap. 4, n. 22. The pamphlet is only attributed to Williams, but his authorship is generally accepted (though Dexter questions it, *Biographical Sketches,* 1 : 634). The comparison with Wise and Otis is made by Shipton, *Harvard Graduates,* 5 : 593. Stiles is quoted by Morgan, *Stiles,* p. 18.

CHAPTER 6

1 Louis Leonard Tucker, *Puritan Protagonist: President Thomas Clap of Yale College* (Chapel Hill, N.C., 1962), pp. 47–59. Tucker's is a good biography of Clap, containing much useful information on Yale during his presidency. Though it does not quite penetrate the complexity of the man, it is probably the best we can expect in the face of the loss of Clap's personal papers. The best biographical sketch is in Shipton, *Harvard Graduates*, 7 : 27–49. Since Ezra Stiles attended Yale and served as a tutor there during Clap's presidency, Morgan, *Stiles*, also contains much that is interesting on Clap.

2 Tucker, *Clap*, p. 61. Shipton believes that most of the trustees who selected Clap were "Arminian or liberal" in their theological inclinations (*Harvard Graduates*, 7 : 31). But the constant rumors must still have been a problem.

3 For the Great Awakening, see Edwin Gaustad, *The Great Awakening in New England* (New York, 1957); Morgan, *Stiles*, and Miller, *Jonathan Edwards*. On Puritanism and the conversion experience, Alan Simpson, *Puritanism in Old and New England* (Chicago, 1955) is particularly good.

4 Stokes, *Memorials*, 1 : 31.

5 Tucker, *Clap*, pp. 124–25.

6 Dexter, *Biographical Sketches*, 1 : 662.

7 Osterweis, *New Haven*, p. 88.

8 Dexter, *Biographical Sketches*, 1 : 663; Schneider, *Johnson*, 1 : 663. There is no evidence that any undergraduates were refused degrees this year, so it appears this must refer to M.A.s. One of them seems to have been Amos Munson of the class of 1738 (see Dexter, *Biographical Sketches*, 1 : 608–09).

9 Thomas Jefferson Wertenbaker, *Princeton, 1746–1896* (Princeton, N.J., 1946), p. 18; Stokes, *Memorials*, 1 : 36–43. Brainerd confessed to making the remark about Whittelsey but did not recall having said anything about Clap—though he admitted he might have (Dexter, *Biographical Sketches*, 1 : 698).

10 Dexter, *Biographical Sketches*, 1 : 698; Tucker, *Clap*, pp. 129–30; see also Hofstadter, *Academic Freedom*, p. 167.

11 Dexter, *Biographical Sketches*, 1 : 86, 531; Tucker, *Clap*, p. 35. That Burr did preach in New Haven is clear from the diary of John Cleaveland for March 1742. A photostat of the diary is in the Yale University Library.

12 Dexter, *Documentary History*, pp. 355–56; Morgan, *Stiles*, p. 39.

13 Dexter, *Documentary History*, pp. 356–58; idem, *Biographical*

Sketches, 1 : 698. On the Shepherd's Tent, see Morgan, *Stiles,* p. 42; and Bainton, *Yale and the Ministry,* p. 34. (Bainton is also good on the general subject of the Great Awakening and Yale's part in it.)

14   Morgan, *Stiles,* pp. 41, 42.

15   Dexter, *Biographical Sketches,* 1 : 771; Tucker, *Clap,* pp. 139–41; *The Judgement of the Rector and Tutors of Yale College, Concerning Two of the Students Who were Expelled; Together with the Reasons of It* (New London, 1745) is printed in Richard Hofstadter and Wilson Smith, *American Higher Education, A Documentary History,* 2 vols. (Chicago, 1961), 1 : 75–82.

16   Morison, *Three Centuries,* p. 87; Tucker, *Clap,* p. 141; Dexter, *Biographical Sketches,* 1 : 30, 772.

17   Hofstadter and Smith, *American Higher Education,* p. 81.

18   Tucker, *Clap,* p. 71; Anna Monrad, "Historical Notes on the Catalogues and Classifications of the Yale University Library," *Papers in Honor of Andrew Keogh,* pp. 251–56.

19   Clap, *Annals,* p. 44; Dexter, *Biographical Sketches,* 1 : 772, 2 : 1. For the opinion that the new charter converted a "powerless rector" into a powerful president, see Tucker, *Clap,* p. 74. The rector as moderator can be seen in the minutes of the trustees meetings, printed in Dexter, *Documentary History.*

20   Clap, *Annals,* p. 42; Dexter, *Biographical Sketches,* 2 : 2–18; Tucker says the volume on customs was either lost or destroyed when the British attacked New Haven (*Clap,* p. 59). For Clap's legalistic mind, see his *Religious Constitution of Colleges* (New London, 1754) and his argument before the General Assembly, which is printed in his *Annals,* pp. 70–76. Clap said he got his new laws partly from the old college statutes and customs, partly from Harvard, and partly from Oxford. His reference to Woods Institutes is in "Judgements of the President and Tutors of Yale College" (hereafter cited as Faculty Judgements), vol. 1, 8 March 1754 (MS, Yale University Library).

21   Tucker, *Clap,* p. 68.

22   Faculty Judgements, vol. 1, 21 January 1752, 7 February 1752; Clap, *Annals,* p. 86; Dexter, *Biographical Sketches,* 2 : 296–97.

23   Shipton, *Harvard Graduates,* 7 : 48; Rudolph, *American College and University,* p. 105.

24   Clap, *Annals,* p. 54; Dexter, *Biographical Sketches,* 2 : 140; Philip Gardiner Nordell, "The Yale Lottery," *Yale Alumni Magazine* (hereafter cited as *YAM*), May 1965. The first colonial legislative act authorizing a lottery was passed by Rhode Island in 1744 (ibid.). George P. Schmidt, *The Old Time College President* (New York, 1930), p. 66; Dexter, *Biographical Sketches,* 2 : 227, 275.

25 Clap, *Annals*, pp. 55–57; *Report of the President of Yale University and of the Deans and Directors . . . 1904–1905* (New Haven, 1905), p. 79; Tucker, *Clap*, p. 75; Shipton, *Harvard Graduates*, 7 : 37; Morison, *Founding of Harvard*, pp. 280–81; "Room and Board," *YAM*, December 1951; the sketch of the room layout is based on the Trumbull drawing printed in the *Yale University Library Gazette* 9 (1935) : 16.

26 Benjamin Trumbull, *A Complete History of Connecticut*, 2 vols. (New Haven, 1818), 2 : 261.

27 Nearly every commentator refers to Noyes's dullness. Henry Bamford Parkes called him "the dullest preacher of the generation" (quoted in Tucker, *Clap*, p. 184). See also Dexter, *Biographical Sketches*, 1 : 87.

28 Tucker, *Clap*, pp. 171–75; Clap, *Annals*, pp. 60–65. We do not know what Clap said at the special meeting in November 1753, but his concerns are made clear in ibid.; Morgan, *Stiles*, p. 104; and Tucker, *Clap*, p. 173. Dexter, *Biographical Sketches*, 2 : 442, says these reasons were used later to persuade Woodbridge and Whitman of the·need to set up a separate church.

29 Dexter, *Documentary History*, p. 233; Clap, *Annals*, pp. 65–66.

30 Dexter, *Biographical Sketches*, 2 : 322.

31 Morgan, *Stiles*, pp. 107–09; Ralph Henry Gabriel, *Religion and Learning at Yale: The Church of Christ in the College and University, 1757–1957* (New Haven, 1958), p. 27. On Clap's *Religious Constitution of Colleges*, see Tucker, *Clap*, p. 195; and Hofstadter, *Academic Freedom*, pp. 171–72. For the hesitation of the Assembly, see Dexter, *Biographical Sketches*, 2 : 322.

32 Tucker, *Clap*, pp. 175–82; Schneider, *Johnson*, 1 : 174–82.

33 Dexter, Biographical Sketches, 2 : 354, 355; "Records of the Yale Corporation," 26 November 1754 (MSS, Yale University Library) (hereafter cited as Corporation Records); Morgan, *Stiles*, pp. 103–08. Morgan believes Clap's attack on Noyes actually allowed the Old Lights to regain strength.

34 Dexter, *Biographical Sketches*, 2 : 442.

35 Tucker, *Clap*, pp. 201 ff.; Dexter, *Biographical Sketches*, 2 : 357.

36 Dexter, *Biographical Sketches*, 2 : 358, 71–72.

37 Morison, *Three Centuries*, pp. 66–67, 201–02.

38 At graduation in 1759, the freshman class numbered 49, the largest class until 1777. In the fall of 1760, 165 students were enrolled. Between 1753 and 1760 Yale awarded 254 B.A.s to Harvard's 205. Dexter, *Biographical Sketches*, 2 : 401; Tucker, *Clap*, p. 77.

39 Gabriel, *Religion and Learning at Yale*, pp. 26–27; Dexter, *Biographical Sketches*, 2 : 400.

40 Dexter, *Biographical Sketches,* 2 : 400, 441, 442; Gabriel, *Religion and Learning at Yale,* pp. 3–6.

41 Dexter, *Biographical Sketches,* 2 : 442–43.

42 Ibid., pp. 443, 507. The lack of sufficient votes is my assumption. The continuation of the pamphlet war may be followed in Tucker, *Clap,* pp. 211–22. The difficulties of raising money for the new chapel are revealed by the fact that as late as June 1763, of the £800 already spent, £300 had come from the college treasury (Dexter, *Biographical Sketches,* 3 : 1). Though not completely finished, the chapel began to be used in June 1763 (ibid.).

43 Faculty Judgements, vol. 1, 11 April 1758.

44 The collapse of discipline and its complex causes can be followed in Dexter, *Biographical Sketches,* vol. 2 for the years 1759–63 and vol. 3 for the last years of Clap's presidency. See also Tucker (*Clap,* pp. 236–57), who feels that the change from pranks to rebellion occurred about 1756. For the monitor's bills and Nichols's behavior, see Faculty Judgements, vol. 2, 18 March and 26 August 1761.

45 Faculty Judgements, vol. 2, 9 November 1761; Dexter, *Biographical Sketches,* 2 : 723, 777–81.

46 Clap, *Annals,* pp. 70–77. Clap was so persuasive that Yale's 150th anniversary was celebrated in 1850.

47 Dexter, *Documentary History,* pp. 261, 271, 279, 280, 293, 303, 363.

48 Dexter, *Biographical Sketches,* 2 : 781; Morgan, *Stiles,* p. 317.

49 Dexter, *Biographical Sketches,* 3 : 94, 170. The stamp distributor for Connecticut was Jared Ingersoll (B.A. 1742). His treatment is mentioned in ibid., 1 : 713; and in more detail in Lawrence H. Gipson, *Jared Ingersoll: A Story of American Loyalism in Relation to British Colonial Government* (New Haven, 1920), pp. 158–228.

50 Faculty Judgements, vol. 3, August [?] 1765; Kenneth Scott, "A 'Dust' at Yale and a 'Blessing' for President Clap," *Bulletin of the Connecticut Historical Society* 23, no. 2 (January 1958): 46–49; Corporation Records, 31 July 1765.

51 Dexter, *Biographical Sketches,* 3 : 167–70, 209.

52 Shores, *Origins of the American College Library,* p. 176 (italics omitted).

53 Tucker, *Clap,* pp. 83 ff.; Florian J. Cajori, *The Teaching and History of Mathematics in the United States* (Washington, D.C., 1890), pp. 31–32. According to Cajori, Clap was the first to mention the study of conic sections and fluxions in an American college (p. 32). Arithmetic was first required for admission in 1745 (see Edwin C. Broome, *A Historical and Critical Discussion of College Admission Requirements* [New York, 1903], p. 30). Algebra appeared at Yale

as early as 1718 under Samuel Johnson and Daniel Browne: "The first evidence of this subject being taught in the colonies," according to Warch, *School of the Prophets,* p. 220. It may have lapsed under Williams, only to return under Clap, where it is mentioned in the 1742 curriculum (see Tucker, *Clap,* p. 83). For the scientific instruments, see ibid., pp. 89–91. Johnson's comment is in Schneider, *Johnson,* 1 : 102–03.

54 Corporation Records, 30 November 1762; *Historical Register of Yale University, 1701–1937,* p. 54. A fourth tutor was added in 1759 (Dexter, *Biographical Sketches,* 2 : 635). Clap speaks of "a publick Examination of each Class, about once a Quarter" (*Annals,* p. 87).

55 Shipton, *Harvard Graduates,* 7 : 34–35.

56 Clap, *Annals,* pp. 84–85.

57 Ibid., pp. 97–103. The only person to give more money was Richard Jackson, who donated £100 in 1765 for "finishing the Chapel." This was the largest single gift in Clap's entire term in office.

58 Franklin B. Dexter, *Extracts from the Itineraries and other Miscellanies of Ezra Stiles . . . with a Selection from His Correspondence* (New Haven, 1916), p. 461. Tucker, *Clap,* p. 270, gives the student's epitaph, which was written in a library book. For other examples this sort of marginalia, see Richard Warch's delightful "Graffiti Olde and Bolde," *YAM,* November 1969.

59 Shipton, *Harvard Graduates,* 7 : 49.

CHAPTER 7

1 Dexter, *Biographical Sketches,* 3 : 210. Dexter says only about 100 students were in attendance, and even this number was "materially reduced" by the end of the year 1766–67. Clap says the average for 1753–63 was about 170 (*Annals,* p. 77). By spring 1767, according to Edmund Morgan, there were only 50 students at Yale (*Stiles,* p. 318).

2 Dexter, *Biographical Sketches,* 3 : 169, 207. Dexter says that he died at the age of fifty-seven and a half "after a long and painful decline" (ibid., 1 : 539).

3 Ibid., 3 : 207.

4 A biographical sketch of Daggett is in ibid., 2 : 153–57; William B. Sprague, *Annals of the American Pulpit,* 1 : 480, quoted in "Daggett," *DAB,* gives the description of Daggett's person; Gipson, *Jared Ingersoll,* pp. 158–59, describes Daggett's attack on Ingersoll; Morgan, *Stiles,* p. 332, has an excellent description of Daggett fighting the British.

5 Dexter, *Biographical Sketches,* 3 : 208.

6   Ibid., pp. 208, 263; Corporation Records, 17 October 1769.

7   Faculty Judgements, vol. 3, 28 January 1767; Morgan, *Stiles,* p. 362, lists the amounts of fines collected from 1756 through June 1766. He notes that "after 1766 scarcely any income from fines was recorded."

8   On placing in general, see Franklin B. Dexter, "On Some Social Distinctions at Harvard and Yale before the Revolution," *Selected Papers,* pp. 203–22; and Clifford K. Shipton, "Ye Mystery of Ye Ages Solved, or, How Placing Worked at Colonial Harvard & Yale," *Harvard Alumni Bulletin* 57 (1954–55) : 258–63. Samuel Eliot Morison commented on Shipton's article in a letter to the editor (ibid., p. 417).

9   Dexter, "Social Distinctions," pp. 210–11; idem, *Biographical Sketches,* 2 : 305, 415.

10 My description of the way the system worked is based on a study of numerous classes. There were differences from the Harvard system described by Shipton. He does not mention sons of college presidents, who were very important at Yale. Sons of justices of the peace were placed in the top group at Harvard; Dexter is not very informative on this matter in *Biographical Sketches,* and though he points to one case where the designation of justice of the peace may have been important ("Social Distinctions," p. 214), it does not generally seem to have been as significant at Yale as at Harvard. The quotation is from ibid., p. 213.

11 The information on this class is all from Dexter, *Biographical Sketches,* 2 : 247–74.

12 For the class position of tutors and Berkeley scholars, see the various classes in Dexter, *Biographical Sketches,* vols. 1–3.

13 Ibid., 3 : 168.

14 *Harvard Alumni Bulletin* 57 (1954–55) : 417.

15 Dexter, "Social Distinctions," p. 218.

16 Shipton, "Ye Mystery," p. 258.

17 Quoted in E. H. Gillette, "Yale College One Hundred Years Ago," *Hours at Home,* February 1870, p. 333. Professor Morison says that since the Yale class of 1768 was placed alphabetically only just before it graduated, while the Harvard class of 1773 was placed alphabetically when it entered in 1769, the "action was practically simultaneous at Yale and Harvard" (Morison to the editor, *Harvard Alumni Bulletin* 57 [1954–55] : 417.) Morison does not indicate where he got this information, but as Avery's letter shows, as far as the students were concerned, the change at Yale had taken place some nine months prior to commencement.

18 Kingsley, *Yale College,* 1 : 315–16.

19 I am so indebted to Richard Warch, *School of the Prophets*, pp. 208–18, for the material in this paragraph that in many places I have merely paraphrased him. Anyone who wishes detailed information on the Yale curriculum between 1701 and 1740 is advised to see the two excellent chapters in his book.

20 For the science curriculum under Clap, see Tucker, *Clap*, pp. 83–93; and Morgan, *Stiles*, pp. 51–86, 386. For the lack of change between Clap and Stiles, see ibid., pp. 385–86.

21 This section on the curriculum, the courses, and the hours is created from numerous sources. The curriculum under Clap is given in Clap, *Annals*, pp. 81–82; and Tucker, *Clap*, pp. 77–92. Also useful is Kingsley, *Yale College*, 2 : 495–502; and Franklin B. Dexter, "Student Life at Yale in the Early Days of Connecticut Hall," *Selected Papers*, p. 266. See also College Laws, 1745, in Dexter, *Biographical Sketches*, 2 : 2–18. For the times of the college bell, see ibid., p. 13; Morgan, *Stiles*, p. 385; and Tucker, *Clap*, p. 266. This schedule lasted well into the nineteenth century; see William Griswold Lane, "Extracts of Letters, 1839–1843" (typed copies, Yale University Library); and Franklin B. Dexter, "Student Life at Yale under the First President Dwight (1795–1817)," *Selected Papers*, pp. 382–94.
    Daggett's introduction of English grammar is described by Morgan (*Stiles*, p. 320), who also states that "the subjects recited when Stiles became President were about the same as when he was a student, and many of the same textbooks were in use" (ibid., p. 385). Daggett's attempt to have the seniors attend afternoon recitations is in Corporation Records, 9 September 1772.
    On courses in metaphysics and ethics, see Rudolph, *American College and University*, p. 140; and Morgan, *Stiles*, pp. 65, 390.

22 Baldwin, "The Ecclesiastical Constitution of Colleges," p. 433; Dexter, *Biographical Sketches*, 1 : 349, 2 : 5, 276; Morgan, *Stiles*, p. 392.

23 Clap, *Annals*, p. 82; Tucker, *Clap*, p. 77, says forensic disputes were introduced in the 1750s. David Potter says, citing Naphtali Daggett's notebook, that disputes in English seem to have appeared as early as 1747 (*Debating in the Colonial Chartered Colleges: An Historical Survey 1642–1900* [New York, 1944], p. 26); Dexter, Biographical Sketches, 2 : 276.

24 Alexander Cowie, *Educational Problems at Yale College in the Eighteenth Century* (New York, 1936), p. 15; this form lasted well into the nineteenth century. By the 1840s the answer had become "Not Prepared," see [Journal of Caleb Lamson], 17 February 1846 (MS, Yale University Library); and Julian M. Sturtevant, ed., *Julian M. Sturtevant, An Autobiography* (New York, 1896), pp. 84–85, 90–91,

reprinted in Hofstadter and Smith, *American Higher Education,*
1 : 274–75. Clap, *Annals,* pp. 81–82, says, "The Tutor explains it, as
far as there is Occasion."

25   "Daniel N. Brinsmade's Book of Disputes Both Forensic and Syllogistic, May 9th AD 1771" (MS, Yale University Library); Morgan, *Stiles,*
48, 79–80; Clap, *Annals,* p. 82.

26   Charles E. Cuningham, *Timothy Dwight, 1752–1817: A Biography*
(New York, 1942), pp. 36–41; Leon Howard, *The Connecticut Wits*
(Chicago, 1943), p. 30; Stokes, *Memorials,* 1 : 119–20, 220; Morgan,
Stiles, p. 320; *The Laws of Yale College in New Haven, Connecticut;
enacted by the President and Fellows,* 1774, 1787, 1800.

27   Corporation Records, 23 October 1776, in "Yale College Register,
1701–1704 & 1717–1800" (MS, Yale University Library) (hereafter
cited as College Register, 1), p. 211; Morgan, *Stiles,* p. 350.

28   Samuel Purviance, Jr., thought both Harvard and Yale failed in
teaching the classics (Dexter, *Itineraries and Miscellanies of Stiles,* p.
559); Jonathan Trumbull, *The Progress of Dulness,* Part I (1772).

29   Morgan, *Stiles,* pp. 315–16. Morgan says that anticlericalism also
"furnished an atmosphere in which deism could grow," and that
both of them were directed against Yale because of the part it had
played "in the religious quarrels of the preceding decades."

30   Dexter, *Biographical Sketches,* 3 : 303.

31   Ibid., p. 513.

32   Ibid., p. 545; Stokes, *Memorials,* 2 : 191; A. C. Goodyear, "Some His-
toric Yale Letters Edited from the Original Manuscripts in his Own
Collection," *YAW,* 9 April 1926; Morison, *Three Centuries,* p. 141;
Thwing, *Higher Education,* p. 173.

33   Stokes, *Memorials,* 1 : 313.

34   Gipson, *Jared Ingersoll,* pp. 336, 350, 360–61; Osterweis, *New
Haven,* p. 130–31.

35   Henry Phelps Johnston, *Yale and Her Honor-Roll in the American
Revolution, 1775–1783* (New York, 1888), pp. 8–9; Dexter, *Biographical Sketches,* 3 : 545.

36   Stokes, *Memorials,* 1 : 312.

37   Dexter, *Biographical Sketches,* 3 : 546. Stokes, *Memorials,* 2 : 95–101,
contains a biographical sketch of Bushnell. Tutor John Lewis reported the invention in a letter to Ezra Stiles (ibid., p. 96).

38   The last grant before the war appears to have been made in May
1774 (Dexter, *Biographical Sketches,* 3 : 513). Since Connecticut was
not a royal colony, Yale did not have to worry about its charter
(Whitehead, *The Separation of College and State,* p. 36). Corporation Records, 25 July 1[77]5, 13 September 1775, Dexter, *Biographical Sketches,* 3 : 598.

39 George W. Pierson, *The Education of American Leaders: Compara-tive Contributions of U.S. Colleges and Universities* (New York, 1969), p. 17. Harvard had the best ratio, with 8 out of 1,224 living graduates, Yale was next with 4 out of some 900, and Princeton was last with 2 from its "fewer than eight hundred" graduates (Morison, *Three Centuries*, p. 147; Johnston, *Yale in the Revolution*, p. 1; Wertenbaker, *Princeton*, p. 116.

40 Ellen D. Larned, ed., "Yale Boys of the Last Century, 'The Journal of Elijah Backus Junior, at Yale College from Jan. ye first to Dec. 31, 1777,'" *Connecticut Quarterly* 1, no. 4 (December 1895) : 355 (here-after cited as "Backus Journal"); Johnston, *Yale in the Revolution*, p. 69.

41 Larned, "Backus Journal," p. 357.

42 Stokes, *Memorials*, 2 : 191–92; Larned, "Backus Journal," p. 357.

43 Dexter, *Biographical Sketches*, 3 : 641; College Register, 1 : 213 (Cor-poration minutes, 1 April 1777). Stiles reported in his diary on 23 June 1779, "The Library of Yale College consists of about three Thous^d Volumes; of which three Quarters have been removed to Northford, Durham, and Westbury, to be out of the Way of the Enemy. I find there still remain a Thous^d Volumes in the Library Room. The Air pump, Apparatus, and Museum still here" (Franklin B. Dexter, *The Literary Diary of Ezra Stiles* [New York, 1901], 2 : 348).

44 College Register, 1 : 215 (Corporation minutes, 30 April 1777); Larned, "Backus Journal," p. 360.

45 Corporation Records, 13 January 1778.

46 Stokes, *Memorials*, 2 : 191; Dexter, *Biographical Sketches*, 1 : 616–20.

47 A brief biography of Hale is in Stokes, *Memorials*, 2 : 317–31.

48 For Barlow, see the biographical sketch in *DAB*; Howard, *Connecti-cut Wits*, pp. 133–34; and Stokes, *Memorials*, 1 : 126–35. On the class as a whole, consult ibid., pp. 128–29, and Dexter, *Biographical Sketches*, 4 : 2–88.

49 Ibid., 3 : 691–94; Larned, "Backus Journal," p. 357.

50 Johnston, *Yale in the Revolution*, pp. 98–99; Dexter, *Biographical Sketches*, 3 : 545–46. In 1776 Camp's father and Ralph Isaacs (B.A. 1761) were forced to leave New Haven and move to Glastonbury be-cause they were considered dangerous loyalists (Osterweis, *New Haven*, p. 128).

51 Schneider, *Johnson*, 1 : 406; Larned, "Backus Journal," p. 360. How-ard says there is some evidence that Timothy Dwight encouraged the revolt by the students because he had hopes of becoming president himself (*Connecticut Wits*, p. 21); cf. Morgan, *Stiles*, pp. 345–47.

CHAPTER 8

1 Morgan, *Stiles,* pp. 299–300.

2 On Stiles's life, see Morgan, *Stiles.* Brief sketches may be found in
   Dexter, *Biographical Sketches,* 2 : 92–97; Stokes, *Memorials,*
   1 : 298–307; *DAB.*

3 Dexter, *Biographical Sketches,* 3 : 713; Morgan, *Stiles,* p. 295. Stiles
   wrote in his diary, "The Fellows have elected me to prevent the Assembly's building another college" (Whitehead, *The Separation of
   College and State,* p. 37).

4 Morgan, *Stiles,* pp. 292–307, 321–24.

5 Ibid., pp. 304, 307. Stiles's letter is recorded in College Register,
   1 : 231–32.

6 Morgan, *Stiles,* pp. 308–10; Dexter, *Biographical Sketches,* 3 : 714;
   College Register, 1 : 237–38; Gabriel, *Religion and Learning at Yale,*
   p. 39.

7 Morgan, *Stiles,* p. 329; Johnston, *Yale in the Revolution,* pp. 93–95;
   Dexter, *Biographical Sketches,* 4 : 89.

8 Dexter, *Biographical Sketches,* 4 : 89; Johnston, *Yale in the Revolution,* pp. 94–95; Morgan, *Stiles,* p. 331.

9 Dexter, *Literary Diary of Stiles,* 2 : 327.

10 For the invasion of New Haven, see Morgan, *Stiles,* pp. 331–35; Dexter, *Biographical Sketches,* 4 : 89; Osterweis, *New Haven,* pp.
   138–49; Johnston, *Yale in the Revolution,* pp. 106–09.

11 Johnston, *Yale in the Revolution,* pp. 108–09.

12 Dexter, *Biographical Sketches,* 4 : 89, 135.

13 Morgan, *Stiles,* pp. 335–36.

14 See the collection of Yale diplomas, University Archives, Yale University Library.

15 Morgan, *Stiles,* pp. 328, 463. Enrollment increased steadily from 1778
   to 1785 while the size of the graduating classes dropped from 1778 to
   1782, indicating that it was in the entering classes that increases
   came. In the class of 1780 (which entered in 1776), a typical wartime
   class, the median entering age was sixteen, but three were nineteen,
   two were twenty-one, and one each twenty-two and twenty-three
   (Dexter, *Biographical Sketches,* 4 : 136–74). The median age was seventeen for the class of 1782 and sixteen for 1785. A study of selected
   classes from 1776 to 1815 indicates that the median entering age was
   generally sixteen. The student "for the time being," Ebenezer Fitch,
   was due to receive his degree in "a few weeks," in any case (Dexter,
   Itineraries and Miscellanies of Stiles, pp. 485–86).

16 Dexter, *Literary Diary of Stiles,* 2 : 458.

17 Johnston, *Yale in the Revolution,* pp. 1, 183, 349; *Catalogue of the Officers and Graduates of Yale University, 1701–1924,* pp. 130–32. A few of those who served were from classes later than 1779, but since the number was so small, I have not included later classes in the total number of graduates because it would badly distort that figure. My statistics for Yale graduates are from Johnston, *Yale in the Revolution.* Unfortunately, he decided that loyalists were not fit to be included in his roll of honor, so we have no figures for that benighted group. Howard H. Peckham, *The War for Independence: A Military History* (Chicago, 1958), pp. 199–200.

18 Stokes, *Memorials,* 2 : 289–90; Morison, *Three Centuries,* p. 148.

19 Morgan, *Stiles,* pp. 315–16, 318–19.

20 See ibid., pp. 337–38, 350–51 for the details of the Corporation's treatment of the tutors.

21 Ibid., pp. 341–42.

22 Ibid., pp. 338–39, 351; Corporation Records, 27 April 1779.

23 Morgan, *Stiles,* pp. 339–41.

24 Dexter, *Biographical Sketches,* 4 : 213, 375; *Catalogue of the Officers and Graduates of Yale University, 1701–1924,* p. 144; Morgan, *Stiles,* p. 463; Johnston, *Yale in the Revolution,* pp. 138–39.

25 Dexter, *Literary Diary of Stiles,* 3 : 12–13. Dexter incorrectly puts this event in October 1781 (*Biographical Sketches,* 4 : 213). The Faculty Judgements, 28 March 1755, defined "rustification" as follows: "The Punishment commonly called *Rustification,* i.e. shall be sent from College into some Place in the Country and there be put under the Care of some Minister . . . to whom he shall Recite. . . . And if he shall produce a Certificate from such Minister that, during that Time, he has diligently attended his Studies, and been Guilty of no Misdemeanours or Disorders, he may then probably be Restored."

26 Corporation Records, 11 June 1782; College Register, 1 : 313; *The Buildings of Yale University* (New Haven, 1965), p. 80.

27 Dexter, *The Literary Diary of Ezra Stiles,* 2 : 348, 3 : 46–47. Monrad, "Catalogues of the Yale Library," *Papers in Honor of Andrew Keogh,* p. 279. *The Laws of Yale-College,* 1774, pp. 22–23, 1817, p. 34.

28 The best account of the Parnassus articles and the other attacks is Morgan, *Stiles,* pp. 349–55. Morgan states that Stiles thought four or five individuals working together composed the Parnassus articles, but Morgan himself seems to think Timothy Dwight was involved. He says that "though no evidence connects him with the letters, he had the ability, the access to inside information, and, if Stiles's estimate of him was correct, the inclination."

29 Ibid., pp. 356–59; on the effect of democracy, see also Rudolph, *American College and University,* pp. 34–35.

30 Morgan, *Stiles,* pp. 409–17, 463.

31 Ibid., pp. 417–20; Dexter, *Biographical Sketches,* 4 : 740; Dexter, *Literary Diary of Stiles,* 3 : 460–64. On the grant, see also M. Louise Greene, *The Development of Religious Liberty in Connecticut* (Boston, 1905), pp. 379–80. A copy of the report of the committee is in College Register, 1 : 345.

32 Dexter, *Biographical Sketches,* 5 : 52; Morgan, *Stiles,* pp. 423–24; College Register, 1 : 357–58; Dexter, *Literary Diary of Stiles,* 3 : 491–92. The building was later known as South College.

33 Morgan, *Stiles,* pp. 96, 360–65, 369–73, 441.

34 McClure to Eleazar Wheelock, 30 October 1765, printed in Gillette, "Yale College One Hundred Years Ago," *Hours at Home,* February 1870, p. 331.

35 Stokes, *Memorials,* 2 : 16; Morgan, *Stiles,* pp. 369–71.

36 Faculty Judgements, vol. 1, 18 June 1752.

37 Stokes, *Memorials,* 1 : 215–16.

38 Ibid., 1 : 215–16; 2 : 190.

39 Stokes, *Memorials,* 1 : 51–52; Morgan, *Stiles,* pp. 367–68, 402–03.

40 Kingsley, *Yale College,* 1 : 308–17; Morgan, *Stiles,* pp. 365–66, 405; Rudolph, *American College and University,* p. 137.

41 Faculty Judgements, vol. 1, 10 December 1754, 2 July 1755.

42 Stokes, *Memorials,* 2 : 256.

43 Kingsley, *Yale College,* 1 : 324–25.

44 Osterweis, *New Haven,* pp. 174–75; Morgan, *Stiles,* pp. 364–65, 421–22.

45 Morison, *Three Centuries,* p. 152.

46 Stokes, *Memorials,* 2 : 237, 239–40.

47 College Register, 1 : 345; Anna Haddow, *Political Science in American Colleges and Universities, 1636–1900* (New York, 1939), p. 28; Morgan, *Stiles,* pp. 376–78, 386–88.

48 Morgan, *Stiles,* pp. 400–02; Corporation Records, 14 September 1785; Dexter, *Biographical Sketches,* 3 : 393, 417, 442. While Dwight examined students (Cuningham, *Dwight,* pp. 239–40), I can find no evidence of grades such as Stiles used until 1813 (see Mary L. Smallwood, *An Historical Study of Examination and Grading Systems in Early American Universities* [Cambridge, Mass., 1935], p. 43).

49 Morgan, *Stiles,* pp. 402–03.

50 Ibid., pp. 325, 380, 406–07, 423, 427, 463.

51 Ibid., p. 428.

52 Ibid., pp. 461, 463. In 1778 Yale graduated forty and in 1794, twenty-two; the class of 1795 had thirty-three members (*Catalogue of the Officers and Graduates of Yale University, 1701–1924,* pp. 131, 138).

53 Stokes, *Memorials,* 1 : 306–07; Morgan, *Stiles,* p. 72.

54 Gabriel, *Religion and Learning at Yale,* pp. 47–48.

CHAPTER 9

1 Dexter, *Biographical Sketches,* 5 : 130; for Dwight's life, see Cuningham, *Dwight.* Brief sketches are in Dexter, *Biographical Sketches,* 3 : 321–33; *DAB;* and Howard, *Connecticut Wits.* On Stiles's opinion of Dwight's Northampton school see Morgan, *Stiles,* pp. 347–48.

2 S. G. Goodrich, *Recollections of a Lifetime* (New York, 1856), 1 : 348–49, 352–53; Cuningham, *Dwight,* p. 350.

3 "Rev. Dr. John Pierce's Manuscript Journal," *Proceedings of the Massachusetts Historical Society,* 2d ser., vol. 3 (1886–87) : 46–47; Cuningham, *Dwight,* pp. 171–72.

4 Cuningham, *Dwight,* p. 166; Howard, *Connecticut Wits,* p. 342; Osterweis, *New Haven,* p. 193. Morgan states that the depression did not lift in Connecticut until the 1790s (*Stiles,* p. 410).

5 Gabriel, *Religion and Learning at Yale,* p. 66; Edmund S. Morgan, "Ezra Stiles and Timothy Dwight," *Proceedings of the Massachusetts Historical Society* 72 (1958) : 102; Stokes, *Memorials,* 1 : 224.

6 Rudolph, *American College and University,* p. 38 (cf. Hofstadter, *Academic Freedom,* p. 210); Morgan, *Stiles,* pp. 394, 451, 461; idem, "Stiles and Dwight," pp. 109–15; Cuningham, *Dwight,* p. 293.

7 Stokes, *Memorials,* 1 : 224; Gabriel, *Religion and Learning at Yale,* pp. 65–71.

8 Morgan, "Stiles and Dwight," pp. 101–17; Gabriel, *Religion and Learning at Yale,* p. 72. A moral society was formed as early as 1795, but apparently it lapsed for a time and was re-formed in 1797 (Morgan, *Stiles,* p. 427).

9 Cuningham, *Dwight,* pp. 179–80, 242–46; Morgan, *Stiles,* pp. 395–98; Timothy Dwight, Jr., *President Dwight's Decisions of Questions Discussed by the Senior Class of Yale College in 1813 and 1814* (New York, 1833).

10 College Register, 1 : 345; Morgan, *Stiles,* p. 371.

11 Cuningham, *Dwight,* p. 255; Morgan, *Stiles,* p. 372; *Laws of Yale College,* 1800, p. 11; Morison, *Three Centuries,* p. 184. *At the An-*

nual Session of the President and Fellows of Yale-College, September 12, 1804 [New Haven, 1804], p. 5.

12 *Laws of Yale College*, 1800, p. 27; Dexter, "Student Life at Yale College under the First President Dwight," *Selected Papers*, p. 391. Commencement and quarter balls, not being "in term time," were still allowed.

13 Cuningham, *Dwight*, p. 258; Rudolph, *American College and University*, p. 107; Gabriel, *Religion and Learning at Yale*, p. 62; Dexter, "Student Life at Yale College under the First President Dwight," p. 393. As late as 1870 there was still a fine for playing ball in the college yard or throwing anything against the college buildings (*Laws of Yale College*, 1870, pp. 13–14); Records of the Faculty, 30 January 1839 (MSS, Yale University Library; hereafter cited as Faculty Records).

14 Kingsley, *Yale College*, 1 : 119; Rudolph, *American College and University*, pp. 103–04; Cuningham, *Dwight*, pp. 252–60, 388; Morgan, *Stiles*, pp. 326, 368, 345, 425.

15 See Dexter, *Biographical Sketches*, vols. 4, 5, 6. At Harvard the median entering age fell to fifteen and a half around 1810 according to Morison (*Three Centuries*, p. 184); at Yale the median entering age never seems to have fallen below sixteen.

16 Cuningham, *Dwight*, p. 388.

17 *At the Annual Session of the President and Fellows of Yale College, September 12, 1804*, p. 4; Corporation Records, 11 September 1810.

18 Cuningham, *Dwight*, pp. 259, 387; Laura Hadley Moseley, ed., *Diary (1843–1852) of James Hadley, Tutor and Professor of Greek in Yale College, 1845–1872* (New Haven, 1951), p. 1 (hereafter cited as Hadley, *Diary*).

19 Cuningham, *Dwight*, p. 259; Stokes, *Memorials*, 1 : 137.

20 Cuningham, *Dwight*, pp. 293–94; Gabriel, *Religion and Learning at Yale*, pp. 68–69. According to Gabriel, this was a crusade which "revealed the man. . . . Timothy Dwight was not a scholar, he was a prophet" (p. 66).

21 Gabriel, *Religion and Learning at Yale*, pp. 72, 75; Perry Miller, *The Life of the Mind in America from the Revolution to the Civil War* (New York, 1965), p. 4; Morgan, "Stiles and Dwight," p. 109.

22 Chauncey Allen Goodrich, "Narrative of Revivals of Religion in Yale College from its Commencement to the Present Time," *American Quarterly Register* 10 (1838) : 295.

23 Ibid., pp. 295–96; Cuningham, *Dwight*, pp. 328–29.

24 Goodrich, "Narrative of Revivals," p. 296. Goodrich must have been referring only to those converted during this revival who later became ministers, for Dexter reveals that 68 became ministers (*Bio-*

graphical Sketches, vol. 5, classes of 1802, 1803, 1804, and 1805). The proportion was higher in the classes of 1804 and 1805 than in the classes 1802 or 1803. For just Dwight's years 1796–1805, the figure was about 25 percent (Dexter, *Biographical Sketches,* 5 : 386–87, 428–29). On professional distribution, see ibid., appendixes at the end of each volume; and Cuningham, *Dwight,* pp. 332–34. For the period 1792–1805, the number dropped to 20 percent.

25 Dexter, *Biographical Sketches,* 5 : 275.

26 George P. Fisher, *Life of Benjamin Silliman,* 2 vols. (Philadelphia, 1866), 1 : 114–15, 117.

27 Rudolph, *American College and University,* p. 98; Cuningham (*Dwight,* pp. 264, 274–75) makes much of the 1805 "Bread and Butter Rebellion" at Harvard, but despite this instance, Harvard was relatively untroubled by student disorders (cf. Morison, *Three Centuries,* pp. 175 ff.).

28 Kingsley, *Yale College,* 1 : 120.

29 Cuningham, *Dwight,* p. 389.

30 *A Letter from John Bartlett written at Yale College, August 21, 1806* (New Haven, 1937), pp. 6–7; Kingsley, *Yale College,* 2 : 462–77.

31 Erastus Osborn to unknown correspondent, 1 May 1812 (MS, Yale University Library); Kingsley, *Yale College,* 2 : 463, contains a description of a riot in 1811; I believe this is the riot that actually occurred in 1812.

32 Kingsley, *Yale College,* 2 : 463–65; Dexter, *Biographical Sketches,* 6 : 493–94; Stokes, *Memorials,* 1 : 62–63.

33 Gabriel, *Religion and Learning at Yale,* pp. 77–79.

34 Dexter, *Biographical Sketches,* 5 : 176; J. L. Kingsley, "A Sketch of the History of Yale College in Connecticut," *American Quarterly Register* 8 (1835) : 209.

35 Stokes, *Memorials,* 2 : 14–15; Kingsley, *Yale College,* vol. 1, facing page 199; Cuningham, *Dwight,* p. 184.

36 Dexter, *Biographical Sketches,* 5 : 176; Kingsley, *Yale College,* 1 : 204–05.

37 Cuningham, *Dwight,* p. 182; Corporation Records, 13 March, 25 October 1797.

38 Dexter, *Biographical Sketches,* 5 : 316; Cuningham, *Dwight,* pp. 184–86. Individual classes varied greatly in size, but the general trend of college enrollment was steadily upward during Dwight's presidency (*Catalogue of the Officers and Graduates of Yale University, 1701–1924,* pp. 138–51). Corporation Records, 4 November 1800, 13 September 1803, 11 September 1804. The partition between the studies and the main room was to have "an upright recess" "inclosed with double doors, sufficient in Depth to contain a large

bed and Bedstead . . . in a Perpendicular position" (ibid., 4 November 1800). The new buildings followed plans drawn up by Trumbull and Hillhouse in 1792 (Morgan, *Stiles,* p. 424).

39 Corporation Records, 14 September 1803; Osterweis, *New Haven,* pp. 186–87; Blake, *Chronicles of New Haven Green,* pp. 26, 254.

40 Dexter, *Biographical Sketches,* 5 : 316; Fisher, *Silliman,* 1 : 91–93.

41 Cuningham, *Dwight,* p. 197; Stokes, *Memorials,* 2 : 19; Fisher, *Silliman,* 1 : 91–92; Gabriel, *Religion and Learning at Yale,* p. 55.

42 Rudolph, *American College and University,* p. 139.

43 Biographical sketches of the three may be found in *DAB;* Cuningham, *Dwight,* p. 196.

44 Dexter, *Biographical Sketches,* 4 : 45–46; Morgan, *Stiles,* p. 427; Cuningham, *Dwight,* pp. 192–93, 199; William M. Meigs, *Life of Josiah Meigs* (Philadelphia, 1887), pp. 37–43.

45 Dexter, *Biographical Sketches,* pp. 115–16; Cuningham, *Dwight,* pp. 193–94.

46 Osterweis, *New Haven,* p. 198; Corporation Records, 9 September 1807; Dexter, *Biographical Sketches,* 4 : 115–16; Cuningham, *Dwight,* p. 195.

47 J. L. Chamberlain, ed., *Universities and Their Sons* (New York, 1898), p. 311; Corporation Records, 11 September 1806; Kingsley, *Yale College,* 2 : 61–64; Corporation Records, 31 August 1813; *Catalogue of the Officers and Graduates of Yale University, 1701–1924,* p. 486.

48 Cuningham, *Dwight,* p. 218; "Nathan Smith," *DAB.*

49 Dexter, *Biographical Sketches,* 6 : 616, 728; *The Buildings of Yale University* (1965), p. 81.

50 Osterweis, *New Haven,* pp. 193–94, 201.

51 Ibid., pp. 192, 482.

52 Dexter, *Biographical Sketches,* 6 : 616.

53 Cuningham, *Dwight,* pp. 351–52; Corporation Records, 11 February 1817. Dexter (*Biographical Sketches,* 3 : 324) and Stokes (*Memorials,* 1 : 214) both say Dwight died 11 February 1817; this error is probably due to the fact that the Corporation meeting referring to his death was held on that day. Silliman said it was 11 January (Fisher, *Silliman,* 1 : 266).

54 Stokes, *Memorials,* 1 : 223; John C. Schwab, "The Yale College Curriculum, 1701–1901," *Educational Review* 22 (1901) : 6–7.

55 Thomas A. Thacher, "James L. Kingsley," *New Englander,* November 1852, pp. 640–43; Cuningham, *Dwight,* pp. 241–42.

56 Thacher, "Kingsley," pp. 640–43.

57 Cuningham, *Dwight,* pp. 205–06; "Silliman," *DAB;* Fisher, *Silliman,* 1 : 121.

58 Cuningham, *Dwight,* pp. 205–06.

59 Ibid., p. 204.

60 Ibid., pp. 206–08; "Silliman," *DAB;* Professor Alexander M. Fisher, a brilliant young mathematician, was lost at sea in 1822 (Dexter, *Biographical Sketches,* 6 : 568).

61 Cuningham, *Dwight,* p. 209; John F. Fulton and Elizabeth H. Thomson, *Benjamin Silliman, 1779–1864: Pathfinder in American Science* (New York, 1947), p. 75.

62 Ibid., pp. 76–77.

63 Fisher, *Silliman,* 1 : 215–16, 256–59; Wilmarth S. Lewis, *The Yale Collections* (New Haven, 1946), pp. 27–28.

64 Fulton and Thomson, *Silliman,* pp. 75, 92–94; Kingsley, *Yale College,* 1 : 216.

65 Fisher, *Silliman,* 1 : 257; Cuningham, *Dwight,* p. 313; Gabriel, *Religion and Learning at Yale,* p. 80.

66 Gabriel, *Religion and Learning at Yale,* pp. 56, 81; Hofstadter, *Academic Freedom,* p. 218.

67 Cuningham, *Dwight,* pp. 248–50; Stokes, *Memorials,* 1 : 223. The size of the graduating classes is given in *Catalogue of Officers and Graduates of Yale University, 1701–1924,* the computations are mine.

68 Morison, *Three Centuries,* p. 198; Dexter, *Biographical Sketches,* 6 : 836; Stokes, *Memorials,* 2 : 196, 227. The number of Southerners actually enrolled was probably higher than these figures suggest. My studies of later decades indicate that many boys from the South tended to leave prior to graduation.

69 Cuningham, *Dwight,* pp. 280–81, 286; Gabriel, *Religion and Learning at Yale,* pp. 54–55, 65–71.

70 Vernon Louis Parrington, *The Connecticut Wits* (Hamden, Conn., 1963), p. xi; Morgan, "Stiles and Dwight," p. 102.

CHAPTER 10

1 Theodore Dwight Woolsey, *An Address Commemorative of the Life and Services of Jeremiah Day, Late President of Yale College, Delivered in the Center Church, New Haven, August 26th, 1867* (New Haven, 1867), pp. 10–11 (hereafter cited as *Day*); "Henry Davis," *DAB;* Jeremiah Day to Thomas Day, 11 April 1817, Day Family Papers (MSS, Yale University Library).

2 Corporation Records, 22 April 1817.

3 There is no full-scale biography of Day. Brief sketches may be found in Woolsey's commemorative address, cited above, the *DAB,* and Dexter, *Biographical Sketches,* 5 : 143–49.

4 *Laws of Yale College,* 1817.

5 Franklin B. Dexter, *An Historical Study of the Powers and Duties of the Presidency in Yale College* (Worcester, Mass., 1898), pp. 16–17; Kingsley, *Yale College*, 1 : 126–27. The president, professors, and tutors formally were given the title "the Faculty" in 1804 (Corporation Records, 11 September 1804).

6 Hofstadter and Smith, *American Higher Education*, 1 : 306–07.

7 Dexter, "Student Life at Yale College under the First President Dwight," p. 385; [James Luce Kingsley], *Remarks on the Present Situation of Yale College; for the Consideration of Its Friends and Patrons* (New Haven[?], 1818[?]); Corporation Records, 4 November 1800; Cuningham, *Dwight*, pp. 198, 249, 252.

8 Kingsley, *Yale College*, 1 : 125; Corporation Records, 23 July 1817; *Historical Register of Yale University, 1701–1937*, p. 57.

9 "Report of the President and Fellows to the General Assembly," 13 September 1810 (copy), Accounts, Treasurer's Papers (MSS, Yale University Library); Day to Silliman, 30 September 1805, in Fisher, 1 : 205; Cuningham, *Dwight*, p. 196; Corporation Records, 11 February 1817; Rudolph, *American College and University*, p. 193; Morison, *Three Centuries*, p. 220; Hofstadter, *Academic Freedom*, p. 230.

10 "Statement of the Amount of Principal of the Funds of Yale College," 1 June 1817, Accounts, Treasurer's Papers; [Kingsley], *Remarks on the Present Situation of Yale College* (1818); Cuningham, *Dwight*, p. 269.

11 [Kingsley], *Remarks on the Present Situation of Yale College* (1818).

12 [James Luce Kingsley], *Remarks on the Present Situation of Yale College for its Friends and Patrons* [New Haven, 1823?], p. 14 (this is a revised edition of his 1818 remarks); Ebenezer Baldwin, *History of Yale College, from Its Foundation, A.D. 1700, to the Year 1838* (New Haven, 1841), p. 236. For information on meetings held during the summer seeking ways to raise funds for the college, see also *The Funds of Yale College . . .* ([New Haven?], 23 March 1818); rough draft of resolves of a meeting of citizens of Connecticut in the North Brick Church, 16 June 1817; Report on a meeting "of a large number of the Clergy and other Citizens of this State, . . ." 22 July 1817; Rev. Dr. Lyman to C. Whittelsey, 25 August 1817; and General Meeting of the Friends of Yale College, 10 September 1817 (all in Correspondence, Treasurer's Papers).

13 President and Fellows to the General Assembly to be held May 1, 1821, "Report for the Year Ending 31 August 1820," Accounts, Treasurer's Papers; Baldwin, *History of Yale College*, p. 322–23.

14 Kingsley, *Yale College*, 1 : 121, 2 : 16; *Laws of Yale College*, 1800, p.

14; Morgan, *Stiles,* p. 391; Rudolph, *American College and University,* p. 11.

15 Bainton, *Yale and the Ministry,* p. 79; Kingsley, *Yale College,* 1 : 121.

16 How disturbing the disestablishment was is revealed in Jeremiah Day's letter to his brother, Thomas, 11 April 1817, Day Family Papers. Day said he doubted that it would be "considered an act of kindness to urge any of our friends to settle in Connecticut at the present time. I think Dr. [Henry] Davis may well congratulate himself on his escape from the overturning power of sectarianism."

17 Goodrich, "Narrative of Revivals," pp. 363–65; "A Statement Submitted to the Prudential Committee by the Prof. of Divinity in Yale College dated April 23, 1822," in William C. Fowler, *Origin of the Theological School of Yale College* (n.p., [1870?]) (College Pamphlets, vol. 2174, Yale University Library); Kingsley, *Yale College,* 1 : 127–28. J. T. Wayland, "The Theological Department in Yale College" (Ph.D. dissertation, Yale University, 1933) attributes the need for a department to: (1) the secularization of the college curriculum; (2) the revival of thought and life in the churches after the two Great Awakenings; (3) the appeal of the West in the face of an advancing population; (4) the rapid development of professional schools; and (5) dissatisfaction with contemporary methods of theological education.

18 Kingsley, *Yale College,* 2 : 20; Corporation Records, 10 September 1822.

19 Corporation Records, 10 September 1822; Kingsley, *Yale College,* 2 : 21. Though the Medical Institution was also established as a separate entity, this seems to have been due to the fact that it was a joint venture with the state medical society rather than to a particular economic policy.

20 [Kingsley], *Remarks on the Present Situation of Yale College,* (1823).

21 W. C. Fowler to Jeremiah Day, 8 October 1823, Correspondence, Treasurer's Papers; Kingsley, *Yale College,* 1 : 130, 485–87; "To the Hon. General Assembly . . . May 1825" (copy), Accounts, Treasurer's Papers.

22 For the difficulties of fund-raising, see Samuel Whittelsey to Day, 12 March and 22 June 1824, Correspondence, Treasurer's Papers.

23 "Sheldon Clark," *DAB;* I. Woodbridge Riley, *American Philosophy: The Early Schools* (New York, [1907]), p. 462.

24 On the attempts to found an Episcopal college, see Rev. E. E. Beardsley, *Historical Address Pronounced before the Convocation of*

Trinity College (Hartford [?], 1851); idem, *The History of the Episcopal Church in Connecticut,* 2 vols. (New York, 1868–69), 2 : 66–69, 246–49; Nelson R. Burr, *The Story of The Diocese of Connecticut: A New Branch of the Vine* (Hartford, 1962); Glenn Weaver, *The History of Trinity College,* 2 vols. (Hartford, 1967), 1 : 7–17. Most of the struggle over the founding of Trinity seems to have come *after* the charter; see [Chauncy Allen Goodrich or Roger Sherman Baldwin], *Considerations Suggested by the Establishment of a Second College in Connecticut* (Hartford, 1824); [Nathaniel S. Wheaton], *Remarks on Washington College and on the "Considerations Suggested by Its Establishment"* (Hartford, 1825); and [Roger Sherman Baldwin], *An Examination of the "Remarks" on Considerations Suggested by the Establishment of a Second College in Connecticut,* (Hartford, 1825). Whitehead, *The Separation of College and State,* accepts the traditional interpretation of this action.

25 Jeremiah Day to Thomas Day, 1 May 1823, Day Family Papers.
26 Corporation Records, 7 May 1823; Riley, *American Philosophy,* pp. 462–63; Franklin B. Dexter, "The Benefactors of Yale College," *Selected Papers,* p. 289. On 22 July 1817 the Corporation approved accepting the president, fellows, tutors, and professors into office either by oath or by giving satisfactory evidence of their religious belief and qualifications (Corporation Records, 22 July 1817); see Corporation Records, 10 September 1822, for the provisions relating to the professor of didactic theology.
27 Corporation Records, 9 September 1823; De Forest Scholarships, Treasurer's Papers.
28 Corporation Records, 9 September 1823.
29 Dexter, "The Benefactors of Yale College," p. 289; Corporation Records, 8 September 1824.
30 Fisher, *Silliman,* 1 : 278–79; "Account of Yale College, 1825," Accounts, Treasurer's Papers.
31 Fulton and Thomson, *Silliman,* pp. 143–45; Stokes, *Memorials,* 2 : 200; *To The Friends of Yale College and of American Science* ([New Haven?], 1825); Paine Ward King & Co. to Stephen Twining, 26 September 1827, Correspondence, Treasurer's Papers; Lewis, *The Yale Collections,* p. 28.
32 Osterweis, *New Haven,* p. 259; An Act in addition to an Act entitled "An Act Relative to the Investment of Funds of Certain Corporations in the Banks of the State," true copy, 2 June 1824, Correspondence, Treasurer's Papers; Dexter, *Biographical Sketches,* 5 : 444; Eagle Bank Stock to the President and Fellows of Yale College,

Debtor, by S. Twining, Asst. Treasurer, Accounts, 1830, Treasurer's Papers.

33 Receipts and Expenditures, year ending August 30, 1826, Accounts, Treasurer's Papers. This was, in fact, an overstatement, since the college deducted from its productive funds monies owed for debts. The account actually shows a profit of $3,899.05. If all the debts had to be paid, however, the college would have been in much worse financial condition.

34 Kingsley, *Yale College*, 1 : 381; Memorial of the President and Fellows to the General Assembly, 10 May 1830, and Report of Committee (true copies), bound together in Correspondence, Treasurer's Papers; Circular furnished by Prof. Goodrich, July 1831, ibid.

35 Fisher, *Silliman*, 2 : 68–69.

36 J. Wood to B. Silliman, 3 June 1831, Correspondence, Treasurer's Papers; Fulton and Thomson, *Silliman*, p. 168; Whitehead, says Yale got this money because "supporters of the Episcopal college maneuvered an education bank bonus through the Assembly" (*The Separation of College and State*, p. 111). But Wood in his letter to Silliman says that if the Episcopalians had not presented a petition, he would have proposed giving the entire bonus to Yale, though he still believed that by appropriating part to Washington College, they probably picked up some Episcopal and Hartford votes for the appropriation. As Whitehead notes, this was the last grant Yale received until the Morill Act of 1862.

37 Theodore Sizer, *Autobiography of Col. John Trumbull* (New York, 1970), pp. 284–90, 322–25. Sizer's excellent description of the gallery is in the *YAW*, 4 November 1932. See also Kingsley, *Yale College*, 2 : 153–56.

38 Circular furnished by Prof. Goodrich, July 1831, Correspondence, Treasurer's Papers.

39 *A Statement of Facts Pertaining to the Case of Yale College* (1 December 1831); W. Warner to J. Day, 20 July 1831, 28 July 1831, 5 August 1831, 24 August 1831; J. Day to W. Warner, 23 July 1831; Samuel M. Hopkins to J. Day, 30 July 1831, all in Correspondence, Treasurer's Papers. I have not found the finished circular, but the Circular furnished by Prof. Goodrich, July 1831, appears to be a draft for it.

40 *A Statement of Facts Pertaining to the Case of Yale College.*

41 Ibid.; Wertenbaker, *Princeton*, pp. 217–19. In 1833 Princeton's income from endowment was about what Yale's had been in 1831. Yale then received $2,300 and Princeton a little over $2,000.

42   The first use of the name Centum Millia I have found was in a balance sheet dated 1 May 1833, Accounts, Treasurer's Papers.

43   Roland H. Bainton, "The School of Divinity," in *Seventy-Five: A Study of a Generation in Transition,* ed. the Editors of the *Yale Daily News* (New Haven, 1953), p. 25.

44   Bainton, *Yale and the Ministry,* pp. 96–101.

45   Warner to Day, 21 December 1831, Correspondence, Treasurer's Papers.

46   Warner to Day, 11 February 1832; Grimké to Silliman, 30 October 1832; letter of introduction for Charles U. Shepherd [*sic*] as a fund raiser, 8 November 1832; Day to Warner, 15 February 1832 (all in Correspondence, Treasurer's Papers).

47   Jeremiah Day, *To the Citizens of New Haven,* 26 July 1832; Jeremiah Day, *Case of Yale College,* 30 July 1832.

48   Oliver P. Hubbard to S. A. Law, 21 September 1832, printed in *YAW,* 31 January 1930.

49   Printed announcement, 20 December 1832, Correspondence, Treasurer's Papers; printed report by Wyllys Warner, 15 August 1838, ibid.

50   *Treasurer's Reports,* 1832, 1833, 1834; for later years, see the printed reports.

51   Corporation Records, 19 August 1834. Supreme Court of Errors, Third Judicial District, October Term, 1898. *Yale University, Appellant,* vs *The Town of New Haven, Appellee. Brief and Argument on Behalf of the Appellant.* [New Haven, 1898], pp. 62–63. Whitehead believes that this was purely a punitive act—a blow against special privilege (*The Separation of Church and State,* p. 112). Since the act, for the first time, exempted Yale's invested funds from possible taxation, I believe Yale profited from the change.

52   Corporation Records, 21 January 1835, 18 August 1840. Erastus Colton to W. Warner, 24 January 1836, Correspondence, Treasurer's Papers; Kingsley, *Yale College,* 1 : 187–88; *The Buildings of Yale University* (1965), p. 14; Morison, *Three Centuries,* p. 267.

53   Kingsley, *Yale College,* 1 : 188; Monrad, "Catalogues of Yale Library," *Papers in Honor of Andrew Keogh,* pp. 259–60.

54   Kingsley, *Yale College,* 1 : 187, 498–99; Corporation Records, 15 August 1843.

55   Zara Jones Powers, "Yale Bibliophile in Europe," *Papers in Honor of Andrew Keogh,* pp. 374–75, 411–12.

56   Ibid., p. 374; Morison, *Three Centuries,* p. 267 (Harvard received another bequest of similar size in 1848, ibid., p. 265); Robert H. Bremner, *American Philanthropy* (Chicago, 1960), p. 52; Werten-

baker, *Princeton*, pp. 271, 294–95; Rudolph, *American College and University*, p. 189.

57 *Catalogue of the Officers and Students in Yale College, 1822–1823.* The addition of a chapter with information on the course of instruction and expenses was another of Day's improvements.

58 Stokes, *Memorials*, 1 : 247.

59 Candidates were examined, ordinarily, on the day before commencement (*Catalogue of the Officers and Students, 1822–1823*). The matriculation idea was Dwight's (Cunningham, *Dwight*, p. 237); *At the Annual Session of the President and Fellows of Yale-College, September 12, 1804*, p. 3.

60 *Catalogue of the Officers and Students, 1822–1823*, appendix.

61 Benjamin Silliman, "Report in [*sic*] the Department of Chemistry," 5 September 1818, Correspondence, Treasurer's Papers.

62 Chauncey A. Goodrich, "Report of the Professor of Rhetoric and Oratory," 7 September 1818, ibid.

63 Kingsley, *Yale College*, 2 : 504; Stokes, *Memorials*, 1 : 81, 248–49; Rudolph, *American College and University*, p. 153; according to Day, tutors were allowed to exchange courses so each would have "the opportunity of teaching his favorite branch" (*Reports on the Course of Instruction in Yale College by a Committee of the Corporation and the Academical Faculty* [New Haven, 1828], p. 13 [hereafter cited as *Yale Report of 1828*]).

64 Julian M. Sturtevant, ed., *Julian M. Sturtevant, An Autobiography*, in Hofstadter and Smith, *American Higher Education*, 1 : 274.

65 On Fisher's death, see Kingsley, *Yale College*, 1 : 229. Yale lost its telescope in the same shipwreck (see David F. Musto, "Yale Astronomy in the Nineteenth Century," *Ventures, Magazine of the Yale Graduate School*, Spring 1968, p. 8). For a charming account of Fisher and his fiancée, Catharine Beecher, and the meaning of his death to her, see Martha Bacon, "Miss Beecher in Hell," *Puritan Promenade* (Boston, 1964), pp. 73–93. Fisher's account of his courses is in an untitled document dated 31 August 1818, Correspondence, Treasurer's Papers. On Chauvenet, see *DAB* and Stokes, *Memorials*, 2 : 43–47.

66 *Laws of Yale College*, 1825, p. 18.

67 Hofstadter and Smith, *American Higher Education*, 1 : 274–75, 305.

68 Ibid., p. 275.

69 Ibid.; Rudolph, *American College and University*, p. 113.

70 Kingsley, *Yale College*, 1 : 133; Rudolph, *American College and University*, pp. 113, 115, 125–26.

71 *Yale Report of 1828*, pp. 6 ff.; Kingsley, *Yale College*, 1 : 133–35; Gabriel, *Religion and Learning at Yale*, pp. 98–99; Corporation Rec-

ords, 11 September 1827; a sensitive appreciation of the report is in
Hofstadter and Hardy, *Higher Education,* pp. 16–17.

72   Rudolph, *American College and University,* pp. 132, 134–35; *Yale
     Report of 1828,* p. 6.

73   *Yale Report of 1828,* pp. 21–22; Richard J. Storr, *The Beginnings of
     Graduate Education in America* (Chicago, 1953), p. 31; see ibid., p.
     163, for Kingsley's feelings about German universities.

74   *Yale Report of 1828,* p. 25.

75   Rudolph, *American College and University,* pp. 134–35.

76   Faculty Records, 29 May 1839; Corporation Records, 12 September
     1820, 24 May 1825; Gustav Gruener, "Germanic Department," *YAW,*
     13 March 1925; *Catalogue of the Officers and Students, 1831–32.*

77   Diary of George Edward Day, 2 May 1832 (MS, Yale University Li-
     brary).

78   Bainton, *Yale and the Ministry,* p. 83; see for example, Benjamin Sil-
     liman to Professor Kingsley, 24 December 1836 and enclosure, "To
     the President and Prudential Committee of Yale College," Corre-
     spondence, Treasurer's Papers; Fulton and Thomson, *Silliman,* pp.
     117–23, 147–49.

79   Tucker, *Clap,* p. 84; Morgan, *Stiles,* pp. 151–57, 442; Musto, "Yale
     Astronomy," pp. 8–9; D. J. Struik, *Yankee Science in the Making*
     (Boston, 1948), p. 326.

80   [Journal of Caleb Lamson], 11 April 1846; diary of George W.
     McPhail, 2 November 1834 (MS, Yale University Library); "An
     Early Undergraduate Genius: The Life Story of Ebenezer Porter
     Mason of the Class of 1839," *YAW,* 11 October 1912.

81   Kingsley, *Yale College,* 1 : 235.

82   Lewis Sheldon Welch and Walter Camp, *Yale, Her Campus, Class-
     Rooms, and Athletics* (Boston, 1899), p. 325; Stokes, *Memorials,*
     1 : 240–41.

83   Stokes, *Memorials,* 2 : 84; George W. Pierson, *Yale College, An Edu-
     cational History, 1871–1921* (New Haven, 1952), p. 702.

84   Bainton, *Yale and the Ministry,* p. 87; Corporation Records, 17 Au-
     gust 1841; "Edward E. Salisbury," *DAB.*

85   *Yale Report of 1828,* p. 23; *Catalogue of the Officers and Students,
     1828–29,* p. 23; Corporation Records, 19 August 1845.

86   Kingsley, *Yale College,* 2 : 504–05.

87   Ibid., p. 505.

88   In 1823, for example, Thomas Jefferson complained that the main
     block to an education for college students was "the insubordination
     of our Youth" (Edward Levi, *Points of View: Talks on Education*
     [Chicago, 1969], p. 139); see also Rudolph (*American College and*

University, pp. 97–98), who says the time from 1800 to 1875 was one of rebellions.

89 *A Circular Explanatory of the Recent Proceedings of the Sophomore Class in Yale College* (New Haven, 1830); [*Letter of the Faculty of Yale College*] (New Haven, 7 August 1830); Kingsley, *Yale College*, 1 : 137–38.

90 Kingsley, *Yale College*, 1 : 138. "Combinations" were strictly prohibited by the *Laws of Yale College*, 1817, and cf. [*Letter of the Faculty*], where much is made of the combination.

91 *Catalogue of the Officers and Graduates of Yale University, 1701–1924*, pp. 163–64; the date after the name is the date the degree was received.

92 Woolsey, *Day*, p. 712. While rebellions passed, Day's last years were marred by the killing of a tutor by a student (see chap. 12).

93 Jeremiah Day to the Corporation, 18 August 1846 (copy), Day Family Papers (misdated and filed 15 August 1843).

94 Day to the Corporation, 18 August 1846 (copy), Day Family Papers; Timothy Dwight, *Memories of Yale Life and Men, 1845–1899* (New York, 1903), p. 50.

95 Kingsley, *Yale College*, 1 : 146.

96 Dwight, *Memories*, pp. 20, 41–52. Woolsey refers to Day's caution as being near to a fault (*Day*, pp. 716–17). No doubt this trait increased as he grew older and must have created difficulties for President Woolsey, though Woolsey denied it (see chap. 11, n. 16).

CHAPTER 11

1 Fulton and Thomson, *Silliman*, pp. 204–05; Wm. G. Lane to Hon. E. Lane, 8 April 1843, William Griswold Lane, "Extracts of Letters, 1839–43" (typed copies, Yale University Library). Apparently some of the faculty agreed with student opinion of Silliman, cf. Hadley, *Diary*, pp. 97, 305; Fisher, 2 : 335.

2 Fulton and Thomson, *Silliman*, p. 204.

3 Dwight, *Memories*, pp. 182–83.

4 Corporation Records, 19 August 1846; "Woolsey," *DAB*.

5 T. D. Woolsey to Fellows of the Yale Corporation, 18 September 1846 (rough draft), Woolsey Family Papers (MSS, Yale University Library).

6 Corporation Records, 20 October 1846; Dwight, *Memories*, pp. 192–93; Dexter, "Reminiscences of the Officers of Yale College in 1857," *Selected Papers*, pp. 300, 302, 305.

7 Dexter, "Reminiscences," p. 305; Hadley, *Diary*, p. 76.

8   Hadley, *Diary,* p. 190. There is no full-length biography of Woolsey. The best sketches are in the *DAB* and Stokes, *Memorials,* 1 : 237–246. There is also a specialized volume, George A. King, *Theodore Dwight Woolsey, His Political and Social Ideas* (Chicago, 1956), which contains biographical information.

9   Corporation Records, 20 October 1846; Faculty Records, 31 May 1848. Another motive for listing class rank was to shorten the commencement program; Kingsley, *Yale College,* 2 : 506; Commencement program, 1848; *Catalogue of the Officers and Students of Yale College, 1845–1846, 1846–1847, 1856–1857, 1870–1871;* Faculty Records, 30 November 1853.

10 Kingsley, *Yale College,* 2 : 506; Hadley, *Diary,* pp. 36, 38, 63, 68, 70, 76, 153. Hadley was on the committee that drafted the plan, but he feared written exams. Thacher wanted annual exams from the first. Faculty Records, 12 July 1850; A Graduate of '69 [Lyman H. Bagg], *Four Years at Yale* (New Haven, 1871), p. 568; Faculty Records, 4 March 1868.

11 See *Catalogue of the Officers and Students of Yale College, 1844–1845* and *1870–1871.*

12 Ibid.; Haddow, *Political Science in American Colleges and Universities,* pp. 142–149. Haddow says that "while Yale at the beginning of the period was dominated by the gospel of conservatism, at the end it was fostering the development of courses in political philosophy which produced contributions to the literature of political science and a stimulating influence on other institutions through providing texts and a model for instruction" (p. 114). According to Wilson Smith, the emergence of politics, political economy, and history from the moral philosophy course did not occur at most colleges until the 1870s (*Professors and Public Ethics; Studies of Northern Moral Philosophers before the Civil War* [Ithaca, N.Y., 1956], p. 9).

13 Laurence R. Veysey, *The Emergence of the American University* (Chicago, 1965), p. 8; "Woolsey," *DAB.*

14 Faculty Records, 16 September 1868, 17 February 1869, 17 March 1869; John Hewitt, '59, says classes were divided by scholarship in his day ("College Life at Yale in the Fifties," *YAW,* 22 April 1910), but if so this must have been most unusual. Harvard tried this reform as early as 1825, but most of the faculty opposed it, so it failed (Morison, *Three Centuries,* pp. 232–34).

15 Dwight, *Memories,* p. 185; Morison, *Three Centuries,* p. 264; Theodore Dwight Woolsey, *An Historical Discourse Pronounced before the Graduates of Yale College, August 14, 1850* (New Haven, 1850), p. 127; Hadley, *Diary,* p. 258; *Theological Department of Yale College* (New Haven, 31 July 1865), p. 2.

16 Silliman first tried to resign in 1849, see Corporation Records, 14 August 1849, 13 August 1850, 26 July 1853; Hadley, *Diary*, p. 39. Woolsey's respect for Day's judgment was revealed in a eulogizing article. After Day's resignation as president, Woolsey said, "His judgements were as just and wise, as safe and as much built on principle, as they had ever been. In fact, freed now from the chief responsibility, he was more ready to accept the measures that were new and bordered on innovation" (Theodore Dwight Woolsey, "President Woolsey's Address at the Funeral of President Day, Commemorative of his Life and Services," *New Englander*, October 1867, p. 702).

17 Dwight, *Memories*, p. 166; Hadley, *Diary*, p. 85; see for example Faculty Records, 24 December 1847; Hadley, *Diary*, p. 24; Stokes, *Memorials*, 1 : 154; Dwight, *Memories*, p. 34.

18 Hadley, *Diary*, p. 85; Dwight, *Memories*, p. 20; Faculty Records, 15 July 1859; Morison, *Three Centuries*, p. 296; Faculty Records, 14 September 1859.

19 Kingsley, *Yale College*, 2 : 507.

20 Rudolph, *American College and University*, p. 288.

21 Dexter, "Reminiscences of the Officers of Yale College in 1857," pp. 297–317.

22 Simon Flexner and James Thomas Flexner, *William Henry Welch and the Heroic Age of American Medicine* (New York, 1941), p. 47; Stokes, *Memorials*, 1 : 340–41. White's other memories of his Yale education were not so flattering. He recalled that *De Senectute* was used as "a series of pegs on which to hang Zumpt's rules for the subjunctive mood" (Ernest P. Earnest, *Academic Procession: An Informal History of the American College, 1636–1953* [Indianapolis, 1953], p. 23).

23 Kingsley, *Yale College*, 1 : 149–50. These are the thoughts of the committee (on which Woolsey served), but see also Theodore Dwight Woolsey, "Dr. Hedge's Address to the Alumni of Harvard," *New Englander*, October 1866, pp. 695–710. Storr, *Beginnings of Graduate Education*, pp. 5–6.

24 Fulton and Thomson, *Silliman*, pp. 147–59; Russell H. Chittenden, *History of the Sheffield Scientific School of Yale University, 1846–1922*, 2 vols. (New Haven, 1922), 1 : 28–29 (hereafter cited as *History of SSS*); Kingsley, *Yale College*, 1 : 143, 149; "E. E. Salisbury," *DAB*.

25 Welch and Camp, *Yale*, p. 326; Chittenden, *History of SSS*, 1 : 37–40; Fulton and Thomson, *Silliman*, pp. 207–10. Whitehead notes that Yale approached the state for the needed $20,000. When it failed to support the program, Yale instituted the fee system. With this decision, he believes, "support for professional and scientific

training had shifted from the state to the individual" (*The Separation of College and State,* p. 113).

26 Chittenden, *History of SSS,* 1 : 40–41.
27 Kingsley, *Yale College,* 1 : 150.
28 Ibid., pp. 150–51; Storr, *Beginnings of Graduate Education,* pp. 50–52.
29 Storr, *Beginnings of Graduate Education,* pp. 55–56; Chittenden, *History of SSS,* 1 : 48.
30 Chittenden, *History of SSS,* 1 : 37.
31 Ibid., pp. 44, 46–47, 51, 54. *The Buildings of Yale* (1965), p. 39.
32 Chittenden, *History of SSS,* 1 : 51–54; "John Pitkin Norton," *DAB;* Kingsley, *Yale College,* 2 : 120; Edwin E. Slosson, *Great American Universities* (New York, 1910), pp. 39–40.
33 Chittenden, *History of SSS,* 1 : 56–59.
34 "John Pitkin Norton," *New Englander,* November 1852, p. 631; Kingsley, *Yale College,* 2 : 120; Chittenden, *History of SSS,* 1 : 55–56.
35 Chittenden, *History of SSS,* 1 : 57, 60; Kingsley, *Yale College,* 2 : 108.
36 Chittenden, *History of SSS,* 1 : 62, 71–74; Kingsley, *Yale College,* 2 : 122; "*J. A. Porter,*" *DAB;* George J. Brush, appointed in 1855, was the first professor of metallurgy in the country (*YAM,* April 1955), while John P. Norton was the first professor of agriculture (B. C. Steiner, *The History of Education in Connecticut* [Washington, 1893], p. 187).
37 Chittenden, *History of SSS,* 1 : 65, 74; *Doctors of Philosophy, 1861–1960* (New Haven, 1961), 5 : 224.
38 Hadley, *Diary,* p. 269; Chittenden, *History of SSS,* 1 : 53.
39 Chittenden, *History of SSS,* 1 : 66–67; Charles Schuchert and C. M. LeVene, *O. C. Marsh, Pioneer in Paleontology* (New Haven, 1940), p. 28; Rudolph dates the beginning of the American university movement from Dana's question (*American College and University,* p. 335). Daniel Coit Gilman, who created the first real American university at Johns Hopkins, was hired to prepare the development plan (Abraham Flexner, *Daniel Coit Gilman, Creator of the American Type of University* [New York, 1916], pp. 8–9).
40 Chittenden, *History of SSS,* 1 : 70–71, 86–88.
41 *Catalogue of Officers and Students, 1861–1862,* p. 53. The German was Hanns Oertel, who was dean of the Graduate School from 1911 to 1917.
42 Chittenden, *History of SSS,* 1 : 63, 64, 65, 75, 77, 81, 82.
43 Fabian Franklin, *Life of Daniel Coit Gilman* (New York, 1910), p. 87.

44 Chittenden, *History of SSS*, 1 : 82; Rudolph, *American College and University*, p. 233.

45 *Catalogue of Officers and Students, 1861–1862*, p. 46.

46 Ibid., pp. 47–48.

47 Kingsley, *Yale College*, 2 : 110–11; Chittenden said senior year was "truly a curiosity" (*History of SSS*, 1 : 82).

48 Chittenden, *History of SSS*, 1 : 90–92.

49 "The New Art Museum," *YAW*, 16 April 1926; Kingsley, *Yale College*, 2 : 140–41; "Nathaniel Jocelyn," *DAB* (Jocelyn had his studio in the new art building); Lewis, *The Yale Collections*, pp. 16–17; Edward E. Atwater, ed., *History of the City of New Haven to the Present Time* (New York, 1887), p. 393; "Augustus Russell Street," *DAB*.

50 Kingsley, *Yale College*, 2 : 142; "Street," *DAB*.

51 Kingsley, *Yale College*, 2 : 157–58.

52 Colin Eisler, "*Kunstgeschichte* American Style; A Study in Migration," *Perspectives in American History* 2 (1968) : 549; Francis Steegmuller, *The Two Lives of James Jackson Jarves* (New Haven, 1951), pp. 228–61; Lewis, *The Yale Collections*, pp. 17–18. Thus Jarves received $2,000 after repaying the loan (Ellen Frank, et al., "Introductory Essay," *Italian Primitives: The Case History of a Collection and Its Conservation* [New Haven, 1972], p. 3). There was some reason for the suspicions about the collection. Between 1860 and 1867 twenty-six paintings were removed from the collection by Jarves. Furthermore, there were incorrect attributions. The worst was the description of a nineteenth-century "fabrication" as a genuine Raphael. Such errors were, according to Osvald Sirén, only too common at the time (see Sirén, *A Description of the Pictures in the Jarves Collection Belonging to Yale University* [New Haven, 1916], pp. xviii–xx).

53 Woolsey, *An Historical Discourse*, pp. 122–28; Hadley, *Diary*, p. 267; the second president Timothy Dwight, who was financially well-off, little recognized the discontent of the faculty over their salaries (cf. Dwight, *Memories*, p. 200).

54 Corporation Records, 29 July 1851; *Nearly a quarter of a century since, when in consequence of its poverty, the existence of Yale College was at stake an application was made to its friends to relieve it from its embarrassments . . . a state of things similar to that before 1830 . . . is impending . . . A subscription, with the hope of raising $100,000, is now set on foot* [New Haven, 1852?]; Hadley, *Diary*, p. 296.

55 Hadley, *Diary*, p. 300.

56 Woolsey, *Historical Discourse,* p. 124; Hadley, *Diary,* pp. 300–03; *To the Friends of Yale College* (New Haven, 25 January 1853), pp. 1, 5; Corporation Records, 27 July 1852. As early as 1825 Harvard was charging fifty-five dollars (Morison, *Three Centuries,* p. 210).

57 Corporation Records, 24 July 1855; *Treasurer's Report,* 1 July 1859; Samuel R. Betts, "General Alumni Gifts to Yale," in G. H. Nettleton, ed., *The Book of the Yale Pageant* (New Haven, 1916), p. 235.

58 Corporation Records, 25 July 1854, 29 July 1856; *Treasurer's Report,* 1 July 1856.

59 Dexter, "Benefactors of Yale College," *Selected Papers,* p. 291; idem, *Biographical Sketches,* 6 : 311; College Register, 2 : 556–57 (Corporation minutes, 26 July 1864); Kingsley, *Yale College,* 1 : 490.

60 Dexter, "Benefactors of Yale College," pp. 291–92; College Register, 2 : 546 (Corporation minutes, 29 March 1864); Kingsley, *Yale College,* 1 : 497.

61 Steiner, *History of Education in Connecticut,* p. 181; Kingsley, *Yale College,* 1 : 490–91; Osterweis, *New Haven,* p. 283.

62 Dexter, "Benefactors of Yale College," pp. 291–93; Stokes, *Memorials,* 2 : 71; Chittenden, *History of SSS,* 1 : 107; Kingsley, *Yale College,* 1 : 152. Schuchert and LeVene, *Marsh,* pp. 73–86, has the most complete account of the Peabody gift. A small amount of information on Marett may be found in Arnold Dana, "New Haven—Old and New," 10 : 88 (MS, New Haven Colony Historical Society).

63 Ellsworth Eliot, Jr., *Yale in the Civil War* (New Haven, 1932), p. 14. Hofstadter and Smith, *American Higher Education,* 1 : 466–67, contains, Englehard's letter. See Fulton and Thomson, *Silliman,* pp. 259–61, on Yale and the rifles, which Englehard specifically alludes to. Thwing, *Higher Education,* pp. 254–55, gives attendance of Southerners by states in decennial years 1820–60. My figures on the Yale classes of 1853 and 1856 through 1861 are computed from the college catalogues, class books, and reunion books of the classes of those years. The division of the states into sections follows J. G. Randall and David Donald, *The Civil War and Reconstruction* (Boston, 1961), pp. 4–5.

64 Northern students left as well. See class books for the class of 1863; *Triennial Record of the Class of 1861, of Yale College* (n.p., 1864). A fascinating letter from Simeon Eben Baldwin to a Texas classmate is printed in Frederick H. Jackson, *Simeon Eben Baldwin, Lawyer, Social Scientist, Statesman* (New York, 1955), pp. 47–48. I assume the Southerners must have remained at Yale because of Baldwin's letter and some faculty votes reported in Eliot, *Yale in the Civil War,* p. 14.

65   Faculty Records, "special meeting" and 8 May 1861.

66   Eliot, *Yale in the Civil War*, pp. 13, 16, 22.

67   George W. Pierson, "Democratic War and Our Higher Learning: A Study of Yale's Student Enrollment and Faculty Employment in Nine Wars," *YAM*, December 1942; Stokes, *Memorials*, 1 : 356. The class books are most revealing, both for what is said and for what is not. Stocking's remark is quoted in Eliot, *Yale in the Civil War*, pp. 18–19.

68   My computations for the class of 1865 are from the class books. Eliot lists 17 percent of the class as having served, but he included men who enlisted after the war was over. Morison, *Three Centuries*, p. 303; my computations for the classes 1851–1863 are based on Eliot, *Yale in the Civil War*, p. 124.

69   *Catalogus Senatus Academicus . . .* (New Haven, 1865); my figures are based on Eliot, *Yale in the Civil War*. Of all classes in the period 1804–76, 1,013 graduates served—850 for the North and 163 for the South. Of the nongraduates for whom there are records, 256 entered the service. For Sheff, my figures are based on Eliot, *Yale in the Civil War*, p. 28, and the *Catalogus Senatus Academicus* (1865).

70   Eliot, *Yale in the Civil War*, pp. 24, 26; Stokes, *Memorials*, 2 : 294–95, 353; Bruce Catton, *The Coming Fury* (Garden City, N.Y., 1961), p. 437; Bremner, *American Philanthropy*, p. 77.

71   Bainton, *Yale and the Ministry*, pp. 133–35, 161; Dwight, *Memories*, pp. 253–54.

72   Bainton, *Yale and the Ministry*, pp. 161, 261–63; Dwight, *Memories*, pp. 254–56, 278–83, 285, 287; *Catalogue of the Officers and Graduates of Yale University, 1701–1924*, p. 543. There appears to have been a desire to make sure the school remained orthodox in religion, for when the new appointments were made in 1861, all the men, including Dwight, were examined on "their faith and religious character" and it was voted that "no professor hereafter shall be inducted into office in the theological department without a similar examination" (College Register, 2 : 507 [Corporation minutes, 23 July 1861]).

73   Dwight, *Memories*, p. 254.

74   Dexter, *Biographical Sketches*, 5 : 310–11; Kingsley, *Yale College*, 2 : 91.

75   Kingsley, Yale College, 2 : 91; Dexter, *Biographical Sketches*, 4 : 261; *Catalogue of the Officers and Students in Yale College, November 1824*.

76   Dexter, *Biographical Sketches*, 4 : 261 (Dexter says, incorrectly, that Daggett was made Kent professor in 1826); *Historical Register of*

Yale University, 1701–1937, pp. 63, 223; Corporation Records, 12 September 1826; *Supplement to Report of the Treasurer for the Fiscal Year 1969–1970, Funds* (New Haven, 1970), p. 52.

77   Kingsley, *Yale College,* 2 : 92, 94, 96; J. L. Chamberlain, ed., *Universities and Their Sons* (New York, 1898), 1 : 321–22; Frederick C. Hicks, *Yale Law School: The Founders and Founders' Collection,* Yale Law Library Publication no. 1 (New Haven, 1935), pp. 24–25; *Catalogue of the Officers and Graduates of Yale University, 1701–1924,* p. 505.

78   *Historical Register of Yale University, 1701–1937,* pp. 149, 432, 452.

79   Kingsley, *Yale College,* 2 : 65; *Catalogue of the Officers and Graduates of Yale University, 1701–1924,* pp. 488, 495; Chamberlain, *Universities and Their Sons,* p. 317.

80   William Henry Welch, "Yale in Its Relation to Medicine," *The Record of the Celebration of the Two Hundredth Anniversary of the Founding of Yale College, Held at Yale University in New Haven, Connecticut, October the Twentieth to October the Twenty-third, A.D. Nineteen Hundred and One* (New Haven, 1902), p. 246.

81   Whitfield J. Bell, Jr., "The Medical Institution of Yale College, 1810–1885," *Yale Journal of Biology and Medicine* 33 (1960) : 173–74.

82   Chamberlain, *Universities and Their Sons,* p. 317; Bell, "The Medical Institution of Yale College," p. 173. *Medical Institution of Yale College,* Feb. 1835 (New Haven [?] 1835 [?]) says the course was seventeen weeks. William Henry Welch, *The Relation of Yale to Medicine* (reprinted from *Yale Medical Journal,* November 1901), says that in the beginning the course was six months, though in his later article, "Yale in Its Relation to Medicine," (p. 248) he says it was soon reduced to five months and in 1824 to four, and "in 1832 it was from the second week in November to the last week in February."

83   *Medical Institution of Yale College, Feb. 1835;* Chamberlain, *Universities and Their Sons,* pp. 317–18.

84   Corporation Records, 14 August 1849; Morison, *Three Centuries,* p. 298; Kingsley, *Yale College,* 2 : 188–89; Welch and Camp, *Yale,* p. 387; Wertenbaker, *Princeton,* p. 311. Wertenbaker says that when McCosh retired in 1888 Princeton ranked second among the college libraries in the country. This seems impossible, since in 1884 Princeton had only 81,000 volumes. Yale had 120,000 in 1880 and 180,000 in 1890. Harvard, of course, was still far ahead.

85   Woolsey, *An Historical Discourse,* p. 126; Gilman to President Woolsey, 1 June 1865, Records of the Librarian (MSS, Yale University Library); Dexter, "Reminiscences of the Officers of Yale College

in 1857," *Selected Papers,* pp. 316–317; Chittenden, *History of SSS,* 1 : 84.

86 Kingsley, *Yale College,* 1 : 186; Chamberlain, *Universities and Their Sons,* pp. 371–72.

87 Ruth R. Brown, "George Catlin's Portraits of North American Indians," *Papers in Honor of Andrew Keogh,* pp. 160 61.

88 Kingsley, *Yale College,* 1 : 186; Addison Van Name, "The Yale Library," *Book of the Yale Pageant,* p. 188.

89 Kingsley, *Yale College,* 1 : 189.

90 Corporation Records, 14 August 1849, 13 August 1850; Hadley, *Diary,* p. 267.

91 Chamberlain, *Universities and Their Sons,* p. 363; Morison, *Three Centuries,* p. 265.

92 Corporation Records, 26 July 1853; College Register, 2 : 454–55 (Corporation minutes, 27 July 1858); Chamberlain, *Universities and Their Sons,* pp. 363–64; Kingsley, *Yale College,* 1 : 157–58, 2 : 197.

93 Dwight, *Memories,* pp. 339–40, 342; Welch and Camp, *Yale,* p. 445. I have used Welch and Camp's figure for enrollment in preference to Dwight's.

94 Frederick C. Hicks, *Yale Law School: From the Founders to Dutton, 1845–1869,* Yale Law Library Publication no. 3 (New Haven, 1936), p. 36.

CHAPTER 12

1 Stokes, *Memorials,* 1 : 161.

2 Bacon, *Puritan Promenade,* pp. 143–44.

3 College Register, 2 : 471–73 (Corporation minutes, 26 July 1859); Gabriel, *Religion and Learning at Yale,* pp. 171–72; "The Old Chapel in the Sixties," *YAW,* 7 May 1909; George W. Pierson, *Yale, 1871–1921,* pp. 12–13.

4 30 November 1845 [Lamson Journal].

5 6 December 1834, Diary of George W. McPhail.

6 Faculty Records, 18 December 1850, 14 January 1852.

7 Kingsley, *Yale College,* 1 : 126; Hofstadter and Smith, *American Higher Education,* 1 : 306–07.

8 Corporation Records, 11 September 1804, 17 August 1847.

9 Bagg, *Four Years at Yale,* p. 575. As an article in the *YAW* (29 May 1907) noted, marks were, up to a point, a measure of privilege.

10 Stokes, *Memorials,* 1 : 81; Dwight, *Memories,* p. 32.

11 Stokes, *Memorials,* 1 : 93–95; Henry A. Beers, *The Ways of Yale in*

the Consulship of Plancus (New Haven, 1923), pp. 9–13. Diary of William A. Peck, 13 January 1864 (MS, Yale University Library). The best way to know what the sports were is to read the faculty records, diaries, memoirs, biographies, and the like. Gilman's letter is in Franklin, *Gilman*, p. 59.

12 Cuningham, *Dwight*, pp. 280–281; Daniel Coit Gilman, *Life of James Dwight Dana, Scientific Explorer, Mineralogist, Geologist, Zoologist* (New York, 1899), pp. 154–55; Corporation Records, 12 September 1826; Stokes, *Memorials*, 1 : 77.

13 *YAW*, 24 October 1930.

14 Stokes, *Memorials*, 1 : 51–52; Clarence Deming, *Yale Yesterdays* (New Haven, 1915), p. 209; E. F. Blake, "A Football Prophecy in 1863," *YAW*, 29 November 1912. The rule against playing ball in the college yard was repeated in the *Laws of Yale College* almost without change from at least 1774 through 1870.

15 Deming, *Yale Yesterdays*, pp. 208, 216; Faculty Records, 14 October 1857, 6 October 1858.

16 George Dudley Seymour, *The Old Time Game of Wickets and Some Old Time Wicket Players* (n.p., n.d.), p. 18; Deming, *Yale Yesterdays*, pp. 192–95; Peck Diary, 6 February 1864; Welch and Camp, *Yale*, p. 551.

17 Deming, *Yale Yesterdays*, pp. 25–28; Osterweis, *New Haven*, p. 261; Kingsley, *Yale College*, 2 : 274–76; F. R. Dulles, *America Learns to Play: A History of Popular Recreation* (New York, 1940), p. 142.

18 Kingsley, *Yale College*, 2 : 310–12.

19 Welch and Camp, *Yale*, pp. 492–93; Beers, *The Ways of Yale*, pp. 9–10; Bagg, *Four Years at Yale*, pp. 256–57.

20 Cuningham, *Dwight*, p. 277; Kingsley, *Yale College*, 1 : 132.

21 Mary Hamilton Hadley, "An Old Time Pilgrimage in Pursuit of Science," [*Bits of New England History*] (3 vols., n.p., 1898–1904, in Yale University Library) 3 : 767; Kingsley, *Yale College*, 1 : 302, 304–05 (Kingsley puts this event in 1819, which appears to be an error); Faculty Records, 27 July, 5 August 1828.

22 Faculty Records, 6 February, 9 October 1839; Pierson, *Yale, 1871–1921*, p. 702.

23 See above, pp. 168–69; Woolsey, "Day," *New Englander*, October 1867, p. 712.

24 Faculty Records, 2 August 1837. Students did have weapons even earlier; see *Yale University Library Gazette* 11 (1937) : 12–13, for an account of James H. Wigfall's encounter with James D. Cogdell. Cogdell later killed Wigfall in a duel in Georgia in 1824.

25 Faculty Records, 24 May 1839; Wm. G. Lane to Hon. E. Lane, 30

October, 3 November, 13 December 1841, Lane Letters; Bagg, *Four Years at Yale,* p. 454, pp. 504–05.

26 Faculty Records, 29 December 1841, 3, 5, 9 August 1842.

27 Faculty Records, 1, 20, 25 October 1843; Deming, *Yale Yesterdays,* p. 177. Deming says, incorrectly, that Dwight was stabbed twice.

28 James Gallup to Julia Geer, 25 December 1847 (typewritten excerpt, Yale University Library); Faculty Records, 24 December 1847.

29 Erastus Osborne to Shadrach Osborne, 12, 19 January 1824 (MS, Yale University Library).

30 *The Riot at New Haven Between the Students and Town Boys, on the Night of March 17, 1854, Which Resulted in the Death of Patrick O'Neil, and the Wounding of Several Persons, &c, &c. Together with the Coroner's Investigation and the Verdict* (New Haven, 1854); Allen Nevins, *Ordeal of the Union* (New York, 1947), 2 : 132; Bainton, *Yale and the Ministry,* pp. 156–58, 284.

31 Bainton, *Yale and the Ministry,* 158–60; Faculty Records, 3, 5 March 1856.

32 Bagg, *Four Years at Yale,* pp. 509–12; College Register, 2 : 461 (Corporation minutes, 27 July 1858); Faculty Records, 17 November 1858.

33 Bagg, *Four Years at Yale,* pp. 512–13.

34 On the emergence of the college bully see above, p. 125; Bagg, *Four Years at Yale,* pp. 501–03 (Bagg is incorrect on the name of the "reform party"); Diary of William McKee Dunne, 29 June 1835 (MS, Yale University Library); *YAW,* 21 March 1909; Wm. G. Lane to Hon. E. Lane, 13 October 1839, 25 October 1840, Lane Letters; Faculty Records, 2 October 1840; Corporation Records, 17 August 1841.

35 Bagg, *Four Years at Yale,* pp. 319–26; Faculty Records, 29 November 1848; Garrick Mallery Diary, 1 November 1849 (MS, Yale University Library).

36 Bagg, *Four Years at Yale,* pp. 659–65.

37 Ibid., pp. 405–22; Deming, *Yale Yesterdays,* pp. 86–87; Eli Senex, "Wooden Spoon Memories," *YAW,* 27 May 1908. See also the invitations, entrance cards, etc., in the Memorabilia Collection, Yale University Library.

38 Bagg, *Four Years at Yale,* pp. 479–99. The ceremony in 1832 is described as *"The day of our final separation"* [July 1832], Day Diary.

39 Bagg, *Four Years at Yale,* pp. 275–77.

40 Kingsley, *Yale College,* 1 : 320; Bagg, *Four Years at Yale,* pp. 221–23; Gabriel, *Religion and Learning at Yale,* p. 149. Alumni Hall was built at the behest of the literary societies (Corporation Records, 13 August 1850, 26 July 1853, 24 July 1855).

41   Kingsley, *Yale College,* 1 : 307–23.

42   Stokes, *Memorials,* 1 : 249–50, 254.

43   Kingsley, *Yale College,* 1 : 319–20, 324–27; Stokes, *Memorials,* 1 : 239–40, 337–65; Faculty Records, 9 December 1822. Gilman said the small societies united "those whom the rivalries of the large societies would render hostile" (Gabriel, *Religion and Learning at Yale,* pp. 148–49).

44   Bagg, *Four Years at Yale,* p. 228; Kingsley, *Yale College,* 1 : 327; Wilbur L. Cross, *Connecticut Yankee: An Autobiography* (New Haven, 1943), p. 80.

45   Charles Tracy, *Yale College: Sketches from Memory* (n.p., 1874), pp. 15–16; Bagg, *Four Years at Yale,* p. 146. Bagg says that "some injustice in the conferring of Phi Beta Kappa elections" seems to have led to the founding, but it appears more likely that the end of one secret society and the beginning of another was not coincidental.

46   Faculty Records, 25 December 1833.

47   Bagg, *Four Years at Yale,* pp. 52–53, 142–43, 169.

48   Ibid., pp. 128, 134–35.

49   Ibid., pp. 123, 143–44, 148, 170–74. Tap day as a public ceremony did not take place until the 1870s. It was first mentioned in the *Yale Daily News* in 1879 (see Loomis Havemeyer, *Go to Your Room* [n.p., 1960], p. 62; and *YAW,* 24 June 1905).

50   Faculty Records, 26 June 1844, 30 June 1852, 20 May 1857, 10 December 1862. "Society System," *New Englander,* May 1884, p. 388, says that about one-half of the faculty and Corporation were society members.

51   Kingsley, *Yale College,* 1 : 338–51; F. L. Mott, *A History of American Magazines,* 5 vols. (Cambridge, Mass., 1930–68), 2 : 99.

52   Bagg, *Four Years at Yale,* pp. 454–56, 460–61.

53   Kingsley, *Yale College,* 2 : 282.

54   The description of Yale in summer is from Deming, *Yale Yesterdays,* pp. 4–5.

55   Faculty Records, 22 September 1858, 21 May 1862, 15 September 1866, 9 April 1867; Deming, *Yale Yesterdays,* 5; Bagg, *Four Years at Yale,* pp. 298–99.

56   Kingsley, *Yale College,* 2 : 480; Gabriel, *Religion and Learning at Yale,* p. 146; Horace Reynolds, "Yale Songs of the Sixties," *YAM,* May 1952; Bagg, *Four Years at Yale,* pp. 301–02. Hadley said he feared their music would be hurt by the organ (*Diary,* p. 269).

57   Faculty Records, 31 January 1855; Bagg, *Four Years at Yale,* p. 303; *YAW,* 6 January, 10 February 1909.

58   A Graduate of Yale of the Class of 1821 [John Mitchell], *Reminis-*

cences of Scenes and Characters in College (New Haven, 1847), pp. 123, 125, 127; Jeremiah Day to Sherman Day, 9 January 1822, Day Family Papers; Corporation Records, 8 September 1824; Bagg, *Four Years at Yale*, pp. 519–20; Stokes, *Memorials*, 1 : 78; 2 : 261; Faculty Records, beginning of term [January–February?], 1826.

59 For social life, see especially Mallery Diary, Peck Diary, and McPhail Diary.

60 Henry Seidel Canby, *Alma Mater: The Gothic Age of the American College* (New York, 1936), pp. 30–31; Mallery Diary, 1 June 1849.

61 John William DeForest, *Miss Ravenel's Conversion from Secession to Loyalty* (New York, 1964), pp. 44–45; Canby, *Alma Mater*, pp. 14–15.

62 John Chapin Sanders to William D. Sanders, n.d. [1853?], *YAM*, January 1948.

CHAPTER 13

1 Harris E. Starr, *William Graham Sumner* (New York, 1925), pp. 80–83; Daniel Coit Gilman, "Proposed Change in the Corporation of Yale College," *The Nation*, 25 May 1871, p. 356.

2 Starr, *Sumner*, pp. 84–95; *Historical Register of Yale University, 1701–1937*, p. 23.

3 Pierson, *Yale, 1871–1921*, p. 57; a friendly review of the book appeared in *The Nation*, 27 October 1870, pp. 283–84; Veysey, *The Emergence of the American University*, p. 451. Porter also opposed the addition of alumni to the Corporation (see Whitehead, *The Separation of College and State*, pp. 211–12).

4 Pierson, *Yale, 1871–1921*, p. 57; Gilman, *Life of Dana*, pp. 395 ff, contains Dana's argument.

5 Timothy Dwight, "Yale College: Some Thoughts Respecting Its Future," *New Englander*, July 1870–October 1871; *Yale College. The Needs of the University, Suggested by the Faculties to the Corporation, the Graduates, and the Benefactors and Friends of the Institution, July 10, 1871* [New Haven?, 1871?]; James D. Dana, "What Yale College Needs," *The Nation*, 25 May 1871, pp. 379–80.

6 Gilman, *Life of Dana*, p. 399; *Yale College. The Needs of the University*, p. 22.

7 The first Timothy Dwight was chosen at the age of forty-three; his grandson reached that age in 1871. For the influence of the first president Dwight on the second, see Dwight, *Memories*. When Porter became president, Dwight was nearly the same age as his grandfather, Jeremiah Day, and Woolsey when they took office. The younger

Dwight felt that a president usually should not be over forty-five when elected (ibid., p. 376).

8 "Gilman," *DAB;* Hugh Hawkins, *Pioneer: A History of the Johns Hopkins University, 1874–1889* (Ithaca, 1960), p. 15; Morris Hadley, *Arthur Twining Hadley* (New Haven, 1948), p. 103; Franklin, *Gilman,* p. 102. For some of his thoughts on education at about this time, see the "confession of faith" of the Scientific School written by Gilman (Chittenden, *History of SSS,* 1 : 136–39).

9 Daniel Coit Gilman, "Proposed Change in the Corporation of Yale College," pp. 355–56.

10 Kingsley, *Yale College,* 1 : 161.

11 "Porter," *DAB;* Dexter, *Biographical Sketches,* 5 : 607.

12 Dwight, *Memories,* pp. 343–44; Gabriel, *Religion and Learning at Yale,* p. 162. Cross recalled how, whenever he visited Porter's office, he found him writing: "All was quiet and serene as if he were sitting not in the center of Yale College but in some remote monastery far from the haunts of men" (*Connecticut Yankee,* p. 73).

13 Dwight, "Yale College," *New Englander,* July 1870, p. 461; Cornelius Howard Patton and Walter Taylor Field, *Eight O'Clock Chapel: A Study of New England College Life in the Eighties* (New York, 1927), pp. 98–99; Stokes, *Memorials,* 1 : 332.

14 *Addresses at the Inauguration of Professor Noah Porter, D.D. LL.D., as President of Yale College, Wednesday, October 11, 1871* (New York, 1871), pp. 3, 27 ff.

15 *The Nation,* 21 July 1870; Steiner, *History of Education in Connecticut,* p. 194. For the report of 1828, see above, pp. 162–65.

16 Morison, *Three Centuries,* pp. 329–30.

17 Dwight, "Yale College," *New Englander,* July 1870, p. 466; Pierson, *Yale, 1871–1921,* p. 63.

18 Steiner, *History of Education in Connecticut,* p. 180. These were relatively good professors' salaries for the time, but in 1866, when they reached $2,600 in the college, a Sheffield faculty member (where the salaries were even lower) noted that the amount was "about two-thirds what it costs a family to live economically" (Franklin, *Gilman,* p. 85).

19 Lynde P. Wheeler, *Josiah Willard Gibbs: The History of a Great Mind* (New Haven, 1951), p. 57.

20 Ibid., p. 63, 78–79; "Gibbs," *DAB; Newsweek,* June 1951.

21 Wheeler, *Gibbs,* pp. 91–92, 164; *YAW,* 6 February 1907.

22 Stokes, *Memorials,* 2 : 32; Pierson, *Yale, 1871–1921,* p. 702; Gilman, *Life of Dana,* p. 33; "Herrick," *DAB.* There was a large number of groups and societies meeting for a variety of purposes in New Haven throughout the nineteenth century (see, for example, Hadley, *Diary,*

pp. 39–40, 43, 63, 70, 75, 162–63, 226). It seems clear that the character of a man as an individual, a teacher, and a researcher would have been well known very early in his career through his performance before some of these organizations.

23 "Dana," *DAB;* Gilman, *Dana,* pp. 152, 297; Corporation Records, 13 August 1850; *Supplement to the Report of the Treasurer for the Fiscal Year 1969–1970, Funds,* pp. 51–52.

24 Gilman, *Dana,* pp. 287, 310–11; "Dana," *DAB;* George P. Merrill, *The First One Hundred Years of American Geology* (New Haven, 1924), p. 419; For Dana's 1856 call for a university in New Haven, see above, pp. 185–86.

25 "Marsh," *DAB;* Pierson, *Yale, 1871–1921,* p. 52; Schuchert and LeVene, *Marsh,* 100–01, 120, 132–33, 137–38, 348. Schuchert and LeVene call Marsh and his competitor Cope paleontological pirates (p. 264) and note, "It must be written down . . . that the foundation of Yale's great collection of fossil vertebrates was laid by these four student parties" (p. 138). William H. Goetzmann, *Exploration and Empire: The Explorer and the Scientist in the Winning of the American West* (New York, 1966), pp. 427–28; Stokes, *Memorials,* 2 : 72–73.

26 "Marsh," *DAB;* Schuchert and LeVene, *Marsh,* pp. 269, 323, 331–33.

27 "Silliman," *DAB;* Kingsley, *Yale College,* 2 : 81; see also above, pp. 181–83.

28 "Silliman," *DAB.*

29 Gerald T. White, *Scientists in Conflict: The Beginnings of the Oil Industry in California* (San Marino, Calif., 1968), p. 130; Osterweis, *New Haven,* p. 280.

30 The best account of Silliman's problems is in White, *Scientists in Conflict.* One of Silliman's major difficulties was that members of the Yale faculty thought his mining promotions "unbecoming to a man of science" (ibid., p. 99). Marsh apparently ran into faculty disapproval, too. Merrill quotes a letter from J. D. Dana to F. V. Hayden condemning Marsh for his hasty work, which "must make an earnest zoologist in Europe curse American science" (*One Hundred Years of American Geology,* p. 716). That Silliman's reputation never entirely recovered at Yale may be indicated by the failure to include him in Stokes's *Memorials of Eminent Yale Men.*

31 *YAW,* 10 January 1927; "Verrill," *DAB.*

32 On the decline of astronomy at Yale, see David F. Musto, "Yale Astronomy in the Nineteenth Century," *Ventures, Magazine of the Graduate School,* Spring 1968, pp. 7–17; On Loomis and Lyman, see *DAB.*

33 Chittenden, *History of SSS,* 1 : 95–97; "Eaton," *DAB.*

34   Stokes, *Memorials*, 2 : 55–63; "Johnson," *DAB*.
35   "Whitney" and "Salisbury," *DAB;* Edgar S. Furniss, *The Graduate School of Yale: A Brief History* (New Haven, 1965), p. 32.
36   Chittenden, *History of SSS*, 1 : 156–60; O. W. Firkin, *Cyrus Northrop: A Memoir* (Minneapolis, 1925), p. 220; "Lounsbury," *DAB;* Cross, *Connecticut Yankee*, pp. 74, 112; Canby, *Alma Mater*, pp. 94–95, 216–17.
37   Starr, *Sumner*, pp. 163–67.
38   Ibid., pp. 77–78.
39   Cross, *Connecticut Yankee*, p. 70; *YAW*, 25 March 1910; "Sumner," *DAB*.
40   Hawkins, *Pioneer*, p. 87; Morison, *Three Centuries*, p. 381.
41   Hawkins, *Pioneer*, p. 155; Morison, *Three Centuries*, p. 373.
42   Hadley, *Hadley*, pp. 39–40, 45, 52, 56, 60–61.
43   "Williams," *DAB*.
44   William Adams Brown, *A Teacher and His Times: A Story of Two Worlds* (New York, 1940), p. 63; "Ladd," *DAB; Historical Register of Yale University, 1701–1937*, p. 547.
45   Brown, *A Teacher and His Times*, p. 63; Pierson, *Yale, 1871–1921*, pp. 84, 97; "Tarbell," *DAB;* Cross, *Connecticut Yankee*, pp. 71–72.
46   Earnest, *Academic Procession*, p. 148.
47   Pierson, *Yale, 1871–1921*, pp. 60–65.
48   See above, pp. 199–200. Dwight, *Memories*, p. 350.
49   Bainton, *Yale and the Ministry*, pp. 164–65; Kingsley, Yale College, 2 : 54; Steiner, *History of Education in Connecticut*, pp. 213–14; Chamberlain, *Universities and Their Sons*, pp. 309–10; *Yale College in 1871, Abstract of the Treasurer's Report for the Year Ending May 31, 1871* (New Haven, 1871), pp. 4, 10 (The *Report of the Treasurer* has been published with various titles. It will be cited hereafter as *Treasurer's Report,* with the year the report ends. Thus for 1903–04, the citation would read *1904); Treasurer's Report, 1886*, p. 18; Deming, *Yale Yesterdays*, p. 181.
50   Chamberlain, *Universities and Their Sons*, pp. 317–20; Welch and Camp, *Yale*, pp. 265–66, 416; Bell, "The Medical Institution of Yale College, 1810–1885," pp. 175, 179–181, *Catalogue of the Officers and Graduates of Yale University, 1701–1924*, p. 496; Steiner, *History of Education in Connecticut*, p. 213; *Yale College. The Needs of the University*, pp. 20 ff.; *Treasurer's Report, 1871*, pp. 2–10; *Treasurer's Report, 1886*, p. 25.
51   Hicks, *Yale Law School, 1845–1869*, pp. 36–37, 42–43; idem, *Yale Law School: 1869–1894 Including the County Court House Period*, Yale Law Library Publication no. 4 (April 1937): 8–9, 14.

52 Kingsley, *Yale College,* 2 : 99; Chamberlain, *Universities and Their Sons,* p. 323; Hicks, *Yale Law School, 1845–1869,* p. 43; idem, *Yale Law School, 1869–1894,* p. 11.

53 Hicks, *Yale Law School, 1869–1894,* pp. 3, 8–9, 11, 50, 53, 57; *Catalogue of Officers and Students, 1871–1872,* p. 13.

54 Chamberlain, *Universities and Their Sons,* p. 327; Hicks, *Yale Law School, 1869–1894,* p. 24.

55 Chamberlain, *Universities and Their Sons,* pp. 325–26; Hicks, *Yale Law School, 1869–1894,* pp. 32–35.

56 Furniss, *The Graduate School of Yale,* p. 26.

57 Chamberlain, *Universities and Their Sons,* p. 344.

58 Furniss, *The Graduate School of Yale,* p. 37; Hadley, *Diary,* pp. 126–27; Morison, *Three Centuries,* p. 334; *Historical Register of Yale University, 1701–1937,* p. 23.

59 *Historical Register of Yale University, 1701–1937,* p. 23. Martha Wright, "Ad Eundem Gradum," *AAUP Bulletin* 52, no. 4 (December 1966): 433–36.

60 Morison, *Three Centuries,* pp. 334–35; Rudolph, *American College and University,* pp. 270–71, 335.

61 Camp and Welch, *Yale,* p. 427; Steiner, *History of Education in Connecticut,* p. 212; *Catalogue of the Officers and Graduates of Yale University, 1701–1924,* pp. 453–55; Hawkins, *Pioneer,* p. 286; "Veblen," *DAB;* Osterweis, *New Haven,* p. 229; *Yale College. The Needs of the University,* p. 11.

62 Schuchert and LeVene, *Marsh,* pp. 88, 90, 73–74, 78, 80; Kingsley, *Yale College,* 2 : 178–79.

63 Kingsley, *Yale College,* 2 : 180; Schuchert and LeVene, *Marsh,* p. 90.

64 Musto, "Yale Astronomy in the Nineteenth Century," pp. 13–17; on the Hillhouse and Winchester gifts, see above, p. 206; Chamberlain, *Universities and Their Sons,* p. 364; Welch and Camp, *Yale,* p. 379.

65 Welch and Camp, *Yale,* p. 379.

66 Kingsley, *Yale College,* 2 : 144–45; Welch and Camp, *Yale,* p. 278; Pierson, *Yale, 1871–1921,* p. 63; "Street," *DAB.*

67 Cross, *Connecticut Yankee,* p. 110; Pierson, *Yale, 1871–1921,* p. 67; Starr, *Sumner,* p. 333; Steiner, *History of Education in Connecticut,* p. 215.

68 Chittenden, *History of SSS,* 1 : 123–24, 133–34, 196.

69 Hadley, *Hadley,* p. 149; Chittenden, *History of SSS,* 1 : 166 ff.; Pierson, *Yale, 1871–1921,* p. 64.

70 Chittenden, *History of SSS,* 1 : 177–78, 182.

71 Ibid., p. 207.

72   Ibid., pp. 209–213.

73   Ibid.; Curti, *Philanthropy*, pp. 72–73.

74   Veysey, *The Emergence of the American University*, p. 86; Rudolph, *American College and University*, p. 268; Chittenden, *History of SSS*, 1 : 142, 188, 150, 163–64; Welch and Camp, *Yale*, pp. 250–52; *Catalogue of the Officers and Students, 1870–1871*, p. 62; *Biographical Sketches and Letters of T. Mitchell Prudden, M.D.* (New Haven, 1927), pp. 12–13.

75   *Catalogue of Officers and Students, 1870–1871*, pp. 62, 65–66.

76   Camp and Welch, *Yale*, p. 254.

77   Pierson, *Yale, 1871–1921*, p. 37.

78   "Report of the Professor of Rhetoric and Oratory" [1818](MS, Yale University Library).

79   On the problems of the old curriculum, see Veysey, *The Emergence of the American University*, especially pp. 21–56; Rudolph, *American College and University*, pp. 287–306; George W. Pierson, "The Elective System and the Difficulties of College Planning, 1870–1940," *Journal of General Education* 4, no. 3 (April 1950): 165–74; idem, *Yale, 1871–1921*, pp. 66–73.

80   Morison, *Three Centuries*, p. 365; *Catalogue of Officers and Graduates of Yale University, 1701–1924*, pp. 211, 228, 350, 355; Pierson, *Yale, 1871–1921*, pp. 722–23.

81   Wertenbaker, *Princeton*, p. 304; Starr, *Sumner*, p. 340; Dexter, "Reminiscences of the Officers of Yale College in 1857," *Selected Papers*, p. 313; Pierson, *Yale, 1871–1921*, p. 44.

82   Pierson, *Yale, 1871–1921*, pp. 80–82.

83   William Graham Sumner, "Our Colleges Before the Country," *War and Other Essays* (New Haven, 1911), pp. 355–73.

84   Pierson, *Yale, 1871–1921*, pp. 80–81; Starr, *Sumner*, p. 342.

85   Pierson, *Yale, 1871–1921*, p. 82; Noah Porter, "Greek and a Liberal Education," *Princeton Review* 60, ser. 2 (September 1884) : 193–218.

86   Hadley, *Diary*, p. 272; William Lyon Phelps, *Autobiography with Letters* (New York, 1939), pp. 282–83; Poultney Bigelow, "Personal Notes Among Our Universities," *The Independent* 54 (January–March 1902): 672–73; Cross, *Connecticut Yankee*, p. 66; Bagg, *Four Years at Yale*, pp. 627–47; Pierson, *Yale, 1871–1921*, pp. 233–34; Veysey, *The Emergence of the American University*, p. 299; Harlow Gale, "A Yale Education Versus Culture," *Pedagogical Seminary* 9 (1902): 3–17.

87   Cross, *Connecticut Yankee*, p. 65.

88   Starr, *Sumner*, pp. 346 ff; Walter P. Metzger, *Academic Freedom in the Age of the University* (New York, 1955), p. 63. There was, however, censorship of entire courses; see p. 284.

89 Dwight, *Memories*, pp. 351, 348, 345–46; *The Buildings of Yale* (1965), p. 92; Steiner, *History of Education in Connecticut*, p. 205; *Treasurer's Report, 1886*, pp. 1–28. I compute from this treasurer's report that total funds amounted to $2,203,721.33. Nettleton, *The Book of the Yale Pageant*, p. 133, puts the figure in 1886–87 at $2,990,000, producing an income of $341,000. Pierson says that Dwight gave the figure as just over $2 million, producing an income of $263,000 (*Yale, 1871–1921*, p. 96).

90 Dwight, *Memories*, p. 353; Rudolph, *American College and University*, pp. 264 ff.; Veysey, *The Emergence of the American University*, pp. 1–2.

91 Dexter, "Reminiscences of the Officers of Yale College in 1857," *Selected Papers*, p. 312.

92 Woolsey, *An Historical Discourse*, p. 118; Schuchert and LeVene, *Marsh*, p. 63; Stokes, *Memorials*, 1 : 333.

CHAPTER 14

1 Pierson, *Yale, 1871–1921*, pp. 61–62.

2 Jackson, *Simeon Eben Baldwin*, pp. 96–102 (see p. 99 for passage from *The Nation*); for an opposition argument, see E. M. Bliss, "The Charter of Yale College: The Import and Reach of Its Several Changes," *New Englander*, May 1882, pp. 325–64.

3 "Dwight," *DAB*; Holden, *Profiles and Portraits of Yale University Presidents*, pp. 53–61; Dwight, *Memories*, pp. 107–08; Bainton, *Yale and the Ministry*, p. 175.

4 Dwight, "Yale College—Some Thoughts Respecting its Future," *New Englander*, July 1870–October 1871.

5 Hadley, *Hadley*, pp. 104–05; Pierson, *Yale, 1871–1921*, p. 597.

6 Porter thought changing the name was the "outgrowth of materialistic tendencies," Veysey, *The Emergence of the American University*, p. 51; Steiner, *History of Education in Connecticut*, p. 224; *President's Report, 1887*, p. 9. Porter came to Sheffield board meetings only three times—once to discuss the students' attendance at morning chapel and twice to report on the activities of some Sheff students involved in a riot, Chittenden, *History of SSS*, 2: 300; Pierson, *Yale, 1871–1921*, pp. 65, 96–97.

The *Report of the President of Yale University* first appeared in 1887. It has been published under various titles ever since. Under whatever title, it will be cited hereafter as *President's Report*. For the years 1889 to 1899 the reports covered the academic year. The date I give is, in the case of the academic year, the year the report ends. Thus a report on 1903–04 will be cited as *1904*. From 1899 through 1923–24 the reports of the deans were published with the president's report. If the report of a dean is referred to, the footnote will still read *President's Report,* and the year.

7 Pierson, *Yale, 1871–1921,* p. 65; Dwight, "Yale College," *New Englander,* July 1870, pp. 462–63; *YAW,* 18 June 1909; Wright began, in 1884, as administrative officer for the junior and senior classes; the office of dean was recognized in the catalogue of 1885 but the title Dean of the College Faculty did not appear on the list of officers of the university until 1891; *President's Report, 1904,* pp. 77–80; Arthur Twining Hadley, "His [Henry P. Wright's] Contribution to the University," *YAW,* 5 July 1918.

8 Steiner, *History of Education in Connecticut,* pp. 223–26; Pierson, *Yale, 1871–1921,* p. 97; Cross, *Connecticut Yankee,* pp. 71–72; Phelps, *Autobiography,* p. 142; Phelps also said (p. 141) that Tarbell was too independent.

9 Dwight, *Memories,* pp. 374–75; *President's Report, 1887,* p. 11; Pierson, *Yale, 1871–1921,* p. 96; Dwight, "Yale College," *New Englander,* July 1870, pp. 457–58.

10 *President's Report, 1887,* p. 16; Steiner, *History of Education in Connecticut,* p. 224; Pierson, *Yale, 1871–1921,* p. 96; *Treasurer's Report, 1899,* pp. 1, 7.

11 Pierson, *Yale, 1871–1921,* pp. 62–63.

12 *Historical Register of Yale University, 1701–1937,* p. 24; Curti, *Philanthropy,* pp. 201–02; *Yale Alumni Fund Annual Report, 1965–1966* ([New Haven, 1966]), p. 55. On the beginning of the fund, see George C. Holt, "The Origin of the Alumni Fund," *YAW,* 2 February 1917.

13 *The Buildings of Yale University* (1965), pp. 91–93; *President's Report, 1896,* p. 95.

14 Curti, *Philanthropy,* p. 191; Pierson, *Yale, 1871–1921,* pp. 30, 583; Steven Vincent Benét, *The Beginning of Wisdom* (New York, 1921), p. 64; Welch and Camp, *Yale,* pp. 27–33.

15 Dwight, "Yale College," *New Englander,* October 1871, pp. 639–45; *President's Report, 1896,* p. 8; Pierson, *Yale, 1871–1921,* p. 31.

16 *President's Report, 1896,* p. 95; Canby, *Alma Mater,* p. 4; *President's Report, 1898,* p. 11; *YAW,* 12 January 1899; Supreme Court of Errors, Third Judicial District, October Term, 1898, *Yale University Appellant* vs *The Town of New Haven, Appellee. Brief and Argument on Behalf of the Appellant.*

17 Irwin G. Wyllie, *The Self-Made Man in America* (New Brunswick, N.J., 1954), pp. 102–03; Steiner, *History of Education in Connecti-*

cut, p. 194; as Steiner notes, the students were also older, the average age at entrance being considerably after the eighteenth birthday; Dwight, *Memories,* pp. 60–61; Thwing, *Higher Education,* p. 264; Welch and Camp, *Yale,* p. 244; *YAW,* 8 December 1898, reports that the steady rise of business began with the class of 1839. It rose most rapidly in the late 1840s, during the Civil War, and in the 1870s, but though it became the second most popular career selection (after law) during the Civil War, it still had not displaced law in 1898.

18 Wyllie, *The Self-Made Man,* pp. 95, 106, 107.

19 Welch and Camp, *Yale,* p. 445.

20 Dwight, "Yale College," *New Englander,* October 1870, p. 611, July 1871: 508; Dwight, *Memories,* pp. 213–14.

21 Hadley, *Hadley,* pp. 60–61, 68, 72, 76–77; *Historical Register of Yale University, 1701–1937,* p. 290.

22 Stokes, *Memorials,* 1 : 282–83 (Harper is the only one of the "Eminent Yale Men" Stokes wrote about who never attended Yale College); Phelps, *Autobiography,* p. 277; Richard J. Storr, *Harper's University: The Beginnings* (Chicago, 1966), pp. 19–27, 74–76; Pierson, *Yale, 1871–1921,* pp. 98–99; Rudolph, *American College and University,* p. 350. It may be significant that Dwight makes no mention of Harper in his memoirs.

23 Pierson, *Yale, 1871–1921,* p. 135; Phelps, *Autobiography,* pp. 281–84, 287–89.

24 *YAW,* 5 July 1918.

25 Pierson, *Yale, 1871–1921,* p. 606.

26 Dwight, "Yale College," *New Englander,* October 1870, pp. 603–13; Nettleton, *The Book of the Yale Pageant,* pp. 145–46; Welch and Camp, *Yale,* p. 293, note that the listing of courses was "then more informal, and the courses were often modified greatly to meet the needs of the . . . students."

27 Chamberlain, *Universities and Their Sons,* p. 344; Hadley, *Hadley,* p. 79; Cross, *Connecticut Yankee,* p. 154; Furniss, *The Yale Graduate School,* p. 39.

28 Furniss, *The Yale Graduate School,* p. 39; Steiner, *History of Education in Connecticut,* p. 227; Arthur T. Hadley, "Yale," *Four American Universities: Harvard, Yale, Princeton, Columbia* (New York, 1895), p. 73. Information on the first women graduate students was taken from *Yale University Doctors of Philosophy, 1861–1960* (New Haven, 1961). Though names are not always a clear indication of sex, I believe my computations are more than 99 percent correct.

29 Welch and Camp, *Yale,* p. 293; Cross, *Connecticut Yankee,* p. 154; Nettleton, *The Book of the Yale Pageant,* pp. 145–46.

30   The problems of Phelps are retailed in his *Autobiography*, pp. 298–302, and those of Cross in *Connecticut Yankee*, pp. 116–17.

31   Welch and Camp, *Yale*, p. 295; "University Topics," *New Englander*, July 1887, pp. 60–61; see also Hadley, "Yale," p. 68.

32   Hadley, "Yale," p. 55; Dwight, "Yale College," *New Englander*, April 1871, p. 316. Dwight did recognize the disadvantages but noted that New Haven was growing rapidly (ibid., pp. 327–28). He also thought Connecticut's lack of large cities and men of great wealth helped to promote democracy and "plain living" at Yale (*Memories*, pp. 55–56). On the dispute over city versus country colleges, see Rudolph, *American College and University*, pp. 93–94 (where, by the post–Civil War period, Yale is described as urban compared to Dartmouth); and Beverly McAnear, "The Selection of an Alma Mater by Pre-Revolutionary Students," *Pennsylvania Magazine of History and Biography*, October 1949, pp. 437–38.

33   A majority of the Law School's professors were still judges or practicing lawyers. Welch and Camp, *Yale*, p. 272; *Treasurer's Report, 1899*, p. 1; *Yale College, Needs of the University*, pp. 17 ff.; Steiner, *History of Education in Connecticut*, p. 233; Hicks, *Yale Law School, 1869–1894*, p. 60; Chamberlain, *Universities and Their Sons*, pp. 323–24; *President's Report, 1900*, p. 67, *1901*, p. 93; Frederick C. Hicks, *Yale Law School, 1895–1915: Twenty Years of Hendrie Hall*, Yale Law Library Publication no. 7 (September 1938), pp. 22–23; "Obituary of Dean Wayland," *YAW*, 13 January 1904.

34   Hicks, *Yale Law School: 1895–1915*, pp. 36–37; Welch and Camp, *Yale*, p. 428. The drop in enrollment was not large, but it helps to explain the appointment on 21 June 1898 of a Law School committee to confer with Dwight and the Yale College faculty "with reference to ways and means to control the increasing annual exodus of Yale graduates to Harvard Law School" (Hicks, *Yale Law School, 1895–1915*, p. 40).

35   Chamberlain, *Universities and Their Sons*, p. 326; Hicks, *Yale Law School, 1869–1894*, pp. 28–35.

36   Chamberlain, *Universities and Their Sons*, p. 319; Welch and Camp, *Yale*, pp. 427–28; Yandell Henderson, "The Yale Medical School," *YAW*, 13 February 1907; *President's Report, 1900*, p. 63.

37   Dwight, "Yale College," *New Englander*, October 1871, p. 638; *Treasurer's Report, 1899*, p. 1; Steiner, *History of Education in Connecticut*, p. 234; Welch and Camp, *Yale*, pp. 281, 427–28.

38   Welch and Camp, *Yale*, pp. 283–90; Chamberlain, *Universities and Their Sons*, pp. 366–67; *Treasurer's Report, 1899*, p. 1.

39   Musto, "Yale Astronomy in the Nineteenth Century," p. 17; Deming,

Yale Yesterdays, p. 118; Chamberlain, *Universities and Their Sons,* p. 366.

40 *President's Report, 1900,* p. 92; *YAW,* 6 December 1905. Among other things, Marsh (with F. W. Stevens) gave Yale a fine collection of 4,500 volumes of Japanese literature. Marsh spent about $200,000 on his collections between 1868 and 1882 (Schuchert and LeVene, *Marsh,* pp. 352, 269; Welch and Camp, *Yale,* p. 385).

41 Hadley, "Yale," pp. 63–64.

42 Chittenden, *History of SSS,* 2 : 300–01, 1 : 255–60; *President's Report, 1887,* p. 26.

43 Chittenden, *History of SSS,* 1 : 251–52.

44 Hadley, "Yale," pp. 56, 60; Chittenden, *History of SSS,* 1 : 144, 228.

45 Chittenden, *History of SSS,* 1 : 228, 232.

46 Ibid., pp. 268–69, 199–203, 229–34.

47 Ibid., pp. 235, 267–70.

48 Ibid., pp. 269–74.

49 *President's Report, 1887,* pp. 27–28; Chittenden, *History of SSS,* 2 : 487; Steiner, *History of Education in Connecticut,* p. 231; *Treasurer's Report, 1899;* Pierson, *Yale, 1871–1921,* pp. 201–07.

50 Chittenden, *History of SSS,* 1 : 301. Dwight had given Yale more than $100,000 by the time he retired (Welch and Camp, *Yale,* p. xxii).

51 Dwight, "Yale College," *New Englander,* October 1871, p. 637; Welch and Camp, *Yale,* p. 387; *President's Report, 1887,* p. 16; "Chittenden," *DAB.*

52 Chamberlain, *Universities and Their Sons,* p. 373–74; *President's Report, 1887,* p. 45; J. R. Prentice, "Yale Library," (MS, Yale University Library), vol. 1, "Chittenden Library," quoting *Yale Daily News,* 22 March 1889, 7 April 1891, 11 October 1895, 3 December 1895; Hicks, *Yale Law School, 1895–1915,* p. 11. Like many "partial" buildings at Yale—such as the first Peabody Museum, the 1928 Art Gallery, and Dunham Laboratory—the building was never completed according to the original plans. If it had been finished, the old library (now Dwight Hall) would have been destroyed.

53 Chamberlain, *Universities and Their Sons,* p. 376; W. W. Phelps was a classmate of O. C. Marsh and had married J. E. Sheffield's daughter (Schuchert and LeVene, *Marsh,* p. 147); *President's Report, 1896,* pp. 86–87.

54 *Treasurer's Report, 1899; The Buildings of Yale* (1965), pp. 92–93; Morison, *Three Centuries,* p. 389; *President's Report, 1887,* p. 23; Steiner, *History of Education in Connecticut,* p. 196; Hadley, "Yale," p. 79.

55 Pierson, *Yale, 1871–1921*, pp. 83–88, 208, 708. In what appears to be a misprint, Pierson actually says it was the first time since "1710" that physics could be avoided.

56 Ibid., pp. 83–84, 321–22; *President's Report, 1896* p. 36.

57 Pierson, *Yale, 1871–1921*, pp. 212–13.

58 Chamberlain, *Universities and Their Sons*, p. 300; Chittenden, *History of SSS*, 2 : 504–05.

59 *Yale Daily News*, 5, 19, 21 April 1898.

60 Chamberlain, *Universities and Their Sons*, pp. 438–39.

61 Welch and Camp, *Yale*, pp. 161–67.

62 *President's Report, 1898, with supplement for 1899 January to June*, p. 7.

63 Pierson, *Yale, 1871–1921*, p. 98.

64 Ibid., pp. 65, 96–106; see, for example, Slosson, *Great American Universities*, pp. 36–72, 523.

CHAPTER 15

1 Pierson, *Yale, 1871–1921*, p. 256.

2 Beers, *The Ways of Yale*, p. 12.

3 Owen Johnson, *Stover at Yale* (New York, 1912), pp. 242–44.

4 Pierson, *Yale, 1871–1921*, pp. 100–01, 103–04; for the new students, see above, pp. 279–80.

5 Bagg, *Four Years at Yale*, p. 314; Dulles, *America Learns to Play*, p. 189; Welch and Camp, *Yale*, p. 551. There were organized urban clubs and playing schedules even before the war according to Harvey Wish, *Society and Thought in Modern America* (New York, 1952), p. 277.

6 Deming, *Yale Yesterdays*, p. 197.

7 Kingsley, *Yale College*, 2 : 373; John M. Stevenson says the Yale and Harvard classes of 1869 played the first game between the two colleges at the 1866 boat races. Yale won 36 to 33 ("When Baseball Started at Yale," *YAW*, 28 March 1913).

8 Stokes, *Memorials*, 2 : 309; Rudolph, *American College and University*, p. 387; Herman Liebert, "The Story of Yale Blue," *YAM*, October 1951; Bagg, *Four Years at Yale*, pp. 383–84. Liebert dates the appearance of the flag in 1853, but see Harrison B. Freeman's letter to the editor, *YAW*, 9 February 1912, claiming it was given to the Yale Navy on 26 May 1858.

9 Kingsley, *Yale College*, 2 : 430; Patton and Field call baseball "king of intercollegiate sports in the eighties," *Eight O'Clock Chapel*, p.

277. On the old football game, see above, pp. 106–07, 213. See also Faculty Records, 5 October 1859; Peck Diary, 6 October 1864; Deming, *Yale Yesterdays*, pp. 217–18. Hamilton Park, which no longer exists, was on Whalley Avenue near Edgewood Park.

10 Kingsley, *Yale College*, 2 : 445; Deming, *Yale Yesterdays*, p. 218; Welch and Camp, *Yale*, p. 514; Tim Cohane, *The Yale Football Story* (New York, 1951), pp. 18–20, 21–22; Welch and Camp, *Yale*, p. 515.

11 Cohane, *Yale Football*, pp. 21–24, 27, 34; "Camp," *DAB;* Harford Powel, Jr., *Walter Camp, The Father of American Football: An Authorized Biography* (Boston, 1926), p. 110.

12 Brown, *A Teacher and His Times*, p. 61; *YAW*, 14 January 1916; Powel, *Camp*, pp. 89–90, 110; Cohane, *Yale Football*, pp. 58–60. Welch and Camp, *Yale*, pp. 455–56, say that one man was always unofficially but completely in charge.

13 Powel, *Camp*, p. 88; Welch and Camp, *Yale*, pp. 540–45; Cohane, *Yale Football*, lists all team members 1872–1950 and has much information on the "greats."

14 Cohane, *Yale Football*, p. 179; Pierson, *Yale, 1871–1921*, p. 347; *YAW*, 24 December 1909, 4 February 1910.

15 Cohane, *Yale Football*, pp. 181–82, 189–92, 195; *YAW*, 11 November 1897, 16 June 1916. In 1927, football gate receipts reached $1 million (*YAW*, 3 February 1928). As early as 29 November 1892 the *YAW* criticized professionalism and especially the tendency of Yale men to go elsewhere and coach for a salary: "We do not mean to say that the game should be restricted, but that other teams should gain their knowledge through contests on the field or through their own inventions, but not by a *purchase* from a Yale graduate of what has been entrusted to him for the benefit of his *alma mater.*"

16 Welch and Camp, *Yale*, pp. 495–96, 562–70, 577; Pierson, *Yale, 1871–1921*, p. 34; *YAW*, 15 January 1926.

17 Pierson, *Yale, 1871–1921*, 240–41, 348; Welch and Camp, *Yale*, p. 452; D. W. Learned, " 'Lits' and 'Pops' of Fifty Years Ago," *YAW*, 5 January 1917; Kingsley, *Yale College*, 1 : 327.

18 Veysey, *The Emergence of the American University*, p. 281; Gabriel, *Religion and Learning at Yale*, pp. 189–90.

19 Gabriel, *Religion and Learning at Yale*, pp. 191–92, 202, 203; Reuben Holden, *Yale-in-China: The Mainland, 1901–1951* (New Haven, 1964), p. 4.

20 Gabriel, *Religion and Learning at Yale*, pp. 203–06.

21 Ibid., pp. 177–78, 199, 202.

22 Pierson, *Yale, 1871–1921*, pp. 13–14; Welch and Camp, *Yale*, pp.

60–61; Holden, *Yale-in-China,* pp. 6–43; Gabriel, *Religion and Learning at Yale,* p. 201.

23 Chamberlain, *Universities and Their Sons,* p. 438; General Joseph C. Jackson, "Educational Spirit as Viewed by an American Graduate," *YAW,* 19 November 1909.

24 Bagg, *Four Years at Yale,* p. 521; Steiner, *History of Education in Connecticut,* p. 219; and see p. 193.

25 Pierson, *Yale, 1871–1921,* p. 36; *YAW,* 29 May 1907; "A Graduate of the Seventies" to the editor, *YAW,* 24 June 1905; Chamberlain, *Universities and Their Sons,* p. 435; Hadley, "Yale," p. 83; cf. Johnson, *Stover at Yale,* pp. 373–74. In 1901 Hadley said that the college was now so large the societies could no longer reward all kinds of prominence. "They will fall into their true function as clubs for mutual improvement rather than as prizes for remorseless competition" (*President's Report, 1901,* p. 8).

26 Norris G. Osborne, "The Moriarity's of Yale," *YAW,* 3 March 1911; Elmer P. Howe to Col. Norris G. Osborne, *YAW,* 7 July 1911; *YAW,* 13 March 1898; *YAM,* June 1948.

27 *YAW,* 24 May 1899, 16 May 1900; Pierson, *Yale, 1871–1921,* p. 236. Pierson puts Thermopylae in Phelps gateway, where it may have moved later.

28 Pierson, *Yale, 1871–1921,* p. 350–51; Steiner, *History of Education in Connecticut,* p. 198; John Chester Grenville, "An Englishman at Yale in '69," *YAW,* 15 December 1911; Veysey, *The Emergence of the American University,* pp. 277–78. See for example *YAW,* 6 February 1894, for the events of prom week: 29 January, glee club and banjo concert, sophomore German and junior German; 30 January, junior German; 31 January, junior promenade.

29 Loomis Havemeyer, *Sheff Days and Ways: Undergraduate Activities in the Sheffield Scientific School Yale University, 1847–1945* [New Haven?, 1958?], pp. 53–62; idem, *"Go to your Room": A Story of Undergraduate Societies and Fraternities at Yale* ([New Haven?], 1960), pp. 73–77.

30 George Santayana, *The Middle Span* (New York, 1945), p. 175; idem, "A Glimpse of Yale," *The Harvard Monthly* 15, no. 3 (December 1882): 89–97.

31 Pierson, *Yale, 1871–1921,* pp. 232–42; Welch and Camp, *Yale,* pp. 154, 427–28; *YAW,* 6 December 1905; "Is Yale a Rich Men's College," *Yale Review,* August 1894, pp. 117–20; Steiner, *History of Education in Connecticut,* p. 219. College Register, 2 : 471–73 (Corporation minutes, 26 July 1859) notes that more than half the students lived off campus. Total enrollment rose from 1,076 in 1885–86 to

2,511 in 1898–99. In the same period the college increased from 563 to 1,224.

32 Johnson, *Stover at Yale,* pp. 28, 27, 29, 68, 79, 182, 198.

33 "Is Yale a Rich Men's College," pp. 117–20; Dwight, *Memories,* pp. 57–60.

34 *YAW,* 9 December 1910, 12 November 1909, 15 November 1912, Pierson, *Yale, 1871–1921,* pp. 412–13.

35 Pierson, *Yale, 1871–1921,* pp. 243–57; Bagg, *Four Years at Yale,* p. 651.

36 Pierson, *Yale, 1871–1921,* p. 346; *The Record of the Celebration of the Two Hundredth Anniversary of the Founding of Yale College, Held at Yale University in New Haven, Connecticut, October the Twentieth to October the Twenty-third, A.D. Nineteen Hundred and One* (New Haven, 1902); Nettleton, *Book of the Yale Pageant;* Stokes, *Memorials,* 1 : 109. William Henry Welch confessed to a friend after being asked to speak on "The Relation of Yale to Medicine" that it was "about the most barren theme which I ever tackled. The relation is so slight that I shall have to beat around the bush and talk on side issues. If they had only asked me to talk on the Relation of Yale to Calvinism or Football there would have been something to say" (Flexner and Flexner, *William Henry Welch,* p. 58).

37 Pierson, *Yale, 1871–1921,* p. 347.

38 Ibid., pp. 347–67.

39 Wilmarth Sheldon Lewis, *One Man's Education* (New York, 1967), pp. 94–95.

40 Pierson, *Yale, 1871–1921,* p. 348.

CHAPTER 16

1 *YAW,* 12 March 1909; Hadley, *Hadley,* pp. 105–06. *YAW,* 7 June 1899, says the Corporation also considered Henry W. Farnam, Bernadotte Perrin, Theodore S. Woolsey, Henry P. Wright, Simeon E. Baldwin, E. B. Coe, and George E. Vincent.

2 Hadley, *Hadley,* pp. 106–07.

3 Ibid., pp. 107–09.

4 "James Hadley," *DAB;* Hadley, *Hadley,* pp. 11 ff.

5 Hadley, *Hadley,* pp. 69–73; Pierson, *Yale, 1871–1921,* p. 111; Burton J. Hendrick, "President Hadley," *World's Work,* June 1914, pp. 141–48.

6 Hadley, *Hadley,* pp. 69, 73–74, 134, 184. Morris Hadley says that while he does not believe the streetcar story is true, it is "inherently plausible."

7   Pierson, *Yale, 1871–1921*, pp. 110, 113; Cross, *Connecticut Yankee*, p. 142.

8   Hadley, *Hadley*, p. 101.

9   *President's Report, 1898, with supplement*, p. 136, and see chap. 14 above.

10 *President's Report, 1897*, pp. 92–112; Hadley, *Hadley*, pp. 114–15.

11 *Record of the Celebration of the Two Hundredth Anniversary*, pp. 378–415; *Yale Daily News*, 23 October 1901; *YAW*, August, n.d., 1901; Hadley, *Hadley*, pp. 118–21.

12 *Record of the Celebration of the Two Hundredth Anniversary*; Wheeler, *Gibbs*, pp. 144, 150, 152.

13 Veysey, *The Emergence of the American University*, pp. 267–68, 306, 311.

14 Pierson, *Yale, 1871–1921*, pp. 129–39; *YAW*, 11 October 1899.

15 *Inauguration of Arthur Twining Hadley, LL.D., as President of Yale University, October Eighteenth A.D. Eighteen Hundred and Ninety-Nine* (New Haven, n.d.), p. 17.

16 *YAW*, 11 October 1899.

17 Brown, *A Teacher and His Times*, p. 277. The habit of analyzing questions from various angles "was called by the younger men of the faculty merely boxing the compass without using the instrument to steer the ship" (Pierson, *Yale, 1871–1921*, pp. 137–39).

18 *YAW*, 11 October 1899; Cross, *Connecticut Yankee*, p. 143.

19 *Inauguration of Arthur Twining Hadley*, pp. 8, 42.

20 Pierson, *Yale, 1871–1921*, p. 121; Brown, *A Teacher and His Times*, pp. 276–77; *YAW*, 14 March 1930.

21 Pierson, *Yale, 1871–1921*, pp. 121, 540; Brown, *A Teacher and His Times*, p. 276; W. W. Farnam to M. C. D. Borden, n.d., printed in *YAW*, 10 May 1940; George W. Pierson, *Yale: The University College, 1921–1937* (New Haven, 1955), p. 5; Hadley, *Hadley*, p. 131.

22 *Treasurer's Report, 1902*, pp. 1–2, *1905*, pp. 1–6, *1907*, pp. 1–2, *1909*, pp. 17–18, *1912*, pp. 12–14, *1913*, pp. 1–2; *YAW*, 19 October 1917.

23 *President's Report, 1902*, p. 4. Woodbridge Hall was so named because it was a gift of his descendants and "not with any claim that the bearer of the name was more helpful and earnest than others" (*Record of the Celebration of the Two Hundredth Anniversary*, p. 421).

24 *President's Report, 1902*, p. 4; *YAW*, 15 January 1915.

25 Pierson, *Yale, 1871–1921*, pp. 61, 100; Hadley, *Hadley*, p. 109; Brown, *A Teacher and His Times*, pp. 274–76. *President's Report, 1919*, p. 49, reveals that Rev. Edwin Pond Parker believed he was largely responsible for changing the makeup of the successor trustees.

26 *YAW,* 17 April 1907; *President's Report, 1909,* p. 117; Pierson, *Yale, 1871–1921,* p. 139.

27 *YAW,* n.d. July 1904, 5 December 1906, 13 November 1907, 30 December 1908; *Historical Register of Yale University, 1701–1937,* p. 25.

28 Hadley, *Hadley,* pp. 171–72; *YAW,* 16 January 1914; *Historical Register of Yale University, 1701–1937* and *Catalogue of Officers and Graduates of Yale University, 1701–1924* both incorrectly date this event in 1913; *YAW,* n.d., July 1905.

29 Hadley, *Hadley,* p. 308.

30 Pierson, *Yale, 1871–1921,* pp. 126, 286; *President's Report, 1898, with supplement,* pp. 42–43; *YAW,* n.d. July 1906; Veysey, *The Emergence of the American University,* pp. 174–75, 151, 153; Slosson, *Great American Universities,* pp. 46–47.

31 Quoted in Pierson, *Yale, 1871–1921,* p. 126.

32 Ibid., pp. 606–07; the retirement rule was to go into effect three years later; between 1906 and 1910 one-third of the entire body of college professors retired, resigned, or died (ibid., p. 276); *YAW,* n.d., July 1906.

33 *YAW,* n.d., July 1906; Pierson, *Yale, 1871–1921,* p. 290; Hadley, *Hadley,* pp. 164–65.

34 *President's Report, 1911,* p. 11; Hadley, *Hadley,* pp. 165–66.

35 Hadley, *Hadley,* p. 164; *YAW,* 23 September 1910.

36 *President's Report, 1910,* pp. 42–43.

37 Pierson, *Yale, 1871–1921,* p. 291; even the first non-Yale appointment had attended Yale for two years (*President's Report, 1907,* pp. 66–70); by 1908 of a total faculty of 134 holding Ph.D. degrees, 30 had no degree from Yale (*YAW,* 4 March 1908).

38 Hadley, *Hadley,* p. 167; Pierson, *Yale, 1871–1921,* pp. 288–89.

39 Slosson, *Great American Universities,* p. 9; *YAW,* 2 December 1910.

40 Slosson, *Great American Universities,* pp. 45–48. On the other hand, Slosson wrote, "no faculty is more fertile of original and progressive ideas, which if taken up and developed, would make it the foremost university of America in many lines" (p. 44).

41 *President's Report, 1902,* pp. 4–5, *1904,* pp. 17–18, *1911,* pp. 50–51.

42 Chittenden, *History of SSS,* 2 : 442; *YAW,* 17 May 1905, n.d. Sept. 1905, 8 July 1910; Pierson, *Yale, 1871–1921,* pp. 369–79.

43 Chittenden, *History of SSS,* 2 : 442–43.

44 Pierson, *Yale, 1871–1921,* pp. 372–76, 656–57.

45 Chittenden, *History of SSS,* 2 : 542, 544–45. In 1919 the *YAW* of 10 January complained that Sheff had been losing money since 1911 and asked how long the university would have to meet these losses.

46   Pierson, *Yale, 1871–1921*, p. 162.

47   George Blumer, "Brief Recollections of the Yale Medical School
     (1906–1920)," *Yale Journal of Biology and Medicine* 21 (1949):
     365–76; Henderson, "Yale Medical School," *YAW*, 13 February 1907;
     President's Report, 1900, p. 63.

48   *President's Report, 1906*, p. 30; *1900*, pp. 61–62, 64–65; *The Build-
     ings of Yale* (1965), p. 21; Pierson, *Yale, 1871–1921*, p. 223.

49   John F. Fulton, "The School of Medicine," *Seventy-Five*, p. 24; Blu-
     mer, "Brief Recollections," p. 370.

50   Blumer, "Brief Recollections," p. 369; *YAW*, 8 October 1909; Had-
     ley, *Hadley*, p. 156; *YAW*, 13 February 1907, 17 June 1910.

51   *The Past, Present, and Future of the Yale Medical School* (New
     Haven, 1915), pp. 29 ff.; *President's Report, 1912*, pp. 23–24.

52   *YAW*, 1 March 1918.

53   Ibid.; *Memorial of the Centennial of the Yale Medical School* (New
     Haven, 1915), pp. 59–60.

54   *YAW*, 1 March 1918, 23 January 1920.

55   *President's Report, 1913*, p. 18; *YAW*, 12 January 1912, 21 February
     1913.

56   Furniss, *The Graduate School of Yale*, p. 42; Cross, *Connecticut Yan-
     kee*, pp. 152, 155.

57   Cross, *Connecticut Yankee*, pp. 152, 156–57; Furniss, *The Graduate
     School of Yale*, pp. 42–43, 47. Strangely, Furniss, who was dean of
     the Graduate School from 1930 to 1950, seems to have thought Cross
     called it Gibbs Hall because he believed Gibbs might have lived
     there.

58   Cross, *Connecticut Yankee*, p. 157.

59   Cross, *Connecticut Yankee*, p. 157; *YAW*, 24 November 1916.

60   *President's Report, 1900*, p. 58; *YAW*, 2 January 1907, 22 March
     1905; Bainton, *Yale and the Ministry*, p. 200.

61   Bainton, *Yale and the Ministry*, pp. 198–204; *YAW*, 27 March 1907.

62   Bainton, *Yale and the Ministry*, pp. 204, 207.

63   Ibid., pp. 203, 206–07; *YAW*, 20 October 1911, 31 May 1912, 24
     April 1914, 5 March 1920.

64   *YAW*, 13 January 1904; "Rogers," *DAB*; Thomas W. Swan, "Yale
     Law School: A Century of Progress Places Yale at the Forefront of
     Legal Education," *YAW*, 1 June 1923; *President's Report, 1904*, p.
     10; Charles P. Sherman, *Academic Adventures* (New Haven, 1944),
     pp. 92–93; Robert Stevens, "Two Cheers for 1870: The American
     Law School," *Perspectives in American History* 5 (1971): 439–40;
     Pierson, *Yale, 1871–1921*, p. 220. Hadley had opposed the require-
     ment of a degree (Hadley, *Hadley*, pp. 158–60).

65 Swan, "Yale Law School"; Stevens, "Two Cheers for 1870," pp. 439–40; Pierson, *Yale, 1871–1921*, p. 221. Many of the faculty were unhappy about having a dean from Harvard. Before the end of Swan's first year, several members of the faculty had resigned. On Alice Rufie Jordan, see Hicks, *Yale Law School, 1869–1894*, pp. 72 ff.

66 *YAW*, 21 March 1900; *President's Report, 1900*, pp. 8, 14, 16; Pierson, *Yale, 1871–1921*, pp. 227–28.

67 *YAW*, 20 February 1907; Gifford Pinchot, "Yale in Forestry," *The Book of the Yale Pageant*, pp. 213–16.

68 *President's Report, 1901*, pp. 3–7; Pierson, *Yale, 1871–1921*, pp. 260–63; Veysey, *The Emergence of the American University*, p. 235.

69 On the liberal culture movement in general, see Veysey, *The Emergence of the American University*, chap. 14.

70 Ibid., p. 233; Pierson, *Yale, 1871–1921*, pp. 207, 377.

71 Quoted in Pierson, *Yale, 1871–1921*, pp. 249–50.

72 *YAW*, 9 April 1903, 26 March 1909, 23 November 1928; Pierson, *Yale, 1871–1921*, p. 250.

73 Pierson, *Yale, 1871–1921*, pp. 263, 218–31; Veysey, *The Emergence of the American University*, p. 236.

74 Pierson, *Yale, 1871–1921*, pp. 341–42, 307, 310–11, 327–38; *YAW*, 10 June, 8 July 1910.

75 Pierson, *Yale, 1871–1921*, pp. 337–38.

76 Ibid., pp. 313–18, 726.

77 Ibid., pp. 313–17.

78 Ibid., pp. 420–26.

79 Ibid., pp. 426–31.

80 Ibid., pp. 392, 404. A list of Yale enrollment by sections, 1900–09 is in *YAW*, 6 January 1909. Part of Jones's speech was published in *YAW*, 26 May 1911.

81 Pierson, *Yale, 1871–1921*, pp. 393–411, 414, 510. Pierson says the alumni were "mollified" by the 1916 decisions (p. 410).

82 Ibid., pp. 417, 428–31.

CHAPTER 17

1 Pierson, *Yale, 1871–1921*, pp. 448, 454; *YAW*, 2 October 1914; *President's Report, 1915*, p. 10.

2 *President's Report, 1915*, p. 76; Pierson, *Yale, 1871–1921*, p. 460.

3 *President's Report, 1915*, pp. 13–16.

4 Pierson, *Yale, 1871–1921*, pp. 457, 460; Hadley, *Hadley*, pp. 202–04; *YAW*, 10 March 1916.

5 Pierson, *Yale, 1871–1921*, pp. 458–59; Hadley, *Hadley*, p. 204; Dean

Acheson, "Range Practice," *YAM*, February 1969, reprinted from *American Heritage*, February 1968.

6   Pierson, *Yale, 1871–1921*, pp. 464–65; Frederick Trubee Davison, "The First Yale Naval Aviation Unit," G. H. Nettleton, ed., *Yale in the World War*, 2 vols. (New Haven, 1925), 1 : 433–36; *YAW*, 14 April 1916; Phelps, *Autobiography*, pp. 642–43.

7   Pierson, *Yale, 1871–1921*, p. 461–63; Hadley, *Hadley*, p. 205.

8   *YAW*, 19 January 1917; Pierson, *Yale, 1871–1921*, p. 463.

9   *YAW*, 9 March 1917.

10 Pierson, *Yale, 1871–1921*, pp. 456–66.

11 Ralph D. Paine, *The First Yale Unit: A Story of Naval Aviation, 1916–1919*, 2 vols. (Cambridge, Mass., 1925), 1 : 34; *YAW*, 13 April 1917, 30 March 1917, 20 April 1917; John Jay Schieffelin, "The Second Yale Naval Aviation Unit," *Yale in the World War*, 1 : 449; Davison, "The First Yale Naval Aviation Unit," p. 447.

12 Pierson, *Yale, 1871–1921*, p. 467; *YAW*, 20 April 1917.

13 *YAW*, 20 April 1917; George Jenks Shively, "The Yale Ambulance Unit [S.S.U. 585]," *Yale in the World War*, 1 : 455.

14 Joseph Marshall Flint, "The Yale Mobile Hospital Unit," *Yale in the World War*, 1 : 437, 440.

15 Pierson, *Yale, 1871–1921*, pp. 468–70.

16 *YAW*, 5 October 1917; E. B. Reed, "The Yale Today," *YAW*, 23 November 1917; Pierson, *Yale, 1871–1921*, p. 471.

17 Pierson, *Yale, 1871–1921*, p. 471; *YAW*, 15 February 1918.

18 Pierson, *Yale, 1871–1921*, pp. 472–73.

19 *YAW*, 11 October 1918.

20 W. A. Brown, "Yale's Educational Contribution to the War," *Yale in the World War*, 1 : 395; Lt. Col. Charles Franklin Craig, "The Yale Army Laboratory School," ibid., pp. 469 ff.; Frank Pell Underhill, "The Yale Chemical Warfare Unit," ibid., pp. 459 ff.; *YAW*, 21 December 1934.

21 Harold Veatch Bozell, "The Yale Signal Corps School for Officer Candidates," ibid., pp. 463 ff.

22 Hadley, "Yale's War-Time Contributions," *YAW*, 1 March 1918.

23 Nettleton, *Yale in the World War*, 2 : vii, xi.

24 On the conversion of the universities to war, see Pierson, *Yale, 1871–1921*, pp. 435–46; Hadley, *Hadley*, p. 211. *President's Report, 1913*, p. 72, gives alumni fund contributions from 1891 through 1912. The best year prior to the war had been 1911, when $132,000 was given. *YAW*, 5 July 1918, 7 January 1916; *Treasurer's Report, 1919*, pp. 2, 8.

25 *President's Report, 1919*, p. 24; *YAW*, 23 March 1917, 6 April 1917,

19 March 1920. For the return on the investment in dormitories, see *Treasurer's Report, 1909*, p. 11.

26 Pierson, *Yale, 1871–1921*, pp. 475, 479–80; *YAW*, 19 April 1918, 8 July 1908; *President's Report, 1918*, p. 22, *1912*, pp. 15–16, *1914*, p. 24.

27 Pierson, *Yale, 1871–1921*, pp. 385, 480–82; Samuel H. Fisher, "The Alumni Committee," *YAW*, 2 January 1920.

28 *President's Report, 1918*, p. 52.

29 *YAW*, 23 August 1918; Pierson, *Yale, 1871–1921*, p. 480.

30 *YAW*, 22 November 1918; Pierson, *Yale, 1871–1921*, p. 482.

31 Pierson, *Yale, 1871–1921*, pp. 483–84.

32 *YAW*, 20 December 1918.

33 Brown, *A Teacher and His Times*, p. 278.

34 Pierson, *Yale, 1871–1921*, p. 278; *YAW*, 24 January 1919, 7 March 1919; Chittenden, *History of SSS*, 2 : 574–75; *Report of the Committee on Educational Policy to the Yale Corporation, March 17, 1919* (New Haven, 1919).

35 Chittenden, *History of SSS*, 2 : 575–80; *YAW*, 7 March 1919.

36 *YAW*, 28 February 1919; Pierson, *Yale, 1871–1921*, p. 485. Bushnell made it clear that the alumni were tired of paying off deficits.

37 *YAW*, 14 March 1930; Hadley, *Hadley*, pp. 212–13; *YAW*, 28 February 1919.

38 *YAW*, 7 March 1919. According to Pierson, Hadley's summer work suggestion brought down on him alumni, deans, and faculty, all together. "So Mr. Hadley 'came around' and Reorganization was pushed forward again, regardless of its inevitable cost" (*Yale, 1871–1921*, p. 489).

39 *Report of the Committee on Educational Policy*, pp. 9–10.

40 Ibid., pp. 10–11; *Memorandum for Alumni Committee of Corporation Committee's Reasons for Disagreeing with Some of the Former's Recommendations* (New Haven, 1919). At least one professor approved the alumni's idea of a chancellor. In a letter to *YAW*, 7 March 1919, B. B. Boltwood said, "To have a single official, namely the Chancellor, whose sole duty would be to promote and supervise the educational interests of the university, would seem to offer advantages so great as to require no further emphasis. The last matter which is given serious consideration in Yale University (so far as I can discover from my own observation) is the determination of a definite educational policy with a clear aim in view and a comprehensive plan for its accomplishment."

41 Pierson, *Yale, 1871–1921*, p. 499; *Report of the Committee on Educational Policy*, p. 11. The report, in what appears to be a deliberate

slap, referred to the Yale College faculty meeting as an "informal meeting."

42 *Report of the Committee on Educational Policy,* pp. 15, 25.

43 Pierson, *Yale, 1871–1921,* pp. 491, 487; Chittenden, *History of SSS,* 2 : 568–69.

44 Brown, *A Teacher and His Times,* pp. 273–81; Pierson, *Yale, 1871–1921,* pp. 385, 483.

45 Hadley, *Hadley,* pp. 216–20; *YAW,* 16 April 1920; *The Buildings of Yale* (1965), pp. 93–95; *YAW,* 10 June 1921.

Chapter 18

1 Brown, *A Teacher and His Times,* p. 391; Pierson, *Yale, 1921–1937,* p. 3.

2 Pierson, *Yale, 1921–1937,* pp. 4–6; idem, *Yale, 1871–1921,* p. 676.

3 Pierson, *Yale, 1921–1937,* pp. 3–15, covers this complicated election in a most thorough and interesting fashion.

4 As with the election campaign—and so much of this period of Yale's history—I am indebted to the work of George W. Pierson for this analysis. See ibid., pp. 16–29, 164–65. Professor Pierson does not draw the parallel, but it is interesting to note a certain similarity between Angell *père et fils* in their unwillingness to push things. The *DAB* notes of James B. Angell, "He was not a dictator, because he was not an egotist. He never sought to impose a policy upon his faculty, or to make some new departure upon a mere majority vote."

5 Pierson, *Yale, 1921–1937,* pp. 26–29; *YAW,* 8 July 1921.

6 Pierson says the sciences and the graduate and professional schools felt this way because of the election of Angell (*Yale, 1921–1937,* p. 21). I assume they felt the same way after the inaugural address. See ibid., p. 29, for college reaction to the inaugural. Phelps's remark and change is referred to in ibid., p. 20.

7 *President's Report, 1937,* p. 8; *YAW,* 19 March, 9 July 1920; *Treasurer's Report, 1920,* pp. 2, 8, *1921,* p. 9. The problem of keeping the Sterling bequest from stopping other gifts was constantly referred to in the *YAW* from 1918 on. See also Angell's speech to the alumni on Alumni University Day, 22 February 1926, published in *YAW,* 26 February 1926.

8 Pierson, *Yale, 1871–1921,* p. 492; idem, *Yale, 1921–1937,* p. 172. As late as 1926 more than twice as much was spent on Yale College as on any other school. A full 27 percent of the total university income went to the college (*YAW,* 19 November 1926). Angell referred to

the alumni's major concern in his inaugural, printed in *YAW*, 8 July 1921.

9 *President's Report, 1937*, p. 8; Pierson, *Yale, 1921–1937*, pp. 71–75.

10 *YAW*, 8 July 1921.

11 On the development plans, see James G. Rogers III, "James Gamble Rogers—Yale Architect" (American Studies Senior Essay, Yale University, 1968); *Treasurer's Report, 1920*, pp. 33–34; Pierson, *Yale, 1921–1937*, pp. 566, 600; *YAW*, 1 February 1924; *President's Report, 1924*, pp. 27–28; *The Buildings of Yale* (1965), pp. 96–98.

12 *YAW*, 16 November 1928; Pierson, *Yale, 1921–1937*, pp. 208–12, 242.

13 *YAW*, 1 May 1907; Pierson, *Yale, 1921–1937*, pp. 229, 216.

14 Pierson, *Yale, 1921–1937*, pp. 112, 211, 213, 214; *YAW*, 5 December 1924; *The Buildings of Yale* (1965), pp. 6, 20, 36.

15 Pierson, *Yale, 1921–1937*, pp. 215–16.

16 Ibid., pp. 216–17, 233–36; *President's Report, 1926*, pp. 3–4. The campaign was for $20 million, which was pledged (*YAW*, 30 December 1927). A newspaper clipping (in a box of endowment materials in the University Archives) dated 23 December [1927] has an A.P. report that, counting the $20 million as paid in (which of course it was not) Yale with $69,354,737 had drawn $284,828 ahead of Harvard. In fact, by 1931, because of the Depression, only a little less than $17.5 million had been collected (Pierson, *Yale, 1921–1937*, pp. 661).

17 The foregoing discussion of dealings between Harkness and Yale is based on Pierson, *Yale, 1921–1937*, pp. 231–32, 236–45, 252, 506, 592, 595–96.

18 Lewis, *The Yale Collections*, p. 5; Pierson, *Yale, 1921–1937*, pp. 506–08; Angell did say it was only "the *spectacular* Yale" and that the greater growth was inside.

19 *President's Report, 1937*, p. 11.

20 Furniss, *The Graduate School of Yale*, pp. 53–54, 96.

21 Ibid., p. 127.

22 *President's Report, 1928*, p. 14.

23 Furniss, *The Graduate School of Yale*, pp. 66, 96, 99–104. Furniss does not identify the department as sociology, but from the description it seems doubtful it could be any other.

24 Ibid., p. 67; Pierson, *Yale, 1921–1937*, pp. 182–83, 673, 675, 677.

25 Furniss, *The Graduate School of Yale*, p. 108; Pierson, *Yale, 1871–1921*, p. 578. On the improvement in programs and admissions procedures, see Furniss, *The Graduate School of Yale*, pp. 104–08. On some of the more entertaining architectural features of the new Hall of Graduate Studies, see ibid., pp. 69–72.

26 *YAW,* 17 January 1936. *YAW,* 20 April 1934, reported that the
    American Council of Education rated Yale, as an institution for
    study for the Ph.D. degree, as distinguished in fifteen fields and qual-
    ified in ten. Another earlier study is R. M. Hughes et al., *A Study of
    the Graduate Schools of America* (Oxford, Ohio, 1925).

27 For a sympathetic review of education's rocky path at Yale, see Com-
    mittee of the Post-Doctoral Seminar, *The Department of Education
    at Yale University, 1891–1958* (New Haven, 1960). On the attitude of
    Yale professors, see *YAW,* n.d., July, 1904.

28 *Treasurer's Report, 1919,* p. 19, *1921,* pp. 16–17; *YAW,* 2 January
    1920, 23 January 1920; Milton C. Winternitz, "The New Era at the
    Medical School," *YAW,* 12 January 1923.

29 *President's Report, 1920,* p. 27; C.–E. A. Winslow, *Dean Winternitz
    and the Yale School of Medicine* (New Haven, 1935), p. 3.

30 *President's Report,* 1935, p. 15; *Treasurer's Report, 1920,* p. 6; Abra-
    ham Flexner, *I Remember* (New York, 1940), p. 258. Flexner called
    Winternitz "one of the most energetic, keen, and able administrators
    that I encountered in the whole course of my dealings with medical
    schools."

31 *The Past, Present and Future of the Yale University School of Medi-
    cine* (New Haven, 1922), pp. 12–14; Winslow, *Dean Winternitz,* pp.
    5–9.

32 Winslow, *Dean Winternitz,* pp. 6–7.

33 *The Past Present and Future of the Yale School of Medicine,* p. 6;
    Winslow, *Dean Winternitz,* p. 10; *YAW,* 29 January 1932. This
    study and examination program is often referred to as the "Yale Sys-
    tem."

34 Winslow, *Dean Winternitz,* pp. 15, 17.

35 See *President's Report, 1928,* pp. 17–19, and James R. Angell,
    "Yale's Institute of Human Relations," *YAW,* 19 April 1929; Furniss,
    The Graduate School of Yale, pp. 54–55; Cross, *Connecticut Yankee,*
    pp. 180–81.

36 Furniss, *The Graduate School of Yale,* pp. 55–56. Furniss says that
    Otto Bannard told Hutchins, "You must remember that Mr. Sterling
    was a law graduate; the Trustees of his Estate know that the new
    Law Building was his prize baby, and you mustn't try to pinch it."

37 Winslow, *Dean Winternitz,* p. 19; *President's Report, 1929,* p. 5;
    YAW, 7 March 1930; Furniss, *The Graduate School of Yale,* p. 56.

38 *The Past, Present, and Future of the Yale University School of Medi-
    cine,* p. 69; *YAW,* 27 April 1923, 2 February 1934. See also "Twenty-
    fifth Anniversary Exercises of the Yale University School of Nurs-
    ing," *Yale Journal of Biology and Medicine* 21 (1949) : 263–92.

39 *YAW*, 29 February 1924.

40 *YAW*, 1 February 1929; *President's Report, 1933,* p. 30; *YAW*, 8 December 1933.

41 Pierson, *Yale, 1921–1937,* p. 577; *Historical Register of Yale University, 1701–1937,* pp. 52, 569.

42 On developments in the law schools of the day, see Stevens, "The American Law School," *Perspectives in American History,* 5 : 470–93; *YAW*, 9 October 1931.

43 *YAW*, 5 December 1924; Morison, *Three Centuries,* p. 432; on the fight over Woolley, see Pierson, *Yale, 1921–1937,* pp. 96–99.

44 *YAW*, 7 December 1928, 17 January 1930; *Historical Register of Yale University, 1701–1937,* p. 29; *YAW*, 4 July 1930; *Treasurer's Report, 1930,* p. 33.

45 *YAW*, 10 June 1932; *President's Report, 1932,* pp. 13–14.

46 Pierson, *Yale, 1871–1921,* p. 492; idem, *Yale 1921–1937,* pp. 177, 267–73.

47 Pierson, *Yale, 1921–1937,* pp. 172, 177, 267–80; *President's Report, 1937,* p. 11.

48 Pierson, *Yale, 1921–1937,* pp. 403, 531–33, 606–07.

49 *YAW*, 14 April 1922.

50 Pierson, *Yale, 1921–1937,* pp. 30, 56–70, 143, 153, 260–62. Professor Pierson estimates that between the time of Porter and the end of Angell's term, "the education of undergraduate Yale had gained almost three years in general maturity" (p. 376).

51 Ibid., pp. 315, 377.

52 *YAW*, 2 October, 13 November 1925; Pierson, *Yale, 1921–1937,* pp. 86–93.

53 Pierson, *Yale, 1921–1937,* pp. 423–44. Pierson also deals with the question of teaching in the colleges, pp. 445–74.

54 *YAW*, 29 February 1924; Pierson, *Yale, 1921–1937,* pp. 34–35, 622, 521.

55 *YAW*, 15 December 1922, 7 May 1926; Pierson, *Yale, 1921–1937,* pp. 32–33, 521–22, 663–64. See *YAW*, 5 March 1926, for the report of the Committee on University Affairs of the Yale Engineering Association. Edward S. Robinson, "Recent Developments at the Senior College Level in Yale University," *Recent Trends in American College Education,* Proceedings of the Institute of Administrative Officers of Higher Institutions, 3 (1931) : 131–42.

56 Pierson, *Yale, 1921–1937,* pp. 51–52; *President's Report, 1930,* pp. 18–19. I recall my father (B.A. 1924) saying that he never attended one of his science courses at all, and in the other all he learned was how to make a penny serve as a dime in a coin telephone.

57 *President's Report, 1931,* pp. 4–7, *1926,* p. 1.
58 *YAW,* 29 January, 26 February, 25 November 1932; *Treasurer's Report, 1932,* p. 12.
59 *YAW,* 6 February 1925, 26 February 1926; *Yale Alumni Fund Annual Report, 1965–1966,* p. 27.
60 Pierson, *Yale, 1921–1937,* pp. 265–67, 280–83, 655–56. The financial picture can be followed through the *Treasurer's Reports.* On taxation, see *YAW,* 3 February, 3 March 1933, 18 December 1936, 12 February, 23 April 1937; *President's Report, 1933,* pp. 6–8, *1937,* pp. 5–6.
61 Pierson, *Yale, 1921–1937,* pp. 426–28.
62 Ibid., pp. 265–66, 283, 524.
63 *Treasurer's Report, 1921,* p. 45, *1937,* pp. 8, 101.
64 Pierson, *Yale, 1921–1937,* pp. 181–82, 577; John Fulton, *Harvey Cushing, A Biography* (Springfield, Ill., 1946), p. 683.

CHAPTER 19

1 *YAW,* 19 February 1937; Holden, *Profiles and Portraits of Yale University Presidents,* pp. 121–22.
2 Holden, *Yale Presidents,* pp. 119–20; *Historical Register of Yale University, 1937–1951* (New Haven, 1952), p. 276; Pierson, *Yale, 1921–1937,* pp. 627, 402 ff.; Furniss, *The Graduate School of Yale,* p. 113.
3 *YAM,* 15 October 1937; *President's Report, 1945,* p. 22; football and crew box, Seymour Papers (MSS, Yale University Library); BMK conversation with William H. Dunham, 1 December 1972; Furniss, *The Graduate School of Yale,* p. 114; Pierson, *Yale, 1921–1937,* pp. 405, 634.
4 Pierson, *Yale, 1921–1937,* p. 381; Robert D. Heinl, Jr., "Presidency of Yale, Its Past, Present, and Future Problems," *Yale Literary Magazine,* April 1937, pp. 31–32, 45–49; *YAM,* 8 March 1940.
5 BMK conversation with Mrs. William C. DeVane, 8 December 1972, Mrs. William C. DeVane to BMK, 20 March 1973.
6 *President's Report, 1938,* p. 13; Pierson, *Yale, 1921–1937,* pp. 464, 470–71.
7 *President's Report, 1939,* p. 3.
8 Lewis, *One Man's Education,* p. 320; Lewis's letters, Lewis folder, Seymour MSS, do not reveal this concern.
9 *YAM,* January 1951; *President's Report, 1940,* pp. 2, 3.
10 *YAW,* 1 May 1936, 7 May 1937; Wayne S. Cole, *America First: The Battle against Intervention, 1940–1941* (Madison, Wisc., 1953), pp.

10–13; *YAM*, 8 November, 7 June 1940. For student attitudes, see Kingman Brewster, Jr., "Pre-War Uncertainty," *Seventy-Five,* p. 67.

11 *YAM*, 27 September, 25 October 1940, 28 November 1941; *President's Report, 1941*, pp. 2, 5.

12 *YAM*, 19 December 1941, 23 January, 6 February, 10 April, 22 May, 6 March 1942.

13 *President's Report, 1942*, p. 7.

14 *YAM*, n.d., August, 20 February, 10 April 1942. Required physical education was also instituted (*YAM*, 20 February 1942). *President's Report, 1942*, pp. 10–11.

15 *President's Report, 1942*, p. 6; *YAM*, October 1942.

16 *President's Report, 1942*, pp. 11–14.

17 *YAM*, October 1942; *President's Report, 1943*, p. 3; Seymour to H. S. Coffin, 15 September 1942, Coffin folder, Seymour MSS.

18 *President's Report, 1943*, p. 3, *1942*, pp. 14–16; George W. Pierson to BMK, 13 December 1972; George W. Pierson, "Democratic War and Our Higher Learning," *YAM*, December 1942.

19 *President's Report, 1942*, p. 16; *YAM*, January 1943; Coffin to Seymour, 21, 23 December 1942, Coffin folder, Seymour MSS.

20 *YAM*, February 1943.

21 *YAM*, March 1943; *President's Report, 1943*, p. 4.

22 *YAM*, May 1943.

23 *President's Report, 1943*, pp. 6–7; *YAM*, August, September 1943.

24 *President's Report, 1943*, pp. 8–9, *1944*, pp. 3–4.

25 *YAM*, January 1946; *President's Report, 1944*, p. 4.

26 *YAM*, August 1943.

27 Ibid.

28 *YAM*, April 1944.

29 *President's Report, 1944*, pp. 1, 3; D. M. Marshman, Jr., "The Undergraduate Month," *YAM*, April 1944; Norman S. Buck, "The Yale Scene Today," *YAM*, May 1944.

30 *YAM*, November 1944, January 1945.

31 *President's Report, 1945*, pp. 1–3; Charles Seymour, "A Living University in Time of War," (statement of Charles Seymour, 8 December 1942, copy, Yale University Library); *Undergraduate Courses, Spring and Summer 1945*, pp. 13–14.

32 *YAM*, December 1945, December 1942, April 1945; *Historical Register of Yale University, 1937–1951*, p. 8; Eugene H. Kone, "History of the 39th General Hospital," *YAM*, March 1947.

33 *President's Report, 1942*, p. 23, *1943*, p. 27. Also in 1942 the art gallery had received the Collection of the Society Anonyme, the gift of Katherine S. Dreier and Marcel Duchamp (ibid., *1942*, p. 23).

34   Ibid., *1929*, p. 10; *YAM,* December 1944; Furniss, *The Graduate School of Yale,* pp. 85–88.

35   *YAM,* March 1942; *President's Report, 1942,* p. 25.

36   *University Catalogue Number for the Academic Year 1941–2, 1942–3, 1943–4, 1944–5; Treasurer's Report, 1942, 1943, 1944, 1945,* all p. 9.

37   *Treasurer's Report, 1943,* pp. 1, 8, *1944,* p. 8; Charles Seymour, "Yale's Job in this War," *YAM,* 6 March 1942; Lawrence Tighe to Reeve Schley, 9 August 1943, Tighe to Marcus Robbins, 8 September 1943, Treasurer's Office folder, Seymour MSS.

38   *President's Report, 1950,* pp. 7–8.

39   Edward S. Noyes, "Admission and Readmission to Yale," *YAM,* March 1946. Noyes said the government told Yale it would be three to six years before all the troops were demobilized.

40   *President's Report, 1946,* p. 4; *YAM,* October 1946; James G. Leyburn, "Pierson College, War and Peace, 1943–1946" (mimeographed), p. 8. At Pierson they tried silver and china, but most colleges used metal trays.

41   *President's Report, 1946,* pp. 6–7.

42   Ibid., pp. 7–8; *YAM,* December 1954; George W. Pierson, in a conversation with BMK, said he had estimated faculty members were contributing about $1,000 a year each in lost salary. I had one friend who found sleeping in the gymnasium just too much—so he went home and never returned.

43   Pierson, *Yale, 1921–1937,* pp. 499–504.

44   Ibid., pp. 500–01; *YAM,* 13 October 1939, March 1947.

45   "Yale College Report of the Committee on the Course of Study," Yale College folder, Seymour MSS.

46   Ralph Gabriel, "The Search for a Curriculum," *Seventy-Five,* pp. 148–49; "Yale College Report of the Committee on the Course of Study," Yale College folder, Seymour MSS; *Courses Offered at Yale University in the Undergraduate Schools, 1946–1947.*

47   "Yale College Report of the Committee on the Course of Study," Yale College folder, Seymour MSS; Gabriel, "The Search for a Curriculum," p. 150; Maynard Mack, "Directed Studies," *YAM,* May 1949. DeVane had outlined a course similar to Directed Studies and specifically referred to the "Our Town" commentator in "American Education after the War," *Yale Review* reprint, n.d. [September 1943], Yale College folder, Seymour MSS.

48   *YAM,* December 1945; *University Catalogue, 1946–1947,* pp. 113–14; "To the Faculty of Yale College," 20 December 1947, Yale College Course of Study folder, Seymour MSS.

49 John Sirjamaki, "A Sociologist's View," *Seventy-Five*, p. 87; Richard B. Sewall, "An Educator Evaluates," ibid., p. 59; H. Richard Niebuhr, "Our Conservative Youth," ibid., p. 89. See also Charles Fenton, "Social Solemnity," ibid., pp. 43–44; *President's Report, 1947*, pp. 1–2.

50 *President's Report, 1947*, p. 4, *1950*, p. 12.

51 *YAM*, May 1950.

52 Tighe was appointed associate treasurer in 1938 to help with the "ever-increasing problems which center in management of a great endowment like Yale's" (*YAM*, 4 March 1938). Investing was left to Tighe, but his acts had to be confirmed by the Finance Committee, which also approved the investment plan. The plan was first explained publicly by Tighe in *YAM*, 12 April 1940. See also Laurence G. Tighe, *The Management of Yale's Endowment Funds*, excerpts from remarks at the 51st annual meeting of the class agents of the Yale Alumni Fund (New Haven [?], 1941). Therein Tighe said that Yale was putting money into bonds because "it has been thought that with the threat of higher and higher taxes, stocks have questionable attraction either for price enhancement or larger dividends, but that with increased national industrial activity, good companies should have no difficulty in servicing their bond issues." For Yale's endowment in 1950, see *Treasurer's Report, 1950*, p. 8. Yale's sale of real estate during these years was called to my attention by both George Pierson and Gaddis Smith. The changes in holdings were not publicized but may be followed in the *Treasurer's Reports*. My figures are from *Treasurer's Report, 1941*, p. 193, and *1950*, p. 161. By 1953 the value of Yale's real estate had fallen to $1,873,168.71 only to rebound, the following year, to $2,400,456.71. *Treasurer's Report, Investments, 1953*, p. 22, *1954*, p. 23. On Hadley's sales, see *YAW*, 30 October, 28 November 1906, 7 October 1908; *Treasurer's Report, 1906*, p. 6, *1907*, p. 11, *1909*, p. 9; *President's Report, 1910*, pp. 11–12.

53 Seymour to Sherrill, 23 March 1945 (copy), Sherrill folder, Seymour MSS.

54 *YAM*, February 1947; A series of pamphlets on Yale's needs began to appear that year. The first was *A Generation of Great Teachers*, the second, *Science and the Humanities, Yale's Program*, which said that though large amounts of money were needed, it was not a request for direct financial assistance. Seymour to Sherrill, 13 August 1946 (copy), Sherrill folder, Seymour MSS; Sherrill to Seymour, n.d., (marked "Received, Aug. 28, 1946"), Sherrill folder, Seymour MSS.

55 *President's Report, 1947*, p. 25; *YAM*, April 1948.

56 *YAM,* January 1948.

57 *President's Report, 1949,* pp. 1–2, 3.

58 Yale University Council, *A Report of the Committee on the Division of Medical Affairs, 1 Aug. 1953* [New Haven, 1953], p. 3; George B. Darling, "Review of Medical Affairs, Yale University, 1946–47—1949–50" (carbon copy), Division of Medical Affairs box, Seymour MSS.

59 Yale University Council, *A Report of the Committee on the Division of Medical Affairs, 1 Aug. 1953,* pp. 4–7.

60 Ibid., pp. 7–8.

61 *YAM,* April 1949.

62 *President's Report, 1948,* p. 17, *1949,* p. 27; Yale University Council, *A Report on the Division of Medical Affairs, 1 Aug. 1953,* p. 9.

63 *President's Report, 1949,* pp. 3–4; *YAM,* May 1953.

64 *President's Report, 1949,* p. 5; Edith Kerr, "The Physics Department—Its Problems and Opportunities in an Atomic Age," *YAM,* February 1951.

65 Lyman Spitzer, Jr., "The Division of the Sciences," *YAM,* November 1948.

66 There has always been a certain amount of talk around Yale about the element of anti-Semitism in its past, but the clearest revelation of it may be in the failure of Yale's name to appear much in "The Intellectual Migration: Europe and America, 1930–1960," *Perspectives in American History,* 2 (1968); Colin Eisler, "*Kunstgeschichte* American Style: A Study in Migration," ibid., p. 624. Charles Weiner, "A New Site for the Seminar: The Refugees and American Physics in the Thirties," ibid., p. 216.

67 Edith Kerr, "The Physics Department," Three grants were made to Yale by the U.S. government in 1946—the first peacetime payments I have found. The largest, from the Public Health Service, was for $9,172.00 (*Treasurer's Report, 1946,* pp. 25, 27). See also Howard W. Haggard, "The Challenge Facing Endowed Universities," *YAM,* November 1948. Haggard, director of the Office of University Development, defined science as objective and history and other similar fields as not.

68 *President's Report, 1949,* pp. 5–7.

69 *Treasurer's Report, 1949,* p. 1; *President's Report, 1949,* p. 1; *YAM,* November 1949, January, July, 1950. During the fall and winter of 1949–50 Seymour wrote three letters to the alumni explaining the university's financial problems and needs. I have not been able to find copies of any of these letters.

To give an example of the university's hesitation to be specific:

George Darling wrote Seymour on 3 February 1950 after talking to Carlos Stoddard of the Office of University Development about the financial goals for the Schools of Medicine and Nursing. Darling wrote, "While I can appreciate the problems involved, I am not entirely certain that the substitution of 'many millions' for a specific sum is the best solution" (Division of Medical Affairs folder, Seymour MSS).

70 *YAM*, May 1949. Griswold was later to dismantle some of this administrative apparatus.

71 *Treasurer's Report, 1950*, p. 1, announced that part of the year's deficit had been financed from principal "from which all future deficits must be financed." On income, expenses, and endowment, see Yale University and the Board of Trustees of the Sheffield Scientific School, dated "Received Oct. 22, 1948," Treasurer's Office folder, Seymour MSS; and *Treasurer's Report, 1937*, pp. 8–9, *1951*, pp. 10–11. For numbers of faculty members see *YAM*, April 1949; *University Catalogue, 1937–38*, p. 622, and *1949–50*, p. 401.

72 *President's Report, 1945*, p. 27, *1946*, pp. 30–31, *1947*, pp. 20–21, *1948*, pp. 29–30; *YAM*, June 1949; William H. Jordy, "The Aftermath of the Bauhaus in America: Gropius, Mies, and Breuer," *Perspectives in American History* 2 (1968) : 507–08.

73 *President's Report, 1945*, p. 15; *Yale University Library Gazette* 43 (1969) : 168; *YAM*, February 1950, November 1946; Herman W. Liebert, "The Boswell Papers," *YAM*, October 1949.

74 "Report of the Committee on the Yale College Deanship," 25 March 1948, Yale College folder, Seymour MSS. BMK conversations with Georges May, 6 December 1972, John Perry Miller, 18 December 1972, Howard Lamar, 19 December 1972.

75 *President's Report, 1950*, p. 19.

76 Ibid., *1948*, p. 13, *1947*, p. 11, *1940*, p. 11; Colin Eisler, "*Kunstgeschichte* American Style," p. 624.

77 *President's Report, 1950*, pp. 21–22.

78 Ibid., pp. 13, 18, 19–20, 22; *YAM*, May 1946, February 1950.

79 *YAM*, July 1950.

CHAPTER 20

1 Lewis, *One Man's Education*, pp. 433–34.

2 Ibid., pp. 434–35.

3 Ibid., pp. 434, 436–37. It is rumored that Lewis himself was strongly opposed to DeVane.

4 Holden, *Yale Presidents*, p. 133; Lewis, *One Man's Education*, p. 436; *President's Report, 1950*, p. 41.

5 Dean Acheson, *Present at the Creation: My Years in the State Department* (New York, 1969), pp. 371–72. Lewis, Blair, and Acheson were clearly for Griswold. I have not been able to identify the fourth man.

6 H. S. Coffin to Seymour, 21 February 1950, Coffin folder, Seymour MSS.

7 BMK conversations with various faculty members and wives of faculty members; *A. Whitney Griswold, 1906–1963: In Memoriam* (Stamford, Conn., 1964), p. 23; Lewis, *One Man's Education,* p. 434; *YAM,* March 1960, *Time,* 11 June 1951.

8 Holden, *Yale Presidents,* p. 131; *YAM,* May 1957.

9 Holden, *Yale Presidents,* p. 136; Pierson, *Yale, 1921–1937,* p. 141.

10 BMK conversation with Howard Lamar, 19 December 1972; Holden, *Yale Presidents,* p. 131; *Life,* 3 May 1963.

11 *Newsweek,* 11 June 1951; Lewis, *One Man's Education,* p. 437. There seems to be no solid basis for the "kitchen cabinet" rumor. Perhaps it grew out of the fact that since Griswold was somewhat remote from most of his faculty, they believed those who were closer to him must be advising him.

12 Holden, *Yale Presidents,* p. 140.

13 *President's Report, 1951,* p. 4; *YAM,* November 1950; A. Whitney Griswold, *Essays in Education* (New Haven, 1954), pp. 1–10.

14 *Newsweek,* 11 June 1951.

15 Ibid.; *Time,* 11 June 1951.

16 George P. Fisher, *Life of Benjamin Silliman,* 1 : 401.

17 *YAM,* June 1951; *President's Report, 1951,* p. 1; *University Catalogue, 1951–1952,* pp. 324–25; *Historical Register of Yale University, 1937–1951,* pp. 9–10. The *Historical Register* placed the endowment at $141,208,881. I have used President Griswold's figure.

18 Yale University Council, *Report of the Committee on the Division of the Humanities* (New Haven, 1949), p. 42; Pierson, *Yale, 1921–1937,* p. 106; Clements C. Fry, "A Psychiatrist Evaluates," *Seventy-Five,* p. 62.

19 Prosser Gifford, "A Student Evaluates," *Seventy-Five,* p. 56; see also Richard C. Carroll, "Extra-Curricular Proficiency," ibid., p. 48; George W. Pierson, *The Education of American Leaders, Comparative Contributions of U.S. Colleges and Universities.*

20 *YAM,* November 1942.

21 *The 250th Anniversary of Yale University* (New Haven, 1952), p. 147.

22 Archibald S. Foord, "Studies that Build Men of Character," *YAM,* December 1951; *Treasurer's Report, 1952,* pp. 10–11, 21–28.

23   *The 250th Anniversary of Yale University,* p. 110; George H. Walker, "Remarks of the New Alumni Fund Chairman at the Dinner on November 3," *YAM,* December 1950.

24   William F. Buckley, Jr., *God and Man at Yale* (Chicago, 1951), pp. xiv–xviii.

25   Griswold, *Essays in Education,* pp. 79–80.

26   "A. Whitney Griswold, 1906–1963," *YAM,* May 1963; *New York Times,* 12 June 1951; *Griswold,* p. 21.

27   Griswold, *Essays in Education,* p. 53; *Treasurer's Report, 1927,* p. 48; Official Register of Harvard University, *Statement of the Treasurer, 1926–1927* (Cambridge, Mass.), pp. 6, 10 (hereafter cited as *Harvard Treasurer,* with year in which the report ends); *Treasurer's Report, 1937,* pp. 37, 38; *Harvard Treasurer, 1937,* p. 8; *Treasurer's Report, 1950,* pp. 8, 10; *Harvard Treasurer, 1950,* p. 8. I have used total assets and income as my basis for comparison because differing methods of handling funds make the more normally used endowment figures not very useful. Market values in the earlier years were not usually given, but they do not seem to have been far from book values until recent years. In 1939 Harvard reported the market value of its General Investments as 97.5 percent of book value. In 1949, when Cabot first signed the Harvard Treasurer's Report, the market value of the General Investment Account was 105.6 percent of book. Yale did not report its market values that year, but the results were probably not too different from Harvard's.

28   *Great Scholars and Teachers Fund* (New Haven, 1951); "The Case for Endowed Professorships," *For the Arts and Sciences at Yale* (New Haven, 1960); *YAM,* January 1960; "Economic Status of the Profession," *AAUP Bulletin,* June 1962, p. 126.

29   *YAM,* February, November 1951.

30   *President's Report, 1952,* p. 17, *1957,* p. 22.

31   *President's Report, 1956,* pp. 5–8, *1957,* p. 19.

32   *YAM,* June 1960.

33   I assume the physics building was the major cause, but other buildings were involved. See *President's Report, 1957,* p. 22, *1959,* pp. 22–23, and Griswold, *For the Arts and Sciences at Yale,* pp. 17–18.

34   The drive actually took in $52 million (*President's Report, 1962,* p. 1). In 1963 the alumni fund received $3,001,139 (*Treasurer's Report, 1963,* p. 1). Griswold had put Yale's need at $147 million for the decade of the sixties, and this, he said, was a conservative estimate. He expected each of the professional schools to raise the funds for their own needs (Griswold, *For the Arts and Sciences at Yale,* p. 20).

35   "A. Whitney Griswold, 1906–1963," *YAM,* May 1963. The market

value of bonds and stocks of all funds was $387,880,178 (*Treasurer's Report, 1964,* p. 8). See the Yale and Harvard treasurer's reports, 1950–63; E. J. Kahn, Jr., *Harvard: Through Change and Through Storm* (New York, 1969), pp. 327–28.

36 *Treasurer's Report, 1950,* p. 10, *1964,* p. 10; *President's Report, 1957,* pp. 29, 34 (there are also extended comments about public and private support in *President's Report, 1952,* pp. 6–8); *Treasurer's Report, 1964,* p. 10; *Treasurer's Report, 1967,* p. 18; *President's Report, 1964,* p. 9.

37 *President's Report, 1951,* p. 1; *University Catalogue, 1951–1952,* p. 324; *University Catalogue, 1962–1963,* p. 410.

38 *President's Report, 1962,* pp. 13–14; Griswold, *For the Arts and Sciences at Yale,* p. 14; *YAM,* December 1960.

39 *President's Report, 1959,* p. 17; this is a criticism I have even heard from many nonscientists. *President's Report, 1962,* pp. 14, 37–38.

40 *YAM,* May 1963; *The Buildings of Yale* (1965), pp. 99–101; A. Whitney Griswold, "Society's Need for Man," Baccalaureate, 9 June 1957, *In the University Tradition* (New Haven, 1957), p. 156; *Architectural Forum,* June 1963, quoted in *Griswold,* p. 27.

41 *President's Report, 1955,* pp. 18–19.

42 *President's Report, 1956,* p. 10; *YAM,* March 1956; Holden, *Yale Presidents,* p. 136.

43 *President's Report, 1953,* pp. 7, 20–23; A Committee of the Post-Doctoral Seminar, *The Department of Education at Yale University, 1891–1958,* p. 44. The Department of Education was to teach the necessary pedagogical courses to the M.A.T. students.

44 *Department of Education at Yale,* pp. 43, 44, 48–49.

45 Ibid., pp. 49–50. As this study points out, there was "severe criticism . . . generally" of public education and teacher training after World War II (p. 47). On the end of M.A.T., see Daniel McIntyre, "M.A.T.: Or Becoming a Part of Institutional History," *New Journal,* 22 February 1970, pp. 12–14.

46 *The 250th Anniversary of Yale University,* pp. 33–36; Pierson, *The Education of American Leaders,* pp. 190–92.

47 *President's Report, 1955,* pp. 12–14, *1957,* p. 2. It was to go into effect for the School of Music in 1958.

48 *President's Report, 1955,* p. 9; Donna Diers, "It's a Good Time for Nursing," *YAM,* December 1972.

49 Holden, *Yale Presidents,* p. 135; *Newsweek,* 11 June 1951. When Yale announced it would no longer support the Alcohol Study Center and the Laboratory of Applied Biodynamics, the reasons given were the diversity of the disciplines involved, which made it difficult

to locate the organizations in the traditional departments, and the fact that the university could not increase its financial support (*YAM*, January 1961). On the other hand, if a center did seem to "fit," like the Center for Quantitative Study of Economic Structure and Growth, it was welcomed (see *YAM*, March 1961).

50 *President's Report, 1962*, pp. 16–21.

51 Eugene V. Rostow, "The Yale Law School Today," *YAM*, March 1961; *YAM*, February 1956.

52 Yale University Council, *A Report of the Committee on the Division of Medical Affairs, 1 Aug. 1953;* Vernon W. Lippard, "The Yale–New Haven Medical Center," An Address Given to the American Institute of Banking, 25 February 1961; *YAM*, October 1962; *Treasurer's Report, 1963*, p. 18.

53 *YAM*, June 1967.

54 Allan M. Cartter, "As Others View Yale: An Assessment of Graduate Education," *Ventures, Magazine of the Yale Graduate School*, Fall 1966, pp. 15–20; Gale D. Johnson, "What Does It Mean, Number Three?" *The University of Chicago Magazine*, March–April 1971, pp. 8–11.

55 *Griswold*, pp. 43–44.

56 Edith Kerr, "Yale Engineering: 100 Years of Progress," *YAM*, October 1952; *The Buildings of Yale* (1965), pp. 45–46.

57 *President's Report, 1962*, p. 22, *1955*, pp. 9–12; "Report of the Committee on Engineering," *Yale Scientific Magazine*, December 1961. The members of the committee were Caryl P. Haskins, president of the Carnegie Foundation; Frederick C. Lindvall, chairman of the division of engineering at California Institute of Technology; Harvey Brooks, dean of engineering and applied physics at Harvard; J. William Hinkley, president of Research Corporation and chairman of the Yale University Council's committee on engineering; Newman Hall, chairman of mechanical engineering at Yale; William D. Robertson, chairman of metallurgy at Yale; and Barnett Dodge, recently retired dean of the Yale School of Engineering.

58 "Report of the Committee on Engineering"; "Y.E.A. Newsletter," *Yale Scientific Magazine*, October 1966; William A. Weber, "A View of Yale Engineering," ibid., January 1967; *YAM*, February 1967; Merritt A. Williamson to the editor, *YAM*, June 1967.

59 *President's Report, 1954*, p. 3, *1956*, pp. 13–18, *1958*, pp. 23–24.

60 "The College Master: A Collective Portrait," *YAM*, March 1953; *YAM*, November 1954; Thomas K. Swing and A. Bartlett Giamatti, eds., *Master Pieces from the Files of T. G. B.* (New Haven, 1964), p. 28.

61   *Report of the President's Committee on General Education* (New Haven, 1953).

62   Course of Study Committee, *Report of the Committee on the Course of Study to the General Faculty of Yale College, April 1955* [New Haven, 1955]. Dean DeVane was on leave for the first year the committee met, so he was able to avoid at least some of the responsibility for the report.

63   *President's Report, 1955,* pp. 3–9; *YAM,* November 1961.

64   Norman S. Buck, "The Freshman Year," *Seventy-Five,* p. 37; Pierson, *Yale, 1921–1937,* p. 625.

65   *President's Report, 1962,* p. 31; "Report of the President's Committee on the Freshman Year," *YAM,* June 1962; Pierson, *Yale, 1921–1937,* p. 376.

66   "Report of the President's Committee on the Freshman Year," *YAM,* June 1962.

67   Alfred B. Fitt observed in a highly entertaining letter to the editor (*YAM,* November 1962) that the magazine was using up two "gut" issues at one time. The attitudes of many Yale graduates are wonderfully presented in the letters to the editor of the *YAM* for the months after June 1962.

68   Furniss, *The Graduate School of Yale,* p. 118; *YAM,* July 1950.

69   *YAM,* December 1950, June 1951.

70   Yale University Council, *A Report of the Committee on the Division of Medical Affairs, Aug. 1, 1953,* p. 16; *President's Report, 1957,* p. 4; *YAM,* December 1959; BMK conversation with John Perry Miller, 18 December 1972, and John Perry Miller to BMK, 3 April 1973.

71   Quoted in Pierson, *Yale, 1921–1937,* p. 607.

72   *President's Report, 1962,* pp. 37–40; *YAM,* May 1963.

73   *A. Whitney Griswold, 1906–1963: In Memoriam,* contains these and many more comments about the president.

74   *President's Report, 1961,* p. 9, *1964,* p. 7.

Index

Abbreviations: SSS (Sheffield Scientific School); YC (Yale College); YU (Yale University)